CAMBRIDGE LIBRARY COLLECTION

Books of enduring scholarly value

Classics

From the Renaissance to the nineteenth century, Latin and Greek were compulsory subjects in almost all European universities, and most early modern scholars published their research and conducted international correspondence in Latin. Latin had continued in use in Western Europe long after the fall of the Roman empire as the lingua franca of the educated classes and of law, diplomacy, religion and university teaching. The flight of Greek scholars to the West after the fall of Constantinople in 1453 gave impetus to the study of ancient Greek literature and the Greek New Testament. Eventually, just as nineteenth-century reforms of university curricula were beginning to erode this ascendancy, developments in textual criticism and linguistic analysis, and new ways of studying ancient societies, especially archaeology, led to renewed enthusiasm for the Classics. This collection offers works of criticism, interpretation and synthesis by the outstanding scholars of the nineteenth century.

Sophocles: The Plays and Fragments

Sir Richard Jebb's seven-volume edition of the works of Sophocles, published between 1883 and 1896, remains a landmark in Greek scholarship. Jebb (1841–1905) was the most distinguished classicist of his generation, a Fellow of Trinity College, Cambridge, and University Orator, subsequently Professor of Greek at Glasgow University and finally Regius Professor of Greek at Cambridge, and a Member of Parliament for the University. Each volume of the edition contains an introductory essay, a metrical analysis, an indication of the sources used to establish the text, and the ancient summaries ('arguments') of the play. The text itself is given with a parallel English translation, textual collation and explanatory notes, and an appendix consisting of expanded notes on some of the textual issues. The quality of Jebb's work means that his editions are still widely consulted today. This volume contains *Oedipus Tyrannus*.

D0880512

Cambridge University Press has long been a pioneer in the reissuing of out-of-print titles from its own backlist, producing digital reprints of books that are still sought after by scholars and students but could not be reprinted economically using traditional technology. The Cambridge Library Collection extends this activity to a wider range of books which are still of importance to researchers and professionals, either for the source material they contain, or as landmarks in the history of their academic discipline.

Drawing from the world-renowned collections in the Cambridge University Library, and guided by the advice of experts in each subject area, Cambridge University Press is using state-of-the-art scanning machines in its own Printing House to capture the content of each book selected for inclusion. The files are processed to give a consistently clear, crisp image, and the books finished to the high quality standard for which the Press is recognised around the world. The latest print-on-demand technology ensures that the books will remain available indefinitely, and that orders for single or multiple copies can quickly be supplied.

The Cambridge Library Collection will bring back to life books of enduring scholarly value (including out-of-copyright works originally issued by other publishers) across a wide range of disciplines in the humanities and social sciences and in science and technology.

Sophocles: The Plays and Fragments

With Critical Notes, Commentary and Translation in English Prose

VOLUME 1: THE OEDIPUS TYRANNUS

EDITED BY RICHARD CLAVERHOUSE JEBB

CAMBRIDGE UNIVERSITY PRESS

CAMBRIDGE UNIVERSITY PRESS

Cambridge, New York, Melbourne, Madrid, Cape Town, Singapore,
São Paolo, Delhi, Dubai, Tokyo

Published in the United States of America by Cambridge University Press, New York

www.cambridge.org
Information on this title: www.cambridge.org/9781108008389

© in this compilation Cambridge University Press 2010

This edition first published 1883
This digitally printed version 2010

ISBN 978-1-108-00838-9 Paperback

SOPHOCLES

THE PLAYS AND FRAGMENTS.

PART I.

THE OEDIPUS TYRANNUS.

London: C. J. CLAY, M.A. & SON,
CAMBRIDGE UNIVERSITY PRESS WAREHOUSE,
17, PATERNOSTER ROW.

Cambridge: DEIGHTON, BELL, AND CO.
Leipzig: F. A. BROCKHAUS.

SOPHOCLES

THE PLAYS AND FRAGMENTS

WITH CRITICAL NOTES, COMMENTARY, AND
TRANSLATION IN ENGLISH PROSE,

BY

R. C. JEBB, M.A., LL.D. Edin.,

PROFESSOR OF GREEK IN THE UNIVERSITY OF GLASGOW,
FORMERLY FELLOW OF TRINITY COLLEGE AND PUBLIC ORATOR IN THE
UNIVERSITY OF CAMBRIDGE.

PART I.

THE OEDIPUS TYRANNUS.

EDITED FOR THE SYNDICS OF THE UNIVERSITY PRESS.

CAMBRIDGE:
AT THE UNIVERSITY PRESS.
1883

𝖢𝖺𝗆𝖻𝗋𝗂𝖽𝗀𝖾:

PRINTED BY C. J. CLAY, M.A. AND SON,

AT THE UNIVERSITY PRESS.

NOTE.

IT is intended that in the present edition of Sophocles each play should form a separate volume. While the volumes subsequent to the first will necessarily contain occasional references to the earlier portion of the work, care will be taken to render each volume, in all essentials, an independent book, available for the use of readers who possess no other part of the edition.

The *Oedipus Coloneus* will follow the present volume at as short an interval as may be found possible. Of the remaining five plays, the *Antigone* will be the first. An eighth volume will contain (1) the Fragments: (2) short Essays on subjects of general interest in relation to Sophocles: (3) a General Index, for all the volumes, of 1. Greek, 2. Matters, 3. Authors quoted.

PREFACE.

As long ago as 1867, I contributed to the *Catena Classicorum* a commentary on the *Electra* of Sophocles, followed in 1868 by one on the *Ajax*. At that time I already meditated a complete edition of Sophocles on a larger scale,— a design which I have never abandoned, though various causes have delayed its execution.

One of these causes may be briefly noticed here. In the course of preparing the commentaries on the *Electra* and the *Ajax*, I had been led to see more clearly the intimate relation which in certain respects exists between Greek tragic dialogue and Greek rhetorical prose, and to feel the desire of studying more closely the whole process by which Greek oratory had been developed. The result of this study was a treatise on the historical development of Attic prose style, which in 1876 was published under the title of *The Attic Orators from Antiphon to Isaeos*. The reception accorded to it has been most gratifying, and has more than repaid the labour which it had cost. It was, however, as a preparation, in one department, for the task of editing Sophocles that the special studies embodied in the *Attic Orators* had originally been undertaken: and, though they necessarily extended beyond that immediate scope, I do not regard the time bestowed on them as lost to the pur-

b 2

poses of the present work. I may say this here, because,—if
I can at all judge from my own feeling in such a case,—
it is sometimes of interest for readers to know that works not
obviously related to each other have been connected, in the
writer's own mind, by a definite unity of purpose. However
much he may have failed of his aim in either task or in both,
at any rate the point of view from which he approached
each may thus be more clearly suggested.

In offering to the public the first part of a new edition
of Sophocles, the editor may reasonably be expected to state
the general characteristics which he intends to be distinctive
of it. In this case, they are chiefly two.

1. First, I aim at showing fully and exactly how the
work of Sophocles is understood by me, both in its larger
aspects, and at every particular point. For this purpose, the
first requisite is a translation, the principle of which shall be
absolute fidelity to the original; not to the letter of the
original at the cost of the spirit, but to the spirit as expressed
in the letter. And, for this end, prose has two advantages
over verse, even though the verse be that of a poet. (i) Metre
will often exact sacrifices precisely at those points which test
the higher fidelity of translation—fidelity to light touches by
which the genius and art of the original are most delicately
marked. (ii) A modern verse translation has necessarily a
more or less modern spirit of its own, due to its very form,
and to the associations with which the form is invested. Thus,
however little he may desire it, the metrical translator is un-
avoidably placed in competition with his original.

The value of verse translations as substantive literary works
is not here in question. Translation is here being considered
solely from the stand-point of the *commentator*, as an indispensable instrument of lucid interpretation. In supplement to a
prose translation, a commentary has a special part to perform,

though this is only one of several functions which a commentary ought to aim at discharging. There are places where a translation, although in prose, cannot combine literal with essential accuracy. A version which subordinates the letter to the spirit will sometimes involve a mental process of which the result bears no visible trace. If the version is sound, this process is not only morally sensitive, but has also a scrupulously logical march. A version which, while brilliant, is unsound, is one which seizes on a smooth compromise or a glittering resemblance, which may imply an unconscious misrepresentation or an undetected fallacy. 'This rendering, I can see, is not literal'—we may suppose a reader to say. 'In what sense, then, and *why*, is it equivalent to the Greek?' Here —supposing the translation to be sound—is the opportunity of the commentary. It comes in to show that there is no flaw in the process by which an advance has been made from a literal rendering to one which, though less literal, is more faithful.

This, then, is the first object for which I have striven—the vivid exposition of my own mind in relation to Sophocles ; so that, even where my understanding of him is defective or mistaken, at least it may seldom be ambiguous. This is an endeavour which appeals more directly to classical students : it is by them, if any of them should use this book in their work, that the measure of failure or success will be most correctly judged.

2. The second object which has been proposed to this edition regards educated readers generally, not classical students alone. It is my hope—whether a vain one or not, I hardly know—that the English version facing the Greek text may induce some persons to read a play of Sophocles as they would read a great poem of a modern poet,—with no such interposing nightmare of τύπτω as at Athens came between Thackeray and his instinctive sense of what was admirable in the nature

and art around him,—but with free exercise of the mind and taste, thinking only of the drama itself, and of its qualities as such. Surely that is, above all things, what is to be desired by us just now in regard to all the worthiest literature of the world—that people should know some part of it (the quantity matters much less) *at first hand*,—not merely through manuals of literary history or magazine articles. Summaries, when the work of scholars, may be valuable as introductions and as retrospects; but only the breath of the great literature itself can make the dry bones live. Any one who had read thoroughly and intelligently a single play such as the *Oedipus Tyrannus* would have derived far more intellectual advantage from Greek literature, and would comprehend far better what it has signified in the spiritual history of mankind, than if he had committed to memory the names, dates, and abridged contents of a hundred Greek books ranging over half-a-dozen centuries.

'Explanatory notes ought to be written in one's own 'language, critical in the Latin.'...'The traditionary Latin of 'scholars' has 'created in a manner a vocabulary of its own.' This is the principle laid down by Shilleto in the preface to his edition of Demosthenes *On the Embassy*, and it could not have been better exemplified than by his own practice in that celebrated book. He felt, as everyone must, the occasional difficulty of drawing the line between 'critical' and 'explanatory.' But the fact is that the difficulty becomes serious only if we try to make the line a hard-and-fast one. Practically, it can nearly always be solved by a little exercise of discretion. When both sets of notes are on the same page, no real inconvenience can arise in cases where either department slightly overlaps the other.

In a later part of this edition, when dealing in short essays with other matters of general interest in relation to Sophocles,

I propose to give an outline of Sophoclean bibliography, with some attempt to estimate the distinctive excellences of the principal works. The subject is a large one, as a single fact may serve to show. In 1874 Dr Hermann Genthe, the reviser of Ellendt's lexicon, published an index to writings illustrative of Sophocles which had appeared, chiefly in Germany, since 1836. The index, a book of 134 pages, does not include editions, whether of single plays, or of all; yet the author can enumerate 801 books, dissertations, or critical articles, all published between 1836 and 1874, and representing upwards of 430 writers. Even in 1874 it would have been possible to make numerous additions to this catalogue from English sources, which Dr Genthe had left nearly untouched : now, in 1883, the increment from all sources would be very considerable. Here, I must be content to mention those editions which, out of a larger number, have in this play been my more constant companions. They are those of Hermann, Wunder, Dindorf, Schneidewin (as revised by Nauck), Blaydes, Campbell, Kennedy. Other editions, commentaries, and writings of various kinds will be found cited on particular points in the critical notes, the commentary, or the appendix.

It is a particular pleasure to me here—and all the greater, because on a few points I have ventured to differ from its interpretations—to commend to all students of this play the edition of Professor Kennedy, in which, as it is unnecessary for me to say, they will trace the hand of the master.

Nor can I mention the most recent English edition of Sophocles without saying how far it is alike from my anticipation and from my desire that the present edition should divert a single reader from the work, in so many senses admirable, of Professor Campbell. The high place which he has justly won among the English scholars who have deserved well of Sophocles is one from which no successor could remove him, and which every worthy successor will most earnestly desire that he should retain. Students will find in his work much which the present does not give,—much which it could not give; they will also recognise the impress of personal qualities which are not more appreciated by his friends than they are significant of the best graces which humane studies can impart to the mind and character.

In the Metrical Analysis I notice my obligations to Dr J. H. Heinrich Schmidt's *Kunstformen*, and more especially to the fourth volume of that work, the *Griechische Metrik;* also to the aids given by the translator of Schmidt's *Leitfaden*, Dr J. W. White, Assistant Professor of Greek in Harvard University, in his able edition of this play.

To the Librarians of the Bibliothèque Nationale, Paris, the Biblioteca Mediceo-Lorenziana, Florence, the Biblioteca Marciana, Venice, and the Bodleian Library, Oxford, I desire to express my thanks for the courtesy with which every facility was afforded to me for consulting manuscripts of Sophocles.

The proof-sheets of the commentary and of the appendix have been read by Mr C. A. M. Fennell, editor of Pindar, and formerly Fellow of Jesus College, Cambridge; whom I have to thank, not only for the care with which a laborious office was performed, but also for several valuable suggestions made during the progress of the work.

I should be very ungrateful if I closed this preface without recording my sense of the combined rapidity and precision which, in printing a volume of somewhat complex form, have sustained the well-known repute of the Cambridge University Press.

THE COLLEGE, GLASGOW.
November, 1883.

CONTENTS.

INTRODUCTION . . . . page xiii—lii

§ 1. General characteristics of the play and of the fable. § 2. References in the Homeric Poems. § 3. Other epic versions. § 4. Pindar. § 5. The logographers. § 6. The dramatists.—Aeschylus.

§ 7. Sophocles. Original features of his plot. § 8. Imagined antecedents. § 9. Analysis. § 10. Aristotle's criticisms. The element of improbability. § 11. The characters. § 12. Oedipus. § 13. Iocasta. § 14. Teiresias. Creon. § 15. Supposed allusions to contemporary events. Alleged defeat of the play. § 16. The actor Polus. Significance of a story concerning him.

§ 17. Other plays on the subject. § 18. The *Oedipus* of Seneca. § 19. His relation to Sophocles. § 20. The *Oedipe* of Corneille. § 21. The *Oedipus* of Dryden. § 22. The *Oedipe* of Voltaire. § 23. His criticisms. § 24. Essential difference between Sophocles and the moderns. § 25. Their references to a prophetic instinct in Oedipus and Iocasta. § 26. The improbable element—how managed by the moderns.

§ 27. Recent revivals of Greek plays. § 28. The *Oedipus Tyrannus*—a crucial experiment. § 29. The result at Harvard. § 30. *Oedipe Roi* at the Théâtre Français.—Conclusion.

THE TEXT. . . . . liii—lxiii

§ 1. MSS. used. § 2. Deviations from L. § 3. Scope of the critical annotation. § 4. The use of conjecture. § 5. Our text— how transmitted. Its general condition. § 6. Textual criticism should have no bias. § 7. Conjectures of former critics, adopted in this edition. § 8. Conjectures by the editor. § 9. Notation.

METRICAL ANALYSIS . . . . lxiv—xcviii

Preliminary remarks on metre and rhythm . . . lxv—lxviii
The lyrics of the *Oedipus Tyrannus* . . . . lxix—xcvi
Relations of lyric form and matter . . . . xcvi—xcviii

CONTENTS.

ANCIENT ARGUMENTS TO THE PLAY; DRAMATIS PERSONAE;
    STRUCTURE . . . . PP. 3—9

TEXT 10

APPENDIX . . . . 279—310

  Note I. *The Oedipus Tyrannus at Harvard.*—Note II. *V.* 2.
On the meaning of θοᾴετε.—Note III. *Vv.* 44 f.—Note IV. *Vv.*
198 f.— Note V. *Vv.* 219—221.—Note VI. *Vv.* 227 f.— Note VII.
The proposed transposition of vv. 246—251.—Note VIII. *V.* 305.
εἰ καί and καὶ εἰ.—Note IX. *Vv.* 628 f.—Note X. *V.* 361. *The
forms* γνωτός *and* γνωστός.—Note XI. *V.* 478. *The reading of
the first hand in the Laurentian* MS., πετραῖος ὁ ταῦρος.—Note
XII. *V.* 508. *The Sphinx.*—Note XIII. *Vv.* 622—626.—Note
XIV. *V.* 762. ἄποπτος.—Note XV. *V.* 1137. *The significance of
Arcturus in the popular Greek calendar.*—Note XVI. *V.* 1505. περί
before a vowel in composition.—Note XVII. *V.* 1526.

INDICES . . . . 311—327

CORRIGENDA.

PAGE 8, lines 5, 6. For 463—511, read 463—512 (as also in p. 97, l. 3 from
      bottom, and p. 98, l. 14 from bottom): and for 512—862 read 513—
      862 (as also on p. 106, l. 11 from bottom).

,, 82, critical note, l. 2. For γέ μου read γ᾽ ἐμοῦ.

,, 102, line 6 of Greek text. Transfer the second ἤ to the beginning of the next
     line.

,, 115, bottom line. After 'cp.', insert 133.

,, 164, crit. note, l. 2, *first word.* For ἄποτμον read ἀπότομον.

,, 169, crit. note, l. 1, for θεῷ read θυμῷ.

,, 176, crit. note, l. 2, insert του after τέθνηκε.

,, 203, crit. note, l. 1, for *de monstrare* read *demonstrare.*

,, 225, bottom line, for περιστύλον read περίστυλον.

INTRODUCTION.

§ 1. THE *Oedipus Tyrannus* is in one sense the masterpiece of Attic Tragedy. No other shows an equal degree of art in the development of the plot; and this excellence depends on the powerful and subtle drawing of the characters. Modern drama, where minor parts can be multiplied and scene changed at will, can more easily divorce the two kinds of merit. Some of Voltaire's plays, for instance, not first-rate in other ways, are models of ingenious construction. The conditions of the Greek stage left less room for such a result. In the *Oedipus Tyrannus* the highest constructive skill is seen to be intimately and necessarily allied with the vivid delineation of a few persons. Here it is peculiarly interesting to recover, so far as we can, the form in which the story of Oedipus came to Sophocles; to remark what he has altered or added; and to see how the same subject has been handled by other dramatists.

The essence of the myth is the son slaying his unknown father, and thereby fulfilling a decree of fate. The subsequent marriage, if not an original part of the story, seems to have been an early addition. The central ideas are, (1) the irresistible power of destiny, and (2) the sacredness of the primary natural ties, as measured by the horror of an unconscious sin against it. The direct and simple form in which these ideas are embodied gives the legend an impress of high antiquity. This might be illustrated by a comparison with the story of Sohrab and Rustum as told in Mr Matthew Arnold's beautiful poem. The slaying of the unknown son by the father is there surrounded with a pathos and a chivalrous tenderness which

have no counterpart in the grim simplicity of the Oedipus myth,
as it appears in its earliest known shape.

§ 2.   The *Iliad*, which knows the war of Polyneices and his
allies against Thebes (4. 378), once glances at the tale of
Oedipus—where Mecisteus, father of Euryalus, is said to have
visited Thebes in order to attend the funeral games which were
celebrated after the death of Oedipus (23. 679 f.) :—

> ὅς ποτε Θήβασδ' ἦλθε δεδουπότος Οἰδιπόδαο
> ἐς τάφον,—

—'who came to Thebes of yore, when Oedipus had fallen, to his
burying.'

The word δεδουπότος plainly refers to a violent death in
fight, or at the hand of an assassin ; it would not be in accord
with the tone of epic language to understand it as a figurative
phrase for a sudden fall from greatness.   But more than this the
Iliad does not tell.   The poet of the 23rd book imagines
Oedipus as having died by violence, and received burial at
Thebes, in the generation before the Trojan war.

The Nekyia in the *Odyssey* gives the earliest sketch of an
integral story (11. 271 ff.) :—

> Μητέρα τ' Οἰδιπόδαο ἴδον, καλὴν Ἐπικάστην,
> ἣ μέγα ἔργον ἔρεξεν ἀϊδρείῃσι νόοιο
> γημαμένη ᾧ υἱεῖ· ὃ δ' ὃν πατέρ' ἐξεναρίξας
> γῆμεν· ἄφαρ δ' ἀνάπυστα θεοὶ θέσαν ἀνθρώποισιν.
> ἀλλ' ὁ μὲν ἐν Θήβῃ πολυηράτῳ ἄλγεα πάσχων
> Καδμείων ἤνασσε θεῶν ὀλοὰς διὰ βουλάς·
> ἡ δ' ἔβη εἰς Ἀΐδαο πυλάρταο κρατεροῖο,
> ἀψαμένη βρόχον αἰπὺν ἀρ' ὑψηλοῖο μελάθρου,
> ᾧ ἄχεϊ σχομένη· τῷ δ' ἄλγεα κάλλιπ' ὀπίσσω
> πολλὰ μάλ', ὅσσα τε μητρὸς Ἐρινύες ἐκτελέουσιν.

'And I saw the mother of Oedipodes, fair Epicastè, who wrought a
dread deed with unwitting mind, in that she wedded her son ; but he
had slain his father ere he wedded her ; and presently the gods made
these things known among men.   Yet he still ruled over the Cadmeans
in lovely Thebes, suffering anguish by the dire counsels of the gods ;
but she went to the house of Hades, the strong warder, when she had
fastened a noose on high from the roof-beam, possessed by her pain ;

and to him she bequeathed sorrows full many, even all that a mother's Avengers bring to pass.'

With regard to this outline in the *Odyssey*, it is to be noted that it ignores (*a*) the deliverance of Thebes from the Sphinx—though this may be implied in the marriage with Epicastè : (*b*) the self-blinding of Oedipus : (*c*) the expulsion of Oedipus from Thebes—herein agreeing with the indication in the *Iliad*. It further seems to exclude the notion of Epicastè having borne children to Oedipus, since the discovery followed 'presently' on the union,—unless, indeed, by ἄφαρ the poet merely meant 'suddenly.'

§ 3. Lost poems of Hesiod may have touched on the story of Oedipus; but in his extant work there is only a passing reference to the war at Thebes (between Polyneices and Eteocles), in which heroes fell, 'fighting for the flocks of Oedipus.' Hesiod knows the Sphinx as the daughter of Echidna and as the pest of Thebes[1]. Other epic versions.

But the story of Oedipus was fully treated in some of those lost epics which dealt with the Theban cycle of myths. One of these was the '*Oedipodeia*,' Οἰδιπόδεια (ἔπη). According to this, the four children of Oedipus were not borne by Iocasta, but by a second wife, Euryganeia. Pausanias, who follows this account, does not know the author of the poem[2]. It will be observed that this epic agrees with the *Odyssey* in not making Iocasta bear issue to Oedipus. It is by Attic writers, so far as we know, that she was first described as doing so. Poets or logographers who desired to preserve the favour of Dorians had a reason for avoiding that version. There were houses which traced their line from the children of Oedipus,—as Theron, tyrant of Acragas,

---

[1] Hes. *Op.* 162: war slew the heroes, τοὺς μὲν ἐφ' ἑπταπύλῳ Θήβῃ...μαρναμένους μήλων ἕνεκ' Οἰδιπόδαο. The Sphinx: *Theog.* 326, ἡ δ' (Echidna) ἄρα Φῖκ' ὀλοὴν τέκε, Καδμείοισιν ὄλεθρον. The hill near Thebes on which the Sphinx sat was called Φίκειον ὄρος. References in lost Hesiodic poems: schol. on *Il.* 23. 680.

[2] He speaks merely of ὁ τὰ ἔπη ποιήσας ἃ Οἰδιπόδεια ὀνομάζουσι (9. 5. 11). But the inscription known as the 'marmor Borgianum' refers it to Cinaethon, a Lacedaemonian poet who treated epically the Dorian family legends, and who is said to have flourished about 775 B.C. Pausanias, however, who quotes Cinaethon on several points of genealogy, certainly did not regard the *Oedipodeia* as his work.

claimed descent from Thersandros, son of Polyneices[1]. To represent these children as the offspring of an incestuous union would have been to declare the stream polluted at its source.

We learn from Proclus that in the epic called the *Cyprian Lays* (Κύπρια), which included the preparations for the Trojan war, Nestor related 'the story of Oedipus' (τὰ περὶ Οἰδίπουν) in the course of a digression (ἐν παρεκβάσει) which comprised also the madness of Heracles, as well as the story of Theseus and Ariadne. This was probably one of the sources used by the Attic dramatists. Another source, doubtless more fertile in detail, was the epic entitled the *Thebaid* (Θηβαΐς), and now usually designated as the 'Cyclic Thebaid,' to distinguish it from a later epic of the same name by Antimachus of Colophon, the contemporary of Euripides. Only about 20 verses remain from it[2]. The chief fragment relates to the curse pronounced by Oedipus on his sons. They had broken his strict command by setting on his table the wine-cups (ἐκπώματα) used by Laïus; and he invoked a curse upon them:—

αἶψα δὲ παισὶν ἑοῖσι μετ' ἀμφοτέροισιν ἐπαρὰς
ἀργαλέας ἠρᾶτο· θεὸν δ' οὐ λάνθαν' Ἐρινῦν·
ὡς οὔ οἱ πατρώϊ' ἐνηείῃ φιλότητος
δάσσαιντ', ἀμφοτέροισι δ' ἔοι πόλεμός τε μάχαι τε.

'And straightway, while his two sons were by, he uttered dire curses,—and the Avenging goddess failed not to hear them,—that they should divide their heritage in no kindly spirit, but that war and strife should be ever between them.'

This *Thebaid*—tracing the operation of a curse through the whole history of the house—must have had an important share in moulding the conception of the Aeschylean trilogy.

Pindar. §4. Pindar touches on the story of Oedipus in *Ol.* 2. 35 ff. Destiny has often brought evil fortune after good,—

ἐξ οὗπερ ἔκτεινε Λᾷον μόριμος υἱὸς
συναντόμενος, ἐν δὲ Πυθῶνι χρησθὲν
παλαίφατον τέλεσσεν.

---

[1] Pind. *Ol.* 2. 35.
[2] See the Didot ed. of the Cyclic fragments, p. 587.

ἰδοῖσα δ᾽ ὀξεῖ᾽ Ἐρινὺς
ἔπεφνέ οἱ σὺν ἀλλαλοφονίᾳ γένος ἀρήιον—

'— from the day when his doomed son met Laïus and killed him, and accomplished the word given aforetime at Pytho. But the swift Erinnys beheld it, and slew his warlike sons, each by the other's sword.'

Here the Fury is represented as destroying the sons in direct retribution for the parricide, not in answer to the imprecation of Oedipus. A fragment of Pindar alludes to the riddle of the Sphinx, and he uses 'the wisdom of Oedipus' to denote counsel wrapped in dark sayings,—since the skill which solves riddling speech can weave it[1].

§ 5. The logographers could not omit the story of Oedipus The logo-in a systematic treatment of the Theban myths. Hellanicus of graphers. Mitylene (circ. 450 B.C.) is mentioned by the scholiast on the *Phoenissae* (61) as agreeing with Euripides in regard to the self-blinding of Oedipus[2]. The contemporary Pherecydes of Leros (usually called 'Athenian' since Athens was his home) treated the legends of Thebes in the fifth of ten books forming a comprehensive survey of Greek tradition[3]. According to him, Iocasta bore two sons to Oedipus, who were slain by the Minyae: but, as in the *Oedipodeia*, his second wife Euryganeia bore Eteocles and Polyneices, Antigone and Ismene. This seems to be the earliest known version which ascribes issue to the marriage of Iocasta with Oedipus.

§ 6. However incomplete this sketch may be relatively to The dram-the materials which existed in the early part of the fifth century atists. B.C., it may at least serve to suggest the general conditions under which Tragedy entered on the treatment of the subject. The story of Oedipus, defined in its main features by a tradition older than the *Odyssey*, had been elaborated in the epics of later poets

---

[1] Pind. fr. 62 αἴνιγμα παρθένου | ἐξ ἀγριᾶν γνάθων: *Pyth.* 4. 263 τὰν Οἰδιπόδα σοφίαν. Pindar's elder contemporary Corinna had sung of Oedipus as delivering Thebes not only from the Sphinx but also from τὴν Τευμησσίαν ἀλώπεκα—a fox from the Boeotian village of Teumessus: but we hear no more of this less formidable pest. (Bergk, *Poet. Lyr.* p. 949.)

[2] Müller, *Frag. Histor.* I. 85.

[3] Müller, *ib.* I. 48.

and the prose of chroniclers. There were versions differing in detail, and allowing scope for selection. While the great outlines were constant, minor circumstances might be adapted to the dramatist's chosen view.

Aeschylus, Sophocles, and Euripides agree in a trait which does not belong to any extant version before theirs. Iocasta, not Euryganeia, is the mother of Eteocles and Polyneices, Antigone and Ismene. They agree also in connecting the doom of the two brothers with a curse pronounced by Oedipus. Neither the scanty fragments[1] which alone represent the *Oedipus* of Euripides, nor the hints in the *Phoenissae*, enable us to determine the distinctive features of his treatment. With regard to Aeschylus, though our knowledge is very meagre, it suffices at least to show the broad difference between his plan and that of Sophocles.

Aeschylus. Aeschylus treated the story of Oedipus as he treated the story of Agamemnon. Oedipus became the foremost figure of a trilogy which traced the action of an inherited curse in the house of Labdacus, even as the Oresteia traced the action of such a curse in the house of Pelops. That trilogy consisted of the

---

[1] Nauck *Eur. Fragm.* 544—561, to which Unger adds Soph. *fr. incert.* 663, Meineke *adespota* 107, 309, others *adesp.* 6. Almost all the verses are commonplaces. From fr. 546, 547 I should conjecture that the Creon of Eur. defended himself against a charge of treason in a passage parallel with Soph. *O. T.* 583—615. One fragment of two lines is curious (545): ἡμεῖς δὲ Πολύβου παῖδ' ἐρείσαντες πέδῳ | ἐξομματοῦμεν καὶ διόλλυμεν κόρας. Quoting these, the schol. on Eur. *Ph.* 61 says: ἐν δὲ τῷ Οἰδίποδι οἱ Λαΐου θεράποντες ἐτύφλωσαν αὐτόν. This would seem to mean that, after the discovery, the old retainers of Laïus blinded Oedipus—for the schol. is commenting on the verse which says that he was blinded by *himself.* But the tragic force of the incident depends wholly on its being the king's own frantic act. I incline to suspect some error on the scholiast's part, which a knowledge of the context might possibly have disclosed.

From the prologue of the *Phoenissae* it appears that Eur. imagined Oedipus to have been found on Cithaeron by the ἱπποβούκολοι of Polybus, and taken by them to the latter's wife. The Iocasta of Eur. herself relates in that play how, when the sons of Oed. grew up, they held him a prisoner in the palace at Thebes—that the disgrace might be hidden from men's eyes. It was then that he pronounced a curse upon them. When they have fallen, fighting for the throne, Iocasta kills herself over their bodies, and Creon then expels Oedipus from Thebes. The mutilated ὑπόθεσις to the *Phoenissae* does not warrant us in supposing that the *Oenomaus* and *Chrysippus* of Eur.,—the latter containing the curse of Pelops on Laïus—formed a trilogy with his *Oedipus.*

Laïus, the *Oedipus*, and the extant *Seven against Thebes;* the satyric drama being the *Sphinx.* From the *Laïus* only a few words remain; from the *Oedipus*, three verses; but some general idea of the *Oedipus* may be gathered from a passage in the *Seven against Thebes* (772—791). Oedipus had been pictured by Aeschylus, as he is pictured by Sophocles, at the height of fame and power. He who had delivered Thebes from 'the devouring pest' (τὰν ἁρπαξάνδραν κῆρα) was admired by all Thebans as the first of men. 'But when, hapless one, he came to knowledge of his ill-starred marriage, impatient of his pain, with frenzied heart he wrought a twofold ill': he blinded himself, and called down on his sons this curse, that one day they should divide their heritage with the sword. 'And now I tremble lest the swift Erinnys bring it to pass.'

Hence we see that the *Oedipus* of Aeschylus included the imprecation of Oedipus upon his sons. This was essential to the poet's main purpose, which was to exhibit the continuous action of the Erinnys in the house. Similarly the *Laïus* doubtless included the curse called down on Laïus by Pelops, when bereft by him of his son Chrysippus. The true climax of the Aeschylean *Oedipus* would thus have consisted, not in the discovery alone, but in the discovery followed by the curse. And we may safely infer that the process of discovery indicated in the *Seven against Thebes* by the words ἐπεὶ δ᾽ ἀρτίφρων | ἐγένετο...γάμων (778) was not comparable with that in the play of Sophocles. It was probably much more abrupt, and due to some of those more mechanical devices which were ordinarily employed to bring about a 'recognition' on the stage. The *Oedipus* of Aeschylus, however brilliant, was only a link in a chain which derived its essential unity from 'the mindful Erinnys.'

§ 7. The *Oedipus Tyrannus* of Sophocles was not part of a Sophocles. trilogy, but a work complete in itself. The proper climax of such a work was the discovery, considered in its immediate effects, not in its ulterior consequences. Here the constructive art of the dramatist would be successful in proportion as the discovery was naturally prepared, approached by a process of rising interest, and attended in the moment of fulfilment with the most

J. S.   *c*

astounding reversal of a previous situation. In regard to the
structure of the plot, this is what Sophocles has achieved. Before
giving an analysis of his plot, we must notice two features of it
which are due to his own invention.

(1) According to previous accounts, the infant Oedipus,
when exposed on Mount Cithaeron, had been found by herds-
men, and reared either in Southern Boeotia, or at Sicyon, a place
associated with the worship of the Eumenides. Sophocles
makes the Theban herd of Laïus give the babe to the herd
of Polybus, king of Corinth, who rears it as his own. Thus are
prepared the two convergent threads of evidence which meet in
the final discovery. And thus, too, the belief of Oedipus concerning his own parentage becomes to him a source, first of
anxiety, then of dread, then of hope—in contrast, at successive
moments, with that reality which the spectators know.

(2) The only verses remaining from the *Oedipus* of Aeschylus
show that in that drama Oedipus encountered and slew Laïus at
a meeting of three roads near Potniae, a place in Boeotia, on the
road leading from Thebes to Plataea. At the ruins of this place
Pausanias saw 'a grove of Demeter and Persephone'[1]. It appears to have been sacred also to those other and more terrible
goddesses who shared with these the epithet of πότνιαι,—the
Eumenides (ποτνιάδες θεαί, Eur. *Or.* 318). For the purpose of
Aeschylus, no choice of a scene could have been more fitting.
The father and son, doomed by the curse in their house, are
brought together at a spot sacred to the Erinnyes:—

ἐπῆμεν τῆς ὁδοῦ τροχήλατον
σχιστῆς κελεύθου τρίοδον, ἔνθα συμβολὰς
τριῶν κελεύθων Ποτνιάδων ἠμείβομεν[2].

'We were coming in our journey to the spot from which three high-
roads part, where we must pass by the junction of triple ways at Potniae.'

But for Sophocles this local fitness did not exist. For him,
the supernatural agency which dominates the drama is not that
of the Furies, but of Apollo. He transfers the scene of the
encounter from the 'three roads' at Potniae to the 'three roads'

---

[1] ἄλσος Δήμητρος καὶ Κόρης, 9. 8. 1.
[2] Aesch. fr. 167 (Nauck).

near Daulia[1] in Phocis. The 'branching ways' of Potniae can no longer be traced. But in the Phocian pass a visitor can still feel how the aspect of nature is in unison with the deed of which Sophocles has made it the theatre[2]. This change of locality has something more than the significance of a detail. It symbolises the removal of the action from the control of the dark Avenging Powers to a region within the influence of that Delphian god who is able to disclose and to punish impurity, but who will also give final rest to the wanderer, final absolution to the weary mourner of unconscious sin.

§ 8. The events which had preceded the action of the *Oedipus Tyrannus* are not set forth, after the fashion of Euripides, in a formal prologue. They have to be gathered from incidental hints in the play itself. It is an indispensable aid to the full comprehension of the drama that we should first connect these hints into a brief narrative of its antecedents as imagined by Sophocles.

Supposed anteced-ents of the plot.

Laïus, king of Thebes, being childless, asked the oracle of Apollo at Delphi whether it was fated that a son should be born to him. The answer was, 'I will give thee a son, but it is doomed that thou leave the sunlight by the hands of thy child : for thus hath spoken Zeus, son of Cronus, moved by the dread curse of Pelops, whose own son (Chrysippus) thou didst snatch from him; and he prayed all this for thee.' When a son was indeed born to Laïus of Iocasta his wife, three days after the birth he caused it to be exposed in the wilds of Mount Cithaeron. An iron pin was driven through the feet of the babe, fastening them together, —that, if perchance it should live to be found by a stranger, he might have the less mind to rear a child so maimed ; from which maiming the child was afterwards called *Oedipus*[3].

The man chosen to expose the babe received it from the hands of the mother, Iocasta herself, with the charge to destroy it. This man was a slave born in the house of Laïus, and so belonging to the class of slaves whom their masters usually treated

---

[1] *Daulis* was the Homeric form of the name, *Daulia* the post-homeric (Strabo 9. 423).

[2] See the note on verse 733.

[3] The incident of the pierced feet was evidently invented to explain the name Οἰδίπους ('Swellfoot,' as Shelley renders it). In v. 397 ὁ μηδὲν εἰδὼς Οἰδίπους suggests a play on οἶδα.

with most confidence. He was employed in tending the flocks of Laïus on Mount Cithaeron, where they were pastured during the half-year from March to September.

In the glens of Cithaeron he had consorted with another herdsman, servant to Polybus, king of Corinth. Seized with pity for the babe, the Theban gave it to this herdsman of Polybus, who took it to Corinth. Polybus and his wife Meropè were childless. They reared the child as their own; the Corinthians regarded him as heir to the throne; and he grew to man's estate without doubting that he was the true son of the Corinthian king and queen.

But one day it chanced that at a feast a man heated with wine threw out a word which sank into the young prince's mind; he questioned the king and queen, whose resentment of the taunt comforted him; yet he felt that a whisper was creeping abroad; and he resolved to ask the truth from Apollo himself at Delphi. Apollo gave him no answer to the question touching his parentage, but told him these things—that he was doomed to slay his father, and to defile his mother's bed.

He turned away from Delphi with the resolve never again to see his home in Corinth; and took the road which leads eastward through Phocis to Boeotia.

At that moment Laïus was on his way from Thebes to Delphi, where he wished to consult the oracle. He was not escorted by the usual armed following of a king, but only by four attendants. The party of five met Oedipus at a narrow place near the 'Branching Roads' in Phocis; a quarrel occurred; and Oedipus slew Laïus, with three of his four attendants. The fourth escaped, and fled to Thebes with the tale that *a band of robbers* had fallen upon their company. This sole survivor was the very man who, long years before, had been charged by Laïus and Iocasta to expose their infant son on Cithaeron.

The Thebans vainly endeavoured to find some clue to the murder of Laïus. But, soon after his death, their attention was distracted by a new trouble. The goddess Hera—hostile to Thebes as the city of her rival Semelè—sent the Sphinx to afflict it,—a monster with the face of a maiden and the body of a winged lion; who sat on a hill near Thebes (the Φίκειον ὄρος), and chanted a riddle. 'What is the creature which is two-footed, three-footed, and four-footed; and weakest when it has most feet?' Every failure to find the answer cost the Thebans a life. Hope was deserting them; even the seer Teiresias had no help to give; when the wandering stranger, Oedipus, arrived. He solved the enigma by the word *man*: the Sphinx hurled herself from a rock; and the grateful Thebans gave the vacant throne to their deliverer as a free gift. At the same time he married Iocasta, the widow of Laïus, and sister of Creon son of Menoeceus.

The sole survivor from the slaughter of Laïus and his company was at Thebes when the young stranger Oedipus ascended the throne. The man presently sought an audience of the queen Iocasta, knelt to her, and, touching her hand in earnest supplication, entreated that he might be sent to his old occupation of tending flocks in far-off pastures. It seemed a small thing for so old and faithful a servant to ask; and it was readily granted.

An interval of about sixteen years may be assumed between these events and the moment at which the *Oedipus Tyrannus* opens. Iocasta has borne four children to Oedipus: Eteocles, Polyneices, Antigone, Ismene. Touches in the closing scene of the play forbid us to suppose that the poet imagines the daughters as much above the age of thirteen and twelve respectively. Oedipus has become thoroughly established as the great king, the first of men, to whose wisdom Thebans turn in every trouble.

And now a great calamity has visited them. A blight is upon the fruits of the earth; cattle are perishing in the pastures; the increase of the womb is denied; and a fiery pestilence is ravaging the town. While the fumes of incense are rising to the gods from every altar, and cries of anguish fill the air, a body of suppliants—aged priests, youths, and children—present themselves before the wise king. He, if any mortal, can help them. It is here that the action opens.

§ 9. The drama falls into six main divisions or chapters. Analysis The following analysis exhibits in outline the mechanism of the of the plot, which deserves study.

I. *Prologue:* 1—150. Oedipus appears as the great prince whom the Thebans rank second only to the gods. He pledges

himself to relieve his afflicted people by seeking the murderer of
Laïus.

Parodos: 151—215. The Chorus bewail the pestilence and
invoke the gods.

II. *First Episode:* 216—462. Oedipus publicly invokes a
solemn curse upon the unknown murderer of Laïus. At Creon's
suggestion he sends for the seer Teiresias, who refuses to speak,
but finally, stung by taunts, denounces Oedipus himself as the
slayer.

First Stasimon: 463—512. The Chorus forebode that the
unknown murderer is doomed; they refuse to believe the
unproved charge brought by the seer.

III. *Second Episode:* 513—862. Creon protests against the
suspicion that he has suborned Teiresias to accuse Oedipus.
Oedipus is unconvinced. Iocasta stops the quarrel, and Creon
departs. Oedipus then tells her that he has been charged with
the murder of Laïus. She replies that' he need feel no dis-
quietude. Laïus, according to an oracle, was to have been slain
by his own son; but the babe was exposed on the hills; and
Laïus was actually slain by *robbers, at the meeting of three roads.*

This mention of *three roads* (v. 716) strikes the first note of
alarm in the mind of Oedipus.

He questions her as to (1) the place, (2) the time, (3) the person and the company of Laïus. All confirm his fear that *he*
has unwittingly done the deed.

He tells her his whole story—the taunt at Corinth—the visit
to Delphi—the encounter in Phocis. But he has still one hope.
The attendant of Laïus who escaped spoke of *robbers*, not of one
robber.

Let this survivor—now a herdsman—be summoned and
questioned.

Second Stasimon: 863—910. The Chorus utter a prayer
against arrogance—such as the king's towards Creon; and
impiety—such as they find in Iocasta's mistrust of oracles.

IV. *Third Episode:* 911—1085. A messenger from Corinth
announces that Polybus is dead, and that Oedipus is now king

designate. Iocasta and Oedipus exult in the refutation of the oracle which had destined Oedipus to slay his sire.

But Oedipus still dreads the other predicted horror—union with his mother.

The messenger, on learning this, discloses that Polybus and Meropè were not the parents of Oedipus. The messenger himself, when a herdsman in the service of Polybus, had found the infant Oedipus on Cithaeron, and had brought him to Corinth. Yet no—not *found* him; had *received* him *from another herdsman* (v. 1040).

Who was this other herdsman? The Corinthian replies:— He was said to be one of the people of Laïus.

Iocasta implores Oedipus to search no further. He answers that he cares not how lowly his birth may prove to be—he will search to the end. With a cry of despair, Iocasta rushes away.

Third Stasimon: 1086—1109. The Chorus joyously foretell that Oedipus will prove to be a native of the land—perchance of seed divine.

V. *Fourth Episode:* 1110—1185. The Theban herdsman is brought in[1].

'There,' says the Corinthian, 'is the man who gave me the child.' Bit by bit, the whole truth is wrung from the Theban. 'The babe was the son of Laïus; the wife of Laïus gave her to me.' Oedipus knows all, and with a shriek of misery he rushes away.

Fourth Stasimon: 1186—1222. The Chorus bewail the great king's fall.

VI. *Exodus:* 1223—1530. A messenger from the house announces that Iocasta has hanged herself, and that Oedipus has put out his eyes. Presently Oedipus is led forth. With passionate lamentation he beseeches the Chorus of Theban Elders to banish or slay him.

Creon comes to lead him into the house. Oedipus obtains

---

[1] The original object of sending for him had been to ask,—'Was it the deed of several men, or of one?'—a last refuge. But he is not interrogated on that point. Voltaire criticised this as inconsistent. It is better than consistent; it is natural. A more urgent question has thrust the other out of sight.

from him a promise of care for his young daughters; they are presently brought to their father, who takes what he intends to be a last farewell. For he craves to be sent out of the land; but Creon replies that Apollo must pronounce.

As Creon leads Oedipus within, the Chorus speak the closing words: No mortal must be called happy on this side death.

The method of discovery.
With reference to the general structure of the plot, the first point to observe is the skill with which Sophocles has managed those two threads of proof which he created by his invention of the second herdsman.

We have :—

(1) The thread of evidence from the reported statement of the Theban herdsman as to the *place* of the murder, in connection with Iocasta's statement as to the time, the person of Laïus, and the retinue. This tends to show that Oedipus has slain Laïus—*being presumably in no wise his kinsman.* The proof of Oedipus having slain Laïus is so far completed at 754 (αἰαῖ, τάδ᾽ ἤδη διαφανῆ) as to leave no longer any moral doubt on the mind of Oedipus himself.

(2) The thread of evidence from the Corinthian, showing, in the first instance, that Oedipus is *not* the son of Polybus and Meropè, and so relieving him from the fear of parricide and incest. Hence the confident tone of Oedipus (1076 ff.), which so powerfully contrasts with the despair of Iocasta : *she* has known the worst from v. 1044.

(3) The convergence of these two threads, when the Theban herdsman is confronted with the Corinthian. This immediately follows the moment of relief just noticed. It now appears that the slayer of Laïus has *also* committed parricide and incest.

Aristotle's criticisms.
§ 10. The frequent references of Aristotle to the *Oedipus Tyrannus* indicate its value for him as a typical masterpiece, though the points for which he commends it concern general analysis of form, not the essence of its distinctive excellence. The points are these :—

1. The 'recognition' (ἀναγνώρισις) is contrived in the best way; *i.e.*, it is coincident with a reversal of fortunes (περιπέτεια).

2. This reversal is peculiarly impressive, because the Corinthian messenger had come to bring tidings of the honour in store for Oedipus.

3. Oedipus is the most effective kind of subject for such a reversal, because he had been (*a*) great and glorious, (*b*) *not* preeminently virtuous or just, (*c*) and, again, one whose reverses are not due to crime, but only to unconscious error.

4. The story is told in such a manner as to excite pity and terror by hearing without seeing (as in regard to the exposure of the child, the killing of Laïus, the death of Iocasta).

5. If there is any improbability in the story, this is not in the plot itself (ἐν τοῖς πράγμασιν), but in the supposed antecedents (ἔξω τῆς τραγῳδίας).

In this last comment, Aristotle indicates a trait which is certainly open to criticism — the ignorance of Oedipus as to the story of Laïus. He knows, indeed, the name of his predecessor—though Creon does not think it unnecessary to remind him of the name (103). He also knows that Laïus had met a violent death: but he does not know whether this had befallen at Thebes, or in its neighbourhood, or abroad (109—113). Nor does he know that Laïus was reported to have been slain by robbers, and that only one of his followers had escaped (116—123): and he asks if no search had been made at the time (128, 566). Iocasta, who has now been his wife for many years, tells him, as if for the first time, the story of the oracle given to Laïus, and he tells her the story of his own early fortunes— though here we need not press the fact that he even names to her his Corinthian parents : that may be regarded as merely a formal preface to a connected narrative. It may be conceded that the matters of which Oedipus is supposed ignorant were themes of which Iocasta, and all the persons about the new king, might well have been reluctant to speak. Still it is evident that the measure of past reticence imagined, both on their part and on his, exceeds the limit of verisimilitude. The true defence of this improbability consists in frankly recognising it. Exquisite as was the dramatic art exercised within the scope of the action (ἐν τοῖς πράγμασι), this art was still so far naïve as to feel no offence at some degree of freedom in the treatment of that

Improbability in the antecedents.

thus a negative witness to the mastery shown by the artist who could construct such a drama as the *Oedipus Tyrannus* with such materials. The modern dramatists, as we shall see, teach the same lesson in a more positive form. Walter Scott's estimate of Seneca's *Oedipus* needs modification, but is just in the main. 'Though devoid of fancy and of genius,' he says, it 'displays the masculine eloquence and high moral sentiment of its author; and if it does not interest us in the scene of fiction, it often compels us to turn our thoughts inward, and to study our own hearts.' Seneca's fault, however, so far as the plot is concerned, seems less that he fails to interest, than that, by introducing the necromantic machinery, and by obliterating the finer moral traits of his Greek original, he has rendered the interest rather 'sensational' than properly dramatic[1].

The *Oedipe* of Corneille.
§ 20. The *Oedipe* of Corneille was produced at Paris in 1657. After an interval which followed the unfavourable reception of his *Pertharite* in 1653, it was with the *Oedipe* that Corneille returned to the theatre, at the instance of his patron, Nicolas Fouquet, to whom it is dedicated. It is immaterial for our purpose that this play is far from exhibiting Corneille at his best; nor need we here inquire what precise rank is to be assigned to it among his less successful works. For the student of Sophocles, it has the permanent interest of showing how the subject of the *Oedipus Tyrannus* was adapted to the modern stage by a typical artist of the French classical school. The severely simple theme of Sophocles, with its natural elements of pity and terror, is found too meagre by the modern dramatist. He cannot trust to that alone; he feels that he needs some further source of variety and relief. To supply this, he interweaves an underplot of secondary persons—'the happy episode of the loves of Theseus and Dircè.' Theseus is the king of Athens; Dircè is a daughter of the deceased Laïus.

The drama opens with a love-scene, in which Theseus is

---

[1] A small trait may be noticed as amusingly characteristic of the Roman poet of the Empire. The Laïus of Sophocles goes to Delphi βαιός—with only four attendants (752). Seneca makes Laïus *set out* with the proper retinue of a king;—but most of them lose their way. *Plures fefellit error ancipitis viae: Paucos fidelis curribus iunxit labor.*

so heavily upon both. Sophocles had found in human nature itself the sanction of 'the unwritten laws,' and the seal of faith in a beneficence immortal and eternal; but his personal attitude towards the 'sceptical' currents of thought in his age was never, so far as we can judge, that of admonitory protest or dogmatic reproof. It was his temperament to look around him for elements of conciliation, to evoke gentle and mediating influences, rather than to make war on the forces which he regarded as sinister:—it might be said of him, as of a person in one of his own plays, οὔτοι συνέχθειν ἀλλὰ συμφιλεῖν ἔφυ. But is there any reason to think that the *Oedipus Tyrannus* marks a moment when this mind—'which saw life steadily, and saw it whole'—was partly shaken in its self-centred calm by the consciousness of a spiritual anarchy around it which seemed fraught with ultimate danger to the cohesion of society, and that a note of solemn warning, addressed to Athens and to Greece, is meant to be heard throughout the drama? Our answer must depend upon the sense in which we conceive that he places Oedipus or Iocasta at issue with religion.

§ 12. As regards Oedipus, it might be said that, in this par-ticular aspect, he is a modern character, and more especially, perhaps, a character of the nineteenth century. The instinct of reverence for the gods was originally fundamental in his nature: it appears in the first act of his manhood—the journey to Delphi. Nor did he for a moment mistrust the gods because the doom assigned to him was bitter. Then he achieved a great intellectual success, reached the most brilliant prosperity, and was ranked by his fellow-men as second to the gods alone. He is not spoiled by his good fortune. We find him, at the opening of the play, neither arrogant nor irreverent; full, rather, of tenderness for his people, full of reverence for the word of Apollo. Suddenly, however, the prophet of Apollo denounces *him*. Instantly his appeal is to the intellect. If it comes to that, what claim has any other human mind to interpose between *his* mind and Heaven? Is he not Oedipus, who silenced the Sphinx? Yes, but presently, gradually, his own mind begins to argue on the other side. No one is so acute as he, and of course he must be the first to see any facts which tell against himself. And now, when he is face to face with the gods, and no prophet stands between, the instinct of reverence inborn in his noble nature finds voice in the prayer, 'Forbid, forbid, ye pure and awful gods, that I should see that day!' After varying hopes and fears, his own mind is convinced of the worst. Reason, which had been the arbiter of faith, now becomes the inexorable judge of sin, the most instant and most rigorous claimant for his absolute abasement before the gods.

Iocasta.

§ 13. Plainly, it would be a mis-reading to construe the fate of Oedipus as a dramatic nemesis of impiety; but the case of Iocasta is at first sight less clear. She, at least, is one who openly avows scorn for oracles, and urges her lord to share it. It may often be noticed—where the dramatist has known how to draw from life—that the true key-note of a dominant mood is struck by a short utterance on which no special emphasis is thrown, just as, in life itself, the sayings most truly significant of character are not always long or marked. For Iocasta, such a key-note is given in the passage where she is telling Oedipus that a response from the Delphian temple had warned Laïus that he was destined to be slain by the child whom she bore to him. 'An oracle came to Laïus once—*I will not say from Phoebus himself, but from his ministers*' (v. 712). Iocasta thoroughly believes in the power of the gods to effect their will (724),—to punish or to save (921). But she does not believe that any mortal—be he priest or prophet—is permitted by them to read the future. Had not the Delphian priests doomed her to sacrifice her first-born child,—and this, without saving the life of her husband, Laïus? The iron which years ago had entered into the soul of the wife and mother has wrought in her a result similar to that which pride of intellect has produced in Oedipus. Like Oedipus, she still believes in the wise omnipotence of the gods; like him also, she is no longer prepared to accept any mortal interpreter of their decrees. Thus are the two foremost persons of this tragedy separated from the offices of human intercession, and directly confronted in spirit—one by his self-reliance, the other by her remembered anguish—with the inscrutable powers which control their fate. It is as a study of the human heart, true for every age, not as a protest against tendencies of the poet's own, that the *Oedipus Tyrannus* illustrates the relation of faith to reason.

§ 14. The central figure of the drama is brought into clearer relief by the characters of Teiresias and Creon. Teiresias exists only for the god whom he serves. Through him Apollo speaks. As opposed to Oedipus, he *is* the divine knowledge of Apollo, opposed to human ignorance and blindness. While 'the servant of Loxias' thus stands above the king of Thebes, Creon stands below him, on the humbler but safer ground of ordinary humanity. Creon is shrewd, cautious, practical, not sentimental or demonstrative, yet of a fervid self-respect, and with a strong and manly kindliness which comes out in the hour of need[1]. It might be said that the Creon of the *Oedipus Tyrannus* embodies a good type of Scottish character, as the Creon of the *Antigone* —an earlier sketch—is rather of the Prussian type, as it is popularly idealised by some of its neighbours. Teiresias is the gauge of human insight matched against divine; Creon, of fortune's heights and depths, compared with the less brilliant but more stable lot of commoner men. 'Crave not to be master in all things; for the mastery which thou didst win hath not followed thee through life'—are his words to Oedipus at the end ; and his own position at the moment exemplifies the sense in which 'the god ever gives the mastery to the middle state'[2].

§ 15. There is no external evidence for the time at which the *Oedipus Tyrannus* was first acted. Internal evidence warrants the belief that it was composed after the *Antigone*, and before the *Oedipus Coloneus*. The probable limits thus indicated might be roughly given as about 439—412 B.C. More than this we cannot say. Modern ingenuity has recognised Pericles in

Teiresias. Creon.

Supposed references to contemporary events.

---

[1] Lest it should be thought that in the note on p. 106 the harsher aspect of Creon's character is unduly prominent, I may observe that this note relates to vv. 512—862, and deals with Creon only as he appears *there*. The scene which begins at v. 1422—and more especially vv. 1476 f.—must of course be taken into account when we offer, as here, a more general estimate of the character.

[2] παντὶ μέσῳ τὸ κράτος θεὸς ὤπασεν, Aesch. *Eum.* 528.

Oedipus,—the stain of Alcmaeonid lineage in his guilt as the
slayer of Laïus,—the 'Dorian war, and a pestilence therewith'
in the afflictions of Thebes. This allegorical hypothesis need
not detain us. But it may be well briefly to remark the difference, for drama, between association of ideas and direct allusion.
If Sophocles had set himself to describe the plague at Athens as
he had known it, it might have been held that, in an artistic
sense, his fault was graver than that of Phrynichus, when, by
representing the capture of Miletus, he ' reminded the Athenians
of their own misfortunes.' If, however, writing at a time subsequent to the pestilence which he had survived, he wished to
give an ideal picture of a plague-stricken town, it would have
been natural and fitting that he should borrow some touches
from his own experience. But the sketch in the play is far too
slight to warrant us in saying that he even did this; perhaps
the reference to the victims of pestilence *tainting the air* (θανατ-
αφόρα v. 180) is the only trait that might suggest it. Thucydides
(II. 50), in describing the plague of 429 B.C., notices the number
of the unburied dead. The remarks just made apply equally to
the supposed allusion in vv. 883 ff. to the mutilation of the
Hermae (see the note on 886).

Alleged
defeat of
the play.

A tradition, dating at least from the 2nd century B.C.[1],
affirmed that, when Sophocles produced the *Oedipus Tyrannus*,
he was defeated for the first prize by Philocles,—a poet of
whose work we know nothing. Philocles was a nephew of
Aeschylus, and, as Aristeides observes[2], achieved an honour which
had been denied to his uncle. The surprise which has been
expressed by some modern writers appears unnecessary; the
composition of Philocles was probably good, and it has never
been held that the judges of such prizes were infallible.

[1] The words in the prose ὑπόθεσις (given on p. 4) are simply, ἡττηθέντα ὑπὸ
Φιλοκλέους, ὥς φησι Δικαίαρχος. The Dicaearchus who wrote ὑποθέσεις τῶν Εὐριπίδου
καὶ Σοφοκλέους μύθων has been generally identified with Dicaearchus of Messana, the
Peripatetic, a pupil of Aristotle and a friend of Theophrastus. We might place
his 'floruit,' then, somewhere about 310 B.C.; there are indications that he survived
296 B.C. If, on the other hand, the ὑποθέσεις were ascribed to the grammarian
Dicaearchus of Lacedaemon, a pupil of Aristarchus, this would bring us to about
140 B.C.
[2] II. 256.

§ 16. The name of an actor, once famous in the chief part of The actor
Polus.
this play, is of interest also on more general grounds. Polus, a
native of Aegina, is said to have been the pupil of another tragic
actor, Archias of Thurii,—the man who in 322 B.C. was sent to
arrest Demosthenes and the other orators whose surrender was
demanded of Athens by Antipater[1]. It would seem, then, that
Polus flourished in the middle or latter part of the 4th century B.C.
—only some 50 or 60 years after the death of Sophocles. Physic-
ally well-gifted, and of versatile grace, he was equally successful
as Oedipus the King, and in the very different but not less difficult
part of Oedipus at Colonus[2]. Like the poet whose masterpieces
he interpreted, he enjoyed a vigorous old age; and it is recorded
that, at seventy, he acted 'eight tragedies in four days'[3]. It will
be remembered that, in the *Electra* of Sophocles, an urn, supposed
to contain the ashes of Orestes, is placed in the hands of his
sister, who makes a lament over it. Polus once acted Electra
not long after the death of his son. An urn, containing the
youth's ashes, was brought from the tomb; the actor, in the
mourning garb of Electra, received it, and, on the scene, suffered
a natural grief to have vehement course[4].

---

[1] Plut. *Dem.* 28 τοῦτον δὲ [Archias] Θούριον ὄντα τῷ γένει λόγος ἔχει τραγῳδίας
ὑποκρίνεσθαί ποτε, καὶ τὸν Αἰγινήτην Πῶλον, τὸν ὑπερβαλόντα τῇ τέχνῃ
πάντας, ἐκείνου γενέσθαι μαθητὴν ἱστοροῦσιν.

[2] Stobaeus *Floril.* p. 522 (XCVII. 28), in an extract from the προτρεπτικαὶ
ὁμιλίαι of Arrian: ἢ οὐχ ὁρᾷς ὅτι οὐκ εὐφωνότερον οὐδὲ ἥδιον ὁ Πῶλος τὸν τύραννον
Οἰδίποδα ὑπεκρίνετο ἢ τὸν ἐπὶ Κολωνῷ ἀλήτην καὶ πτωχόν; (οὐδὲ ἥδιον is Gaisford's
emendation of οὐδὲν δι' ὧν.)

[3] Plut. *Mor.* 785 C Πῶλον δὲ τὸν τραγῳδὸν 'Ερατοσθένης καὶ Φιλόχορος ἱστοροῦσιν
ἑβδομήκοντα ἔτη γεγενημένον ὀκτὼ τραγῳδίας ἐν τέτταρσιν ἡμέραις διαγωνίσασθαι μικρὸν
ἔμπροσθεν τῆς τελευτῆς.

[4] Aulus Gellius 7. 5 Histrio in terra Graecia fuit fama celebri qui gestus et
vocis claritudine ceteris antestabat....Polus lugubri habitu Electrae indutus ossa
atque urnam a sepulcro tulit filii, et quasi Orestis amplexus opplevit omnia non
simulacris neque imitamentis sed luctu atque lamentis veris et spirantibus.

Lucian *Iupp. Tragoed.* § 3 οὐχ ὁρῶ...ἐφ' ὅτῳ Πῶλος ἢ 'Αριστόδημος ἀντὶ Διὸς
ἡμῖν ἀναπέφηνας. Id. *Menippus* § 16 (on the contrast between the life of actors
on and off the stage) ἤδη δὲ πέρας ἔχοντος τοῦ δράματος, ἀποδυσάμενος ἕκαστος αὐτῶν
τὴν χρυσόπαστον ἐκείνην ἐσθῆτα καὶ τὸ προσωπεῖον ἀποθέμενος καὶ καταβὰς ἀπὸ
τῶν ἐμβατῶν πένης καὶ ταπεινὸς περιέρχεται, οὐκέτ' 'Αγαμέμνων ὁ "Ατρεως οὐδὲ
Κρέων ὁ Μενοικέως, ἀλλὰ Πῶλος Χαρικλέους Σουνιεὺς ὀνομαζόμενος ἢ
Σάτυρος Θεογείτονος Μαραθώνιος. ['Polus, son of Charicles, *of Sunium,*' is not
inconsistent with τὸν Αἰγινήτην in Plut. *Dem.* 28, for the great actor may have
been a native of Aegina who was afterwards enrolled in the Attic deme of Sunium.]

Little as such an incident may accord with modern feeling or taste, it is at least of very clear significance in relation to the tone of the Attic stage as it existed for a generation whose grandfathers were contemporary with Sophocles. Whether the story was true or not, it must have been conceived as possible. And, this being so, nothing could better show the error of supposing that the old Greek acting of tragedy was statuesque in a cold or rigid sense,—in a sense excluding declamation and movement suitable to the passions which the words expressed. Play of feature, indeed, was excluded by the use of masks; but this very fact would have increased the need for appropriate gesture. The simple grouping—as recent revivals have helped us to feel—must have constantly had a plastic beauty rarely seen on our more crowded stage[1]; but it is inconceivable, and the story just noticed affords some direct ground for denying, that this result was obtained at any sacrifice of life and truth in the portrayal of emotion. Demosthenes tells us that some of the inferior tragedians of his time were called 'ranters'[2]. It might be said, of course, that this indicates a popular preference for an undemonstrative style. But it might with more force be replied that 'ranting' is not a fault which a coldly 'statuesque' tradition would have generated.

§ 17. The story of Oedipus was one of a few subjects which the Greek dramatists never tired of handling. Some eight or nine tragedies, entitled *Oedipus*, are known by the names of their authors, and by nothing else[3]. Plato, the poet of the Old

---

Id. *De mercede conduct.* § 5 τοῖς τραγικοῖς ὑποκριταῖς....οἱ ἐπὶ μὲν τῆς σκηνῆς Ἀγα-
μέμνων ἕκαστος αὐτῶν ἢ Κρέων ἢ αὐτὸς Ἡρακλῆς εἰσιν, ἔξω δὲ Πῶλος ἢ Ἀριστόδημος,
ἀποθέμενοι τὰ προσωπεῖα, γίγνονται.
    The Aristodemus coupled by Lucian with Polus is the actor mentioned by Aeschines and Demosthenes; the latter specially notices that he and Theodorus had both often acted the Antigone of Sophocles (or. 19. § 246)ᵒ Satyrus is the comic actor mentioned by the same orators (Aeschin. 2. § 156, Dem. or. 19. § 193). Thus we see how, in later Greek literature, Polus had become one of a small group of names typical of the best histrionic art of the classical age.

[1] On the sense in which a 'plastic' character is common to Greek Sculpture, Tragedy, and Oratory, cp. my *Attic Orators*, vol. I. pp. xcviii—ciii.

[2] Dem. or. 18. § 262 μισθώσας αὐτὸν τοῖς βαρυστόνοις ἐπικαλουμένοις ἐκείνοις ὑποκριταῖς, Σιμύλῳ καὶ Σωκράτει, ἐτριταγωνίστεις.

[3] An Οἰδίπους by the Carcinus whom Aristophanes ridicules is quoted by Arist. *Rhet.* 5. 16. 11. Xenocles is said to have been victorious, with a series of plays

Comedy, wrote a *Laïus*, which was perhaps a parody of the Aeschylean play; and the Middle Comedy was indebted to Eubulus for an *Oedipus* from which a few verses are left—a travesty of the curse pronounced upon the unknown criminal[1]. Julius Caesar, like the younger Pitt, was a precocious dramatist, and Oedipus was his theme[2]. The self-blinded Oedipus was a part which Nero loved to act[3], and the last public recitation which he ever gave, we are told, was in this character. The Greek verse at which he stopped is on record: whose it was, we know not[4]. Of all the Greek versions, not one remains by which to gauge the excellence of Sophocles. But the literatures of other languages make some amends.

Nothing can better illustrate the distinctive qualities of the Sophoclean Oedipus than to compare it with the treatment of the same theme by Seneca, Corneille, Dryden and Voltaire. So far as the last three are concerned, the comparison has a larger value. The differences between the spirit of the best Greek Tragedy and that of modern drama are not easily expressed in formulas, but can be made clearer by a particular example. Perhaps the literature of drama hardly affords any example so apposite for this purpose as the story of Oedipus.

§ 18. Seneca has followed, and sometimes paraphrased, The *Oedipus* including an Οἰδίπους, against Euripides, one of whose pieces on that occasion was of Seneca. the *Troades*, probably in 415 B.C. An Οἰδίπους is also ascribed to Achaeus (Nauck *Trag. fr.* p. 584), Theodectes (p. 623), and, more doubtfully, to Diogenes of Sinope (p. 627); also by Suidas to Philocles, and to each of two poets named Nicomachus (one of Athens, the other of the Troad).

[1] Meineke *Com. Frag.* pp. 231 (Plato), Eubulus (451). Of the latter's five verses, the last three are—ὅστις δ' ἐπὶ δεῖπνον ἢ φίλον τιν' ἢ ξένον | καλέσας ἔπειτα συμβολὰς ἐπράξατο, | φυγὰς γένοιτο μηδὲν οἴκοθεν λαβών. It seems quite possible, as has been suggested, that Eubulus was parodying verses from the *Oedipus* of Euripides.

[2] Sueton. *Iul. Caes.* 56 Feruntur et a puero et ab adolescuntulo quaedam scripta, ut laudes Herculis, tragoedia Oedipus.

[3] Sueton. *Nero* 21 Tragoedias quoque cantavit personatus. Inter cetera cantavit Canacen parturientem, Orestem matricidam, Oedipodem excaecatum, Herculem insanum.

[4] *ib.* 46 Observatum etiam fuerat novissimam fabulam cantasse eum [Neronem] publice *Oedipum exsulem*, atque in hoc desisse versu, οἰκτρῶς θανεῖν μ' ἄνωγε σύγγαμος πατήρ. Dio Cassius (63. 28) also quotes the verse as one on which Nero's mind dwelt: τὸ ἔπος ἐκεῖνο συνεχῶς ἐνενόει.

Sophocles with sufficient fidelity to heighten the contrast between the original and the rhetorical transcript. For the comparative student of drama, however, the Roman piece is by no means devoid of instruction or of interest. Seneca's plot diverges from that of Sophocles in three main points. (i) Teiresias does not intuitively know the murderer of Laïus. When his aid is invoked by Oedipus, he has recourse to the arts of divination. Manto, the daughter of the blind seer, reports the signs to him, and he declares that neither voice of birds nor inspection of victims can reveal the name. Laïus himself must be called up from the shades. In a grove near Thebes, Teiresias performs the awful rites which evoke the dead; the ghastly shape of Laïus rises—

> Stetit per artus sanguine effuso horridus—

and denounces his son. This scene is related to Oedipus by Creon in a long and highly-wrought speech (530—658). Here, as in the earlier scene with Manto (303—402), copious use is made of detail from Roman augural lore, as well as of the Nekyia in the eleventh book of the *Odyssey*—suggesting a contrast with the lightness of touch which marks that passage of the Sophoclean *Antigone* (998—1011) where Teiresias describes the failure of his appeal to augury. There, the technical signs are briefly but vividly indicated; in Seneca, the erudition is heavy and obtrusive.

(ii) After the discovery of the parricide and the incest, and when Oedipus has now blinded himself, Iocasta meets and thus accosts him :—

> Quid te vocem?
> Natumne? dubitas? natus es, natum pudet.
> Invite, loquere, nate: quo avertis caput
> Vacuosque vultus?
> *Oed.*   Quis frui et tenebris vetat?
> Quis reddit oculos? matris, heu, matris sonus.
> Perdidimus operam. Congredi fas amplius
> Haud est. Nefandos dividat vastum mare...

Iocasta presently kills herself on the stage. Here, at least, Seneca has the advantage of Euripides, whose Iocasta speaks the prologue of the *Phoenissae,* and coldly recites the horrors of her past life,—adding that Oedipus has been imprisoned by his sons, 'in order that his fate might be forgotten—for it needs much art to hide it'.[1] The Iocasta of Sophocles rushes from the scene, not to re-appear, at the moment when she finds Oedipus resolved to unbare that truth of which she herself is already certain, and leaves the terrible cry thrilling in our ears—

> ἰού, ἰού, δύστηνε· τοῦτο γάρ σ’ ἔχω
> μόνον προσειπεῖν, ἄλλο δ’ οὔποθ’ ὕστερον.

In the truth and power of this touch, Sophocles is alone. Neither Seneca, nor any later dramatist, has managed this situation so as to express with a similar union of delicacy and strength the desperate anguish of a woman whom fate has condemned to unconscious crime.

(iii) Seneca had no 'Oedipus at Colonus' in view. He was free to disregard that part of the legend according to which Oedipus was expelled from Thebes by Eteocles and Polyneices, and can therefore close his play by making Oedipus go forth into voluntary exile:—

> Mortifera mecum vitia terrarum extraho.
> Violenta fata et horridus morbi tremor
> Maciesque et atra pestis et tabidus dolor
> Mecum ite, mecum: ducibus his uti libet.

§ 19. The closeness with which Seneca has studied Sophocles can be judged from several passages[2]. It is instructive to notice that, while Seneca has invented rhetorical ornament (as in the opening dialogue, 1—105, and the Nekyia, 530—568), he has not known how to vary the natural development of the action. He has compressed the incidents of Sophocles into the smallest compass; and hence, notwithstanding the rhetorical episodes, the whole play consists only of 1060 lines, and would not have occupied more than an hour and a half in representation. Seneca is

Seneca's relation to Sophocles.

---

[1] Eur. *Phoen.* 64 ἵν’ ἀμνήμων τύχη | γένοιτο, πολλῶν δεομένη σοφισμάτων.

[2] Such are, the scene in which Oedipus upbraids Creon (Sen. 678—708, cp. Soph. 532—630); the questioning of Iocasta by Oedipus (Sen. 773—783, cp. Soph. 740—755); the scene with the messenger from Corinth, and the final discovery (Sen. 783—881, cp. Soph. 955—1185).

thus a negative witness to the mastery shown by the artist who could construct such a drama as the *Oedipus Tyrannus* with such materials. The modern dramatists, as we shall see, teach the same lesson in a more positive form. Walter Scott's estimate of Seneca's *Oedipus* needs modification, but is just in the main. 'Though devoid of fancy and of genius,' he says, it 'displays the masculine eloquence and high moral sentiment of its author; and if it does not interest us in the scene of fiction, it often compels us to turn our thoughts inward, and to study our own hearts.' Seneca's fault, however, so far as the plot is concerned, seems less that he fails to interest, than that, by introducing the necromantic machinery, and by obliterating the finer moral traits of his Greek original, he has rendered the interest rather 'sensational' than properly dramatic[1].

The *Oedipe* of Corneille.

§ 20. The *Oedipe* of Corneille was produced at Paris in 1657. After an interval which followed the unfavourable reception of his *Pertharite* in 1653, it was with the *Oedipe* that Corneille returned to the theatre, at the instance of his patron, Nicolas Fouquet, to whom it is dedicated. It is immaterial for our purpose that this play is far from exhibiting Corneille at his best; nor need we here inquire what precise rank is to be assigned to it among his less successful works. For the student of Sophocles, it has the permanent interest of showing how the subject of the *Oedipus Tyrannus* was adapted to the modern stage by a typical artist of the French classical school. The severely simple theme of Sophocles, with its natural elements of pity and terror, is found too meagre by the modern dramatist. He cannot trust to that alone; he feels that he needs some further source of variety and relief. To supply this, he interweaves an underplot of secondary persons—'the happy episode of the loves of Theseus and Dircè.' Theseus is the king of Athens; Dircè is a daughter of the deceased Laïus.

The drama opens with a love-scene, in which Theseus is

---

[1] A small trait may be noticed as amusingly characteristic of the Roman poet of the Empire. The Laïus of Sophocles goes to Delphi βαιός—with only four attendants (752). Seneca makes Laïus *set out* with the proper retinue of a king;—but most of them lose their way. *Plures fefellit error ancipitis viae: Paucos fidelis curribus iunxit labor.*

urging Dircè not to banish him from her presence at
Thebes :—

> N'écoutez plus, madame, une pitié cruelle,
> Qui d'un fidèle amant vous feroit un rebelle...

To the end, the fortunes of this pair divide our attention
with those of Oedipus and Iocasta. Corneille does not bring
Teiresias on the scene ; but Nérine, 'lady of honour to Iocasta,'
relates how the seer has called forth the shade of Laïus. The
ghost does not (as with Seneca) denounce Oedipus, but declares
that the woes of Thebes shall cease only 'when the blood of
Laïus shall have done its duty.' The discovery is brought about
nearly as in Sophocles, though the management of the process is
inferior in a marked degree. The herdsman of Laïus—whom
Corneille, like Dryden and Voltaire, names Phorbas, after
Seneca's example—kills himself on the stage ; Iocasta, snatching
the poniard from him, plunges it in her own breast. Oedipus
blinds himself. No sooner have the gory drops flowed from his
eyes, than the pest which is ravaging Thebes ceases : the message of the spirit is fulfilled :—'the blood of Laïus has done its
duty.' Theseus and Dircè, we understand, are made happy.

The chief character, as drawn by Corneille, shows how an
artificial stoicism can destroy tragic pathos. The Oedipus of
Corneille is an idealised French king of the seventeenth century
—one of those monarchs concerning whom Dircè says,

> Le peuple est trop heureux quand il meurt pour ses rois ;

he learns the worst with a lofty serenity ; and his first thought is
to administer a stately rebuke to the persons whose misdirected
forethought had saved him from perishing in infancy :—

> Voyez où m'a plongé votre fausse prudence.

Dircè admires his impassive fortitude :—

> La surprenante horreur de cet accablement
> Ne coûte à sa grande âme aucun égarement.

Contrast with this the life-like and terrible power of the delineation in Sophocles, from the moment when the cry of despair
bursts from the lips of Oedipus (1182), to the end.

§ 21.   Twenty-two years after Corneille, Dryden essayed the
same theme.   His view was that his French predecessor had
failed through not rendering the character of Oedipus more
noble and attractive.   On the other hand, he follows Corneille
in the essential point of introducing an underplot.   Dryden's
Eurydicè answers to Corneille's Dircè, being, like her, the
daughter of Laïus.   Corneille's Theseus is replaced by Adrastus,
king of Argos,—a personage less likely, in Dryden's opinion, to
eclipse Oedipus.   When the play opens, Oedipus is absent from
Thebes, and engaged in war with Argos.   Meanwhile plots are
being laid against his throne by Creon—a hunch-backed villain
who makes love to Eurydicè, and is rejected by her much as
Shakspeare's Richard, Duke of Gloster—who has obviously
suggested some traits—is repulsed by the Lady Ann.   Presently Oedipus returns, bringing the captive Adrastus, whom
he chivalrously sets free to woo Eurydicè.   From this point, the
piece follows the general lines of Sophocles, so far as the discovery is concerned.   Oedipus is denounced, however, not by
Teiresias, but, as in Seneca, by the ghost,—which Dryden, unlike
Seneca, brings on the stage.

It is singular that Dryden should have committed the same
mistake which he perceived so clearly in Corneille.   Eurydicè
and Adrastus are less tiresome than Dircè and Theseus, but
their effect is the same.   The underplot spoils the main plot.
The tragic climax is the death of Eurydicè, who is stabbed by
Creon.   Creon and Adrastus next kill each other; then Iocasta
slays herself and her children; and finally Oedipus throws himself from an upper window of the palace.   'Sophocles,' says
Dryden, 'is admirable everywhere; and therefore we have followed him as close as we possibly could.'   In a limited verbal
sense, this is true.   There are several scenes, or parts of scenes, in
which Dryden has almost transcribed Sophocles[1].   But the difference of general result is complete.   The *Oedipus* of Sophocles
does perfectly that which Tragedy, according to Aristotle, ought
to do.   It effects, by pity and terror, the 'purgation' of such

---

[1] As in the scene with the suppliants (Act I. Sc. i.); that between Oedipus and
Iocasta (Act III. Sc. i.); and that between Oedipus and Aegeon (the messenger from
Corinth, Act IV. Sc. i.).

feelings; that is, it separates them from the alloy of mean accident, and exercises them, in their pure essence, on great objects
—here, on the primary instincts of natural affection. In relation
to pity and terror, Tragedy should be as the purgatorial fire,—

> exemit labem, purumque reliquit
> Aetherium sensum atque aurai simplicis ignem.

Now, Dryden's play first divides our sympathy between
the fate of Eurydicè and that of Oedipus; next, it involves it
with feelings of a different order,—loathing for the villainy of
Creon, and disgust at the wholesale butchery of the end. Instead of 'purging' pity and terror, it stupefies them; and the
contrast is the more instructive because the textual debt of
Dryden to Sophocles has been so large.

It is right to add that, while the best parts of the play—the
first and third Acts—are wholly Dryden's, in the rest he was
assisted by an inferior hand[1]. And, among the places where
Dryden's genius flashes through, it is interesting to remark one
in which he has invented a really Greek touch,—not in the
manner of Sophocles, certainly, yet such as might occur in
Euripides. Oedipus is pronouncing the curse on the unknown
murderer :—

> But for the murderer's self, unfound by man,
> Find him, ye powers celestial and infernal!
> And the same fate, or worse than Laïus met,
> Let be his lot: his children be accurst;
> His wife and kindred, all of his, be cursed!

Both Priests. Confirm it, heaven!

> Enter JOCASTA, *attended by Women.*

Joc. At your devotions? Heaven succeed your wishes;
> And bring the effect of these your pious prayers
> On you, and me, and all.

Pr. Avert this omen, heaven!

Oedip. O fatal sound! unfortunate Jocasta!

---

[1] 'What Sophocles could undertake alone, Our poets found a work for more than
one' (Epilogue). Lee must be held accountable for the worst rant of Acts IV. and
V.; but we are not concerned here with the details of execution, either in its merits or
in its defects.

What hast thou said? an ill hour hast thou chosen
For these foreboding words! why, we were cursing!
Joc. Then may that curse fall only where you laid it.
Oedip. Speak no more!
For all thou say'st is ominous: we were cursing;
And that dire imprecation hast thou fasten'd
On Thebes, and thee, and me, and all of us.

The *Oedipe* of Voltaire. § 22. More than either Dryden or Corneille, Voltaire has treated this subject in the spirit of the antique. His *Oedipe* was composed when he was only nineteen. It was produced in 1718 (when he was twenty-four), and played forty-six times consecutively—a proof, for those days, of marked success. In 1729, the piece having kept its place on the stage meanwhile, a new edition was published. It is not merely a remarkable work for so young a man; its intrinsic merit, notwithstanding obvious defects, is, I venture to think, much greater than has usually been recognised. The distinctive 'note' of the modern versions —the underplot—is there, no doubt; but, unlike Corneille and Dryden, Voltaire has not allowed it to overshadow the main action.

The hero Philoctetes revisits Thebes, after a long absence, to find Oedipus reigning in the seat of Laïus. The Thebans are vexed by pestilence, and are fain to find a victim for the angry god; Philoctetes was known to have been the foe of the late king, and is now accused of his murder. Iocasta had been betrothed to Philoctetes in youth, and loves him still. She urges him to fly, but he resolves to remain and confront the false charge. At this moment, the seer Teiresias denounces Oedipus as the criminal. Philoctetes generously protests his belief in the king's innocence; and from this point (the end of the third Act) appears no more.

Thenceforth, the plot is mainly that of Sophocles. The first scene of the fourth Act, in which Iocasta and Oedipus inform each other of the past, is modelled on *Oed. Tyr.* 698—862, with some characteristic differences. Thus, in Sophocles, the first doubt of Oedipus as to his parentage springs from a taunt uttered at a feast (779). Here is Voltaire's substitute for that incident (the scene, of course, being Corinth):—

Un jour, ce jour affreux, présent à ma pensée,
Jette encore la terreur dans mon âme glacée ;
Pour la première fois, par un don solennel,
Mes mains, jeunes encore, enrichissaient l'autel :
Du temple tout-à-coup les combles s'entr'ouvrirent ;
De traits affreux de sang les marbres se couvrirent ;
De l'autel, ébranlé par de longs tremblemens,
Une invisible main repoussait mes présens ;
Et les vents, au milieu de la foudre éclatante,
Portèrent jusqu'à moi cette voix effrayante :
"Ne viens plus des lieux saints fouiller la pureté ;
"Du nombre des vivans les dieux t'ont rejeté ;
"Ils ne reçoivent point tes offrandes impies ;
"Va porter tes présens aux autels des Furies ;
"Conjure leurs serpens prêts à te déchirer ;
"Va, ce sont là les dieux que tu dois implorer."

This is powerful in its way. But where Voltaire has introduced a prodigy—the supernatural voice heard amid lightnings—Sophocles was content to draw from common life, and to mark how a random word could sink into the mind with an effect as terrible as that of any portent. Voltaire has managed the final situation on Corneille's plan, but with infinitely better effect. The High Priest announces that Oedipus has blinded himself, thereby appeasing the gods ; and the play closes with the death of Iocasta :—

IOCASTE.

O mon fils! hélas! dirai-je mon époux?
O des noms les plus chers assemblage effroyable!
Il est donc mort?

LE GRAND PRÊTRE.

Il vit, et le sort qui l'accable
Des morts et des vivans semble le séparer[1] ;

---

[1] Voltaire borrowed this verse from Corneille,—'parcequ' ayant précisément la même chose à dire,...il m'était impossible de l'exprimer mieux'; and Corneille was himself translating Seneca's *' nec vivis mixtus, nec sepultis.'* Voltaire was perhaps unconscious that the ground which he assigns here was exactly that on which the repetition of passages in the Greek orators was defended—viz. that τὸ καλῶς εἰπεῖν ἅπαξ περιγίγνεται, δὶς δὲ οὐκ ἐνδέχεται (Theon, προγυμνάσματα 1 : see my *Attic Orators*, vol. I. p. lxxii.).

Il s'est privé du jour avant que d'expirer.
Je l'ai vu dans ses yeux enfoncer cette épée,
Qui du sang de son père avait été trempée;
Il a rempli son sort, et ce moment fatal
Du salut des Thébains est le premier signal.
Tel est l'ordre du ciel, dont la fureur se lasse;
Comme il veut, aux mortels il fait justice ou grâce;
Ses traits sont épuisés sur ce malheureux fils:
Vivez, il vous pardonne.

IOCASTE.

Et moi je me punis.   (*Elle se frappe.*)
Par un pouvoir affreux réservée à l'inceste,
La mort est le seul bien, le seul dieu qui me reste.
Laïus, reçois mon sang, je te suis chez les morts:
J'ai veçu vertueuse, et je meurs sans remords.

LE CHOEUR.

O malheureuse reine! ô destin que j'abhorre!

IOCASTE.

Né plaignez que mon fils, puisqu'il respire encore.
Prêtres, et vous Thébains qui fûtes mes sujets,
Honorez mon bûcher, et songez à jamais
Qu'au milieu des horreurs du destin qui m'opprime
J'ai fait rougir les dieux qui m'ont forcée au crime.

Voltaire's criticisms. § 23. Voltaire was conscious of the objections to his own episode of Philoctetes; no one, indeed, could have criticised it with more wit or force. 'Philoctetes seems to have visited Thebes only for the purpose of being accused': not a word is said of him after the third Act, and the catastrophe is absolutely independent of him. In a letter to the Jesuit Porée, with whom he had read the classics, Voltaire apologises for Philoctetes by saying that the Parisian actors would not hear of an *Oedipus* with no love in it; 'I spoiled my piece,' he says, 'to please them.'

But it is certain, from what he says more than once elsewhere, that he regarded *some* underplot as a necessity. His remarks on this point are worth noting, because they touch an essential difference between the old Greek view of drama and that which has prevailed on our stage. 'The subject (Oedipus)

did not, in itself, furnish me with matter for the first three Acts;
indeed, it scarcely gave me enough for the last two. Those who
know the theatre—that is, who are as much alive to the difficulties
as to the defects of composition—will agree with what I say.'
'In strictness, the play of Oedipus ought to end with the first
Act.' Oedipus is one of those ancient subjects 'which afford
only one scene each, or two at most—not an entire tragedy.'
In short, to demand a modern drama on the *simple* story of
Oedipus was like setting one to make bricks without straw.
Corneille found himself constrained to add the episode of
Theseus and Dircè; Dryden introduced Adrastus and Eurydicè[1].

§ 24. Now, why could Sophocles dispense with any such addition, and yet produce a drama incomparably more powerful?
The masterly art of Sophocles in the structure and development
of the plot has already been examined, and is properly the first
attribute of his work which claims attention. But this is not the
only, or the principal, source to which the *Oedipus Tyrannus*
owes its greatness; the deeper cause is, that Sophocles, in the
spirit of Greek Tragedy, has known how to make the story of
Oedipus an ideal study of character and passion. Corneille,
Dryden, Voltaire—each in his own way—were thinking, 'How

Essential difference between Sophocles and the moderns.

---

[1] 'All we could gather out of Corneille,' says Dryden, 'was that an episode must
be, but not his way.' Dryden seems to have felt, however, that it was demanded
rather by convention than by artistic necessity. The following passage is interesting as an indication that his instinct was better than his practice :—'The Athenian
theatre (whether more perfect than ours, is not now disputed), had a perfection
differing from ours. You see there in every act a single scene, (or two at most),
which manage the business of the play; and after that succeeds the chorus, which
commonly takes up more time in singing, than there has been employed in speaking.
The principal person appears almost constantly through the play; but the inferior
parts seldom above once in the whole tragedy. The conduct of our stage is much
more difficult, where we are obliged never to lose any considerable character, which
we have once presented.' [Voltaire's Philoctetes broke this rule.] 'Custom likewise
has obtained, that we must form an underplot of second persons, which must be
depending on the first; and their bye-walks must be like those in a labyrinth, which
all of them lead into the great parterre; or like so many several lodging chambers,
which have their outlets into the same gallery. Perhaps, after all, if we could think
so, the ancient method, as it is the easiest, is also the most natural and the best. For
variety, as it is managed, is too often subject to breed distraction; and while we
would please too many ways, for want of art in the conduct, we please in none.'
(*Preface to Oedipus.*)

am I to keep the audience amused? Will they not find this horrible story of Oedipus rather too painful and monotonous? Will they not desire something lighter and pleasanter—some love-making, for instance, or some intrigue?' 'What an insipid part would Iocasta have played,' exclaims Voltaire, 'had she not retained at least the memory of a lawful attachment, and trembled for the existence of a man whom she had once loved!' There is the secret frankly told.

Sophocles, on the other hand, *concentrates* the attention of the audience on the destiny of Oedipus and Iocasta. The spectators are enchained by the feelings which this destiny moves at each step in its course. They are made to see into the depths of two human souls. It is no more possible for them to crave minor distractions than it would be for our eyes or thoughts to wander, if we were watching, without the power of arresting, a man who was moving blind-fold towards a precipice. The interest by which Sophocles holds us is continuous and intense; but it is not monotonous, because alternations of fear lead up to the worst; the exciting causes of pity and terror are not unworthy or merely repulsive, for the spectacle offered is that of a noble and innocent nature, a victim to unknown and terrible forces which must be counted among the permanent conditions of life, since the best of mankind can never be sure of escaping them. When the worst has befallen, *then* Sophocles knows how to relieve the strain; but it is a relief of another order from that which Corneille affords by the prospect of Theseus being made happy with Dircè. It is drawn from the natural sources of the tragedy itself; the blind king hears the voices of his children.

References to a prophetic instinct.

§ 25. A comparison may fitly close with a glance at two points in which the modern dramas illustrate Sophocles, and which have more than the meaning of details. Dryden has represented Oedipus and Iocasta as haunted, from the first, by a mysterious instinct of their true relationship. Thus she says to him :—

> When you chid, methought
> A mother's love start[1] up in your defence,

---

[1] = 'started,' as again in this scene: 'Nature herself start back when thou wert born.'

And bade me not be angry. Be not you;
For I love Laïus still, as wives should love,
But you more tenderly, as part of me[1].

Voltaire has the same thought (Act II. Sc. ii.), where Iocasta is speaking of her marriage with Oedipus :

je sentis dans mon âme étonnée
Des transports inconnus que je ne conçus pas :
Avec horreur enfin je me vis dans ses bras.

There is a similar touch in Corneille. Oedipus is watching Dircè—whom he believes to be his step-daughter, but who is in fact his sister—with her lover Theseus (Act III. Sc. iv.):

Je ne sais quelle horreur me trouble à leur aspect ;
Ma raison la repousse, et ne m'en peut défendre.

Such blind warnings of nature are indeed fitted to make the spectator shudder ; but they increase the difficulty of explaining why the truth was not divined sooner ; and they also tend to lessen the shock of the discovery. In other words, they may be poetical,—they may be even, in the abstract, tragic,—but they are not, for this situation, dramatic ; and it is due to the art of Sophocles to observe that he has nowhere admitted any hint of this kind.

§ 26. Next, it should be noticed that no one of the later dramatists has been able to avoid leaving a certain element of improbability in the story. We saw above that Aristotle alludes to the presence of such an element, not in the plot itself, but in the supposed antecedents. It consists in the presumed ignorance of Oedipus and Iocasta regarding facts with which they ought to have been familiar. Sophocles tacitly accepts this condition, and, by doing so, minimizes its prominence ; so much so, that it may be doubted whether many readers or spectators of the *Oedipus Tyrannus* would think of it, if their attention had not been drawn to it previously. Seneca has not attempted to improve on that example. But the moderns have sought various ways of evading a critical censure which they foresaw ; and it is instructive to consider the result. The Oedipus of Corneille

The improbable element— how managed by the moderns.

---

[1] Act I. Sc. i. : cp. what Oedipus says in Act II. Sc. i.

knows that Laïus was said to have been killed by robbers; he
also knows the place and the date. Further, he distinctly re-
members that, at the same place and at the same date, he himself
had slain three wayfarers. Strange to say, however, it never
occurs to him that these wayfarers could possibly have been
Laïus and his attendants. He mildly suggests to Iocasta that
they may have been *the robbers* (Act I. Sc. i.); though, as appears
from the circumstances which he himself afterwards relates
(Act IV. Sc. iv.), he had not the slightest ground for such a supposition. This device cannot be deemed an improvement on
Sophocles. Dryden's expedient is simpler :—

> Tell me, Thebans,
> How Laïus fell; for a confused report
> Pass'd through my ears, when first I took the crown ;
> *But full of hurry, like a morning dream,*
> *It vanish'd in the business of the day.*

That only serves to show us that the dramatist has an uneasy
conscience. Voltaire's method is subtler. Oedipus thus excuses
himself for having to question Iocasta concerning the death
of Laïus :—

> Madame, jusqu' ici, respectant vos douleurs,
> Je n'ai point rappelé le sujet de vos pleurs ;
> Et de vos seuls périls chaque jour alarmée
> Mon âme à d'autres soins semblait être fermée.

But, as the author admits, the king ought not to have been
so long deterred, by the fear of displeasing his wife, from inform-
ing himself as to the death of his predecessor: 'this is to have
too much discretion and too little curiosity.' Sophocles, according to Voltaire, ought to have suggested some explanation of
the circumstance that Oedipus, on hearing how Laïus perished,
does not at once recollect his own adventure in the narrow pass.
The French poet seeks to explain it by hinting at a miraculous
suspension of memory in Oedipus :—

> Et je ne conçois pas par quel enchantement
> J'oubliais jusqu' ici ce grand événement ;
> La main des dieux sur moi si long-temps suspendue
> Semble ôter le bandeau qu'ils mettaient sur ma vue.

But this touch, though bold and not unhappy, must be classed with the transparent artifices of the stage. The true answer to the criticisms on this score which Voltaire directs against Sophocles, Corneille, and himself is contained in a remark of his own, that a certain amount of improbability is inherent in the story of Oedipus[1]. If that improbability is excluded at one point, it will appear at another. This being so, it is not difficult to choose between the frank treatment of the material by Sophocles, and the ingenious but ineffectual compromises of later art.

§ 27. The recent revivals of Greek plays have had their great reward in proving how powerfully the best Greek Tragedy can appeal to modern audiences. Those who are furthest from being surprised by the result will be among the first to allow that the demonstration was needed. The tendency of modern study had been too much to fix attention on external contrasts between the old Greek theatre and our own. Nor was an adequate corrective of this tendency supplied by the manner in which the plays have usually been studied; a manner more favourable to a minute appreciation of the text than to apprehension of the play as a work of art. The form had been understood better than the spirit. A vague feeling might sometimes be perceived that the effectiveness of the old Greek dramas, *as such*, had depended essentially on the manners and beliefs of the people for whom they were written, and that a successful Sophocles presupposed a Periclean Athens. Some wonderment appeared to greet the discovery that a masterpiece of Aeschylus, when acted, could move the men and women of to-day. Now that this truth has been so profoundly impressed on the most cultivated audiences which England or America could furnish,—in Germany and France it had been less unfamiliar,—it is not too much to say that a new life has been breathed into the modern study of the Greek drama.

§ 28. Recent representations of the *Oedipus Tyrannus* have

Revivals of Greek plays.

The Oedipus

---

[1] In the fifth letter to M. de Genonville:—'Il est vrai qu'il y a des sujets de tragédie où l'on est tellement gêné par la bizarrerie des événemens, qu'il est presqu' impossible de réduire l'exposition de sa pièce à ce point de sagesse et de vraisemblance. Je crois, pour mon bonheur, que le sujet d'Œdipe est de ce genre.'

INTRODUCTION.

1

Tyrannus —a crucial experiment. a peculiar significance, which claims notice here. The incestuous relationship—the entrance of Oedipus with bleeding eyes—these are incidents than which none could be imagined more fitted to revolt a modern audience. Neither Corneille nor Voltaire had the courage to bring the self-blinded king on the stage; his deed is related by others. Voltaire, indeed, suggested[1] that the spectacle might be rendered supportable by a skilful disposition of lights,—Oedipus, with his gore-stained face, being kept in the dim back-ground, and his passion being expressed by action rather than declamation, while the scene should resound with the cries of Iocasta and the laments of the Thebans. Dryden dared what the others declined ; but his play was soon pronounced impossible for the theatre. Scott quotes a contemporary witness to the effect that, when Dryden's *Oedipus* was revived about the year 1790, 'the audience were unable to support it to an end ; the boxes being all emptied before the third act was concluded.'

The result at Harvard. § 29. In May, 1881, after seven months of preparation, the *Oedipus Tyrannus* was acted in the original Greek by members of Harvard University. Archaeology, scholarship, and art had conspired to make the presentation perfect in every detail ; and the admirable record of the performance which has been published has a permanent value for every student of Sophocles[2]. References to it will be found in the following commentary. But it is the impression which the whole work made on the spectators of which we would speak here. Nothing of the original was altered or omitted ; and at the last Oedipus was brought on the scene, 'his pale face marred with bloody stains.' The performances were seen by about six thousand persons,—the Harvard theatre holding about a thousand at a time. As an English version was provided for those who needed it, it cannot be said that the language veiled what might else have offended. From first to last, these great audiences, thoroughly representative of the most cul-

---

[1] In one of his notes on Corneille's Preface to the *Oedipe* (Oeuvres de Corneille, vol. VII. p. 262, ed. 1817).

[2] *An Account of the Harvard Greek Play. By Henry Norman.* Boston : James R. Osgood and Co., 1882. The account is illustrated by 15 photographs of characters and groups, and is dedicated by the Author (who acted the part of Creon) to Professor J. W. White. See Appendix, Note 1, p. 280.

tivated and critical judgment, were held spell-bound. 'The ethical situation was so overwhelming, that they listened with bated breath, and separated in silence.' 'The play is over. There is a moment's silence, and then the theatre rings with applause. It seems inappropriate, however, and ceases almost as suddenly as it began. The play has left such a solemn impression that the usual customs seem unfitting, and the audience disperses quietly[1].' There is the nineteenth century's practical interpretation of Aristotle. This is Tragedy, 'effecting, by means of pity and terror, the *purgation* of such feelings.'

§ 30. A few months later in the same year (1881), the *Oedipe Roi at the* Oedipus Tyrannus was revived in a fairly close French transla- *Théâtre* tion at the Théâtre Français. When the version of Jules *Français.* Lacroix was played there in 1858, the part of Oedipus was filled by Geoffroy; but on this occasion an artist was available whose powers were even more congenial. Probably no actor of modern times has excelled M. Mounet-Sully in the union of all the qualities required for a living impersonation of the Sophoclean Oedipus in the entire series of moods and range of passions which the part comprises; as the great king, at once mighty and tender; the earnest and zealous champion of the State in the search for hidden guilt; the proud man startled by a charge which he indignantly repels, and embittered by the supposed treason of a friend; tortured by slowly increasing fears, alternating with moments of reassurance; stung to frenzy by the proof of his unspeakable wretchedness; subdued to a calmer despair; finally softened by the meeting with his young daughters. The scene between Oedipus and Iocasta (vv. 700 —862) should be especially noticed as one in which the genius of Sophocles received the fullest justice from that of M. Mounet-Sully. In the words of a critic who has finely described the performance[2]:—

'Every trait of the tragedian's countenance is now a witness to the inward dread, always increasing upon him, as he relates his own adven-

---

[1] *Account of the Harvard Greek Play*, pp. 36, 103.

[2] *Saturday Review*, Nov. 19, 1881. The article was written by Sir Frederick Pollock.

J. S.   *e*

ture, and questions her for more minute details of the death of Laius. His voice sometimes sinks to a trembling gasp of apprehension, as the identity of the two events becomes more and more evident. He seems to be battling with fate.'

With a modern audience, the moment at which the self-blinded Oedipus comes forth is that which tests the power of the ancient dramatist; if, at that sight, repugnance overpowers compassion, the spell has been imperfect; if all other feelings are absorbed in the profound pathos of the situation, then Sophocles has triumphed. We have seen the issue of the ordeal in the case of the representation at Harvard. On the Paris stage, the traditions of the French classical drama (represented on this point by Corneille and Voltaire) were apt to make the test peculiarly severe. It is the more significant that the moment is thus described in the excellent account which we have cited above :—

'Oedipus enters, and in the aspect of the man, his whole history is told. It is not the adjunct of the bleeding eyes which now most deeply stirs the spectators. It is the intensity of woe which is revealed in every movement of the altered features and of the tottering figure whose bearing had been so majestic, and the tone of the voice,—hoarse, yet articulate. The inward struggle is recognised in its necessary outward signs. The strain on the audience might now become too great but for the relief of tenderness which almost immediately succeeds in the parting of Oedipus from his children. Often as pathetic farewells of a similar kind have been presented on the stage, seldom has any made an appeal so forcible.'

Conclusion.

In the presence of such testimonies, it can no longer be deemed that the Tragedy of ancient Greece has lost its virtue for the modern world. And, speaking merely as a student of Sophocles, I can bear witness that the representation of the *Ajax* at Cambridge (1882) was to me a new revelation of meaning and power. Of that performance, remarkable in so many aspects, I hope to say something in a later part of this edition. Here it must suffice to record a conviction that such revivals, apart from their literary and artistic interest, have also an educational value of the very highest order.

THE TEXT.

§ 1. The manuscripts of the *Oedipus Tyrannus* which have been MSS. used. chiefly used in this edition are the following [1]

In the Biblioteca Mediceo-Lorenziana, Florence.

L, cod. 32. 9, commonly known as the Laurentian MS., 11th century.

In the Bibliothèque Nationale, Paris.

A, cod. 2712, 13th century.
B, cod. 2787, ascribed to the 15th cent. (Catal. II. 553).
E, cod. 2884, ascribed to the 13th cent. (? *ib.* II. 565).
T, cod. 2711, 15th cent.

In the Biblioteca Marciana, Venice.

V, cod. 468, late 13th century or early 14th.
V², cod. 616, probably of the 14th cent.
V³, cod. 467, 14th cent.
V⁴, cod. 472, 14th cent.

---

[1] There is no doubt that L is of the 11th century, and none (I believe) that A is of the 13th. These are the two most important dates. In the case of several minor MSS., the tendency has probably been to regard them as somewhat older than they really are. The dates indicated above for such MSS. are given on the best authority that I could find, but I do not pretend to vouch for their precision. This is, in fact, of comparatively small moment, so long as we know the general limits of age. Excluding L and A, we may say broadly that almost all other known MSS. of Sophocles belong to the period 1300—1600 A.D.

In the Bodleian Library, Oxford.

Cod. Laud. Misc. 99 (now Auct. F. 3. 25), late 14th century.
Cod. Laud. 54, early 15th cent.
Cod. Barocc. 66, 15th cent.

In the Library of Trinity College, Cambridge.

Cod. R. 3. 31, mainly of the late 14th century, in parts perhaps of the early 15th.

These MSS. I have myself collated.

The following are known to me in some cases by slighter personal inspection, but more largely from previous collations, especially from those of Prof. L. Campbell (2nd ed., 1879):—Pal. = Palat. 40, Heidelberg: Vat. a = cod. 40 in the Vatican, 13th cent. (ascribed by some to the 12th): Vat. b, cod. Urbin. 141, *ib.*, 14th cent.: Vat. c, cod. Urbin. 140, *ib.*, 14th cent.: M, cod. G. 43 sup., in the Biblioteca Ambrosiana, Milan, 13th or early 14th cent.: M², cod. L. 39 sup., *ib.*, early 14th cent.: L², cod. 31. 10 (14th cent.) in the Bibliot. Med.-Lor., Florence; Γ, cod. Abbat. 152, late 13th, *ib.*: Δ, cod. Abbat. 41, 14th cent., *ib.*: Ricc. cod. 34, in the Biblioteca Riccardiana, Florence, sometimes ascribed to the 14th cent., but really of the 16th (see P. N. Papageorgius, 'cod. Laurent. von Soph.,' etc., p. 406, Leipzig, Teubner, 1883).

In making a first selection of MSS. to be collated, I was guided chiefly by what I already knew of their character and of their relations to each other, as these might be inferred from the previous reports; and this list was afterwards modified by such light as I gradually gained from my own experience. L and A being placed apart, several MSS. exist, equal in age and quality to some of those named above; but, so far as I am able to judge, the list which has been given may be said to be fairly representative. In the present state of our knowledge, even after all that has been done in recent years, it would, I think, be generally allowed that the greatest reserve must still be exercised in regard to any theory of the connections existing, whether by descent or by contamination, between our MSS. of Sophocles. We have not here to do with well-marked families, in the sense in which this can be said of the manuscript authorities for some other ancient texts; the data are often exceedingly complex, and such that the facts could be equally well explained by any one of two, or sometimes more, different suppositions. This is a subject with which I hope to deal more fully on a future occasion; even a slight treatment of it would carry me far beyond the limits which must be kept here. Meanwhile, it may be useful to give a few notes regarding some of the MSS. mentioned above, and to add some general remarks.

Codex A, no. 2712 in the National Library of Paris, is a parchment of the 13th century[1]. It is a volume of 324 pages, each about 11½ inches by 9 in size, and contains (1) Eur. *Hec., Or., Phoen., Androm., Med., Hipp.:* (2) p. 117—214, the seven plays of Soph.: (3) Ar. *Plut., Nub., Ran., Eq., Av., Acharn., Eccl.* (imperfect). The text of each page is in three columns; the writing goes continuously from left to right along all three, so that, *e.g.*, vv. 1, 2, 3 of a play are respectively the first lines of columns 1, 2, 3, and v. 4 is the second line of col. 1. The contractions are naturally very numerous, since the average breadth of each column (*i.e.* of each verse) is only about 2 inches; but they are regular, and the MS. is not difficult to read.

Codex B, no. 2787, in the same Library, written on thick paper, contains (1) Aesch. *P. V., Theb., Pers.:* (2) Soph. *O. T., Trach., Phil., O. C.* Codex E, no. 2884, written on paper, contains (1) the same three plays of Aesch., (2) Soph. *Ai., El., O. T.,* (3) Theocr. *Idyll.* 1—14. Both these MSS. have short interlinear notes and scholia. In E the writing is not good, and the rather frequent omissions show the scribe to have been somewhat careless. Though the Catalogue assigns E to the 13th cent., the highest date due to it seems to be the middle or late 14th. T, no. 2711, on thick paper, a MS. of the 15th cent., exhibits the seven plays of Sophocles in the recension of Demetrius Triclinius, the grammarian of the 14th cent. The single-column pages, measuring about 11½ by 7½, contain copious marginal scholia, which are mainly Triclinian. The general features of the Triclinian recension are well-known. He occasionally gives, or suggests, improved readings, but his ignorance of classical metre was equalled by his rashness, and especially in the lyrics he has often made havoc.

Of the Venetian MSS., V, no. 468, a paper folio of the late 13th or early 14th cent., contains (1) Oppian; (2) Aesch., *P. V., Theb., Pers., Agam.* (imperfect): (3) Soph., the 7 plays (but *Trach.* only to 18, *O. C.* only from 1338). V², no. 616, a parchment in small folio, probably of the 14th cent., contains (1) Soph., the 7 plays: (2) Aesch., 5 plays (*Cho.* and *Suppl.* wanting). V³, no. 467, a paper 8vo. of the 14th cent., has the 7 plays of Sophocles. V⁴, no. 472, a paper 8vo. of the 14th cent., has (1) Ar. *Plut., Nub., Ran.;* (2) Soph. *Ai., El., Ant.* (imperfect), *O. T.,* with marginal scholia.

---

[1] It contains the entry, 'Codex optimae notae. Codex Memmianus. Anno D. 1731 Feb. 16 Die.' In 1740 it had not yet been collated (Catal. II. 542).

Of the Bodleian MSS., Laud. Misc. 99 (Auct. F. 3. 25), late 14th cent., contains Soph. *O. T.*, *El.*, *Ai.:* Laud. 54 (early 15th cent.) the same three: Barocc. 66, 15th cent., the same three, with Eur. *Phoen.* The MS. of Trin. Coll. Camb. (late 14th—early 15th) has *El.*, *Ai.*, *O. T.*

Of the Florentine MSS., the famous L, cod. 32. 9 (parchment, 11th cent.), contains, as is well known, besides the 7 plays of Soph., also the 7 plays of Aesch., and the *Argonautica* of Apollonius Rhodius. The first corrector, sometimes distinguished as the διορθωτής, who compared the first hand with the archetype, is generally believed to have been of the 11th century. It continued to receive corrections, conjectures, annotations, from various hands, down at least to the 16th century[1]. L², cod. 31. 10 (14th cent.), contains the 7 plays of Soph., while Γ (cod. Abbat. 152), of the late 13th cent., has only *Ai.*, *El.*, *O. T.*, *Phil.*, and Δ (cod. Abbat. 41), of the 14th cent., only *Ai.*, *El.*, *O. T.*

As regards the relation of L to our other MSS., while much else is obscure or disputable, two facts, at least, are clear.

(1) It seems to be established beyond reasonable doubt that L cannot be regarded as the archetype of all the other MSS. which are known to exist. Some of these evidently represent a tradition, not only independent of, but presumably older than, L. Two particular pieces of evidence to this effect occur in the *Oedipus Tyrannus ;* (i) verse 800, omitted in the text of L, and only inserted in the margin by a hand certainly later than several of the MSS. which have the verse in the text: (ii) the words πονεῖν ἢ τοῖς θεοῖς written at v. 896 in the text of L,—these being corrupted from a gloss πανηγυρίζειν τοῖς θεοῖς which exists in full in the Trinity MS. and elsewhere[2].

(2) Taken as a whole, L is decidedly superior to any other MS. of Sophocles which we possess. On the other hand, it often shares particular errors from which some of the other MSS. are free, and these errors are sometimes of the grosser sort. It is safe to conclude that the scribe who wrote the text of Sophocles in L was not of high intelligence, being much inferior in this respect, apparently, to the first corrector, or 'διορθωτής': though allowance may also be made for the

---

[1] Under the auspices of the London 'Society for the Promotion of Hellenic Studies,' it is proposed to publish a photographic facsimile of the text of Sophocles in this MS., with an Introduction in which its palaeographic character will be described by Mr E. Maunde Thompson, of the British Museum.

[2] A valuable discussion of this point is given by Prof. Campbell, vol. I. pp. xxv—xli.

supposition that the former took a view of his office which precluded him from amending even the more palpable mistakes of the archetype which he transcribed.

§ 2. The subjoined table shows the principal cases in which the reading adopted in my text is not that of L, but is found in some other MS. or MSS.; or, if not in any MS., in a citation of Sophocles by an ancient author[1]. The reading of L is placed first; after it, that of my text. Note L's faults in vv. 332, 337, 657, 730, 1387, 1474. *Deviations from L.*

43 τοῦ] που. 182 παραβώμιον] παρὰ βῶμιον. 221 αὐτό] αὐτός. 229 ἀσφαλής] ἀβλαβής. 240 χέρνιβας] χέρνιβος. 290 τά τ'] τά γ'. 296 οὐξελέγχων] οὐξελέγξων. 315 πόνος] πόνων. 332 ἐγώ τ'] ἐγὼ οὖτ'. 337 ὁρμήν] ὀργήν. 347 εἰργάσθαι δ'] εἰργάσθαι θ'. 396 τοῦ] τον. 466 ἀελλοπόδων] ἀελλάδων Hesychius. 528 ἐξ ὀμμάτων ὀρθῶν δὲ (τε A)] ἐξ ὀμμάτων δ' ὀρθῶν τε Suidas. 598 αὐτοῖς ἅπαν] αὐτοῖσι πᾶν. 631 κυρίαν] καιρίαν. 635 ἐπήρατ'] ἐπήρασθ'. 657 λόγον...ἐκβαλεῖν] λόγῳ...βαλεῖν. 713 ἥξει] ἥξοι. 730 διπλαῖς] τριπλαῖς. 749 ἃ δ' ἂν] ἂν δ'. 800 The verse is wanting in the text of L, having being supplied in the margin by a late hand. 870 κατακοιμάσῃ] κατακοιμάσει. 903 ὀρθόν] ὄρθ'. 926 κάτοισθ'] κάτισθ'. 957 σημήνας] σημάντωρ. 967 κτανεῖν] κτενεῖν. 976 λέχος] λέκτρον. 1055 τόν θ'] τόνδ'. 1075 ἀναρρήξῃ sic] ἀναρρήξει. 1170 ἀκούων] ἀκούειν Plutarch. 1197 ἐκράτησας] ἐκράτησε (ν). 1260 ὑφ' ἡγητοῦ] ὑφηγητοῦ. 1264 ἐμπεπληγμένην] ἐμπεπλεγμένην. 1320 φορεῖν] φέρειν. 1387 ἀνεσχόμην] ἂν ἐσχόμην. 1474 ἐγγόνοιν] ἐκγόνοιν.

§ 3. In relation to a text, the report of manuscript readings may be valuable in either, or both, of two senses, the palaeographical and the critical. For example, in *O. T.* 15 L reads προσήμεθα, and in 17 στένοντες. These facts have a palaeographical interest, as indicating the kind of mistakes that may be expected in MSS. of this age and class. But they are of no critical interest, since neither προσήμεθα nor στένοντες is a possible variant : they in no way affect the certainty that we must read προσήμεθα and σθένοντες. In a discussion on the characteristics and tendencies of a particular MS., such facts have a proper (and it may happen to be, an important) place, as illustrating how, for instance, ι may have been wrongly added, or θ wrongly altered, elsewhere. The editor of a text has to consider how far he will report facts of which the direct interest is palaeographical only. *Scope of the critical annotation.*

The rule which I have followed is to report only those readings of MSS. which have a direct critical interest, that is, which affect the

---

[1] On p. 164, in crit. note line 2, the first word should be read ἀπότομον, not ἄποτμον: v. 877, then, is not an instance in which my text deviates from L.

question as to what should be read in that place of the text; except in
the instances, not numerous in this play, where a manuscript error, *as
such,* appeared specially significant. Had I endeavoured to exhibit all, or
even a considerable part, of the mere mis-spellings, errors of accentuation, and the like, which I have found in the MSS. which I have collated,
my critical notes must have grown to an enormous bulk, without any
corresponding benefit, unless to the palaeographical student of the
particular codex and its kindred. On the other hand, I have devoted
much time, care, and thought to the endeavour not to omit in my critical
notes any point where the evidence of the MSS. known to me seemed to
have a direct bearing on the text.

The use of
conjecture.
§ 4. The use of conjecture is a question on which an editor must be
prepared to meet with large differences of opinion, and must be content
if the credit is conceded to him of having steadily acted to the best of
his judgment. All students of Sophocles would probably agree at least
in this, that his text is one in which conjectural emendation should
be admitted only with the utmost caution. His style is not seldom
analogous to that of Vergil in this respect, that, when his instinct felt a
phrase to be truly and finely expressive, he left the logical analysis of it
to the discretion of grammarians then unborn. I might instance νῦν
πᾶσι χαίρω (*O. T.* 596). Such a style may easily provoke the heavy
hand of prosaic correction; and, if it requires sympathy to interpret and
defend it, it also requires, when it has once been marred, a very tender
and very temperate touch in any attempt to restore it. Then in the lyric
parts of his plays Sophocles is characterised by tones of feeling and
passion which change with the most rapid sensibility—by boldness and
sometimes confusion of metaphor—and by occasional indistinctness of
imagery, as if the figurative notion was suddenly crossed in his mind by
the literal.

Our text—
how trans-
mitted.
§ 5. Now consider by what manner of process the seven extant plays
of this most bold and subtle artist have come down to us through about
23 centuries. Already within some 70 years after the death of Sophocles,
the Athenian actors had tampered in such wise with the texts of the
three great dramatists that the orator Lycurgus caused a standard copy
to be deposited in the public archives of Athens, and a regulation to be
made that an authorised person should follow in a written text the
performances given on the stage, with a view to controlling unwarranted
change[1]. Our oldest manuscript dates from 1400 to 1500 years after
the time of Lycurgus. The most ancient sources which existed for the

---

[1] [Plut.] *Vit. Lycurg.* § 11.

writers of our MSS. were already, it cannot be doubted, seriously corrupted. And with regard to these writers themselves, it must not be forgotten what their ordinary qualifications were. They were usually men who spoke and wrote the Greek of their age (say from the 11th to the 16th century) as it was commonly spoken and written by men of fair education. On the other hand, as we can see, they were usually very far from being good scholars in old classical Greek; of classical metres they knew almost nothing; and in respect of literary taste or poetical feeling they were, as a rule, no less poorly equipped. In the texts of the dramatists they were constantly meeting with things which they did not understand, and in such cases they either simply transmitted a fault of the archetype, or tried to make sense by some expedient of their own. On the whole, the text of Sophocles has fared better in the MSS. than that of either Aeschylus or Euripides. This needs no explanation in the case of Aeschylus. The style of Euripides, apparently so near to common life, and here analogous to that of Lysias, is, like the orator's, full of hidden snares and pitfalls for a transcriber: λείη μὲν γὰρ ἰδεῖν, as the old epigram says of it, εἰ δέ τις αὐτὴν | εἰσβαίνοι, χαλεποῦ τρηχυτέρη σκόλοπος. Where, however, our MSS. of Sophocles do fail, the corruption is often serious and universal. His manuscript text resembles a country with generally good roads, but an occasional deficiency of bridges.

Its general condition.

Is there reason to hope that, in such places, more light will yet be obtained from the manuscripts or scholia now known to exist? It appears hardly doubtful that this question must be answered in the negative. The utmost which it seems prudent to expect is a slightly increased certitude of minor detail where the text is already, in the main, uncorrupted. I need scarcely add that the contingency of a new MS. being discovered does not here come into account.

§ 6. Such, then, are the general conditions under which an editor of Sophocles is required to consider the treatment of conjectural emendation. It would seem as if a conservative *tendency* were sometimes held to be desirable in the editor of a text. When a text has been edited, we might properly speak of the *result* as 'conservative' or the contrary. But an editor has no more right to set out with a conservative tendency than with a tendency of the opposite kind. His task is simply to give, as nearly as he can ascertain it, what the author wrote. Each particular point affecting the text must be considered on its own merits. Instances have not been wanting in which, as I venture to think, editors of Sophocles have inclined too much to the side of unnecessary or even disastrous

Textual criticism should have no bias.

alteration. On the other hand, it is also a serious fault to place our manuscripts above the genius of the ancient language and of the author, and to defend the indefensible by 'construing,' as the phrase is, 'through thick and thin.' Who, then, shall be the judge of the golden mean? The general sense, it must be replied, of competent and sympathetic readers. This is the only tribunal to which in such a case an editor can go, and in the hands of this court he must be content to leave the decision.

Con-jectures of former critics, adopted in the text. § 7. The following table exhibits the places where the reading adopted in my text is found in no MS., but is due to conjecture. The reading placed first is one in which L agrees with some other MS. or MSS., except where it is differently specified. After each conjecture is placed the name of the critic who (to the best of my knowledge) first proposed it: where the priority is unknown to me, two or more names are given.

198 τέλει] τελεῖν Hermann.　200 A long syllable wanting. < ταῦ > Hermann.　2 – ◡ ◡ wanting.　< σύμμαχον > Kennedy.　248 ἄμοιρον] ἄμορον Porson.　351 προσεῖπας] προεῖπας Brunck.　360 λέγειν] λέγων Hartung.　376 με...γε σοῦ] σε...γ᾽ ἐμοῦ[1] Brunck.　478 πέτρας ὡς ταῦρος (πετραῖος ὁ ταῦρος first hand of L)] πέτρας ἰσόταυρος E. L. Lushington.　537 ἐν ἐμοί] ἔν μοι Reisig.　537 κοὐκ] ἢ οὐκ A. Spengel and Blaydes.　538 γνωρίσοιμι] γνωριοῖμι Elmsley.　657 σ᾽ inserted by Hermann after λόγῳ.　666 καὶ τάδ᾽] τὰ δ᾽ Kennedy (τάδ᾽ Herm.). 672 ἐλεεινὸν] ἐλεινὸν Porson.　693 εἴ σε νοσφίζομαι] εἴ σ᾽ ἐνοσφιζόμαν Hermann, Hartung, Badham.　696 εἰ δύναιο γενοῦ (δύνᾳ first hand in L)] ἂν γένοιο Blaydes.　741 τίνα δ᾽] τίνος Nauck.　763 ὁ δέ γ᾽ (ὅ γ᾽ L)] οἳ Hermann.　790 προὐφάνη] προὔφηνεν Hermann.　815 τίς τοῦδέ γ᾽ ἀνδρὸς νῦν ἔστ᾽ ἀθλιώτερος (others τίς τοῦδέ γ᾽ ἀνδρός ἐστιν ἀθλιώτερος)] τίς τοῦδε νῦν ἔστ᾽ ἀνδρὸς ἀθλιώτερος. I had supposed this obvious remedy to be my own, but find that P. N. Papageorgius (*Beiträge* p. 26, 1883) ascribes it to Dindorf in the *Poet. Scen.*: this then must be some former edit., for it is not in that of 1869 (the 5th), and in the Oxford ed. of 1860 Dind. ejected the verse altogether: see my crit. note on the place.　817 ᾧ...τινα] ὅν...τινι Wunder.　825 μήτ᾽ (μῆστ᾽ first hand in L)] μηδ᾽ Dindorf.　876 ἀκροτάταν] ἀκρότατον Wunder.　891 ἕξεται (ἐξεται, sic, L)] θίξεται Blaydes.　893 θυμῶι (others θυμῶ or θυμοῦ)] θεῶν Hermann.　906 – ◡ – ◡ or ◡ – ◡ ◡ wanting.　παλαίφατα Linwood. 943 f. ἢ τέθνηκε Πόλυβος; εἰ δὲ μὴ | λέγω γ᾽ ἐγὼ τἀληθὲς] Triclinius

---

[1] On p. 82, in crit. note, line 2, for γέ μου read γ᾽ ἐμοῦ.

conjectured ἢ τέθνηκέ που[1] Πόλυβος γέρων; | εἰ μὴ λέγω τἀληθές, which Erfurdt improved by substituting Πόλυβος, ὦ γέρον for που Πόλυβος γέρων. 987 μέγας] μέγας γ' Porson. 993 ἢ οὐ θεμιτὸν] ἢ οὐχὶ θεμιτὸν Brunck. 1002 ἔγωγ' οὐ (ἔγωγ' οὐχὶ A)] ἐγὼ οὐχὶ Porson. 1025 τεκὼν] τυχὼν Bothe, Foertsch. 1062 οὐκ ἂν ἐκ τρίτης] οὐδ' ἐὰν τρίτης Hermann. 1099 τῶν] τᾶν Nauck. 1100 προσπελασθεῖσ'] πατρὸς πελασθεῖσ' Lachmann. 1109 Ἑλικωνιάδων] Ἑλικωνίδων Porson. 1137 ἐμμήνους (ἐκμήνους cod. Trin.)] ἐκμήνους Porson. 1193 τὸ σόν τοι] τὸν σόν τοι Joachim Camerarius. 1196 οὐδένα] οὐδὲν Hermann. 1205 τίς ἐν πόνοις, τίς ἄταις ἀγρίαις] τίς ἄταις ἀγρίαις, τίς ἐν πόνοις Hermann. 1216 A long syllable wanting. <ὦ> Erfurdt. 1218 ὀδύρομαι] δύρομαι Seidler. 1244 ἐπιρρήξασ'] ἐπιρράξασ' Dobree. 1245 κάλει] καλεῖ Erfurdt. 1264 πλεκταῖς ἐώραις ἐμπεπλεγμένην (L ἐμπεπληγμένην)· ὁ δὲ | ὅπως δ' (A omits δ'). πλεκταῖσιν αἰώραισιν ἐμπεπλεγμένη ὁ δὲ | ὅπως δ' also occurs.] πλεκταῖσιν αἰώραισιν ἐμπεπλεγμένην. | ὁ δ' ὡς Campbell. 1279 αἵματος (others αἵματός τ')] αἱματοῦς Heath. 1310 διαπέταται] διαπωτᾶται Musgrave, Seidler. 1315 ἀδάμαστον] ἀδάματον Hermann. *ib.* A syllable ⌣ wanting. <ὸν> Hermann. 1341 τὸν ὀλέθριον μέγαν (others μέγα)] τὸν μέγ' ὀλέθριον Erfurdt. 1348 μήδ' ἀναγνῶναί ποτ' ἄν (or ποτε)] μηδέ γ' ἂν γνῶναί ποτε Hermann. 1350 νομάδος] νομάδ' Elmsley. 1360 ἄθλιος] ἄθεος Erfurdt. 1365 ἔφυ] ἔτι Hermann. 1401 μέμνησθ' ὅτι] μέμνησθέ τι Elmsley. 1495 γονεῦσιν] γόνοισιν Nauck. 1505 μή σφε παρίδῃς] μή σφε περιίδῃς Dawes. 1513 ἀεὶ] ἐᾷ Dindorf. 1517 εἰμὶ] εἶμι Brunck. 1521 νῦν...νῦν] νυν...νυν Brunck. 1526 ὅστις...καὶ τύχαις ἐπιβλέπων] οὐ τίς...ταῖς τύχαις ἐπέβλεπεν Hartung, partly after Martin and Ellendt.

§ 8. The following emendations, adopted in the text, are due to the present editor. The grounds on which they rest are in each case stated in the commentary :— Conjectures by the editor.

227 ὑπεξελὼν | αὐτὸς] ὑπεξελεῖν αὐτὸν.
624 ὅταν] ὡς ἂν.
640 δρᾶσαι...δυοῖν] δυοῖν...δρᾶν.
1091 Οἰδίπου] Οἰδίπουν.
1218 ὡς περίαλλα ἰαχέων (vv. ll. περίαλα, ἀχέων)] ὥσπερ ἰάλεμον χέων.
1280 κακὰ] κάτα.
1405 ταὐτὸν] ταὐτοῦ.

Two conjectural supplements are also the editor's:
493 <βασανίζων>
877 <ἄκρον>

[1] On p. 176, crit. note, line 2, insert που after τέθνηκε.

In a few other places, where I believe the text to be corrupt, I have remedies to suggest. But these are cases in which the degree of probability for each mind must depend more on an ἄλογος αἴσθησις. Here, then, the principles of editing which I have sought to observe would not permit me to place the conjectures in the text. In the commentary they are submitted to the consideration of scholars, with a statement of their grounds in each case. 1090 οὐκ ἔσῃ τὰν αὔριον] τὰν ἐπιοῦσαν ἔσῃ. 1101 ἢ σέ γέ τις θυγάτηρ | Λοξίου ;] ἢ σέ γ᾽ ἔφυσε πατὴρ | Λοξίας ; 1031 ἐν καιροῖς (others, ἐν κακοῖς)] ἐγκυρῶν. 1315 δυσούριστον ⚥] δυσούριστ᾽ ἰόν. 1350 νομάδ᾽] μονάδ᾽.

Notation. § 9. In my text, a conjecture is denoted by open type, as τελεῖν for τέλει in 198: except in those cases where a slight correction, which at the same time appears certain, has been so generally adopted as to have become part of the received text; as ἄμορον for ἄμοιρον in 248. In such cases, however, no less than in others, the fact that the reading is due to conjecture is stated in the critical note.

The marks † † signify that the word or words between them are believed by the editor to be unsound, but that no conjecture seemed to him to possess a probability so strong as to warrant its insertion in the text.

It was only after my text had been printed that I received, through the kindness of Mr P. N. Papageorgius, his *Beiträge zur Erklärung und Kritik des Sophokles.* Pars Prima. Iena, Fromann (H. Pohle) 1883 : pp. 40. I gladly take this opportunity of mentioning his emendations of the *O. T.*, which, had his work reached me earlier, would have been recorded in my critical notes :—

(1) 329 τἄμ᾽ ὡς ἂν εἴπω] τἄμ᾽ ἐς σ᾽ ἀνείπω. (2) 360 καὶ τοὔργον ἂν σοῦ τοῦτ᾽ ἔφην εἶναι μόνου, where εἶναι, though found in A and others, has come in L from a later hand. For εἶναι he proposes ἐγώ. (3) 815 τίς τοῦδέ γ᾽ ἀνδρὸς νῦν ἔστ᾽ ἀθλιώτερος (L)] τίς τοῦδέ γ᾽ ἀνδρὸς νῦν ὃς

ο

ἀθλιώτερος ; (4) 360 ἢ ᾽κπειρᾷ λέγειν (L)] ἢ ᾽κπειρᾷ λόγοις ; I am glad to find him confirming the remark made in my critical note (p. 80),

ο

that the λέγειν of L points to λόγων, which, as he notices, occurs in a gloss by a late hand, εἰ [wanting in L] πεῖραν λόγων κινεῖς.

In 1881 the same author published his *Kritische und palaeographische Beiträge zu den alten Sophokles-Scholien*, and in supplement to it (1883), *Codex Laur. von Soph. und eine neue Kollation in Scholien-Texte* (37 pp.), giving in many places the true readings of the old scholia in the MS., and also some old lemmata and scholia hitherto unpublished[1].

---

[1] His transcript of an old schol. on v. 35, p. 20, enables me to supplement my crit. note on ὅς γ' in 35. An old schol. there in L runs, ὅς τε μολὼν ἄστυ Καδμεῖον, ἵνα καὶ ἡ ἀπὸ ξένης αὐτοῦ ἄφιξις δηλωθῇ (the parent, doubtless, of the corrupt ὥστε μολεῖν ἄστυ Καδμεῖον). The reading ὅς τ', then, claims such weight as is due to the fact that it was recognised by the scholiast : but this circumstance does not affect the preference which, on other grounds, seems due to ὅς γ'.

METRICAL ANALYSIS.

In my text, I have exhibited the lyric parts with the received division of verses, for convenience of reference to other editions, and have facilitated the metrical comparison of strophe with antistrophe by prefixing a small numeral to each verse.

Here, in proceeding to analyse the metres systematically, I must occasionally depart from that received division of verses—namely, wherever it differs from that which (in my belief) has been proved to be scientifically correct. These cases are not very numerous, however, and will in no instance cause difficulty.

The researches of Dr J. H. Heinrich Schmidt into the Rhythmic and Metric of the classical languages have thrown a new light on the lyric parts of Greek Tragedy[1]. A thorough analysis of their structure shows how inventive and how delicate was the instinct of poetical and musical fitness which presided over every part of it. For the criticism of lyric texts, the gain is hardly less important. Conjectural emendation can now in many cases be controlled by more sensitive tests than were formerly in use. To take one example from this play, we shall see further on how in v. 1214 the δικάζει τὸν of the MSS. is corroborated, as against Hermann's plausible conjecture δικάζει τ'. The work of Dr Schmidt might be thus described in general terms. Setting out from the results of Rossbach and Westphal, he has verified, corrected, and developed these by an exhaustive study of the Greek metrical texts themselves. The essential strength of his position con-

---

[1] Dr Schmidt's work, 'Die Kunstformen der Griechischen Poesie und ihre Bedeutung,' comprises four volumes, viz. (1) 'Die Eurhythmie in den Chorgesängen der Griechen,' &c. Leipzig, F. C. Vogel, 1868. (2) 'Die antike Compositionslehre,' &c. *ib.* 1869. (3) 'Die Monodien und Wechselgesänge der attischen Tragödie,' &c. *ib.* 1871. (4) 'Griechische Metrik,' *ib.* 1872.

sists in this, that his principles are in the smallest possible measure hypothetical. They are based primarily on internal evidence afforded by Pindar, Aeschylus, Sophocles, Euripides and Aristophanes. To Professor J. W. White, Assistant Professor of Greek at Harvard University, is due the credit of having introduced Dr Schmidt's system to English readers[1].

With regard to the lyric parts of this play, were I to give merely a skeleton scheme of them, the application of it to the Greek text might prove a little difficult for those who are not already acquainted with the results indicated above. For the sake, therefore, of greater clearness, I give the Greek text itself, with the scheme applied to it. Such notes as appeared requisite are added.

A few explanatory remarks must be premised.

A syllable of speech, like a note of music, has three conditions of utterance: (1) *length of tone*, (2) *strength of tone*, (3) *height of tone*.

Preliminary remarks.

(1) *Length of tone*—according as the voice dwells a longer or shorter time on the syllable—is the affair of *Quantity*. A 'short' syllable, as distinguished from a 'long,' is one which is pronounced in a shorter time. (2) *Strength of tone*—according to the stronger or weaker 'beat,' *ictus*, which the voice gives to the syllable—is the affair of *Rhythm*. 'Rhythm' is measured movement. The unity of a rhythmical sentence depends on the fact that one syllable in it has a stronger ictus than any other. (3) *Height of tone*—according as the voice has a higher or lower pitch—is the affair of *Accent*.

In modern poetry, Accent is the basis of Rhythm. In old Greek poetry, Quantity is the basis of Rhythm, and Accent has no influence which we can perceive. The facts which we have now to notice fall, then, under two heads: I. Quantity, as expressed in *Metre:* and II. *Rhythm*.

I. *Metre.* § 1. In Greek verse, the short syllable, denoted by ᴗ, is the unit of measure, and is called 'a time' (Lat. *mora*): a long

Metre.

---

[1] By his excellent translation, made conjointly with Prof. Dr Riemenschneider, and revised by Dr Schmidt, of the 'Leitfaden in der Rhythmik und Metrik der Classischen Sprachen' (Leipzig, 1869)—an epitome, for schools, of the principles established in the 'Kunstformen.' The 'Introduction to the Rhythmic and Metric of the Classical Languages' was published at Boston, by Ginn and Heath, 1878; and in Prof. White's edition of this play (*ib.* 1879) the lyrics are constituted in conformity with it. Here, I have felt it necessary to assume that few of my English readers would be familiar with Dr Schmidt's results, and have therefore deemed it expedient to give fuller explanations than would otherwise have been necessary.

syllable, –, has twice the value of a short; so that – ⏑ is a foot of 'three times.' The short syllable has the musical value of a quaver ♪ or $\frac{1}{8}$ note (*i.e.* eight of which make 𝅝). The long syllable has therefore the value of ♩ or a $\frac{1}{4}$ note.

§ 2. As in music ♩. signifies that the $\frac{1}{4}$ note has been made one-half as long again (*i.e.* $\frac{1}{4}+\frac{1}{8}=\frac{3}{8}$), so in Greek verse the long syllable could be prolonged by a pause, and made equal to *three* short syllables. When it has this value, instead of – we write └.

§ 3. In a metrical foot, there is always one syllable on which the chief strength of tone, or ictus, falls. This syllable is called the *arsis* of the foot. The rest of the foot is called the *thesis*[1]. When a long syllable forms the *arsis* of a measure, it can have the value of even *more* than three short syllables. When it becomes equivalent to *four* (=𝅗𝅥, a $\frac{1}{2}$ note), it is written thus, ⊔. When to *five* (= ♩.♩, $\frac{5}{8}$ note), thus, ш.

§ 4. When the long syllable (written └) is made equal to *three* short, it can be used, alone, as a metrical substitute for a whole foot of three short 'times,' viz. for – ⏑ (trochee), ⏑ – (iambus), or ⏑ ⏑ ⏑ (tribrach). So, when (written ⊔) it has the value of *four* short, it can represent a whole foot in $\frac{4}{8}$ ($\frac{1}{2}$) measure, viz. – ⏑ ⏑ (dactyl), ⏑ ⏑ – (anapaest), or – – (spondee). And so ш can replace any $\frac{5}{8}$ measure, as – ⏑ –, – ⏑ ⏑ ⏑, ⏑ ⏑ ⏑ – (paeons), ⏑ – –, – – ⏑ (bacchii). This representation of *a whole foot* by one prolonged syllable is called *syncope*, and the foot itself is 'a *syncopated* trochee,' &c.

§ 5. When two short syllables are used, by 'resolution,' for a long one (♪♪ for ♩) this is denoted by ⏕. Conversely the sign ⏖ means that one long syllable is used, by 'contraction,' for two short ones.

§ 6. An '*irrational syllable*' (συλλαβὴ ἄλογος) is one which has a *metrical* value to which its actual *time-value* does not properly entitle it. The most frequent case is when a long stands for a short in the thesis of a foot, which is then 'an irrational foot.' The irrational syllable is

[1] This is the reverse of the old Greek usage, in which θέσις meant 'putting down *the foot*' (and so the syllable which has the ictus), ἄρσις, the 'lifting' of it. Roman and modern writers applied *arsis* to 'the raising of the *voice*,' *thesis*, to the lowering of it. Dr Schmidt has reverted to the Greek use, which is intrinsically preferable, since the modern use of the term 'arsis' tends to confuse *ictus* with *accent*. But the modern use has become so general that, in practice, it appears more convenient to retain it; and I have done so.

marked >. Thus in the trochaic verse (*O. T.* 1524), ὦ πάτρ | ᾶς
θήβᾱ|ης, the syllable θή is irrational, and ᾱς θηβ is an irrational
trochee. The converse use of an irrational short syllable instead of a
long is much rarer, occurring chiefly where – ᴗ ᴗ is replaced by an
apparent ᴗ ᴗ ᴗ (written ᴗ ᴗ >), or – – by an apparent – ᴗ̆ (written
–>̆). In a metrical scheme ⸗ means that a long syllable is admitted as
an irrational substitute for a short one.

§ 7. When a dactyl takes the place of a trochee, it is called a
cyclic dactyl, and written –ᴗ ᴗ. The true dactyl (– ᴗ ᴗ) = ♩♫ : the
cyclic = ♩.♪♩ : *i.e.* the long syllable loses ¼ of its value, and the first
short loses ½, so that we have $\frac{1\frac{1}{2}}{8} + \frac{1}{16} + \frac{1}{8} = \frac{3}{8}$. So the cyclic anapaest,
ᴗ ᴗ–, can replace an iambus.

§ 8. A measure can be introduced by a syllable external to it, and
having no ictus. This syllable is called the *anacrusis* (ἀνάκρουσις,
'upward beat'). It can never be longer than the thesis of the measure,
and is seldom less. Thus, before – ᴗ, the anacrusis would properly
be ᴗ (for which an irrational syllable > can stand). Before – ᴗ ᴗ, it
would be ᴗ ᴗ or –. The anacrusis is divided from the verse by three
vertical dots :

§ 9. It will be seen that in the Parodos, 2nd strophe, 1st period,
3rd verse, the Greek letter ω is printed over the syllables στόλος which
form the anacrusis. This means that they have not the full value
of ᴗ ᴗ or two ⅛ notes (♪♪), but only of two $\frac{1}{16}$ notes (♬).

§ 10. *Pauses.* The final measure of a series, especially of a verse,
might always be incomplete. Then a pause represented the thesis of
the unfinished foot. Thus the verse νῦν δ' ἐπὶ|κεκλὄμὲν|ᾱ ᴗ ᴗ is in-
complete. The lacking syllables ᴗ ᴗ are represented by a pause. The
signs for the pause, according to its length, are as follows :—

A pause equal to ᴗ is denoted by ∧ , musically ᴖ for ♪

,,	,,	–	,,	,,	⊼,	,,	ᴦ	,, ♩
,,	,,	– ᴗ	,,	,,	⊼,	,,	ᴦ·	,, ♩.
,,	,,	– –	,,	,,	⊼,	,,	ᴖ·	,, 𝅝

II. *Rhythm.* § 11. Metre having supplied feet determined by Rhythm.
quantity, Rhythm combines these into groups or 'sentences' determined
by ictus. Thus in verse 151, ὦ Διὸς ἁδυεπὲς φάτι, || τίς ποτε τᾶς
πολυχρύσου, there are two rhythmical sentences. The first owes its
rhythmical unity to the chief ictus on ὦ, the second to the chief ictus

J. S.

f

on τίς.   Such a rhythmical κῶλον or sentence almost always consists of feet equal to each other.   The end of a sentence is denoted by the sign ‖.

§ 12.   Rhythmical *sentences* are again combined in the higher unity of the rhythmical *period.*   Here the test of unity is no longer the presence of a chief ictus on one syllable, but the accurate correspondence with each other of the sentences which the period comprises.   The period is seen to be such by the fact that it is neither less nor more than an artistic and symmetrical whole.

§ 13.   In the choric type of lyrics, which Tragedy uses, we find, as in other Greek lyric types, the rhythmical sentence and period.   Their correspondence is subordinate to that of strophe and antistrophe. Each strophe contains usually (though not necessarily) more than one rhythmical period.   Each period of the strophe has its rhythmical counterpart in a period of the antistrophe.   And, within each period, the rhythmical 'sentences' (κῶλα) accurately correspond with each other.

§ 14.   In the choric dance which accompanied the choric song, the *antistrophe* brought the dancer back to the position from which, at the beginning of the *strophe,* he set out.   Hence the necessity for strict metrical correspondence, *i. e.* for equal duration in time.   When any part of a choric song is non-antistrophic, this means that, while that part was being sung, the dancers stood still.   A non-antistrophic element could be admitted in any one of three forms : viz. (1) as a verse prefixed to the first strophe—a 'proöde' or *prelude,* τὸ προῳδικόν, ἡ προῳδός, denoted by πρ.: (2) as a verse inserted between strophe and antistrophe—a 'mesode' or *interlude,* τὸ μεσῳδικόν, ἡ μεσῳδός : (3) as a verse following the last antistrophe—an ' epode' or *postlude,* τὸ ἐπῳδικόν, ἡ ἐπῳδός[1].

During the pause at the end of a verse in a choric ode of Tragedy, the dance and song momentarily ceased ; but instrumental music probably filled the brief interval.   Such pauses correspond no less exactly than the other rhythmical divisions.

We will now see how these principles are exemplified in the lyrics of the *Oedipus Tyrannus.*   Under each line of a strophe I give in smaller type the corresponding line of the antistrophe, since the comparison is often instructive, especially with regard to irrational syllables.

---

[1] Distinguish the masc. ὁ ἐπῳδός, a refrain, esp. the epodic distichon as used by Archilochus and Horace.

I. Parodos, vv. 151—215.

FIRST STROPHE.

(I., II., denote the *First* and *Second Rhythmical Periods.* The sign ‖ marks the end of a *Rhythmical Sentence;* ⟧ marks that of a *Period.*)

```
    ‾ ◡◡   ‾◡◡   ‾,  ◡◡   ‾  ◡ ◡   ‾  ◡◡   ‾ ‾
```
I. 1. ω διος | αδυεπ | ες φατι ‖ τις ποτε | τας πολυ | χρυσου‖

πρωτα σε | κεκλομεν | ος θυγατ ‖ ερ   διος | αμβροτ αθ | ανα ‖

```
    ∟◡   ∟◡   ∟◡   ∟◡
```
2. πυ ⋮ θωνος | αγλα | ας εβ | ας ‾⋀ ‖

γαι ⋮ αοχ | ον τ αδ | ελφε | αν ‖

```
    ‾ ◠◠  ‾ ◡◡   ‾ ◡ ◡  ‾   ◡◡  ‾◡◡  ‾ ‾
```
3. θηβας | εκτεταμ | αι φοβερ ‖αν φρενα | δειματι | παλλων ‖

αρτεμιν | α κυκλο | εντ αγορ ‖ας θρονον | ευκλεα | θασσει ‖

```
    ‾   ‾◡◡   ‾◡◡ ∟ ‾
```
4. ι ⋮ ηιε | δαλιε | παι | αν ‾⋀ ⟧

και ⋮φοιβον εκ | αβολον | ι | ω ⟧

```
    ‾ ◡ ◡‾◡◡ ‾ ◡ ◡‾◡◡ ‾ ◡◡ ‾ ◡◡ ‾◠ ‾ ◡◡
```
II. 1. αμφι σοι|αζομεν|ος τι μοι| η νεον ‖ η περι|τελλομεν|αις ωρ | αις παλιν ‖

τρισσοι α | λεξιμορ | οι προφαν| ητε μοι ‖ ειποτε | και προτερ| ας ατ | ας υπερ ‖

```
    ‾◡◡  ‾ ◡◡ ‾◡ ◡ ◡ ◡‾ ◡ ◡ ‾ ◡◡ ‾  ◡◡ ‾ ‾
```
2. εξαννσ | εις χρεος | ειπε μοι | ω χρυσε ‖ ας τεκνον | ελπιδος|αμβροτε |φαμα⟧

ορνυμεν | ας πολει | ηνυσατ | εκ τοπι ‖ αν φλογα | πηματος | ελθετε |και νυν⟧⟧

I. *First Period:* 4 verses. Metre, *dactylic.* Verse 1. The comma after ‾ in the 3rd foot denotes caesura. Verse 2. The dots ⋮ after πυ show that it is the *anacrusis:* see § 8. The sign

└─ means that the long syllable here has the time-value of − ∪ or a
¾ note, so that θωνος = a dactyl, − ∪∪ : see § 2. This verse forms a
rhythmical sentence of 3 dactyls, a dactylic tripody. It is known as a
'Doric sentence,' because characteristic of Doric melodies: Pind. *Ol.*
8. 27 κίονα | δαιμονί | αν ⌒ || : *ib.* 40 εἰς δ᾽ ἐσόρ | ουσε βο | άσαις ||.
The sign ⌒ marks a *pause* equal to ∪∪ : see § 10.   Verse **3.**
∪∪ shows that ᾱς represents, by contraction, ∪∪.   Verse **4.** π ᾱ ι has
the time-value of a whole dactyl − ∪∪, or ¼ note: this is therefore a
case of *syncope*, see § 4.   When syncope occurs thus in the *penultimate* measure of a rhythmical sentence or of a verse, it imparts to it a
melancholy cadence: and such is called a '*falling*' sentence or verse.

Now count the sentences marked off by ||. In v. **1**, we have 2
sentences of 3 feet each; 3, 3.   In v. **2** one sentence of 4 feet; 4.
In v. **3**, the same as in v. **1**.   In v. **4**, the same as in v. **2**.   The series
thus is 3 3. 4. 3 3. 4.   This determines the *form* of the entire *Rhythmical
Period*, which is expressed thus :—

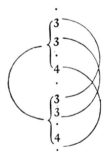

Here the curve on the *left* means that one whole
group (verses 1, 2) corresponds with the other whole
group (verses 3, 4).   The curves on the *right* mean
that the 1st *sentence* of the 1st group corresponds to
the 1st of the 2nd, the 2nd of the 1st to the 2nd of
the 2nd, the 3rd of the 1st to the 3rd of the 2nd.
The vertical dots mean that the figure or figures between any two of them relate to a single verse.

This is called the *palinodic* period : meaning that
a group of rhythmical sentences *recurs once, in the
same order.*

II. *Second Period:* 2 verses. Metre, still *dactylic.*   Verse **1.**   The
last foot, ᾱις παλιν, is a true dactyl (not a 'cyclic,' see § 7); it is not
contracted into − −; and it *closes a rhythmical sentence.*   Now, when
this happens, it is a rule that the immediately preceding foot should be
also an *uncontracted* dactyl.   Why do not ᾱις ωρ, ᾱς ατ, break this rule?
Because, in singing, two ⅛ notes, ♫, instead of one ¼ note, ♩, were
given to the syllable ωρ, and likewise to ατ.   This is expressed by
writing ω͡ρ, and not merely ω̄ρ.

In v. **1** we have two rhythmical sentences of 4 feet each : 4, 4.   In

v. 2, the same. The series, then, is 4 4. 4 4., and the form of the Rhythmical Period is again *palinodic*:—

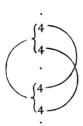

SECOND STROPHE.

I. 1.   ω ⋮ ποποι αν | αριθμα | γαρ φερ ¦ ω ∧ ‖
       ων ⋮ πολις αν | αριθμος | ολλυ | ται

 2.   πη ⋮ ματα νοσ | ει δε | μοι προ | πας ∧ ‖
      νη ⋮ λε α δε | γενεθλα | προς πεδ | ω

 3.   στολος ⋮ ουδ ενι | φροντιδος | εγχ | ος ∧ ⟧
      θανατ ⋮ αφορα | κειται αν | οικτ | ως

II. 1.   ω τις α | λεξεται | ουτε γαρ | εκγονα ‖
       ενδ αλοχ | οι πολι | αιτ επι | ματερες

 2.   κλυτ ⋮ ας χθονος | αυξεται | ουτε τοκ | οισιν ‖
      ακτ ⋮ αν παρα | βωμιον | αλλοθεν | αλλαι

 3.   ι ⋮ η ι | ων καματ | ων ανεχ ‖ ουσι γυν | αικ | ες ∧ ‖
      λυγρ ⋮ ων πον | ων ικτ | ηρες επ ‖ ι στεναχ | ους | ιν

 4.   αλλ ⋮ ουδ αν | αλλ | ω προσιδ ‖ οις απερ | ευπτερον | ορνιν ‖
      παι ⋮ αν δε | λαμπ | ει στονο ‖ εσσα τε | γηρυς ομ | αυλος

 5.   κρεισσον α | μαιμακετ | ου πυρος | ορμενον ‖
      ων υπερ | ω χρυσε | α θυγατ | ερ διος

 6.   ακτ ⋮ αν προς | εσπερ | ου | θεου ∧ ⟧
      ευ ⋮ ω πα | πεμψον | αλκ | αν

I. *First Period:* 3 verses. The metrical basis of the rhythm is the *choree* (or 'trochee,' – ◡), for which the *cyclic* dactyl (–◡ ◡, see § 7) and tribrach (◡ ◡◡) can be substituted. The rhythm itself is *logaoedic*[1]. When chorees are arranged in ordinary *choreic* rhythm, the ictus of arsis is to that of thesis as 3 to 1 (∸ ◡): when in *logaoedic*, as 3 to 2 (∸ ◡̇). The latter has a lighter and livelier effect. Verse 1. The anacrusis ω is marked >, since it is an 'irrational' syllable (§ 6),—a long serving for a short. The anacrusis can here be no more than ◡, since it can never be longer than the thesis (§ 8), which is here ◡, since ◡ ◡ ◡ represents – ◡. Verse 3. ω written over στολος means that the two short syllables here have only the time-value of ◡, or , not of ◡ ◡ or ♩: see § 9. ουδενι and φροντιδος are *cyclic* dactyls (–◡ ◡ = – ◡), not true ones (– ◡ ◡), see § 7. The second syllable of εγχος is marked *long*, because the last syllable of a verse (*syllaba anceps*, συλλαβὴ ἀδιάφορος) always can be so, and here ος is the first of a choree, – ◡, which the pause ∧ completes.

Verses 1, 2, 3 contain each one rhythmical sentence of 4 feet; the series is therefore . 4 . 4 . 4 ., and the form of the period is:—

4⟩
.⟩
4⟨   When *two* rhythmical sentences of equal length correspond to
.⟩   each other, they form a 'stichic' period (στίχος, a line or verse);
4⟩   when, as here, *more than two*, they form a *repeated stichic period*.

---

[1] The name λογαοιδικός, 'prose-verse,' meant simply that, owing to the apparently lawless interchange of measures (–◡◡, ◡◡◡, – >, for – ◡) in this rhythm, the old metrists looked upon it as something intermediate between prose and verse. It should be borne in mind that the essential difference between choreic and logaoedic rhythm is that of *ictus*, as stated above. The admission of the cyclic dactyl is also a specially logaoedic trait, yet not *exclusively* such, for it is found occasionally in pure choreics also. The question, 'Is this rhythm choreic or logaoedic?' can often be answered only by appeal to the whole poetical and musical character of the lyric composition,— the logaoedic *ictus* being always more vivacious than the choreic. See, on this subject, *Griech. Metrik* § 19. 3. Students will remember that 'logaoedic verse' is a *generic* term.

Three kinds of it have special names: (1) the logaoedic *dipodia*, as κᾰμπῠλον | ᾱρμᾰ‖, is an 'Αδώνιον μέτρον: (2) the *tripodia*, βῠρσοτον | ον κῠκλ | ωμα‖, a Φερεκράτειον: (3) the *tetrapodia*, which is very common, νῠνγαρεμ | οι μελ | ει χορ | ευσαι‖, is the 'glyconic,' Γλυκώνειον. (2) and (3) can vary the place of the cyclic dactyl, and can be catalectic. The logaoedic (5) *pentapodia* and (6) *hexapodia*, both of which occur in tragedy, are not commonly designated by special names.

II. *Second Period:* 6 verses. Metre, dactylic, Verse 2. The anacrusis κλυτ is marked ≥ since it is a really short syllable serving 'irrationally' (§ 6) as a long: for, the measure being – ◡ ◡, the anacrusis should properly be ◡ ◡ or – (as ακτ in the antistr. actually is). Verse 3. $\overleftrightarrow{αικ}$ = – ◡ ◡ (§ 4). This *syncope* (§ 4) in the penult. measure makes a 'falling' verse: see on Str. I., Per. I., v. 4. $\overline{\wedge}$ = a *pause* equal to ◡ ◡ (§ 10).

Verse I contains I rhythmical sentence of 4 feet: v. 2, the same: v. 3, two sentences each of 3 feet: v. 4, the same: vv. 5, 6, the same as I, 2. Series : .4.4. 3 3.4. 4, and the form of period is:—

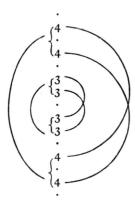

The curves on the *left* show the correspondence of whole rhythmical groups; those on the *right*, that of rhythmical sentences.

If the second group of ·3 3· had followed the second of ·4·4·, this would have been a simple palinodic period, like the 1st of Strophe I. But as the groups are repeated in *reversed* order, it is called a *palinodic-antithetic* period.

THIRD STROPHE.

I. I. αρ : εα τε | τον | μαλερον | ος ‖ νυν α | χαλκος | ασπιδ | ων ∧ ‖

λυκ : ει αν | αξ | τα τε σα | χρυσ ‖ οστροφ | ων απ | αγκυλ | αν

2. φλεγ : ει με | περιβο | ατος | αντι | αξ | ων ∧ ‖

βελ : εα θελ | οιμ αν | αδαματ | ενδατ | εισθ | αι

3. παλ : ισσυτ | ον δραμ | ημα | νωτισ | αι πατρ | ας ∧ ‖

αρ : ωγα | προσταθ | εντα | τας τε | πυρφορ | ους

4. επ : ουρον | ειτ | ες μεγ | αν ‖ θαλαμον | αμφι | τριτ | ας ∧ ⟧

αρτ : εμιδος | αιγλ | ας ξυν | αις ‖ λυκι ορ | η δι | ϙσσ | ει

$$
\begin{array}{l}
\overset{>}{}\quad \smile\ \smile\quad \overset{\smile}{}\smile\quad \llcorner\quad\ \ \llcorner\quad\quad -\smile\ -\quad \smile\quad \llcorner\quad - \\
\end{array}
$$

II. 1. ειτ : ες του απ | οξενον | ορμ | ον ‖ θρηκι | ον κλυδ | ων | α ∧ ‖

      τον : χρυσομιτρ | αν τε κι | κλησκ | ω ‖ τασδ επ | ωνυμ | ον | γας

$$
\overset{>}{-}\quad\smile\quad -\ \smile\quad -\ \smile\quad \llcorner\quad -\ \smile\quad -\ \smile\quad -\ \smile\quad -
$$

2. τελ : ειν γαρ | ει τι | νυξ αφ | η ‖ τουτ επ | ημαρ | ερχετ | αι ∧′‖

      οιν : ωπα | βακχον | ευι | ον ‖ μαιναδ | ων ομ | οστολ | ον

$$
\smile\quad \llcorner\quad \llcorner\quad -\ \smile\quad \llcorner\quad -\ \smile\quad -\ \smile\quad -\ \smile\quad -
$$

3. τον : ω | ταν | πυρφορ | ων ‖ αστραπ | αν κρατ | η νεμ | ων ∧ ‖

      πελ : ασθ | ην | αι φλεγ | οντ ‖ αγλα | ωπι | συμμαχ | ον

$$
\overset{>}{-}\quad -\ \smile\quad \smile\ \smile\ \smile\quad -\quad \smile\quad -\ \smile\quad \llcorner\quad -\quad -
$$

4. ω : ζευ πατ | ερ υπο | σω φθισ | ον κερ | αυν | ω ∧]

      πευκ : α | πι | τον απο | τιμον | εν θε | οις | θεον

I. *First Period :* 4 verses. The *choree* $-\smile$ is again the fundamental measure, as in Str. II. Per. I., but the choreic rhythm here expresses greater excitement. Verse 1. The place of the *syncope* ($\llcorner$, § 4) at τον and ος, each following a tribrach, makes a '*rising*' rhythmical sentence, in contrast with the '*falling*' sentence (see Str. I. Per. I. v. 4), such as verse 4. This helps to mark the strong agitation. Verse 4. $\overset{\gt}{\underset{\smile}{}}$ επ means that the proper anacrusis, $\smile$, can be represented by an 'irrational' syllable (as αρτ in the antistr.).

Verse 1 has 2 sentences of 4 feet each: 2, 1 of 6: 3, the same: 4, the same as 1. Series: .4 4 . 6 . 6 . 4 4. Form of period :—

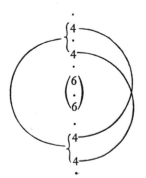

A palinodic-antithetic period, like the last.

II. *Second Period :* 4 verses. Metre, still *choreic.* Note the weighty effect given by syncope ($\llcorner$) in the 'falling' sentences of v. 1, and in

v. 3. In v. 1, ειτ is marked > ('irrational'), because the following dactyl is only *cyclic* (equal to $-\cup$), and the thesis being $\cup$, the anacrusis cannot be more: cp. v. 4.

Verses 1, 2, 3, have each 2 sentences of 4 feet each. Verse 4 forms 1 sentence of 6 feet, to which nothing corresponds : *i.e.* it is an *epode* (§ 14), during the singing of which the dancers *stood still.* (This was dramatically suitable, since Oedipus came on the scene as the last period began, and his address immediately follows its conclusion.) Series :—4 4 . 4 4 . 4 4. 6 = ἐπῳδικόν. Form of period :—

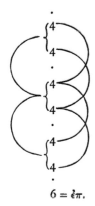

6 = ἐπ.

The period is generically palinodic, since a group recurs, with the sentences in the same order. But the group recurs *more than once.* This is therefore called a *repeated palinodic period,* with 'epode' or postlude.

II. First Stasimon, vv. 463—512.

FIRST STROPHE.

I. 1.   τις : οντιν | α | θεσπιεπ | εια ‖ δελφις | ειπε | πετρ | α ⋀ ‖

ε : λαμψε | γαρ | του νιφο | εντος ‖ αρτι | ως φαν | εισ | α

2.   αρρητ | αρρητ | ων τελε | σαντα ‖ φοινι | αισι | χερσ | ιν ⋀ ⟧

φαμα | παρνασσ | ου τον α | δηλον ‖ ανδρα | παντ ιχν | ευ | ειν

II. 1.   ωρ : α νιν α | ελλαδ | ων ⋀ ‖

φοιτ : α γαρ υπ | αγρι | αν

2.   ιππ : ων σθεναρ | ωτερ | ον ⋀ ‖

υλ : αν ανα τ | αντρα | και

3.   φυγ : ᾳ ποδα | νωμ | αν ⋀ ⟧

πετρ : ας ισο | ταυρ | ος

III. 1.   ενοπλ : ος γαρ επ | αυτον επ | ενθρωσκ | ει ⋀ ‖

μελε : ος μελε | ω ποδι | χηρευ | ων

2.   πυρι : και στεροπ | αις ο δι | ος γενετ | ας ⋀ ‖

τα μεσ : ομφαλα | γας απο | νοσφιζ | ων

3.   δειν : αι δ αμεπ | ονται | κηρες | αναπλακ | ητ | οι ⋀ ⟧

μαντ : εια ταδ | αει | ζωντα | περιποτ | ατ | αι

I.   *First Period:* 2 verses.   Rhythm, *logaoedic,* based on the choree, – ∪ : see Parodos Str. I. Period I.   Each verse has 2 sentences of 4 feet each.   Series: . 4 4 . 4 4.   Form of period:—

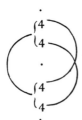

A palinodic period, like the 1st of Parod. Str. I.

II.   *Second Period:* 3 verses.   Rhythm, the same, but in shorter, more rapid sentences.   Each verse has 1 sentence of 3 feet.   Series : . 3 . 3 . 3.   Form of period :—

A repeated stichic period: see Parod. Str. II. Per. I.

III.   *Third Period:* 3 verses.   Rhythm, the same: remark the weighty hexapody of v. 3, expressing how the hand of the avenging god will be heavy on the criminal.   In v. 2, ω written over γενετ (see § 9) means that the time-value of the two syllables was here ♫ : *i.e.* ος γενετ was not a true cyclic dactyl, = ♪♫, but = ♩♫.   In the antistr., the corresponding νοσφιζ is – > for – ∪.

Verses 1 and 2 have each 1 sentence of 4 feet: v. 3 has 1 of 6 feet, an ἐπῳδικόν, during which the dance ceased.   Series : . 4 . 4 . 6 . = ἐπ. Form of period:—

$\left.\begin{matrix} \bullet \\ 4 \\ \bullet \\ 4 \\ \bullet \end{matrix}\right)$ A stichic period (see Parod. Str. II. Per. I.), with postlude.

6 = ἐπ.
•

Second Strophe.

$$- \cup \cup - \quad - \cup \ \cup - \quad - \quad \cup \cup \ - \ - \cup \cup -$$

I. 1. δεινα μεν ουν | δεινα ταρασσ ‖ ει σοφος οι | ωνοθετας ‖

αλλ ο μεν ουν | ζευς οτ απολλ ‖ ων ξυνετοι | και τα βροτων

$$- \cup \cup - \quad - \ \cup \cup - \quad - \ \cup \cup - \quad - \ \cup \cup -$$

2. ουτε δοκουντ | ουτ αποφασκ ‖ οντ οτι λεξ | ω δ απορω ⟧

ειδοτες ανδρ | ων δ οτι μαντ ‖ ις πλεον η | γω φερεται

$$\cup \cup \quad - \ - \cup \cup \quad - \ - \cup \cup \quad - \ - \quad \cup \cup \quad \sqcup$$

II. 1. πετομ : αιδ ελπισιν | ουτ ενθαδορ ‖ ων ουτ οπισ | ω $\overline{\wedge}$ ‖

κρισις : ουκ εστιν αλ | ηθης σοφι ‖ ᾳ δ᾽ αν σοφι | αν

$$- \ - \quad \cup \cup \quad \sqcup$$

2. τι γαρ : η λαβδακιδ | αις $\overline{\wedge}$ ‖

παρα : μειψειεν αν | ηρ

$$- \ - \ \cup \cup \ | \ \cup - \cup \cup \ | \ - \cup \cup \ - \ - \ \cup \cup \ - \ - \cup \cup \ - \ -$$

3. η τω πολυβ | ου νεικος εκ | ειτ ουτε παρ ‖ οιθεν ποτεγ | ωγ ουτε τα | νυν πω $\overline{\wedge}$ ‖

αλλ ουποτ εγ | ωγαν πριν ιδ | οιμ ορθον επ ‖ ος μεμφομεν | ων αν κατα | φαιην

$$\cup \cup \quad \sqcup \quad \cup \cup \ - \ - \quad \cup \cup \quad - \ - \quad \cup \cup \quad \sqcup$$

4. εμαθ : ον προς οτ | ου δη βασαν ‖ ιζων βασαν | ω $\overline{\wedge}$ ‖

φανερ : α γαρ επ | αυτω πτερο ‖ εσσ ηλθε κορ | α

$$\cup \cup \quad \sqcup \ \cup \cup \quad - \ -$$

5. επι : ταν επι | δαμον $\overline{\wedge}$ ‖

ποτε : και σοφος | ωφθη

$$\cup \cup \quad - \ - \cup \cup \quad - \ - \quad \cup \cup \quad \sqcup , \cup \cup \quad \sqcup \cup \cup \quad - \ - \quad \cup \cup \quad \sqcup$$

6. φατιν : ειμ οιδιποδ | α λαβδακιδ ‖ αις επι ‖ κουρος α | δηλων θανατ | ων $\overline{\wedge}$ ⟧

βασαν : ῳ θ αδυπολ | ις τω απ εμ | ας φρενος ‖ ουποτ οφλ | ησει κακι | αν

I. *First Period;* 2 verses. Metre, *choriambic* ($- \cup \cup -$). This measure suits passionate despair or indignation : here it expresses the feeling with which the Chorus hear the charge against their king. Choriambics do not admit of anacrusis.

Each verse has 2 sentences of 2 feet each. Series: . 2 2 . 2 2. Form of period :—

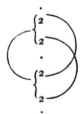

A palinodic period.

II. *Second Period:* **6** verses. Metre, *ionic* ($- - \cup \cup$), an animated, but less excited, measure than the preceding choriambic. Note that *one* verse (**3**) has *no anacrusis*. Such an ionic verse is most nearly akin to a choriambic, in which anacrusis is never allowed. Here we see the consummate skill of Sophocles in harmonising the character of the two periods. Verse 1. $\overline{\cup\cup} = - -$ (§ 4): $\overline{\wedge}$ = a pause equal to $\cup \cup$ (§ 10): the whole is thus $- - \cup \cup$.

Verse 1 has 2 sentences of 2 feet each : v. 2, 1 of 2 feet : v. 3, 2 of 3 feet : v. 4, same as 1 ; v. 5, same as 2 ; v. 6, same as 3. Series : . 2 2 . 2 . 3 3 . 2 2 . 2 . 3 3. Form of period :—

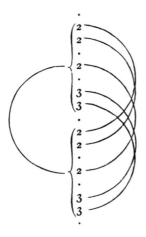

A palinodic period.

III. First Kommos, vv. 649—697 [1].

I πιθ : ου θελ | ησ | ας φρον | ης ‖ ας ταν | αξ | λισσομ | αι ∧]]
   γυν : αι τι | μελλ | εις κομ | ιϛ ‖ ειν δομ | ων | τονδ εσ | ω
   [Here follows an iambic dimeter.]

II. τον : ουτε | πριν | νηπι | ον ‖νυν τ εν| ορκ ‖ ω μεγ | αν κατ | αιδεσ | αι ∧]]
    δοκ : ησις | αγν | ως λογ | ων ‖ ηλθε | δαπτ ‖ ει δε | και το | μη νδικ | ον
    [Here follows an iambic trimeter.]

III. 1. τον : εναγη φιλ | ον μη ‖ ποτ εν αι τι | ᾳ ∧ ‖
      αλ : ις εμοιγ αλ | ις γας ‖ προπονουμεν | ας
   2. συν : αφανει λογ | ωσα ‖ ιμον βαλ | ειν ∧]]
      φαιν : εται ενθ ε | ληξεν ‖ αυτου μεν | ειν
      [Here follow two iambic trimeters.]

[1] The received constitution of this κομμός—which, for convenience of reference to other editions, I have indicated in my text of the play—is as follows: (1) *1st strophe*, 649—659, (2) *2nd strophe*, 660—668; (3) *1st antistr.*, 678—688, (4) *2nd antistr.*, 689—697. The division exhibited above is, however, in stricter accord with scientific method. Here, Periods I. II. III. correspond to the 1st strophe and 1st antistrophe of the traditional arrangement: Period IV. corresponds to the 2nd strophe and 2nd antistrophe. Thus the whole κομμός, so far as it is lyric, might be conceived as forming a single strophe and antistrophe. These terms, however, are not applicable to the κομμοί, nor to the μονῳδίαι (lyrics sung by individual actors, μέλη ἀπὸ σκηνῆς), in the same accurate sense as to the odes sung by the Chorus, since here there was no regular dance accompanying the song. Consequently there was no need for the same rigour in the division of the composition. The principles which governed the structure of the κομμοί and μονῳδίαι have been fully explained by Dr Schmidt in vol. III. of his *Kunstformen*, '*Die Monodien und Wechselgesänge der Attischen Tragödie.*'

IV. 1. $\overset{\scriptstyle >}{\underset{\scriptstyle\smile}{}}$ $\llcorner$ $\llcorner$ $-$ $\smile$ $-$ $\smile$ $-$ $\smile$ $-$

ου : τον | παντ | ων θε | ων θε | ον προμ | ον $\wedge$ ||

ων : αξ | ειπ | ον μεν | ουχ α | παξ μον | ον

2. $-\smile$ $\smile$ $\smile$ $\smile$ $\smile$ $\smile$ $\smile$ $\smile$ $\smile$ $\smile$ $\smile$ $\smile$ $\smile$ $\smile$ $\smile$

αλι | ον επει | αθεος | αφιλος | οτι πυμ | α τον $\wedge$ ||

ισθι | δε παρα | φρονιμον | απορον | επι φρον | ιμα

3. $\smile$ $-$ $-$ $\smile$ $-\smile$ $-$ $\smile$ $-$

ολ : οιμαν φρον | ησιν ει | τανδ εχω ||

πε : φανθαι μ αν | ει σ ενοσφ | ιζομαν

4. $\smile$ $-$ $-$ $\smile$ $-$ $-$ $\smile$ $-$ $-$

αλλ : α μοι δυσ | μορω γα | φθινουσα ||

οστ : εμαν γαν | φιλαν εν | πονοισιν

5. $\overset{\scriptstyle >}{\underset{\scriptstyle\smile}{}}$ $\llcorner$ $\llcorner$ $-$ $\smile$ $-$ $\smile$ $-$ $\smile$ $-$

τρυχ : ει | ψυχ | αν ταδ | ει κακ | οις κακ | α ||

αλ : υ | ουσ | αν κατ | ορθον | ουρισ | ας

6. $\smile$ $\llcorner$ $\llcorner$ $-$ $\smile$ $-$ $\smile$ $-$ $\smile$ $-$

προσ : αψ | ει | τοις παλ | αι τα | προς | σφων $\wedge$]

τα : νυν | ευ | πομπος | αν γεν | οι | ο

I. *First Period:* 1 verse, *choreic.* Two sentences of 4 feet each, forming :—

$$\left.\begin{array}{c} 4 \\ 4 \end{array}\right) \quad \text{A stichic period.}$$

II. *Second Period :* 1 verse, *choreic.* The rhythmical sentence of 2 feet νυν τ εν ορκ || has nothing corresponding with it, but stands between 2 sentences of 4 feet each : *i.e.* it is a μεσῳδός or *interlude.* The form of the period is thus :—

$$\left.\begin{array}{c} 4 \\ 2 \\ 4 \end{array}\right) \quad \text{A mesodic stichic period.}$$

III. *Third Period:* 2 verses. Rhythm, *dochmiac.* When an interchange of measures occurs in Greek verse, it is nearly always between measures of equal length: as when the ionic, $--\smile\smile$, in $\frac{3}{4}$ time, is interchanged with the dichoree, $-\smile-\smile$, in $\frac{6}{8}$ time. The peculiarity of the *dochmius* (ποῦς δόχμιος, 'oblique' foot) is that it is an interchange of measures *not* equal to each other,—viz. the bacchius ∪ – – or – – ∪ (with anacrusis), and shortened choree, – ∧. The fundamental form is ∪ ⋮ – – ∪ | – ∧ ‖. The varieties are due to resolution of long syllables, or to the use of 'irrational' instead of short syllables. Seidler reckoned 32 forms; but, as Schmidt has shown, only 19 actually occur, and some of these very rarely. With resolution, the commonest form is that seen here, ∪ ⋮ ∪ ∪ – ∪ | – ∧ ‖. Each verse contains two dochmiac sentences: *i.e.* we have

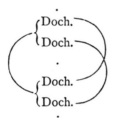

A palinodic period.

  IV. *Fourth Period:* 6 verses. In **1, 2, 5, 6**, the metre is *choreic* (– ∪). In **3, 4**, the metrical basis is the *paeon*, here in its primary form, the 'amphimacer' or 'cretic,' – ∪ –, combined with another measure of the same time-value ($\frac{5}{8}$), the bacchius (∪ – – or – – ∪)[1].

  Verse 1 has 1 sentence of 6 feet; v. 2, the same; v. 3, 1 of 3 feet; v. 4, the same; vv. 5, 6 the same as 1, 2. Series: . 6 . 6 . 3 . 3 . 6 . 6 .: *i.e.*

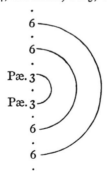

Here we have no repetition of whole groups, but only of single sentences. The period is not therefore palinodic. And the single sentences correspond in an inverted order. This is called simply an *antithetic period.*

---

[1] In v. 4, if Dindorf's conjecture φθινὰς for φθίνουσα is received, we should write:

$$\overline{\alpha\lambda\lambda\alpha} \; \breve{\mu o\iota} \; \overline{} \mid \overline{\delta\upsilon\sigma}\breve{\mu o}\rho\overline{\hat{\omega}} \mid \overline{\gamma\bar{a}} \; \phi\overline{\theta\acute{\iota}}\nu\breve{a}\overline{\varsigma} \;\|$$

οστ εμαν | γαν φιλαν | εν πονοις.

The ear will show anyone that this is *rhythmically* better than what I obtain with the MS. φθίνουσα and πόνοισιν, and the conjecture φθινὰς is entitled to all the additional weight which this consideration affords. On other grounds—those of language and of diplomatic evidence—no less distinct a preference seems due to φθίνουσα.

IV. Second Stasimon, vv. 863—910.

FIRST STROPHE.

I.
>   − ∪   − ∪   − ∪,   − ∪ −   − ∪ − >

εἰ : μοι ξυν | ει | η φερ | οντι ‖ μοιρα | ταν ευ ‖ σεπτον | αγνει |

υβρ : ις φυτ | ευ | ει τυρ | αννον ‖ υβρις | ˙ει πολλ ‖ ων υπ | ερπλησθ |

αν λογ | ων Λ

η ματ | αν

II. 1. εργ : ων τε | παντων | ων νομ | οι προ | κειντ | αι Λ ‖

α : μη πι | καιρα | μηδε | συμφερ | οντ | α

2. υψ : ιποδες | ουρανι | αν Λ ‖

ακρ : οτατον | εισανα | βασ

3. δι : αιθερα | τεκνωθ | εντες | ων ο | λυμπ | ος Λ ⟧

ακρ : ον απο | τομον ωρ | ουσεν | εις αν | αγκ | αν

III. 1. πα : τηρμονος | ουδε | νιν θνα | τα φυσις | ανερ | ων Λ ‖

ενθ : ου ποδι | χρησι | μω χρη | ται το καλ | ως δεχ | ων

2. ε : τικτεν | ουδε | μαν ποτε | λαθ ‖ α κατα | κοιμ | ασ | ει Λ ‖

πολ : ει παλ | αισμα | μη ποτε | λυσ ‖ αι θεον | αιτ | ου | μαι

3. μεγας : εν τουτ | οις θεος | ουδε | γηρ | ασκ | ει Λ ⟧

θεον : ου ληξ | ω ποτε | προστατ | αν | ισχ | ων

J. S.   *g*

I. *First Period:* 1 verse. Rhythm, *logaoedic.*

Two sentences, of 4 feet each, are separated by a *mesode* or inter‑
lude, consisting of the sentence of 2 feet μοιρα | ταν ευ : *i.e.*

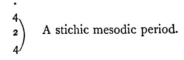

A stichic mesodic period.

II. *Second Period:* 3 verses. Rhythm the same[1].

Verse 1 has 1 sentence of 6 feet: v. 2 is a mesode of 3 feet: v. 3,
the same as 1 : *i.e.*

A mesodic stichic period.

III. *Third Period:* 3 verses. Rhythm the same. For the mark
ω over μεγας and θεον in 3, see § 9, and Parod. Str. ii. Per. i. v. 3.

Verses 1, 3 have each 1 sentence of 6 feet: v. 2, 2 of 4 each : *i.e.*

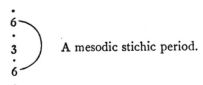

An antithetic period. (See First Kommos, Per. iv.)

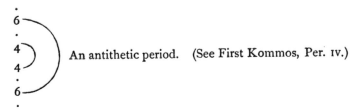

---

[1] The conjectural reading οὐρανίᾳ | αἰθέρι, adopted by Prof. White and (as I
suppose) by Dr Schmidt, would give in v. 3

$$\overset{>}{αιθ} : \overset{\cup\cup}{θερι} \ \overset{\cup}{τεκν} \ | \ \overset{L}{ωθ} \ | \ \overset{-\cup}{εντες} \ | \ \overset{-}{ων} \ \overset{\cup}{ο} \ | \ \overset{L}{λυμπ} \ | \ \overset{-}{ος} \ \wedge \ \|$$

In the antistrophe, Prof. White reads simply ἀκρότατον εἰσαναβᾶσ | ἀπότομον
ὤρουσεν εἰς ἀνάγκαν, which similarly would give

$$\overset{\cup}{απ} : \overset{\cup\cup\cup}{οτομον} \ | \ \overset{L}{ωρ} \ | \ \overset{-\cup}{ουσεν} \ | \ \overset{-}{εις} \ \overset{\cup}{αν} \ | \ \overset{L}{αγκ} \ | \ \overset{-}{αν} \ \wedge \ \|$$

Now, there is no apparent reason for doubting the genuineness of the reading on
which the MSS. agree, οὐρανίαν | δι᾽ αἰθέρα: while in the antistr. the sense affords the
strongest reason (as it seems to me) for holding, as has so generally been held, that
something has fallen out before ἀπότομον. That something I believe to be ἄκρον,
which I have conjecturally supplied. Whether, however, τομον ωρ can properly be
treated as a cyclic anapaest (∪ ∪—, equal in *time*-value to — ∪ or a ⅔ note) seems

SECOND STROPHE.

‒ ◡   ◡ ◡ ◡   ‒ ◡   ‒ ◡

I. 1. ειδε | τις υπερ | οπτα | χερσιν ‖
  ουκετ | ι τον α | θικτον | ειμι

‒   ◡   ‒   ◡   ‒◡

 2. η λογ | ω πορ | ευετ | αι Λ ‖
  γας επ | ομφαλ | ον σεβ | ων

⋛   ◡ ◡   ‒◡   L   ‒

 3. δικ : ας αφοβ | ητος | ου | δε Λ ‖
  ουδ : ες τον αβ | αισι | να | ον

‒◡   ‒   ◡   ‒   ◡   ‒

 4. δαιμον | ων εδ | η σεβ | ων Λ ‖
  ουδε | ταν ο | λυμπι | αν

⋛   ◡ ◡   ‒◡   L   ‒

 5. κακ : α νιν ελ | οιτο | μοιρ | α Λ ‖
  ει : μη ταδε | χειρο | δεικτ | α

‒   ◡   ‒   ◡   ‒   ◡   ‒

 6. δυσποτμ | ου χαρ | ιν χλιδ | ας Λ ‖
  πασιν | αρμοσ | ει βροτ | οις

>   ‒ ◡   ‒ >   ‒ ◡   ‒ ◡   L   ‒

II. 1. ει : μη το | κερδος | κερδαν | ει δικ | αι | ως Λ ‖
  αλλ : ω κρατ | υνων | ειπερ | ορθ ακ | ου | εις

>   ‒ ◡   ‒ >   ‒ ◡   ‒

 2. και : των α | σεπτων | ερξετ | αι Λ ‖
  ζευ : παντ αν | ασσων | μηλαθ | οι

>   ‒ ◡   ‒ >   ◡◡   ‒ ◡   L   ‒

 3. η : των α | θικτων | θιξετ | αι ματ | αζ | ων Λ ⟧
  σε : ταν τε | σαν α | θανατον | αιεν | αρχ | αν

◡   ◡◡ ◡   L   ‒   ◡   ‒   ◡   ‒

III. 1. τις : ετι ποτ | εν | τοισδ αν | ηρ θε | ων βελ | η Λ ‖
  φθιν : οντα | γαρ | λαϊ | ου παλ | αιφατ | α

‒◡   ‒ >   ‒ ◡   ‒ ‒

 2. ευξετ | αι ψυχ | ας αμ | υνειν ‖
  θεσφατ | εξαιρ | ουσιν | ηδη

‒ ◡   ‒ ⋛   ‒◡   ‒ >   ‒ ◡   ‒

 3. ει γαρ | αι τοι | αιδε | πραξεις | τιμι | αι Λ ‖
  κουδαμ | ου τιμ | αις α | πολλων | εμφαν | ης

⋛   ◡◡ ◡   ‒◡

 4. τι : δει με χορ | ευειν ⟧
  ερρ : ει δε τα | θεια

a doubtful point. An alternative would perhaps be to write ακρον‿ : αποτομ | ον ωρ | ,
treating ον ωρ as an inverted choree.

g 2

I. *First Period:* 6 verses. Rhythm, *logaoedic.*

Each verse contains 1 sentence of 4 feet : and the six verses fall into 3 groups : *i.e.*

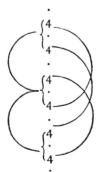

[A repeated palinodic period.

II. *Second Period:* 3 verses. Rhythm, the same. In v. 3 ⌣⌣ over θιξ means that in the antistrophe θᾰνᾰτ represents, by resolution, a long syllable, see § 5.

Verses 1 and 3 have each one sentence of 6 feet : v. 2 is a mesode of 4 feet : *i.e.*

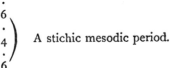

A stichic mesodic period.

III. *Third Period:* 4 verses. Rhythm, the same. In v. 4, the last syllable of χορευειν is marked *short*, because, being the last of a verse, it can be either long or short; and here it is the second of a choree, − ⌣.

Verses 1 and 3 have each 1 sentence of 6 feet : v. 2 is a mesode of 4 feet : v. 4 is an epode of 2 feet. Thus, in this period, the dancers stood still during the alternate verses, 2 and 4. The form is :—

A stichic mesodic period, with postlude.

2 = ἐπ.

V. Third Stasimon (properly a Hyporcheme[1]), vv. 1086—1109.

I. 1. ⌣ ⌣ L – ⌣ –⌣ – ⌣ – > – ⌣ –
   ειπερ εγ | ω | μαντις | ειμι ‖ και κατ | α γνωμ | αν ιδρ | ις ⋀ ‖
   τις σε τεκν | ον | τις σ ε | τικτε ‖ των μακρ | αι ων | ων αρ | α

   ⌣ ⌣ ⌣ ⌣ – > – ⌣ L –
2. ου τον ο | λυμπον α | πειρων | ω κιθ | αιρ | ων ⋀ ‖
   πανος ορ | εσσιβατ | α πα | τρος πελ | ασθ | εισ

   – ⌣ – > – ⌣ L – ⌣ – > –– ⌣ –
3. † ουκ εσ | η ταν | αυρι | ον † ‖ πανσελ | ηνον | μηου σε | γε ⋀]
   † η σε γε τις | θυγατηρ † ‖ λοξι | ου τῳ | γαρ πλακ | ες

   ⌣ ⌣ – > – ⌣ –
II. 1. και πατρι | ω ταν | οιδιπ | ουν ⋀ ‖
    αγρονομ | οι πασ | αι φιλ | αι

    – ⌣ – > – ⌣ – ⌣
2. και τροφ | ον και | ματερ | αυξειν ‖
   ειθ ο | κυλλαν | ας αν | ασσων

---

[1] ὑπόρχημα, 'a dance-song,' merely denotes a melody of livelier movement than the ordinary στάσιμα of the tragic Chorus, and is here expressive of delight. Thus Athenaeus says (630 E) ἡ δ' ὑπορχηματικὴ (ὄρχησις) τῇ κωμικῇ οἰκειοῦται, ἥτις καλεῖται κόρδαξ· παιγνιώδεις δ' εἰσὶν ἀμφότεραι: 'the hyporchematic dance is akin to the comic dance called 'cordax,' and both are sportive.' Fragments of ὑπορχήματα, which were used from an early age in the worship of Apollo, have been left by several lyric poets,—among whom are Pratinas (who is said to have first adapted them to the Dionysiac cult),—Bacchylides, and Pindar.

3. καὶ χορ | ευεσθ | αι προς | ημων ‖ ως επι | ηρα φερ | οντα ‖ τοις εμ |

   ειθ ο | βακχει | ος θε | ος ναι ‖ ων επ ακρ | ων ορε | ων ευρ ‖ ημα |

                                οις τυρ | ανν | οις ∧ ‖

                                δεξατ | εκ | του

4. ι : ηιε | φοιβε | σοι | δε ∧ ‖

   νυμφ : αν ελικ | ωνιδ | ων | αις

5. ταυτ αρ | εστ | ει | η ∧]

   πλειστα | συμ | παιζ | ει

I. *First Period:* 3 verses. Rhythm, *logaoedic.* If in the first sentence of v. 3 we adopt for the antistrophe Arndt's conjecture, ἢ σέ γ' εὐνάτειρά τις (which is somewhat far from the MSS.), then verses 1 and 3 have each 2 sentences of 4 feet, and verse 2 has 1 of 6 feet ; *i.e.*

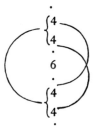
A palinodic period, with mesode.

If, on the other hand, we should hold that ἢ σέ γέ τις θυγάτηρ represents the true *metre* (being corrupted from ἢ σέ γ' ἔφυσε πατήρ), and that οὐκ ἔσῃ τὰν αὔριον should be amended to τὰν ἐπιοῦσαν ἔσῃ, the rhythmical correspondence of sentences would be different. The rhythmical division of verses 2 and 3 would then be :—

2. ου τον ο | λυμπον α | πειρ | ων ‖ ω κιθ | αιρ | ων | ταν ∧ ‖

   πανος ορ | εσσιβατ | α | πα ‖ προς πελ | ασθ : εισ | η

3. επι : ουσαν εσ | η | πανσελ | ηνον | μη ου σε | γε ∧

   σε γε : φυσε πα | τηρ | λοξι | ας τῳ | γαρ πλακ | ες

and v. 3 would be an epode, the form being :—

A palinodic period, with postlude.

II. *Second Period:* 5 verses. Rhythm, the same. Verses **1, 2, 4, 5** have each one sentence of 4 feet: v. **3** has 3 sentences, the first and third of 4 feet each, the second of 3 (the words ὡς ἐπὶ ἦρα φέροντα). Series : . 4. 4 . 4 3 4 . 4 . 4 ., *i.e.*

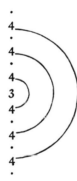

Here, single sentences correspond in an *inverted* order, while the middle sentence of v. 3 has nothing corresponding to it, but forms a mesode or interlude. This is therefore a *mesodic period.* We need not add 'antithetic,' because, where more than two *single sentences* (and not groups) are arranged about a mesode, their arrangement is *normally* inverted.

VI. Fourth Stasimon, vv. 1186—1222.

FIRST STROPHE

(forming a single period).

$$- \quad - \quad \cup\cup \quad - \quad - \quad \cup \quad -$$

1. ι | ω γενε | αι βροτ | ων ∧ ‖

   οσ | τις καθ υπ | ερ βολ | αν

$$- \quad > \quad - \quad \cup\cup \quad - \quad \overset{\smile}{>} \quad \llcorner \quad - \quad > \quad - \quad \cup\cup \quad \llcorner \quad -$$

2. ως υμ | ας ισα | και το | μη | δεν ζωσ | as εναρ | ιθμ | ω ∧ ‖

   τοξευσ | as εκρατ | ησε | του | παντ ευ | δαιμονος | ολβ | ου

$$\llcorner \quad \overset{\smile}{\smile} \quad \cup \quad - \quad \cup \quad -$$

3. τις | γαρ τις αν | ηρ πλε | ον ∧ ‖|

   ω | ξευ κατα | μεν φθισ | as

$$- \quad > \quad \overset{\smile}{\smile} \quad \cup \quad - \quad \cup \quad -$$

4. τας ευ | δαιμονι | as φερ | ει ∧ ‖

   ταν γαμψ | ωνυχα | παρθεν | ον

$$- \quad \overset{\smile}{>} \quad - \quad \cup \quad \cup \quad - \quad \cup \quad -$$

5. η τοσ | ουτον οσ | ον δοκ | ειν ∧ ‖

   χρησμωδ | ον θανατ | ωνδ εμ | α

$$- \quad > \quad \overset{\smile}{\smile} \quad \cup \quad - \quad -$$

6. και δοξ | αντ απο | κλιν | αι ∧ ‖

   χωρα | πυργος αν | εστ | α

$$\overset{\smile}{>} \quad \llcorner \quad \overset{\smile}{\smile} \quad \cup \quad - \quad \cup \quad -$$

7. τον : σον | τοι παρα | δειγμ εχ | ων ∧ ‖

   εξ : ου | και βασιλ | ευς καλ | ει

$$\overset{\smile}{>} \quad \llcorner \quad \overset{\smile}{\smile} \quad \cup \quad - \quad \cup \quad \llcorner \quad - \quad \overset{\smile}{>} \quad - \quad \cup\cup \quad - \quad \cup \quad -$$

8. τον : σον | δαιμονα | τον σον | ω ‖ τλαμον | οιδιποδ | α βροτ | ων ∧ ‖

   εμ : os | και τα μεγ | ιστ ε | τιμ ‖ αθης | ταις μεγαλ | αισιν | εν

$$\llcorner \quad \overset{\smile}{\smile} \quad \cup \quad \llcorner$$

9. ου | δεν μακαρ | ιζ | ω ∧ ‖

   θη | βαισιν αν | ασσ | ων

Rhythm, *logaoedic.* Verse 1 contains 1 sentence of 4 feet: v. 2, 2 of 4 feet each: v. 3, 1 of 4 feet; to which answer respectively vv. 7, 8, 9. Verses 4, 5, 6 also contain each 1 sentence of 4 feet, v. 4 answering to v. 6, and v. 5 forming a mesode.   The series . 4 . 4 4 . 4 ., 4 . 4 . 4 ., 4 . 4 4 . 4 . thus forms the period :—

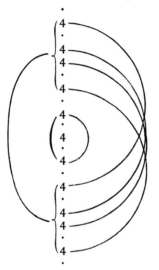

Since the whole group, consisting of vv. **1, 2, 3**, recurs once, the period is *palinodic;* since the sentences formed by vv. **4** and **6** are grouped about the interlude formed by v. **5**, it is also *mesodic.*

SECOND STROPHE.

I. 1. $\smile$ $-$ $\smile$ $\llcorner$ $-$ $\smile$ $-$ $\smile$ $-$ $\smile$ $-$
   τα ⁝ νυν δ ακ | ου | ειν τις ⁝ αθλι | ωτερ | ος Λ ‖
   εφ ⁝ ευρε σ | α | κονθ ο | πανθ ορ |ων χρον| ος

2. $\smile$ $\llcorner$ $\llcorner$ $\underset{\smile}{\smile}$ $-$ $\smile$ $-$ $\smile$ $-$
   τις ⁝ατ | αις | αγρι | αις τις | εν πον | οις Λ ‖
   δικ ⁝ αζ | ει | τον αγαμ | ον γαμ | ον παλ | αι

3. $\smile$ $-\smile$ $-$ $\smile$ $-\smile$ $-$
   ξυν ⁝ οικος | αλλαγ | α βι | ου Λ]]
   τεκν ⁝ ουντα | και τεκν | ουμεν | ον

II. 1. $\llcorner$ $\llcorner$ $-$ $\smile$ $-\smile$ $-$ $\smile$ $-$
   ι | ω | κλεινον | οιδιπ | ου καρ | α Λ ‖
   ι | ω | λαϊ | ειον | ω τεκν | ον

2. $-$ $\smile$ $-$ $\smile$ $-$
   ω μεγ | ας λιμ | ην Λ ‖
   ειθε σ | ειθε | σε

3. $-\smile$ $-$ $\smile$ $-$
   αυτος | ηρκεσ | εν Λ ‖
   μηποτ | ειδομ | αν

4. $-$ $\smile$ $-$ $\smile$ $\smile$ $\smile\smile$ $-$ $\smile$ $-$ $\smile$ $-$
   παιδι | και πα | τρι θαλαμ | ηπολ | ω πεσ | ειν Λ]]
   δυρο | μαι γαρ | ωσπερ ι | αλεμ | ον χε | ων

$$- \;\; \cup\cup \;\; - \;\; \cup \;\; - \;\; \cup \;\; \llcorner \;\; - \;\; \cup\cup \;\; - \;\; \cup \;\; - \;\; \cup \;\; -$$

III. 1. πως ποτε | πως ποθ | αι πατρ | ω ‖ αι σ αλοκ | ες φερ | ειν ταλ | ας ∧ ‖

     εκ στοματ | ων το δ | ορθον | ειπ ‖ ειν ανεπν | ευσα τ | εκ σεθ | εν

$$- \;\; \cup\cup \;\; \llcorner \;\; - \;\; \cup \;\; - \;\; \cup \;\; \llcorner \;\; -$$

   2. σιγ εδυν | α | θησαν | ες τοσ | ον | δε ∧]

     και κατε | κοιμ | ησα | τουμον | ομμ | α

I. *First Period:* 3 verses. Rhythm, *choreic.* Verses **1** and **2** have each 1 sentence of 6 feet: v. **3** forms an epode or postlude of 4 feet: *i.e.*

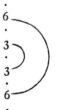

A stichic period, with postlude.

II. *Second Period:* 4 verses. Rhythm, the same. In v. **4** τρῐ θᾰλᾰμ is an *apparent* tribrach, representing a cyclic dactyl, $\sim \cup$, and having the time-value of ♩♪♪ (see § 7). This denoted by writing $\gtrsim \cup \cup$, because the 'irrational' character, though in strictness shared by the first and second short syllables, is more evident in the first.

Verses **1, 4** have each 1 sentence of 6 feet, vv. **2, 3** each 1 of 3: *i.e.*

6 ⎞
. ⎟
3 ⎞
. ⎟   An antithetic period: see First Kommos, Per. IV.
3 ⎠
.
6 ⎠
.

III. *Third Period:* 2 verses. Rhythm, the same. Verse **1** has 2 sentences, each of 4 feet: v. **2** has 1 of 6 feet, and forms an epode or postlude: *i.e.*

.
4 ⎞
4 ⎠   A stichic period, with postlude: see Parod.
.   Str. II. Per. I., Stas. I. Str. I. Per. III.
6 = *ἐπ.*
.

VII.   Second Kommos [1], vv. 1297—1368.

(After the anapaests of the Chorus, 1297—1306, and of Oedipus, 1307—1311, followed by one iambic trimeter of the Chorus, 1312, the strophic system of lyrics begins at 1313.)

First Strophe

(forming a single period).

1. ⏑ ⌐ ⏑ —
    ι ⋮ ω σκοτ | ου ⋀ ‖

    ι ⋮ ω φιλ | ος

2. ⏑ ⏑ ⏑⏑ ⏑⏑ ⏑⏑ ⏑ ⏑ ⏑⏑⏑ ⏑ ⏑⏑
    νεφ ⋮ ος εμον απο | τροπον επ ‖ ιπλομενον α | φατον ⋀ ‖

    συ ⋮ μεν εμος επι | πολος ετ ‖ ι μονιμος ετ | ι γαρ

3. ⏑ ⏑ ⏑ ⏑— ⏑ —, ⏑   — — ⏗ —
    α ⋮ δαματον τε | και δυσ ‖ ουριστον | ον ⋀ ⟧

    υπ ⋮ ομενεις με | τον τυφλ ‖ ον κη δευ | ων

[Here follow four iambic trimeters.]

Rhythm, *dochmiac:* see First Kommos, Period III.   It will be seen that every dochmiac metre here is a variation of the ground-form ⏑ ⋮ — — ⏑ | — ⋀ ‖, by substitution either of ⏑ ⏑ for —, or of > (an irrational syllable, *apparently* long) for ⏑, as in v. 3, κη̄δε͞υῶν.   Verse 1

---

[1] At v. 1336, and in the corresponding 1356, an iambic dimeter is given to the Chorus (Period III., v. 3).   With this exception, the Chorus speaks only iambic trimeters, which follow a lyric strophe or antistrophe assigned to Oedipus.   Since, then, the lyrics belong all but exclusively to Oedipus, the passage might be regarded as his μονῳδία, interrupted by occasional utterances, in the tone of dialogue, by the Chorus.   If, however, regard is had to the character and matter of the whole composition, it will be felt that it may be properly designated as a κομμός, the essence of which was the alternate lament.   On a similar ground, I should certainly consider it as beginning at 1297, though the properly lyric form is assumed only at 1313.

is a dochmiac used as a *prelude* (προῳδικόν), ω being prolonged to the time-value of – –. Vv. **2, 3** have each 2 dochmiac sentences : *i.e.*

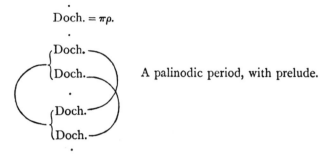

Doch. = πρ.

A palinodic period, with prelude.

SECOND STROPHE.

I. 1.   α ⫶ πολλων ταδ | ην α ‖ πολλων φιλ | οι ⋀ ‖

    ολ ⫶ οιθ οστις | ην ος ‖ αγριας πεδ | ας

2.   ο ⫶ κακα κακα τελ | ων εμ ‖ α ταδ εμα παθ | ε α ⋀ ⫽

    νομ ⫶ αδ επιποδι | ας ε ‖ λυσ απο τε | φονου

II.   ε ⫶ παισε δ | αυτο | χειρ νιν | ουτις ‖ αλλ εγ | ω | τλαμ | ων ⋀ ⫽

    ερρ ⫶ υτο | κανεσ | ωσε μ | ουδεν ‖ ες χαρ | ιν | πρασσ | ων

III. 1.   τι ⫶ γαρ εδει μ ορ | αν ⋀ ‖

    τοτ ⫶ ε γαρ αν θαν | ων

2.   οτ ⫶ ῳ γ ορ | ωντι | μηδεν | ην ιδ | ειν γλυκ | υ ⋀ ‖

    ουκ ⫶ ην φιλ | οισιν | ουδ εμ | οι τοσ | ονδ αχ | ος

3.   ην ⫶ ταυθ οπ | ωσπερ | και συ | φης ⋀ ‖

    θελ ⫶ οντι | καμοι | τουτ αν | ην

4.   τι ⫶ δητ εμ | οι | βλεπτον | η ‖ στερκτον | η προσ | η γορ | ον ⋀ ‖

    ουκ ⫶ ουν πα | τρος γ | αν φον | ευσ ‖ ηλθον | ουδε | νυμφι | ος

5.   ετ ⫶ εστ ακ | ου | ειν | αδον | α φιλ | οι ⋀ ⫽

    βροτ ⫶ οις ε | κληθ | ην | ων ε | φυν απ | ο

IV. 1. ᷄υ υυ — υ ᷍υυ υ υ υ — υ —

1. απ ⋮ αγετ εκ τοπ | ιον οτ ‖ ι ταχιστ α | με ⋏ ‖

   νυν δ ⋮ αθεος μεν | ειμ αν ‖ οσιων δε | παις

   υ υυ — υ —, υ υ υ — υ —

2. απ ⋮ αγετ ω φιλ | οι τον ‖ μεγ ολεθρι | ον ⋏ ‖

   ομ ⋮ ογενης δ αφ | ων αυτ ‖ οσ εφυν ταλ | ας

   ᷄υ υυ — υ υυ υ υ υ — υ —

3. τον ⋮ καταρατο | τατον ετ ‖ ι δε και θε | οις ⋏ ‖

   ει ⋮ δε τι πρεσβυ | τερον ετ ‖ ι κακου κακ | ον

   > υυ — υ —

4. εχθρ ⋮ οτατον βροτ | ων ⋏]

   τουτ ⋮ ελαχ οιδιπ | ους

   [Here follow two iambic trimeters.]

I. *First Period:* 2 verses. Rhythm, *dochmiac*. In verse 1 (antistrophe), we have ἀγρίας: observe that if we read ἀπ' ἀγρίας the dochmiac would have one υ too much, and see my note on v. 1350. In v. 2, the MS. reading νομάδος is *impossible*, as the metre shows. φόνου, by resolution for —, as in the strophe, since the last syllable of a verse can be either long or short: see on Parod. Str. II. Per. I. v. 1, and cp. χορευεῖν, Stas. II. Str. II. Per. III. v. 4. Metre would admit ἔλαβέ μ' or ἔλαβεν, but not, of course, ἔλυσέ μ' or ἔλυσεν.

Each verse has 2 dochmiac sentences, *i.e.*

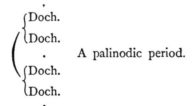

A palinodic period.

II. *Second Period:* 1 verse. Rhythm, *choreic.* Two sentences, each of 4 feet: *i.e.*

$$\left.\begin{array}{l} 4 \\ 4 \end{array}\right)$$ A stichic period.

III. *Third Period:* 5 verses. Rhythm, *choreic,* except in verse 1, which is a dochmiac, serving as prelude (προῳδικόν).

Verse 2 has 1 sentence of 6 feet : v. 3, 1 of 4 feet : v. 4, 2 of 4 feet each: v. 5, 1 of 6 feet. The first of the 2 sentences in v. 4 forms a *mesode;* which can either (as here) begin a verse, or close it, or stand within it, or, form a separate verse. Series : . 6 . 4 . 4 . 4 . 6 . : form :—

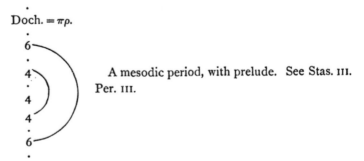

Doch. = πρ.

A mesodic period, with prelude. See Stas. III. Per. III.

IV. *Fourth Period :* 4 verses. Rhythm, *dochmiac.* Verses 1, 2, 3 have each two dochmiac sentences : v. 4 has one, which forms an epode : *i.e.*

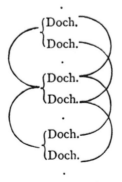

A repeated palinodic period, with postlude.

Doch. = ἐπ.

RELATIONS OF LYRIC FORM AND MATTER.

In the lyric parts of Tragedy, the poet was a composer, setting words to music. Words, music, and dance were together the expression of the successive feelings which the course of the drama excited in the Chorus, or typical spectator. It is obvious, then, that the choice of lyric rhythms necessarily had an ethical meaning, relative to the mood which in each case sought utterance. It is everywhere characteristic of Sophocles that he has been finely sensitive to this relation. So much, at least, moderns can see, however far they may be from adequately appreciating the more exquisite secrets of his skill. Without attempting minute detail, we may glance here at some of the chief traits in which this skill is exemplified by the lyrics of the *Oedipus Tyrannus.*

I. PARODOS. *First Strophe.* The Theban Elders are reverentially awaiting the message from Delphi, and solemnly entreating the gods for deliverance from their woes. With this mood the *dactylic* rhythm is in unison. The Greek dactylic measure was slow and solemn, the fitting utterance of lofty and earnest warning—as when oracles spoke—or, as here, of exalted faith in Heaven.

Second Strophe. Period I. The chorees, in *logaoedic* rhythm, express the lively sense of personal suffering (ἀνάριθμα γὰρ φέρω | πήματα). Per. II. *Dactyls,* somewhat less stately than those of the opening, again express trust in the gods who will banish the pest.

Third Strophe. *Choreic* rhythms of the strongest and most excited kind embody the fervid prayer that the Destroyer may be quelled by the Powers of light and health.

II. FIRST STASIMON. The doom has gone forth against the unknown criminal; and the prophet has said that this criminal is Oedipus. *First Strophe.* While the rhythm is *logaoedic* throughout, the fuller measures of Period I. are suited to the terrible decree of Delphi; those of Per. II. to the flight of the outlaw; those of III. to the rapid pursuit, and, finally, to the crushing might, of the Avenger.

Second Strophe. Period I. The *choriambic* rhythm—the most passionate of all, adapted to vehement indignation or despair—interprets the intensity of emotion with which the Theban nobles have heard the charge against their glorious king. Period II. Passing to their reasons for discrediting that charge, the Chorus pass at the same time from the choriambic rhythm to the kindred but less tumultuous *ionic,* which is here (as we have seen) most skilfully linked on to the former.

III.   The FIRST KOMMOS, in its 3rd and 4th Periods, shows how *dochmiac* measures, and *paeonic* combined with choreic, can suit varying tones of piteous entreaty or anxious agitation; an effect which, as regards dochmiacs, the SECOND KOMMOS (VII) also exhibits in a still more impressive manner.

IV.   In the SECOND STASIMON, *logaoedics* are the vehicle of personal reflection and devotion; the lively measures of the Hyporcheme which holds the place of THIRD STASIMON (V) speak for themselves.

VI.   In the FOURTH STASIMON we have a highly-wrought example of lyric art comparable with the First Stasimon, and with the Parodos.   The utter ruin of Oedipus has just been disclosed.   *First Strophe.* It was a general rule that, when a verse was opened with a *syncope*, anacrusis must precede.   By the *disregard* of this rule here, an extraordinary weight and solemnity are imparted to the first accent of the lament:

⌞ ‿‿ ‿ — ‿ —

ι | ω γενε | αι βροτ | ων ∧ ‖.   (See the musical rendering of this, Appendix, Note 1, § 10, p. 284.)   So, again, in the profoundly sorrowful conclusion

⌞ ‿‿ ‿ —

drawn from the instance of Oedipus, ουδ | εν μακαρ | ιζω ∧ ‖. And, since his unhappy fate is here contemplated in its entirety, the whole strophe forms a single rhythmical period.

The *Second Strophe*—reflecting on *particular aspects* of the king's destiny—is appropriately broken up into three short periods; and the choreic rhythm is here so managed as to present a telling.contrast with the logaoedic rhythm of the first strophe.   The weightiest verses are those which form the conclusion.

I have but briefly indicated relations of which the reader's own ear and feeling will give him a far more vivid apprehension.   There are no metrical texts in which it is more essential than in those of ancient Greece never to consider the measures from a merely mechanical point of view, but always to remember *what* the poet is saying.   No one who cultivates this simple habit can fail to attain a quicker perception of the delicate sympathies which everywhere exist between the matter and the form of Greek lyrics.

ΣΟΦΟΚΛΕΟΥΣ

ΟΙΔΙΠΟΥΣ ΤΥΡΑΝΝΟΣ

ΣΟΦΟΚΛΕΟΥΣ

ΟΙΔΙΠΟΥΣ ΤΥΡΑΝΝΟΣ

I.

ΑΡΙΣΤΟΦΑΝΟΥΣ ΓΡΑΜΜΑΤΙΚΟΥ ΥΠΟΘΕΣΙΣ.

Λιπὼν Κόρινθον Οἰδίπους, πατρὸς νόθος
πρὸς τῶν ἀπάντων λοιδορούμενος ξένος,
ἦλθεν πυθέσθαι Πυθικῶν θεσπισμάτων
ζητῶν ἑαυτὸν καὶ γένους φυτοσπόρον.
εὑρὼν δὲ τλήμων ἐν στεναῖς ἁμαξιτοῖς   5
ἄκων ἔπεφνε Λάιον γεννήτορα.
Σφιγγὸς δὲ δεινῆς θανάσιμον λύσας μέλος
ᾔσχυνε μητρὸς ἀγνοουμένης λέχος.
λοιμὸς δὲ Θήβας εἷλε καὶ νόσος μακρά.
Κρέων δὲ πεμφθεὶς Δελφικὴν πρὸς ἑστίαν,   10
ὅπως πύθηται τοῦ κακοῦ παυστήριον,
ἤκουσε φωνῆς μαντικῆς θεοῦ πάρα,
τὸν Λάιειον ἐκδικηθῆναι φόνον.
ὅθεν μαθὼν ἑαυτὸν Οἰδίπους τάλας
δισσάς τε χερσὶν ἐξανάλωσεν κόρας,   15
αὐτὴ δὲ μήτηρ ἀγχόναις διώλετο.

ΑΡΙΣΤΟΦΑΝΟΥΣ......ΥΠΟΘΕΣΙΣ] 'Αριστοφάνους ἐπίγραμμα εἰς τὸν τύραννον
οἰδίπουν A. Vox ἐπίγραμμα melius de titulo libri quam de argumento dicitur.
3 θεσπισμάτων] νόμων θέλει A, unde patet fuisse qui ἐλθὼν pro ἦλθεν legerent.
11 πύθηται codd., notissima structura: nihil causae erat quod Brunck. πύθοιτο
scriberet.   15 δισσάς τε ·χερσὶν] Optimorum codd. lectionem δισσαῖς τε χερσὶν
sic corrigere malo quam Brunckii coniecturam sequi, elegantem illam quidem sed
prorsus incertam, πόρπαισι δισσάς.   16 αὐτὴ δὲ] Quod Elmsl. coniecit αὐτή τε
dubito recipere: poterat enim grammaticus eos tragicorum locos de industria imitari
ubi post τε codd. δὲ exhibent, ut *El.* 1099, *Ai.* 836.

4 ΣΟΦΟΚΛΕΟΥΣ

ΑΡΙΣΤΟΦΑΝΟΥΣ ΓΡΑΜΜΑΤΙΚΟΥ] The first of the three prose ὑποθέσεις to the *Antigone* is also ascribed in the MSS. to Aristophanes of Byzantium (flor. 200 B.C.). His name is likewise given in the MSS. to the metrical ὑποθέσεις prefixed to all the extant comedies of his namesake except the *Thesmophoriazusae*. All these ascriptions are now generally held to be false. There is no reason to think that the fashion of metrical arguments existed in the Alexandrian age; and the language in every case points more or less clearly to a lower date. The verses above form no exception to the rule, though they are much more correct than the comic ὑποθέσεις. See Nauck's fragments of the Byzantine Aristophanes, p. 256 : Dindorf agrees with him, *Schol. Soph.* vol. II. p. xxii.

II.

ΔΙΑ ΤΙ ΤΥΡΑΝΝΟΣ ΕΠΙΓΕΓΡΑΠΤΑΙ.

Ο ΤΥΡΑΝΝΟΣ ΟΙΔΙΠΟΥΣ ἐπὶ διακρίσει θατέρου ἐπιγέγραπται. χαριέντως δὲ ΤΥΡΑΝΝΟΝ ἅπαντες αὐτὸν ἐπιγράφουσιν, ὡς ἐξέχοντα πάσης τῆς Σοφοκλέους ποιήσεως, καίπερ ἡττηθέντα ὑπὸ Φιλοκλέους, ὥς φησι Δικαίαρχος. εἰσὶ δὲ καὶ οἱ ΠΡΟΤΕΡΟΝ, οὐ ΤΥΡΑΝΝΟΝ, αὐτὸν ἐπιγράφ-
5 οντες, διὰ τοὺς χρόνους τῶν διδασκαλιῶν καὶ διὰ τὰ πράγματα· ἀλήτην γὰρ καὶ πηρὸν Οἰδίποδα τὸν ἐπὶ Κολωνῷ εἰς τὰς Ἀθήνας ἀφικνεῖσθαι. ἴδιον δέ τι πεπόνθασιν οἱ μεθ᾽ Ὅμηρον ποιηταὶ τοὺς πρὸ τῶν Τρωϊκῶν βασιλεῖς ΤΥΡΑΝΝΟΥΣ προσαγορεύοντες, ὀψέ ποτε τοῦδε τοῦ ὀνόματος εἰς τοὺς Ἕλληνας διαδοθέντος, κατὰ τοὺς Ἀρχιλόχου χρόνους, καθάπερ
10 Ἱππίας ὁ σοφιστής φησιν. Ὅμηρος γοῦν τὸν πάντων παρανομώτατον Ἔχετον βασιλέα φησὶ καὶ οὐ τύραννον·

Εἰς Ἔχετον βασιλῆα, βροτῶν δηλήμονα.

προσαγορευθῆναι δέ φασι τὸν τύραννον ἀπὸ τῶν Τυρρηνῶν· χαλεποὺς γάρ τινας περὶ λῃστείαν τούτους γενέσθαι. ὅτι δὲ νεώτερον τὸ τοῦ τυράννου
15 ὄνομα δῆλον. οὔτε γὰρ Ὅμηρος οὔτε Ἡσίοδος οὔτε ἄλλος οὐδεὶς τῶν παλαιῶν τύραννον ἐν τοῖς ποιήμασιν ὀνομάζει. ὁ δὲ Ἀριστοτέλης ἐν Κυμαίων πολιτείᾳ τοὺς τυράννους φησὶ τὸ πρότερον αἰσυμνήτας προσαγορεύεσθαι. εὐφημότερον γὰρ ἐκεῖνο τοὔνομα.

2 ἐπιγράφουσιν] Sic cum cod. Laurentiano Dindorf.: vulg. ἐπέγραφον.
4 ΠΡΟΤΕΡΟΝ, οὐ ΤΥΡΑΝΝΟΝ, αὐτὸν] L, Dind.: vulg. ΠΡΟΤΕΡΟΝ αὐτὸν, οὐ ΤΥΡΑΝΝΟΝ.

---

2 τύραννον ..ἐπιγράφουσιν] The distinguishing title was suggested by v. 514 of the play, τὸν τύραννον Οἰδίπουν, v. 925 τὰ τοῦ τυράννου...Οἰδίπου. Sophocles doubtless called it simply Οἰδίπους. 9 κατὰ τοὺς Ἀρχιλόχου χρόνους] circ. 670 B.C. It is about 679 B.C. that Orthagoras is said to have founded his dynasty at Sicyon, and ' the despots of Sikyôn are the earliest of whom we have any distinct mention,' Grote III, 43.

12 Ἔχετον] *Od.* 18. 85. 15 οὔτε γὰρ Ὅμηρος] For the writer of this ὑπόθεσις, then (unless he made an oversight), 'Homer' was not the author of the 'Homeric hymn' to Ares, 8. 5, ἀντιβίοισι τύραννε, δικαιοτάτων ἀγὲ φωτῶν. The earliest occurrences of the word τύραννος which can be approximately dated are (1) Alcaeus fr. 37 Bergk, circ. 606 B.C., referring to Pittacus; see below on 17: (2) Pind. *Pyth.* 3. 85, where it is convertible with βασιλεύς, *ib.* 70 (Hiero of Syracuse), date perh. 474 B.C. (see Fennell's introd.): and (3) Aesch. *P. V.* 736 ὁ τῶν θεῶν τύραννος (Zeus), date circ. 472—469 B.C. On the question as to the origin of τύραννος, scholars will read with interest the opinion of the author of *Greek and Latin Etymology.* Mr Peile has kindly communicated to me the following note :—"There seems no reason to doubt the usual connection of τύραννος with √*tur*, a by-form of √TAR. It does not occur, I think, in Greek, but it is used in Vedic,—as is also the common epithet *tur-a*, 'strong,' applied chiefly to Indra, but also to other gods. Rarer cognates are *turvaṇ*, ='victory,' and *turvaṇi*='victorious,' also of Indra. The primary meaning of the root was ' to bore '—then ' to get to the end ' of a thing—then 'to get the better of' it. There is another family of words, like in form, with the general sense of 'haste'; e.g. *turvaṇya*, a verb-stem in Vedic='to be eager,' and *turaṇyu* an adjective. These, I think, are distinct in origin. In form they come nearer to τύραννος. But I think that they are *late* Vedic forms, and therefore cannot be pressed into the service. The form in Greek is difficult to explain in either case. If there were an Indo-Eur. *turvan* (whence the Sanskrit word), the Greek might have formed a secondary *turan-yo:* but one would expect this to have taken the form τυραινο. Taking into account the entire absence of all cognates in Greek, I think that it is probably a borrowed word, and that from being an adjective (?='mighty'), it became with the Greeks a title." 16 ἐν Κυμαίων πολιτείᾳ] Cp. schol. in Eur. *Med.* 19 (Dind. vol: IV. p. 8) αἰσυμνᾷ· ἡγεῖται καὶ ἄρχει· ἰδίως δέ φησιν Ἀριστοτέλης ὑπὸ Κυμαίων αἰσυμνήτην τὸν ἄρχοντα λέγεσθαι. 'αἰσυμνῆται δὲ κριτοὶ ἐννέα πάντες ἀνέσταν' [*Od.* 8. 258] τοὺς ἄρχοντας τῶν ἀγώνων (sc. ὁ ποιητὴς λέγει). 17 The αἰσυμνητεία resembled the τυραννίς in being *absolute*, but differed from it in being *elective;* hence it is called by Arist. αἱρετὴ τυραννίς, *Pol.* 3. 14. Alluding to the choice of Pittacus as αἰσυμνήτης by the Mityleneans, Alcaeus said ἐστάσαντο τύραννον, *ib.*: but this was *ad invidiam.*

III.

ΑΛΛΩΣ.

Ὁ Τύραννος Οἰδίπους πρὸς ἀντιδιαστολὴν τοῦ ἐν τῷ Κολωνῷ ἐπι-γέγραπται. τὸ κεφάλαιον δὲ τοῦ δράματος γνῶσις τῶν ἰδίων κακῶν Οἰδίποδος, πήρωσίς τε τῶν ὀφθαλμῶν, καὶ δι᾽ ἀγχόνης θάνατος Ἰοκάστης.

'Haec in fine fabulae habet L, om. A, qui de sequentibus nihil habet praeter aenigma Sphingis,' Dind. *Schol.* II. 13.

ΧΡΗΣΜΟΣ Ο ΔΟΘΕΙΣ ΛΑΙΩι ΤΩι ΘΗΒΑΙΩι.

Λάιε Λαβδακίδη, παίδων γένος ὄλβιον αἰτεῖς.
δώσω τοι φίλον υἱόν· ἀτὰρ πεπρωμένον ἐστὶν
παιδὸς ἑοῦ χείρεσσι λιπεῖν φάος. ὣς γὰρ ἔνευσε

Ζεὺς Κρονίδης, Πέλοπος στυγεραῖς ἀραῖσι πιθήσας,
οὗ φίλον ἥρπασας υἱόν· ὁ δ᾽ ηὔξατό σοι τάδε πάντα.

ΧΡΗΣΜΟΣ Ο ΔΟΘΕΙΣ] Aegre careas articulo, quem L praebet, τῷ Θηβαίῳ
addens: vulg. χρησμὸς δοθεὶς Λαΐῳ.   2 δώσω...ἐστίν] Legebatur etiam τέξεις
μὲν φίλον υἱόν· ἀτὰρ τόδε σοι μόρος ἔσται· Valckenaer. Eur. *Phoen.* p. xvi.   3 παιδὸς
ἐοῦ] Vulg. σοῦ παιδὸς.   Reposui lectionem multo elegantiorem, quam ex cod. Augus-
tano affert Valck. l. c.   Vix opus est ut moneam ἐοῦ hoc loco *tui* significare, non
sui.   Pronomen ἑός (=σϝος, anglice '*own*'), pariter ut Sanscr. *sva* ('*self*'), trium erat
personarum.   Fortasse reponendum, quod Zenodotus probavit, ἑοῖο, *tui,* pro ἑῆος in
Il. I. 393, 15. 138, 24. 422, 550.

ΤΟ ΑΙΝΙΓΜΑ ΤΗΣ ΣΦΙΓΓΟΣ.

Ἔστι δίπουν ἐπὶ γῆς καὶ τετράπον, οὗ μία φωνή,
καὶ τρίπον· ἀλλάσσει δὲ φυὴν μόνον ὅσσ᾽ ἐπὶ γαῖαν
ἑρπετὰ κινεῖται ἀνά τ᾽ αἰθέρα καὶ κατὰ πόντον.
ἀλλ᾽ ὁπόταν πλείστοισιν ἐρειδόμενον ποσὶ βαίνῃ,
ἔνθα τάχος γυίοισιν ἀφαυρότατον πέλει αὐτοῦ.

2 φυὴν] φύσιν Athen. 456 b, βοὴν L, A.   3 κινεῖται] γίνηται L.   4 ἐρειδόμενον Athen. et Euripidis codd. meliores: ἐπειγόμενον L, A, quae lectio, quamvis
primo aspectu placeat, vera non est.   Neque enim festinationi tarditas opponitur, sed
numero pedum imbecillitas.

Athenaeus 456 b introduces his quotation of the riddle thus : Καὶ τὸ τῆς Σφιγγὸς
δὲ αἴνιγμα Ἀσκληπιάδης ἐν τοῖς Τραγῳδουμένοις τοιοῦτον εἶναι φησίν. Asclepiades
of Tragilus in Thrace, a pupil of Isocrates, wrote (circ. 340 B.C.) a work called
Τραγῳδούμενα ('Subjects of Tragedy') in six books, dealing with the legendary
material used by the tragic poets, and their methods of treatment. The Αἴνιγμα,
in this form, is thus carried back to at least the earlier part of the fourth century B.C.

ΛΥΣΙΣ ΤΟΥ ΑΙΝΙΓΜΑΤΟΣ.

Κλῦθι καὶ οὐκ ἐθέλουσα, κακόπτερε Μοῦσα θανόντων,
φωνῆς ἡμετέρης σὸν τέλος ἀμπλακίης.
ἄνθρωπον κατέλεξας, ὃς ἡνίκα γαῖαν ἐφέρπει,
πρῶτον ἔφυ τετράπους νήπιος ἐκ λαγόνων·
5   γηραλέος δὲ πέλων τρίτατον πόδα βάκτρον ἐρείδει,
αὐχένα φορτίζων, γήραϊ καμπτόμενος.

5 ἐρείδει] ἔχει vel ἐπάγει codd.: correxit Gale.

The Λύσις is not in the MSS. of Sophocles, but is given by the schol. on Eur.
Phoen. 50 (αἴνιγμ᾽ ἐμὸς παῖς Οἰδίπους Σφιγγὸς μαθών)...τὴν δὲ λύσιν τοῦ αἰνίγματος
οὕτω τινές φασιν· 'Κλῦθι' κ.τ.λ. Valckenaer, *Schol. Phoen.* p. 28, gives it as above
from a collation of three MSS.

ΤΑ ΤΟΥ ΔΡΑΜΑΤΟΣ ΠΡΟΣΩΠΑ.

<table>
<tr><td>ΟΙΔΙΠΟΥΣ.</td><td>ΙΟΚΑΣΤΗ.</td></tr>
<tr><td>ΙΕΡΕΥΣ.</td><td>ΑΓΓΕΛΟΣ.</td></tr>
<tr><td>ΚΡΕΩΝ.</td><td>ΘΕΡΑΠΩΝ Λαΐου.</td></tr>
<tr><td>ΧΟΡΟΣ γερόντων Θηβαίων.</td><td>ΕΞΑΓΓΕΛΟΣ.</td></tr>
<tr><td>ΤΕΙΡΕΣΙΑΣ.</td><td></td></tr>
</table>

The ἰκέται in the opening scene (like the προπομποί at the close of the *Eumenides* of Aeschylus) would come under the general designation of a παραχορήγημα—which properly meant (not, of course, 'an auxiliary chorus,' but) anything which the choragus provided *in supplement* to the ordinary requirements of a drama, and was specially applied to a fourth actor, according to Pollux 4. 110 παραχορήγημα εἰ τέταρτος ὑποκριτής τι παραφθέγξαιτο. The distribution of the parts among the three actors would be as follows:—

OEDIPUS, πρωταγωνιστής.

IOCASTA,
PRIEST OF ZEUS,
MESSENGER from the house (ἐξάγγελος), } δευτεραγωνιστής.
SERVANT OF LAÏUS,

CREON,
TEIRESIAS, } τριταγωνιστής.
MESSENGER from Corinth (ἄγγελος),

Structure of the Play.

1. πρόλογος, verses 1—150.
2. πάροδος, 151—215.

3. ἐπεισόδιον πρῶτον, 216—462.
4. στάσιμον πρῶτον, 463—511.

5. ἐπεισόδιον δεύτερον, 512—862, with κομμός, 649—697.
6. στάσιμον δεύτερον, 863—910.

7. ἐπεισόδιον τρίτον, 911—1085.
8. στάσιμον τρίτον, 1086—1109.

9. ἐπεισόδιον τέταρτον, 1110—1185.
10. στάσιμον τέταρτον, 1186—1222.

11. ἔξοδος, 1223—1530.

In reference to a Greek tragedy, we cannot properly speak of 'Acts'; but the πάροδος and the στάσιμα mark the conclusion of chapters in the action. The *Oedipus Tyrannus* falls into six such chapters.

The parts named above are thus defined by Aristotle (*Poet.* 12):—

1. πρόλογος = μέρος ὅλον τραγῳδίας τὸ πρὸ χοροῦ παρόδου, 'all that part of a tragedy which precedes the parodos' (or 'entrance' of the Chorus into the orchestra).

2. πάροδος = ἡ πρώτη λέξις ὅλου χοροῦ, 'the first utterance of the whole Chorus.'

3. ἐπεισόδιον = μέρος ὅλον τραγῳδίας τὸ μεταξὺ ὅλων χορικῶν μελῶν, 'all that part of a tragedy which comes between whole choric songs.'

4. στάσιμον = μέλος χοροῦ τὸ ἄνευ ἀναπαίστου καὶ τροχαίου, 'a song of the Chorus without anapaests or trochaics.' στάσιμον is 'stationary': στάσιμον μέλος, a song by the Chorus at its *station*—after it has taken up its place in the orchestra—as distinguished from the πάροδος or entrance-song. [I do not now think that the notion of 'unbroken'—by anapaests or dialogue—can be included in the term.]

Aristotle's definition needs a few words of explanation. (1) The anapaestic was especially a marching measure. Hence the πάροδος of the older type often began with anapaests (*e.g.* Aesch. *Agam.* 40—103, *Eum.* 307—320), though, in the extant plays of Soph., this is so with the *Ajax* alone (134—171). But a στάσιμον never *begins* with anapaests. Further, the antistrophic arrangement of a στάσιμον is never *interrupted* by anapaests. Yet, after an antistrophic στάσιμον, the choral utterance may *end* with anapaests: thus the third στάσιμον of the *Antigone* is antistrophic from 781 to 800, after which come immediately the choral anapaests 801—805: and we should naturally speak of 781—805 as the third stasimon, though, according to Arist., it strictly consists only of 781—800. (2) By τροχαίου Arist. plainly means the trochaic *tetrameter: i.e.* a στάσιμον must not be interrupted by dialogue (such as that which the Chorus holds in trochaic tetrameters with Aegisthus and Clytaemnestra, Aesch. *Ag. ad fin.*). Measures into which trochaic rhythms enter are, of course, frequent in στάσιμα.

5. ἔξοδος = μέρος ὅλον τραγῳδίας μεθ᾽ ὃ οὐκ ἔστι χοροῦ μέλος, 'all that part of a tragedy after which there is no song of the Chorus.'

Verses 649—697 of the second ἐπεισόδιον form a short κομμός. The Chorus are pleading with Oedipus, lyric measures being mingled with iambic trimeters. Arist. (*Poet.* 12) defines the κομμός as θρῆνος κοινὸς χοροῦ καὶ ἀπὸ σκηνῆς, *i.e.* a lamentation in which the Chorus (in the orchestra) took part with the actor on the stage. An example of the κομμός on a larger scale is Soph. *El.* 121—250.

ΟΙΔΙΠΟΥΣ.

Ὦ ΤΕΚΝΑ, Κάδμου τοῦ πάλαι νέα τροφή,
τίνας ποθ' ἕδρας τάσδε μοι θοάζετε
ἱκτηρίοις κλάδοισιν ἐξεστεμμένοι;
πόλις δ' ὁμοῦ μὲν θυμιαμάτων γέμει,
ὁμοῦ δὲ παιάνων τε καὶ στεναγμάτων·   5
ἀγὼ δικαιῶν μὴ παρ' ἀγγέλων, τέκνα,

Scene:—*Before the palace of Oedipus at Thebes. In front of the large central doors* (βασίλειος θύρα) *there is an altar; a smaller altar stands also near each of the two side-doors:* see verse 16. *Suppliants—old men, youths, and young children—are seated on the steps of the altars. They are dressed in white tunics and cloaks,—their hair bound with white fillets. On the altars they have laid down olive-branches wreathed with fillets of wool. The* PRIEST OF ZEUS, *a venerable man, is alone standing, facing the central doors of the palace. These are now thrown open: followed by two attendants* (πρόσπολοι), *who place themselves on either side of the doors,* OEDIPUS *enters, in the robes of a king: for a moment he gazes silently on the groups at the altars, and then speaks.* See Appendix, Note 1, § 1.

1—77 Oedipus asks why they are suppliants. The Priest of Zeus, speaking for the rest, prays him to save them, with the gods' help, from the blight and the plague. Oedipus answers that he has already sent Creon to consult Apollo at Delphi, and will do whatever the god shall bid. **1 νέα,** last-born (not '*young*,' for τέκνα includes the old men, v. 17), added for contrast with τοῦ πάλαι. Oedipus,—who believes himself a Corinthian (774)—marks his respect for the ancient glories of the Theban house to whose throne he has been called: see esp. 258 f. So the Thebans are στρατὸς Καδμογενής Aesch. *Theb.* 303, Καδμογενὴς γέννα Eur. *Phoen.* 808, or Καδμεῖοι. τροφή = θρέμματα (abstract for concrete): Eur. *Cycl.* 189 ἀρνῶν τροφαί = ἄρνες ἐκτεθραμμέναι. Cadmus, as guardian genius of Thebes, is still τροφεύς of all who are reared in the δῶμα Καδμεῖον (v. 29). Campbell understands, 'my last-born care derived from ancient Cadmus,'—as though the τροφεύς were Oedipus. But could Κάδμου τροφή mean '[*my*] nurslings [*derived*

OEDIPUS.

My children, latest-born to Cadmus who was of old,
why are ye set before me thus with wreathed branches
of suppliants, while the city reeks with incense, rings
with prayers for health and cries of woe? I deemed it
unmeet, my children, to hear these things at the mouth

---

from] Cadmus'? It is by the word τέκνα that Oedipus expresses his
own fatherly care. **2 ἕδρας.** The word ἕδρα = 'posture,' here, as usu.,
sitting: when *kneeling* is meant, some qualification is added, as Eur.
Ph. 293 γονυπετεῖς ἕδρας προσπίτνω σ᾽, 'I supplicate thee on my
knees.' The suppliants are sitting on the steps (βάθρα) of the altars, on
which they have laid the κλάδοι: see 142: cp. 15 προσήμεθα, 20 θακεῖ:
Aesch. *Eum.* 40 (Orestes a suppliant in the Delphian temple) ἐπ᾽ ὀμφαλῷ
(on the omphalos) ἕδραν ἔχοντα προστρόπαιον... ἐλαίας θ᾽ ὑψιγέννητον
κλάδον. **θοάζετε** prob. = θάσσετε, 'sit,' ἕδρας being cognate acc. In
Eur. θοάζω (θοός) always = 'to hasten' (transitive or intrans.). But
Empedocles and Aesch. clearly use θοάζω as = θάσσω, the sound
and form perh. suggesting the epic θαάσσω, θόωκος. See Appendix,
Note 2. **3 ἱκτηρίοις κλάδοισιν.** The suppliant carried a branch of olive
or laurel (ἱκετηρία), round which were twined festoons of wool (στέφη,
στέμματα,—which words can stand for the ἱκετηρία itself, *infra* 913, *Il.* 1.
14): Plut. *Thes.* 18 ἦν δὲ [ἡ ἱκετηρία] κλάδος ἀπὸ τῆς ἱερᾶς ἐλαίας, ἐρίῳ
λευκῷ κατεστεμμένος. He laid his branch on the altar (Eur. *Her.* 124
βωμὸν καταστέψαντες), and left it there, if unsuccessful in his petition
(Eur. *Suppl.* 259); if successful, he took it away (*ib.* 359, *infra* 143).
ἱκτ. κλ. ἐξεστεμμένοι = ἱκτηρίους κλάδους ἐξεστεμμένους ἔχοντες: Xen.
Anab. 4. 3. 28 διηγκυλωμένους τοὺς ἀκοντιστὰς καὶ ἐπιβεβλημένους
τοὺς τοξότας, 'the javelin-throwers *with* javelins *grasped* by the thong
(ἀγκύλη), and the archers *with* arrows *fitted* to the string.' So 18 ἐξεστεμμένον absol., = provided with στέφη (*i.e.* with ἱκετηρίαι: see last note).
Triclinius supposes that the suppliants, besides carrying boughs, wore
garlands (ἐστεφανωμένοι), and the *priests* may have done so: but ἐξεστεμμ.
does not refer to this. **4 ὁμοῦ μέν ... ὁμοῦ δὲ.** The verbal contrast is

ἄλλων ἀκούειν αὐτὸς ὧδ' ἐλήλυθα,
ὁ πᾶσι κλεινὸς Οἰδίπους καλούμενος.
ἀλλ', ὦ γεραιέ, φράζ', ἐπεὶ πρέπων ἔφυς
πρὸ τῶνδε φωνεῖν, τίνι τρόπῳ καθέστατε,   10
δείσαντες ἢ στέρξαντες; ὡς θέλοντος ἂν
ἐμοῦ προσαρκεῖν πᾶν· δυσάλγητος γὰρ ἂν

11 In cod. Laur. 32. 9 (L) pr. manus στέρξαντες scripserat; quod recentior
in στέξαντες mutavit, littera ε talem in modum grandiore facta ut vicinam
ρ obscuraret.   In margine schol. στέρξαντες interpretatur per ἤδη πεπονθότες.

merely between the *fumes* of incense burnt on the altars as a propi-
tiatory offering (*Il*. 8. 48 τέμενος βωμός τε θυήεις), and the *sounds*—
whether of invocations to the Healer, or of despair. **7 ἄλλων.** Redundant, but serving to contrast ἀγγέλων and αὐτός, as if one said, 'from
messengers,—at second hand.' Blaydes cp. Xen. *Cyr*. I. 6. 2 ὅπως μὴ
δι' ἄλλων ἑρμηνέων τὰς τῶν θεῶν συμβουλίας συνείης, ἀλλ' αὐτὸς...γιγνώσκοις.
ὧδε = δεῦρο, as in vv. 144, 298, and often in Soph.: even with βλέπειν,
ὁρᾶν, as in *Trach*. 402 βλέφ' ὧδε = βλέπε δεῦρο. **8 ὁ πᾶσι κλεινὸς...καλού-
μενος.** πᾶσι with κλεινός (cp. 40 πᾶσι κράτιστον), not with καλούμενος:
'called Oedipus famous in the sight of all,' not 'called famous Oed. by all.'
Cp. πασίγνωστος, πασίδηλος, πασιμέλουσα, πασίφιλος. The tone is Homeric
(*Od*. 9. 19 εἴμ' Ὀδυσεύς...καί μευ κλέος οὐρανὸν ἵκει, imitated by Verg.
Aen. I. 378 *sum pius Aeneas...fama super aethera notus*): Oedipus is a
type, for the frank heroic age, of Arist.'s μεγαλόψυχος—ὁ μεγάλων αὐτὸν
ἀξιῶν, ἄξιος ὤν (*Eth. N*. 4. 3). **9 ἔφυς,** which is more than εἶ, refers,
not to appearance (φυή), but to the natural claim (φύσις) of age and
office combined. **10 πρὸ τῶνδε,** 'in front of,' and so 'on behalf of,'
'*for*' these. Ellendt: 'Non est ἀντὶ τῶνδε, nec ὑπὲρ τῶνδε, sed μᾶλλον s.
μάλιστα τῶνδε, *prae ceteris dignus* propter auctoritatem et aetatem.'
Rather ἀντὶ τῶνδε = 'as their deputy': ὑπὲρ τῶνδε = 'as their champion':
πρὸ τῶνδε = 'as their spokesman.' **τίνι τρόπῳ** with **καθέστατε** only :
δείσαντες ἢ στέρξαντες = εἴτε ἐδείσατέ τι, εἴτε ἐστέρξατε (not πότερον δείσαντες; ἢ στέρξαντες;), 'in what mood are ye set here, whether it be one of
fear or of desire?' **11 στέρξαντες,** 'having formed a desire': the aor. part.,
as *Ai*. 212 ἐπεί σε... | στέρξας ἀνέχει 'is constant to the love which he
hath formed for thee.' *El*. 1100 καὶ τί βουληθεὶς πάρει; *Ai*. 1052 αὐτὸν
ἐλπίσαντες...ἄγειν. Cp. *O. C*. 1093 καὶ τὸν ἀγρευτὰν Ἀπόλλω | καὶ κα-

of others, and have come hither myself, I, Oedipus renowned of all.

Tell me, then, thou venerable man—since it is thy natural part to speak for these—in what mood are ye placed here, with what dread or what desire? Be sure that I would gladly give all aid; hard of heart were I,

Cod. Paris. 2787 (B) στέρξαντες, superscripto παθόντες. Cod. Paris. 2884 (E) στέξαντες habet in στέρξαντες mutatum (non στέρξ. in στέξ.), cum gloss. παθόντες, ὑπομείναντες. Biblioth. Bodleianae cod. Laud. 54 στέξαντες cum gl. ὑπομείναντες. στέξαντες A: quae l. librariis procul dubio debetur mirantibus quo pacto

---

σιγνῆταν... | στέργω διπλᾶς ἀρωγὰς | μολεῖν, 'I desire': where, in such an invocation (ἰὼ...Ζεῦ,...πόροις, κ.τ.λ.), στέργω surely cannot mean, 'I am content.' Oed. asks: Does this supplication mean that some new dread has seized you (δείσαντες)? Or that ye have set your hearts (στέρξαντες) on some particular boon which I can grant?'—Others render στέρξαντες 'having acquiesced.' This admits of two views. (i) 'Are ye afraid of suffering? Or have ye already learned to bear suffering?' To this point the glosses ὑπομείναντες, παθόντες. But this seems unmeaning. He knows that the suffering has come, and he does not suppose that they are resigned to it (cp. v. 58). (ii) Professor Kennedy connects ἢ στέρξαντες ὡς θέλοντος ἂν | ἐμοῦ προσαρκεῖν πᾶν; i.e. are ye come in vague terror, or in contentment, as believing that I would be willing to help you? This is ingenious and attractive. But (a) it appears hardly consonant with the kingly courtesy of this opening speech for Oedipus to assume that their belief in his good-will would reconcile them to their present miseries. (b) We seem to require some direct and express intimation of the king's willingness to help, such as the words ὡς θέλοντος...πᾶν give only when referred to φράζε. (c) The rhythm seems to favour the question at στέρξαντες.—στέξαντες, explained as 'having endured,' may be rejected, because (1) the sense is against it—see on (i) above: (2) στέγειν in classical Greek = 'to be proof against,' not 'to suffer': (3) στέξω, ἔστεξα are unknown to Attic, which has only the pres. and the imperf. ὡς θέλοντος ἂν (to be connected with φράζε) implies the apodosis of a conditional sentence. Grammatically, this might be either (a) εἰ δυναίμην, θέλοιμι ἄν, or (b) εἰ ἠδυνάμην, ἤθελον ἄν: here, the sense fixes it to (a). ὡς, thus added to the gen. absol., expresses the supposition on which the agent acts. Xen. Mem. 2. 6, 32 ὡς οὐ προσοίσοντος (ἐμοῦ) τὰς χεῖρας,...δίδασκε: 'as

εἴην τοιάνδε μὴ οὐ κατοικτείρων ἕδραν.

ΙΕΡΕΥΣ.

ἀλλ', ὦ κρατύνων Οἰδίπους χώρας ἐμῆς,
ὁρᾷς μὲν ἡμᾶς ἡλίκοι προσήμεθα   15
βωμοῖσι τοῖς σοῖς, οἱ μὲν οὐδέπω μακρὰν
πτέσθαι σθένοντες, οἱ δὲ σὺν γήρᾳ βαρεῖς,
ἱερῆς, ἐγὼ μὲν Ζηνός, οἵδε τ' ἠθέων
λεκτοί· τὸ δ' ἄλλο φῦλον ἐξεστεμμένον
ἀγοραῖσι θακεῖ, πρός τε Παλλάδος διπλοῖς   20

παθόντες, ὑπομείναντες in στέρξαντες quadrarent. **13** μὴ κατοικτείρων Par.
2712 (A), B. **18** ἱερεῖς codd.: edd. plerique cum Brunck. ἱερῆς. Gratior
sane post βαρεῖς formae Atticae veterioris sonus. Bentleium frustra ἱερεὺς scri-
bentem secutus est Nauck., qui ἐγὼ μὲν in ἔγωγε mutavit.   οἱ δέ τ' ἠϊθέων,
L, A. In L accessit signum elisionis (') post rasuram; litterae π tamen, ex qua

---

(you may be sure) I will not lay hands on you, teach me.' **13 μὴ
οὐ κατοικτείρων.** An infinitive or participle, which for any reason would
regularly take μή, usually takes μὴ οὐ if the principal verb of the
sentence is negative. Here, δυσάλγητος = οὐκ εὐάλγητος: Dem. *Fals.
Legat.* § 123 (πόλεις) χαλεπαὶ λαβεῖν...μὴ οὐ χρόνῳ καὶ πολιορκίᾳ (*sc.*
λαμβάνοντι), where χαλεπαί = οὐ ῥᾴδιαι: 'cities *not easy* to take, *unless
by a protracted siege.*' The participial clause, μὴ οὐ κατοικτείρων, is
equivalent to a protasis, εἰ μὴ κατοικτείροιμι. Prof. Kennedy holds that
the protasis is εἰ μὴ θέλοιμι understood, and that μὴ οὐ κατοικτείρων is
epexegetic of it :—' Yes (γάρ) I should be unfeeling, *if I did not wish*
(to help you): that is, if I refused to pity such a supplication as this.'
But the double negative μὴ οὐ could not be explained by a negative in
the *protasis* (εἰ μὴ θέλοιμι): it implies a negative in the *apodosis* (δυσάλγητος ἂν εἴην). Since, then, the resolution into οὐκ εὐάλγητος ἂν εἴην is
necessary, nothing seems to be gained by supposing a suppressed
protasis, εἰ μὴ θέλοιμι. **16 βωμοῖσι τοῖς σοῖς.** The altars of the προστατήριοι θεοί in front of the palace, including that of Apollo Λύκειος (919).
μακρὰν πτέσθαι. So Andromache to her child—νεοσσὸς ὡσεὶ πτέρυγας
ἐσπίτνων ἐμάς Eur. *Tro.* 746. The proper Attic form for the aor. of
πέτομαι was ἐπτόμην, which alone was used in prose and Comedy.
Though forms from ἐπτάμην sometimes occur in Tragedy, as in
the Homeric poems, Elms. had no cause to wish for πτάσθαι here.

did I not pity such suppliants as these.

PRIEST OF ZEUS.

Nay, Oedipus, ruler of my land, thou seest of what years we are who beset thy altars,—some, nestlings still too tender for far flights,—some, bowed with age, priests, as I of Zeus,—and these, the chosen youth; while the rest of the folk sit with wreathed branches in the market-places, and before the two shrines of Pallas,

factum τ Duebner. suspicatus est, ne levissimum quidem vestigium deprehendere potui. Cod. Venet. 472 (V⁴), quocum consentit B, οἱ δ' ἠϊθέων. Wunder. coni. οἱ δ' ἐπ' ἠθέων, quod recepit Dindorf. (ed. 1860), collato *Antig.* v. 787 ἐπ' ἀνθρώπων: Musgrav. cf. Aristid. *Pan.* I. 96 μόνῃ τῇ πόλει ἐπὶ τῶν Ἑλληνικῶν. Equidem vereor ut Graece dicatur ἐπ' ἠθέων λεκτοί hoc sensu, *ex omni iuventute delecti* ('*chosen to repre-*

---

17 σὺν γήρᾳ βαρεῖς = βαρεῖς ὡς γήρᾳ συνόντες. *O. C.* 1663 σὺν νόσοις | ἀλγεινός: *Ai.* 1017 ἐν γήρᾳ βαρύς. **18** ἐγὼ μὲν. The answering clause, οἱ δὲ ἄλλων θεῶν, must be supplied mentally: cp. *Il.* 5. 893 τὴν μὲν ἐγὼ σπουδῇ δάμνησ' ἐπέεσσι (*sc.* τὰς δὲ ἄλλας ῥᾳδίως). It is slightly different when μέν, used alone, emphasizes the personal pronoun, as in ἐγὼ μὲν οὐκ οἶδα Xen. *Cyr.* I. 4. 12. ἠθέων, unmarried youths: *Il.* 18. 593 ἠΐθεοι καὶ παρθένοι: Eur. *Phoen.* 944 Αἵμονος...γάμοι | σφαγὰς ἀπείργουσ'· οὐ γάρ ἐστιν ἠθέος: Plut. *Thes.* 15 ἠθέους ἑπτὰ καὶ παρθένους. **19** ἐξεστεμμένον: see on 3. **20** ἀγοραῖσι, local dative, like οἰκεῖν οὐρανῷ Pind. *Nem.* 10. 58. Thebes was divided from N. to S. into two parts by the torrent called Strophia. The W. part, between the Strophia and the Dircè, was the upper town or Cadmeia: the E. part, between the Strophia and the Ismenus, was ἡ κάτω πόλις. The name Καδμεία was given especially to the S. eminence of the upper town, the acropolis. (1) One of the ἀγοραί meant here was on a hill to the north of the acropolis, and was the ἀγορὰ Καδμείας. See Paus. 9. 12. 3. (2) The other was in the lower town. Xen. *Hellen.* 5. 2. 29 refers to this—ἡ βουλὴ ἐκάθητο ἐν τῇ ἐν ἀγορᾷ στοᾷ, διὰ τὸ τὰς γυναῖκας ἐν τῇ Καδμείᾳ θεσμοφοριάζειν: unless Καδμεία has the narrower sense of 'acropolis.' Cp. Arist. *Pol.* 4. (7) 12. 2 on the Thessalian custom of having two ἀγοραί—one, ἐλευθέρα, from which everything βάναυσον was excluded. πρός τε Παλλάδος...ναοῖς. Not '*both*' at the two temples,' &c., as if this explained ἀγοραῖσι, but '*and*,' &c.: for the ἀγοραί

ναοῖς, ἐπ' Ἰσμηνοῦ τε μαντεία σποδῷ.
πόλις γάρ, ὥσπερ καὐτὸς εἰσορᾷς, ἄγαν
ἤδη σαλεύει κἀνακουφίσαι κάρα
βυθῶν ἔτ' οὐχ οἷά τε φοινίου σάλου,
φθίνουσα μὲν κάλυξιν ἐγκάρποις χθονός,   25

sent the youth'). 21 μαντείᾳ L, ex μαντείας radendo factum: manet litterae σ pars superior. A μαντεῖα (sic). E μαντεία.

would have their own altars of the ἀγοραῖοι θεοί, as of Artemis (161). One of the διπλοῖ ναοί may be that of Παλλὰς Ὄγκα, near the Ὀγκαία πύλη on the W. side of Thebes (πύλας | Ὄγκας Ἀθάνας Aesch. *Theb.* 487, Ὄγκα Παλλάς *ib.* 501), whose statue and altar ἐν ὑπαίθρῳ Paus. mentions (9. 12. 2). The other temple may be that of Athene Καδμεία or of Athene Ἰσμηνία—both mentioned by the schol., but not by Paus. Athene Ζωστηρία, too, had *statues* at Thebes (Paus. 9. 17. 3). The schol. mentions also Ἀλαλκομενία, but her shrine was at the village of Alalcomenae neâr Haliartus (Paus. 9. 23. 5). It was enough for Soph. that his Athenian hearers would think of the Erechtheum and the Parthenon—the shrines of the Polias and the Parthenos—above them on the acropolis. **21 ἐπ' Ἰσμ. μ. σποδῷ.** 'The oracular ashes of Ismenus' = the altar in the temple of Apollo Ἰσμήνιος, where divination by burnt offerings (ἡ δι' ἐμπύρων μαντεία) was practised. So the schol., quoting Philochorus (in his περὶ μαντικῆς, circ. 290 B.C.). σποδῷ: the embers dying down when the μαντεῖον has now been taken from the burnt offering: cp. *Ant.* 1007. Soph. may have thought of Ἀπόλλων Σπόδιος, whose altar (ἐκ τέφρας τῶν ἱερείων) Paus. saw to the left of the Electrae gates at Thebes: 9. 11. 7. Ἰσμηνοῦ, because the temple was by the river Ismenus: Paus. 9. 10. 2 ἔστι δὲ λόφος ἐν δεξιᾷ τῶν πυλῶν (on the right of the Ἠλέκτραι πύλαι on the S. of Thebes, within the walls) ἱερὸς Ἀπόλλωνος· καλεῖται δὲ ὅ τε λόφος καὶ ὁ θεὸς Ἰσμήνιος, παραρρέοντος τοῦ ποταμοῦ ταύτῃ τοῦ Ἰσμηνοῦ. Ismenus (which name Curtius, *Etym.* 617, connects with rt ἱς, to wish, as = 'desired') was described in the Theban myths as the son of Asopus and Metope, or of Amphion and Niobe. The son of Apollo by Melia (the fountain of the Ismenus) was called Ismenius. Cp. Her. 8. 134 (the envoy of Mardonius in the winter of 480—79) τῷ Ἰσμηνίῳ Ἀπόλλωνι ἐχρήσατο· ἔστι δὲ κατάπερ ἐν Ὀλυμπίῃ ἱροῖσι χρηστηριάζεσθαι: Pind. *Olymp.* 8. *init.* Οὐλυμπία | ...ἵνα μάντιες ἄνδρες | ἐμπύροις τεκμαιρόμενοι παραπειρῶνται Διός. In Pind. *Pyth.*

and where Ismenus gives answer by fire.

For the city, as thou thyself seest, is now too sorely vexed, and can no more lift her head from beneath the angry waves of death; a blight is on her in the fruitful blossoms of the land,

---

11. 4 the Theban heroines are asked to come πὰρ Μελίαν (because she shared Apollo's temple) 'to the holy treasure-house of golden tripods, which Loxias hath honoured exceedingly, and hath named it *Ismenian*, a truthful seat of oracles' (MSS. μαντείων, not μαντίων, Fennell): for the tripod dedicated by the δαφναφόρος, or priest of Ismenian Apollo, see Paus. 9. 10. 4. Her. saw offerings dedicated by Croesus to Amphiaraus ἐν τῷ νηῷ τοῦ Ἰσμηνίου Ἀπόλλωνος (1. 52), and notices inscriptions there (5. 59). The Ἰσμήνιον, the temple at Abae in Phocis, and that on the hill Πτῶον to the E. of Lake Copais, were, after Delphi, the chief shrines of Apollo in N. Greece. **24 βυθῶν,** 'from the depths,' *i.e.* out of the trough of the waves which rise around. Cp. *Ant.* 337 περιβρυχίοισιν | περῶν ὑπ' οἴδμασιν, *under* swelling waves which threaten to engulf him. Arat. 426 ὑπόβρυχα ναυτίλλονται. φοινίου here merely poet. for θανασίμου, as *Tr.* 770 φοινίας | ἐχθρᾶς ἐχίδνης ἰός. But in *Ai.* 351 φοινία ζάλη = the madness which drove Ajax to *bloodshed*. ἔτ' οὐχ οἷά τε: for position of ἔτι, cp. *Trach.* 161 ὡς ἔτ' οὐκ ὤν, *Phil.* 1217 ἔτ' οὐδέν εἰμι. With οἷός τε the verb is often omitted, as 1415, *O. C.* 1136, *Tr.* 742, Ar. *Eq.* 343. **25 φθίνουσα μὲν κ.τ.λ.** The anger of heaven is shown (1) by a *blight* (φθίνουσα) on the fruits of the ground, on flocks and on child-birth: (2) by a *pestilence* (λοιμός) which ravages the town. Cp. 171 ff. For the threefold blight, Her. 6. 139 ἀποκτείνασι δὲ τοῖσι Πελασγοῖσι τοὺς σφετέρους παῖδάς τε καὶ γυναῖκας οὔτε γῆ καρπὸν ἔφερε οὔτε γυναῖκές τε καὶ ποῖμναι ὁμοίως ἔτικτον καὶ πρὸ τοῦ: Aeschin. *In Ctes.* § 111 μήτε γῆν καρποὺς φέρειν μήτε γυναῖκας τέκνα τίκτειν γονεῦσιν ἐοικότα, ἀλλὰ τέρατα, μήτε βοσκήματα κατὰ φύσιν γονὰς ποιεῖσθαι. Schneid. and Blaydes cp. Philostratus *Vit. Apoll.* 3. 20, p. 51. 21 ἡ γῆ οὐ ξυνεχώρει αὐτοῖς ἵστασθαι· τήν τε γὰρ σπορὰν ἣν ἐς αὐτὴν ἐποιοῦντο, πρὶν ἐς κάλυκα ἥκειν, ἔφθειρε, τούς τε τῶν γυναικῶν τόκους ἀτελεῖς ἐποίει, καὶ τὰς ἀγέλας πονηρῶς ἔβοσκεν. **25 κάλυξιν ἐγκάρποις.** The datives mark the points or parts in which the land φθίνει. **κάλυξ ἔγκαρπος** is the shell or case which encloses immature fruit,—whether the blossom of fruit-trees, or the ear of wheat or barley: Theophr. *Hist. Plant.* 8. 2. 4 (of κριθή and πυρός) πρὶν ἂν προαυξηθεὶς (ὁ

φθίνουσα δ᾽ ἀγέλαις βουνόμοις τόκοισί τε
ἀγόνοις γυναικῶν· ἐν δ᾽ ὁ πυρφόρος θεὸς
σκήψας ἐλαύνει, λοιμὸς ἔχθιστος, πόλιν,
ὑφ᾽ οὗ κενοῦται δῶμα Καδμεῖον· μέλας δ᾽
Ἀιδης στεναγμοῖς καὶ γόοις πλουτίζεται.   30
θεοῖσι μέν νυν οὐκ ἰσούμενόν σ᾽ ἐγὼ
οὐδ᾽ οἵδε παῖδες ἑζόμεσθ᾽ ἐφέστιοι,
ἀνδρῶν δὲ πρῶτον ἔν τε συμφοραῖς βίου
κρίνοντες ἔν τε δαιμόνων συναλλαγαῖς·

29 Καδμείων A, et codd. aliquot recentiores. Cf. v. 35.

στάχυς) ἐν τῇ κάλυκι γένηται.   26 ἀγέλαι βουνόμοι (paroxyt.) = ἀγέλαι
βοῶν νεμομένων : but ἀκτὴ βούνομος, proparoxyt., a shore on which
oxen are pastured, *El.* 181. Cp. *El.* 861 χαλαργοῖς ἐν ἀμίλλαις =
ἀμίλλαις ἀργῶν χηλῶν: Pind. *Pyth.* 5. 28 ἀρισθάρματον...γέρας = γέρας
ἀρίστου ἅρματος. The epithet marks that the blight on the flocks
is closely connected with that on the pastures: cp. Dionys. Hal.
1. 23 (describing a similar blight) οὔτε πόα κτήνεσιν ἐφύετο διαρ-
κής. τόκοισι, the labours of child-bed: Eur. *Med.* 1031 στερρὰς ἐνεγκοῦσ᾽
ἐν τόκοις ἀλγηδόνας: *Iph. T.* 1466 γυναῖκες ἐν τόκοις ψυχορραγεῖς.
Dionys. Hal. 1. 23 ἀδελφὰ δὲ τούτοις (*i.e.* to the blight on fruits
and crops) ἐγίνετο περί τε προβάτων καὶ γυναικῶν γονάς· ἢ γὰρ ἐξημ-
βλοῦτο τὰ ἔμβρυα, ἢ κατὰ τοὺς τόκους διεφθείρετο ἔστιν ἃ καὶ τὰς φερού-
σας συνδιαλυμηνάμενα. 27 ἀγόνοις, abortive, or resulting in a still
birth. ἐν δ᾽, adv., 'and among our other woes,' 'and withal': so
183, *Tr.* 206, *Ai.* 675. Not in 'tmesis' with σκήψας, though Soph. has
such tmesis elsewhere, *Ant.* 420 ἐν δ᾽ ἐμεστώθη, *ib.* 1274 ἐν δ᾽ ἔσεισεν. For
the simple σκήψας, cp. Aesch. *Ag.* 308 εἶτ᾽ ἔσκηψεν, 'then it swooped.'
So *Pers.* 715 λοιμοῦ τις ἦλθε σκηπτός. ὁ πυρφόρος θεὸς, the bringer of
the plague which spreads and rages *like* fire (176 κρεῖσσον ἀμαιμακέτου
πυρός, 191 φλέγει με): but also with a reference to *fever*, πυρετός.
Hippocrates 4. 140 ὁκόσοισι δὲ τῶν ἀνθρώπων πῦρ (= πυρετὸς) ἐμπίπτῃ:
Il. 22. 31 καί τε φέρει (Seirius) πολλὸν πυρετὸν δειλοῖσι βροτοῖσι (the
only place where πυρετός occurs in *Il.* or *Od.*). In *O. C.* 55 ἐν δ᾽ ὁ
πυρφόρος θεὸς | Τιτὰν Προμηθεύς refers to the representation of Prometheus
with the narthex, or a torch, in his right hand (Eur. *Phoen.* 1121 δεξιᾷ
δὲ λαμπάδα | Τιτὰν Προμηθεὺς ἔφερεν ὥς). Cp. Aesch. *Theb.* 432 ἄνδρα
πυρφόρον, | φλέγει δὲ λαμπάς, κ.τ.λ. Here also the Destroyer is

in the herds among the pastures, in the barren pangs of women; and withal the flaming god, the malign plague, hath swooped on us, and ravages the town; by whom the house of Cadmus is made waste, but dark Hades rich in groans and tears.

It is not as deeming thee ranked with gods that I and these children are suppliants at thy hearth, but as deeming thee first of men, both in life's common chances, and when mortals have to do with more than man:

31 οὐκ ἰσούμενον L, sed κ, ut videtur, ex χὶ facto.

---

imagined as *armed with a deadly brand*,—against which the Chorus presently invoke the holy fires of Artemis (206) and the 'blithe torch' of Dionysus (214). For θεός said of λοιμός, cp. Simonid. Amorg. fr. 7. 101 οὐδ᾽ αἶψα λιμὸν οἰκίης ἀπώσεται, | ἐχθρὸν συνοικητῆρα, δυσμενέα θεόν. Soph. fr. 837 ἀλλ᾽ ἡ φρόνησις ἀγαθὴ θεὸς μέγας. 29 μέλας δ᾽: elision at end of verse, as 785 ὅμως δ᾽, 791 γένος δ᾽, 1184 ξὺν οἷς τ᾽, 1224 ὅσον δ᾽: *El.* 1017 καλῶς δ᾽: *Ant.* 1031 τὸ μανθάνειν δ᾽: Ar. *Av.* 1716 θυμιαμάτων δ᾽. Besides δ᾽ and τ᾽, the only certain example is ταῦτ᾽, 332; in *O. C.* 1164 μολόντ᾽ is doubtful. 30 πλουτίζεται with allusion to Πλούτων, as Hades was called by an euphemism (ὑποκοριστικῶς, schol. Ar. *Plut.* 727), ὅτι ἐκ τῆς κάτωθεν ἀνίεται ὁ πλοῦτος (crops and metals), as Plato says, *Crat.* 403 A. Cp. Sophocles fr. 252 (from the satyric drama *Inachus*) Πλούτωνος (="Αιδου) ἥδ᾽ ἐπείσοδος: Lucian *Timon* 21 (Πλοῦτος speaks), ὁ Πλούτων (Hades) ἀποστέλλει με παρ᾽ αὐτοὺς ἅτε πλουτοδότης καὶ μεγαλόδωρος καὶ αὐτὸς ὤν· δηλοῖ γοῦν καὶ τῷ ὀνόματι. Schneid. cp. Statius *Theb.* 2. 48 *pallentes devius umbras Trames agit nigrique Iovis vacua atria* ditat Mortibus. 31 οὐκ ἰσούμενόν σ᾽, governed by κρίνοντες in 34. But the poet began the sentence as if he were going to write, instead of ἐζόμεσθ᾽ ἐφέστιοι, a verb like ἱκετεύομεν: hence ἰσούμενον instead of ἴσον. It is needless to take ἰσούμενον (1) as accus. absol., or (2) as governed by ἐζόμεσθ᾽ ἐφέστιοι in the sense of ἱκετεύομεν,—like φθορὰς...ψήφους ἔθεντο Aesch. *Ag.* 814, or γένος...νέωσον αἶνον *Suppl.* 533. Musgrave conj. ἰσούμενοι as = 'deeming equal,' but the midd. would mean 'making *ourselves* equal,' like ἀντισουμένου Thuc. 3. 11. Plato has ἰσούμενον as passive in *Phaedr.* 238 E, and ἰσοῦσθαι as passive in *Parm.* 156 B: cp. 581 ἰσοῦμαι. 34 δαιμόνων συναλλαγαῖς = dealings (of men) with immortals, = ὅταν ἄνθρωποι συναλλάσσωνται δαίμοσιν, as opposed to the *ordinary* chances

ὅς γ᾽ ἐξέλυσας, ἄστυ Καδμεῖον μολών,   35
σκληρᾶς ἀοιδοῦ δασμὸν ὃν παρείχομεν·
καὶ ταῦθ᾽ ὑφ᾽ ἡμῶν οὐδὲν ἐξειδὼς πλέον
οὐδ᾽ ἐκδιδαχθείς, ἀλλὰ προσθήκῃ θεοῦ
λέγει νομίζει θ᾽ ἡμὶν ὀρθῶσαι βίον·
νῦν τ᾽, ὦ κράτιστον πᾶσιν Οἰδίπου κάρα,   40
ἱκετεύομέν σε πάντες οἵδε πρόστροποι
ἀλκήν τιν᾽ εὑρεῖν ἡμίν, εἴτε του θεῶν
φήμην ἀκούσας εἴτ᾽ ἀπ᾽ ἀνδρὸς οἶσθά που·

35 ὅς γ᾽ codd. omnes. Elmsl. coni. ὅς τ᾽, quasi responderet νῦν τ᾽ in v. 40: quod
recepit Campb. Vulgatam tueor, neque coniecturae satis opitulari credo quod annotavit schol. in cod. Laur. ὥστε μολεῖν ἄστυ Καδμεῖον: qua sententia, parum liquet.

of life (συμφοραῖς βίου).   Such συναλλαγαί were the visit of the Sphinx
(130) and of the πυρφόρος θεός (27).   Cp. 960 νόσου συναλλαγῇ, Trach.
845 οὐλίαισι συναλλαγαῖς, 'in fatal converse.'   But in Ant. 156 θεῶν συν-
τυχίαι = fortunes sent by gods.   The common prose sense of συναλλαγή
is 'reconciliation,' which Soph. has in Ai. 732.   35 ὅς γ᾽. The γε of the
MSS. suits the immediately preceding verses better than the conjectural
τε, since the judgment (κρίνοντες) rests solely on what Oed. has done, not
partly on what he is expected to do.   Owing to the length of the first
clause (35—39) τ᾽ could easily be added to νῦν in 40 as if another τε
had preceded.   ἐξέλυσας...δασμόν. The notion is not, 'paid it in full,'
but 'loosed it,'—the thought of the tribute suggesting that of the riddle
which Oed. solved.   Till he came, the δασμός was as a knotted cord in
which Thebes was bound.   Cp. Trach. 653 Ἄρης...ἐξέλυσ᾽ | ἐπίπονον
ἀμέραν, 'has burst the bondage of the troublous day.'   Eur. Phoen. 695
ποδῶν σῶν μόχθον ἐκλύει παρών, 'his presence dispenses with (solves the
need for) the toil of thy feet.'   This is better than (1) 'freed the city
from the songstress, in respect of the tribute,' or (2) 'freed the city from
the tribute (δασμόν by attraction for δασμοῦ) to the songstress.'   36 σκληρᾶς,
'hard,' stubborn, relentless.   Eur. Andr. 261 σκληρὸν θράσος.   In 391
κύων expresses a similar idea.   37 καὶ ταῦθ᾽, 'and that too': Ant. 322
(ἐποίησας τὸ ἔργον) καὶ ταῦτ᾽ ἐπ᾽ ἀργυρῷ γε τὴν ψυχὴν προδούς.   οὐδὲν πλέον,
nothing more than anyone else knew, nothing 'that could advantage
thee.'   Plat. Crat. 387 A πλέον τι ἡμῖν ἔσται, we shall gain something.
Sympos. 217 C οὐδὲν γάρ μοι πλέον ἦν, it did not help me.   ἐξειδὼς—ἐκδιδαχθείς: not having heard (incidentally)—much less having been
thoroughly schooled.   38 προσθήκη θεοῦ, 'by the aid of a god.' [Dem.] In

seeing that thou camest to the town of Cadmus, and didst quit us of the tax that we rendered to the hard songstress; and this, though thou knewest nothing from us that could avail thee, nor hadst been schooled; no, by a god's aid, 'tis said and believed, didst thou uplift our life.

And now, Oedipus, king glorious in all eyes, we beseech thee, all we suppliants, to find for us some succour, whether by the whisper of a god thou knowest it, or haply as in the power of man;

Καδμεῖον L, Καδμείων A. Καδμεῖον ex Καδμείων factum B: contraria in V⁴ ratio. Ut in v. 29, ita hic quoque genit. pluralem librariis commendavit locutio pedestri propior. **40** νῦν δ' Blaydes. **43** που A, cod. Ven. 468 (V), cum codd. plerisque. του L, superscr. που a manu admodum recenti: B τ⁸ in π⁸ mutatum a manu recenti. του Schneidewin., Dindorf., Blaydes.

Aristog. I. § 24 ἡ εὐταξία τῇ τῶν νόμων προσθήκῃ τῶν αἰσχρῶν περίεστι, 'discipline, with *the support* of the laws, prevails against villainy.' Dionys. Hal. 5. 67 προσθήκης μοῖραν ἐπεῖχον οὗτοι τοῖς ἐν φάλαγγι τεταγμένοις, 'these served as *supports* to the main body of the troops.' προστίθεσθαί τινι, to take his side: Thuc. 6. 80 τοῖς ἀδικουμένοις... προσθεμένους: so Soph. *O. C.* 1332 οἷς ἂν σὺ προσθῇ. (The noun προσθήκη does not occur as = '*mandate*,' though Her. 3. 62 has τό τοι προσέθηκα ·πρῆγμα.) The word is appropriate, since the achievement of Oed. is viewed as essentially a triumph of human wit: a divine agency prompted him, but remained in the background. **40** νῦν τ': it is unnecessary to read νῦν δ': see on 35. πᾶσιν, ethical dat. masc. (cp. 8), 'in the eyes of all men.' *Tr.* 1071 πολλοῖσιν οἰκτρόν. **42** εἴτε οἶσθα ἀλκήν, ἀκούσας φήμην θεῶν του (*by* having heard a voice from some god), εἴτε οἶσθα ἀλκήν ἀπ' ἀνδρός που (help obtainable from a man, haply). Not, 'knowest from a man' (as thy informant): this would be παρὰ or πρὸς ἀνδρός. So in *Od.* 6. 12 θεῶν ἄπο μήδεα εἰδώς = 'with wisdom inspired by gods,' not 'having learned wisdom from (the lips of) gods.' **43** φήμην, any message (as in a dream, φήμη ὀνείρου, Her. 1. 43), any rumour, or speech casually heard, which might be taken as a hint from the god. *Od.* 20. 98 Ζεῦ πάτερ... | φήμην τίς μοι φάσθω...(Odysseus prays), 'Let some one, I pray, show me *a word of omen*.' Then a woman, grinding corn within, is heard speaking of the suitors, '*may they now sup their last*': χαῖρεν δὲ κληδόνι δῖος Ὀδυσσεύς, 'rejoiced in the sign of the voice.' ὀμφή was esp. the voice of an oracle; κληδών comprised *inarticulate* sounds

ὡς τοῖσιν ἐμπείροισι καὶ τὰς ξυμφορὰς
ζώσας ὁρῶ μάλιστα τῶν βουλευμάτων.   45
ἴθ', ὦ βροτῶν ἄριστ', ἀνόρθωσον πόλιν·
ἴθ', εὐλαβήθηθ'· ὡς σὲ νῦν μὲν ἥδε γῆ
σωτῆρα κλῄζει τῆς πάρος προθυμίας·
ἀρχῆς δὲ τῆς σῆς μηδαμῶς μεμνώμεθα
στάντες τ' ἐς ὀρθὸν καὶ πεσόντες ὕστερον,   50
ἀλλ' ἀσφαλείᾳ τήνδ' ἀνόρθωσον πόλιν.

48 πάρος L, ρος a manu recentiore, deletis litteris quas λαι fuisse neque negare

---

(κλ. δυσκρίτους, Aesch. *P. V.* 486). **44—45 ὡς τοῖσιν...βουλευμάτων.** I
take these two verses with the whole context from v. 35, and not
merely as a comment on the immediately preceding words εἴτ' ἀπ'
ἀνδρὸς οἶσθά που. Oedipus has had practical experience (ἐμπειρία) of
great troubles; when the Sphinx came, his wisdom stood the trial.
Men who have become thus ἔμπειροι are apt to be *also* (καί) prudent
in regard to the future. Past *facts* enlighten the *counsels* which they
offer on things still uncertain; and we observe that the issues of their
counsels are not usually futile or dead, but effectual. Well may we
believe, then, that he who saved us from the Sphinx can tell us how
to escape from the plague. Note these points. (1) The words
ἐμπείροισι and βουλευμάτων imply the antithesis (*a*) between past and
future, (*b*) between ἔργα and λόγοι. Cp. Thuc. I. 22 ὅσοι δὲ βουλή-
σονται τῶν τε γενομένων τὸ σαφὲς σκοπεῖν καὶ τῶν μελλόντων ποτὲ
αὖθις κατὰ τὸ ἀνθρώπειον τοιούτων καὶ παραπλησίων ἔσεσθαι. (2) τὰς
ξυμφορὰς τῶν βουλευμάτων, the events, issues, of their counsels: Thuc.
I. 140 ἐνδέχεται γὰρ τὰς ξυμφορὰς τῶν πραγμάτων οὐχ ἧσσον
ἀμαθῶς χωρῆσαι ἢ καὶ τὰς διανοίας τοῦ ἀνθρώπου: *the issues of human
affairs* can be as incomprehensible in their course as the thoughts
of man: *ib.* πρὸς τὰς ξυμφορὰς καὶ τὰς γνώμας τρεπομένους, altering
their views according to the *events.* 3. 87 τῆς ξυμφορᾶς τῷ ἀποβάντι,
by the *issue* which has resulted. (3) ζώσας is not 'successful,' but
'operative,'—effectual for the purpose of the βουλεύματα: as v. 482
ζῶντα is said of the oracles which remain operative against the guilty,
and *Ant.* 457 ζῇ ταῦτα of laws which are ever in force. Conversely
λόγοι θνήσκοντες μάτην (Aesch. *Cho.* 845) are threats which come to
nothing. See Appendix, Note 3. **47 εὐλαβήθητι,** have a care *for thy*

for I see that, when men have been proved in deeds past, the issues of their counsels, too, most often have effect.

On, best of mortals, again uplift our State! On, guard thy fame,—since now this land calls thee saviour for thy former zeal; and never be it our memory of thy reign that we were first restored and afterward cast down: nay, lift up this State in such wise that it fall no more!

potest quisquam neque affirmare; totae evanuerunt.   **49** μεμνώμεθα codd.: μεμνώμεθα Eustath., Herm., Erfurdt., Dobraeus: vide annot.   **50** στάντες γ' Triclinius, Elms., Blaydes.

---

repute—as the next clause explains.   Oed. is supposed to be above personal risk; it is only the degree of his future glory (55) which is in question;—a fine touch, in view of the destined sequel.   **48** τῆς πάρος προθυμίας, causal genit.: Plat. *Crito* 43 B πολλάκις μὲν δή σε...εὐδαιμόνισα τοῦ τρόπου.   **49** μεμνώμεθα. This subjunctive occurs also in *Od.* 14. 168 πῖνε καὶ ἄλλα παρὲξ μεμνώμεθα, Plat. *Politicus* 285 C φυλάττωμεν...καὶ... μεμνώμεθα, *Phileb.* 31 A μεμνώμεθα δὴ καὶ ταῦτα περὶ ἀμφοῖν.   Eustathius (1303. 46, 1332. 18) cites the word here as μεμνῷμεθα (optative).   We find, indeed, μεμνῷο Xen. *Anab.* I. 7. 5 (*v. l.* μεμνῇο), μεμνεῷτο *Il.* 23. 361, μεμνῷτο Xen. *Cyr.* I. 6. 3, but these are rare exceptions.   On the other hand, μεμνήμην *Il.* 24. 745, μεμνῆτο Ar. *Plut.* 991, Plat. *Rep.* 518 A.   If Soph. had meant the optative he would have written μεμνήμεθα: cp. *Philoct.* 119 ἄν...κεκλῇο.   See Curtius *Greek Verb* II. 226 (Eng. tr. p. 423).   The personal appeal, too, here requires the subjunct., not optat.: cp. *O. C.* 174 μὴ δῆτ' ἀδικηθῶ, *Trach.* 802 μηδ' αὐτοῦ θάνω.   **50** στάντες τ' κ.τ.λ. For partic. with μέμνημαι cp. Xen. *Cyr.* 3. 1. 31 ἐμέμνητο γὰρ εἰπών: Pind. *Nem.* 11. 15 θνατὰ μεμνάσθω περιστέλλων μέλη: for τε...καί, *Ant.* 1112 αὐτός τ' ἔδησα καὶ παρὼν ἐκλύσομαι, as I bound, so will I loose.   **51** ἀσφαλείᾳ, 'in steadfastness': a dative of manner, equivalent to ἀσφαλῶς in the proleptic sense of ὥστε ἀσφαλῆ εἶναι.   Thuc. 3. 56 οἱ μὴ τὰ ξύμφορα πρὸς τὴν ἔφοδον αὐτοῖς ἀσφαλείᾳ πράσσοντες, those who *securely* made terms on their own account which were not for the common good in view of the invasion.   3. 82 ἀσφαλείᾳ δὲ τὸ ἐπιβουλεύσασθαι (where ἀσφάλεια is a false reading), to form designs *in security*, opp. to τὸ ἐμπλήκτως ὀξύ, fickle impetuosity.   The primary notion of ἀσφαλής ('not slipping') is brought out by πεσόντες and ἀνόρθωσον.

ὄρνιθι γὰρ καὶ τὴν τότ' αἰσίῳ τύχην
παρέσχες ἡμῖν, καὶ τανῦν ἴσος γενοῦ.
ὡς εἴπερ ἄρξεις τῆσδε γῆς, ὥσπερ κρατεῖς,
ξὺν ἀνδράσιν κάλλιον ἢ κενῆς κρατεῖν·   55
ὡς οὐδέν ἐστιν οὔτε πύργος οὔτε ναῦς
ἔρημος ἀνδρῶν μὴ ξυνοικούντων ἔσω.

ΟΙ. ὦ παῖδες οἰκτροί, γνωτὰ κοὐκ ἄγνωτά μοι
προσήλθεθ' ἱμείροντες· εὖ γὰρ οἶδ' ὅτι
νοσεῖτε πάντες, καὶ νοσοῦντες, ὡς ἐγὼ   60
οὐκ ἔστιν ὑμῶν ὅστις ἐξ ἴσου νοσεῖ.
τὸ μὲν γὰρ ὑμῶν ἄλγος εἰς ἕν' ἔρχεται

---

52 ὄρνιθι...αἰσίῳ, like *secunda alite* or *fausta avi* for *bono omine*. A bird of omen was properly οἰωνός: *Od.* 15. 531 οὔ τοι ἄνευ θεοῦ ἔπτατο δεξιὸς ὄρνις· | ἔγνων γάρ μιν ἐσάντα ἰδὼν οἰωνὸν ἐόντα: Xen. *Cyr.* 3. 3. 22 οἰωνοῖς χρησάμενος αἰσίοις. But cp. Eur. *I. A.* 607 ὄρνιθα μὲν τόνδ' αἴσιον ποιούμεθα: *Her.* 730 ὄρνιθος οὕνεκα: Ar. *Av.* 720 φήμη γ' ὑμῖν ὄρνις ἐστί, πταρμόν τ' ὄρνιθα καλεῖτε, | ξύμβολον ὄρνιν, φωνὴν ὄρνιν, θεράποντ' ὄρνιν, ὄνον ὄρνιν. For dat., Schneid. cp. Hippônax fr. 63 (Bergk) δεξιῷ...ἐλθὼν ῥωδιῷ (heron). In Bergk *Poet. Lyr.* p. 1049 fr. incerti 27 δεξιῇ σιττῇ (woodpecker) is a conject. for δεξιῇ σιττῇ. καὶ is better taken as = 'also' than as 'both' (answering to καὶ τανῦν in 53). **54** ἄρξεις...κρατεῖς...κρατεῖν. κρατεῖν τινός, merely to hold in one's power; ἄρχειν implies a constitutional rule. Cp. Plat. *Rep.* 338 D οὐκοῦν τοῦτο κρατεῖ ἐν ἑκάστῃ πόλει, τὸ ἄρχον; Her. 2. 1 ἄλλους τε παραλαβὼν τῶν ἦρχε καὶ δὴ καὶ Ἑλλήνων τῶν ἐπεκράτεε, *i.e.* the Asiatics who were his lawful subjects, and the Greeks over whom he could exert force. But here the poet intends no stress on a verbal contrast: it is as if he had written, εἴπερ ἄρξεις, ὥσπερ ἄρχεις. Cp. *Trach.* 457 κεἰ μὲν δέδοικας, οὐ καλῶς ταρβεῖς: below 973 προὔλεγον... | ηὔδας. **55** ξὺν ἀνδράσιν, not 'with the help of men,' but 'with men in the land,' = ἄνδρας ἐχούσης γῆς. Cp. 207 ξὺν αἷς = ἃς ἔχουσα. *El.* 191 ἀεικεῖ σὺν στολᾷ. *Ai.* 30 σὺν νεορράντῳ ξίφει. *Ant.* 116 ξὺν θ' ἱπποκόμοις κορύθεσσι. **56** ὡς οὐδέν ἐστιν κ.τ.λ. Thuc. 7. 77 ἄνδρες γὰρ πόλις, καὶ οὐ τείχη οὐδὲ νῆες ἀνδρῶν κεναί. Dio Cass. 56. 6 ἄνθρωποι γάρ που πόλις ἐστίν, οὐκ οἰκίαι, κ.τ.λ. Her. 8. 61 (Themistocles, taunted by Adeimantus after the Persian occupation of Athens in 480 B.C. with being ἄπολις, re-

With good omen didst thou give us that past happiness; now also show thyself the same. For if thou art to rule this land, even as thou art now its lord, 'tis better to be lord of men than of a waste: since neither walled town nor ship is anything, if it is void and no men dwell with thee therein.

OE. Oh my piteous children, known, well known to me are the desires wherewith ye have come: well wot I that ye suffer all; yet, sufferers as ye are, there is not one of you whose suffering is as mine. Your pain comes on each one of you

---

torted) ἑωυτοῖσι...ὡς εἴη καὶ πόλις καὶ γῆ μέζων ἤπερ κείνοισι, ἔστ' ἂν διηκόσιαι νῆές σφι ἔωσι πεπληρωμέναι. πύργος = the city wall with its towers: the sing. as below, 1378: *Ant.* 953 οὐ πύργος, οὐχ ἁλίκτυποι | ... νᾶες: Eur. *Hec.* 1209 πέριξ δὲ πύργος εἶχ' ἔτι πτόλιν. 57 Lit., 'void of men, when they do not dwell with thee in the city': ἀνδρῶν depends on ἔρημος, of which μὴ ξυνοικούντων ἔσω is epexegetic. Rhythm and Sophoclean usage make this better than to take ἀνδρῶν μὴ ξυνοικ. ἔ. as a gen. absol. Cp. *Ai.* 464 γυμνὸν φανέντα τῶν ἀριστείων ἄτερ: *Phil.* 31 κένην οἴκησιν ἀνθρώπων δίχα: Lucret. 5. 841 *muta sine ore etiam, sine voltu caeca.* 58 γνωτὰ κοὐκ ἄγνωτα. This formula is used when the speaker feels that he has to contend against an opposite impression in the mind of the hearer: 'known, and not, (*as you perhaps think*,) unknown.' *Il.* 3. 59 ἐπεί με κατ' αἶσαν ἐνείκεσας οὐδ' ὑπὲρ αἶσαν, duly, and not,—as you perhaps expect me to say,—unduly. Her. 3. 25 ἐμμανής τε ἐὼν καὶ οὐ φρενήρης—being mad,—for it must be granted that no man in his right mind would have acted thus. *O. C.* 397 βαιοῦ κοὐχὶ μυρίου χρόνου, soon, and not after such delay as thy impatience might fear. 60 νοσοῦντες...νοσεῖ. We expected καὶ νοσοῦντες οὐ νοσεῖτε, ὡς ἐγώ. But at the words ὡς ἐγώ the speaker's consciousness of his own exceeding pain turns him abruptly to the strongest form of expression that he can find—οὐκ ἔστιν ὑμῶν ὅστις νοσεῖ, *there is not one of you* whose pain is as mine. In Plat. *Phileb.* 19 B (quoted by Schneid.) the source of the anacolouthon is the same: μὴ γὰρ δυνά-μενοι τοῦτο κατὰ παντὸς ἑνὸς καὶ ὁμοίου καὶ ταὐτοῦ δρᾶν καὶ τοῦ ἐναντίου, ὡς ὁ παρελθὼν λόγος ἐμήνυσεν, οὐδεὶς εἰς οὐδὲν οὐδενὸς ἂν ἡμῶν οὐδέ-ποτε γένοιτο ἄξιος,—instead of the tamer οὐκ ἂν γενοίμεθα. 62 εἰς ἕνα... μόνον καθ' αὑτόν. καθ' αὑτόν, 'by himself' (*O. C.* 966), is strictly only an emphatic repetition of μόνον: but the whole phrase εἰς ἕνα μόνον καθ' αὑτόν is virtually equivalent to εἰς ἕνα ἕκαστον καθ' αὑτόν, each several

26 ΣΟΦΟΚΛΕΟΥΣ

μόνον καθ' αὐτόν, κοὐδέν' ἄλλον· ἡ δ' ἐμὴ
ψυχὴ πόλιν τε κἀμὲ καὶ σ' ὁμοῦ στένει.
ὥστ' οὐχ ὕπνῳ γ' εὕδοντά μ' ἐξεγείρετε,   65
ἀλλ' ἴστε πολλὰ μέν με δακρύσαντα δή,
πολλὰς δ' ὁδοὺς ἐλθόντα φροντίδος πλάνοις.
ἣν δ' εὖ σκοπῶν εὕρισκον ἴασιν μόνην,
ταύτην ἔπραξα· παῖδα γὰρ Μενοικέως
Κρέοντ', ἐμαυτοῦ γαμβρόν, ἐς τὰ Πυθικὰ   70
ἔπεμψα Φοίβου δώμαθ', ὡς πύθοιθ' ὅ τι
δρῶν ἢ τί φωνῶν τήνδε ῥυσαίμην πόλιν.
καί μ' ἦμαρ ἤδη ξυμμετρούμενον χρόνῳ

67 πλάνοισ L, οι ex αι facto: superscriptum est ἀντὶ πλάναις θηλυντικῶς. T
πλάνοις habet: ubi schol. in marg. formae masculinae suffragatur, τοὺς φυγαδικοὺς

one apart from the rest. **64 πόλιν τε κἀμὲ καὶ σ'.** The king's soul grieves
for the whole State,—for himself, charged with the care of it,—and for
each several man (σέ). As the first contrast is between public and
private care, κἀμέ stands between πόλιν and σέ. For the elision of σέ,
though accented, cp. 329 τἄμ', ὡς ἂν εἴπω μὴ τὰ σ': 404 καὶ τὰ σ': El.
1499 τὰ γοῦν σ': Phil. 339 οἴμοι μὲν ἀρκεῖν σοί γε καὶ τὰ σ': Eur. Hipp.
323 ἔα μ' ἁμαρτεῖν· οὐ γὰρ ἐς σ' ἁμαρτάνω. **65** The modal dat. ὕπνῳ is
more forcible than a cognate accus. ὕπνον, and nearly = 'deeply,'
'soundly.' Cp. Trach. 176 φόβῳ, φίλαι, ταρβοῦσαν: Eur. Tro. 28
κωκυτοῖσιν... | βοᾷ: [Eur.] fr. 1117. 40 ὀργῇ χολωθείς (where Nauck,
rashly, I think, conjectures ἔργει). Verg. Aen. 1. 680 sopitum somno. εὕδειν,
καθεύδειν (Xen. An. 1. 3. 11) were familiar in the fig. sense of 'to be at
ease' (cp. ἔνθ' οὐκ ἂν βρίζοντα ἴδοις, of Agam., Il. 4. 223): the addition
of ὕπνῳ raises and invigorates a trite metaphor. **67 πλάνοις** has
excellent manuscript authority here; and Soph. uses πλάνου O. C.
1114, πλάνοις Phil. 758, but πλάνη nowhere. Aesch. has πλάνη
only: Eur. πλάνος only, unless the fragment of the Rhadamanthus be
genuine (660 Nauck, v. 8, οὕτω βίοτος ἀνθρώπων πλάνη). Aristoph. has
πλάνος once (Vesp. 872), πλάνη never. Plato uses both πλάνη and
πλάνος, the former oftenest: Isocrates has πλάνος, not πλάνη. **68 εὕρισκον**, 'could find' (impf.). Elmsley ηὕρισκον. Curtius (Verb I. 139, Eng.
tr. 93) justly says that we cannot lay down any definite rules on the
omission of the temporal augment in such forms. While the omission

for himself alone, and for no other; but my soul mourns at once for the city, and for myself, and for thee.

So that ye rouse me not, truly, as one sunk in sleep: no, be sure that I have wept full many tears, gone many ways in wanderings of thought. And the sole remedy which, well pondering, I could find, this I have put into act. I have sent the son of Menoeceus, Creon, mine own wife's brother, to the Pythian house of Phoebus, to learn by what deed or word I might deliver this town. And already, when the lapse of days is reckoned,

πλάνους citans. πλάνοις, non πλάναις, indicat script. compendiaria in B. Multi tamen codd. recentiorum πλάναις praebent.

---

of the syllabic augment was an archaic and poetical license, that of the temporal was 'a sacrifice to convenience of articulation, and was more or less common to all periods.' Thus εἴκαζον could exist in Attic by the side of ἤκαζον, εὕρισκον by the side of ηὕρισκον. On such a point our MSS. are rarely safe guides. **69** ταύτην ἔπραξα, a terse equivalent for ταύτῃ ἔργῳ ἐχρησάμην. **71** ὅ τι δρῶν...τί φωνῶν. Cp. Plat. *Rep.* 414 D οὐκ οἶδα ὁποίᾳ τόλμῃ ἢ ποίοις λόγοις χρώμενος ἐρῶ. These are exceptions to the rule that, where an interrogative pronoun (as τίς) and a relative (as ὅστις) are both used in an indirect question, the former stands first: cp. Plat. *Crito* 48 A οὐκ ἄρα...φροντιστέον, τί ἐροῦσιν οἱ πολλοὶ ἡμᾶς, ἀλλ' ὅ τι ὁ ἐπαΐων, κ.τ.λ.: *Gorg.* 448 E οὐδεὶς ἐρωτᾷ ποία τις εἴη ἡ Γοργίου τέχνη, ἀλλὰ τίς, καὶ ὅντινα δέοι καλεῖν τὸν Γοργίαν: *ib.* 500 A ἐκλέξασθαι ποῖα ἀγαθὰ καὶ ὁποῖα κακά: *Phileb.* 17 B (ἴσμεν) πόσα τέ ἐστι καὶ ὁποῖα. **72 δρῶν ἢ φωνῶν:** there is no definite contrast between *doing* and *bidding others to do*: rather 'deed' and 'word' represent the two chief forms of agency, the phrase being equivalent to 'in what possible way.' Cp. Aesch. *P. V.* 659 θεοπρόπους ἴαλλεν, ὡς μάθοι τί χρὴ | δρῶντ' ἢ λέγοντα δαίμοσιν πράσσειν φίλα. **ῥυσαίμην.** The direct deliberative form is πῶς ῥύσωμαι; the indirect, ἐρωτῶ ὅπως (or πῶς) ῥύσωμαι, ἠρώτων. ὅπως (or πῶς) ῥυσαίμην. ῥυσοίμην (oblique for ῥύσομαι) would imply that he was confident of a successful *result*, and doubtful only concerning the *means;* it is therefore less suitable. **73 καί μ' ἧμαρ...χρόνῳ.** Lit., 'and already the day, compared with the lapse of time [since his departure], makes me anxious what he doth': *i.e.* when I think what day this is, and how many days ago he started, I feel anxious. **ἤδη,** showing that *to-day* is meant, sufficiently defines ἧμαρ. χρόνῳ is not

λυπεῖ τί πράσσει· τοῦ γὰρ εἰκότος πέρα
ἄπεστι πλείω τοῦ καθήκοντος χρόνου.   75
ὅταν δ' ἵκηται, τηνικαῦτ' ἐγὼ κακὸς
μὴ δρῶν ἂν εἴην πάνθ' ὅσ' ἂν δηλοῖ θεός.

ΙΕ. ἀλλ' εἰς καλὸν σύ τ' εἶπας οἵδε τ' ἀρτίως
Κρέοντα προσστείχοντα σημαίνουσί μοι.

ΟΙ. ὦναξ Ἄπολλον, εἰ γὰρ ἐν τύχῃ γέ τῳ   80
σωτῆρι βαίη λαμπρὸς ὥσπερ ὄμματι.

ΙΕ. ἀλλ' εἰκάσαι μέν, ἡδύς. οὐ γὰρ ἂν κάρα
πολυστεφὴς ὧδ' εἷρπε παγκάρπου δάφνης.

ΟΙ. τάχ' εἰσόμεσθα· ξύμμετρος γὰρ ὡς κλύειν.

74 πέραι L, et placuit quidem Porsono, v. 75 delendum censenti, περᾷ legere:
vide tamen annot.   79 προσστείχοντα codd., sed verbum cum πρός non cum

---

for τῷ χρόνῳ, *the* time since he left,—though this is implied,—but is
abstract,—time in its course. **ξυμμετρούμενον**: cp. Her. 4. 158 συμμετρη-
σάμενοι τὴν ὥρην τῆς ἡμέρης, νυκτὸς παρῆγον, 'having *calculated* the time,
they led them past the place by night': lit., 'having compared the season
of the day (with the distance to be traversed).' Eur. *Or.* 1214 καὶ δὴ
πέλας νιν δωμάτων εἶναι δοκῶ | τοῦ γὰρ χρόνου τὸ μῆκος αὐτὸ συντρέχει
'for the length of time (since her departure) just tallies (with the time
required for the journey).' **74 λυπεῖ τί πράσσει**: *Ai.* 794 ὥστε μ' ὠδίνειν
τί φῄς. **τοῦ γὰρ εἰκότος πέρα**. τὸ εἰκός is *a reasonable estimate* of the
time required for the journey. Porson conjectured τοῦ γὰρ εἰκότος περᾷ,
as = 'for he overstays the due limit'—thinking v. 75, ἄπεστι...χρόνου, to
be a spurious interpolation. The same idea had occurred to Bentley.
But (1) περᾶν with the genitive in this sense is strange (in 674 θυμοῦ
περᾶν is different), and would not be readily understood as referring to
time; (2) it is Sophoclean to explain and define τοῦ εἰκότος πέρα by
πλείω τοῦ καθήκοντος χρόνου. **78 εἰς καλόν**, to fit purpose, 'opportunely':
Plat. *Symp.* 174 E εἰς καλὸν ἥκεις. *Ai.* 1168 καὶ μὴν ἐς αὐτὸν καιρὸν... |
πάρεισιν. Cp. Ar. *Ach.* 686 εἰς τάχος = ταχέως, *Av.* 805 εἰς εὐτέλειαν
= εὐτελῶς. **οἵδε**: some of those suppliants who are nearer to the stage
entrance on the spectators' left—the conventional one for an arrival
from the country—have made signs to the Priest. Creon enters, wearing a wreath of bay leaves bright with berries, in token of a favourable
answer. See Appendix, Note 1, § 2. **80 ἐν τύχῃ...ὄμματι**: may his

it troubles me what he doth ; for he tarries strangely, beyond the fitting space. But when he comes, then shall I be no true man if I do not all that the god shows.

PR. Nay, in season hast thou spoken ; at this moment these sign to me that Creon draws near.

OE. O king Apollo, may he come to us in the brightness of saving fortune, even as his face is bright!

PR. Nay, to all seeming, he brings comfort ; else would he not be coming crowned thus thickly with berry-laden bay.

OE. We shall know soon : he is at range to hear.—

πρό compositum, credo, significantes : ne enim in talibus duplex σ scriberetur, inferiorum temporum Graecis Latina suadere poterant exempla, ut *astare, postemplum*.

---

radiant look prove the herald of good news. λαμπρὸς with ἐν τύχῃ κ.τ.λ.,
—being applicable at once to *brilliant* fortune and (in the sense of φαιδρός) to a *beaming* countenance. ἐν τύχῃ, nearly = μετὰ τύχης, 'invested with,' 'attended by': cp. 1112 ἔν τε γὰρ μακρῷ | γήρᾳ ξυνᾴδει: *Ai.* 488 σθένοντος ἐν πλούτῳ. τύχη σωτήρ (Aesch. *Ag.* 664), like χεὶρ πράκτωρ (*ib.* 111), θέλκτωρ πειθώ (Aesch. *Suppl.* 1040), καρανιστῆρες δίκαι (*Eum.* 186). 82 εἰκάσαι μέν, ἡδύς (*sc.* βαίνει). Cp. *El.* 410 ἐκ δείματός του νυκτέρου, δοκεῖν ἐμοί. *O. C.* 151 δυσαίων | μακραίων τ', ἐπεικάσαι. ἡδύς, not 'joyous,' but 'pleasant to us,' 'bringing good news': as 510 ἡδύπολις, pleasant to the city: *El.* 929 ἡδὺς οὐδὲ μητρὶ δυσχερής, a guest welcome, not grievous, to her. In *Trach.* 869 where ἀηδὴς καὶ συνωφρυωμένη is said of one who approaches with bad news, ἀηδής is not 'unwelcome,' but rather 'sullen,' 'gloomy.' 83 πολυστεφὴς...δάφνης. The use of the gen. after words denoting fulness is extended to the notions of encompassing or overshadowing: *e.g.* περιστεφῆ | ...ἀνθέων θήκην (*El.* 895), στέγην...ῆς [*v. l.* ῇ] κατηρεφεῖς δόμοι (Eur. *Hipp.* 468). But the *dat.* would stand: cp. *Od.* 9. 183 σπέος...δάφνῃσι κατηρεφές: Hes. *Op.* 513 λάχνῃ δέρμα κατάσκιον. παγκάρπου, covered with berries: Plin. 15. 30 *maximis baccis atque e viridi rubentibus* (of the Delphic laurel). Cp. *O. C.* 676. In Eur. *Hipp.* 806 Theseus, returning from the oracle at Delphi to find Phaedra dead, cries τί δῆτα τοῖσδ' ἀνέστεμμαι κάρα | πλεκτοῖσι φύλλοις, δυστυχὴς θεωρὸς ὤν; So Fabius Pictor returned from Delphi to Rome *coronatus laurea corona* (Liv. 23. 11). 84 ξύμμετρος γὰρ ὡς κλύειν. He is at a just distance for hearing: ξύμμετρος = *commensurate* (in respect of his distance) *with* the range of our

ἄναξ, ἐμὸν κήδευμα, παῖ Μενοικέως,   85
τίν' ἡμὶν ἥκεις τοῦ θεοῦ φήμην φέρων;

ΚΡΕΩΝ.

ἐσθλήν· λέγω γὰρ καὶ τὰ δύσφορ', εἰ τύχοι
κατ' ὀρθὸν ἐξελθόντα, πάντ' ἂν εὐτυχεῖν.

OI. ἔστιν δὲ ποῖον τοὔπος; οὔτε γὰρ θρασὺς
οὔτ' οὖν προδείσας εἰμὶ τῷ γε νῦν λόγῳ.   90

ΚΡ. εἰ τῶνδε χρῄζεις πλησιαζόντων κλύειν,
ἕτοιμος εἰπεῖν, εἴτε καὶ στείχειν ἔσω.

OI. ἐς πάντας αὔδα. τῶνδε γὰρ πλέον φέρω
τὸ πένθος ἢ καὶ τῆς ἐμῆς ψυχῆς πέρι.

ΚΡ. λέγοιμ' ἂν οἷ' ἤκουσα τοῦ θεοῦ πάρα.   95
ἄνωγεν ἡμᾶς Φοῖβος ἐμφανῶς ἄναξ
μίασμα χώρας, ὡς τεθραμμένον χθονὶ
ἐν τῇδ', ἐλαύνειν, μηδ' ἀνήκεστον τρέφειν.

---

88 ἐξελθόντα codd. Quod Suidas et Zonaras s.v. δύσφορα legunt ἐξιόντα, id mera negligentia factum esse putes.

---

voices (implied in κλύειν). 85 κήδευμα, 'kinsman' (by marriage), = κηδεστής, here = γαμβρός (70). *Ant.* 756 γυναικὸς ὢν δούλευμα μὴ κώτιλλέ με. Eur. *Or.* 928 τἄνδον οἰκουρήματα = τὰς ἔνδον οἰκουρούσας. 87 λέγω γὰρ...εὐτυχεῖν. Creon, unwilling to speak plainly before the Chorus, hints to Oedipus that he brings a clue to the means by which the anger of heaven may be appeased. 88 ἐξελθόντα, of the *event*, 'having issued'; cp. 1011 μή μοι Φοῖβος ἐξέλθῃ σαφής: so 1182 ἐξήκοι. The word is chosen by Creon with veiled reference to the duty of *banishing* the defiling presence (98 ἐλαύνειν). πάντα predicative with εὐτυχεῖν, 'will all of them (= altogether)· be well.' λέγω εὐτυχεῖν ἄν = λέγω ὅτι εὐτυχοίη ἄν. 89 τοὔπος, the actual oracle (τοὔπος τὸ θεοπρόπον, *Tr.* 822): λόγῳ (90), Creon's own saying (λέγω, 87). προδείσας, alarmed beforehand. Cp. Her. 7. 50 κρέσσον δὲ πάντα θαρσέοντα ἥμισυ τῶν δεινῶν πάσχειν μᾶλλον ἢ πᾶν χρῆμα προδειμαίνοντα μηδαμὰ μηδὲν παθεῖν. No other part of προδείδω occurs: προταρβεῖν, προφοβεῖσθαι = 'to fear beforehand,' but ὑπερδέδοικά σου, I fear *for* thee, *Ant.* 82. In compos. with a verb of *caring for*, however, πρό sometimes = ὑπέρ, e.g. προκήδομαι *Ant.* 741. 91 πλησιαζόντων here = πλησίον ὄντων: usu. the verb = either (1) to approach, or (2) to *consort with* (dat.), as below, 1136. 92 εἴτε

Prince, my kinsman, son of Menoeceus, what news hast thou brought us from the god?

CREON.

Good news: I tell thee that even troubles hard to bear,—if haply they find the right issue,—will end in perfect peace.

OE. But what is the oracle? So far, thy words make me neither bold nor yet afraid.

CR. If thou wouldest hear while these are nigh, I am ready to speak; or else to go within.

OE. Speak before all: the sorrow which I bear is for these more than for mine own life.

CR. With thy leave, I will tell what I heard from the god. Phoebus our lord bids us plainly to drive out a defiling thing, which (he saith) hath been harboured in this land, and not to harbour that which is past cure.

καὶ στείχειν ἔσω (χρῄζεις), (ἕτοιμός εἰμι τοῦτο δρᾶν). So Eur. *Ion* 1120 (quoted by Elms., etc.) πεπυσμέναι γάρ, εἰ θανεῖν ἡμᾶς χρεών, | ἥδιον ἂν θάνοιμεν, εἶθ' ὁρᾶν φάος: *i.e.* εἴτε ὁρᾶν φάος (χρή), (ἥδιον ἂν ὁρῷμεν αὐτό). εἰ...εἴτε, as Aesch. *Eum.* 468 σὺ δ', εἰ δικαίως εἴτε μή, κρῖνον δίκην. 93 ἐς πάντας. Her. 8. 26 οὔτε ἠνέσχετο σιγῶν εἰπέ τε ἐς πάντας τάδε: Thuc. I. 72 ἐς τὸ πλῆθος εἰπεῖν (before the assembly). πλέον adverbial, as in *Ai.* 1103, etc.: schol. περὶ τούτων πλέον ἀγωνίζομαι ἢ περὶ τῆς ἐμαυτοῦ ψυχῆς. τῶνδε, object. gen. with τὸ πένθος (not with περί): cp. *El.* 1097 τᾷ Ζηνὸς εὐσεβείᾳ. 94 ἢ καί, 'than *even*.' This must not be confounded with the occasional use of ἢ καί in *negative* sentences containing a comparison: *e. g. Ai.* 1103 οὐκ ἔσθ' ὅπου σοὶ τόνδε κοσμῆσαι πλέον | ἀρχῆς ἔκειτο θεσμὸς ἢ καὶ τῷδε σέ: *El.* 1145 οὔτε γάρ ποτε | μητρὸς σύ γ' ἦσθα μᾶλλον ἢ κἀμοῦ φίλος: Antiphon *de caed. Her.* § 23 ἐζητεῖτο οὐδέν τι μᾶλλον ὑπὸ τῶν ἄλλων ἢ καὶ ὑπ' ἐμοῦ (where καί is redundant, = 'on my part'). 95 λέγοιμ' ἄν, a deferential form, having regard to the permission just given. Cp. *Phil.* 674 χωροῖς ἂν εἴσω: *El.* 637 κλύοις ἂν ἤδη. 97 ὡς marks that the partic. τεθραμμένον expresses the view held by the subject of the leading verb (ἄνωγεν): *i.e.*, 'as having been harboured' = 'which (*he says*) has been harboured.' Cp. Xen. *An.* I. 2. 1 ἔλεγε θαρρεῖν ὡς καταστησομένων τούτων εἰς τὸ δέον: he said, 'Take courage, *in the assurance that*' &c. 98 ἐλαύνειν for ἐξελαύνειν was regular in this context: Thuc. I. 126 τὸ ἄγος ἐλαύνειν τῆς θεοῦ (*i.e.* to banish the Alcmaeonidae): and so I. 127, 128, 135, 2. 13. μηδ' ἀνήκεστον τρέφειν. The μίασμα was

ΟΙ. ποίῳ καθαρμῷ; τίς ὁ τρόπος τῆς ξυμφορᾶς;
ΚΡ. ἀνδρηλατοῦντας, ἢ φόνῳ φόνον πάλιν   100
λύοντας, ὡς τόδ' αἷμα χειμάζον πόλιν.
ΟΙ. ποίου γὰρ ἀνδρὸς τήνδε μηνύει τύχην;
ΚΡ. ἦν ἡμίν, ὦναξ, Λάϊός ποθ' ἡγεμὼν
γῆς τῆσδε, πρὶν σὲ τήνδ' ἀπευθύνειν πόλιν.
ΟΙ. ἔξοιδ' ἀκούων· οὐ γὰρ εἰσεῖδόν γέ πω.   105
ΚΡ. τούτου θανόντος νῦν ἐπιστέλλει σαφῶς
τοὺς αὐτοέντας χειρὶ τιμωρεῖν τινας.

101 χειμάζον A, superscripto a m. recentiore ἤτοι χειμάζοντος τοῦ αἵματος: simile in Bodl. Laud. 54 schol., χειμάζοντος ἀντὶ τοῦ ταράττοντος. Qui talia annotaverunt, χειμάζον accus. absolutum esse intellexerant. Lectionis χειμάζει, in paucis sequioris notae codd. inventae, nulla est auctoritas; quanquam L

ἀνήκεστον in the sense that it could not be expiated *by anything else than* the death or banishment of the blood-guilty. The version, 'and not to cherish it *till past cure*' (*i.e.* ὥστε ἀνήκεστον εἶναι), suits the context less well, since the guilt was incurred long ago, and Thebes has already suffered. Cp. Antiphon *Tetr.* Γ. γ. § 7 ἀντὶ τοῦ παθόντος (in the cause of the dead) ἐπισκήπτομεν ὑμῖν τῷ τούτου φόνῳ τὸ μήνιμα τῶν ἀλιτηρίων ἀκεσαμένους πᾶσαν τὴν πόλιν καθαρὰν τοῦ μιάσματος καταστῆσαι, 'to heal with this man's blood the deed which angers the avenging spirits, and so to purge the whole city of the defilement.' **99 ποίῳ... ξυμφορᾶς.** By what purifying rite (does he command us ἐλαύνειν τὸ μίασμα)? What is the manner of our misfortune (*i.e.* our defilement)? Eur. *Phoen.* 390 τίς ὁ τρόπος αὐτοῦ; τί φυγάσιν τὸ δυσχερές; 'what is the manner thereof?' (*sc.* τοῦ κακοῦ, exile). **ξυμφορᾶς**, euphemistic for guilt, as Plat. *Legg.* 934 B λωφῆσαι πολλὰ μέρη τῆς τοιαύτης ξυμφορᾶς, to be healed in great measure of such a malady (viz., of evil-doing): *ib.* 854 D ἐν τῷ προσώπῳ καὶ ταῖς χερσὶ γραφεὶς τὴν ξυμφοράν, with his *misfortune* [the crime of sacrilege] branded on his face and hands.' Her. I. 35 συμφορῇ ἐχόμενος = ἐναγής, under a ban. Prof. Kennedy understands: 'what is the mode of *compliance* (with the oracle)?' He compares *O. C.* 641 τῇδε γὰρ ξυνοίσομαι ('for with that choice I will comply'). But elsewhere, at least, συμφορά does not occur in a sense parallel with συμφέρεσθαι, 'to agree with.' **100 ἀνδρηλατοῦντας.** As if, instead of ποίῳ καθαρμῷ, the question had been τί ποιοῦντας; **101 ὡς**

OE. By what rite shall we cleanse us? What is the manner of the misfortune?

CR. By banishing a man, or by bloodshed in quittance of bloodshed, since it is that blood which brings the tempest on our city.

OE. And who is the man whose fate he thus reveals?

CR. Laïus, king, was lord of our land before thou wast pilot of this State.

OE. I know it well—by hearsay, for I saw him never.

CR. He was slain; and the god now bids us plainly to wreak vengeance on his murderers—whosoever they be.

χειμάζον exhibet, ubi ει non a prima manu profectum videtur. Cod. in biblioth. Coll. SS. Trin. Cant. R. 3. 31, qui χειμάζει habet, ipse se refellit, non suae sed verae lectionis interpretatione adiecta καθὰ χειμάζοντος. In V⁴ autem χειμάζει factum est ex χειμάζον.

107 τινασ L sine accentu; litteram σ damnaverat librarius, puncto superposito,

___

τόδ' αἷμα χειμάζον πόλιν, since it is this blood [τόδε, viz. that implied in φόνον] which brings the storm on Thebes. χειμάζον, acc. absol. ὡς presents the fact as the ground of belief on which the Thebans are commanded to act: 'Do thus, assured that it is this blood,' &c. Xen. Hellen. 2. 4. 1 οἱ δὲ τριάκοντα, ὡς ἐξὸν ἤδη αὐτοῖς τυραννεῖν ἀδεῶς, προεῖπον, κ.τ.λ. Cp. Eur. Suppl. 268 πόλις δὲ πρὸς πόλιν | ἔπτηξε χειμασθεῖσα, 'city with city seeks shelter, when vexed by storms.' **104** ἀπευθύνειν, to steer in a right course. The infin. is of the imperf., = πρότερον ἢ ἀπηύθυνες, before you were steering (began to steer). Oedipus took the State out of angry waters into smooth: cp. 696 ἐμὰν γᾶν φίλαν | ἐν πόνοις ἀλύουσαν κατ' ὀρθὸν οὔρισας: fr. 151 πλήκτροις ἀπευθύνουσιν οὐρίαν τρόπιν, 'with the helm (πλῆκτρα, the blades of the πηδάλια) they steer their bark before the breeze.' **105** οὐ γὰρ εἰσεῖδόν γέ πω. As Oed. knows that Laïus is dead, the tone of unconcern given by this colloquial use of οὔπω (instead of οὔποτε) is a skilful touch. Cp. El. 402 ΧΡ. σὺ δ' οὐχὶ πείσει...; ΕΛ. οὐ δῆτα· μήπω νοῦ τοσόνδ' εἴην κενή: Eur. Hec. 1278 μήπω μανείη Τυνδαρὶς τοσόνδε παῖς: Il. 12. 270 ἀλλ' οὔπω πάντες ὁμοῖοι | ἀνέρες ἐν πολέμῳ: cp. our (ironical) 'I have yet to learn.' **107** τοὺς αὐτοέντας... τινας. τούς implies that the death had human authors; τινας, that they are unknown. So in O. C. 290 ὅταν δ' ὁ κύριος | παρῇ τις, 'the master—whoever he be.' τιμωρεῖν, 'punish.' The act., no less than the midd., is

J. S.   3

ΟΙ. οἱ δ' εἰσὶ ποῦ γῆς; ποῦ τόδ' εὑρεθήσεται
    ἴχνος παλαιᾶς δυστέκμαρτον αἰτίας;
ΚΡ. ἐν τῇδ' ἔφασκε γῇ. τὸ δὲ ζητούμενον   110
    ἁλωτόν, ἐκφεύγει δὲ τἀμελούμενον.
ΟΙ. πότερα δ' ἐν οἴκοις ἢ 'ν ἀγροῖς ὁ Λάϊος
    ἢ γῆς ἐπ' ἄλλης τῷδε συμπίπτει φόνῳ;
ΚΡ. θεωρός, ὡς ἔφασκεν, ἐκδημῶν πάλιν
    πρὸς οἶκον οὐκέθ' ἵκεθ', ὡς ἀπεστάλη.   115
ΟΙ. οὐδ' ἄγγελός τις οὐδὲ συμπράκτωρ ὁδοῦ
    κατεῖδ', ὅτου τις ἐκμαθὼν ἐχρήσατ' ἄν;
ΚΡ. θνῄσκουσι γάρ, πλὴν εἷς τις, ὃς φόβῳ φυγὼν

quod aut ipse aut alius postea delere voluit. In cod. A, qui pariter τινασ habet, simile punctum non ad σ pertinere existimo, sed spiritum lenem esse litterae ι in οἰδ., quod, Oedipi personam indicans, voci τινασ proximum est. τινασ sine accentu praebent etiam Bodl. codd. Laud. 54, Barocc. 66. τινὰσ T, E, V, V², V³, V⁴. Lectionem τινά codex quod sciam nullus, sola habet Suidae editio Mediolanensis,

---

thus used even in prose: Lysias *In Agor.* § 42 τιμωρεῖν ὑπὲρ αὑτοῦ ὡς φονέα ὄντα, to punish (Agoratus), on his own account, as his murderer. χειρὶ τιμωρεῖν, here, either 'to slay' or 'to expel by force,' as distinguished from merely fining or disfranchising: in 140 τοιαύτῃ χειρὶ τιμωρεῖν is explained by κτανὼν in 139. **108** ποῦ τόδ'...αἰτίας; τόδε ἴχνος αἰτίας = ἴχνος τῆσδε αἰτίας, cp. τοὐμὸν φρενῶν ὄνειρον *El.* 1390. **αἰτίας**, 'crime': *Ai.* 28 τήνδ' οὖν ἐκείνῳ πᾶς τις αἰτίαν νέμει. For **δυστέκμαρτον**, hard to track, cp. Aesch. *Eum.* 244 (the Furies hunting Orestes) εἶεν· τόδ' ἐστὶ τἀνδρὸς ἐκφανὲς τέκμαρ. The poet hints a reason for what might else have seemed strange—the previous inaction of Oedipus. Cp. 219. **110 ἔφασκε**, *sc.* ὁ θεὸς (εὑρεθήσεσθαι τὸ ἴχνος). τὸ δὲ ζητούμενον: δὲ has a sententious force, = 'now.' The γνώμη, though uttered in an oracular tone, is not part of the god's message. Cp. Eur. fr. 435 αὐτός τι νῦν δρῶν εἶτα δαίμονας κάλει· | τῷ γὰρ πονοῦντι καὶ θεὸς συλλαμβάνει. **113 συμπίπτει**. The vivid historic present suits the alertness of a mind roused to close inquiry: so below, 118, 716, 1025, etc. Cp. *Ai.* 429 κακοῖς τοιοῖσδε συμπεπτωκότα. **114 θεωρός**: Laïus was going to Delphi in order to ask Apollo whether the child (Oedipus), formerly exposed by the god's command, had indeed perished: Eur. *Phoen.* 36 τὸν ἐκτεθέντα παῖδα μαστεύων μαθεῖν | εἰ μηκέτ' εἴη. **ὡς ἔφασκεν**, as Laïus told

OE. And where are they upon the earth? Where shall the dim track of this old crime be found?

CR. In this land,—said the god. What is sought for can be caught; only that which is not watched escapes.

OE. And was it in the house, or in the field, or on strange soil that Laïus met this bloody end?

CR. 'Twas on a visit to Delphi, as he said, that he had left our land; and he came home no more, after he had once set forth.

OE. And was there none to tell? Was there no comrade of his journey who saw the deed, from whom tidings might have been gained, and used?

CR. All perished, save one who fled in fear, and

---

cum ceterae τινάς tueantur (s.v. ἐπιστέλλει). Mirum mihi quidem quod τινά receperunt Elmsleius, Erfurdt., Dindorf., Blaydes.   **117** ὅτου cum ceteri codd. tum etiam L. Versantur enim in re minime probabili qui primam Laurentiani manum ὅπου, ὅτου nonnisi recentem dedisse affirmant. Factum est sane τ post deletam litteram quae π esse potuit, tota autem interiit: quam delevisse non recentior manus videtur, sed vel prima ipsa vel certe antiqua.

---

the Thebans at the time when he was leaving Thebes. **ἐκδημῶν**, not *going* abroad, but *being* [= having gone] abroad: cp. Plat. *Legg.* 864 E οἰκείτω τὸν ἐνιαυτὸν ἐκδημῶν. **ὡς = ἐπεί:** Xen. *Cyr.* I. 3. 2 ὡς δὲ ἀφίκετο τάχιστα...ἠσπάζετο. Cic. *Brut.* 5 ut *illos libros edidisti, nihil a te postea accepimus.* **116** οὐδ᾽ ἄγγελος...ἐχρήσατ᾽ ἄν; The sentence begins as if ἄγγελός τις were to be followed by ἦλθε: but the second alternative, συμπράκτωρ ὁδοῦ, suggests κατεῖδε [had *seen*, though he did not *speak*]: and this, by a kind of zeugma, stands as verb to ἄγγελος also. Cp. Her. 4. 106 ἐσθῆτα δὲ φορέουσι τῇ Σκυθικῇ ὁμοίην, γλῶσσαν δὲ ἰδίην. **οὐδ᾽ ἄγγελος:** *Il.* 12. 73 οὐκέτ᾽ ἔπειτ᾽ ὀίω οὐδ᾽ ἄγγελον ἀπονέεσθαι. **ὅτου,** gen. masc.: from whom having gained knowledge one might have used it. **117 ἐκμαθὼν** = a protasis, εἰ ἐξέμαθεν, ἐχρήσατ᾽ ἄν, *sc.* τούτοις ἃ ἐξέμαθεν. Plat. *Gorg.* 465 E ἐὰν μὲν οὖν καὶ ἐγὼ σοῦ ἀποκρινομένου μὴ ἔχω ὅ τι χρήσωμαι, if, when you answer, I also do not know what use to make [of your answer, *sc.* τούτοις ἃ ἂν ἀποκρίνῃ],—where shortly before we have οὐδὲ χρῆσθαι τῇ ἀποκρίσει ἥν σοι ἀπεκρινάμην οὐδὲν οἷός τ᾽ ἦσθα. **118 φόβῳ φυγὼν,** 'having fled in fear': φόβῳ, modal dative; cp. Thuc. 4. 88 διά τε τὸ ἐπαγωγὰ εἰπεῖν τὸν Βρασίδαν καὶ περὶ τοῦ καρποῦ φόβῳ

ὧν εἶδε πλὴν ἓν οὐδὲν εἶχ᾽ εἰδὼς φράσαι.

ΟΙ. τὸ ποῖον; ἓν γὰρ πόλλ᾽ ἂν ἐξεύροι μαθεῖν,   120
ἀρχὴν βραχεῖαν εἰ λάβοιμεν ἐλπίδος.

ΚΡ. λῃστὰς ἔφασκε συντυχόντας οὐ μιᾷ
ῥώμῃ κτανεῖν νιν, ἀλλὰ σὺν πλήθει χερῶν.

ΟΙ. πῶς οὖν ὁ λῃστής, εἴ τι μὴ ξὺν ἀργύρῳ
ἐπράσσετ᾽ ἐνθένδ᾽, ἐς τόδ᾽ ἂν τόλμης ἔβη;   125

ΚΡ. δοκοῦντα ταῦτ᾽ ἦν· Λαΐου δ᾽ ὀλωλότος
οὐδεὶς ἀρωγὸς ἐν κακοῖς ἐγίγνετο.

ΟΙ. κακὸν δὲ ποῖον ἐμποδὼν τυραννίδος
οὕτω πεσούσης εἶργε τοῦτ᾽ ἐξειδέναι;

ΚΡ. ἡ ποικιλῳδὸς Σφὶγξ τὸ πρὸς ποσὶ σκοπεῖν   130
μεθέντας ἡμᾶς τἀφανῆ προσήγετο.

ἔγνωσαν: 5. 70 ἐντόνως καὶ ὀργῇ χωροῦντες. **119 εἰδὼς**, with sure knowledge (and not merely from confused recollection, ἀσαφὴς δόξα): so 1151 λέγει γὰρ εἰδὼς οὐδὲν ἀλλ᾽ ἄλλως πονεῖ: *El.* 41 ὅπως ἂν εἰδὼς ἡμῖν ἀγγείλῃς σαφῆ. Iocasta says (849), in reference to this same point in the man's testimony, κοὐκ ἔστιν αὐτῷ τοῦτό γ᾽ ἐκβαλεῖν πάλιν. **120 τὸ ποῖον;** Cp. 291: *El.* 670 πρᾶγμα πορσύνων μέγα. | ΚΛ. τὸ ποῖον, ὦ ξέν᾽; εἰπέ. Ar. *Pax* 696 εὐδαιμονεῖ· πάσχει δὲ θαυμαστόν. ΕΡΜ. τὸ τί; **ἐξεύροι μαθεῖν.** One thing would find out *how* to learn many things, *i.e.* would prove a clue to them. The infin. μαθεῖν as after a verb of *teaching* or *devising:* Her. 1. 196 ἄλλο δέ τι ἐξευρήκασι νεωστὶ γενέσθαι. Plat. *Rep.* 519 E ἐν ὅλῃ τῇ πόλει τοῦτο μηχανᾶται ἐγγενέσθαι. **122 ἔφασκε** sc. ὁ φυγών (118). **οὐ μιᾷ ῥώμῃ** = οὐχ ἑνὸς ῥώμῃ, in the strength not of one man. Cp. Her. 1. 174 πολλῇ χειρὶ ἐργαζομένων τῶν Κνιδίων. *Ant.* 14 διπλῇ χερί = by the hands of twain. So perh. χερὶ διδύμᾳ Pind. *Pyth.* 2. 9. **123 σὺν πλήθει:** cp. on 55. **124 εἴ τι μὴ κ.τ.λ.** if some intrigue, aided by (ξὺν) money, had not been working from Thebes. τι is subject to ἐπράσσετο: distinguish the adverbial τι (= 'perchance') which is often joined to εἰ μή in diffident expressions, as 969 εἴ τι μὴ τὠμῷ πόθῳ | κατέφθιτ᾽, 'unless *perchance*': *Tr.* 586 εἴ τι μὴ δοκῶ | πράσσειν μάταιον, etc. Schneid. cp. Thuc. 1. 121 καί τι αὐτῷ καὶ ἐπράσσετο ἐς τὰς πόλεις ταύτας προδοσίας πέρι: and 5. 83 ὑπῆρχε δέ τι αὐτοῖς καὶ ἐκ τοῦ Ἄργους αὐτόθεν πρασσόμενον. **125 ἐπράσσετο...ἔβη:** the imperf. refers here to a *continued act* in past time, the aor. to an act done at a definite past moment. Cp. 402 ἐδόκεις—ἔγνως: 432 ἱκόμην—ἐκάλεις. **126 δοκοῦντα...**

could tell for certain but one thing of all that he saw.

OE. And what was that? One thing might show the clue to many, could we get but a small beginning for hope.

CR. He said that robbers met and fell on them, not in one man's might, but with full many hands.

OE. How, then, unless there was some trafficking in bribes from here, should the robber have dared thus far?

CR. Such things were surmised; but, Laïus once slain, amid our troubles no avenger arose.

OE. But, when royalty had fallen thus, what trouble in your path can have hindered a full search?

CR. The riddling Sphinx had made us let dark things go, and was inviting us to think of what lay at our doors.

ἦν expresses the vivid presence of the δόξα more strongly than ταῦτα ἐδόκει would have done: (cp. 274 τάδ' ἔστ' ἀρέσκονθ'): Her. 1. 146 ταῦτα δὲ ἦν γινόμενα ἐν Μιλήτῳ. **128** ἐμποδὼν sc. ὄν, with κακόν, not with εἴργε, 'what trouble (being) in your path.' Cp. 445 παρὼν...ἐμποδὼν | ὀχλεῖς. **τυραννίδος.** Soph. conceives the Theban throne as having been vacant from the death of Laïus—who left no heir—till the election of Oed. The abstract τυραννίδος suits the train of thought on which Oed. has already entered,—viz. that the crime was the work of a Theban faction (124) who wished to destroy, not the king merely, but the kingship. Cp. Aesch. *Cho.* 973 ἴδεσθε χώρας τὴν διπλῆν τυραννίδα (Clytaemnestra and Aegisthus). **130** ποικιλῳδός, singing ποικίλα, *subtleties*, αἰνίγματα: cp. Plat. *Symp.* 182 A ὁ περὶ τὸν ἔρωτα νόμος ἐν μὲν ταῖς ἄλλαις πόλεσι νοῆσαι ῥάδιος· ἁπλῶς γὰρ ὥρισται· ὁ δ' ἐνθάδε καὶ ἐν Λακεδαίμονι ποικίλος. Her. 7. 111 πρόμαντις δὲ ἡ χρέουσα, κατάπερ ἐν Δελφοῖσι, καὶ οὐδὲν ποικιλώτερον, 'the chief prophetess is she who gives the oracles, as at Delphi, and in no wise of darker speech.' **131** The constr. is προσήγετο ἡμᾶς, μεθέντας τὰ ἀφανῆ, σκοπεῖν τὸ πρὸς ποσί. προσήγετο, was drawing us (by her dread song), said with a certain irony, since προσάγεσθαι with infin. usually implies a *gentle* constraint (though, as a milit. term, ἀνάγκῃ προσηγάγοντο, *reduced* by force, Her. 6. 25): cp. Eur. *Ion* 659 χρόνῳ δὲ καιρὸν λαμβάνων προσάξομαι | δάμαρτ' ἐᾶν σε σκῆπτρα τἄμ' ἔχειν χθονός. τὸ πρὸς ποσί (cp. ἐμποδὼν 128), the *instant*, *pressing* trouble, opp. to τὰ ἀφανῆ, obscure questions (as to the death of Laïus) of no present or practical interest. Pind. *Isthm.* 7. 12 δεῖμα μὲν παροιχόμενον | καρτερὰν ἔπαυσε μέριμναν· τὸ δὲ πρὸς ποδὸς ἄρειον ἀεὶ σκοπεῖν | χρῆμα

ΟΙ. ἀλλ᾽ ἐξ ὑπαρχῆς αὖθις αὔτ᾽ ἐγὼ φανῶ.
ἐπαξίως γὰρ Φοῖβος, ἀξίως δὲ σὺ
πρὸ τοῦ θανόντος τήνδ᾽ ἔθεσθ᾽ ἐπιστροφήν·
ὥστ᾽ ἐνδίκως ὄψεσθε κἀμὲ σύμμαχον,   135
γῇ τῇδε τιμωροῦντα τῷ θεῷ θ᾽ ἅμα.
ὑπὲρ γὰρ οὐχὶ τῶν ἀπωτέρω φίλων
ἀλλ᾽ αὐτὸς αὑτοῦ τοῦτ᾽ ἀποσκεδῶ μύσος.
ὅστις γὰρ ἦν ἐκεῖνον ὁ κτανὼν τάχ᾽ ἂν
κἄμ᾽ ἂν τοιαύτῃ χειρὶ τιμωρεῖν θέλοι.   140
κείνῳ προσαρκῶν οὖν ἐμαυτὸν ὠφελῶ.
ἀλλ᾽ ὡς τάχιστα, παῖδες, ὑμεῖς μὲν βάθρων
ἵστασθε, τούσδ᾽ ἄραντες ἱκτῆρας κλάδους,

---

134 πρὸ habent optimi duo codd., L, A : inter reliquos, V³, Bodl. Laud. 54
(cum interpr. ὑπὲρ uterque), Barocc. 66, Misc. 99. πρὸς codd. aliquot, inter quos B,
E, T, V, V², V⁴: vide annot.   τήνδ᾽ ἔθεσθ᾽ ἐπιστροφήν. Variam lect. τήνδε
θεσπίζει γραφήν notat schol. in marg. L, quae cum plane supervacua et eadem insulsa

---

πᾶν. Ant. 1327 τᾶν ποσὶν κακά. 132 ἐξ ὑπαρχῆς, i.e. taking up anew
the search into the death of Laïus. Arist. de Anim. 2. 1 πάλιν δ᾽ ὥσπερ
ἐξ ὑπαρχῆς ἐπανίωμεν: so πάλιν οὖν οἷον ἐξ ὑπαρχῆς Rhet. 1. 1. 14 : [Dem.]
or. 40 § 16 πάλιν ἐξ ὑπαρχῆς λαγχάνουσί μοι δίκας.   The phrase ἐν
τῇ τῆς ἐπιστήμης ὑπαρχῇ occurs in the paraphrase by Themistius of
Arist. περὶ φυσικῆς ἀκροάσεως 8. 3 (Berlin ed. vol. 1. 247 b 29): elsewhere the word occurs only in ἐξ ὑπαρχῆς. Cp. El. 725 ἐξ ὑποστροφῆς =
ὑποστραφέντες : Her. 5. 116 ἐκ νέης : Thuc. 3. 92 ἐκ καινῆς. αὖθις, as he
had done in the case of the Sphinx's riddle : αὐτά = τὰ ἀφανῆ. 133 ἐπαξίως
(which would usually have a genitive) implies the standard—worthily of
his *own godhead*, or *of the occasion*—and is slightly stronger than ἀξίως.
Cp. Eur. Hec. 168 ἀπώλεσατ᾽, ὠλέσατ᾽: Or. 181 διοιχόμεθ᾽, οἰχόμεθ᾽:
Alc. 400 ὑπάκουσον, ἄκουσον. 134 πρὸ, *on behalf of,* cp. πρὸ τῶνδε
10, O. C. 811: Xen. Cyr. 8. 8. 4 εἴ τις...διακινδυνεύσειε πρὸ βασιλέως:
1. 6. 42 ἀξιώσουσι σὲ πρὸ ἑαυτῶν βουλεύεσθαι. Campb. reads πρὸς
τοῦ θανόντος, which here could mean only ‘ *at the instance of* the dead.’
πρός never = ‘on behalf of,’ ‘for the sake of,’ but sometimes ‘ *on the
side of* ’: e. g. Her. 1. 124 ἀποστάντες ἀπ᾽ ἐκείνου καὶ γενόμενοι πρὸς σέο,
‘ranged themselves on your side’: 1. 75 ἐλπίσας πρὸς ἑωυτοῦ τὸν χρησμὸν
εἶναι, that the oracle was on his side: below, 1434 πρὸς σοῦ...φράσω, I

OE. Nay, I will start afresh, and once more make dark things plain. Right worthily hath Phoebus, and worthily hast thou, bestowed this care on the cause of the dead; and so, as is meet, ye shall find me too leagued with you in seeking vengeance for this land, and for the god besides. On behalf of no far-off friend, no, but in mine own cause, shall I dispel this taint. For whoever was the slayer of Laïus might wish to take vengeance on me also with a hand as fierce. Therefore, in doing right to Laïus, I serve myself.

Come, haste ye, my children, rise from the altar-steps, and lift these suppliant boughs;

sit, docet quanta mutandi licentia grammatici interdum uterentur. **138** αὐτοῦ recte B, T, alii; eorum in quibus αὐτοῦ legitur sunt L et A. **139** ἐκεῖνον L (ex ἐκεῖνοσ factum), A: ἐκεῖνον B. Pravam l. ἐκεῖνος deteriorum codd. unus et alter admisit.

will speak on your side,—in your interest: *Trach.* 479 καὶ τὸ πρὸς κείνου λέγειν, to state his side of the case also. ἐπιστροφή, a turning round (*O. C.* 1045), hence, attention, regard: ἐπιστροφὴν τίθεσθαι (like σπουδήν, πρόνοιαν τίθ., *Ai.* 13, 536) = ἐπιστρέφεσθαί (τινος), *Phil.* 599. Dem. *In Aristocr.* § 136 οὐκ ἐπεστράφη 'heeded not' = οὐδὲν ἐφρόντισε *ib.* § 135. **137** ὑπὲρ γὰρ οὐχὶ κ.τ.λ., *i.e.* not merely in the cause of Laïus, whose widow he has married. The arrangement of the words is designed to help a second meaning of which the speaker is unconscious: 'in the cause of a friend who is *not* far off' (his own father). The reference to Laïus is confirmed by κείνῳ προσαρκῶν in 141. **138** αὐτοῦ = ἐμαυτοῦ: so κλαίω...αὐτὴ πρὸς αὐτήν, *El.* 285: τούς γ' αὐτὸς αὑτοῦ πολεμίους (οὐκ ἐῶ θάπτειν) *Ai.* 1132. ἀποσκεδῶ, dispel, as a taint in the air: cp. *Od.* 8. 149 σκέδασον δ' ἄπο κήδεα θυμοῦ: Plat. *Phaed.* 77 D μὴ...ὁ ἄνεμος αὐτὴν (τὴν ψυχὴν) ἐκβαίνουσαν ἐκ τοῦ σώματος διαφυσᾷ καὶ διασκεδάννυσιν. **139** ἐκεῖνον ὁ κτανών. ἐκεῖνον is thus placed for emphasis: cp. 820. **140** τοιαύτη, referring to κτανών, implies φονία: on τιμωρεῖν see 107. The spectator thinks of the time when Oed. shall be blinded by his own hand. **142** παῖδες. The king here, as the priest in 147, addresses *all* the suppliants. ἄλλος (144) is one of the king's attendants. βάθρων | ἵστασθε κ.τ.λ. Cp. *Ant.* 417 χθονὸς...ἀείρας: *Phil.* 630 νεὼς ἄγοντα. Prose would require a compound verb: Xen. *Symp.* 4. 31 ὑπανίστανται...θάκων. ἄραντες. Aesch. *Suppl.* 481 κλάδους γε τούτους αἶψ' ἐν ἀγκάλαις λαβὼν | βωμοὺς

ἄλλος δὲ Κάδμου λαὸν ὧδ' ἀθροιζέτω,
ὡς πᾶν ἐμοῦ δράσοντος· ἢ γὰρ εὐτυχεῖς   145
σὺν τῷ θεῷ φανούμεθ', ἢ πεπτωκότες.
ΙΕ. ὦ παῖδες, ἱστώμεσθα. τῶνδε γὰρ χάριν
καὶ δεῦρ' ἔβημεν ὧν ὅδ' ἐξαγγέλλεται.
Φοῖβος δ' ὁ πέμψας τάσδε μαντείας ἅμα
σωτήρ θ' ἵκοιτο καὶ νόσου παυστήριος.   150

ΧΟΡΟΣ.

στρ. α΄. ὦ Διὸς ἀδυεπὲς φάτι, τίς ποτε τᾶς πολυχρύσου
2 Πυθῶνος ἀγλαὰς ἔβας

ἐπ' ἄλλους δαιμόνων ἐγχωρίων | θές. **145** πᾶν...δράσοντος, to do every-
thing = to leave nothing untried: for ὡς cp. 97. Plat. *Apol.* 39 A
ἐάν τις τολμᾷ πᾶν ποιεῖν καὶ λέγειν. Xen. *Hellen.* 7. 4. 21 πάντα
ἐποίει ὅπως, εἰ δύναιτο, ἀπαγάγοι. εὐτυχεῖς...πεπτωκότες: 'fortunate,' if
they succeed in their search for the murderer, who, as they now
know, is in their land (110): 'ruined,' if they fail, since they will then
rest under the ἀνήκεστον μίασμα (98). The unconscious speaker,
in his last word, strikes the key-note of the destined περιπέτεια. **147**
ὦ παῖδες: see on 142. **148** καὶ δεῦρ' ἔβημεν, we e'en came here: i.e. this
was the motive of our coming in the first instance. *Phil.* 380 ἐπειδὴ
καὶ λέγεις θρασυστομῶν: Lys. *In Eratosth.* § 29 παρὰ τοῦ ποτε καὶ λήψεσθε δίκην; ἐξαγγέλλεται, proclaims on his own part (midd.), of himself:
i.e. promises unasked, *ultro pollicetur.* Cp. *Ai.* 1376 ἀγγέλλομαι...εἶναι
φίλος, 'I offer friendship.' Eur. has thus used ἐξαγγ. even where metre
permitted the more usual ἐπαγγέλλομαι: *Heracl.* 531 κἀξαγγέλλομαι |
θνήσκειν, I offer to die. **149** ἅμα: i.e. may the god, who has summoned
us to put away our pollution, *at the same time* come among us as a
healing presence.

151—215 The Chorus consists of Theban elders—men of noble
birth, 'the foremost in honour of the land' (1223)—who represent the
Κάδμου λαός just summoned by Oedipus (144). Oedipus having now
retired into the palace, and the suppliants having left the stage, the
Chorus make their entrance (πάροδος) into the hitherto vacant ὀρχήστρα.
For the metres, see the Analysis which follows the Introduction.

1st strophe (151—158). Is the god's message indeed a harbinger
of health? Or has Apollo some further pain in store for us?

and let some other summon hither the folk of Cadmus, warned that I mean to leave nought untried ; for our health (with the god's help) shall be made certain—or our ruin.

PR. My children, let us rise ; we came at first to seek what this man promises of himself. And may Phoebus, who sent these oracles, come to us therewith, our saviour and deliverer from the pest.

CHORUS.

O sweetly-speaking message of Zeus, in what spirit hast thou come from golden Pytho unto glorious   1st strophe.

1st *antistrophe* (159—166). May Athene, Artemis and Apollo succour us !

2nd *strophe* (167—178). The fruits of the earth and the womb perish.

2nd *antistrophe* (179—189). The unburied dead taint the air : wives and mothers are wailing at the altars.

3rd *strophe* (190—202). May Ares, the god of death, be driven hence : may thy lightnings, O Zeus, destroy him.

3rd *antistrophe* (203—215). May the Lycean Apollo, and Artemis, and Dionysus fight for us against the evil god.

151 φάτι, of a god's utterance or oracle (1440), a poet. equivalent for φήμη : cp. 310 ἀπ' οἰωνῶν φάτιν. Διὸς, because Zeus speaks by the mouth of his son ; Aesch. *Eum.* 19 Διὸς προφήτης δ' ἐστὶ Λοξίας πατρός. ἀδυεπὲς, merely a general propitiatory epithet : the Chorus have not yet heard whether the response is comforting or not. It is presently told to them by Oed. (242). Cp. *El.* 480 ἀδυπνόων...ὀνειράτων, dreams breathing comfort (from the gods). τίς ποτε...ἔβας; What art thou that hast come? *i.e.* in what spirit hast thou come? bringing us health or despair? 152 Πυθῶνος, *from* Pytho (Delphi): for the gen., see on 142 βάθρων | ἵστασθε. τᾶς πολυχρύσου, 'rich in gold,' with allusion to the costly ἀναθήματα dedicated at Delphi, and esp. to the treasury of the temple, in which gold and silver could be deposited, as in a bank, until required for use. *Iliad* 9. 404 οὐδ' ὅσα λάϊνος οὐδὸς ἀφήτορος ἐντὸς ἐέργει | Φοίβου Ἀπόλλωνος, Πυθοῖ ἐνὶ πετρηέσσῃ. Thuc. I. 121 ναυτικόν τε ἀπὸ τῆς ὑπαρχούσης τε οὐσίας ἐξαρτυσόμεθα, καὶ ἀπὸ τῶν ἐν Δελφοῖς καὶ Ὀλυμπίᾳ χρημάτων. Athen. 233 F τῷ μὲν οὖν ἐν Δελφοῖς Ἀπόλλωνι τὸν πρότερον ἐν τῇ Λακεδαίμονι χρυσὸν καὶ ἄργυρον [πρότερον = before the time of Lysander] ἱστοροῦσιν ἀνατεθῆναι. Eur. *Andr.* 1093 θεοῦ | χρυσοῦ γέμοντα γύαλα (recesses), θησαυροὺς βροτῶν. *Ion* 54 Δελφοί σφ'

3 Θήβας ; ἐκτέταμαι, φοβερὰν φρένα δείματι πάλλων,
4 ἰήιε Δάλιε Παιάν,
5 ἀμφὶ σοὶ ἀζόμενος τί μοι ἢ νέον   155
6 ἢ περιτελλομέναις ὥραις πάλιν ἐξανύσεις χρέος.
7 εἰπέ μοι, ὦ χρυσέας τέκνον Ἐλπίδος, ἄμβροτε Φάμα.

ἀντ. ά. πρῶτά σε κεκλόμενος, θύγατερ Διός, ἄμβροτ᾽ Ἀθάνα,
2 γαιάοχόν τ᾽ ἀδελφεὰν   160

159 κεκλομενοσ͞ L (ω a manu admodum recenti), A, E : κεκλόμενος V, V⁴, B, al. :

ἔθεντο (the young Ion) χρυσοφύλακα τοῦ θεοῦ, | ταμίαν τε πάντων.
Pind. *Pyth.* 6. 8 ἐν πολυχρύσῳ Ἀπολλωνίᾳ...νάπᾳ (*i.e.* ἐν Πυθοῖ).
153 The bold use of **ἐκτέταμαι** is interpreted by **φοβερὰν φρένα δείματι
πάλλων**, which is to be taken in close connection with it. **ἐκτείνεσθαι**
is not found elsewhere of *mental tension* (though Dionys. *De Comp. Verb.*
c. 15 *ad fin.* has ἡ τῆς διανοίας ἔκτασις καὶ τὸ τοῦ δείματος ἀπροσ-
δόκητον) : and Triclinius wrongly explains here, 'I am *prostrated* by
dread' (ἐκπέπληγμαι, παρ᾽ ὅσον οἱ ἐκπλαγέντες ἔκτασιν σώματος καὶ
ἀκινησίαν πάσχουσιν : cp. Eur. *Med.* 585 ἐν γὰρ ἐκτενεῖ σ᾽ ἔπος). Cp.
Xen. *Cyr.* I. 3. 11 ἕως παρατείναιμι τοῦτον, ὥσπερ οὗτος ἐμὲ παρα-
τείνει ἀπὸ σοῦ κωλύων,—'*rack*,' '*torture*' him. But παρατείνεσθαι,
when used *figuratively*, usually meant 'to be worn out,' 'fatigued
to death' : *e. g.* Plato *Lysis* 204 c παραταθήσεται ὑπὸ σοῦ ἀκούων θαμὰ
λέγοντος, *enecabitur*, he will be tired to death of hearing it. So
Xen. *Mem.* 3. 13. 6 παρατέταμαι μακρὰν ὁδὸν πορευθείς. **πάλλων**,
transitive, governing φρένα, *making my heart to shake;* not intransitive, for παλλόμενος, with φρένα as accus. of the part affected. An
intransitive use of πάλλω in this figurative sense is not warranted by
such instances as Ar. *Lys.* 1304 κοῦφα πάλλων, 'lightly leaping in
the dance': Eur. *El.* 435 ἔπαλλε δελφίς (= ἐσκίρτα), 'the dolphin
leaped': *ib.* 477 ἵπποι ἔπαλλον 'quivered' (in death). Cp. Aesch. *P. V.*
881 κραδία φόβῳ φρένα λακτίζει : so, when the speaker is identified
with the troubled spirit within him, we can say φρένα πάλλω,—where
φρένα has a less distinctly physical sense than in Aesch. *l.c.*, yet has
physical associations which help to make the phrase less harsh. **154 Δάλιε.**
The Delphian Apollo is also Delian—having passed, according to the
Ionic legend, from his native Delos, through Attica, to Delphi (Aesch.
Eum. 9). A Boeotian legend claimed Tegyra as the birthplace of

Thebes? I am on the rack, terror shakes my soul, O thou
Delian Healer to whom wild cries rise, in holy fear of thee,
what thing thou wilt work for me, perchance unfelt before,
perchance returning in the fulness of the years: tell me, thou
immortal Voice, born of golden Hope!

First call I on thee, daughter of Zeus, divine   1st anti-
Athene, and on thy sister, guardian of our land,   strophe.

κεκλομένῳ V³, Bodl. Barocc. 66: κεκλομένω V², Bodl. Laud. 54 : κέκλομαι, ὦ Blaydes.

Apollo : Plut. *Pelop.* 16 ἐνταῦθα μυθολογοῦσι τὸν θεὸν γενέσθαι, καὶ τὸ
μὲν πλησίον ὄρος Δῆλος καλεῖται. We can scarcely say, however, with
Schneidewin that Δάλιε here ‘bewrays the Athenian,’ when we remember
that the Theban Pindar hails the Delphian Apollo as Λύκιε καὶ Δάλου
ἀνάσσων Φοῖβε (*Pyth.* I. 39). ἰήιε (again in 1096), invoked with the cry
ἰή : cp. *Tr.* 221 ἰὼ ἰὼ Παιάν. Soph. has the form παιών, παιήων as = ‘a
healer’ (not with ref. to Apollo), *Phil.* 168, 832. **155** ἁζόμενος (rt. ἁγ,
whence ἅγιος) implies a *religious* fear: cp. *Od.* 9. 478 σχέτλι', ἐπεὶ ξείνους
οὐχ ἅζεο σῷ ἐνὶ οἴκῳ | ἐσθέμεναι. ἢ νέον ἢ...πάλιν. Are we to suffer some
new plague, for some recent impiety? Or are we to be visited by a
recurrence of plagues suffered in past years, on account of some old
defilement? The second guess is right: it is the old curse in the
house of Labdacus that is at work. πάλιν recalls Aesch. *Ag.* 154
μίμνει γὰρ φοβερὰ παλίνορτος | οἰκονόμος δολία μνάμων μῆνις τεκνόποινος.
νέον, adjective with χρέος: πάλιν, adverb with ἐξανύσεις. τί μοι νέον
χρέος ἐξανύσεις; ἢ τί χρέος πάλιν ἐξανύσεις; The *doubling* of ἢ harshly
co-ordinates νέον and πάλιν, as if one said τίνας ἢ μαχομένους ἢ ἀμαχεὶ
ἐνίκησαν; **156** περιτελλομ. ὥραις, an epic phrase which Ar. *Av.* 697 also
has. *Od.* 14. 293 ἀλλ' ὅτε δὴ μῆνές τε καὶ ἡμέραι ἐξετελεῦντο | ἂψ περι-
τελλομένου ἔτεος, καὶ ἐπήλυθον ὧραι. **157** χρυσέας κ.τ.λ. The answer
(not yet known to them) sent by Apollo is personified as Φάμα, a divine
Voice,—‘the daughter of golden hope,’ because—whether favourable or
not—it is the *issue* of that hope with which they had awaited the god’s
response. **159** κεκλόμενος is followed in 164 by προφάνητέ μοι instead of
εὔχομαι προφανῆναι. Cp. Plat. *Legg.* 686 D ἀποβλέψας γὰρ πρὸς τοῦτον
τὸν στόλον οὗ πέρι διαλεγόμεθα ἔδοξέ μοι πάγκαλος...εἶναι. Antiphon *Tetr.*
Β. β. § 10 ἀπολυόμενος δὲ ὑπό τε τῆς ἀληθείας τῶν πραχθέντων ὑπό τε
τοῦ νόμου καθ' ὃν διώκεται, οὐδὲ τῶν ἐπιτηδευμάτων εἵνεκα δίκαιοι τοιούτων κακῶν ἀξιοῦσθαί ἐσμεν. Xen. *Cyr.* 8. 8. 10 ἦν δὲ αὐτοῖς νόμιμον
...νομίζοντες. **160** γαιάοχον has this sense only here. In *O. C.* 1072

44 ΣΟΦΟΚΛΕΟΥΣ

3 Ἄρτεμιν, ἃ κυκλόεντ᾽ ἀγορᾶς θρόνον εὐκλέα θάσσει,
4 καὶ Φοῖβον ἑκαβόλον, ἰὼ
5 τρισσοὶ ἀλεξίμοροι προφάνητέ μοι,
6 εἴ ποτε καὶ προτέρας ἄτας ὕπερ ὀρνυμένας πόλει 165
7 ἠνύσατ᾽ ἐκτοπίαν φλόγα πήματος, ἔλθετε καὶ νῦν.

στρ. β'. ὦ πόποι, ἀνάριθμα γὰρ φέρω
2 πήματα· νοσεῖ δέ μοι πρόπας στόλος, οὐδ᾽ ἔνι φροντίδος ἔγχος
3 ᾧ τις ἀλέξεται. οὔτε γὰρ ἔκγονα   171
4 κλυτᾶς χθονὸς αὔξεται οὔτε τόκοισιν

it is the Homeric epithet of Poseidon, 'girdling the earth,' τὸν πόντιον
γαιάοχον. Cp. Παλλὰς πολιοῦχος Ar. Eq. 581 (πολιάοχος Pind. Ol. 5.
10), πολισσοῦχοι θεοί Aesch. Theb. 69. 161 κυκλόεντ᾽ ἀγορᾶς θρόνον =
κυκλοέσσης ἀγορᾶς θρόνον, a throne in the centre of the agora; cp.
Ant. 793 νεῖκος ἀνδρῶν ξύναιμον, Trach. 993 ὦ Κηναία κρηπὶς βωμῶν.
κυκλόεντα should not be pressed as if asserting a definitely circular
form for the agora; the notion is not so much 'round' as 'sur-
rounding,'—the epithet marking that the sitting statue of Artemis
is the central object. The phrase may have been partly suggested
by the familiarity of the word κύκλος in connection with the Athenian
agora, of which it perhaps denoted a special part; schol. Ar. Eq.
137 ὁ δὲ κύκλος Ἀθήνησίν ἐστι καθάπερ μάκελλος, ἐκ τῆς κατασκευῆς
(form) τὴν προσηγορίαν λαβών. ἔνθα δὴ πιπράσκεται χωρὶς κρεῶν τὰ
ἄλλα ὤνια, καὶ ἐξαιρέτως δὲ οἱ ἰχθύες. Cp. Eur. Or. 919 ὀλιγάκις
ἄστυ κἀγορᾶς χραίνων κύκλον, 'the circle of the agora,' i.e. 'its
bounds': cp. Thuc. 3. 74 τὰς οἰκίας τὰς ἐν κύκλῳ τῆς ἀγορᾶς, 'all
round' the agora. In Il. 18. 504, cited by Casaubon on Theophr.
Char. 2. 4, ἱερῷ ἐνὶ κύκλῳ refers merely to the γέροντες in council. I
prefer my version above to (1) 'her round throne, (consisting) of the
agora,'—a strained metaphor, for θρόνος is the chair of the statue:
(2) 'her round seat in the agora'—κυκλόεντα meaning that the pedestal
of the statue was circular: (3) 'her throne in the agora, round which
κύκλιοι χοροί range themselves.' This last is impossible. εὐκλέα, alluding to Artemis Εὔκλεια, the virgin goddess of Fair Fame, worshipped

Artemis, who in the centre of our agora holds her throne of fame, and on Phoebus the far-darter: O shine forth on me, my threefold help against death! If ever aforetime, in arrest of ruin hurrying on the city, ye drove a fiery pest beyond our borders, come now also!

Woe is me, countless are the sorrows that I bear; a plague is on all our host, and thought can find no weapon for defence. The fruits of the glorious earth grow not; by no birth of children 2nd strophe.

---

esp. by Locrians and Boeotians: Plut. *Arist.* 20 βωμὸς γὰρ αὐτῇ καὶ ἄγαλμα παρὰ πᾶσαν ἀγορὰν ἴδρυται, καὶ προθύουσιν αἵ τε γαμούμεναι καὶ οἱ γαμοῦντες: also at Corinth, Xen. *Hellen.* 4. 4. 2. Pausanias saw a temple of Ἄρτεμις Εὔκλεια, with a statue by Scopas, near the Προιτίδες πύλαι on the N. E. side of Thebes. Near it were statues of Apollo Boedromios and Hermes Agoraios. The latter suggests that the Agora of the Lower Town (which was deserted when Pausanias visited Thebes) may have been near. In mentioning the ἀγορά, Soph. may have been further influenced by the fact that Artemis was worshipped as Ἀγοραία: thus in the altis at Olympia there was an Ἀρτεμίδος Ἀγοραίας βωμός near that of Ζεὺς Ἀγοραῖος (Paus. 5. 15. 4). **165** ἄτας ὕπερ, '*on account of* ruin' (*i.e.* 'to avert it'): cp. *Ant.* 932 κλαύμαθ' ὑπάρξει βραδυτῆτος ὕπερ. So Aesch. *Theb.* 111 ἴδετε παρθένων ἱκέσιον λόχον δουλοσύνας ὕπερ, 'to avert slavery.' Cp. **187**. ὀρνυμένας πόλει: the dat. (poet.) as after verbs of *attacking, e.g.* ἐπιέναι, ἐπιτίθεσθαι. Musgrave's conj. ὑπερορνυμένας πόλει (the compound nowhere occurs) has been adopted by some editors. **166** ἤνύσατ' ἐκτοπίαν, *made* ἐκτοπίαν, = ἐξωρίσατε, a rare use of ἀνύω like ποιεῖν, καθιστάναι, ἀποδεικνύναι: for the ordinary use, cp. 720 ἐκεῖνον ἤνυσεν | φονέα γενέσθαι, *effected that* he should become. In *Ant.* 1178 τοὔπος ὡς ἄρ' ὀρθὸν ἤνυσας, the sense is not 'made right,' but '*brought* duly *to pass.*' ἔλθετε καὶ νῦν, an echo of προφάνητέ μοι, προτέρας having suggested καὶ νῦν: as in 338 ἀλλ' ἐμὲ ψέγεις repeats ὀργὴν ἐμέμψω τὴν ἐμήν. **167** ὦ πόποι is merely a cry like παπαῖ: *Trach.* 853 κέχυται νόσος, ὦ πόποι, οἷον, κ.τ.λ. **170** στόλος, like στρατός (Pind. *Pyth.* 2. 46, etc.) = λαός. ἔνι = ἔνεστι, is available. φροντίδος ἔγχος, not, a weapon *consisting in* a device, but a weapon *discovered by* human wit, ἔγχος ᾧ τις ἀλέξεται being a bold equivalent for μηχανὴ ἀλεξητηρία. **173** τόκοισιν, *by* births: *i.e.* the mother dies, or the child is still-born:

5 ἰηίων καμάτων ἀνέχουσι γυναῖκες· 174
6 ἄλλον δ' ἂν ἄλλῳ προσίδοις ἅπερ εὔπτερον ὄρνιν
7 κρεῖσσον ἀμαιμακέτου πυρὸς ὄρμενον
8 ἀκτὰν πρὸς ἑσπέρου θεοῦ·

ἀντ. β'. ὧν πόλις ἀνάριθμος ὄλλυται·
2 νηλέα δὲ γένεθλα πρὸς πέδῳ θανατᾱφόρα κεῖται
ἀνοίκτως·
3 ἐν δ' ἄλοχοι πολιαί τ' ἐπὶ ματέρες
4 ἀκτὰν παρὰ βώμιον ἄλλοθεν ἄλλαι 182
5 λυγρῶν πόνων ἱκτῆρες ἐπιστενάχουσιν. 185
6 παιὰν δὲ λάμπει στονόεσσά τε γῆρυς ὅμαυλος·
7 ὧν ὕπερ, ὦ χρυσέα θύγατερ Διός,
8 εὐῶπα πέμψον ἀλκάν·

180 Veram l. θανατᾱφόρα, quam ex cod. Palat. 40 et Laur. 31. 10 (L.²) affert Campb., inveni etiam in V. L θανατᾱφόρω (sic), a m. rec. in -α correctum:

---

see on 26, and cp. Hes. *Op*. 244 οὐδὲ γυναῖκες τίκτουσιν. If τόκοισιν = '*in* child-bed' (and so the schol., ἐν τοῖς τόκοις), the meaning implied would be that *all* the women perished in their travail, since οὐχ ἀνέχουσι could not be explained as merely = 'do not *soon* or *easily* surmount.' 175 ἄλλον δ'...ἄλλῳ, 'one *after* another.' The dative here seems to depend mainly on the notion of adding implied by the iteration itself; though it is probable that the neighbourhood of πρός in προσίδοις may have been felt as softening the boldness. That προσορᾶν could be used as = 'to see *in addition*' is inconceivable ; nor could such use be justified by that of ἐνορᾶν τινι as = ὁρᾶν ἔν τινι. And no one, I think, would be disposed to plead lyric license for ἄλλῳ πρὸς ἴδοις on the strength of ἀκτὰν πρὸς ἑσπέρου θεοῦ in 177. Clearly there was a tendency (at least in poetry) to use the dative thus, though the *verb* of the context generally either (*a*) helps the sense of 'adding,' or (*b*) leaves an alternative. Under (*a*) I should put *El*. 235 τίκτειν ἄταν ἄταις: Eur. *Helen*. 195 δάκρυα δάκρυσί μοι φέρων. Under (*b*), Eur. *Or*. 1257 πήματα πήμασιν ἐξεύρῃ: *Phoen*. 1496 φόνῳ φόνος | Οἰδιπόδα δόμον ὤλεσε: where the datives *might* be instrumental. On the whole, I forbear to recommend ἄλλον δ' ἂν ἄλλᾳ προσίδοις, though easy and tempting; cp. Thuc. 2. 4 ἄλλοι δὲ ἄλλῃ τῆς πόλεως σποράδην ἀπώλλυντο. 177 ὄρμενον, aor.

do women surmount the pangs in which they shriek ; and life on life mayest thou see sped, like bird on nimble wing, aye, swifter than resistless fire, to the shore of the western god.

By such deaths past numbering, the city perishes : unpitied, 2nd anti-strophe. her children lie on the ground, spreading pestilence, with none to mourn: and meanwhile young wives, and grey-haired mothers with them, uplift a wail at the steps of the altars, some here, some there, entreating for their weary woes. The prayer to the Healer rings clear, and, blent therewith, the voice of lamentation : for these things, golden daughter of Zeus, send us the bright face of comfort.

θανατηφόρῳ (sic) A. Dativus, voci πέδῳ debitus, in codd. fere omnes irrepsit. **182** παραβώμιον L, A, plerique. παρὰ βῶμον, B, T, V², V⁴, al. αὐδὰν παραβώμιον Hartung., ἀχὰν παραβώμιον Nauck. ἄλλαι codd.: ἄλλαν Dindorf.

---

part. (*Il.* 11. 571 δοῦρα...ὄρμενα πρόσσω), 'sped,' 'hurried,' since the life is quickly gone. κρεῖσσον...πυρὸς, because the πυρφόρος λοιμός drives all before it. **178** ἀκτὰν πρὸς for πρὸς ἀκτάν, cp. 525 : *O. C.* 126 ἄλσος ἐς τᾶνδ' ἀμαιμακετᾶν κορᾶν. ἑσπέρου θεοῦ : as the Homeric Erebos is in the region of sunset and gloom (*Od.* 12. 81), and Hades is ἐννυχίων ἄναξ *O. C.* 1559. **179** ὧν...ἀνάριθμος. ὧν, masc., referring to ἄλλον ...ἄλλῳ,—'to such (deaths) knowing no limit': cp. ἀνάριθμος θρήνων *El.* 232, μηνῶν | ἀνήριθμος *Ai.* 602, where the gen. depends on the substantival notion (ἀριθμός) in the compound. **180** γένεθλα (πόλεως), 'her sons': cp. 1424 τὰ θνητῶν γένεθλα, the sons of men. νηλέα, un-pitied ; ἀνοίκτως, without οἶκτος, lament, made for them : they receive neither ταφή nor θρῆνος. Cp. Thuc. 2. 50 πολλῶν ἀτάφων γιγνομένων (in the plague, 430 B.C.). **181** ἐν δ', cp. on 27. ἐπὶ, adv.: Her. 7. 65 τόξα δὲ καλάμινα εἶχον,...ἐπὶ δέ, σίδηρον (v. l. -ος) ἦν. But ἔπι = ἔπεστι, *Il.* 1. 515. **182** ἀκτὰν παρὰ βῶμον, 'at the steps of the altars': Aesch. *Cho.* 722 ἀκτῇ χώματος, the edge of the mound : Eur. *Her. F.* 984 ἀμφὶ βωμίαν | ἔπτηξε κρηπῖδ', at the base of the altar. **185** ἱκτῆρες with λυγρῶν πόνων, entreating on account of (for release from) their woes, causal gen.: cp. ἀλγεῖν τύχης, Aesch. *Ag.* 571. **186** λάμπει: 473 ἔλαμ-ψε...φάμα : Aesch. *Theb.* 104 κτύπον δέδορκα. ὁμαυλος, i. e. heard at the same time, though not σύμφωνος with it. **188** ὧν ὕπερ: see on 165. **189** εὐῶπα ἀλκάν: cp. ἀγανὴ σαίνουσ' | ἐλπίς, Aesch. *Ag.* 101 (where Weil

στρ. γ´. Ἀρεά τε τὸν μαλερόν, ὃς νῦν ἄχαλκος ἀσπίδων

2 φλέγει με περιβόατος ἀντιάζων,   191

3 παλίσσυτον δράμημα νωτίσαι πάτρας

4 ἔπουρον εἴτ᾽ ἐς μέγαν

5 θάλαμον Ἀμφιτρίτας   195

6 εἴτ᾽ ἐς τὸν ἀπόξενον ὅρμον

7 Θρήκιον κλύδωνα·

8 τελεῖν γάρ, εἴ τι νὺξ ἀφῇ,

194 ἄπουρον L (cum interpr. μακράν): est tamen α a manu recentiore. Prima ἔπουρον scripsit, quod primo loco scholiasta interpretatur; deinde ἄπουρον (ἄπορον scribens) ita explicat ut significet ἀπὸ τῶν ὅρων τῆς πάτρας. In V, ut in L, ἄπουρον factum est ex ἔπουρον. T ἔπουρον. A et ceteri ἄπουρον. **198** τελεῖν. τέλη Bodl.

___

προφανεῖσ᾽), ἱλαρὸν φέγγος Ar. *Ran.* 455. **190** Ἀρεά τε κ.τ.λ. The acc. and infin. Ἀρεα...νωτίσαι depend on δός or the like, suggested by the preceding words. Cp. *Il.* 7. 179 Ζεῦ πάτερ, ἢ Αἴαντα λαχεῖν ἢ Τυδέος υἱόν (grant that). Aesch. *Theb.* 253 θεοὶ πολῖται, μή με δουλείας τυχεῖν. **μαλερόν**, raging: cp. μαλεροῦ πυρός *Il.* 9. 242: μαλερῶν...λεόντων Aesch. *Ag.* 141. Ares is for Soph. not merely the *war-god*, but generally βροτολοιγός, the *Destroyer*: cp. *Ai.* 706. Here he is identified with the fiery plague. **ἄχαλκος ἀσπίδων** (cp. *El.* 36 ἄσκευον ἀσπίδων: Eur. *Phoen.* 324 ἄπεπλος φαρέων): Ares comes not, indeed, as the god of *war*, yet shrieks of the dying surround him with a cry (βοή) as of battle. **191** περιβόατος could not mean 'crying loudly': the prose use ('famous' or 'notorious,' Thuc. 6. 31) confirms the pass. sense here. **ἀντιάζων**, attacking: Her. 4. 80 ἠντίασάν μιν (acc.) οἱ Θρήϊκες. Aesch. has the word once only, as = 'to meet' (not in a hostile sense), *Ag.* 1557 πατέρ᾽ ἀντιάσασα: Eur. always as = 'to entreat'; and so Soph. *El.* 1009. Dindorf reads φλέγει με περιβόατον (the accus. on his own conject.), ἀντιάζω (suggested by Herm.), 'I *pray* that' etc. But the received text gives a more vivid picture. **192** νωτίσαι, to turn the back in flight (Eur. *Andr.* 1141 πρὸς φυγὴν ἐνώτισαν), a poet. word used by Aesch. with acc. πόντον, to *skim* (*Ag.* 286), by Eur. *Ph.* 651 (Dionysus) κισσὸς ὄν...ἐνώτισεν as = 'to cover the back of.' **δράμημα**, cognate acc.: **πάτρας**, gen. after verb of parting from: see on βάθρων, 142. **194** ἔπουρον = ἐπουριζόμενον (ironical). Lidd. and Scott *s. v.* refer to Clemens Alexandr. *Paed.* 130 τῷ τῆς ἀληθείας πνεύματι ἔπουρος ἀρθείς, 'lifted *on a prospering gale* by the spirit of Truth.' So *Trach.* 815 οὖρος

And grant that the fierce god of death, who now with no _{3rd} brazen shields, yet amid cries as of battle, wraps me in the ^{strophe.} flame of his onset, may turn his back in speedy flight from our land, borne by a fair wind to the great deep of Amphitritè, or to those waters in which none find haven, even to the Thracian wave; for if night leave aught undone,

Barocc. 66, seu dormitante librario, seu sensum expediri putante si accus. ad ἀφῇ referretur. *el. ἦν* V².

ὀφθαλμῶν ἐμῶν | αὐτῇ γένοιτ᾽ ἄπωθεν ἑρπούσῃ καλῶς : *ib.* 467 ἀλλὰ ταῦτα μὲν | ῥείτω κατ᾽ οὖρον. *Active* in *Trach.* 954 ἔπουρος ἑστιῶτις αὔρα (schol. ἄνεμος οὔριος ἐπὶ τῆς οἰκίας), 'wafting.' The *v. l.* ἄπουρον would go with πάτρας, '*away from* the *borders* of my country'—from Ionic οὖρος=ὅρος, like ὅμουρος (Her. 1. 57), πρόσουρος (*Phil.* 691), ξύνουρος (Aesch. *Ag.* 495), τηλουρός. Pollux 6. 198 gives ἔξορος, ἐξόριος, but we nowhere find an Ionic ἄπουρος: while for Attic writers ἄφορος (from ὅρος) would have been awkward, since ἄφορος 'sterile' was in use. **194 μέγαν | θάλαμον Ἀμφιτρίτας**, the Atlantic. θάλαμος Ἀμφιτρίτης *alone* would be merely 'the sea' (*Od.* 3. 91 ἐν πελάγει μετὰ κύμασιν Ἀμφιτρίτης), but μέγαν helps to localise it, since the Atlantic (ἡ ἔξω στηλέων θάλασσα ἡ Ἀτλαντὶς καλεομένη, Her. 1. 202) was esp. ἡ μεγάλη θάλασσα. Thus Polyb. 3. 37 calls the *Mediterranean* τὴν καθ᾽ ἡμᾶς,—the *Atlantic*, τὴν ἔξω καὶ μεγάλην προσαγορευομένην. In Plat. *Phaedo* 109 B the limits of the known habitable world are described by the phrase, τοὺς μέχρι τῶν Ἡρακλείων στηλῶν ἀπὸ Φάσιδος (which flows into the Euxine on the E.), Eur. *Hipp.* 3 ὅσοι τε πόντου (the Euxine) τερμόνων τ᾽ Ἀτλαντικῶν | ναίουσιν εἴσω : *Herc. F.* 234 ὥστ᾽ Ἀτλαντικῶν πέρα | φεύγειν ὅρων ἄν. **196 ἀπόξενον**. Aesch. has the word as = 'estranged from' (γῆς, *Ag.* 1282), cp. ἀποξενοῦσθαι. Here it means '*away from* strangers,' in the sense of 'keeping them at a distance.' Such compounds are usu. *passive* in sense: cp. ἀπόδειπνος (Hesych., = ἄδειπνος), ἄποθεος, ἀπόμισθος, ἀπόσιτος, ἀπότιμος (215), ἀποχρήματος. ἀπόξενος ὅρμος, the Euxine : an oxymoron, = ὅρμος ἄνορμος, as in *Phil.* 217 ιαὸς ἄξενον ὅρμον. Strabo 7. 298 ἄπλουν γὰρ εἶναι τότε τὴν θάλατταν ταύτην καὶ καλεῖσθαι Ἄξενον διὰ τὸ δυσχείμερον καὶ τὴν ἀγριότητα τῶν περιοικούντων ἐθνῶν καὶ μάλιστα τῶν Σκυθικῶν, ξενοθυτούντων, κ.τ.λ. The epithet Θρῇκιον here suggests the savage folk to whom Ares is ἀγχίπτολις on the W. coast of the Euxine (*Ant.* 969). Ovid *Trist.* 4. 4. 55 *Frigida me cohibent Euxini litora Ponti: Dictus ab antiquis Axenus ille fuit.* **198 τελεῖν γὰρ...ἔρχεται.** Reading τελεῖν, as Herm. suggested,

9 τοῦτ᾽ ἐπ᾽ ἦμαρ ἔρχεται·
10 τόν, ὦ < τᾶν > πυρφόρων   200
11 ἀστραπᾶν κράτη νέμων,
12 ὦ Ζεῦ πάτερ, ὑπὸ σῷ φθίσον κεραυνῷ.

ἀντ. γ΄. Λύκει᾽ ἄναξ, τά τε σὰ χρυσοστρόφων ἀπ᾽ ἀγκυλᾶν
2 βέλεα θέλοιμ᾽ ἂν ἀδάματ᾽ ἐνδατεῖσθαι   205
3 ἀρωγὰ προσταθέντα, τάς τε πυρφόρους

200 τὸν ὦ πυρφόρων codd. Syllabam longam desiderari docet versus 213 (πελασθῆναι φλέγοντα). τὸν ὦ τᾶν πυρφόρων Hermann. Praebet autem cod. Flor. Abb. 152
(Γ) τᾶν ὦ πυρφόρων. In voce πυρφόρων o super ω scriptum a m. rec. habent L, A, al. :
κράτει (v. 201) A, al. Hinc conflata est lectio quam E sine ulla varietatis mentione

instead of τέλει, I construe thus :—εἰ τι νὺξ ἀφῇ, ἦμαρ ἐπέρχεται τελεῖν
τοῦτὸ, 'If night omit anything (in the work of destruction), day comes
after it to accomplish this.' τελεῖν is the infin. expressing purpose, as
often after a verb of going or sending, where the fut. participle might
have been used: cp. Her. 7. 208 ἔπεμπε...κατάσκοπον ἱππέα, ἰδέσθαι
[= ὀψόμενον] ὁκόσοι τέ εἰσι, κ.τ.λ.: Thuc. 6. 50 δέκα δὲ τῶν νεῶν προὔπεμψαν
ἐς τὸν μέγαν λιμένα πλεῦσαί τε καὶ κατασκέψασθαι...καὶ κηρῦξαι.
Here the *pres.* inf. is right, because the act is not single but repeated.
Observe how strongly τελεῖν is supported by the *position* of the word
('To accomplish,—if night omit aught,—day follows'). No version of
τέλει explains this. The most tolerable is :—'*In fulness*—if night omit
aught—day attacks (ἐπέρχεται) this': but I do not think that such a
rendering can stand. See Appendix, Note 4. **εἰ...ἀφῇ.** Cp. 874
εἰ ὑπερπλησθῇ (lyric): O. C. 1443 εἰ στερηθῶ (dialogue): Ant. 710
κεἴ τις ᾖ (do.): In using εἰ with subjunct., the Attic poets were influenced by the epic usage, on which see Monro, *Homeric Grammar*
§ 292. The instances in classical prose are usu. doubtful, but in Thuc.
6. 21 εἰ ξυστῶσιν has good authority. **199 ἐπ᾽...ἔρχεται**: for the adverbial
ἐπί separated from ἔρχεται; cp. O. C. 1777 μηδ᾽ ἐπὶ πλείω | θρῆνον ἐγείρετε.
This is 'tmesis' in the larger sense: tmesis proper is when the prep. is
essential to the sense of the verb : Il. 8. 108 οὓς ποτ᾽ ἀπ᾽ Αἰνείαν ἑλόμην
= οὓς ἀφειλόμην Αἰνείαν: cp. Monro H. G. § 176. **200 τόν = ὅν,** sc.
Ἄρεα (190). **203 Λύκει᾽,** Apollo, properly the god of light (λυκ), whose
image, like that of Artemis, was sometimes placed before houses (El.
637 Φοῖβε προστατήριε, Aesch. Theb. 449 προστατηρίας | Ἀρτέμιδος), so
that the face should catch the first rays of the morning sun (δαίμονες...

day follows to accomplish this. O thou who wieldest the powers of the fire-fraught lightning, O Zeus our father, slay him beneath thy thunder-bolt.

Lycean King, fain were I that thy shafts also, from thy bent bow's string of woven gold, should go abroad in their might, our champions in the face of the foe; yea, and the flashing

3rd anti-strophe.

offert, ὦ πυρφόρον ἀστραπὰν | κράτει νέμων.   **205** ἀδάμαστ' codd.: ἀδάματ' Erfurdt. **206** Super προσταθέντα scriptum est et in L et in A προϊστάμενα, unde videas librarios participium duxisse a verbo προΐστημι, non a προστείνω. Dindorfius προσταχθέντα scribere iubet, tanquam coniecturae debitum. Ipsum autem προσταχθέντα illud in cod. Par. B inveni. Verumtamen minor est huius codicis fides quam ut contra ceteros valeat, praesertim cum lectionis προσταθέντα salva sit ratio.

ἀντήλιοι *Agam.* 519): then, through Λύκειος being explained as λυκο-κτόνος (Soph. *El.* 7), Apollo the *Destroyer* of foes: Aesch. *Theb.* 145 Λύκει' ἄναξ, Λύκειος γενοῦ | στρατῷ δαΐῳ. Cp. below, 919. **204** ἀγκυλᾶν. ἀγκύλη, a cord brought round on itself, a noose or loop, here = the νευρά of the *bent* bow. ἀγκύλων, the reading of L and A, was taken by Eustath. 33. 3 of the *bow* (ἄγκυλα τόξα). **205** ἐνδατεῖσθαι, pass., to be distributed, *i.e. showered abroad* on the hostile forces. The order of words, and the omission of σέ, are against making ἐνδατ. midd., though elsewhere the pass. occurs only in δέδασμαι: Appian, however, has γῆς διαδατουμένης 1. 1. It is possible that Soph. may have had in mind *Il.* 18. 263 ἐν πεδίῳ, ὅθι περ Τρῶες καὶ Ἀχαιοί | ἐν μέσῳ ἀμφό-τεροι μένος Ἄρηος δατέονται, 'share the rage of war,' give and take blows. Others understand, 'I would fain *celebrate*,' a sense of ἐνδα-τεῖσθαι derived from that of *distributing words* (λόγους ὀνειδιστῆρας ἐνδατούμενος, Eur. *Herc. F.* 218). The bad sense occurs in *Trach.* 791 τὸ δυσπάρευνον λέκτρον ἐνδατούμενος: the good, only in Aesch. fr. 340 ὁ δ' ἐνδατεῖται τὰς ἑὰς εὐπαιδίας, 'celebrates his happy race of children.' **206** προσταθέντα from προΐστημι, not προστείνω. Cp. *Ai.* 803 πρόστητ' ἀναγκαίας τύχης. *El.* 637 Φοῖβε προστατήριε. *O. T.* 881 θεὸν οὐ λήξω προστάταν ἴσχων. For 1st aor. pass. part., cp. καταστασθείς Lys. or. 24. 9, συσταθείς Plato *Legg.* 685 c. The conject. προσταλέντα (as = 'launched') is improbable (1) because it would mean rather 'having set out on a journey'; cp. *O. C.* 20: (2) on account of the metaphor in ἀρωγά. προσταθέντα from προστείνω (a verb which does not occur) would scarcely mean 'directed against the enemy,' but rather 'strained against the bow-string.' προσταχθέντα, found in one MS., would make

4 Ἀρτέμιδος αἴγλας, ξὺν αἷς
5 Λύκι' ὄρεα διᾴσσει·
6 τὸν χρυσομίτραν τε κικλήσκω,
7 τᾶσδ' ἐπώνυμον γᾶς,   210
8 οἰνῶπα Βάκχον εὔιον,
9 Μαινάδων ὁμόστολον
10 πελασθῆναι φλέγοντ'
11 ἀγλαῶπι < σύμμαχον >
12 πεύκᾳ 'πὶ τὸν ἀπότιμον ἐν θεοῖς θεόν.   215

214 ἀγλαῶπι πεύκᾳ codd.: vide annot.

ἀρωγά prosaic, while προσταθέντα—if not strictly suitable—is at least poetical: the difference is like that between speaking of 'auxiliary forces' and of 'champions.' 207 Ἀρτέμιδος αἴγλας, the torches with which Artemis was represented,—holding one in each hand (Ar. *Ran.* 1362 διπύρους ἀνέχουσα λαμπάδας, *Trach.* 214 Ἄρτεμιν ἀμφίπυρον),—in her character of Διἴλύκη, σελασφόρος, φωσφόρος, ἀνθήλιος,—names marking her connection with Selene; cp. Aesch. fr. 164 ἀστερωπὸν ὄμμα Λητῴας κόρης. 208 Λύκι' ὄρεα διᾴσσει as ἐλαφηβόλος, ἀγροτέρα, huntress: *Od.* 6. 102 οἴη δ' Ἄρτεμις εἶσι κατ' οὔρεος ἰσχέαιρα, | ...τερπομένη κάπροισι καὶ ὠκείῃς ἐλάφοισιν· | τῇδέ θ' ἅμα νύμφαι. Λύκια: the *Lycian* hills are named here in order to associate Artemis more closely with her brother under his like-sounding name of Λύκειος. At Troezen there was even a temple of Ἄρτεμις Λυκεία: Paus. says (2. 31. 4) that he could not learn why she was so called (ἐς δὲ τὴν ἐπίκλησιν οὐδὲν εἶχον πυθέσθαι παρὰ τῶν ἐξηγητῶν), and suggests that this may have been her title among the Amazons—a guess which touches the true point, viz. that the Λυκεία was a feminine counterpart of the Λύκειος. 209 τὸν χρυσομίτραν. μίτρα, a snood: Eur. *Bacch.* 831 ΔΙ. κόμην μὲν ἐπὶ σῷ κρατὶ ταναὸν ἐκτενῶ. ΠΕΝΘΕΥΣ. τὸ δεύτερον δὲ σχῆμα τοῦ κόσμου τί μοι; ΔΙ. πέπλοι ποδήρεις· ἐπὶ κάρᾳ δ' ἔσται μίτρα. 210 τᾶσδ' ἐπώνυμον γᾶς. As he is Βάκχος, so is Thebes called Βακχεία (*Trach.* 510), while he, on the other hand, was Καδμείας νύμφας ἄγαλμα (1115). The *mutual* relation of the names is intended here by ἐπώνυμον. The word usually means *called after* (τινός). But ἄρχων ἐπώνυμος, ἥρωες ἐπώνυμοι were those who *gave* names to the year, the tribes: and so Soph. *Ai.* 574 (σάκος) ἐπώνυμον, the shield which *gave* its name to Eurysaces. Cp. Eur. *Ion* 1555 where Athene says, ἐπώνυμος δὲ σῆς ἀφικόμην χθονός, *giving* my name to

fires of Artemis wherewith she glances through the Lycian hills. And I call him whose locks are bound with gold, who is named with the name of this land, ruddy Bacchus to whom Bacchants cry, the comrade of the Maenads, to draw near with the blaze of his blithe torch, [our ally] against the god unhonoured among gods.

---

thy land. **211** οἰνῶπα...εὔιον, 'ruddy'—'to whom Bacchants cry εὐοῖ.' Note how in this passionate ode all bright colours (χρυσέας, εὐῶπα, χρυσοστρόφων, αἴγλας, χρυσομίτραν, οἰνῶπα, ἀγλαῶπι), and glad sounds (ἰήιε Παιάν, εὔιον), are contrasted with the baleful fires of pestilence and the shrieks of the dying. **212** Μαινάδων ὁμόστολον = στελλόμενον ἅμα ταῖς Μαινάσιν, setting forth, roaming with the Maenads : Apoll. Rhod. 2. 802 ὁμόστολος ὑμῖν ἕπεσθαι. The nymphs attendant on Dionysus, who nursed the infant god in Nysa, and afterwards escorted him in his wanderings, are called Μαινάδες, Θυιάδες, Βάκχαι. *Il.* 6. 132 μαινομένοιο Διωνύσοιο τιθήνας | σεῦε κατ' ἠγάθεον Νυσήιον· αἱ δ' ἅμα πᾶσαι | θύσθλα (*i.e.* thyrsi and torches) χαμαὶ κατέχευαν. Aesch. fr. 397 πάτερ Θέοινε, Μαινάδων ζευκτήριε, who bringest the Maenads under thy spell. *Il.* 22. 460 μεγάροιο διέσσυτο, μαινάδι ἴση, | παλλομένη κραδίην. Catullus 63. 23 *capita Maenades vi iaciunt hederigerae*: as Pind. fr. 224 ῥιψαύχενι σὺν κλόνῳ. Lucian may have had our passage in mind, when he mentions the μίτρα and the *Maenads* together: *Dial. D.* 18 θῆλυς οὕτω,...μίτρᾳ μὲν ἀναδεδεμένος τὴν κόμην, τὰ πολλὰ δὲ μαινομέναις ταῖς γυναιξὶ συνών. **214** ἀγλαῶπι. A cretic has been lost. Prof. Kennedy's σύμμαχον is simple and appropriate. Arndt's conjecture, δαΐᾳ ('destroying, consuming,' prob. from rt. δαϜ, to kindle, Curt. *Etym.* § 258) is supported by the possibility of a corruption ΔΑΙΔΙ having been rejected as a gloss on πεύκα. Cp. *Il.* 9. 347 δήιον πῦρ, Aesch. *Theb.* 222 πυρὶ δαΐῳ. But in connection with the 'blithe torch' of Dionysus so sinister an epithet seems unsuitable. **215** τὸν ἀπότιμον. See on ἀπόξενον 196. Ares is 'without honour' among the gentler gods : cp. *Il.* 5. 31 (Apollo speaks), Ἄρες, Ἄρες βροτολοιγέ, μιαιφόνε, τειχεσιπλῆτα : and *ib.* 890 where Zeus says to Ares, ἔχθιστός τέ μοι ἔσσι θεῶν, κ.τ.λ. So the Erinyes are στύγη θεῶν (*Eum.* 644); and the house of Hades is hateful even to the gods (*Il.* 20. 65).

216—462 First ἐπεισόδιον. Oedipus re-enters from the palace. He solemnly denounces a curse on the unknown murderer of Laïus. The prophet Teiresias declares that the murderer is Oedipus.

54 ΣΟΦΟΚΛΕΟΥΣ

ΟΙ. αἰτεῖς· ἃ δ' αἰτεῖς, τἄμ' ἐὰν θέλῃς ἔπη
κλύων δέχεσθαι τῇ νόσῳ θ' ὑπηρετεῖν,
ἀλκὴν λάβοις ἂν κἀνακούφισιν κακῶν·
ἀγὼ ξένος μὲν τοῦ λόγου τοῦδ' ἐξερῶ,
ξένος δὲ τοῦ πραχθέντος· οὐ γὰρ ἂν μακρὰν   220
ἴχνευον αὐτός, μὴ οὐκ ἔχων τι σύμβολον.

221 αὐτὸ L, nullam indicans lectionis varietatem. αὐτὸς A. Cum ceterorum

216 αἰτεῖς: Oedipus had entered in time to hear the closing strains of the prayer for aid against the pestilence which the Chorus had been addressing to the gods. ἃ δ' αἰτεῖς. The place of λάβοις is against taking ἀλκὴν κἀνακούφισιν κακῶν as in apposition with ἅ: rather the construction changes, and ἅ is left as an accus. of general reference.   217 κλύων not strictly = πειθαρχῶν, 'obediently' (in which sense κλύειν takes gen., τῶν ἐν τέλει, Ai. 1352), but simply, 'on hearing them': δέχεσθαι, as Phil. 1321 κοὔτε σύμβουλον δέχει. τἄμ' emphatic by place: 'you pray (to the gods): hear me and (with their help) you shall have your wish.' τῇ νόσῳ ὑπηρετεῖν, = θεραπεύειν τὴν νόσον, to do that which the disease requires (for its cure), like ὑπηρετοίην τῷ παρόντι δαίμονι El. 1306. In Eur. fr. 84. 7 οὐδ' αὖ πενέσθαι κἀξυπηρετεῖν τύχαις | οἷοί τε, Nauck now gives with Athenaeus 413 C καὶ ξυνηρετμεῖν. Acc. to the commoner use of the word, the phrase would mean to humour the disease, i.e. obey morbid impulses: cp. Lysias In Eratosth. § 23 τῇ ἑαυτοῦ παρανομίᾳ προθύμως ἐξυπηρετῶν, eagerly indulging the excess of his own lawlessness. 218 ἀλκὴν, as well as ἀνακούφισιν, with κακῶν: Hes. Op. 199 κακοῦ δ' οὐκ ἔσσεται ἀλκή: Eur. Med. 1322 ἔρυμα πολεμίας χερός: below 1200 θανάτων ...πύργος. 219—223 ἀγὼ ξένος μὲν...τάδε. Oedipus has just learned from Creon that Laïus was believed to have been murdered by robbers on his way to Delphi, but that, owing to the troubles caused by the Sphinx, no effective search had been made at the time (114—131). He has at once resolved to take up the matter—both because Apollo enjoins it, and as a duty to the Theban throne (255). But the murder occurred before he had come to Thebes. He must therefore appeal for some clue—σύμβολον—to those who were at Thebes when the rumour was fresh. οὐ γὰρ ἂν μακρὰν | ἴχνευον αὐτός κ.τ.λ. justifies ἐξερῶ: 'As one who has no personal knowledge of the matter, I must make this appeal to you Thebans for any information that you can give me; for I could not have tracked the matter far alone (αὐτός), μὴ οὐκ ἔχων τι σύμβολον, if I had

Oe. Thou prayest; and in answer to thy prayer,—if thou wilt give a loyal welcome to my words and minister to thine own disease,—thou mayest hope to find succour and relief from woes. These words will I speak publicly, as one who has been a stranger to this report, a stranger to the deed; for I could not have tracked it far by myself, if I had not had some clue.

codd. alii hoc alii illud habeant, idcirco praeferendum est αὐτὸς quod sententiam clarius enuntiat : vide annot.

---

not had some clue : **νῦν δ'**, but as it is (having *no* clue),—**ὕστερος γὰρ κ.τ.λ.**, for it was only subsequently to the date of the crime that I became a Theban—I address myself to *you.*' **219 ξένος**, 'a stranger' to the affair, is tinged with the notion, 'unconnected with Thebes' : and this is brought out by **ἀστός** in 222. **220 οὐ γὰρ ἂν | ἴχνευον…μὴ οὐκ ἔχων.** μὴ οὐκ, not μή, is used, because the principal verb ἴχνευον has οὐ before it. Two views of the conditional sentence are admissible. I prefer (*a*) to regard the protasis as εἰ μὴ εἶχον implicit in μὴ οὐκ ἔχων. As ἴχνευον ἄν, μὴ ἔχων (if I had not), could represent ἴχνευον ἄν, εἰ μὴ εἶχον, so οὐκ ἴχνευον ἄν, μὴ οὐκ ἔχων, could represent οὐκ ἴχνευον ἄν, εἰ μὴ εἶχον. So in 13 μὴ οὐ κατοικτείρων = εἰ μὴ κατοικτείροιμι. The other view (*b*) would regard the protasis as suppressed, and μὴ οὐκ ἔχων as exempting a special case from the effect of the negative condition : (εἰ γὰρ μὴ ἐξεῖπον) οὐκ ἴχνευον ἄν, μὴ οὐκ ἔχων κ.τ.λ., 'for (if I had *not* appealed to you) I could not have tracked the crime far,—*unless, indeed, I had had some clue.*' But the word **ξένος** has already intimated that Oed. looks to *Thebans* for the needful σύμβολον. It seems, therefore, an inappropriate refinement to reserve the hypothesis of his being able to dispense with their aid, because possessed of a σύμβολον from some independent source. For other explanations of the passage, see Appendix, Note 5. **τοῦ πραχθέντος**, the murder. We cannot, I think, understand 'what was *done* at the time by way of search': for (*a*) τὸ πραχθέν, as opp. to ὁ λόγος, must surely mean the ἔργον to which the λόγος is related : (*b*) Oed. has lately expressed his surprise that *nothing* effective was done (128), and could hardly, therefore, refer with such emphasis to τὸ πραχθέν in this sense. **221 αὐτός**, 'by myself,' unaided: cp. *Il.* 13. 729 ἀλλ' οὔπως ἅμα πάντα δυνήσεαι αὐτὸς ἑλέσθαι: (not, 'even I myself, with all my insight.') **αὐτό** (*sc.* τὸ πραχθέν) would stand: and αὐτός is so far tautological that it really implies the protasis. Yet its emphasis helps to bring out the sense more forcibly: and cumulative

νῦν δ', ὕστερος γὰρ ἀστὸς εἰς ἀστοὺς τελῶ,
ὑμῖν προφωνῶ πᾶσι Καδμείοις τάδε·
ὅστις ποθ' ὑμῶν Λάϊον τὸν Λαβδάκου
κάτοιδεν ἀνδρὸς ἐκ τίνος διώλετο,   225
τοῦτον κελεύω πάντα σημαίνειν ἐμοί·
κεἰ μὲν φοβεῖται, τοὐπίκλημ' ὑπεξελεῖν
αὐτὸν καθ' αὑτοῦ· πείσεται γὰρ ἄλλο μὲν
ἀστεργὲς οὐδέν, γῆς δ' ἄπεισιν ἀβλαβής·
εἰ δ' αὖ τις ἄλλον οἶδεν ἐξ ἄλλης χθονὸς   230
τὸν αὐτόχειρα, μὴ σιωπάτω· τὸ γὰρ

227, 228 ὑπεξελὼν | αὐτὸς codd. ὑπεξελεῖν praeeuntibus K. Halmio et Blaydesio,
αὐτὸν ex mea coniectura scripsi.   229 ἀσφαλής L (ascripto γρ. ἀβλαβής a manu
rec.), cum paucis codd., quorum est V⁴. ἀβλαβής A, E (cui ἀσφαλής errore tribuit

---

expression is not in such cases foreign to the manner of Soph.
222 **νῦν δ'** reverts to the statement that he is ξένος to the matter: 'but
as it is,—as I have *no σύμβολον*,—(and it was impossible that I should
have had one,) *for* it was only subsequently to the date of the deed and
of the rumour that my first connection with Thebes was formed.'
ὕστερος sc. τοῦ πραχθέντος: for the adj. instead of an adv. ὕστερον, cp.
Ai. 217 νύκτερος...ἀπελωβήθη: *Il.* 1. 424 χθιζὸς ἔβη: *Xen. An.* 1. 4. 12
τοῖς προτέροις (= πρότερον) μετὰ Κύρου ἀναβᾶσι. **εἰς ἀστοὺς τελῶ** *inter
cives censeor*: a metaphor from being *rated* (for taxation) in a certain
class: *Her.* 6. 108 εἰς Βοιωτοὺς τελέειν: *Eur. Bacch.* 822 ἐς γυναῖκας
ἐξ ἀνδρὸς τελῶ. **ἀστὸς εἰς ἀστοὺς** like *Ai.* 267 κοινὸς ἐν κοινοῖσι: *ib.* 467
ξυμπεσὼν μόνος μόνοις: *Ph.* 135 ἐν ξένᾳ ξένον: *ib.* 633 ἴσος ὢν ἴσοις ἀνήρ.
227 f. κεἰ μὲν φοβεῖται τοὐπίκλημ' ὑπεξελὼν | αὐτὸς καθ' αὑτοῦ is the reading of
all the MSS.: for the ὑπεξελθὼν of the first hand in one Milan MS. of
the early 14th cent. (Ambros. L 39 sup., Campbell's M²) is a mere
slip. I feel certain that we should read **ὑπεξελεῖν | αὐτὸν καθ' αὑτοῦ**,
the change of **αὐτὸν** into **αὐτὸς** having necessarily followed that of
ὑπεξελεῖν into **ὑπεξελὼν**, due to an interpretation which took the latter
with **φοβεῖται**. I find the key to the true sense in *Thuc.* 4. 83
(Arrhibaeus, the enemy of Perdiccas, makes overtures to Brasidas, and
the Chalcidians exhort Brasidas to listen): ἐδίδασκον αὐτὸν μὴ ὑπεξελεῖν τῷ Περδίκκᾳ τὰ δεινά, 'they impressed upon him that he must
not *remove the dangers from the path of Perdiccas*'—by repulsing the
rival power of Arrhibaeus. ὑπεξελεῖν τὰ δεινά = to take them *away* (ἐκ)

But as it is,—since it was only after the time of the deed that I was numbered a Theban among Thebans,—to you, the Cadmeans all, I do thus proclaim.

Whosoever of you knows by whom Laïus son of Labdacus was slain, I bid him to tell all to me. And if he is afraid, I bid him to remove the danger of the charge from his own path; for he shall suffer nothing else unlovely, but only leave the land, unhurt. Or if anyone knows an alien, from another land, as the assassin, let him not keep silence; for

Campb.), et codd. plerique. ἀβλαβής Ald., Brunck., Herm., Linwood., Wunder., Blaydes., Kennedius: ἀσφαλής Dindorf. (qui tamen in annot. ἀβλαβής, ut aptius, verum esse suspicatur), Schneidewin., Campbell., J. W. White.

---

from under (ὑπό) the feet,—from the path immediately before him : τῷ Περδίκκᾳ being a dat. commodi. So here: κεἰ μὲν φοβεῖται, *and if he is afraid* (as knowing *himself* to be the culprit), *then I bid him* (κελεύω continued from 226) ὑπεξελεῖν τὸ ἐπίκλημα *to take the peril of the charge out of his path* αὐτὸν καθ' αὑτοῦ (*by speaking*) *himself against himself.*' If the culprit is denounced by another person, he will be liable to the extreme penalty. If he denounces himself, he will merely be banished. By denouncing himself, he forestalls the danger of being denounced by another. Instead of a dat. commodi αὑτῷ (corresponding to τῷ Περδίκκᾳ in Thuc.), Soph. has written καθ' αὑτοῦ, because self-accusation is the mode of doing the act expressed by ὑπεξελεῖν, which implies κατηγορῆσαι. The pregnant καθ' αὑτοῦ is rendered still less harsh by the fact that τοὐπίκλημα precedes. There is no 'aposiopesis' or 'suppressed clause': we have simply to carry on κελεύω. For other explanations, see Appendix, Note 6. **229** ἀβλαβής, the reading of A and most MSS., 'without damage,' ἀζήμιος, is far more suitable than ἀσφαλής to this context: and Soph. has the word as a cretic in *El.* 650 ζῶσαν ἀβλαβεῖ βίῳ. Although in L ἀσφαλής appears as the older reading, so common a word was very likely to be intruded; while it would be difficult to explain how the comparatively rare ἀβλαβής could have supplanted it. A metrical doubt may have first brought ἀσφαλής in. **230** ἄλλον...ἐξ ἄλλης χθονός, 'another [*i.e.* other than one of yourselves, the Thebans] from a strange land': an alien, whether resident at Thebes, or not: cp. 451 οὗτός ἐστιν ἐνθάδε, | ξένος λόγῳ μέτοικος. The cases contemplated in the proclamation (223—235) are (1) a Theban denouncing another Theban, (2) a Theban denouncing himself, (3) a Theban denouncing an alien. **231** τὸ κέρδος,

κέρδος τελῶ 'γὼ χἠ χάρις προσκείσεται.
εἰ δ' αὖ σιωπήσεσθε, καί τις ἢ φίλου
δείσας ἀπώσει τοὖπος ἢ χαὑτοῦ τόδε,
ἃκ τῶνδε δράσω, ταῦτα χρὴ κλύειν ἐμοῦ.   235
τὸν ἄνδρ' ἀπαυδῶ τοῦτον, ὅστις ἐστί, γῆς
τῆσδ', ἧς ἐγὼ κράτη τε καὶ θρόνους νέμω,
μήτ' ἐσδέχεσθαι μήτε προσφωνεῖν τινα,
μήτ' ἐν θεῶν εὐχαῖσι μήτε θύμασιν
κοινὸν ποιεῖσθαι, μήτε χέρνιβος νέμειν·   240
ὠθεῖν δ' ἀπ' οἴκων πάντας, ὡς μιάσματος
τοῦδ' ἡμὶν ὄντος, ὡς τὸ Πυθικὸν θεοῦ
μαντεῖον ἐξέφηνεν ἀρτίως ἐμοί.
ἐγὼ μὲν οὖν τοιόσδε τῷ τε δαίμονι
τῷ τ' ἀνδρὶ τῷ θανόντι σύμμαχος πέλω   245

240 χέρνιβασ L (quod tamen a χέρνιβοσ levi tactu fecit manus antiqua, fortasse prima), A, reliqui fere omnes. Lectionem certe elegantiorem χέρνιβος solus videtur

---

the (expected) gain, τὰ μήνντρα. *Trach.* 191 ὅπως | πρὸς σοῦ τι κερδά-ναιμι καὶ κτώμην χάριν. **232** προσκείσεται, will be stored up *besides* (cp. Eur. *Alc.* 1039 ἄλγος αλγει...προσκείμενον, *added*). χάρις κεῖται is perf. pass. of χάριν τίθεμαι or κατατίθεμαι (τινί or παρά τινί),—a metaphor from deposits of money: τὰ χρήματα...κείσθω παρ' οἷς τισιν ἂν ὑμῖν δοκῇ [Plat.] *Epist.* 346 C. **233** φίλου, αὑτοῦ with ἀπώσει only (*Il.* 15. 503 ἀπώσασθαι κακὰ νηῶν). **234** δείσας φίλου as = δείσας ὑπὲρ φίλου (like κήδομαι, φροντίζειν) would be too harsh, and rhythm is against it. τοὖπος...τόδε, this command to give up the guilty. **236—240** ἀπαυδῶ (ἀπ-, because the first clauses are negative), I command, (μή) τινα γῆς τῆσδε that no one belonging to this land μήτ' ἐσδέχεσθαι μήτε προσφωνεῖν shall either entertain or accost τὸν ἄνδρα τοῦτον, ὅστις ἐστί. For the gen. γῆς, cp. Plat. *Prot.* 316 B Ἱπποκράτης ὅδε ἐστὶ μὲν τῶν ἐπιχωρίων, Ἀπολλο-δώρου υἱός, οἰκίας μεγάλης καὶ εὐδαίμονος. Since μήτε...μήτε in 238 connect ἐσδέχεσθαι and προσφωνεῖν, we require either (a) separate verbs for εὐχαῖσι and θύμασιν, or (b) as Elms. proposed and Blaydes reads, μηδὲ instead of μήτε before θύμασιν. As the text stands, we must suppose a μήτε suppressed before εὐχαῖσι, the constr. being μήτε κοινὸν ποιεῖσθαι [μήτε] ἐν...εὐχαῖσι μήτε θύμασιν. Cp. Aesch. *Ag.* 532 Πάρις γὰρ οὔτε

I will pay his guerdon, and my thanks shall rest with him besides.

But if ye keep silence—if anyone, through fear, shall seek to screen friend or self from my behest—hear ye what I then shall do. I charge you that no one of this land, whereof I hold the empire and the throne, give shelter or speak word unto that murderer, whosoever he be,—make him partner of his prayer or sacrifice,—or serve him with the lustral rite ; but that all ban him their homes, knowing that *this* is our defiling thing, as the oracle of the Pythian god hath newly shown me. I then am on this wise the ally of the god and of the slain.

praebere cod. Laur. 31. 10 (L²): nam in cod. V⁴, ubi Campb. χέρνιβος agnovit, χέρνιβας, nisi me oculi mei fefellerunt, legi.

συντελὴς πόλις : *Cho.* 294 δέχεσθαι δ᾽ οὔτε συλλύειν τινά. 240 κοινὸν here = κοινωνόν, cp. *Ai.* 267 ἢ κοινὸς ἐν κοινοῖσι λυπεῖσθαι ξυνών. Plat. *Legg.* 868 E (the slayer) ξυνέστιος αὐτοῖς μηδέποτε γιγνέσθω μηδὲ κοινωνὸς ἱερῶν. χέρνιβος (partitive gen.) is more suitable than χέρνιβας to the idea of exclusion from all fellowship in ordinary worship : χέρνιβας νέμειν would rather suggest a special κάθαρσις of the homicide. When sacrifice was offered by the members of a household (κοινωνὸν εἶναι χερνίβων...κτησίου βωμοῦ πέλας Aesch. *Ag.* 1037) or of a clan (χέρνιψ φρατέρων *Eum.* 656), a brand taken from the altar was dipped in water, and with the water thus consecrated (χέρνιψ) the company and the altar were sprinkled : then holy silence was enjoined (εὐφημία ἔστω): and the rite began by the strewing of barley meal (οὐλοχύται) on altar and victim. (Athenaeus 409: Eur. *H. F.* 922 ff.) Acc. to Dem. *Adv. Lept.* § 158 a law of Draco prescribed χέρνιβος [so the best MSS.: *v. l.* χερνίβων] εἴργεσθαι τὸν ἀνδροφόνον, σπονδῶν, κρατήρων, ἱερῶν, ἀγορᾶς. This was a sentence of excommunication (1) from the life of the family and the clan, (2) from the worship common to all Hellenes, who, as opposed to βάρβαροι, are (Ar. *Lys.* 1129) οἳ μιᾶς ἐκ χέρνιβος | βωμοὺς περιρραίνοντες, ὥσπερ ξυγγενεῖς, | Ὀλυμπίασιν, ἐν Πύλαις, Πυθοῖ. The mere presence of the guilty could render sacrifice inauspicious: Antiph. *De Caed. Her.* § 82 ἱεροῖς παραστάντες πολλοὶ δὴ καταφανεῖς ἐγένοντο οὐχ ὅσιοι ὄντες καὶ διακωλύοντες τὰ ἱερὰ μὴ γίγνεσθαι (*bene succedere*) τὰ νομιζόμενα. 241 ὠθεῖν δὲ, sc. αὐδῶ, understood from the negative ἀπαυδῶ: cp. Her. 7. 104 οὐκ ἐῶν φεύγειν...ἀλλὰ ἐπικρατέειν. 246—251 These six verses are placed by some editors between 272 and 273. See Appendix, Note 7.

κατεύχομαι δὲ τὸν δεδρακότ', εἴτε τις
εἷς ὢν λέληθεν εἴτε πλειόνων μέτα,
κακὸν κακῶς νιν ἄμορον ἐκτρῖψαι βίον.
ἐπεύχομαι δ', οἴκοισιν εἰ ξυνέστιος
ἐν τοῖς ἐμοῖς γένοιτ' ἐμοῦ συνειδότος,　　　　　　250
παθεῖν ἅπερ τοῖσδ' ἀρτίως ἠρασάμην.
ὑμῖν δὲ ταῦτα πάντ' ἐπισκήπτω τελεῖν
ὑπέρ τ' ἐμαυτοῦ τοῦ θεοῦ τε τῆσδέ τε
γῆς ὧδ' ἀκάρπως κἀθέως ἐφθαρμένης.
οὐδ' εἰ γὰρ ἦν τὸ πρᾶγμα μὴ θεήλατον,　　　　　　255
ἀκάθαρτον ὑμᾶς εἰκὸς ἦν οὕτως ἐᾶν,
ἀνδρός γ' ἀρίστου βασιλέως τ' ὀλωλότος,

248 ἄμορον A et plerique codd.: κἄμοιρον B, et in L erasa est ante ἄμορον littera quae κ procul dubio fuerat: νιν ἄμοιρον E, T: νιν ἄμορον Porson. 257 βασιλέως τ'. Sic recte L, A, et codd. meliores aliquot: alii τ' omittunt. Fatendum

246 κατεύχομαι. Suidas κατεύχεσθαι· τὸ καταρᾶσθαι. οὕτω Πλάτων. καὶ Σοφοκλῆς, κατεύχομαι δὲ τὸν δεδρακότα τάδε. Phot. *Lex.* p. 148. 7 κατεύχεσθαι τῶν Ἀχαιῶν· ἀντὶ τοῦ κατὰ τῶν Ἀχαιῶν εὔχεσθαι. οὕτως Σοφοκλῆς. Here the ref. is to Plato *Rep.* 393 E τὸν δὲ (the Homeric Chryses, priest of Apollo)...κατεύχεσθαι τῶν Ἀχαιῶν πρὸς θεόν. But Photius prefixes the words, κατεύχεσθαι· τὸ καταρᾶσθαι. οὕτως Πλάτων. It is clear, then, that in Photius οὕτως Σοφοκλῆς and οὕτως Πλάτων have changed places. The 'Soph. fr. 894,' quoted by Lidd. and Scott under κατεύχομαι as =*imprecari*, thus vanishes (Nauck *Fragm. Trag.* p. 283). Cp. Aesch. *Theb.* 632 πόλει | οἵας ἀρᾶται καὶ κατεύχεται τύχας. But where, as here, **κατεύχομαι** is used without gen. (or dat.), it is rather *to pray solemnly:* often, however, in a context which *implies* imprecation: *e.g.* Plat. *Legg.* 935 A κατεύχεσθαι ἀλλήλοις ἐπαρωμένους: *Rep.* 394 A κατεύχετο τῖσαι τοὺς Ἀχαιοὺς τὰ ἃ δάκρυα. **εἴτε τις**: whether the unknown man (τις) who has escaped discovery is **εἷς**, alone in the crime, or one of several. τις, because the person is indefinite: cp. 107. **248 νιν ἄμορον**: Porson (*praef. Hec.* p. ix) defends the redundant **νιν** by *Trach.* 287 αὐτὸν δ' ἐκεῖνον, εὖτ' ἂν ἁγνὰ θύματα | ῥέξῃ πατρῴῳ Ζηνὶ τῆς ἁλώσεως, | φρόνει νιν ὡς ἥξοντα. The form ἄμορος occurs in Eur. *Med.* 1395 (where ἄμοιρος is a *v. l.*); ἄμμορος in Hec. 421, Soph. *Phil.* 182. **κακὸν κακῶς**: *Phil.* 1369 ἔα κακῶς αὐτοὺς ἀπόλλυσθαι κακούς. Ar. *Plut.* 65 ἀπό σ' ὀλῶ κακὸν κακῶς. **249 ἐπεύχομαι**,

And I pray solemnly that the slayer, whoso he be, whether his hidden guilt is lonely or hath partners, evilly, as he is evil, may wear out his unblest life. And for myself I pray that if, with my privity, he should become an inmate of my house, I may suffer the same things which even now I called down upon others. And on you I lay it to make all these words good, for my sake, and for the sake of the god, and for our land's, thus blasted with barrenness by angry heaven.

For even if the matter had not been urged on us by a god, it was not meet that ye should leave the guilt thus un-purged, when one so noble, and he your king, had perished;

est in ipso L τ' non a prima manu scriptum fuisse: accessit tamen a manu, ut Duebnerus quoque vidit, antiqua. Vide annot.

imprecate on *myself:* Plato *Critias* 120 B ταῦτα ἐπευξάμενος ἕκαστος αὐτῶν αὐτῷ καὶ τῷ ἀφ' αὑτοῦ γένει. οἴκο:σιν...ξυνέστιος: not tautological, since ξυνέστιος is more than ἔνοικος, implying admission to the family worship at the ἑστία and to the σπονδαί at meals. Plat. *Legg.* 868 E ἱερῶν μὴ κοινωνείτω μηδὲ...ξυνέστιος αὐτοῖς μηδέποτε γιγνέσθω μηδὲ κοινωνὸς ἱερῶν. Plat. *Euthyphro* 4 B καὶ εἰ μὲν ἐν δίκῃ [ἔκτεινεν], ἐᾶν, if he slew the man justly, forbear; εἰ δὲ μή, ἐπεξιέναι (prosecute the slayer), ἐάνπερ ὁ κτείνας συνέστιός σοι καὶ ὁμοτράπεζος ᾖ. ἴσον γὰρ τὸ μίασμα γίγνεται, ἐὰν ξυνῇς τῷ τοιούτῳ ξυνειδὼς καὶ μὴ ἀφοσιοῖς σεαυτόν τε καὶ ἐκεῖνον τῇ δίκῃ ἐπεξιών. 251 τοῖσδ', the slayer or slayers (247): see on 246. 254 ἀκάρπως κάθέως: *El.* 1181 ὦ σῶμ' ἀτίμως κάθέως ἐφθαρμένον: below 661 ἄθεος, ἄφιλος, forsaken by gods and men. 256 εἰκὸς ἦν. The imperfect indic. of a verb denoting obligation (ἔδει, χρῆν, προσῆκεν, εἰκὸς ἦν), when joined *without* ἄν to an infinitive, often implies a conditional sentence with imperfect indic. in protasis and apodosis: *e.g.* οὐκ εἰκὸς ἦν ἐᾶν = οὐκ ἂν εἴατε (εἰ τὰ δέοντα ἐποιεῖτε), you would not (now) be neglecting it, (if you did your duty): Xen. *Mem.* 2. 7. 10 εἰ μὲν τοίνυν αἰσχρόν τι ἔμελλον ἐργάσεσθαι [if I were now intending—as I am not], θάνατον ἀντ' αὐτοῦ προαιρετέον ἦν, = προῃρούμην ἂν (εἰ τὰ δέοντα ἐποίουν). Thuc. 6. 78 καὶ μάλιστα εἰκὸς ἦν ὑμᾶς ...προορᾶσθαι, = προεωρᾶτε ἂν εἰ τὰ εἰκότα ἐποιεῖτε. So ἐβουλόμην, ἠξίουν, without ἄν, of that which one wishes were true, but which is not so. 257 βασιλέως τ': τε is to be retained after βασιλέως, because (1) there is a climax, which is destroyed if βασιλέως stands merely in apposition with ἀνδρὸς ἀρίστου: (2) ἀνδρὸς ἀρίστου represents the claim of birth

ἀλλ' ἐξερευνᾶν· νῦν δ', ἐπεὶ κυρῶ τ' ἐγὼ
ἔχων μὲν ἀρχὰς ἃς ἐκεῖνος εἶχε πρίν,
ἔχων δὲ λέκτρα καὶ γυναῖχ' ὁμόσπορον,   260
κοινῶν τε παίδων κοίν' ἄν, εἰ κείνῳ γένος
μὴ 'δυστύχησεν, ἦν ἂν ἐκπεφυκότα,
νῦν δ' ἐς τὸ κείνου κρᾶτ' ἐνήλαθ' ἡ τύχη·
ἀνθ' ὧν ἐγὼ τάδ', ὡσπερεὶ τοὐμοῦ πατρός,
ὑπερμαχοῦμαι, κἀπὶ πάντ' ἀφίξομαι   265

258 κυρῶ τ' codd.: κυρῶ γ' T. F. Benedict. (Observationes in Soph., Lips. 1820),
ap. Blaydes. ad loc.; Campb.

---

and personal merit,—βασιλέως, the special claim of a king on his
people. Cp. *Phil.* 1302 ἄνδρα πολέμιον | ἐχθρόν τε. **258** κυρῶ τ' ἐγὼ
= ἐγώ τε κυρῶ, answered by κοινῶν τε, κ.τ.λ. For τε so placed cp. *El.*
249 ἔρροι τ' ἂν αἰδὼς | ἁπάντων τ' εὐσέβεια θνατῶν. **260** ὁμόσπορον =
ὁμοίως σπειρομένην, *i.e.* ἦν καὶ ἐκεῖνος ἔσπειρε: but in 460 πατρὸς |
ὁμόσπορος = ὁμοίως (τὴν αὐτὴν) σπείρων. ὁμογενής in 1361 is not similar.
261 κοινῶν παίδων κοινὰ ἦν ἂν ἐκπεφυκότα, common things *of* (= *ties* consisting *in*) kindred children would have been generated : = κοινῶν παίδων
κοινὴ φύσις ἐγένετο ἄν, a brood, common to Laïus and Oedipus, of
children akin to each other (as having the same mother, Iocasta) would
have issued : 'children born of one mother would have made ties
between him and me.' For ἄν doubled cp. 139, 339. κοινῶν = ἀδελφῶν,
ὁμαίμων (*Ant.* 1 ὦ κοινὸν αὐτάδελφον Ἰσμήνης κάρα). The language of
this passage is carefully framed so as to bear a second meaning, of
which the speaker is unconscious, but which the spectators can feel:
Iocasta has actually borne children to her own son Oedipus : thus in
κοινῶν παίδων κοινά...ἐκπεφυκότα, the obvious sense of κοινά, '*common to
Laïus and Oedipus,*' has behind it a second sense, in which it hints at a
brood who are *brothers and sisters of their own sire:* see below 1403 f.
This subtle emphasis—so ghastly, ξυνετοῖσιν—of the iteration in κοινῶν
κοινά must not be obliterated by amending κοίν' ἄν into κύματ' (Nauck)
or σπέρματ' (Blaydes). Similarly, εἰ κείνῳ γένος | μὴ 'δυστύχησεν, is sus-
ceptible of the sense—'if his son (Oed. himself) had not been ill-fated.'
κείνῳ γένος ἐδυστύχησε (his hope of issue was disappointed) is here a
bold phrase for κεῖνος ἐδυστύχησε τὰ περὶ γένος : for Oed. is not *now*
supposed to know the story of the exposed babe (see 717 f.). Cp. Eur.
Andr. 418 πᾶσι δ' ἀνθρώποις ἄρ' ἦν | ψυχὴ τέκν'· ὅστις δ' αὖτ' ἄπειρος ὢν

rather were ye bound to search it out. And now, since 'tis I who hold the powers which once he held, who possess his bed and the wife who bare seed to him; and since, had his hope of issue not been frustrate, children born of one mother would have made ties betwixt him and me—but, as it was, fate swooped upon his head; by reason of these things will I uphold his cause, even as the cause of mine own sire, and will leave nought untried

---

ψέγει, | ἧσσον μὲν ἀλγεῖ, δυστυχῶν δ' εὐδαιμονεῖ: *ib.* 711 ἢ στεῖρος οὖσα μόσχος οὐκ ἀνέξεται | τίκτοντας ἄλλους, οὐκ ἔχουσ' αὐτὴ τέκνα· | ἀλλ' εἰ τὸ κείνης δυστυχεῖ παίδων πέρι, κ.τ.λ.: *Suppl.* 66 εὐτεκνία opp. to δυστυχία. 263 νῦν δ', 'but as it is,' with aor. equivalent to a *perf.*, as *O. C.* 84, 371. Cp. below 948 καὶ νῦν ὅδε | πρὸς τῆς τύχης ὄλωλε. So with *historic* pres., Lys. *In Erat.* § 36 εἰ μὲν οὖν ἐν τῷ δικαστηρίῳ ἐκρίνοντο, ῥᾳδίως ἂν ἐσώζοντο...νῦν δ' εἰς τὴν βουλὴν εἰσάγουσιν. ἐνήλατο: *i.e.* he was cut off by a timeless fate, leaving no issue, cp. 1300: *Ant.* 1345 ἐπὶ κρατί μοι | πότμος...εἰσήλατο: so the Erinyes say, μάλα γὰρ οὖν ἀλομένα | ἀνέκαθεν βαρυπεσῆ | καταφέρω ποδὸς ἀκμάν Aesch. *Eum.* 369, *Ag.* 1175 δαίμων ὑπερβαρὴς ἐμπίτνων: *Pers.* 515 ὦ δυσπόνητε δαῖμον, ὡς ἄγαν βαρὺς | ποδοῖν ἐνήλλου παντὶ Περσικῷ γένει. 264 ἀνθ' ὧν, *therefore.* The protasis ἐπεὶ κυρῶ (258) required an apodosis introduced by ἀντὶ τούτων: but the parenthesis νῦν δ' ἐς τὸ κείνου κ.τ.λ. (263) has led to ὧν being irregularly substituted for τούτων. Cp. 1466: Antiphon *De Caed. Herod.* § 11 δέον σε διομόσασθαι κ.τ.λ....ἃ σὺ παρελθών, where the length of the protasis has similarly caused ἃ to be substituted for ταῦτα. Distinguish from this the use of ἀνθ' ὧν, by ordinary attraction, for ἀντὶ τούτων ἃ or ὅτι, = *because*, *Ant.* 1068. τάδ', cogn. acc. to ὑπερμαχοῦμαι, as *Ai.* 1346 σὺ ταῦτ' Ὀδυσσεῦ τοῦδ' ὑπερμαχεῖς ἐμοί; Cp. *Il.* 5. 185 οὐχ ὅ γ' ἄνευθε θεοῦ τάδε μαίνεται. Brunck, Nauck and Blaydes adopt the conj. τοῦδ'. But the MSS. agree in the harder and more elegant reading. 265 ὑπερμαχοῦμαι only here: in *Ant.* 194, *Ai.* 1346 Soph. uses ὑπερμαχεῖν. But we need not therefore, with Elms. and Blaydes, read ὑπὲρ μαχοῦμαι. The derivative form ὑπερμαχέω, to be a champion, implies ὑπέρμαχος, as συμμαχέω is from σύμμαχος, προμαχέω from πρόμαχος: ὑπερμάχομαι is a simple compound, like συμμάχομαι (Plat., Xen.) προμάχομαι (*Iliad*, Diod., Plut.). κἀπὶ πάντ' ἀφίξομαι with ζητῶν, will leave nothing untried in seeking: a poetical variation of ἐπὶ πᾶν ἐλθεῖν (Xen. *Anab.* 3. 1. 18 ἆρ' οὐκ ἂν ἐπὶ πᾶν ἔλθοι...ὡς φόβον παράσχοι), as in Eur. *Hipp.* 284 εἰς πάντ' ἀφῖγμαι, 'I have tried all means.' In prose ἀφικνεῖσθαι εἴς τι

ζητῶν τὸν αὐτόχειρα τοῦ φόνου λαβεῖν
τῷ Λαβδακείῳ παιδὶ Πολυδώρου τε καὶ
τοῦ πρόσθε Κάδμου τοῦ πάλαι τ᾽ Ἀγήνορος.
καὶ ταῦτα τοῖς μὴ δρῶσιν εὔχομαι θεοὺς
μήτ᾽ ἄροτον αὐτοῖς γῆς ἀνιέναι τινὰ　　　　　270
μήτ᾽ οὖν γυναικῶν παῖδας, ἀλλὰ τῷ πότμῳ
τῷ νῦν φθερεῖσθαι κἄτι τοῦδ᾽ ἐχθίονι·
ὑμῖν δὲ τοῖς ἄλλοισι Καδμείοις, ὅσοις
τάδ᾽ ἔστ᾽ ἀρέσκονθ᾽, ἥ τε σύμμαχος Δίκη
χοἱ πάντες εὖ ξυνεῖεν εἰσαεὶ θεοί.　　　　　275
ΧΟ. ὥσπερ μ᾽ ἀραῖον ἔλαβες, ὧδ᾽, ἄναξ, ἐρῶ.

270 γῆς, quod Vauvillers. coniecit, ne unius quidem codicis fide niti vulgo
traditum est.　Certe γῆν habènt L, A, reliqui fere omnes.　Inveni tamen in cod.
Venet. 468 (V) clare scriptum γῆς, quod nemo dubitabit qui formas litterarum ν et σ,

---

usu. = to be *brought* to a situation, as Her. 8. 110 ἐς πᾶσαν βάσανον
ἀπικνεομένοισι, though put to any torment; Plat. *Euthyd.* 292 E εἰς πολ-
λήν γε ἀπορίαν ἀφίκεσθε.　267 τῷ Λαβδακείῳ παιδὶ, a dat. following ζητῶν
κ.τ.λ. as = τιμωρούμενος.　For Λαβδακείῳ—Πολυδώρου τε cp. Eur. *Med.*
404 τοῖς Σισυφείοις τοῖς τ᾽ Ἰάσονος γάμοις: for the adj., *Od.* 3. 190
Φιλοκτήτην Ποιάντιον [= Ποίαντος] ἀγλαὸν υἱόν: Her. 7. 105 τοῖς Μασκα-
μείοισι ἐκγόνοισι.　Her. (5. 59) saw in the temple of the Ismenian Apollo
at Thebes an inscription which he assigns to the age of Laïus : ταῦτα
ἡλικίην ἂν εἴη κατὰ Λᾶιον τὸν Λαβδάκου τοῦ Πολυδώρου τοῦ Κάδμου.　Cadmus, in the myth, is the son of Agenor king of Phoenicia, whence
Carthage is ʻAgenor's city' (Verg. *Aen.* 1. 338): Polydorus, son of
Cadmus and Harmonia, was king of Thebes.　269 f. construe: καὶ
εὔχομαι τοῖς ταῦτα μὴ δρῶσιν [*for* them, *Ph.* 1019 καί σοι πολλάκις τόδ᾽
ηὐξάμην] θεοὺς ἀνιέναι αὐτοῖς μήτ᾽ ἄροτόν τινα γῆς, μήτ᾽ οὖν γυναικῶν παῖδας.
The acc. θεοὺς as subject to ἀνιέναι is better than a dat. θεοῖς with
εὔχομαι would be: Xen. *Anab.* 6. 1. 26 εὔχομαι δοῦναί μοι τοὺς θεοὺς
αἴτιόν τινος ὑμῖν ἀγαθοῦ γενέσθαι: Ar. *Thesm.* 350 ταῖς δ᾽ ἄλλαισιν ὑμῖν
τοὺς θεοὺς | εὔχεσθε πάσαις πολλὰ δοῦναι κἀγαθά.　271 μήτ᾽ οὖν: ʻ *no, nor.*'
Aesch. *Ag.* 474 μήτ᾽ εἴην πτολιπόρθης, | μήτ᾽ οὖν αὐτὸς ἁλούς, κ.τ.λ.　Soph.
Phil. 345 εἴτ᾽ ἀληθὲς εἴτ᾽ ἄρ᾽ οὖν μάτην: cp. above v. 90.　But οὖν with
the *first* clause, below, 1049 : *El.* 199, 560 : see on 25.　272 φθερεῖσθαι,
a fut. found also in Eur. *Andr.* 708 (φθερεῖ 2 sing.): Thuc. 7. 48
φθερεῖσθαι: Ionic φθαρέομαι Her. 9. 42, 8. 108. (φθαρήσομαι in

in seeking to find him whose hand shed that blood, for the honour of the son of Labdacus and of Polydorus and elder Cadmus and Agenor who was of old.

And for those who obey me not, I pray that the gods send them neither harvest of the earth nor fruit of the womb, but that they be wasted by their lot that now is, or by one yet more dire. But for all you, the loyal folk of Cadmus to whom these things seem good, may Justice, our ally, and all the gods be with you graciously for ever.

CH. As thou hast put me on my oath, on my oath, O king, I will speak.

ut ab illo librario scribuntur, semel contulerit. In cod. Venet. 467 (V³) ambigi sane potest de extrema vocabuli littera; postquam vero diligenter inspexeram quomodo utramque eadem manus alibi scribere soleret, satis mihi persuasum habui, non γῆν sed γῆς huic quoque libro iure vindicari.

Hippocr., Arist., Plut.). The schol. says, φθαρῆναι δεῖ γράφειν, οὐ φθερεῖσθαι, distinguishing εὔχομαι with fut. infin., 'I vow' (to do), from εὔχομαι with pres. or aor. infin., 'I pray.' But verbs of wishing or praying sometimes take a fut. infin. instead of pres. or aor.: Thuc. 6. 57 ἐβούλοντο...προτιμωρήσεσθαι: 6. 6 ἐφιέμενοι μὲν...τῆς πάσης ἄρξειν: 1. 27 ἐδεήθησαν...ξυμπροπέμψειν: 7. 56 διενοοῦντο κλῄσειν. See Goodwin, Moods and Tenses § 27. N. 2. a. 273 τοῖς ἄλλοισι. The loyal, as opp. to οἱ μὴ ταῦτα δρῶντες (269). 274 ἔστ' ἀρέσκοντ', cp. 126. ἥ τε σύμμαχος Δίκη, Justice who ever helps the righteous cause; Blaydes needlessly writes ἡ Δίκη τε σύμμαχος. O. C. 1012 ἐλθεῖν ἀρωγοὺς συμμάχους τε (τὰς θεάς). 275 εὖ: cp. Trach. 229 ἀλλ' εὖ μὲν ἵγμεθ', εὖ δὲ προσφωνούμεθα. 276 ὥσπερ μ' ἀραῖον κ.τ.λ. As you have brought me into your power under a curse [if I speak not the truth], so (ὧδε, i.e. ἔνορκος) I will speak. Aeschin. In Ctes. § 90 μίαν ἐλπίδα λοιπὴν κατεῖδε σωτηρίας, ἔνορκον λαβεῖν τὸν Ἀθηναίων δῆμον...βοηθήσειν, to bind them by an oath that they would help. λαβεῖν here has nearly the same force as in λαβεῖν αἰχμάλωτον etc.: Lys. or. 4 § 5 ὑποχείριον λαβὼν τὸ σῶμα, having got his person into my power. ἀραῖον = τῇ ἀρᾷ ἔνοχον, cp. ὄρκιος...λέγω Ant. 305. The paraphrase of Eustath. 1809. 14 ὥσπερ με εἷλες διὰ τῆς ἀρᾶς is substantially right. The use of καταλαβεῖν is not really similar (Her. 9. 106 πίστι τε καταλαβόντες καὶ ὁρκίοισι, Thuc. 4. 85 ὅρκοις...καταλαβὼν τὰ τέλη), since the κατά in comp. gives the sense of overtaking, and so of binding. Nor can we compare O. C. 284 ὥσπερ ἔλαβες τὸν ἱκέτην ἐχέγγυον, where the sense is,

J. S.   5

οὔτ' ἔκτανον γὰρ οὔτε τὸν κτανόντ' ἔχω
δεῖξαι. τὸ δὲ ζήτημα τοῦ πέμψαντος ἦν
Φοίβου τόδ' εἰπεῖν, ὅστις εἴργασταί ποτε.

ΟΙ. δίκαι' ἔλεξας· ἀλλ' ἀναγκάσαι θεοὺς   280
ἂν μὴ θέλωσιν οὐδ' ἂν εἷς δύναιτ' ἀνήρ.

ΧΟ. τὰ δεύτερ' ἐκ τῶνδ' ἂν λέγοιμ' ἁμοὶ δοκεῖ.

ΟΙ. εἰ καὶ τρίτ' ἐστί, μὴ παρῇς τὸ μὴ οὐ φράσαι.

ΧΟ. ἄνακτ' ἄνακτι ταῦθ' ὁρῶντ' ἐπίσταμαι
μάλιστα Φοίβῳ Τειρεσίαν, παρ' οὗ τις ἂν   285
σκοπῶν τάδ', ὦναξ, ἐκμάθοι σαφέστατα.

ΟΙ. ἀλλ' οὐκ ἐν ἀργοῖς οὐδὲ τοῦτ' ἐπραξάμην.
ἔπεμψα γὰρ Κρέοντος εἰπόντος διπλοῦς
πομπούς· πάλαι δὲ μὴ παρὼν θαυμάζεται.

281 Codices vel ἀν sine accentu praebent (ut L et A) vel ἂν: vera lectio ἄν, a Brunckio restituta, in nullo, quod sciam, extat.

' As thou hast *received* the (self-surrendered) suppliant under thy pledge.' **277** γάρ after ἔκτανον merely prefaces the statement: Plat. *Prot.* 320 C δοκεῖ τοίνυν...μῦθον ὑμῖν λέγειν. ἦν γάρ ποτε κ.τ.λ. **278** δεῖξαι, 'point to.' Note the emphatic place of the word: the speaker knows not that he is face to face with the slayer. τὸ ζήτημα, acc. of general reference. The simpler form would have been, ἦν τοῦ πέμψαντος τὸ ζήτημα καὶ λῦσαι: but, instead of a verb which could govern ζήτημα, τόδ' εἰπεῖν is substituted, because it conveniently introduces the clause ὅστις εἴργασται, explaining what the ζήτημα itself was. τὸ ζήτημα is then left much as ἃ αἰτεῖς is left in 216 when the insertion of ἀλκὴν κ.τ.λ. has modified the construction. **281** ἂν μὴ θέλωσιν κ.τ.λ. Cp. *Phil.* 1366 κἄμ' ἀναγκάζεις τάδε. ἂν as 580, 749: *O. C.* 13, *Ant.* 1057, *Phil.* 1276, *Ai.* 1085. οὐδ' ἂν εἷς: *Ant.* 884 οὐδ' ἂν εἷς παύσαιτ' ἄν: *O.C.* 1656 οὐδ' ἂν εἷς | θνητῶν φράσειε. In this emphatic form even a prep. could be inserted (Xen. *Hellen.* 5. 4. 1 οὐδ' ὑφ' ἑνός, *Cyr.* 4. 1. 14 μηδὲ πρὸς μίαν), and in prose οὐδὲ εἷς stood without elision: in Ar. *Ran.* 927 etc., where the MSS. have οὐδὲ ἕν (Dind. writes οὐδεὲν), οὐδ' ἂν ἕν is a possible *v. l.* **282** ἐκ τῶνδε = μετὰ τάδε: Dem. *de Cor.* § 313 λόγον ἐκ λόγου λέγων. For δεύτερα, second-*best*, cp. the proverb δεύτερος πλοῦς: Plat. *Legg.* 943 C τὴν τῶν ἀριστείων κρίσιν...καὶ τὴν τῶν δευτέρων καὶ τρίτων. ἂκ λέγοιμι: see on 95. **283** τὸ μὴ οὐ, not τὸ μή, because the sentence is negative: below, 1232: *Ant.* 544 μή

I am not the slayer, nor can I point to him who slew. As for the question, it was for Phoebus, who sent it, to tell us this thing—who can have wrought the deed.

OE. Justly said ; but no man on the earth can force the gods to what they will not.

CH. I would fain say what seems to me next best after this.

OE. If there is yet a third course, spare not to show it.

CH. I know that our lord Teiresias is the seer most like to our lord Phoebus; from whom, O king, a searcher of these things might learn them most clearly.

OE. Not even this have I left out of my cares. On the hint of Creon, I have twice sent a man to bring him ; and this long while I marvel why he is not here.

μ' ἀτιμάσῃς τὸ μὴ οὐ | θανεῖν. But even in such a negative sentence the simple τὸ μή occurs, below, 1387 : *Ant.* 443. 284 ἄνακτ' : *Od.* 11. 151 Τειρεσίαο ἄνακτος. ταὐτὰ ὁρῶντα, not = ταὐτὰ φρονοῦντα or γιγνώσκοντα, 'taking the same views,' but *seeing in the same manner, i.e.* with equal clearness : ὁρῶντα absol., as *O. C.* 74 ὅσ' ἂν ·λέγοιμι, πάνθ' ὁρῶντα λέξομαι : ταὐτὰ adverbial = κατὰ ταὐτά : the dat. ἄνακτι as *Her.* 4. 119 τωὐτὸ ἂν ὑμῖν ἐπρήσσομεν. 287 οὐκ ἐν ἀργοῖς τοῦτο κατέλιπον would have meant, ·' I did not leave this among things neglected.' Soph. fuses the negative form with the positive, and instead of κατέλιπον writes ἐπραξάμην : 'I saw to this (midd.) in such a manner that it also should not be among things neglected.' πράσσεσθαι (midd.) elsewhere usu. = 'to exact' (Thuc. 4. 65 etc.): here = διαπράσσεσθαι, effect for oneself. For ἐν cp. οὐκ ἐν ἐλαφρῷ ἐποιεύμην (Her. 1. 118), ἐν εὐχερεῖ | ἔθου (ταῦτα) *Phil.* 875, ταῦτ' οὖν ἐν αἰσχρῷ θέμενος Eur. *Hec.* 806. ἀργοῖς, not things *undone*, but things at which the work is sluggish or tardy ; *O. C.* 1605 κοὐκ ἦν ἔτ' οὐδὲν ἀργὸν ὧν ἐφίετο : Eur. *Phoen.* 766 ἐν δ' ἐστὶν ἡμῖν ἀργόν, εἴ τι θέσφατον | οἰωνόμαντις Τειρεσίας ἔχει φράσαι, *i.e.* 'in one thing our zeal has lagged,—the quest whether' &c.: Theognis however (583 Bergk 3rd ed.) has τὰ μὲν προβέβηκεν ἀμήχανόν ἐστι γενέσθαι | ἀργά, = ἀποίητα, *infecta.* 288 διπλοῦς | πομπούς; he had sent two successive messages—one messenger with each. πομπός = one who is sent to escort (πέμπειν) or fetch a person (*O. C.* 70). The words could mean (as Ellendt takes them) 'two sets of messengers' : but the other view is simpler, and consists equally well with οἶδε in 297. 289 μὴ παρὼν θαυμάζεται = θαυμάζω εἰ μὴ πάρεστι ; but with οὐ, = θαυμάζω ὅτι οὐ πάρεστι : differing nearly as ' I

ΧΟ. καὶ μὴν τά γ᾽ ἄλλα κωφὰ καὶ παλαί᾽ ἔπη.　　　290
ΟΙ. τὰ ποῖα ταῦτα; πάντα γὰρ σκοπῶ λόγον.
ΧΟ. θανεῖν ἐλέχθη πρός τινων ὁδοιπόρων.
ΟΙ. ἤκουσα κἀγώ· τὸν δ᾽ ἰδόντ᾽ οὐδεὶς ὁρᾷ.
ΧΟ. ἀλλ᾽ εἴ τι μὲν δὴ δείματός γ᾽ ἔχει μέρος,
τὰς σὰς ἀκούων οὐ μενεῖ τοιάσδ᾽ ἀράς.　　　295
ΟΙ. ᾧ μή 'στι δρῶντι τάρβος, οὐδ᾽ ἔπος φοβεῖ.
ΧΟ. ἀλλ᾽ οὑξελέγξων αὐτὸν ἔστιν· οἶδε γὰρ
τὸν θεῖον ἤδη μάντιν ὧδ᾽ ἄγουσιν, ᾧ

290 τά τ᾽ ἄλλα L. τά γ᾽ ἄλλα A: ubi γ᾽ non corrector dedit, sed manus prima, quae litteram δ facere inceperat, hanc autem in γ mutavit. 293 τὸν δ᾽ ἰδόντ᾽ codd. omnes. Anonymi coniecturam τὸν δὲ δρῶντ᾽, a Burtono citatam, receperunt Dindorf., Nauck., Blaydes. 294 δείματοσ τ̇ (sic) L, ubi τ̇ non prima scripsit manus, sed ex γ᾽ fecit corrector, facillima mutatione, cum formam Γ haberet: simile exemplum vides in v. 516. δείματός τ᾽ A et ceteri quos quidem cognoverim omnes: unus cod. Urb. 140 (Vat. c) τ᾽ an γ᾽ habeat, in dubio relinquit Campb. Haesisse tamen in illo τ᾽ grammaticos vel inde colligere potes quod in cod.

___

wonder *why*' and 'I wonder *that.*' Xen. *Anab.* 4. 4. 15 (he spoke of) τὰ μὴ ὄντα ὡς οὐκ ὄντα : *i.e.* εἴ τι μὴ ἦν, ἔλεγεν ὅτι οὐκ ἦν. 290 τά γ᾽ ἄλλα ...ἔπη : the rumours which were current—*apart from* the knowledge which the seer may have to give us. Not, '*the other* rumours.' Cp. Plat. *Phaed.* 110 E καὶ λίθοις καὶ γῇ καὶ τοῖς ἄλλοις ζῴοις τε καὶ φυτοῖς. κωφά : the rumour has died down ; it no longer gives a clear sound. Cp. fr. 604 λήθην τε τὴν ἅπαντ᾽ ἀπεστερημένην, | κωφήν, ἄναυδον. *Ai.* 911 ὁ πάντα κωφός, ὁ πάντ᾽ ἄϊδρις, reft of all sense and wit. 291 τὰ ποῖα, cp. 120. 292 ὁδοιπόρων: the survivor had spoken of λῃσταί, 122. The word now used comes nearer to the truth (cp. 801 ὁδοιπορῶν); but, as the next v. shows, Oed. does not regard this rumour as a different one from that which Creon had mentioned. 293 τὸν δ᾽ ἰδόντ᾽: the surviving eye-witness: cp. 119 ὧν εἶδε, πλὴν ἕν κ.τ.λ. Oed. has not yet learned that this witness could be produced: cp. vv. 754 ff. ἰδόντα is better than the conj. δρῶντα (1) as expressing, not merely that the culprit is unknown, but that no eye-witness of the deed is now at hand: (2) because, with ὁρᾷ, it has a certain ironical point,—expressing the king's incredulity as to anything being made of this clue. Cp. 105, 108. 294 δείματός γ᾽. δεῖμα, prop. 'an object of fear,' is used by Her. and the poets as = δέος: Her. 6. 74 Κλεομένεα...δεῖμα ἔλαβε Σπαρτιητέων: Aesch. *Suppl.* 566 χλωρῷ δείματι θυμὸν | πάλλοντ᾽: Eur. *Suppl.* 599 ὡς

CH.   Indeed (his skill apart) the rumours are but faint and old.

OE.   What rumours are they? I look to every story.

CH.   Certain wayfarers were said to have killed him.

OE.   I, too, have heard it, but none sees him who saw it.

CH.   Nay, if he knows what fear is, he will not stay when he hears thy curses, so dire as they are.

OE.   When a man shrinks not from a deed, neither is he scared by a word.

CH.   But there is one to convict him. For here they bring at last the godlike prophet, in whom

Paris. T τοι superscriptum inveni.   Quod et Hartung. et Kennedius coniecerunt, δειμάτων ἔχει μέρος, receperunt Ritter., Van Herwerden., Campb.   Vide annot.   **297** οὐξελλέγχων (sic) L.   Alterum λ erasit manus prima: ξ super γ scripsit aut prima (ut Duebnero visum est) aut antiqua.   οὐξελέγξων A, E, codd. Venet. 616, 467 (V², V³), Bodl. Laud. 54, Misc. 99, alii.   οὐξελέγχων B, T, V, V⁴, al. Codicum igitur auctoritas paullo gravior cum l. οὐξελέγξων facit.   Eodem inclinat maiore etiam, ut opinor, momento Graeci sermonis usus: vide annot.

μοι ὑφ᾽ ἥπατι δεῖμα χλοερὸν ταράσσει: id. *El.* 767 ἐκ δείματος, from fear. Cp. above, 153.   The γε gives emphasis: the ἀραί of Oed. were enough to scare the boldest.   Hartung and, independently, Prof. Kennedy conjecture δειμάτων ἔχει μέρος.   The plur. δείματα means either (*a*) objects of fear, or (*b*) much more rarely, *fears*, with reference to *some particular objects* already specified: as in *El.* 636 δειμάτων ἃ νῦν ἔχω, 'the terrors which I now suffer,' alluding to the *dreams*.   Here we seem to need the sing., 'fear.'   295 τὰς σὰς...ἀράς, thy curses: τοιάσδε, being such as they are.   297 οὐξελέγξων.   The present οὐξελέγχων would mean, 'there is one who convicts him': *i.e.* the supposed criminal, whom threats scare not, is already detected; for the prophet has come.   Cp. Isocr. or. 8. § 139 ὥστ᾽ οὐκ ἀπορήσομεν μεθ᾽ ὧν κωλύσομεν τοὺς ἐξαμαρτάνοντας, ἀλλὰ πολλοὺς ἕξομεν τοὺς ἑτοίμως καὶ προθύμως συναγωνιζομένους ἡμῖν: where, however, the present part. συναγωνιζομένους is relative to the future ἕξομεν.   To this it may be objected: (1) the *present* participle with ἔστιν would not be suitable unless the conviction were in act of taking place: (2) the fut. partic. not only suits the context better—'one *to convict* him' [supposing he is here]—but also agrees with the regular idiom: *e.g. Phil.* 1242 τίς ἔσται μ᾽ οὑπικωλύσων τάδε; *El.* 1197 οὐδ᾽ οὑπαρήξων οὐδ᾽ ὁ κωλύσων πάρα; (cp. *Ant.* 261): Aesch. *P. V.* 27 ὁ λωφήσων γὰρ οὐ πέφυκέ πω: Xen.

τἀληθὲς ἐμπέφυκεν ἀνθρώπων μόνῳ.

ΟΙ. ὦ πάντα νωμῶν Τειρεσία, διδακτά τε   300
ἄρρητά τ', οὐράνιά τε καὶ χθονοστιβῆ,
πόλιν μέν, εἰ καὶ μὴ βλέπεις, φρονεῖς δ' ὅμως
οἵᾳ νόσῳ σύνεστιν· ἧς σε προστάτην
σωτῆρά τ', ὦναξ, μοῦνον ἐξευρίσκομεν.
Φοῖβος γάρ, εἰ καὶ μὴ κλύεις τῶν ἀγγέλων,   305
πέμψασιν ἡμῖν ἀντέπεμψεν, ἔκλυσιν
μόνην ἂν ἐλθεῖν τοῦδε τοῦ νοσήματος,
εἰ τοὺς κτανόντας Λάϊον μαθόντες εὖ

305 εἰ καὶ μὴ codd.: εἴ τι μὴ L. Stephanus, Dindorf., Wunder., Hartung.

Anab. 2. 4. 5 ὁ ἡγησόμενος οὐδεὶς ἔσται. **299 ἐμπέφυκεν**, is implanted,—with reference to the divine gift of prophecy: Her. 9. 94 (of the seer Evenius) καὶ μετὰ ταῦτα αὐτίκα ἔμφυτον μαντικὴν εἶχε. **ἀνθρώπων μόνῳ,** above all other men: cp. *O. C.* 261 μόνας .. | σώζειν οἵας τε κ.τ.λ., Athens, above all other cities, can save: Isocr. or. 14. § 57 ὀφείλετε δὲ μόνοι τῶν Ἑλλήνων τοῦτον τὸν ἔρανον, *unice* (though others owe it also). **300 ὦ πάντα νωμῶν**: νωμάω (νεμ) means (1) to distribute, (2) to dispose, and so to wield, ply, (3) figuratively, to ponder, *animo versare*: ἐνὶ φρεσὶ κέρδε' ἐνώμας *Od.* 18. 216: ἐν ὠσὶ νωμῶν καὶ φρεσὶν πυρὸς δίχα | χρηστηρίους ὄρνιθας ἀψευδεῖ τέχνῃ Aesch. *Theb.* 25 (of Teiresias): (4) then, absolutely, to *observe*: Her. 4. 128 νωμῶντες ...σῖτα ἀναιρεομένους, observing the moment when they were cutting forage. Similarly here,—with the idea of *mental grasp* unaided by eyesight. Plato (*Crat.* 411 D) fancifully connects γνώμη with νώμησις, —τὸ γὰρ νωμᾶν καὶ τὸ σκοπεῖν ταὐτόν. **διδακτά τε | ἄρρητά τε,** cp. the colloquial ῥητὸν ἄρρητόν τ' ἔπος (*O. C.* 1001 *dicenda tacenda*): ἄρρητα = ἀπόρρητα: Her. 6. 135 ἄρρητα ἱρὰ ἐκφήνασαν. **301 οὐράνιά τε καὶ χθονοστιβῆ**: not in apposition with ἄρρητα and διδακτά respectively, but both referring to each, lore that may or that may not be told, whether of the sky or of the earth. Dindorf cp. Nicephorus Gregoras *Hist. Byz.* 695 D ἄκτιστα γενέσθαι πάντα τά τ' οὐράνια τά τε χθονοστιβῆ καὶ ὑδραῖα γένη: where, however, χθονοστιβῆ has its literal sense,—'walking the earth': here it is poet. for ἐπίγεια, 'the lowly things of earth.' **302 πόλιν μέν** is answered by σὺ δ' in 310: the *city's* state you know,—do then *your* part. The δὲ after φρονεῖς introduces

alone of men doth live the truth.

OE. Teiresias, whose soul grasps all things, the lore that may be told and the unspeakable, the secrets of heaven and the low things of earth,—thou feelest, though thou canst not see, what a plague doth haunt our State,—from which, great prophet, we find in thee our protector and only saviour. Now, Phoebus—if indeed thou knowest it not from the messengers—sent answer to our question that the only riddance from this pest which could come was if we should learn aright the slayers of Laïus,

---

the apodosis after a concessive protasis, as Her. 8. 22 εἰ δὲ ὑμῖν ἐστι τοῦτο μὴ δυνατὸν ποιῆσαι, ὑμέες δὲ (then) ἔτι καὶ νῦν ἐκ τοῦ μέσου ἡμῖν ἔζεσθε. Xen. Cyr. 5. 5. 21 ἀλλ' εἰ μηδὲ τοῦτο...βούλει ἀποκρίνασθαι, σὺ δὲ τοὐντεῦθεν λέγε. 303 ἧς sc. νόσου. προστάτην νόσου, a protector from a plague: strictly, one who stands in front of, *shields*, the city's distempered state. Cp. *Ai.* 803 πρόστητ' ἀναγκαίας τύχης, *shelter* my hard fate. In Eur. *Andr.* 220 χεῖρον' ἀρσένων νόσον | ταύτην νοσοῦμεν, ἀλλὰ προὖστημεν καλῶς, 'we suffer this distemper more cruelly than men, but ever rule it well,' the idea is that of *administering* (not protecting), as in προΐστασθαι τῆς ἡλικίας, to regulate one's own early years, Isocr. or. 15. § 290. Cp. 882. 304 μοῦνον: this Ionic form (like κοῦρος, δουρί, ξεῖνος, γούνατα) is used in dialogue by Soph.: Aesch. has not μοῦνος, though in *P. V.* 804 τόν τε μουνῶπα στρατόν. In [Eur.] *Rhes.* 31 μόναρχοι is now restored for μούναρχοι. 305 εἰ καὶ μὴ κλύεις, implying that he probably *has* heard it. *Ai.* 1127 δεινόν γ' εἶπας, εἰ καὶ ζῇς θανών. *Trach.* 71 πᾶν τοίνυν, εἰ καὶ τοῦτ' ἔτλη, κλύοι τις ἄν, if *indeed*. On εἰ καί and καὶ εἰ see Appendix, Note 8. Others would render, 'if you have not heard from the messengers *also*,' supposing it to be a hyperbaton for εἰ μὴ κλύεις καὶ τῶν ἀγγέλων. This is impossible. Prof. Campbell compares Thuc. 5. 45 καὶ ἦν ἐς τὸν δῆμον ταῦτα λέγωσιν, as if put for ἦν καὶ ἐς τὸν δῆμον: but there the passage runs thus; (Spartan envoys had been pleading with effect before the Athenian Βουλή:)—τὸν Ἀλκιβιάδην ἐφόβουν μὴ καί, ἢν ἐς τὸν δῆμον ταῦτα λέγωσιν, ἐπαγάγωνται τὸ πλῆθος καὶ ἀπωσθῇ ἡ Ἀργείων συμμαχία: where the καί before ἢν goes with ἐπαγάγωνται. Dindorf, Nauck and Blaydes are among those who adopt the conj. εἴ τι μή, 'unless *perchance*': for τι so used, see below 969, *O. C.* 1450, *Tr.* 586, 712: but no change is required. 308 μαθόντες εὖ. εὖ = 'with care,' 'aright': cp. *Ai.* 18 ἐπέγνως εὖ: *ib.* 528 ἐὰν τὸ ταχθὲν εὖ τολμᾷ τελεῖν. Meineke's conj. ἤ, adopted by

κτείναιμεν, ἢ γῆς φυγάδας ἐκπεμψαίμεθα.
σὺ δ᾽ οὖν φθονήσας μήτ᾽ ἀπ᾽ οἰωνῶν φάτιν   310
μήτ᾽ εἴ τιν᾽ ἄλλην μαντικῆς ἔχεις ὁδόν,
ῥῦσαι σεαυτὸν καὶ πόλιν, ῥῦσαι δ᾽ ἐμέ,
ῥῦσαι δὲ πᾶν μίασμα τοῦ τεθνηκότος.
ἐν σοὶ γὰρ ἐσμέν· ἄνδρα δ᾽ ὠφελεῖν ἀφ᾽ ὧν
ἔχοι τε καὶ δύναιτο κάλλιστος πόνων.   315

ΤΕΙΡΕΣΙΑΣ.

φεῦ φεῦ, φρονεῖν ὡς δεινὸν ἔνθα μὴ τέλη
λύῃ φρονοῦντι. ταῦτα γὰρ καλῶς ἐγὼ
εἰδὼς διώλεσ᾽· οὐ γὰρ ἂν δεῦρ᾽ ἱκόμην.
ΟΙ. τί δ᾽ ἔστιν; ὡς ἄθυμος εἰσελήλυθας.

310 Errant, credo, qui lectionem σὺ νῦν, nusquam alibi inventam, cod. Laurentiano imputant. Prima manus, nisi fallor, non σὺ νῦν verum σὺ οὖν (omisso δ᾽)
scripserat, δ᾽ recentior supplevit. σύ νυν Blaydes.   315 Mendosa l. ἔχει non
in A solo occurrit, sed etiam in V³, Bodl. Laud. 54, Barocc. 66; videtur in Misc. 99

Nauck, is weak, and against the rhythm. 310 ἀπ᾽ οἰωνῶν φάτιν: for
ἀπό, see 43: φάτιν, 151. 311 ἄλλην ὁδόν, as divination by fire (see on
21), to which Teiresias resorts (Ant. 1005) when the voice of birds fails
him. 312 ῥῦσαι σεαυτὸν κ.τ.λ. ῥύεσθαί τι is to draw a thing to oneself, and
so to protect it. ῥῦσαι μίασμα here = literally, 'take the defilement under
thy care'; i.e. 'make it thy care to remove the defilement.' Cp. πρόστητ᾽
ἀναγκαίας τύχης (Ai. 803), shelter my hard fate, (instead of, 'shelter me from
it'). πᾶν μίασμα, the whole defilement, as affecting not only human life
but also the herds and flocks and the fruits of the earth: cp. 253. τοῦ
τεθνηκότος, gen. of the source from which the μίασμα springs,—more
pathetic than τοῦ φόνου, as reminding the hearer that vengeance is due
for innocent blood. Both πᾶν and the usual sense of μίασμα forbid us
to understand, 'avenge the uncleanness [i.e. the unpunished murder] of
the dead man.' For ῥῦσαι δὲ Blaydes conj. λῦσον δὲ, comparing Eur.
Or. 598 μίασμα λῦσαι. But the triple ῥῦσαι is essential to the force.
314 ἐν σοὶ = penes te: O. C. 248 ἐν ὑμῖν ὡς θεῷ | κείμεθα τλάμονες: Eur.
Alc. 278 ἐν σοὶ δ᾽ ἐσμὲν καὶ ζῆν καὶ μή. ἄνδρα, accus. before, not after,
ὠφελεῖν, as in Ant. 710 ἀλλ᾽ ἄνδρα, κεἴ τις ᾖ σοφός, τὸ μανθάνειν | πόλλ᾽
αἰσχρὸν οὐδέν. In both places ἄνδρα has a certain stress—'for mortal
man.' But in Ai. 1344 ἄνδρα δ᾽ οὐ δίκαιον, εἰ θάνοι, | βλάπτειν τὸν ἐσθλόν,

and slay them, or send them into exile from our land. Do
thou, then, grudge neither voice of birds nor any other way
of seer-lore that thou hast, but rescue thyself and the State,
rescue me, rescue all that is defiled by the dead. For we are
in thy hand; and man's noblest task is to help others by his
best means and powers.

TEIRESIAS.

Alas, how dreadful to have wisdom where it profits not the
wise! Aye, I knew this well, but let it slip out of mind; else
would I never have come here.

OE. What now? How sad thou hast come in!

quoque ἔχοι ab ἔχει ortum esse. πόνοσ L, ubi ων antiqui correctoris est: πόνων A,
B, V⁴, L². πόνων (sic, non πόνοσ πόνων) E. Itaque lectio πόνων, quae elegantior
est, etiam librorum auctoritate plus valet quam πόνος. **317** λύηι L, λύη (sic) L²,
Γ, Pal. Contra A et plerique λύει, quod 'ut gravius dictum' praetulerunt Hermann.
et Erfurdt. Vide tamen annot.

ανδρα is the object, agreeing with τὸν ἐσθλόν. **315** ἀφ' ὧν ἔχοι τε καὶ
δύναιτο, by means of all his *resources* and *faculties*. The optat., as *Ant.*
666 ἀλλ' ὃν πόλις στήσειε, τοῦδε χρὴ κλύειν: Xen. *Cyr.* 1. 6. 19 ἀλλὰ τοῦ
μὲν αὐτὸν λέγειν, ἃ μὴ σαφῶς εἰδείη, φείδεσθαι δεῖ. The force of the mood
may be seen by putting the sentence in a hypothetical form: εἴ τις ὠφε-
λοίη ἀφ' ὧν ἔχοι, κάλλιστα ἂν πονοίη. **317** λύη: for subjunct. without ἄν,
cp. *O. C.* 395 ὃς νέος πέσῃ: *Ai.* 1074 ἔνθα μὴ καθεστήκῃ δέος: *Tr.*
1008 ὅ τι καὶ μύσῃ. On the other hand, the indic. λύει would state
the fact: cp. *O. C.* 839 μὴ 'πίτασσ' ἃ μὴ κρατεῖς: *ib.* 1442 μὴ πεῖθ'
ἃ μὴ δεῖ. But L has λύη and some other MSS. have λύη: and it is
much more likely that this should have become λύει than *vice versa*.
τέλη λύη = λυσιτελῇ, only here: cp. Eur. *Alc.* 627 φημὶ τοιούτους γάμους |
λύειν βροτοῖς. ταῦτα γὰρ (I have to bewail this now), *for,* though I
once knew it, I had forgotten it. Teiresias, twice summoned (288), had
come reluctantly. Only now, in the presence of Oedipus, does he realise
the full horror of the secret which he holds. **318** διώλεσ' = let slip out
of my memory; perh. a common use, though it occurs only here: cp.
σώζεσθαι to *remember*, Plat. *Theaet.* 153 B κτᾶταί τε μαθήματα καὶ σώζεται: *Rep.* 455 B ἃ ἔμαθε, σώζεται: and so Soph. *El.* 993, 1257. So
Terent. *Phormio* 2. 3. 39 *perii hercle: nomen perdidi,* 'have forgotten.'
319 τί δ' ἔστιν; *El.* 920 φεῦ τῆς ἀνοίας...ΧΡΥΣ. τί δ' ἔστιν; and so often in

74 ΣΟΦΟΚΛΕΟΥΣ

ΤΕ. ἄφες μ' ἐς οἴκους· ῥᾷστα γὰρ τὸ σόν τε σὺ   320
κἀγὼ διοίσω τοὐμόν, ἢν ἐμοὶ πίθῃ.

ΟΙ. οὔτ' ἔννομ' εἶπας οὔτε προσφιλῆ πόλει
τῇδ', ἢ σ' ἔθρεψε, τήνδ' ἀποστερῶν φάτιν.

ΤΕ. ὁρῶ γὰρ οὐδὲ σοὶ τὸ σὸν φώνημ' ἰὸν
πρὸς καιρόν· ὡς οὖν μηδ' ἐγὼ ταὐτὸν πάθω.   325

ΟΙ. μὴ πρὸς θεῶν φρονῶν γ' ἀποστραφῇς, ἐπεὶ
πάντες σε προσκυνοῦμεν οἵδ' ἱκτήριοι.

ΤΕ. πάντες γὰρ οὐ φρονεῖτ'. ἐγὼ δ' οὐ μή ποτε
τἄμ', ὡς ἂν εἴπω μὴ τὰ σ', ἐκφήνω κακά.

ΟΙ. τί φῇς; ξυνειδὼς οὐ φράσεις, ἀλλ' ἐννοεῖς   330
ἡμᾶς προδοῦναι καὶ καταφθεῖραι πόλιν;

322 οὔτ' ἐννο μ' (sic) L, in rasura: mox προσφιλῆ, ubi εσ corrector addidit. Prima manus, credo, ἔννομον scripserat, ipsa autem in ἔννομ' correxit, dein recte προσφιλῆ dedit. ἔννομον habent pauci codd.; προσφιλὲς autem A et reliqui fere omnes qui ἔννομ' praebent. Ipsum autem προσφιλὲς ab ἔννομον illo fluxit. Sic primo errore sublato

---

Soph.: δέ marking that the attention is turned to a new point, as in τί δ'; *quid vero?* (941), or to a new person: Isaeus or. 8. § 24 σὺ δὲ τίς εἶ; 321 διοίσω, bear to the end: Eur. *Hipp.* 1143 δάκρυσι διοίσω | πότμον ἄποτμον, *live out* joyless days: Thuc. 1. 11 εἰ ξυνεχῶς τὸν πόλεμον διέφερον. διαφέρειν could not mean 'to bear *apart*' (from each other), though that is implied. **322** οὔτ' ἔννομ' κ.τ.λ. οὐκ ἔννομα, not in conformity with usage, which entitled the State to benefit by the wisdom of its μάντις. The king's first remonstrances are gentle. **323** ἀποστερῶν 'withholding': Arist. *Rhet.* 2. 6. 3 ἀποστερῆσαι παρακαταθήκην, *depositum non reddere*. φάτιν, of a divine message, 151. **324** ὁρῶ γὰρ κ.τ.λ. (*I* do *not* speak), for I see that *neither* dost *thou* speak opportunely: (I am silent) therefore, lest I too should speak unseasonably. **325** πρὸς καιρόν = καιρίως, as with ἐννέπειν *Trach.* 59. ὡς μηδὲ ἐγὼ πάθω is irregular for μὴ καὶ ἐγὼ πάθω, influenced by the *form* of the preceding clause with οὐδὲ σοί. The sense requires that μηδέ should be broken up into μή *not*, δέ *on the other hand*. The final clause ὡς...πάθω depends on σιγῶ, or the like, understood. **326** μὴ πρὸς θεῶν κ.τ.λ. The attribution of these two verses to the Chorus in some MSS. is probably due to the plur. in 327 having misled those who did not see that the king speaks for all Thebes. φρονῶν γ', if thou hast understanding (of this matter): cp. 569 ἐφ' οἷς γὰρ μὴ φρονῶ σιγᾶν φιλῶ: not, 'if thou art sane.' But in 328 οὐ φρονεῖτε = 'are

TE. Let me go home; 'twill be best that thou bear thine own burden to the end, and I mine—if thou wilt heed me.

OE. Thy words are strange, nor kindly to this State which nurtured thee, when thou withholdest this response.

TE. Nay, I see that thou, on thy part, openest not thy lips in season : therefore take I heed lest I, too, have the like hap.

OE. For the love of the gods, turn not away, if thou hast knowledge : all we suppliants implore thee on our knees.

TE. Aye, for ye are all without knowledge; but never will I reveal my griefs—that I say not thine.

OE. How sayest thou? Thou knowest the secret, and wilt not tell it, but art minded to betray us and to destroy the State?

---

secundus mansit. **326, 327** Hos versus Oedipo recte tribuit L: quos quod choro A aliique codd. assignant, versum 327 causae fuisse credo. Parum tempestive se chorus interponit dum crescente sensim ira rex et vates colloquontur. Cum vehemens oratio utrimque iam exarsit, tum demum convenienter intercedit chorus (v. 404).

---

without understanding,' are senseless. **328** ἐγὼ δ' οὐ μή ποτε ἐκφήνω τὰ ἐμὰ (ὡς ἂν μὴ εἴπω τὰ σὰ) κακά: I will never reveal my (not to call them *thy*) griefs. τὰ ἐμὰ κακά, = those secrets touching Oedipus which lie heavy on the prophet's soul: τὰ σὰ κακά, those same secrets in their import for Oedipus. We might render ὡς ἂν εἴπω μὴ τὰ σ' either (i) as above, or (ii) 'in order that I may not utter thy griefs.' But (i) is preferable for these reasons :—(1) The subjunct. εἴπω with μή was familiar in such phrases. Plat. *Rep.* 487 D τοὺς μὲν πλείστους καὶ πάνυ ἀλλοκότους γιγνομένους, ἵνα μὴ παμπονήρως εἴπωμεν, 'becoming very strange persons,—not to use a more unqualified epithet:' *Rep.* 507 D οὐδ' ἄλλαις πολλαῖς, ἵνα μὴ εἴπω οὐδεμιᾷ, τοιούτου προσδεῖ οὐδενός, i. e. few,—not to say none: *Hippias minor* 372 D τοιοῦτός εἰμι οἷός πέρ εἰμι, ἵνα μηδὲν ἐμαυτὸν μεῖζον εἴπω,—to say nothing more of myself. The substitution of ὡς ἂν for the commoner ἵνα in no way alters the meaning. For ὡς ἂν μή, cp. Ar. *Av.* 1508 τουτὶ...τὸ σκιάδειον ὑπέρεχε | ἄνωθεν, ὡς ἂν μή μ' ἴδωσιν οἱ θεοί. For ὡς ἂν εἴπω μὴ instead of ὡς ἂν μὴ εἴπω, cp. 255, *Phil.* 66 εἰ δ' ἐργάσει | μὴ ταῦτα. (2) The emphatic position of τἄμ' suits this version. (3) ἐκφήνω is more forcible than εἴπω. If the meaning were, 'I will not *reveal* my griefs, in order that I may not *mention* (εἴπω) thy griefs,' the clauses would be ill-balanced. See Appendix, Note 9. **330** ξυνειδώς,

ΤΕ. ἐγὼ οὔτ᾽ ἐμαυτὸν οὔτε σ᾽ ἀλγυνῶ. τί ταῦτ᾽
    ἄλλως ἐλέγχεις; οὐ γὰρ ἂν πύθοιό μου.

ΟΙ. οὐκ, ὦ κακῶν κάκιστε, καὶ γὰρ ἂν πέτρου
    φύσιν σύ γ᾽ ὀργάνειας, ἐξερεῖς ποτέ,   335
    ἀλλ᾽ ὧδ᾽ ἄτεγκτος κἀτελεύτητος φανεῖ;

ΤΕ. ὀργὴν ἐμέμψω τὴν ἐμήν, τὴν σὴν δ᾽ ὁμοῦ
    ναίουσαν οὐ κατεῖδες, ἀλλ᾽ ἐμὲ ψέγεις.

ΟΙ. τίς γὰρ τοιαῦτ᾽ ἂν οὐκ ἂν ὀργίζοιτ᾽ ἔπη
    κλύων, ἃ νῦν σὺ τήνδ᾽ ἀτιμάζεις πόλιν;   340

ΤΕ. ἥξει γὰρ αὐτά, κἂν ἐγὼ σιγῇ στέγω.

332 ἐγὼ οὔτ᾽ cum paucis codd. B et Bodl. Barocc. 66: ἐγώ τ᾽ L, A, plerique.
τ᾽ illud tanquam pro οὔτε positum explicabant, ut docent scholiastae verba, ἀπὸ κοινοῦ
τὸ οὐ.   337 ὁρμὴν L. Est γ ab antiqua manu. Credit Duebnerus ipsum illud

---

because ἐκφήνω implied that he knew. Cp. 704 αὐτὸς ξυνειδὼς ἢ
μαθὼν ἄλλου πάρα, *i.e.* of his own knowledge, or on hearsay? Not,
'being an accomplice' (as *Ant.* 266 ξυνειδέναι | τὸ πρᾶγμα βουλεύ-
σαντι): Oed. can still control his rising anger. 332 ἐγὼ οὔτ᾽ κ.τ.λ.
The ruggedness of this verse is perh. designed to express agitation.
Cp. 1002 ἐγὼ οὐχὶ: *O. C.* 939 ἐγὼ οὔτ᾽ ἄνανδρον: *ib.* 998 ἐγὼ οὐδὲ: *Ant.*
458 ἐγὼ οὐκ ἔμελλον. ταῦτ᾽; see on 29. 334 πέτρου | φύσιν: Eur. *Med.*
1279 ὦ τάλαιν᾽, ὡς ἄρ᾽ ἦσθα πέτρος ἢ σίδα|ρος. For the periphrasis cp.
Plat. *Phaedr.* 251 B ἡ τοῦ πτεροῦ φύσις, = τὸ πτερόν, πεφυκὸς ὥσπερ πέφυκε,
being constituted as it is: *Timae.* 45 B τὴν τῶν βλεφάρων φύσιν: 74 D
τὴν τῶν νεύρων φ.: 84 C ἡ τοῦ μυελοῦ φύσις: *Legg.* 145 D τὴν ὕδατος
φύσιν. And so often in Arist., *e.g.* ἡ τοῦ πνεύματος φύσις *Meteor.* 2. 8:
ἡ τῶν νεύρων φύσις *Hist. Anim.* 3. 5. 335 ποτέ, *tandem aliquando: Phil.*
816 μέθες ποτέ: *ib.* 1041 τίσασθ᾽ ἀλλὰ τῷ χρόνῳ ποτέ. 336 ἀτελεύτητος,
not brought to an end: *Il.* 4. 175 ἀτελευτήτῳ ἐπὶ ἔργῳ. Plut. *Mor.* 114 F
τὸ γὰρ δὴ ἀτελεύτητον νομίζειν τὸ πένθος ἀνοίας ἐστὶν ἐσχάτης. Here, a
man 'with whom one cannot make an end,'—who cannot be brought to
the desired issue. In freely rendering, 'Wilt thou never make an end?'
we remember, of course, that the adj. could not literally mean 'not
finishing.' Possibly it is borrowed from the colloquial vocabulary of the
day: the tone is like that of the Latin *odiosus.* 337 ἐμέμψω, aor. referring to the moment just past: so oft. ἐπήνεσα, ξυνῆκα, ἥσθην: ἀπέ-

TE. I will pain neither myself nor thee. Why vainly ask these things? Thou wilt not learn them from me.

OE. What, basest of the base,—for thou wouldest anger a very stone,—wilt thou never speak out? Can nothing touch thee? Wilt thou never make an end?

TE. Thou blamest my temper, but seest not that to which thou thyself art wedded : no, thou findest fault with me.

OE. And who would not be angry to hear the words with which thou now dost slight this city?

TE. The future will come of itself, though I shroud it in silence.

μ prius γ fuisse: equidem vero propius duco primam manum calami lapsu ὁρμὴν scripsisse. Nullum alias eiusdem mendi vestigium. τὴν σὴν δ' L, A, ceteri paene omnes. Dindorfius 'ex duobus apographis' τὴν σοὶ δ' in textum recepit. Hoc in V⁴ quidem inveni: alter Dindorfii codex quis sit, nescio. Sed vide annot.

πτύσα (Eur. *Hec.* 1276) : ἐδεξάμην (Soph. *El.* 668). ὁμοῦ | ναίουσαν, while (or though) it dwells close to thee,—possesses and sways thee. Cp. *O. C.* κηλὶς (1134) and βλάβη (*El.* 785) ξύνοικος: συνναίειν πόνοις (*Ph.* 892): συντρόφοις | ὀργαῖς (*Ai.* 639). But (as Eustathius saw, 755. 14) the words have a second meaning: 'thou seest not that thine own [τὴν σήν, thy kinswoman, thy mother] is dwelling with thee [as thy wife].' The ambiguity of τὴν σήν, the choice of the phrase ὁμοῦ ναίουσαν, the choice of κατεῖδες, leave no doubt of this. Cp. 261. **338 ἀλλ' ἐμὲ ψέγεις** : the thought of ὀργὴν ἐμέμψω τὴν ἐμήν returns upon itself, as if from a sense that the contrast between ἐμέμψω and κατεῖδες would be imperfectly felt without such an iteration : this is peculiarly Sophoclean ; cp. above 166 (ἔλθετε καὶ νῦν): Schneidewin cp. also *Ai.* 1111 οὐ...τῆς σῆς οὕνεκ'... | ἀλλ' οὕνεχ' ὅρκων... | σοῦ δ' οὐδέν : and similarly *Trach.* 431. **339** The emphasis on τοιαῦτα as well as on οὐκ warrants the repeated ἄν: Eur. *Andr.* 934 οὐκ ἄν ἕν γ' ἐμοῖς δόμοις | βλέπουσ' ἂν αὐγὰς τἄμ' ἐκαρποῦτ' ἂν λέχη. **340 ἅ...ἀτιμάζεις πόλιν:** ἅ cogn. accus.: *Ai.* 1107 τὰ σέμν' ἔπη | κόλαζ' ἐκείνους: *Ant.* 550 τί ταῦτ' ἀνιᾶς μ'; ἀτιμάζεις, by rejecting the request that he would speak : *Ant.* 544. **341 ἥξει γὰρ αὐτά.** The subject to ἥξει is designedly left indeterminate : '(the things of which I wot) will come of themselves.' The seer is communing with his own thought, which dwells darkly on the κακά of v. 329. αὐτά = αὐτόματα: *Il.* 17. 252 ἀργαλέον δέ μοί ἐστι διασκοπιᾶσθαι ἕκαστον... | ἀλλά τις αὐτὸς ἴτω. Cp. the phrase αὐτὸ δείξει, *res ipsa arguet*, the result will show :

78 ΣΟΦΟΚΛΕΟΥΣ

ΟΙ. οὐκοῦν ἅ γ᾽ ἥξει καὶ σὲ χρὴ λέγειν ἐμοί.

ΤΕ. οὐκ ἂν πέρα φράσαιμι. πρὸς τάδ᾽, εἰ θέλεις,
θυμοῦ δι᾽ ὀργῆς ἥτις ἀγριωτάτη.

ΟΙ. καὶ μὴν παρήσω γ᾽ οὐδέν, ὡς ὀργῆς ἔχω,   345
ἅπερ ξυνίημ᾽. ἴσθι γὰρ δοκῶν ἐμοὶ
καὶ ξυμφυτεῦσαι τοὔργον, εἰργάσθαι θ᾽, ὅσον
μὴ χερσὶ καίνων· εἰ δ᾽ ἐτύγχανες βλέπων,
καὶ τοὔργον ἂν σοῦ τοῦτ᾽ ἔφην εἶναι μόνου.

ΤΕ. ἄληθες; ἐννέπω σὲ τῷ κηρύγματι   350
ᾧπερ προεῖπας ἐμμένειν, κἀφ᾽ ἡμέρας
τῆς νῦν προσαυδᾶν μήτε τούσδε μήτ᾽ ἐμέ,
ὡς ὄντι γῆς τῆσδ᾽ ἀνοσίῳ μιάστορι.

347 εἰργάσθαι δ᾽ L, quod recepit Hermann., 'perpetrasse *autem*' intelligens:
'i.e. perpetrasse autem non ipsum, sed per alios.' Quo facto perditur sententiae

---

Soph. fr. 355 ταχὺ δ᾽ αὐτὸ δείξει τοὔργον. **342** οὐκοῦν ἅ γ᾽ ἥξει. Elmsley,
Nauck and Hartung read οὐκ οὖν...ἐμοί; but the positive χρὴ is stronger
without the query. 'Then, seeing that they will *come*, thou on thy part
(καὶ σὲ) shouldest *tell* them to me.' The stress of καὶ falls primarily on
σὲ, but serves at the same time to contrast λέγειν with ἥξει. In ἅ γ᾽ ἥξει
the causal force of the relative is brought out by γε: *quippe quae ventura
sint.* **343** οὐκ ἂν πέρα φράσαιμι. The courteous formula (95, 282), just
because it is such, here expresses fixed resolve. **344** ἥτις ἀγριωτάτη: *Il.*
17. 61 ὅτε τίς τε λέων...βοῦν ἁρπάσῃ ἥτις ἀρίστη: Plat. *Apol.* 23 A πολλαὶ
ἀπέχθειαι...καὶ οἷαι χαλεπώταται: Dem. *Olynth.* 2. § 18 εἰ μὲν γάρ τις
ἀνήρ ἐστιν ἐν αὐτοῖς οἷος ἔμπειρος πολέμου καὶ ἀγώνων [*sc.* ἐστί], τούτους,
κ.τ.λ. **345** καὶ μὴν with γε, 'aye verily': cp. *El.* 554 where ἦν ἐφῇς μοι
is answered (556) by καὶ μὴν ἐφίημ᾽. ὡς ὀργῆς ἔχω = ἔχων ὀργῆς ὡς ἔχω,
being so wroth as I am. Thuc. 1. 22 ὡς ἑκατέρων τις εὐνοίας ἢ μνήμης
ἔχοι: Eur. *Hel.* 313 πῶς δ᾽ εὐμενείας τοισίδ᾽ ἐν δόμοις ἔχεις; παρήσω...
οὐδὲν (τούτων) ἅπερ ξυνίημ᾽, I will leave unsaid nothing (of those things)
which I comprehend, *i.e.* I will reveal my whole insight into the plot.
ξυνίημι suits the intellectual pride of Oedipus: he does not say 'think'
or 'suspect': cp. 628. For γὰρ after ἴσθι cp. 277. **347** καὶ ξυμφυτεῦσαι
...εἰργάσθαι θ᾽. καὶ...τε could no more stand for 'and'...'both' than et...
que could. καὶ here (adeo) implies, 'no mere *sympathiser*, but *actually* the

OE. Then, seeing that it must come, thou on thy part should'st tell me thereof.

TE. I will speak no further ; rage, then, if thou wilt, with the fiercest wrath thy heart doth know.

OE. Aye, verily, I will not spare—so wroth I am—to speak all my thought. Know that thou seemest to me e'en to have helped in plotting the deed, and to have done it, short of slaying with thy hands. Hadst thou eye-sight, I would have said that the doing, also, of this thing was thine alone.

TE. In sooth?— I charge thee that thou abide by the decree of thine own mouth, and from this day speak neither to these nor to me: *thou* art the accursed defiler of this land.

---

gradatio sive κλῖμαξ: forti enim dicto non iam fortius sed lenius subicitur. **351**
προσεῖπας codd.: προεῖπας Brunck.

---

plotter.' ξυμφυτεῦσαι: Pind. *Isth.* 5 (6) 12 σύν τε οἱ δαίμων φυτεύει δόξαν: *Ai.* 953 Παλλὰς φυτεύει πῆμα: *El.* 198 δεινὰν δεινῶς προφυτεύσαντες | μορφάν (of crime). ὅσον (εἶχες εἰργάσθαι) μὴ καίνων, so far as you could be the author of the deed without slaying: Thuc. 4. 16 φυλάσσειν δὲ καὶ τὴν νῆσον Ἀθηναίους μηδὲν ἧσσον, ὅσα μὴ ἀποβαίνον-τας: I. 111 τῆς γῆς ἐκράτουν ὅσα μὴ προϊόντες πολὺ ἐκ τῶν ὅπλων: *Trach.* 1214 | ὅσον γ' ἂν (sc. δρῷην τοῦτο) αὐτὸς μὴ ποτιψαύων χεροῖν. **349** καὶ τοὔργον...τοῦτο, the *doing* of this thing also, αὐτὴν τὴν πρᾶξιν, as dist. from the plotting and the direction of the act. **350** ἄληθες; κ.τ.λ. The same word marks the climax of Creon's anger in *Ant.* 758: cp. Ar. *Av.* 393 ἐτεόν; etc. ἐννέπω σὲ...ἐμμένειν I command that thou abide: so *Phil.* 101 λέγω σε...λαβεῖν. **351** ᾧπερ προεῖπας (sc. ἐμμένειν), by which thou didst proclaim that (all) should abide: this is better than taking ᾧπερ as by attraction for ὅπερ, since προεῖπον could take an acc. of *the thing proclaimed* (e.g. ξενίαν, πόλεμον, θάνατον), but not of the edict itself (as κήρυγμα). **353** ὡς ὄντι...μιάστορι, an anacolouthon for ὡς ὄντα...μιάστορα, as if ἐννέπω σοί had preceded. ἐμέ just before made this necessary. In Eur. *Med.* 57 most MSS. give ὥσθ' ἵμερός μ' ὑπῆλθε γῆ τε κοὐρανῷ | λέξαι μολούσῃ δεῦρο δεσποίνης τύχας, where Porson, reading μολοῦσαν, admits that the dat. stands in Philemon's parody (Athenaeus 288 D) ὡς ἵμερός μ' ὑπῆλθε γῆ τε κοὐρανῷ | λέξαι μολόντι τοὔψον ὡς ἐσκεύασα. Elms. cp. Eur. *I. A.* 491 ἄλλως τέ μ' ἔλεος τῆς

ΟΙ. οὕτως ἀναιδῶς ἐξεκίνησας τόδε
τὸ ῥῆμα; καὶ ποῦ τοῦτο φεύξεσθαι δοκεῖς;   355
ΤΕ. πέφευγα· τἀληθὲς γὰρ ἰσχῦον τρέφω.
ΟΙ. πρὸς τοῦ διδαχθείς; οὐ γὰρ ἔκ γε τῆς τέχνης.
ΤΕ. πρὸς σοῦ· σὺ γάρ μ' ἄκοντα προὐτρέψω λέγειν.
ΟΙ. ποῖον λόγον; λέγ' αὖθις, ὡς μᾶλλον μάθω.
ΤΕ. οὐχὶ ξυνῆκας πρόσθεν; ἢ 'κπειρᾷ λέγων;   360
ΟΙ. οὐχ ὥστε γ' εἰπεῖν γνωστόν· ἀλλ' αὖθις φράσον.

360 ἢ ἐκπειρᾷι λέγειν L. Littera o, quae super ἐ scripta a manu rec.
iam paene evanuit, coniecturam λόγων videtur indicare. Lectionis λέγοι nullum
vestigium est. ἢ 'κπειρᾷ (sic) λέγειν A, et ceteri, scripto in quibusdam 'κ

ταλαιπώρου κόρης | εἰσῆλθε συγγένειαν ἐννοουμένῳ. **354 ἐξεκίνησας.** ἐκκινεῖν
is used of *starting* game, *El.* 567 ἐξεκίνησεν ποδοῖν | ...ἔλαφον: of *rousing*
one from rest, *Trach.* 1242, and fig. of *exciting* pain which had been
lulled, *ib.* 979. Here the notion is that of a sudden and startling
utterance. But the choice of the word has also been influenced by the
common use of κινεῖν in the sense of mooting subjects which should not
have been touched: Eur. *El.* 302 ἐπεὶ δὲ κινεῖς μῦθον, *i.e.* since thou
hast broached this theme: cp. *O. C.* 1526 ἃ δ' ἐξάγιστα μηδὲ κινεῖται
λόγῳ. In Eur. *Med.* 1317 τί τάσδε κινεῖς κἀναμοχλεύεις πύλας; Porson,
with the author of the *Christus Patiens*, reads λόγους, thinking that
Ar. *Nub.* 1399 ὦ καινῶν ἐπῶν | κινητὰ καὶ μοχλευτά alluded to that place.
So ἀκίνητα (ἔπη) = ἀπόρρητα *O. C.* 624, *Ant.* 1060 ὄρσεις με τἀκίνητα
διὰ φρενῶν φράσαι. | κίνει, κ.τ.λ. **355 καὶ ποῦ κ.τ.λ.** And on what ground
dost thou think to escape (punishment for) this thing? For ποῦ cp.
390: *Ai.* 1100 ποῦ σὺ στρατηγεῖς τοῦδε; Distinguish καὶ (1) *prefixed* to
interrogative particles, when it expresses an objection: Aesch. *Ag.* 280
καὶ τίς τόδ' ἐξίκοιτ' ἂν ἀγγέλων τάχος; Dem. *Fals. Legat.* § 257 (with
Shilleto's note), and καὶ πῶς; *passim*: (2) *suffixed*, where, granting a
fact, it asks for further information: *Agam.* 278 ποίου χρόνου δὲ καὶ
πεπόρθηται πόλις; (assuming it to be taken, *when was* it taken?) Eur.
Alc. 834 ποῦ καί σφε θάπτει; **τοῦτο φεύγειν** here = τούτου τὴν δίκην
ἐκφεύγειν: Eur. *Med.* 795 παίδων φόνον | φεύγουσα, fleeing from (the
penalties of) the murder: Cic. *Pro Cluent.* 59 § 163 *calumniam* (=*crimen
calumniae*) *non effugiet.* But in Lys. *In Erat.* § 34 τοῦτο...οὐ φεύγω = 'I
do not avoid this point.' **356 ἰσχῦον** expresses the living strength of the
divine instinct within him: cp. ζῶντα 482. **τρέφω:** see on ἐμπέφυκεν
299. **357 τέχνης,** slightly contemptuous; cp. 388, 562, 709. **358 προὐ-**

OE. So brazen with thy blustering taunt? And wherein dost thou trust to escape thy due?

TE. I have escaped: in my truth is my strength.

OE. Who taught thee this? It was not, at least, thine art.

TE. Thou: for thou didst spur me into speech against my will.

OE. What speech? Speak again that I may learn it better.

TE. Didst thou not take my sense before? Or art thou tempting me in talk?

OE. No, I took it not so that I can call it known :—speak again.

πειρᾷ (sic). ἢ πειρᾷ λέγων; Hartung.: ἢ 'κπειρᾷ λόγῳ; Campb.: οὐχὶ ξυνῆκας; πρὸς τί μου 'κπειρᾷ λέγειν; proposuit Blaydes.

τρέψω: the midd., as 1446: but the act., *Ant.* 270, *El.* 1193. 360 ἢ 'κπειρᾷ λέγων; or (while you *do* understand my meaning already) are you merely trying by your talk (λέγων) to provoke a still fuller statement of it? Her. 3. 135 δείσας μή εὖ ἐκπειρῷτο Δαρεῖος, was making trial of him: Ar. *Eq.* 1234 καί σου τοσοῦτο πρῶτον ἐκπειράσομαι· 'thus far make trial of thee' (test thee by one question). The notion of ἐκ in the compound is that of *drawing forth* something from the person tested. λέγων here implies *idle* talk, cp. 1151 λέγει γὰρ εἰδὼς οὐδέν: *Phil.* 55 τὴν Φιλοκτήτου σε δεῖ | ψυχὴν ὅπως λόγοισιν ἐκκλέψεις λέγων: where, as here, the partic. denotes the process. If we read λέγειν, we must supply ὥστε: 'tempting me so that I should speak': a weak sense. λόγῳ could only mean, 'by thy talk': whereas it would naturally mean 'in word' (only, and not ἔργῳ). Musgrave conj. λοχῶν (laying a snare for me); Arndt μ' ἑλεῖν; (to catch me): Madvig ἐκ πείρας λέγεις; But, with λέγων, all is, I think, sound. 361 οὐχ ὥστε γ' κ.τ.λ. οὐ (ξυνῆκα) οὕτω γ' ἀκριβῶς ὥστε εἰπεῖν: cp. 1131. γνωστόν: 'known.' So the MSS: but γνωτά 58, γνωτόν 396. In fr. 262 ἐκ κάρτα βαιῶν γνωτὸς ἂν γένοιτ' ἀνήρ, γνωτός = 'well-known,' γνώριμος: but Soph. used γνωστός in the same sense in the *Hermione* (Antiatticista 87. 25). It has been held that, where a sigmatic form of the verbal (as γνωστός) existed along with the non-sigmatic (as γνωτός), Attic usage distinguished γνωστός as = 'what *can* be known' from γνωτός as = 'what *is* known.' But there is no ground for assuming

ΤΕ. φονέα σε φημὶ τἀνδρὸς οὗ ζητεῖς κυρεῖν.

ΟΙ. ἀλλ' οὔ τι χαίρων δίς γε πημονὰς ἐρεῖς.

ΤΕ. εἴπω τι δῆτα κἄλλ', ἵν' ὀργίζῃ πλέον ;

ΟΙ. ὅσον γε χρήζεις· ὡς μάτην εἰρήσεται.   365

ΤΕ. λεληθέναι σε φημὶ σὺν τοῖς φιλτάτοις
αἴσχισθ' ὁμιλοῦντ', οὐδ' ὁρᾶν ἵν' εἶ κακοῦ.

ΟΙ. ἦ καὶ γεγηθὼς ταῦτ' ἀεὶ λέξειν δοκεῖς ;

ΤΕ. εἴπερ τί γ' ἐστὶ τῆς ἀληθείας σθένος.

ΟΙ. ἀλλ' ἔστι, πλὴν σοί· σοὶ δὲ τοῦτ' οὐκ ἔστ', ἐπεὶ   370
τυφλὸς τά τ' ὦτα τόν τε νοῦν τά τ' ὄμματ' εἶ.

ΤΕ. σὺ δ' ἄθλιός γε ταῦτ' ὀνειδίζων, ἃ σοὶ
οὐδεὶς ὃς οὐχὶ τῶνδ' ὀνειδιεῖ τάχα.

ΟΙ. μιᾶς τρέφει πρὸς νυκτός, ὥστε μήτ' ἐμὲ
μήτ' ἄλλον, ὅστις φῶς ὁρᾷ, βλάψαι ποτ' ἄν.   375

ΤΕ. οὐ γάρ σε μοῖρα πρός γ' ἐμοῦ πεσεῖν, ἐπεὶ

---

376 Sursum deorsum rem versant codd. omnes, με...γε σοῦ praebentes, excepto Flor. Abb. 41 (Δ), qui σε...γε σοῦ habet: σε...γέ μου Brunck.

---

that such a distinction was observed. See Appendix, Note 10. **362** οὗ ζητεῖς κ.τ.λ. φημί σε φονέα κυρεῖν (ὄντα) τοῦ ἀνδρὸς οὗ (τὸν φονέα) ζητεῖς. **363** πημονὰς: *i.e.* such charges are downright πημοναί, calamities, infamies. There is something of a colloquial tone in the phrase: cp. *Ai.* 68 μηδὲ συμφορὰν δέχου | τὸν ἄνδρα: *El.* 301 ὁ πάντ' ἄναλκις οὗτος, ἡ πᾶσα βλάβη. Cp. 336 ἀτελεύτητος. **364** εἴπω, delib. subjunct.: Eur. *Ion* 758 εἴπωμεν ἢ σιγῶμεν ἢ τί δράσομεν ; **366** σὺν τοῖς φιλτάτοις κ.τ.λ. = σὺν τῇ φιλτάτῃ (Iocasta): since ὁμιλοῦντ' implies wedlock, and not merely the companionship denoted by ξυνών in 457: for the allusive plural, cp. Aesch. *Cho.* 53 δεσποτῶν θανάτοισι (Agamemnon's murder). **367** ἵν' εἶ κακοῦ: cp. 413, 1442. *Trach.* 375 ποῦ ποτ' εἰμὶ πράγματος ; **368** ἦ καὶ: 'dost thou *indeed*?' Aesch. *Eum.* 402 ἦ καὶ τοιαύτας τῷδ' ἐπιρροιζεῖς φυγάς ; **370** πλὴν σοί· σοὶ δὲ κ.τ.λ. Note in these two vv. (1) the rhetorical iteration (ἐπαναφορά) of σοί, as in *O. C.* 787 οὐκ ἔστι σοι ταῦτ', ἀλλά σοι ταῦτ' ἔστ': *Phil.* 1054 πλὴν εἰς σέ· σοὶ δέ: Isocr. or. 15 § 41 κινδυνεύων τὰ μὲν ὑφ' ὑμῶν τὰ δὲ μεθ' ὑμῶν τὰ δὲ δι' ὑμᾶς τὰ δ' ὑπὲρ ὑμῶν. (2) the ninefold τ (παρήχησις) in 371 ; cp. 425: *Ai.* 528 ἐὰν τὸ ταχθὲν εὖ τολμᾷ τελεῖν: *ib.* 1112 οἱ πόνου πολλοῦ πλέῳ: Eur.

Te.　I say that thou art the slayer of the man whose slayer thou seekest.

Oe.　Now thou shalt rue that thou hast twice said words so dire.

Te.　Would'st thou have me say more, that thou mayest be more wroth?

Oe.　What thou wilt; it will be said in vain.

Te.　I say that thou hast been living in unguessed shame with thy nearest kin, and seest not to what woe thou hast come.

Oe.　Dost thou indeed think that thou shalt always speak thus without smarting?

Te.　Yes, if there is any strength in truth.

Oe.　Nay, there is,—for all save thee; for thee that strength is not, since thou art maimed in ear, and in wit, and in eye.

Te.　Aye, and thou art a poor wretch to utter taunts which every man here will soon hurl at thee.

Oe.　Night, endless night hath thee in her keeping, so that thou canst never hurt me, or any man who sees the sun.

Te.　No, thy doom is not to fall by *me*:

Med. 476 ἔσωσά σ'· ὡς ἴσασιν Ἑλλήνων ὅσοι, κ.τ.λ.: Ennius *O Tite tute Tati tibi tanta tyranne tulisti:* Cic. *Pro Cluent.* 35 § 96 *non fuit igitur illud iudicium iudicii simile, iudices.*　372 ἄθλιος, of wretched *folly.* Cp. the use of ἄνολβος, *Ai.* 1156, *Ant.* 1025 (joined with ἄβουλος), μέλεος (*Ai.* 621), κακοδαίμων, κ.τ.λ.　373 οὐδεὶς (ἔστιν) ὃς οὐχί = πᾶς τις: [Plat.] *Alc.* 1 103 B οὐδεὶς ὃς οὐχ ὑπερβληθεὶς...πέφευγε.　*Ai.* 725 ἤρασσον...οὗτις ἔσθ' ὃς οὔ.　More properly οὐδεὶς ὅστις οὐ, declined (by attraction) in both parts, as Plat. *Phaed.* 117 D οὐδένα ὅντινα οὐ κατέκλαυσε.　374 μιᾶς τρέφει πρὸς νυκτός, thou art cherished by (thy life is passed in) one unbroken night: the pass. form of μία νύξ σε τρέφει. Cp. *Ai.* 859 ὦ φέγγος, ὦ γῆς ἱρὸν οἰκείας πέδον | ...χαίρετ', ὦ τροφῆς ἐμοί: fr. 521 τερπνῶς γὰρ ἀεὶ πάντας ἀνοία τρέφει: *i.e.* folly ever *gives* a joyous *life:* Eur. *Hipp.* ὦ πόνοι τρέφοντες βροτούς cares that *make up the life* of men.　μιᾶς might be simply μόνης, but, in its emphatic place here, rather = 'unbroken,' unvaried by day: cp. Ar. *Rhet.* 3. 9 (λέξιν) εἰρομένην καὶ τῷ συνδεσμῷ μίαν, forming one continuous chain. The ingenious conj. μαίας (nurse) seems to me far less forcible.　376 (οὐκ

6—2

ἱκανὸς Ἀπόλλων, ᾧ τάδ᾽ ἐκπρᾶξαι μέλει.

ΟΙ. Κρέοντος ἢ σοῦ ταῦτα τἀξευρήματα;

ΤΕ. Κρέων δέ σοι πῆμ᾽ οὐδέν, ἀλλ᾽ αὐτὸς σὺ σοί.

ΟΙ. ὦ πλοῦτε καὶ τυραννὶ καὶ τέχνη τέχνης   380
    ὑπερφέρουσα τῷ πολυζήλῳ βίῳ,
    ὅσος παρ᾽ ὑμῖν ὁ φθόνος φυλάσσεται,
    εἰ τῆσδέ γ᾽ ἀρχῆς οὕνεχ᾽, ἣν ἐμοὶ πόλις
    δωρητόν, οὐκ αἰτητόν, εἰσεχείρισεν,
    ταύτης Κρέων ὁ πιστός, οὑξ ἀρχῆς φίλος   385
    λάθρα μ᾽ ὑπελθὼν ἐκβαλεῖν ἱμείρεται,
    ὑφεὶς μάγον τοιόνδε μηχανορράφον,
    δόλιον ἀγύρτην, ὅστις ἐν τοῖς κέρδεσιν

379 Κρέων δὲ codd., recte. Κρέων γε temere dedit Brunck.

ἐγώ σε βλάψω), οὐ γὰρ μοῖρά σε πεσεῖν κ.τ.λ.   377 ἐκπρᾶξαι, 'to accomplish' (not to 'exact'); τάδε has a mysterious vagueness (cp. 341), but includes τὸ πεσεῖν σε, as in 1158 τόδ᾽ refers to ὀλέσθαι.   379 **Κρέων δὲ** = 'Nay, Creon'—introducing an objection, as *Trach.* 729 τοιαῦτα δ᾽ ἂν λέξειεν κ.τ.λ.: *O. C.* 395 γέροντα δ᾽ ὀρθοῦν φλαῦρον.   381 **τῷ πολυζήλῳ βίῳ**, locative dative, defining the sphere of ὑπερφέρουσα, like ἔτι μέγας οὐρανῷ | Ζεύς *El.* 174. **πολυζήλῳ** = full of emulation (ζῆλος). Others understand, 'in the *much-admired* life' (of princes). This is the sense of πολύζηλον (πόσιν) in *Trach.* 185. But (1) βίῳ seems to denote life generally, rather than a particular station: (2) the phrase, following πλοῦτε καὶ τυραννί, would be a weak addition. For the general sense of **τέχνη** cp. *Phil.* 138 τέχνα γὰρ τέχνας ἑτέρας προὔχει | καὶ γνώμα, παρ᾽ ὅτῳ τὸ θεῖον | Διὸς σκῆπτρον ἀνάσσεται: for skill and wit (γνώμη), surpassing those of other men, belong to him by whom is swayed the godlike sceptre which Zeus gives. *Ant.* 365 τὸ μηχανόεν τέχνας, the inventiveness of (human) skill. The phrase here has a reference to that (μαντικὴ) τέχνη of Teiresias which Oed. surpassed when he solved the riddle: cp. 357.   382 **παρ᾽ ὑμῖν...φυλάσσεται**, is guarded, stored, in your keeping: *i.e.* how much envy do ye tend to excite against those who receive your gifts. **φυλάσσεται**, stronger than τρέφεται, represents envy as the *inseparable* attendant on success: cp. *O. C.* 1213 σκαιοσύναν φυλάσσων, stubborn in folly: Eur. *Ion* 735 ἄξι᾽ ἀξίων γεννητόρων | ἤθη φυλάσσεις.   384 **δωρητόν, οὐκ αἰτητόν**, feminine. The adjectives might

Apollo is enough, whose care it is to work that out.

OE. Are these Creon's devices, or thine?

TE. Nay, Creon is no plague to thee; thou art thine own.

OE. O wealth and empire and skill outmatching skill in life's keen rivalries, how great is the envy that cleaves to you, if for the sake, yea, of this power which the city hath put into my hands, a gift unsought, Creon the trusty, Creon mine old friend, hath crept on me by stealth, yearning to thrust me out of it, and hath suborned such a scheming juggler as this, a tricky quack, who hath eyes only for his gains,

---

be neuter: 'a thing given, not asked.' But this use of the neuter adj., when the subject is regarded in its most general aspect, is far most common in *simple* predications, as *Il.* 2. 204 οὐκ ἀγαθὸν πολυκοιρανίη: Eur. *Hipp.* 109 τερπνὸν ἐκ κυναγίας | τράπεζα πλήρης. And γνωτόν in 396—which must agree with ἦν—favours the view that here also the adjectives are fem. Cp. *Il.* 2. 742 κλυτὸς Ἱπποδάμεια: Thuc. 2. 41 γῆν ἐσβατόν: 7. 87 ὀσμαὶ οὐκ ἀνεκτοί: Plat. *Rep.* 573 B μανίας...ἐπακτοῦ: *Eryxias* 398 D ἀρετὴ διδακτός: *O. C.* 1460 πτερωτὸς βροντή: *Trach.* 446 εἰ...μεμπτός εἰμι (Deianeira). **385** ταύτης, redundant, for emphasis: Xen. *Cyr.* 8. 7. 9 τὸ δὲ προβουλεύειν καὶ τὸ ἡγεῖσθαι, ἐφ' ὅτι ἂν καιρὸς δοκῇ εἶναι, τοῦτο προστάττω. **387** ὑφείς, having secretly sent as his agent, 'having suborned.' [Plat.] *Axiochus* 368 E προέδρους ἐγκαθέτους ὑφέντες, 'having privily brought in suborned presidents.' The word μάγος expresses contempt for the rites of divination practised by Teiresias: ἀγύρτης taunts him as a mercenary impostor. So Plut. *Mor.* 165 F joins ἀγύρτας καὶ γόητας, Zosimus 1. 11 μάγοις τε καὶ ἀγύρταις. The passage shows how Asiatic superstitions had already spread among the vulgar, and were scorned by the educated, in Greece. The Persian μάγος (as conceived by the Greeks) was one who claimed to command the aid of beneficent deities (δαίμονες ἀγαθοεργοί), while the γόης was properly one who could call up the dead (Suid. 1. 490: cp. Plut. *De Defect. Orac.* c. 10). So Eur. *Or.* 1496 (Helen has been spirited away) ἢ φαρμάκοισιν (by charms) ἢ μάγων | τέχναισιν ἢ θεῶν κλοπαῖς. **388** ἀγύρτην (ἀγείρω), a priest, esp. of Cybele (μητραγύρτης, or, when she had the lunar attributes, μηναγύρτης), who sought money from house to house (ἐπὶ τὰς τῶν πλουσίων θύρας ἰόντες, Plat. *Rep.* 364 B), or in public places, for predictions or expiatory rites: Maximus Tyrius 19. 3 τῶν ἐν τοῖς κύκλοις ἀγειρόντων..., οἳ δυοῖν ὀβολοῖν τῷ προστυχόντι ἀποθεσπίζουσιν.

μόνον δέδορκε, τὴν τέχνην δ' ἔφυ τυφλός.
ἐπεί, φέρ' εἰπέ, ποῦ σὺ μάντις εἶ σαφής;　　　　390
πῶς οὐχ, ὅθ' ἡ ῥαψῳδὸς ἐνθάδ' ἦν κύων,
ηὔδας τι τοῖσδ' ἀστοῖσιν ἐκλυτήριον;
καίτοι τό γ' αἴνιγμ' οὐχὶ τοὐπιόντος ἦν
ἀνδρὸς διειπεῖν, ἀλλὰ μαντείας' ἔδει·
ἣν οὔτ' ἀπ' οἰωνῶν σὺ προὐφάνης ἔχων　　　　395
οὔτ' ἐκ θεῶν του γνωτόν· ἀλλ' ἐγὼ μολών,
ὁ μηδὲν εἰδὼς Οἰδίπους, ἔπαυσά νιν,
γνώμῃ κυρήσας οὐδ' ἀπ' οἰωνῶν μαθών·
ὃν δὴ σὺ πειρᾷς ἐκβαλεῖν, δοκῶν θρόνοις
παραστατήσειν τοῖς Κρεοντείοις πέλας.　　　　400
κλαίων δοκεῖς μοι καὶ σὺ χὠ συνθεὶς τάδε
ἀγηλατήσειν· εἰ δὲ μὴ 'δόκεις γέρων

396 τοῦ L, T, Barocc. 66: τον A et plerique.

ἐν τοῖς κέρδεσιν, in the case of gains: cp. *Ai.* 1315 ἐν ἐμοὶ θρασύς; rather than, 'on opportunities for gain' (= ὅταν ᾖ κερδαίνειν) as Ellendt takes it. Cicero's *videbat in litteris* (*Tusc.* 5. 38. 112, quoted by Schneid.) seems not strictly similar, meaning rather 'in the region of letters' (like *in tenebris*). **390** ἐπεί = 'for' (if this is *not* true): *El.* 351 οὐ ταῦτα...δειλίαν ἔχει; | ἐπεὶ δίδαξον, κ.τ.λ. ποῦ; where? *i.e.* in what sense? Eur. *Ion* 528 ποῦ δέ μοι πατὴρ σύ; εἰ σαφής = πέφηνας ὤν: cp. 355. **391** κύων, esp. because the Sphinx was the watchful agent of Hera's wrath: cp. 36. Ar. *Ran.* 1287 has a line from the Σφίγξ of Aesch., Σφίγγα δυσαμεριᾶν [vulg. δυσαμερίαν] πρύτανιν κύνα πέμπει, 'the watcher who presides over evil days' (for Thebes). ῥαψῳδός, chanting her riddle (in hexameter verse), as the public reciters chanted epic poems. The word is used with irony: the baneful lay of the Sphinx was not such as the servant of Apollo chants. Cp. 130. **393** τό γ' αἴνιγμ' is nominative: the riddle did not belong to (was not for) the first comer, that he should solve it. *O. C.* 751 οὐ γάμων | ἔμπειρος, ἀλλὰ τοὐπιόντος ἁρπάσαι, Thuc. 6. 22 πολλὴ γὰρ οὖσα [ἡ στρατιά] οὐ πάσης ἔσται πόλεως ὑποδέξασθαι. ὁ ἐπιών, any one who comes up; cp. Plat. *Rep.* 372 D ὡς νῦν ὁ τυχὼν καὶ οὐδὲν προσήκων ἔρχεται ἐπ' αὐτό. **394** διειπεῖν, 'to declare,' (where διά implies the drawing of clear distinctions), 'to solve': cp. 854. **395** ἦν οὔτ' ἀπ' οἰωνῶν ἔχων οὔτ' ἐκ θεῶν του γνωτὸν (ἔχων) προὐφάνης: and thou

but in his art is blind!

Come, now, tell me, where hast thou proved thyself a seer? Why, when the Watcher was here who wove dark song, didst thou say nothing that could free this folk? Yet the riddle, at least, was not for the first comer to read; there was need of a seer's skill; and none such thou wert found to have, either by help of birds, or as known from any god: no, I came, I, Oedipus the ignorant, and made her mute, when I had seized the answer by my wit, untaught of birds. And it is I whom thou art trying to oust, thinking to stand close to Creon's throne. Methinks thou and the plotter of these things will rue your zeal to purge the land. Nay, didst thou not seem to be an old man,

---

wert not publicly seen to have this art either from (ἀπ') birds, or as known through the agency of (ἐκ) any god. προὐφάνης, when brought to a public test. For ἀπό cp. 43: ἐκ with θεῶν του, of the primary or remoter agent (Xen. *Hellen.* 3. 1. 6 ἐκ βασιλέως ἐδόθη), meaning by a φήμη (43) or other sign. γνωτόν: cp. on 384. 396 μολών: he was a mere stranger who chanced to arrive then. ὁ μηδὲν εἰδώς = ὁ ἔχων οὕτως ὥσπερ εἰ μηδὲν ᾔδη, who is as if he knew nothing. So ὁ μηδὲν (*sc.* ὤν *Ai.* 1231) is 'one who exists no more than if he were not' (*Ant.* 1325 τὸν οὐκ ὄντα μᾶλλον ἢ μηδένα). 400 πέλας, adv., so Aesch. *Theb.* 669 παραστατεῖν πέλας. 401 κλαίων: cp. 368, 1152: *Ant.* 754 κλαίων φρενώσεις. ὁ συνθείς, Creon, as whose agent (387) Teir. is regarded: so in Thuc. 8. 68 ὁ τὴν γνώμην εἰπών is contrasted with ὁ τὸ πρᾶγμα ξυνθείς. 402 ἀγηλατεῖν = τὸ ἄγος ἐλαύνειν (see on 98), in this case ἀνδρηλατεῖν (100), to expel the μιάστωρ. Her. 5. 72 Κλεομένης...ἀγηλατέει ἑπτακόσια ἐπίστια (households) Ἀθηναίων. The MSS. of Soph. have ἀγηλατεῖν (L. has no breathing), and so Hesych.; so also the grammarians in Bekker's *Anecdota* Vol. I. p. 328. 32, p. 337. 11: Eustathius, however (1704—5), and Suid. *s. v.*, quoting Soph., give the aspirate. Curtius distinguishes (1) ἄγ-ος, guilt, object of awe, whence ἐναγής: Skt. *ág-as*, vexation, offence: *Etym.* § 116: (2) root ἄγ, ἄζ-ο-μαι reverence, ἅγ-ιο-s, holy, ἁγ-νό-s pure: Skt. *jaĝ* (*jaĝ-â-mi*) reverence, consecrate: *Etym.* § 118. In Aesch. *Cho.* 155 and Soph. *Ant.* 775 he would with Herm. write ἅγος as = 'consecrated offering.' In both places, however, ἄγος *piaculum* will stand: and for ἄγος in the good sense there is no other evidence. But this, at least, seems clear: the compound synonym for τὸ ἄγος ἐλαύνειν (Thuc. I. 126) should be written ἀγηλατεῖν. 'δόκεις is the scornful

εἶναι, παθὼν ἔγνως ἂν οἷά περ φρονεῖς.

ΧΟ. ἡμῖν μὲν εἰκάζουσι καὶ τὰ τοῦδ᾽ ἔπη
ὀργῇ λελέχθαι καὶ τὰ σ᾽, Οἰδίπου, δοκεῖ.   405
δεῖ δ᾽ οὐ τοιούτων, ἀλλ᾽ ὅπως τὰ τοῦ θεοῦ
μαντεῖ᾽ ἄριστα λύσομεν, τόδε σκοπεῖν.

ΤΕ. εἰ καὶ τυραννεῖς, ἐξισωτέον τὸ γοῦν
ἴσ᾽ ἀντιλέξαι· τοῦδε γὰρ κἀγὼ κρατῶ.
οὐ γάρ τι σοὶ ζῶ δοῦλος, ἀλλὰ Λοξίᾳ·   410
ὥστ᾽ οὐ Κρέοντος προστάτου γεγράψομαι.
λέγω δ᾽, ἐπειδὴ καὶ τυφλόν μ᾽ ὠνείδισας·
σὺ καὶ δέδορκας κοὐ βλέπεις ἵν᾽ εἶ κακοῦ,
οὐδ᾽ ἔνθα ναίεις, οὐδ᾽ ὅτων οἰκεῖς μέτα.

405 Οἰδίπου codd. Usitatior vocativi forma Οἰδίπους est, quam Dindorfius, Elmsleium et Reisigium secutus, solam esse veram statuit. Dandum est aliquid tamen librorum consensui, qui etiam in *O. C.* 557, 1346 Οἰδίπου praebent; neque quemquam infitias iturum reor quin hic saltem locus vocativum sigmate carentem auribus magnopere commendet. Post τὰ σ᾽, Οἰδίπους sonum haberet minime gratum. Equidem utramque formam poetae concedendam puto. **413** δέδορκας κοὐ L, A, plerique:

phrase of an angry man ; I know little concerning thee, but from thine aspect I should judge thee to be old : cp. 562 where Oed. asks, τότ᾽ οὖν ὁ μάντις οὖτος ἦν ἐν τῇ τέχνῃ ; Not (1) 'seemed,' as opposed to really being ; nor (2) 'wert felt by me' to be old : a sense which I do not see how the word could yield. **403** παθὼν, by bodily pain, and not merely μαθών, by reproof : cp. 641. οἷά περ φρονεῖς : see on 624 οἷόν ἐστι τὸ φθονεῖν. **405** καὶ τὰ σ᾽ κ.τ.λ., the elision as in 328 : see on 64. **407** τόδε emphatically resumes ὅπως λύσομεν, *this* we must consider : cp. 385 ταύτης : so *Trach.* 458 τὸ μὴ πυθέσθαι, τοῦτό μ᾽ ἀλγύνειεν ἄν. **408** εἰ καὶ κ.τ.λ. For εἰ καὶ see on 305. ἐξισωτέον κ.τ.λ. = δεῖ ἐξισοῦν τὸ γοῦν ἴσα ἀντιλέξαι, one must equalize the right at least of like reply ; *i.e.* you must make me so far your equal as to grant me the right of replying at the same length. The phrase is a pleonastic fusion of (1) ἐξισωτέον τὸ ἀντιλέξαι with (2) συγχωρητέον τὸ ἴσα ἀντιλέξαι. **410** Λοξίᾳ : see note to 853. **411** ὥστ᾽ οὐ Κρέοντος κ.τ.λ. 'You charge me with being the tool of Creon's treason. I have a right to plead my own cause when I am thus accused. I am not like a resident alien, who can plead before a civic tribunal only by the mouth of that patron under

thou should'st have learned to thy cost how bold thou art.

CH. To our thinking, both this man's words and thine, Oedipus, have been said in anger. Not for such words is our need; but to seek how best we shall discharge the mandates of the god.

TE. King though thou art, the right of speech, at least, must be deemed the same for both; of that I too am lord. Not to thee do I live servant, but to Loxias; and so I shall not stand enrolled under Creon for my patron. And I tell thee—since thou hast taunted me even with blindness—that thou hast sight, yet seest not in what misery thou art, nor where thou dwellest, nor with whom.

δεδορκὼς κοὐ B: σύ, καὶ δεδορκώς, οὐ post Reiskium Brunck. Cui coniecturae quod obiecit Hermann., καὶ δεδορκώς non *quamvis videns* sed *etiam videns* significare, id quidem facile potest redargui; quis enim nescit quam saepe καί simplex compositi καίπερ officio fungatur? Immo δέδορκας κοὐ idcirco melius est quam δεδορκὼς οὐ, quod multo fortius: vide annot.

---

whom he has been registered.' Every μέτοικος at Athens was required ἐπιγράφεσθαι προστάτην, *i.e.* to have the name of a citizen, as patron, inscribed over his own. In default, he was liable to an ἀπροστασίου γραφή. Ar. *Pax* 684 αὐτῷ πονηρὸν προστάτην ἐπεγράψατο: *Ach.* 1095 ἐπεγράφου τὴν Γοργόνα, you took the Gorgon for your patron: Lysias or. 31 § 9 ἐν Ὠρωπῷ μετοίκιον κατατιθεὶς (paying the alien's tax) ἐπὶ προστάτου ᾤκει. γεγράψομαι, will *stand* enrolled: cp. Ar. *Eq.* 1370 οὐδεὶς κατὰ σπουδὰς μετεγγραφήσεται, | ἀλλ' ὥσπερ ἦν τὸ πρῶτον ἐγγεγράψεται: Theocr. 18. 47 γράμματα δ' ἐν φλοιῷ γεγράψεται, *remain* written. For the gen. Κρέοντος cp. Ar. *Eq.* 714 τὸν δῆμον σεαυτοῦ νενόμικας. **412** λέγω δ', a solemn exordium, bespeaking attention: cp. 449. τυφλόν μ' ὠνείδισας. As ὠνείδισας could not stand for ἀπεκάλεσας, 'called me reproachfully,' τυφλόν must stand for ὡς τυφλὸν ὄντα. For the ellipse of ὄντα, cp. *El.* 899 ὡς δ' ἐν γαλήνῃ πάντ' ἐδερκόμην τόπον: for that of ὥς, *O. C.* 142 μή μ', ἱκετεύω, προσίδητ' ἄνομον. **413** σὺ καὶ δέδορκας. 'Thou *both* hast sight *and* dost not see,' *i.e.* thou hast sight, and at the same time dost not see. The conject. of Reiske and Brunck, σύ, καὶ δεδορκώς (*though* having sight), οὐ βλέπεις, spoils the direct contrast with τυφλόν. **414** ἔνθα ναίεις might mean, 'in what a situation thou art': but, as distinguished from the preceding and following

ἆρ' οἶσθ' ἀφ' ὧν εἶ; καὶ λέληθας ἐχθρὸς ὢν   415
τοῖς σοῖσιν αὐτοῦ νέρθε κἀπὶ γῆς ἄνω,
καί σ' ἀμφιπλὴξ μητρός τε καὶ τοῦ σοῦ πατρὸς
ἐλᾷ ποτ' ἐκ γῆς τῆσδε δεινόπους ἀρά,
βλέποντα νῦν μὲν ὄρθ', ἔπειτα δὲ σκότον.
βοῆς δὲ τῆς σῆς ποῖος οὐκ ἔσται λιμήν,   420
ποῖος Κιθαιρὼν οὐχὶ σύμφωνος τάχα,
ὅταν καταίσθῃ τὸν ὑμέναιον, ὃν δόμοις
ἄνορμον εἰσέπλευσας, εὐπλοίας τυχών;
ἄλλων δὲ πλῆθος οὐκ ἐπαισθάνει κακῶν,
ἅ σ' ἐξισώσει σοί τε καὶ τοῖς σοῖς τέκνοις.   425

425 Locus varie tentatus nulla eget medicina: quod infra paucis explicare conatus sum.

---

clauses, is best taken literally: 'where thou dwellest'—viz. in thy murdered father's house. **415 ἆρ' οἶσθα κ.τ.λ.** Thy parents are unknown to thee. *Yea, and* (καὶ) thou knowest not how thou hast sinned against them,—the dead and the living. **417 ἀμφιπλὴξ**: as in *Trach.* 930 ἀμφιπλῆγι φασγάνῳ = a sword which smites with both edges, so here ἀμφιπλὴξ ἀρά is properly *a curse which smites on both sides*,—on the mother's and on the father's part. The pursuing Ἀρά must be conceived as bearing a whip with double lash (διπλῇ μάστιξ, *Ai.* 242). Cp. ἀμφίπυρος, carrying two torches (*Trach.* 214). The genitives μητρός, πατρός might be causal, with ἀμφιπλήξ, 'smiting twice—*for* mother and for sire,' but are better taken with ἀρά, which here = Ἐρινύς: cp. Aesch. *Theb.* 70 Ἀρά τ', Ἐρινὺς πατρὸς ἡ μεγασθενής. **418 δεινόπους**, with dread, untiring chase: so the Fury, who chases guilt 'as a hound tracks a wounded fawn' (Aesch. *Eum.* 246), is χαλκόπους (*El.* 491), τανύπους (*Ai.* 837), καμψίπους ('fleet,' Aesch. *Theb.* 791). **419 βλέποντα κ.τ.λ.**, *i.e.* τότε σκότον βλέποντα, εἰ καὶ νῦν ὀρθὰ βλέπεις. The Greek love of direct antithesis often co-ordinates clauses where we must subordinate one to the other: cp. below, 673: Isocr. or. 6 § 54 πῶς οὐκ αἰσχρόν,...τὴν μὲν Εὐρώπην καὶ τὴν Ἀσίαν μεστὴν πεποιηκέναι τροπαίων,...ὑπὲρ δὲ τῆς πατρίδος ...μηδὲ μίαν μάχην φαίνεσθαι μεμαχημένους; βλέπειν σκότον, like ἐν σκότῳ...| ὀψοίατο (1273), Eur. *Bacch.* 510 σκότιον εἰσορᾷ κνέφας. **420 βοῆς δὲ κ.τ.λ.** Of thy cry what haven shall there not be (*i.e.* to what place shall it not be borne),—what part of Cithaeron shall not be resonant with it (σύμφωνος ἔσται sc. αὐτῇ), re-echo it? If we took σύμφωνος ἔσται (and not

Dost thou know of what stock thou art? And thou hast been an unwitting foe to thine own kin, in the shades, and on the earth above; and the double lash of thy mother's and thy father's curse shall one day drive thee from this land in dreadful haste, with darkness then on the eyes that now see true.

And what place shall not be harbour to thy shriek, what of all Cithaeron shall not ring with it soon, when thou hast caught the meaning of the marriage-song wherewith thou wert borne to thy fatal haven in yonder house, after a voyage so fair? And a throng of other ills thou guessest not, which shall make thee level with thy true self and with thine own brood.

ἔσται alone) with λιμήν as well as with Κιθαιρών, the figurative force of λιμήν would be weakened. We must not understand: What haven of the sea or what mountain (as if Cithaeron stood for ὄρος) shall not resound? λιμήν, poet. in the sense of ὑποδοχή, for that in which anything is received: Aesch. *Pers.* 250 ὦ Περσὶς αἶα καὶ μέγας πλούτου λιμήν (imitated by Eur. *Or.* 1077): the augural seat of Teiresias is παντὸς οἰωνοῦ λιμήν *Ant.* 1000: the place of the dead is Ἄιδου λιμήν *ib.* 1284: cp. below, 1208. **421 ποῖος Κιθαιρὼν**, vigorous for ποῖον μέρος Κιθαιρῶνος. **422 ὅταν καταίσθῃ κ.τ.λ.**: ὃν, cognate acc. to εἰσέπλευσας, as if ὑμέναιον had been πλοῦν: **δόμοις**, local dat. (381): ἄνορμον is added predicatively, though it (thy course) led thee to no true haven: εὐπλοίας τυχών, because Oed. *seemed* to have found ὄλβος, and also because the gale of fortune had borne him *swiftly* on: cp. οὔθ᾽ ὁρῶν οὔθ᾽ ἱστορῶν, 1484. **τὸν ὑμέναιον**, sung while the bride and bridegroom were escorted to their home, *Il.* 18. 492 νύμφας δ᾽ ἐκ θαλάμων δαΐδων ὑπὸ λαμπομενάων | ἠγίνεον ἀνὰ ἄστυ, πολὺς δ᾽ ὑμέναιος ὀρώρει, as distinguished from the ἐπιθαλάμιον afterwards sung before the bridal chamber: *Ant.* 813 οὔθ᾽ ὑμεναίων | ἔγκληρον, οὔτ᾽ ἐπινύμφειός πώ μέ τις ὕμνος | ὕμνησεν. **424 ἄλλων δὲ κ.τ.λ.** Verses 422—425 correspond with the actual process of the drama. The words καταίσθῃ τὸν ὑμέναιον refer to the first discovery made by Oed.,—that his wife was the widow of one whom he had himself slain: cp. 821. The ἄλλων πλῆθος κακῶν denotes the further discovery that this wife was his mother, with all the horrors involved (1405). **425 ἅ σ᾽ ἐξισώσει**, which shall make thee level with *thy* (*true*) *self*,—by showing thee to be the son of Laïus, not of Polybus;—and level with *thine own children*, *i.e.* like them, the child of Iocasta, and thus at once ἀδελφὸς καὶ πατήρ (458). For ἅ σ᾽ Markland conject. ἵσ᾽, which

πρὸς ταῦτα καὶ Κρέοντα καὶ τοὐμὸν στόμα
προπηλάκιζε· σοῦ γὰρ οὐκ ἔστιν βροτῶν
κάκιον ὅστις ἐκτριβήσεταί ποτε.

ΟΙ. ἦ ταῦτα δῆτ᾽ ἀνεκτὰ πρὸς τούτου κλύειν;
οὐκ εἰς ὄλεθρον; οὐχὶ θᾶσσον; οὐ πάλιν   430
ἄψορρος οἴκων τῶνδ᾽ ἀποστραφεὶς ἄπει;

ΤΕ. οὐδ᾽ ἱκόμην ἔγωγ᾽ ἄν, εἰ σὺ μὴ 'κάλεις.

ΟΙ. οὐ γάρ τί σ᾽ ᾔδη μῶρα φωνήσοντ᾽, ἐπεὶ
σχολῇ σ᾽ ἂν οἴκους τοὺς ἐμοὺς ἐστειλάμην.

ΤΕ. ἡμεῖς τοιοίδ᾽ ἔφυμεν, ὡς μὲν σοὶ δοκεῖ,   435
μῶροι, γονεῦσι δ᾽, οἵ σ᾽ ἔφυσαν, ἔμφρονες.

ΟΙ. ποίοισι; μεῖνον. τίς δέ μ᾽ ἐκφύει βροτῶν;

434 σχολῇ σ᾽ codd.: σχολῇ γ᾽ Suidas, et sic post Erfurdt. et Hermann. multi
edd.: quo recepto Porsonus post ἐμοὺς intulit σ᾽, et sic Blaydes. Pronomen quidem
σ᾽ facile subaudimus: codicum vero auctoritas contra Suidam eo praecipue argumento

---

shall *be made* equal for thee and for thy children: and so Porson
interpreted, conjecturing ἄσσ᾽ from Agathon fr. 5 ἀγένητα ποιεῖν
ἄσσ᾽ ἂν ᾖ πεπραγμένα. Nauck ingeniously conj. ἅ σ᾽ ἐξισώσει σῷ τοκεῖ
καὶ σοῖς τέκνοις. But the vulgate is sound: for the παρήχησις cp. 371.
426 τοὐμὸν στόμα: *i.e.*, it is Apollo who speaks by my mouth, which
is not, as thou deemest, the ὑπόβλητον στόμα (*O. C.* 794) of Creon.
427 προπηλάκιζε: acc. to Arist. *Top.* 6. 6 προπηλακισμός was defined
as ὕβρις μετὰ χλευασίας, insult expressed by scoffing: so in *Eth.* 5. 2.
13 κακηγορία, προπηλακισμός = libellous language, *gross* abuse: and in
Ar. *Thesm.* 386 προπηλακιζομένας is explained by πολλὰ καὶ παντοῖ᾽ ἀκου-
ούσας κακά. Dem. *In Mid.* § 72 has ἀήθεις...τοῦ προπηλακίζεσθαι as
= 'unused to gross contumely' (generally, but with immediate ref.
to a blow). **428 ἐκτριβήσεται,** rooted out. Eur. *Hipp.* 683 Ζεύς σε γεν-
νήτωρ ἐμὸς | πρόρριζον ἐκτρίψειεν. **430 οὐκ εἰς ὄλεθρον** κ.τ.λ. Ar. *Plut.*
394 οὐκ ἐς κόρακας; *Trach.* 1183 οὐ θᾶσσον οἴσεις; Cratinus Νόμοι fr. 6
(Meineke p. 27) οὐκ ἀπερρήσεις σὺ θᾶττον; Aesch. *Theb.* 252 οὐκ ἐς φθόρον
σιγῶσ᾽ ἀνασχήσει τάδε; **πάλιν ἄψορρος** like *El.* 53 ἄψορρον ἥξομεν πάλιν: the
gen. **οἴκων τῶνδ᾽** with **ἀποστραφείς. 432 ἱκόμην—ἐκάλεις:** cp. 125, 402.
434 σχολῇ σ᾽ ἄν. The simple σχολῇ is stronger than σχολῇ γε would
be: *Ant.* 390 σχολῇ ποθ᾽ ἥξειν (where σχολῇ γ᾽ ἄν is an inferior
v. l.), Plat. *Soph.* 233 B σχολῇ ποτ᾽...ἤθελεν ἄν, *Prot.* 330 E σχολῇ
μέντ᾽ ἂν ἄλλο τι ὅσιον εἴη, and often. **οἴκους:** *O. C.* 643 δόμους στείχειν

Therefore heap thy scorns on Creon and on my message:
for no one among men shall ever be crushed more miserably
than thou.

OE. Are these taunts to be indeed borne from *him?*—
Hence, ruin take thee! Hence, this instant! Back!—away!
—avaunt thee from these doors!

TE. I had never come, not I, hadst thou not called me.

OE. I knew not that thou wert about to speak folly, or
it had been long ere I had sent for thee to my house.

TE. Such am I,—as thou thinkest, a fool; but for the
parents who begat thee, sane.

OE. What parents? Stay...and who of men is my sire?

firmatur, quod addita particula γε vocis σχολῇ vim non modo non auget sed etiam
extenuat.

ἐμούς. ἐστειλάμην=μετεστειλάμην, μετεπεμψάμην. Distinguish στέλλεσθαι, to summon *to oneself*, from στέλλειν said (1) of the messenger,
below 860 πέμψον τινὰ στελοῦντα: (2) of him who sends word by a
messenger, *Phil.* 60 οἵ σ' ἐν λιταῖς στείλαντες ἐξ οἴκου μολεῖν: having
urged thee with prayers to come: *Ant.* 164 ὑμᾶς...πομποῖσιν... | ἔστειλ'
ἱκέσθαι, sent you word to come. 435 τοιοῦ refers back to the taunt
implied in μῶρα φωνήσοντ', and is then made explicit by μῶροι...ἔμφρονες:
cp. *Phil.* 1271 τοιοῦτος ἦσθα (referring to what precedes—thou wert
such *as thou now art*) τοῖς λόγοισι χὦτε μου | τὰ τόξ' ἔκλεπτες, πιστός,
ἀτηρὸς λάθρα. In fr. 700 (quoted by Nauck), καὶ τὸν θεὸν τοιοῦτον
ἐξεπίσταμαι, | σοφοῖς μὲν αἰνικτῆρα,... | σκαιοῖς δὲ φαῦλον, we have not
the preceding words, but doubtless τοιοῦτον referred to them. ὡς μὲν σοὶ
δοκεῖ. σοὶ must be accented; else the contrast would be, not partly between σοὶ and γονεῦσι, but solely between δοκεῖ and some other verbal
notion. σοὶ does not, however, cohere so closely with δοκεῖ as to form a
virtual cretic. It is needless, then, to read (as Elms. proposed) ὡς μέν
σοι or ὡς σοὶ μέν. Cp. *O. C.* 1543 ὥσπερ σφὼ πατρί: Eur. *Heracl.* 641
σωτὴρ νῷν βλάβης. As neither σφὼ nor νῷν adheres to the following
rather than to the preceding word, it seems unnecessary to read with
Porson ὡς πρὶν σφὼ or νῷν σωτήρ. Here we have ὡς μὲν σοὶ instead of ὡς
σοὶ μὲν, because, besides the contrast of persons, there is also a contrast
between semblance (ὡς δοκεῖ) and fact. 436 γονεῦσι, 'for' them, *i.e.* in
their judgment: *Ant.* 904 καίτοι σ' ἐγὼ 'τίμησα, τοῖς φρονοῦσιν, εὖ.
Ar. *Av.* 445 πᾶσι νικᾶν τοῖς κριταῖς. 437 ἐκφύει. The pres. is not

ΤΕ. ἤδ᾽ ἡμέρα φύσει σε καὶ διαφθερεῖ.

ΟΙ. ὡς πάντ᾽ ἄγαν αἰνικτὰ κἀσαφῆ λέγεις.

ΤΕ. οὔκουν σὺ ταῦτ᾽ ἄριστος εὑρίσκειν ἔφυς;   440

ΟΙ. τοιαῦτ᾽ ὀνείδιζ᾽ οἷς ἔμ᾽ εὑρήσεις μέγαν.

ΤΕ. αὕτη γε μέντοι σ᾽ ἡ τύχη διώλεσεν.

ΟΙ. ἀλλ᾽ εἰ πόλιν τήνδ᾽ ἐξέσωσ᾽, οὔ μοι μέλει.

ΤΕ. ἄπειμι τοίνυν· καὶ σύ, παῖ, κόμιζέ με.

ΟΙ. κομιζέτω δῆθ᾽· ὡς παρὼν σύ γ᾽ ἐμποδὼν   445
  ὀχλεῖς, συθείς τ᾽ ἂν οὐκ ἂν ἀλγύναις πλέον.

ΤΕ. εἰπὼν ἄπειμ᾽ ὧν οὕνεκ᾽ ἦλθον, οὐ τὸ σὸν
  δείσας πρόσωπον· οὐ γὰρ ἔσθ᾽ ὅπου μ᾽ ὀλεῖς.
  λέγω δέ σοι· τὸν ἄνδρα τοῦτον, ὃν πάλαι
  ζητεῖς ἀπειλῶν κἀνακηρύσσων φόνον   450

445 σύ γ᾽ A et plerique. Et est γ᾽ quidem in L, erasis duabus quae praecesserant litteris: in marg. autem scripsit manus recentior γρ. σύ γε. Ex uno cod. Vat. 40

---

historic (for ἐξέφυσε), but denotes a permanent character: 'is my sire.' Eur. *Ion* 1560 ἤδε τίκτει σ᾽, is thy mother: so perh. *Heracl.* 208 πατὴρ δ᾽ ἐκ τῆσδε γεννᾶται σέθεν. Xen. *Cyr.* 8. 2. 27 ὁ δὲ μὴ νικῶν (he who was not victorious) τοῖς μὲν νικῶσιν ἐφθόνει: and so φεύγειν = φυγὰς εἶναι *passim*. Shilleto thus takes οἱ ἐπαγόμενοι Thuc. 2. 2, οἱ προδιδόντες *ib.* 5, οἱ διαβάλλοντες 3. 4; which however I should rather take simply as imperfect participles, = οἳ ἐπήγοντο, προὐδίδοσαν, διέβαλλον. He well compares Verg. *Aen.* 9. 266 *quem dat Sidonia Dido* (is the giver): in Persius 4. 2 *sorbitio tollit quem dira cicutae* I find rather a harsh historic pres. **440 οὔκουν κ.τ.λ.** Well (οὖν—if I *do* speak riddles), art not thou most skilled to read them? **441 τοιαῦτ᾽ ὀνείδιζέ (μοι)**, make those things my reproach, in which [οἷς, dat. of circumstance] thou wilt find me great: *i.e.* mock my skill in reading riddles if thou wilt; but thou wilt find (on looking deeper) that it has brought me true honour. **442 αὕτη γε μέντοι.** It was just (γε) that fortune, however (μέντοι), that ruined thee. γε emphasises the preceding word: so 778 σπουδῆς γε μέντοι: 1292 ῥώμης γε μέντοι: *Phil.* 93 πεμφθείς γε μέντοι (since I have been *sent*): 1052 νικᾶν γε μέντοι: *Ant.* 233 τέλος γε μέντοι. τύχη implies some abatement of the king's boast, γνώμῃ κυρήσας, 398. **443 ἐξέσωσ᾽**, 1st pers., not 3rd. **445 κομιζέτω δῆθ᾽.** δῆτα in assent, as Aesch. *Suppl.* 206 Ζεὺς δὲ γεννήτωρ ἴδοι. ΔΑΝ. ἴδοιτο δῆτα.

TE. This day shall show thy birth and shall bring thy ruin.

OE. What riddles, what dark words thou ever dost speak!

TE. Nay, art not thou most skilled to unravel dark speech?

OE. Make that my reproach in which thou shalt find me great.

TE. Yet 'twas just that fortune that undid thee.

OE. Nay, if I delivered this town, I care not.

TE. Then I will go: so do thou, boy, take me hence.

OE. Aye, let him take thee: while here, thou art a hindrance, thou, a trouble: when thou hast vanished, thou wilt not vex me more.

TE. I will go when I have done mine errand, fearless of thy frown: for thou canst never destroy me. And I tell thee— the man of whom thou hast this long while been in quest, uttering threats, and proclaiming a search into the murder of

σύ μ' recepit Campb. Sed lectio σύ γ' ut librorum fide ita sua vi commendatur, quippe quae optime conveniat indignantis fastidio. τά γ' ἐμποδών B.

ἐμποδών with παρών,—present where thy presence irks: cp. 128: γε added to σύ is scornful. The weak conjecture τά γ' ἐμποδών is explained by Brunck and Erfurdt (with Thomas Magister) 'thou hinderest the business before us,' comparing Eur. *Phoen.* 706 ἃ δ' ἐμποδών μάλιστα ('most urgent') ταῦθ' ἥκω φράσων. 448 πρόσωπον: 'thy face,'—thy angry presence: the blind man speaks as though he saw the 'vultus instantis tyranni.' Not, 'thy *person*' (*i.e.* thy royal quality): πρόσωπον is not classical in this sense, for which cp. the Hellenistic προσωποληπ- τεῖν, 'to be a respecter of persons,' and the spurious Phocylidea 10 (Bergk *Poet. Lyr.* p. 361) μὴ ῥίψῃς πενίην ἀδίκως· μὴ κρῖνε πρόσωπον. οὐκ ἔσθ' ὅπου, there is no case in which...: cp. 355, 390. 449 λέγω δέ σοι, cp. 412. τὸν ἄνδρα τοῦτον...οὗτός ἐστιν κ.τ.λ. The antecedent, attracted into the case of the relative, is enclitic thus prefixed to the relative clause, to mark with greater emphasis the subject of a coming statement: *Trach.* 283 τάσδε δ' ἅσπερ εἰσορᾷς | ...χωροῦσι: *Il.* 10. 416 φυλακὰς δ' ἃς εἴρεαι, ἥρως, | οὔτις κεκριμένη ῥύεται στρατόν: *Hom. hym. Cer.* 66 κούρην τὴν ἔτεκον... | τῆς ἀδινὴν ὄπ' ἄκουσα: Ar. *Plut.* 200 τὴν δύναμιν ἣν ὑμεῖς φατὲ | ἔχειν με, ταύτης δεσπότης γενήσομαι. Plaut. *Trinum.* 985 *Illum quem ementitu's, is ego sum ipse Charmides.* 450 ἀνακηρύσσων φόνον, pro- claiming (a search into) the murder: cp. Xen. *Mem.* 2. 10. 2 σῶστρα τούτου ἀνακηρύττων: Andoc. *De Myst.* § 40 ζητητάς τε ἤδη ἡρημένους...

τὸν Λάϊειον, οὗτός ἐστιν ἐνθάδε,
ξένος λόγῳ μέτοικος, εἶτα δ' ἐγγενὴς
φανήσεται Θηβαῖος, οὐδ' ἡσθήσεται
τῇ ξυμφορᾷ· τυφλὸς γὰρ ἐκ δεδορκότος
καὶ πτωχὸς ἀντὶ πλουσίου ξένην ἔπι　　　　　455
σκήπτρῳ προδεικνὺς γαῖαν ἐμπορεύσεται.
φανήσεται δὲ παισὶ τοῖς αὑτοῦ ξυνὼν
ἀδελφὸς αὑτὸς καὶ πατήρ, κἀξ ἧς ἔφυ
γυναικὸς υἱὸς καὶ πόσις, καὶ τοῦ πατρὸς
ὁμόσπορός τε καὶ φονεύς. καὶ ταῦτ' ἰὼν　　　460
εἴσω λογίζου· κἂν λάβῃς ἐψευσμένον,
φάσκειν ἔμ' ἤδη μαντικῇ μηδὲν φρονεῖν.

ΧΟ. στρ. α'.　τίς ὄντιν' ἁ θεσπιέπεια Δελφὶς εἶπε πέτρα

461 λάβῃς ἐψευσμένον L et edd. plerique. λάβῃς μ' ἐψευσμένον A, E, V, al.,
quos secuti sunt Brunck. et Hermann. Placet Blaydesio quoque λάβῃς μ' in hoc
versu, in 462 τότ' ἤδη legere. Dum vero in 462 ἔμ' ἤδη habeamus, in 461 pro-
nomine facile caremus.　　**463** εἶπε factum est in L post deletum verbum quod

καὶ μήνυτρα κεκηρυγμένα ἑκατὸν μνᾶς. **451** τὸν Λάϊειον: cp. 267.
452 ξένος μέτοικος, a foreign sojourner: ξένος, because Oed. was
reputed a Corinthian. In poetry μέτοικος is simply *one who comes
to dwell with* others: it has not the full technical sense which belonged to it at Athens, a resident *alien*: hence the addition of ξένος
was necessary. Cp. *O. C.* 934 μέτοικος τῆσδε γῆς: *Ant.* 868 πρὸς οὓς
(to the dead) ἅδ' ἐγὼ μέτοικος ἔρχομαι. εἶτα δὲ opp. to νῦν μὲν, implied
in ἐνθάδε. ἐγγενὴς, 'native,' as γεννητός is opp. to ποιητός (*adoptivus*).
454 τῇ ξυμφορᾷ: the (seemingly happy) event: cp. *El.* 1230 κἀπὶ
συμφοραῖσί μοι | γεγηθὸς ἕρπει δάκρυον. ἐκ δεδορκότος: Xen. *Cyr.* 3. 1.
17 ἐξ ἄφρονος σώφρων γεγένηται. **455** ξένην ἔπι, sc. γῆν: *O. C.* 184 ξεῖνος
ἐπὶ ξένης: *Ph.* 135 ἐν ξένᾳ ξένον. **456** γαῖαν with προδεικνὺς only: *pointing
to, i.e.* feeling, ψηλαφῶν, the ground *before* him: so of a boxer, χερσὶ
προδεικνύς, sparring, Theocr. 22. 102. Cp. Lucian *Hercules* 1 τὸ τόξον
ἐντεταμένον ἡ ἀριστερὰ προδείκνυσι, *i.e.* holds in front of him:
id. *Hermotimus* 68 θαλλῷ προδειχθέντι ἀκολουθεῖν, ὥσπερ τὰ πρόβατα.
Seneca *Oed.* 656 *repet incertus viae,* | *Baculo senili triste praetentans
iter.* The order of words is against taking ξένην with γαῖαν (when

Laïus—that man is here,—in seeming, an alien sojourner, but anon he shall be found a native Theban, and shall not be glad of his fortune. A blind man, he who now hath sight, a beggar, who now is rich, he shall make his way to a strange land, feeling the ground before him with his staff. And he shall be found at once brother and father of the children with whom he consorts; son and husband of the woman who bore him; heir to his father's bed, shedder of his father's blood.

So go thou in and think on that; and if thou find that I have been at fault, say thenceforth that I have no wit in prophecy.

CHORUS.

Who is he of whom the divine voice from the Delphian rock hath 1st
strophe.

non dubito quin εἶδε fuisset, praesertim cum in Flor. Abb. 152 (Γ) εἶδε a pr. m. scriptum recentior in εἶπε correxerit. Noverat scholiasta εἶδε illud, quod tamen huic loco ita est alienum ut vix aliunde quam ex incuria librariorum gigni potuerit.

---

we should write ἐπὶ), and supplying τὴν ὁδόν with προδεικνύς. **457** ξυνὼν: the idea of daily converse under the same roof heightens the horror. Cp. Andoc. *De Myst.* § 49 οἷς...ἐχρῶ καὶ οἷς συνῆσθα, your friends and associates. **458** ἀδελφὸς αὐτός. If ἀδελφὸς stood alone, then αὐτός would be right: *himself* the brother of *his own* children: but with ἀδελφὸς καὶ πατὴρ we should read αὐτός: *at once* sire and brother of his own children. Cp. *Phil.* 119 σοφός τ᾽ ἂν αὐτὸς κἀγαθὸς κεκλῇ᾽ ἅμα: Eur. *Alc.* 143 καὶ πῶς ἂν αὐτὸς κατθάνοι τε καὶ βλέποι; **460** ὁμόσπορος: here act., = τὴν αὐτὴν σπείρων: but passive above, 260. Acc. to the general rule, verbal derivatives with a short penult. are paroxytone when active in meaning (see on βουνόμοις, v. 26). But those compounded with a preposition (or with a *privativum*) are excepted: hence διάβολος, not διαβόλος. So ὁμόσπορος here no less than in 260. On the other hand πρωτοσπόρος = 'sowing first,' πρωτόσπορος = 'first-sown.' **462** φάσκειν: 'say' (*i.e.* you may be confident): *El.* 9 φάσκειν Μυκήνας τὰς πολυχρύσους ὁρᾶν: *Phil.* 1411 φάσκειν δ᾽ αὐδὴν τὴν Ἡρακλέους | ...κλύειν. μαντικῇ: *in respect* to seer-craft: for the dat. cp. Eur. *I. A.* 338 τῷ δοκεῖν μὲν οὐχὶ χρῄζων, τῷ δὲ βούλεσθαι θέλων.

463—511 First στάσιμον. Teiresias has just denounced Oedipus. Why, we might ask, do not the Chorus *at once* express their horror? The answer is that this choral ode is the first since v. 215, and that

J. S.   7

2 ἄρρητ᾽ ἀρρήτων τελέσαντα φοινίαισι χερσίν;　465
3 ὥρα νιν ἀελλάδων
4 ἵππων σθεναρώτερον
5 φυγᾷ πόδα νωμᾶν.
6 ἔνοπλος γὰρ ἐπ᾽ αὐτὸν ἐπενθρώσκει
7 πυρὶ καὶ στεροπαῖς ὁ Διὸς γενέτας,　470
8 δειναὶ δ᾽ ἅμ᾽ ἕπονται
9 Κῆρες ἀναπλάκητοι.

466 ἀελλοπόδων codd.: ἀελλάδων Hesych.　**472** Veram l. ἀναπλάκητοι habet L, superscripto tamen μ falsam correctionem indicante. Praeter Laur. 31. 10 et

---

therefore, in accordance with the conception of the Chorus as personified reflection, it must furnish a lyric comment on *all* that has been most stirring in the interval. Hence it has two leading themes: (1) 'Who can be the murderer?': 1st strophe and antistrophe, referring to vv. 216—315. (2) 'I will not believe that it is Oedipus': 2nd strophe and antistrophe, referring to vv. 316—462.

1st strophe (463—472). Who is the murderer at whom the Delphic oracle hints? He should fly: Apollo and the Fates are upon him.

1st antistrophe (473—482). The word has gone forth to search for him. Doubtless he is hiding in waste places, but he cannot flee his doom.

2nd strophe (483—497). Teiresias troubles me with his charge against Oedipus: but I know nothing that confirms it.

2nd antistrophe (498—511). Only gods are infallible; a mortal, though a seer, may be wrong. Oedipus has given proof of worth. Without proof, I will not believe him guilty.

463 θεσπιέπεια, giving divine oracles (ἔπη), fem. as if from θεσπιεπής (not found): cp. ἀρτιέπεια, ἡδυέπεια. Since θέ-σπ-ι-ς already involves the stem σεπ (Curt. *E.* § 632), the termination, from ϝεπ (*ib.* 620), is pleonastic. Δελφὶς πέτρα. The town and temple of Delphi stood in a recess like an amphitheatre, on a high platform of rock which slopes out from the south face of the cliff: Strabo 9. 418 οἱ Δελφοί, πετρῶδες χωρίον, θεατροειδές, κατὰ κορυφὴν (*i.e.* at the upper part of the rocky platform, nearest the cliff) ἔχον τὸ μαντεῖον καὶ τὴν πόλιν, σταδίων ἑκκαίδεκα κύκλον πληροῦσαν: *i.e.* the whole sweep of the curve extends nearly two miles. *Hom. hymn. Apoll.* 1. 283 ὕπερθεν | πέτρη ἐπικρέμαται (the rocky platform overhangs the Crisaean plain)

spoken, as having wrought with red hands horrors that no tongue can tell?

It is time that he ply in flight a foot stronger than the feet of storm-swift steeds : for the son of Zeus is springing on him, all armed with fiery lightnings, and with him come the dread, unerring Fates.

Palat. 40, etiam T ἀναπλάκητοι praebet: quo in cod. ascripsit schol. ἀναπλάκητοι χρὴ γράφειν (metri causa)...εὕρηται γὰρ καὶ ἕν τινι τῶν παλαιοτάτων βιβλίων. ἀναμπλάκητοι A et plerique.

κοίλη δ' ὑποδέδρομε βῆσσα (the valley of the Pleistus). 465 ἄρρητ' ἀρρήτων : Blaydes cp. O. C. 1237 πρόπαντα | κακὰ κακῶν, Phil. 65 ἔσχατ' ἐσχάτων, Aesch. Pers. 681 ὦ πιστὰ πιστῶν ἥλικές τ' ἥβης ἐμῆς, | Πέρσαι γέροντες. Cp. also 1301 μείζονα τῶν μακίστων. (But El. 849 δειλαία δειλαίων [κυρεῖς], cited by Blaydes, and by Jelf § 139, is not in point.) 466 ἀελλάδων : O. C. 1081 ἀελλαία ταχύρρωστος πελειάς : fr. 621 ἀελλάδες φωναί. Not 'daughters of the storm,' as if alluding to the mares impregnated by Boreas, Il. 20. 221. For the form cp. θυστάδας λιτάς Ant. 1019. 467 ἵππων, instead of ἵππων ποδός : Her. 2. 134 πυραμίδα δὲ καὶ οὗτος ἀπελίπετο πολλὸν ἐλάσσω τοῦ πατρός : Xen. Cyr. 3. 3. 41 χώραν ἔχετε οὐδὲν ἧττον ἔντιμον τῶν πρωτοστατῶν. 470 στεροπαῖς. The oracular Apollo is Διὸς προφήτης. As punisher of the crime which the oracle denounced, he is here armed with his father's lightnings, not merely with his own arrows (205). γενέτας, one concerned with γένος, either passively, = 'son,' as here (cp. γηγενέτᾳ Eur. Phoen. 128), or actively, = 'father.' Eur. has both senses. Cp. γαμβρός, son-in-law, brother-in-law, or father-in-law : and so κηδεστής or πενθερός could have any one of these three senses. 472 Κῆρες : avenging spirits, identified with the Furies in Aesch. Theb. 1055 Κῆρες Ἐρινύες, αἵ τ' Οἰδιπόδα | γένος ὠλέσατε. Hesiod Theog. 217 (Νὺξ) καὶ Μοίρας καὶ Κῆρας ἐγείνατο νηλεοποίνους... | αἵ τ' ἀνδρῶν τε θεῶν τε παραιβασίας ἐφέπουσαι | οὐδέποτε λήγουσι θεαὶ δεινοῖο χόλοιο, | πρίν γ' ἀπὸ τῷ δώωσι κακὴν ὄπιν, ὅστις ἁμάρτῃ. The Μοῖραι decree, the Κῆρες execute. In Trach. 133 κῆρες = calamities. ἀναπλάκητοι, not erring or failing in pursuit : cp. Trach. 120 ἀλλά τις θεῶν | αἰὲν ἀναμπλάκητον Ἅιδα σφε δόμων ἐρύκει, some god suffers not Heracles to fail, but keeps him from death. Metre requires here the form without μ. ἀμπλακεῖν is prob. a cognate of πλάζω (from stem πλαγ for πλακ, Curtius Etym. § 367), strengthened with an inserted μ; cp.

ἀντ. α΄. ἔλαμψε γὰρ τοῦ νιφόεντος ἀρτίως φανεῖσα

2 φάμα Παρνασοῦ τὸν ἄδηλον ἄνδρα πάντ᾽ ἰχνεύειν.   475

3 φοιτᾷ γὰρ ὑπ᾽ ἀγρίαν

4 ὕλαν ἀνά τ᾽ ἄντρα καὶ

5 πέτρας ἰσόταυρος,

6 μέλεος μελέῳ ποδὶ χηρεύων,

7 τὰ μεσόμφαλα γᾶς ἀπονοσφίζων   480

478 πέτρασ ὡσ ταυροσ (sic) L, quod fecit antiqua manus ex πετραῖοσ ὁ ταῦροσ. πέτρας ὡς ταῦρος A et ceterorum pars maior. V autem et cod. Ambros. G. 56 (M) πετραῖος ὡς ταῦρος exhibent: quod, prima Laurentiani manu adiuvante, eo ducere videtur ut credamus vocem πετραῖος aliqua saltem vetustatis auctoritate niti. Nimirum

---

ἄβροτος, ἄμβροτος. **473 ἔλαμψε**: see on 186. **τοῦ νιφόεντος**: the message flashed forth like a beacon from that snow-crowned range which the Thebans see to the west. I have elsewhere noted some features of the view from the Dryoscephalae pass over Mount Cithaeron :—'At a turn of the road the whole plain of Boeotia bursts upon the sight, stretched out far below us. There to the north-west soars up Helicon, and beyond it, Parnassus; and, *though this is the middle of May, their higher cliffs are still crowned with dazzling snow.* Just opposite, nearly due north, is Thebes, on a low eminence with a range of hills behind it, and the waters of Lake Copais to the north-west, gleaming in the afternoon sun.' (*Modern Greece*, p. 75.) **475** Join τὸν ἄδηλον ἄνδρα, and take πάντα as neut. plur., 'by all means.' The adverbial πάντα is very freq. in Soph., esp. with adj., as *Ai.* 911 ὁ πάντα κωφός, ὁ πάντ᾽ ἄϊδρις : but also occurs with verb, as *Trach.* 338 τούτων ἔχω γὰρ πάντ᾽ ἐπιστήμην ἐγώ. Here, the emphasis on πάντα would partly warrant us in taking it as acc. sing. masc., subject to ἰχνεύειν. But, though the masc. nominative πᾶς sometimes = πᾶς τις, it may be doubted whether Soph. would have thus used the ambiguous πάντα alone for the acc. sing. masc. Ellendt compares 226, but there πάντα is acc. plur. neut. **478** πέτρας ἰσόταυρος is Prof. E. L. Lushington's brilliant emendation of πετραῖος ὁ ταῦρος, the reading of the first hand in L. It is at once closer to the letters, and more poetical, than πέτρας ἄτε ταῦρος (Dorville), πέτρας ἴσα ταύροις (M. Schmidt), or πέτρας ὡς ταῦρος, which last is a prosaic correction found in some MSS. I suppose the corruption to have arisen thus. A transcriber who had before him ΠΕΤΡΑΣΙΣΟΤΑΥΡΟΣ took the first O for the art., and then amended ΠΕΤΡΑΣΙΣ into the familiar word

Yea, newly given from snowy Parnassus, the message hath flashed forth to make all search for the unknown man. Into the wild wood's covert, among caves and rocks he is roaming, fierce as a bull, wretched and forlorn on his joyless path, still seeking to put from him the doom spoken at Earth's central

1st anti-strophe.

lectio quam V et M praestant id agebat ut traditum πετραῖος cum correctione ὡς conciliaret. πετραῖος ὁ ταῦρος legunt Hermann., G. Wolff., Schneidewin.: πέτρας ὡς ταῦρος Campbell. Coniecit πέτρας ἅτε ταῦρος Dorville: receperunt Wunder., Hartung., Dindorf., Nauck., Blaydes. πέτρας ἴσα ταύροις coni. M. Schmidt.: πέτρας ἰσόταυρος elegantissime E. L. Lushington.: vide annot.

ΠΕΤΡΑΙΟΣ. With a cursive MS. this would have been still easier, since in πετρασισοταυροσ the first σ might have been taken for ο (not a rare mistake), and then a simple transposition of ι and the supposed ο would have given πετραιοσ. It is true that such compounds with ἰσο- usu. mean, not merely 'like,' but 'as good as' or 'no better than': e.g. ἰσοδαίμων, ἰσόθεος, ἰσόνεκυς, ἰσόνειρος, ἰσόπαις, ἰσόπρεσβυς. Here, however, ἰσόταυρος can well mean 'wild' or 'fierce of heart' as a bull. And we know that in the lost Κρέουσα Soph. used ἰσοθάνατος in a way which seemed too bold to Pollux (6. 174 οὐ πάνυ ἀνεκτόν),—probably in the sense of 'dread as death' (cp. Ai. 215 θανάτῳ γὰρ ἴσον πάθος ἐκπεύσει). The bull is the type of a savage wanderer who avoids his fellows. Soph. in a lost play spoke of a bull 'that shuns the herd,' Bekk. Anecd. 459. 31 ἀτιμαγέλης· ὁ ἀποστάτης τῆς ἀγέλης ταῦρος· οὕτω Σοφοκλῆς. Verg. Geo. 3. 225 (taurus) Victus abit, longeque ignotis exulat oris. Theocr. 14. 43 αἶνος θὴν λέγεταί τις, ἔβα καὶ ταῦρος ἀν' ὕλαν a proverb ἐπὶ τῶν μὴ ἀναστρεφόντων (schol.). The image also suggests the fierce despair of the wretched outlaw: Aesch. Cho. 275 ἀπόχρημάτοισι ζημίαις ταυρούμενον, 'stung to fury by the wrongs that keep me from my heritage': Eur. Med. 92 ὄμμα ταυρουμένην: Ar. Ran. 804 ἔβλεψε γοῦν ταυρηδὸν ἐγκύψας κάτω: Plat. Phaed. 117 B ταυρηδὸν ὑποβλέψας πρὸς τὸν ἄνθρωπον. On the reading πετραῖος ὁ ταῦρος see Appendix, Note 11. 479 χηρεύων, solitary, as one who is· ἀφρήτωρ, ἀθέμιστος, ἀνέστιος (Il. 9. 63): he knows the doom which cuts him off from all human fellowship (236 f.). Aesch. Eum. 656 ποία δὲ χέρνιψ φρατέρων προσδέξεται; 480 τὰ μεσόμφαλα γᾶς μαντεῖα = τὰ ἀπὸ μέσου ὀμφαλοῦ γᾶς: El. 1386 δωμάτων ὑπόστεγοι = ὑπὸ στέγῃ δωμάτων: Eur. Phoen. 1351 λευκοπήχεις κτύπους χεροῖν. The ὀμφαλός in the Delphian temple (Aesch. Eum. 40), a large white stone in the form of a half globe, was held to mark the spot at which the eagles from east and west had met: hence

8 μαντεῖα· τὰ δ' ἀεὶ
9 ζῶντα περιποτᾶται.

στρ. β'. δεινὰ μὲν οὖν, δεινὰ ταράσσει σοφὸς οἰωνοθέτας, 483
2 οὔτε δοκοῦντ' οὔτ' ἀποφάσκονθ'· ὅ τι λέξω δ' ἀπορῶ. 485
3 πέτομαι δ' ἐλπίσιν οὔτ' ἐνθάδ' ὁρῶν οὔτ' ὀπίσω.
4 τί γὰρ ἢ Λαβδακίδαις ἢ   [οὔτε τανῦν πω
5 τῷ Πολύβου νεῖκος ἔκειτ' οὔτε πάροιθέν ποτ' ἔγωγ'
6 ἔμαθον, πρὸς ὅτου δὴ <βασανίζων> βασάνῳ

493   Excidit aut ionicus a minore post ἔμαθον vel post δή: aut choriambus post
βασάνῳ. βασανίζων conieci: vide annot.   πρὸς ὅτου.   Inveni in Bodl. Laud. 54

Pindar calls Delphi itself μέγαν ὀμφαλὸν εὐρυκόλπου | ...χθονός (*Nem.*
7. 33): Liv. 38. 48 *Delphos, umbilicum orbis terrarum.* ἀπονοσφίζων,
trying to put away (from himself): the midd. (cp. 691) would be more
usual, but poetry admits the active: 894 ψυχᾶς ἀμύνειν: Eur. *Or.* 294
ἀνακάλυπτε...κάρα: Pind. *Pyth.* 4. 106 κομίζων = κομιζόμενος (seeking to
recover): *O. C.* 6 φέροντα = φερόμενον. In *Phil.* 979 ἀπονοσφίζειν τινά
τινος = to rob one of a thing: but here we cannot render 'frustrating.'
482 ζῶντα, 'living,' *i.e.* operative, effectual; see on 45 ζώσας.   περιποτᾶται:
the doom pronounced by Apollo hovers around the murderer as the
οἶστρος around some tormented animal: he cannot shake off its pursuit.
The haunting thoughts of guilt are objectively imaged as terrible
words ever sounding in the wanderer's ears.   **483 f.**   The Chorus have
described the unknown murderer as they imagine him—a fugitive in
remote places.   They now touch on the charge laid against Oedipus,—
but only to say that it lacks all evidence.   δεινὰ μὲν οὖν.   οὖν marks the
turning to a new topic, with something of concessive force: '*it is true*
that the murderer is said to be here': μὲν is answered by δὲ after λέξω:
δεινὰ is adverbial: for (1) ταράσσει could not mean κινεῖ, stirs up, raises,
dread questions: (2) δοκοῦντα, ἀποφάσκοντα are acc. sing. masc., referring to με understood.   The schol., οὔτε πιστὰ οὔτε ἄπιστα, has
favoured the attempt to take the participles as acc. neut. plur.,
ἀποφάσκοντα being explained as 'negative' in the sense of 'admitting
of negation,' ἀπόφασιν καὶ ἀπιστίαν δεχόμενα (Triclinius).   This is
fruitless torture of language.   Nor will the conj. ἀπαρέσκοντ' serve:
for, even if the Chorus found the charge credible, they would
not find it *pleasing*.   δοκοῦντα is not 'believing,' but '*approving*.'

shrine : but that doom ever lives, ever flits around him.

Dreadly, in sooth, dreadly doth the wise augur move me, who 2nd
approve not, nor am able to deny. How to speak, I know not ; strophe.
I am fluttered with forebodings ; neither in the present have I
clear vision, nor of the future. Never in past days, nor in these,
have I heard how the house of Labdacus or the son of Polybus
had, either against other, any grief that I could bring as proof

lectionem a nemine quod sciam prius memoratam, παρ' ὅτου, adiecta interpr. παρ' οὗ,
ἤγουν τοῦ νείκους.

Cp. *Ant.* 1102 καὶ ταῦτ' ἐπαινεῖς καὶ δοκεῖς παρεικαθεῖν; 'and
you recommend this course, and approve of yielding?' The preg-
nant force of δοκοῦντα is here brought out by the direct contrast with
ἀποφάσκοντα. In gauging the rarer uses of particular words by an
artist in language so subtle and so bold as Soph. we must never
neglect the context. **485** λέξω, deliberative aor. subj. **486** ἐνθάδε, the
actual situation, implies the known facts of the past ; ὀπίσω refers to the
seer's hint of the future, v. 453 φανήσεται κ.τ.λ. *Od.* 11. 482 σεῖο δ',
Ἀχιλλεῦ, | οὔτις ἀνὴρ προπάροιθε μακάρτατος, οὔτ' ἄρ' ὀπίσσω (nor will
be hereafter). **487 f.** ἢ Λαβδακίδαις ἢ τῷ Πολύβου. A quarrel might have
originated with either house. This is what the disjunctive statement
marks : since ἔκειτο, 'had been made,' implies 'had been provoked.'
But we see the same Greek tendency as in the use of τε καί where καί
alone would be more natural: Aesch. *P. V.* 927 τό τ' ἄρχειν καὶ τὸ δου-
λεύειν δίχα: cp. Hor. *Ep.* 1. 2. 12 *Inter Priamiden animosum atque inter
Achillen Ira fuit.* **493** πρὸς ὅτου. In the antistr., 509, the words γὰρ
ἐπ' αὐτῷ are undoubtedly sound : here then we need to supply ∪∪——
or – ∪ ∪ –. I incline to believe that the loss has been that of a
participle going with βασάνῳ. Had this been βασανίζων, the iteration
would help to account for the loss. Reading πρὸς ὅτου δὴ βασανίζων
βασάνῳ I should take πρὸς with βασάνῳ: 'testing *on* the touchstone
whereof'—'using which (νεῖκος) as a test.' To Brunck's βασάνῳ χρησά-
μενος (Plat. *Legg.* 946 c βασάνοις χρώμενοι) the objections are (1) the
aorist part. where we need the pres., (2) the tame and prosaic phrase.
Two other courses of emendation are possible: (i) To supply after ἔμαθον
something to express the informant, as τινος ἀστῶν, or προφέροντος, when
πρὸς ὅτου would mean 'at whose suggestion.' This remedy seems to me
improbable. (ii) To supply σὺν and an adj. with βασάνῳ, as σὺν
ἀληθεῖ β., or β. σὺν φανερᾷ. As the mutilated verse stands in the

7 ἐπὶ τὰν ἐπίδαμον φάτιν εἶμ' Οἰδιπόδα Λαβδακίδαις 495
8 ἐπίκουρος ἀδήλων θανάτων.

[βροτῶν

ἀντ. β΄. ἀλλ' ὁ μὲν οὖν Ζεὺς ὅ τ' Ἀπόλλων ξυνετοὶ καὶ τὰ
2 εἰδότες· ἀνδρῶν δ' ὅτι μάντις πλέον ἢ 'γὼ φέρεται, 500
3 κρίσις οὐκ ἔστιν ἀληθής· σοφίᾳ δ' ἂν σοφίαν
4 παραμείψειεν ἀνήρ. [ἂν καταφαίην.

5 ἀλλ' οὔποτ' ἔγωγ' ἄν, πρὶν ἴδοιμ' ὀρθὸν ἔπος, μεμφομένων
6 φανερὰ γὰρ ἐπ' αὐτῷ πτερόεσσ' ἦλθε κόρα
7 ποτέ, καὶ σοφὸς ὤφθη βασάνῳ θ' ἀδύπολις· τῷ ἀπ' ἐμᾶς

509 φανερὰ γὰρ ἐπ' αὐτῷ. Hermannus, cum versui 493 ἔμαθον πρὸς ὅτου δὴ βασάνῳ nihil deesse crederet, hic verba γὰρ ἐπ' αὐτῷ in prima editione omisit, in secunda tamen reposuit: Dindorf. etiamnunc omittit. Iam Triclinius ἐπ' αὐτῷ omiserat, nullam aliam ob causam quam quod ea verba parum convenienter dici censeret: γὰρ autem reliquerat, metri, ut solebat, securus. In A (ubi, ut in L,

MSS., it cannot, I think, be translated without some violence to Greek idiom: the most tolerable version would be this:—'setting out from which (πρὸς ὅτου neut., referring to νεῖκος), I can with good warrant (βασάνῳ) assail the public fame of Oed.' Then βασάνῳ would be an instrumental dative equivalent to βάσανον ἔχων: and πρὸς ὅτου would be like 1236 πρὸς τίνος ποτ' αἰτίας; *Ant.* 51 πρὸς αὐτο-φώρων ἀμπλακημάτων: πρὸς denoting the source back to which the act can be traced. **495** ἐπὶ φάτιν εἶμι, a phrase from war: it is unnecessary to suppose tmesis: Her. 1. 157 στρατὸν ἐπ' ἑωυτὸν ἰόντα: Eur. *I. A.* 349 ταῦτα μέν σε πρῶτ' ἐπῆλθον, ἵνα σε πρῶθ' ηὗρον κακόν, *censured* thee: *Andr.* 688 ταῦτ' εὖ φρονῶν σ' ἐπῆλθον, οὐκ ὀργῆς χάριν. **497** The gen. θανάτων after ἐπίκουρος is not objective, 'against' (as Xen. *Mem.* 4. 3. 7 πῦρ...ἐπίκουρον...ψύχους), but causal, 'on account of'; being softened by the approximation of ἐπίκουρος to the sense of τιμωρός: Eur. *El.* 135 ἔλθοις τῶνδε πόνων ἐμοὶ τᾷ μελέᾳ λυτήρ, | ...πατρί θ' αἱμάτων | ἐχθίστων ἐπίκουρος (= 'avenger'). The allusive plur. θανάτων is like αἱμάτων there, and δεσποτῶν θανάτοισι Aesch. *Ch.* 52: cp. above, 366 τοῖς φιλτάτοις. **498** It is true (οὖν, cp. 483) that *gods* indeed (μὲν) have perfect knowledge. But there is no way of deciding in a strict sense (ἀληθής) that any *mortal* who essays to read the future attains to more than I do—*i. e.* to more than *con-jecture:* though I admit that one man may excel another in the art of interpreting omens according to the general rules of augural lore

in assailing the public fame of Oedipus, and seeking to avenge the line of Labdacus for the undiscovered murder.

Nay, Zeus indeed and Apollo are keen of thought, and know the things of earth; but that mortal seer wins knowledge above mine, of this there can be no sure test; though man may surpass man in lore. Yet, until I see the word made good, never will I assent when men blame Oedipus. Before all eyes, the winged maiden came against him of old, and he was seen to be wise; he bore the test, in welcome service to our State; never, therefore, by the verdict of my

2nd anti-strophe.

verbis φανερὰ γὰρ versus finitur, proximus a verbis ἐπ' αὐτῷ incipit) deleverat librarius duos versus inter φανερὰ γὰρ et ἐπ' αὐτῷ: quod tamen ad nullum textus vitium spectat. Erraverant scribentis oculi, quod ipse simul ac senserat, illatos aliunde versus expulit. **510** ἡδύπολις codd., Hermann., Nauck., Blaydes.: ἀδύπολις Dindorf., Campbell.

(σοφίᾳ: cp. σοφὸς οἰωνοθέτας 484). The disquieted speaker clings to the negative argument: 'Teiresias is more likely to be right than a common man: still, it is not *certain* that he is right.' **500** πλέον φέρεται, achieves a better result,—deserves to be ranked above me: Her. 1. 31 δοκέων πάγχυ δευτερεῖα γῶν οἴσεσθαι, 'thinking that he was sure of the second place at least.' **504** παραμείψειεν: Eur. *I. A.* 145 μή τίς σε λάθῃ | τροχάλοισιν ὄχοις παραμειψαμένη |...ἀπήνη. **506** πρὶν ἴδοιμ'. After an optative of wish or hypothesis in the principal clause, πρίν regularly takes optat.: *Phil.* 961 ὄλοιο μήπω πρὶν μάθοιμ' εἰ καὶ πάλιν | γνώμην μετοίσεις. So after ὅπως, ὅστις, ἵνα, etc.: Aesch. *Eum.* 297 ἔλθοι...|ὅπως γένοιτο: Eur. *Helen.* 435 τίς ἂν...μόλοι | ὅστις διαγγείλειε. ὀρθὸν: the notion is not 'upright,' established, but 'straight,'—*justified* by proof, as by the application of a rule: cp. Ar. *Av.* 1004 ὀρθῷ μετρήσω κανόνι προστιθείς: so below, 853, *Ant.* 1178 τοὔπος ὡς ἄρ' ὀρθὸν ἤνυσας. **507** καταφαίην: Arist. *Metaphys.* 3. 6 ἀδύνατον ἅμα καταφάναι καὶ ἀποφάναι ἀληθῶς. *Defin. Plat.* 413 c ἀλήθεια ἕξις ἐν καταφάσει καὶ ἀποφάσει. **508** πτερόεσσα...κόρα: the Sphinx having the face of a maiden, and the winged body of a lion: Eur. *Phoen.* 1042 ἁ πτεροῦσσα παρθένος. See Appendix, Note 12. **510** βασάνῳ with ἀδύπολις only, which, as a dat. of manner, it qualifies with nearly adverbial force: commending himself to the city under a practical test,—*i.e.* ἔργῳ καὶ οὐ λόγῳ. Pind. *Pyth.* 10. 67 πειρῶντι δὲ καὶ χρυσὸς ἐν βασάνῳ πρέπει | καὶ νόος ὀρθός:

8 φρενὸς οὔποτ' ὀφλήσει κακίαν. 511

ΚΡ. ἄνδρες πολῖται, δείν' ἔπη πεπυσμένος
κατηγορεῖν μου τὸν τύραννον Οἰδίπουν
πάρειμ' ἀτλητῶν. εἰ γὰρ ἐν ταῖς ξυμφοραῖς 515
ταῖς νῦν νομίζει πρός γ' ἐμοῦ πεπονθέναι
λόγοισιν εἴτ' ἔργοισιν εἰς βλάβην φέρον,
οὔτοι βίου μοι τοῦ μακραίωνος πόθος,
φέροντι τήνδε βάξιν. οὐ γὰρ εἰς ἁπλοῦν

516 πρόσ τ' ἐμοῦ L, post factam in littera τ' rasuram; neque dubium videtur quin τ' ex Γ' ortum sit, ut in v. 294 δείματόσ τ', quem vide. πρὸ τ' ἐμ᷇ (=πρός τ' ἐμοῦ) A, cui τῖ litteris rubris super τε scriptum corrector addidit. Indicatur v. l. τι pro τε etiam in B: in V autem, cui Campb. eam tribuit, meis quidem oculis non adfuit. Id autem animadversione dignum est, quod T, cum veram l. πρόσ γ' ἐμοῦ servet,

'an upright mind, like gold, is shown by the touchstone, when one assays it': as base metal τρίβῳ τε καὶ προσβολαῖς | μελαμπαγὴς πέλει | δικαιωθείς Aesch. *Ag.* 391. ἀδύπολις, in the sense of ἀνδάνων τῇ πόλει (cp. Pind. *Nem.* 8. 38 ἀστοῖς ἀδών): boldly formed on the analogy of compounds in which the adj. represents a verb governing the *accus.*, as φιλόπολις = φιλῶν τὴν πόλιν, ὀρθόπολις (epithet of a good dynasty) = ὀρθῶν τὴν πόλιν (Pind. *Olymp.* 2. 7). In *Ant.* 370 ὑψίπολις is analogous, though not exactly similar, if it means ὑψηλὸς ἐν πόλει, and not ὑψηλὴν πόλιν ἔχων (like δικαιόπολις = δικαίας πόλεις ἔχουσα, of Aegina, Pind. *Pyth.* 8. 22). **511** τῷ, 'therefore,' as *Il.* I. 418 etc.; joined with νύ, *Il.* 7. 352 etc.: Plat. *Theaet.* 179 D τῷ τοι, ὦ φίλε Θεόδωρε, μᾶλλον σκεπτέον ἐξ ἀρχῆς. ἀπ', on the part of: *Trach.* 471 κἀπ' ἐμοῦ κτήσει χάριν.

512—862 ἐπεισόδιον δεύτερον, with κομμός (649—697). Oedipus upbraids Creon with having suborned Teiresias. The quarrel is allayed by Iocasta. As she and Oedipus converse, he is led to fear that he may unwittingly have slain Laïus. It is resolved to send for the surviving eye-witness of the deed.

Oedipus had directly charged Creon with plotting to usurp the throne (385). Creon's defence serves to bring out the character of Oedipus by a new contrast. Creon is a man of somewhat rigid nature, and essentially matter-of-fact. In his reasonable indignation, he bases his argument on a calculation of interest (583),—insisting on the substance in contrast with the show of power, as in the *Antigone*

heart shall he be adjudged guilty of crime.

CREON.

Fellow-citizens, having learned that Oedipus the king lays dire charges against me, I am here, indignant. If, in the present troubles, he thinks that he has suffered from *me*, by word or deed, aught that tends to harm, in truth I crave not my full term of years, when I must bear such blame as this. The wrong of this rumour touches me not in one

ipse tamen $\bar{\tau}$ super γε scriptum habet. Equidem credo lectionem τι inde provenisse, quod cum γ' in τ' corruptum fuerat, rudes elisionis legum librarii ipsum illud τ', quasi pro τι positum, ad φέρον rettulerunt. Deinde varia lectio τι iis quoque libris accessit in quibus, ut in T, vera manserat. Praeeunte tamen Hartungio πρός τι μου recepit Dindorf. πρός γ' ἐμοῦ Suidas s. v. βάξιν.

his vindication of the written law ignores the unwritten. His blunt anger at a positive wrong is softened by no power of imagining the mental condition in which it was done. He cannot allow for the tumult which the seer's terrible charge excited in the mind of Oedipus, any more than for the conflict of duties in the mind of Antigone.

515 ἀτλητῶν. The verb ἀτλητέω, found only here, implies an active sense of ἄτλητος, *impatiens:* as μεμπτός, pass. in *O. C.* 1036, is active in *Trach.* 446. So from the *act.* sense of the verbal adj. we find ἀλαστέω, ἀναισθητέω, ἀναισχυντέω, ἀνελπιστέω, ἀπρακτέω. **516 πρός γ' ἐμοῦ,** from *me,* whatever others may have done. The weak correction πρός τί μου was prompted by the absence of τι with φέρον: but cp. Aesch. *Ag.* 261 σὺ δ' εἴτε (*v. l.* εἴ τι) κεδνὸν εἴτε μὴ πεπυσμένη: Plat. *Soph.* 237 C χαλεπὸν ἤρου: *Meno* 97 E τῶν ἐκείνου ποιημάτων λελυμένον μὲν ἐκτῆσθαι οὐ πολλῆς τινος ἄξιόν ἐστι τιμῆς. **517 εἴτε** is omitted before λόγοισιν: Pind. *Pyth.* 4. 78 ξεῖνος αἴτ' ὢν ἀστός: *Trach.* 236 πατρῴας εἴτε βαρβάρου. **φέρον: 519 φέροντι: 520 φέρει:** such repetitions are not rare in the best Greek and Latin writers. Cp. 1276, 1278 (ὁμοῦ), Lucr. 2. 54—59 *tenebris—tenebris—tenebris—tenebras.* **518 βίου τοῦ μακρ.:** *Ai.* 473 τοῦ μακροῦ χρῄζειν βίου: *O. C.* 1214 αἱ μακραὶ | ἁμέραι, where the art. refers to the normal span of human life. For βίος μακραίων cp. *Trach.* 791 δυσπάρευνον λέκτρον. **519 εἰς ἁπλοῦν.** The charge does not hurt him in a *single* aspect only, —*i.e.* merely in his relation to his family and friends (ἰδίᾳ). It touches him also in relation to the State (κοινῇ), since treachery to his kinsman would be treason to his king. Hence it 'tends to the largest result' (φέρει ἐς μέγιστον), bearing on the *sum* of his relations as man and

ἡ ζημία μοι τοῦ λόγου τούτου φέρει,   520
ἀλλ᾽ ἐς μέγιστον, εἰ κακὸς μὲν ἐν πόλει,
κακὸς δὲ πρὸς σοῦ καὶ φίλων κεκλήσομαι.

ΧΟ. ἀλλ᾽ ἦλθε μὲν δὴ τοῦτο τοὔνειδος τάχ᾽ ἂν
ὀργῇ βιασθὲν μᾶλλον ἢ γνώμῃ φρενῶν.

ΚΡ. τοῦ πρὸς δ᾽ ἐφάνθη ταῖς ἐμαῖς γνώμαις ὅτι   525
πεισθεὶς ὁ μάντις τοὺς λόγους ψευδεῖς λέγοι;

ΧΟ. ηὐδᾶτο μὲν τάδ᾽, οἶδα δ᾽ οὐ γνώμῃ τίνι.

ΚΡ. ἐξ ὀμμάτων δ᾽ ὀρθῶν τε κἀξ ὀρθῆς φρενὸς
κατηγορεῖτο τοὐπίκλημα τοῦτό μου;

525 Vulgo legebatur vel πρὸς τοῦδ᾽ (et hoc quidem, non πρὸς τοῦ δ᾽, habet inter aliqs A), vel πρὸς τοῦ δ᾽, quod praetulit Brunckius. Multi autem codd. veram lectionem τοῦ πρὸς δ᾽ servant; quorum sunt L et B, pravo tamen accentu τοῦ πρόσ δ᾽ exhibentes. Cum τοῦπος habeant Γ et L², Nauckius τοῦπος legit, omisso post λέγοι

---

citizen. The thought is, ἡ ζημία οὐχ ἁπλῆ ἐστιν ἀλλὰ πολυειδής (cp. Plat. *Phaedr.* 270 D ἁπλοῦν ἢ πολυειδές ἐστιν): but the proper antithesis to ἁπλῆ is merged in the comprehensive μέγιστον. **523 ἀλλ᾽ ἦλθε...** τάχ᾽ ἂν: 'would perhaps have come' (if he had been in a hasty mood at the moment); a softened way of saying, '*probably came.*' ἂν with ἦλθε: cp. *O. C.* 964 θεοῖς γὰρ ἦν οὕτω φίλον | τάχ᾽ ἄν τι μηνίουσιν εἰς γένος πάλαι: 'for such would perhaps have been (*i.e.* probably was) the pleasure of the gods, wrath against the race from of old': where ἄν belongs to ἦν, and could not go with μηνίουσιν, any more than here with βιασθέν. ἄν can belong to the partic. or infin. only when this answers to an apodosis with ἄν and the finite verb: *e.g.* οἶδα βιασθὲν ἄν = ὅτι ἐβιάσθη ἄν or βιασθείη ἄν: φαίνονται μηνίοντες ἄν = φαίνεται ὅτι ἐμήνιον ἄν or μηνίοιεν ἄν. τάχα, as = 'perhaps,' is commonest with optat. and ἄν, but occurs also with simple indic., as *Phil.* 305 τάχ᾽ οὖν τις ἄκων ἔσχε: Plat. *Legg.* 711 A ὑμεῖς δὲ τάχα οὐδὲ τεθέασθε. We cannot take τάχ᾽ ἂν as = 'perhaps,' and treat ἦλθε as a simple indic. In Plat. *Phaedr.* 265 B τάχα δ᾽ ἂν καὶ ἄλλοσε παραφερόμενοι is explained by an ellipse of a verb. Such a neutralisation of ἄν could not be defended by the instances in which it is irregularly left adhering to a relative word, after a subjunct. verb has become optative (Xen. *An.* 3. 2. 12 ὁπόσους ἂν κατακάνοιεν). But the form of the Greek sentence, by putting ἦλθε first, was able to suggest the virtual equivalence here of the con-

point alone, but has the largest scope, if I am to be called a traitor in the city, a traitor too by thee and by my friends.

CH. Nay, but this taunt would have come under stress, perchance, of anger, rather than from the purpose of the heart.

CR. And by whom was it set forth that *my* counsels won the seer to utter his falsehoods?

CH. Such things were said—I know not with what meaning.

CR. And was this charge laid against me with steady eyes and steady mind?

interrogationis signo. **528** Suidam ἐξ ὀμμάτων δ' ὀρθῶν τε recte legentem confirmare tres tantum videntur codd., Γ, Δ, Trin. Lectionum quae in codicibus praevalebant duae sunt familiae: (1) ἐξ ὀμμάτων ὀρθῶν δὲ L (ubi tamen δὲ ex τε factum est). Sic B, E, V, V⁴, cod. Ven. 467 (V³), alii. (2) ἐξ ὀμμάτων ὀρθῶν τε A: quocum consentiunt T, V², Bodl. Laud. 54, Barocc. 66.

ditional ἦλθεν ἄν to a positive ἦλθε. Cp. the use of the optat. with ἄν in mild assertion of probable fact: εἶησαν δ' ἄν οὗτοι Κρῆτες, Her. I. 2. It is hardly needful to add that ἦλθε cannot be taken with βιασθέν as a mere periphrasis for ἐβιάσθη (Il. 18. 180 αἴ κέν τι νέκυς ᾐσχυμμένος ἔλθῃ). **525** τοῦ πρὸς δ': this order (1) gives an emphasis on τοῦ answering to that on ταῖς ἐμαῖς γν.: (2) avoids a likeness of sound between τοῦ δ' and τοῦδ'. πρὸς follows its case, as above, 177: Aesch. P. V. 653 ποίμνας βουστάσεις τε πρὸς πατρός: Theb. 185 βρέτη πεσούσας πρὸς πολισσούχων θεῶν: Eur. Or. 94 βούλει τάφον μοι πρὸς κασιγνήτης μολεῖν. Cp. Il. 24. 617 θεῶν ἐκ κήδεα πέσσει. ἐφάνθη, 'was set forth' (for the first time). Who *originated* the story which Oedipus repeated? Cp. below, 848: Antig. 620 σοφίᾳ γὰρ ἔκ του | κλεινὸν ἔπος πέφανται: Trach. I λόγος μὲν ἔστ' ἀρχαῖος ἀνθρώπων φανείς. **527** ηὐδᾶτο: these things were *said* (by Oedipus); but I do not know how much the words meant; *i.e.* whether he spoke at random, or from information which had convinced his judgment. **528** The reading ἐξ ὀμμάτων δ' ὀρθῶν τε gives a fuller emphasis than ἐξ ὀμμάτων ὀρθῶν δὲ: when δ' had been omitted, τε was naturally changed to δὲ. The place of τε (as to which both verse and prose allowed some latitude) is warranted, since ὀμμάτων-ὀρθῶν opposed to ὀρθῆς-φρενός forms a single notion. ἐξ='with': El. 455 ἐξ ὑπερτέρας χερός, Trach. 875 ἐξ ἀκινήτου ποδός. ὀμμάτων ὀρθῶν: cp. 1385: Ai. 447 κεἰ μὴ τόδ' ὄμμα καὶ φρένες διάστροφοι | γνώμης ἀπῇξαν τῆς ἐμῆς: Eur. H. F. 931 (when the frenzy comes on Heracles), ὁ δ' οὐκέθ' αὑτὸς ἦν, | ἀλλ' ἐν στροφαῖσιν ὀμμάτων ἐφθαρμένος, κ.τ.λ. In Hor.

ΧΟ. οὐκ οἶδ᾽· ἃ γὰρ δρῶσ᾽ οἱ κρατοῦντες οὐχ ὁρῶ.　530
αὐτὸς δ᾽ ὅδ᾽ ἤδη δωμάτων ἔξω περᾷ.

ΟΙ. οὗτος σύ, πῶς δεῦρ᾽ ἦλθες; ἦ τοσόνδ᾽ ἔχεις
τόλμης πρόσωπον ὥστε τὰς ἐμὰς στέγας
ἵκου, φονεὺς ὢν τοῦδε τἀνδρὸς ἐμφανῶς
λῃστής τ᾽ ἐναργὴς τῆς ἐμῆς τυραννίδος;　535
φέρ᾽ εἰπὲ πρὸς θεῶν, δειλίαν ἢ μωρίαν
ἰδών τιν᾽ ἔν μοι ταῦτ᾽ ἐβουλεύσω ποιεῖν;
ἦ τοὔργον ὡς οὐ γνωριοῖμί σου· τόδε
δόλῳ προσέρπον ἢ οὐκ ἀλεξοίμην μαθών;
ἆρ᾽ οὐχὶ μῶρόν ἐστι τοὐγχείρημά σου,　540

537 ἐν ἐμοὶ codd.; quod cur nolim recipere, rationes allatas infra videbis. ἔν μοι
Reisig., Hermann., Dindorf.　**538** γνωρίσοιμι codd., Schneidewin., Campbell.:

Carm. I. 3. 18 Bentley gave *rectis oculis* for *siccis*.　530 οὐκ οἶδ᾽.
Creon has asked: 'Did any trace of madness show itself in the bearing
or in the speech of Oedipus?'　The Chorus reply: 'Our part is only to
hear, not to criticise.'　These nobles of Thebes (1223) have no eyes
for indiscretion in their sovereign master.　532 Join οὗτος σύ: cp.
1121: Eur. *Hec.* 1280 οὗτος σύ, μαίνει καὶ κακῶν ἐρᾷς τυχεῖν; where
οὗτος, σὺ μαίνει is impossible.　τοσόνδε τόλμης-πρόσωπον, like τοὐμὸν
φρενῶν-ὄνειρον (*El.* 1390), νεῖκος-ἀνδρῶν ξύναιμον (*Ant.* 793).　535 τῆς
ἐμῆς closely follows τοῦδε τἀνδρός, as in *Ai.* 865 μυθήσομαι immediately
follows Αἴας θροεῖ.　If a Greek speaker rhetorically refers to himself in the
third person, he usu. reverts as soon as possible to the first.　537 ἔν μοι.
The MSS. have ἐν ἐμοί.　But when a tribrach holds the second place in a
tragic senarius, we usually find that (*a*) the tribrach is a single word, as
Phil. 1314 ἥσθην | πατέρα | τὸν ἀμὸν εὐλογοῦντά σε: or (*b*) there is a
caesura between the first and the second foot, as Eur. *Tro.* 496 τρυχηρὰ
περὶ | τρυχηρὸν εἱμένην χρόα: Eur. *Phoen.* 511 ἐλθόντα|α σὺν ὅπλ|οις τόνδε
καὶ πορθοῦντα γῆν, if there we should not read ἐλθόντ᾽ ἐν ὅπλοις.　With ἐν
ἐμοί (even though we regard the prep. as forming one word with its case)
the rhythm would at least be exceptional, as well as extremely harsh.
On such a point as ἐμοί *versus* μοι the authority of our MSS. is not
weighty.　And the enclitic μοι suffices: for in this verse the stress is on
the verbal notion (ἰδών),—Creon's supposed *insight:* the reference to
Oedipus is drawn out in the next two verses by the verbs in the 1st

Сн. I know not; I see not what my masters do: but here comes our lord forth from the house.

OEDIPUS.

Sirrah, how camest thou here? Hast thou a front so bold that thou hast come to my house, who art the proved assassin of its master,—the palpable robber of my crown? Come, tell me, in the name of the gods, was it cowardice or folly that thou sawest in me, that thou didst plot to do this thing? Didst thou think that I would not note this deed of thine creeping on me by stealth, or, aware, would not ward it off? Now is not thine attempt foolish,—

γνωριοῖμι Elmsleius, Nauck., edd. plerique: vide annot. **539** ἢ οὐκ con-icientes opem loco necessariam tulerunt A. Spengel. (teste Nauck.) et Blaydes., cum codd. omnes procli vi mutatione κοὐκ praebeant.

---

person, γνωριοῖμι—ἀλεξοίμην. ἰδών...ἐν: prose would say ἐνιδών, either with or without ἐν (Thuc. 1. 95: ὅπερ καὶ ἐν τῷ Παυσανίᾳ ἐνεῖδον: 3. 30 ὅ...τοῖς πολεμίοις ἐνορῶν): cp. Her. 1. 37 οὔτε τινὰ δειλίην παριδών μοι (*remarked* in me) οὔτε ἀθυμίην. **538** ἢ τοὔργον κ.τ.λ. Supply νομίσας or the like from ἰδών: 'thinking that *either* I would not see...*or* would not ward it off': an example of what Greek rhetoric called χιασμός (from the form of X), since the first clause corresponds with μωρία and the second with δειλία. γνωριοῖμι. 'Futures in -ίσω are not common in the good Attic period: but we have no trustworthy collections on this point': Curtius, *Verb* II. 312, Eng. tr. 481. On the other hand, as he says, more than 20 futures in -ιῶ can be quoted from Attic literature. And though some ancient grammarians call the form 'Attic,' it is not exclusively so: instances occur both in Homer (as *Il.* 10. 331 ἀγλαΐεῖσθαι, cp. Monro, *Hom. Gram.* § 63) and in Herodotus (as 8. 68 ἀτρεμιεῖν, besides about ten other examples in Her.). On the whole, the general evidence in favour of γνωριοῖμι decidedly outweighs the preference of our MSS. for γνωρίσοιμι in this passage. **539** ἢ οὐκ. The κοὐκ of the MSS. cannot be defended here—where stress is laid on the dilemma of δειλία or μωρία—by instances of ἤ...τε carelessly put for ἤ—ἤ in cases where there is no such sharp distinction of alternatives: as *Il.* 2. 289 ἢ παῖδες νεαροὶ χῆραί τε γυναῖκες: Aesch. *Eum.* 524 ἢ πόλις βροτός θ' ὁμοίως. ἀλεξοίμην. This future has the support of the best MSS. in Xen. *An.* 7. 7. 3 οὐκ ἐπιτρέψομεν...

ἄνευ τε πλήθους καὶ φίλων τυραννίδα
θηρᾶν, ὃ πλήθει χρήμασίν θ' ἁλίσκεται;

ΚΡ. οἶσθ' ὡς ποίησον; ἀντὶ τῶν εἰρημένων
ἴσ' ἀντάκουσον, κᾆτα κρῖν' αὐτὸς μαθών.

ΟΙ. λέγειν σὺ δεινός, μανθάνειν δ' ἐγὼ κακὸς   545
σοῦ· δυσμενῆ γὰρ καὶ βαρύν σ' εὕρηκ' ἐμοί.

ΚΡ. τοῦτ' αὐτὸ νῦν μου πρῶτ' ἄκουσον ὡς ἐρῶ.

ΟΙ. τοῦτ' αὐτὸ μή μοι φράζ', ὅπως οὐκ εἶ κακός.

ΚΡ. εἴ τοι νομίζεις κτῆμα τὴν αὐθαδίαν
εἶναί τι τοῦ νοῦ χωρίς, οὐκ ὀρθῶς φρονεῖς.   550

ΟΙ. εἴ τοι νομίζεις ἄνδρα συγγενῆ κακῶς
δρῶν οὐχ ὑφέξειν τὴν δίκην, οὐκ εὖ φρονεῖς.

---

541 πλήθους codd. : πλούτου coniecit anonymus in translatione Germanica a.

ὡς πολεμίους ἀλεξόμεθα: and of grammarians, Bekk. *Anecd.* p. 415: the aorist ἀλέξαι, ἀλέξασθαι also occurs. These forms are prob. not from the stem ἀλεξ (whence present ἀλέξω, cp. ἀέξω, ὀδάξω) but from a stem ἀλκ with unconsciously developed ε, making ἀλεκ (cp. ἄλ-αλκον): see Curtius, *Verb*, II. 258, Eng. tr. 445. Homer has the fut. ἀλεξήσω, and Her. ἀλεξήσομαι. **541** πλήθους refers to the rank and file of the aspirant's following,—his popular partisans or the troops in his pay; φίλων, to his powerful connections,—the men whose wealth and influence support him. Thus (542) χρήμασιν is substituted for φίλων. Soph. is thinking of the historical Greek τύραννος, who commonly began his career as a demagogue, or else 'arose out of the bosom of the oligarchies' (Grote III. 25). **542** ὅ, *a thing* which, marking the general category in which the τυραννίς is to be placed: cp. Xen. *Mem.* 3. 9. 8 φθόνον δὲ σκοπῶν ὅ τι εἴη. So the neut. adj. is used, Eur. *Hipp.* 109 τερπνὸν...| τράπεζα πλήρης: Eur. *Hel.* 1687 γνώμης, ὃ πολλαῖς ἐν γυναιξὶν οὐκ ἔνι. **543** οἶσθ' ὡς ποίησον; In more than twelve places of the tragic or comic poets we have this or a like form where a person is eagerly be-speaking attention to a command or request. Instead of οἶσθ' ὡς δεῖ σε ποιῆσαι; or οἶσθ' ὡς σε κελεύω ποιῆσαι; the anxious haste of the speaker substitutes an abrupt imperative: οἶσθ' ὡς ποίησον; That the imperative was here felt as equivalent to '*you are to do*,' appears clearly from the substitutes which sometimes replace it. Thus we find (1) fut. indic.; Eur. *Cycl.* 131 οἶσθ' οὖν ὃ δράσεις; *Med.* 600 οἶσθ' ὡς μετεύξει καὶ σοφωτέρα φανεῖ;

to seek, without followers or friends, a throne,—a prize which followers and wealth must win?

CR. Mark me now,—in answer to thy words, hear a fair reply, and then judge for thyself on knowledge.

OE. Thou art apt in speech, but I have a poor wit for thy lessons, since I have found thee my malignant foe.

CR. Now first hear how I will explain this very thing—

OE. Explain me not one thing—that thou art not false.

CR. If thou deemest that stubbornness without sense is a good gift, thou art not wise.

OE. If thou deemest that thou canst wrong a kinsman and escape the penalty, thou art not sane.

1803, recepit post Nauckium Dindorf. in Poet. Scenicorum ed. quinta (1869). Nollem factum. Sana est vulgata l., quod infra paucis docere conatus sum.

where the conjectures δρᾶσον (Canter) and μέτευξαι (Elmsley) are arbitrary: so with the 1st pers., *I. T.* 759 ἀλλ' οἶσθ' ὃ δράσω; (2) a periphrasis: Eur. *Suppl.* 932 ἀλλ' οἶσθ' ὃ δρᾶν σε βούλομαι τούτων πέρι; Only a sense that the imperat. had this force could explain the still bolder form of the phrase with 3rd pers.: Eur. *I. T.* 1203 οἶσθά νυν ἅ μοι γενέσθω = ἃ δεῖ γενέσθαι μοι: Ar. *Ach.* 1064 οἶσθ' ὡς ποιείτω = ὡς δεῖ ποιεῖν αὐτήν, where ποιεῖτε is a conjecture. The theory of a transposition (ποίησον, οἶσθ' ὡς, like Plaut. *Rud.* 3. 5. 18 *tange, sed scin quomodo?*) would better satisfy syntax; but the natural order of words can itself be a clue to the way in which colloquial breaches of strict grammar really arise. **546** σοῦ, emphatic by place and pause: cp. *El.* 1505 χρῆν δ' εὐθὺς εἶναι τήνδε τοῖς πᾶσιν δίκην | ὅστις πέρα πράσσειν γε τῶν νόμων θέλει, | κτεί νειν· τὸ γὰρ πανοῦργον οὐκ ἂν ἦν πολύ. **547** ὡς ἐρῶ, how I will state this very matter (my supposed hostility to you): *i.e.* in what a light I will place it, by showing that I had no motive for it. **548 f.** τοῦτ' αὐτὸ κ.τ.λ. Oedipus flings back Creon's phrases, as the Antigone of Aeschylus bitterly echoes those of the κῆρυξ (αὐδῶ—αὐδῶ—τραχύς—τράχυν', *Theb.* 1042 f.). An accent of rising passion is similarly given to the dialogue between Menelaus and Teucer (*Ai.* 1142 ἤδη ποτ' εἶδον ἄνδρ' ἐγώ—1150 ἐγὼ δέ γ' ἄνδρ' ὄπωπα). Aristophanes parodies this style, *Ach.* 1097 ΛΑΜΑΧΟΣ. παῖ, παῖ, φέρ' ἔξω δεῦρο τὸν γύλιον ἐμοί. ΔΙΚΑΙΟΠΟΛΙΣ. παῖ, παῖ, φέρ' ἔξω δεῦρο τὴν κίστην ἐμοί. **549** κτῆμα: cp. *Ant.* 1050 ὅσῳ κράτιστον κτημάτων εὐβουλία. **550** τοῦ νοῦ χωρίς: for αὐθαδία is not necessarily devoid of intelligence: as Heracles says (Eur. *H. F.* 1243) αὔθαδες ὁ

ΚΡ. ξύμφημί σοι ταῦτ' ἔνδικ' εἰρῆσθαι. τὸ δὲ
πάθημ' ὁποῖον φῂς παθεῖν δίδασκέ με.

ΟΙ. ἔπειθες, ἢ οὐκ ἔπειθες, ὡς χρείη μ' ἐπὶ   555
τὸν σεμνόμαντιν ἄνδρα πέμψασθαί τινα;

ΚΡ. καὶ νῦν ἔθ' αὐτός εἰμι τῷ βουλεύματι.

ΟΙ. πόσον τιν' ἤδη δῆθ' ὁ Λάϊος χρόνον

ΚΡ. δέδρακε ποῖον ἔργον; οὐ γὰρ ἐννοῶ.

ΟΙ. ἄφαντος ἔρρει θανασίμῳ χειρώματι;   560

ΚΡ. μακροὶ παλαιοί τ' ἂν μετρηθεῖεν χρόνοι.

ΟΙ. τότ' οὖν ὁ μάντις οὗτος ἦν ἐν τῇ τέχνῃ;

ΚΡ. σοφός γ' ὁμοίως κἀξ ἴσου τιμώμενος.

ΟΙ. ἐμνήσατ' οὖν ἐμοῦ τι τῷ τότ' ἐν χρόνῳ;

ΚΡ. οὔκουν ἐμοῦ γ' ἑστῶτος οὐδαμοῦ πέλας.   565

ΟΙ. ἀλλ' οὐκ ἔρευναν τοῦ θανόντος ἔσχετε;

ΚΡ. παρέσχομεν, πῶς δ' οὐχί; κοὐκ ἠκούσαμεν.

555 χρεῖ' ἢ L, ubi spiritum et accentum litterae η addidit manus certe recentior; prima tamen χρείη vel χρειη scripserit necne, propterea dubito quod intervallum est iusto maius inter litteras ι et η. χρεῖ' ἢ A (superscripto χρη`, quo χρῆν, non χρὴ,

---

θεός· πρὸς δὲ τοὺς θεοὺς ἐγώ. 555 ἢ οὐκ: Aesch. *Theb.* 100 ἀκούετ' ἢ οὐκ ἀκούετ' ἀσπίδων κτύπον; *Od.* 4. 682 ἢ εἰπέμεναι δμωῆσιν Ὀδυσσῆος θείοιο. Such 'synizesis' points to the rapidity and ease of ancient Greek pronunciation: see J. H. H. Schmidt, *Rhythmik und Metrik* § 3 (p. 9 of Eng. tr. by Prof. J. W. White). 556 While such words as ἀριστόμαντις, ὀρθόμαντις are seriously used in a good sense, σεμνόμαντις refers ironically to a solemn manner: cp. σεμνολογεῖν, σεμνοπροσωπεῖν, σεμνοπανοῦργος, σεμνοπαράσιτος, etc. 557 αὐτός: 'I am the same man in regard to my opinion' (dat. of respect): not, 'am identical with my former opinion' (when the dat. would be like Φοίβῳ in 285). Thuc. can dispense with a dative, 2. 61 καὶ ἐγὼ μὲν ὁ αὐτός εἰμι καὶ οὐκ ἐξίσταμαι: though he adds it in 3. 38 ἐγὼ μὲν οὖν ὁ αὐτός εἰμι τῇ γνώμῃ. 559 δέδρακε. Creon has heard only what Oedipus said of him: he does not yet know what Teiresias said of Oedipus (cp. 574). Hence he is startled at the mention of Laïus. οὐ γὰρ ἐννοῶ: *i.e.* 'I do not understand what Laïus has to do with this matter.' 560 χειρώματι, deed of a (violent) hand: Aesch. *Theb.* 1022 τυμβόχοα χειρώματα = service of the hands in raising a mound. In the one other place where Aesch. has

CR. Justly said, I grant thee: but tell me what is the wrong that thou sayest thou hast suffered from me.

OE. Didst thou advise, or didst thou not, that I should send for that reverend seer?

CR. And now I am still of the same mind.

OE. How long is it, then, since Laïus—

CR. Since Laïus...? I take not thy drift...

OE. —was swept from men's sight by a deadly violence?

CR. The count of years would run far into the past.

OE. Was this seer, then, of the craft in those days?

CR. Yea, skilled as now, and in equal honour.

OE. Made he, then, any mention of me at that time?

CR. Never, certainly, when I was within hearing.

OE. But held ye not a search touching the murder?

CR. Due search we held, of course—and learned nothing.

significari suspicor), et sic codd. plerique. Bodl. Barocc. 66 χρείμ', superscripto α: Γ, χρεῖ' ἦν. **561** Unus cod. A ἀναμετρηθεῖεν. Confer v. 1348, ubi eodem mendo (vera lectione ἀν γνῶναι in ἀναγνῶναι corrupta) codd. omnes laborant.

---

the word, it means 'prey' (*Ag.* 1326 δούλης θανούσης εὐμαροῦς χειρώματος): Soph. uses it only here (though he has δυσχείρωμα *Ant.* 126): Eur. never. **561 μακροὶ κ.τ.λ.**: long and ancient times would be measured; *i.e.* the reckoning of years from the present time would go far back into the past; μακροὶ denoting the course, and παλαιοί the point to which it is retraced. Some sixteen years may be supposed to have elapsed since the death of Laïus. **562 ἐν τῇ τέχνῃ**: slightly contemptuous. ἐν of a pursuit or calling: Her. 2. 82 τῶν Ἑλλήνων οἱ ἐν ποιήσει γενόμενοι: Thuc. 3. 28 οἱ ἐν τοῖς πράγμασι: Isocr. or. 2. § 18 οἱ ἐν ταῖς ὀλιγαρχίαις καὶ ταῖς δημοκρατίαις (meaning, the *administrators* thereof): Plat. *Phaed.* 59 A ὡς ἐν φιλοσοφίᾳ ἡμῶν ὄντων: *Legg.* 762 A τῶν ἐν ταῖς γεωργίαις: *Protag.* 317 C (Protagoras of himself as a σοφιστής) πολλά γε ἔτη ἤδη εἰμὶ ἐν τῇ τέχνῃ. **565 οὐδαμοῦ** with ἑστῶτος πέλας, 'when I was standing anywhere near'; but equivalent in force to, 'on any occasion when I was standing near': cp. *Ai.* 1281 ὃν οὐδαμοῦ φῇς οὐδὲ συμβῆναι ποδί. **567 παρέσχομεν**, we held it, as in duty bound: παρέχειν, as distinct from ἔχειν, expressing that it was something to be expected *on their part*. Cp. *O. C.* 1498 δικαίαν χάριν παρασχεῖν παθών. For παρέσχομεν after ἔσχομεν cp.

ΟΙ. πῶς οὖν τόθ' οὗτος ὁ σοφὸς οὐκ ηὔδα τάδε;

ΚΡ. οὐκ οἶδ'· ἐφ' οἷς γὰρ μὴ φρονῶ σιγᾶν φιλῶ.

ΟΙ. τοσόνδε γ' οἶσθα καὶ λέγοις ἂν εὖ φρονῶν. 570

ΚΡ. ποῖον τόδ'; εἰ γὰρ οἶδά γ', οὐκ ἀρνήσομαι.

ΟΙ. ὁθούνεκ', εἰ μὴ σοὶ ξυνῆλθε, τὰς ἐμὰς
οὐκ ἄν ποτ' εἶπε Λαΐου διαφθοράς.

ΚΡ. εἰ μὲν λέγει τάδ', αὐτὸς οἶσθ'· ἐγὼ δὲ σοῦ
μαθεῖν δικαιῶ ταῦθ' ἅπερ κἀμοῦ σὺ νῦν. 575

ΟΙ. ἐκμάνθαν'· οὐ γὰρ δὴ φονεὺς ἁλώσομαι.

ΚΡ. τί δῆτ'; ἀδελφὴν τὴν ἐμὴν γήμας ἔχεις;

ΟΙ. ἄρνησις οὐκ ἔνεστιν ὧν ἀνιστορεῖς.

ΚΡ. ἄρχεις δ' ἐκείνῃ ταὐτὰ γῆς ἴσον νέμων;

ΟΙ. ἂν ᾗ θέλουσα πάντ' ἐμοῦ κομίζεται. 580

ΚΡ. οὔκουν ἰσοῦμαι σφῷν ἐγὼ δυοῖν τρίτος;

---

570 τὸ σὸν δέ γ' L: voluit autem corrector gravem vocis σὸν accentum in acutum mutare, utpote qui τοσόνδε veram esse l. censeret. τὸ σὸν δέ γ' [non δε γ'] A: sic etiam V et alii. Veram lectionem, quamvis peccet accentus, praebere vult B, qui τοσόνδέ γ' [sic] habet; ascriptum est enim τοσοῦτον. Cum B consentit cod. Ven. 616 (V²), et codicis T prima manus; recentior, rubro charactere usa, syllabae το gravem

---

ἐπαξίως...ἀξίως: 575 μαθεῖν...576 ἐκμάνθαν'. 570 τοσόνδε γ'. If we read τὸ σὸν δέ γ', the coarse and blunt τὸ σὸν would destroy the edge of the sarcasm. Nor would τὸ σὸν consist so well with the calm tone of Creon's inquiry in 571. τοσόνδε does not need δέ after it, since οἶσθα is a mocking echo of οἶδα. Cp. Eur. I. T. 554 OP. παῦσαί νυν ἤδη, μηδ' ἐρωτήσῃς πέρα. ΙΦ. τοσόνδε γ', εἰ ζῇ τοῦ ταλαιπώρου δάμαρ. Against the conject. τόσον δέ γ' it is to be noted that Soph. has τόσος only in Ai. 185 (lyric, τόσσον), 277 (δὶς τόσ'), and Trach. 53 φράσαι τόσον. 572 The simple answer would have been :—'that you prompted him to make his present charge': but this becomes:—'that, if you had not prompted him, he would never have made it.' ξυνῆλθε: Ar. Eq. 1300 φασὶν ἀλλήλαις συνελθεῖν τὰς τριήρεις ἐς λόγον, 'the triremes laid their heads together': ib. 467 ἰδίᾳ δ' ἐκεῖ τοῖς Λακεδαιμονίοις ξυγγίγνεται. τὰς ἐμὰς: the conject. τάσδ' ἐμὰς mars the passage: 'he would never have described this slaying of L. as mine.' οὐκ ἂν εἶπε τὰς ἐμὰς Λαΐου διαφθοράς = οὐκ ἂν εἶπεν ὅτι ἐγὼ Λάϊον διέφθειρα, but with a certain bitter force added;—'we should never have heard a word of this slaying of Laïus by me.' Soph. has purposely chosen

OE. And how was it that this sage did not tell his story *then?*

CR. I know not; where I lack light, 'tis my wont to be silent.

OE. Thus much, at least, thou knowest, and could'st declare with light enough.

CR. What is that? If I know it, I will not deny.

OE. That, if he had not conferred with thee, he would never have named *my* slaying of Laïus.

CR. If so he speaks, thou best knowest; but I claim to learn from thee as much as thou hast now from me.

OE. Learn thy fill: I shall never be found guilty of the blood.

CR. Say, then—thou hast married my sister?

OE. The question allows not of denial.

CR. And thou rulest the land as she doth, with like sway?

OE. She obtains from me all her desire.

CR. And rank not I as a third peer of you twain?

accentum addidit. Inter editores quibus τὸ σὸν δέ γ' placuit numerantur, quod mireris, Brunck., Hermann., Dindorf., Nauck., Burton. Cum Porsono ad Eur. *Med.* 461 et Elmsleio τοσόνδε γ' probaverunt Erfurdt., Blaydes., Campbell. τόσον δέ γ' cum Reisigio Wunder. **572** τὰς codd.: τάσδ' Doederlein., Wunder., Hartung., Dindorf., Blaydes. **575** ταῦθ' codd.: ταθθ' Brunckius, quem secuti sunt edd.

---

a turn of phrase which the audience can recognise as suiting the fact that Oed. *had* slain Laïus. For διαφθοράς instead of a clause with διαφθείρειν, cp. Thuc. I. 137 γράψας τὴν ἐκ Σαλαμῖνος προάγγελσιν τῆς ἀναχωρήσεως καὶ τὴν τῶν γεφυρῶν...οὐ διάλυσιν. **574** To write σοῦ instead of σου is not indeed necessary; but we thus obtain a better balance to κἀμοῦ. **575** μαθεῖν ταῦθ', to question in like manner and measure. ταῦθ' (MSS.) might refer to the events since the death of Laïus, but has less point. **577** γήμας ἔχεις: simply, I think, = γεγάμηκας, though the special use of ἔχειν (*Od.* 4. 569 ἔχεις Ἑλένην καί σφιν γαμβρὸς Διός ἐσσι) might warrant the version, 'hast married, and hast to wife.' **579** γῆς with ἄρχεις: ἴσον νέμων explains ταὐτά, —'with equal sway' (cp. 201 κράτη νέμων, and 237): γῆς ἴσον νέμων would mean, 'assigning an equal share of land.' **580** ἢ θέλουσα: cp. 126, 274, 747. **581** τρίτος: marking the completion of the lucky number, as *O. C.* 8, *Ai.* 1174, Aesch. *Eum.* 759 (τρίτου | Σωτῆρος): parodied by Menander,

ΟΙ. ἐνταῦθα γὰρ δὴ καὶ κακὸς φαίνει φίλος.

ΚΡ. οὔκ, εἰ διδοίης γ᾽ ὡς ἐγὼ σαυτῷ λόγον.

σκέψαι δὲ τοῦτο πρῶτον, εἴ τιν᾽ ἂν δοκεῖς
ἄρχειν ἑλέσθαι ξὺν φόβοισι μᾶλλον ἢ   585
ἄτρεστον εὕδοντ᾽, εἰ τά γ᾽ αὔθ᾽ ἕξει κράτη.
ἐγὼ μὲν οὖν οὔτ᾽ αὐτὸς ἱμείρων ἔφυν
τύραννος εἶναι μᾶλλον ἢ τύραννα δρᾶν,
οὔτ᾽ ἄλλος ὅστις σωφρονεῖν ἐπίσταται.
νῦν μὲν γὰρ ἐκ σοῦ πάντ᾽ ἄνευ φόβου φέρω,   590
εἰ δ᾽ αὐτὸς ἦρχον, πολλὰ κἂν ἄκων ἔδρων.
πῶς δῆτ᾽ ἐμοὶ τυραννὶς ἡδίων ἔχειν
ἀρχῆς ἀλύπου καὶ δυναστείας ἔφυ;
οὔπω τοσοῦτον ἠπατημένος κυρῶ
ὥστ᾽ ἄλλα χρῄζειν ἢ τὰ σὺν κέρδει καλά.   595
νῦν πᾶσι χαίρω, νῦν με πᾶς ἀσπάζεται,
νῦν οἱ σέθεν χρῄζοντες ἐκκαλοῦσί με·

597 Nisi quod in E mendose legitur καλοῦσι, nulla varietate codd. ἐκκαλοῦσι praebent. Superscripta est in L interpretatio προκαλοῦσι: in A corrector adiecit παρα, ea potius, opinor, sententia ut ἐκ explicaret quam ut variam l. παρακαλοῦσι

(*Sentent.* 231) θάλασσα καὶ πῦρ καὶ γυνὴ τρίτον κακόν. 582 ἐνταῦθα γὰρ: (yes indeed :) *for* (otherwise your treason would be less glaring :) it is just the fact of your virtual equality with us which places your ingratitude in the worst light. 583 διδοίης λόγον: Her. 3. 25 λόγον ἐωυτῷ δοὺς ὅτι...ἔμελλε κ.τ.λ. 'on *reflecting* that,' etc. : [Dem.] or. 45 § 7 (the speech prob. belongs to the time of Dem.) λόγον δ᾽ ἐμαυτῷ διδοὺς εὑρίσκω κ.τ.λ. Distinguish the *plur.* in Plato's ποικίλῃ ποικίλους ψυχῇ... διδοὺς λόγους, applying speeches (*Phaedr.* 277 c). 587 οὔτ᾽ αὐτὸς would have been naturally followed by οὔτ᾽ ἄλλῳ παραινοῖμ᾽ ἄν, but the form of the sentence changes to οὔτ᾽ ἄλλος (ἱμείρει). 590 ἐκ σοῦ: ἐκ is here a correct substitute for παρά, since the king is the ultimate source of benefits: Xen. *Hellen.* 3. 1. 6 ἐκείνῳ δ᾽ αὕτη ἡ χώρα δῶρον ἐκ βασιλέως ἐδόθη. φέρω = φέρομαι, as *O. C.* 6 etc. 591 κἂν ἄκων: he would do much of his own good pleasure, but much *also* (καὶ) against it, under pressure of public duty. 594 οὔπω, ironical: see on 105. 595 τὰ σὺν κέρδει καλά: honours which bring substantial advantage (real power and personal

OE. Aye, 'tis just therein that thou art seen a false friend.

CR. Not so, if thou would'st reason with thine own heart as I with mine, And first weigh this,—whether thou thinkest that any one would choose to rule amid terrors rather than in unruffled peace,—granting that he is to have the same powers. Now I, for one, have no yearning in my nature to be a king rather than to do kingly deeds, no, nor hath any man who knows how to keep a sober mind. For now I win all boons from thee without fear; but, were I ruler myself, I should be doing much e'en against mine own pleasure.

How, then, could royalty be sweeter for me to have than painless rule and influence? Not yet am I so misguided as to desire other honours than those which profit. Now, all wish me joy; now, every man has a greeting for me; now, those who have a suit to thee crave speech with me,

indicaret. Quid autem sibi velit verbum ἐκκαλοῦσι viderat quisquis in B annotavit μεσ[ίτην]ποιοῦσι: ut in E quoque schol. εἰς βοήθειαν μεσοῦντα. αἰκάλλουσι coniecit Musgravius (cui etiam ἐπικαλοῦσι in mentem venerat), recepit Dindorf.: sed vide annot.

---

comfort), as opp. to honours in which outward splendour is joined to heavier care. *El.* 61 δοκῶ μέν, οὐδὲν ῥῆμα σὺν κέρδει κακόν: *i.e.* the sound matters not, if there is κέρδος, solid good. **596** πᾶσι χαίρω, 'all men wish me joy': lit. 'I rejoice with the consent of all men': all are content that I should rejoice. Cp. *O. C.* 1446 ἀνάξιαι γὰρ πᾶσίν ἐστε δυστυχεῖν, all deem you undeserving of misfortune: Ar. *Av.* 445 πᾶσι νικᾶν τοῖς κριταῖς | καὶ τοῖς θεαταῖς πᾶσι. The phrase has been suggested by χαῖρέ μοι, but refers to the meaning rather than to the form of the greeting: *i.e.* πᾶσι χαίρω is not to be regarded as if it meant literally, ' I have the word χαῖρε said to me by all.' This is one of the boldly subtle phrases in which the art of Soph. recalls that of Vergil. Others understand: (1) 'I rejoice in all,'—instead of suspecting some, as the τύραννος does, who φθονέει...τοῖσι ἀρίστοισι...χαίρει δὲ τοῖσι κακίστοισι τῶν ἀστῶν Her. 3. 80: (2) 'I rejoice in relation to all'—*i.e.* am on good terms with all: (3) 'I rejoice in the sight of all': *i.e.* enjoy a happiness which is the greater because men see it: (4) 'I rejoice in all things.' This last is impossible. Of the others, (1) is best, but not in accord with the supposed position of Oedipus ὁ πᾶσι κλεινός. **597** ἐκκαλοῦσι. Those who have a boon to ask of Oed. come to the palace (or to Creon's own house, see on 637) and send in a message, praying Creon to speak

τὸ γὰρ τυχεῖν αὐτοῖσι πᾶν ἐνταῦθ᾽ ἔνι.
πῶς δῆτ᾽ ἐγὼ κεῖν᾽ ἂν λάβοιμ᾽ ἀφεὶς τάδε;
οὐκ ἂν γένοιτο νοῦς κακὸς καλῶς φρονῶν.   600
ἀλλ᾽ οὔτ᾽ ἐραστὴς τῆσδε τῆς γνώμης ἔφυν
οὔτ᾽ ἂν μετ᾽ ἄλλου δρῶντος ἂν τλαίην ποτέ.
καὶ τῶνδ᾽ ἔλεγχον τοῦτο μὲν Πυθώδ᾽ ἰὼν
πεύθου τὰ χρησθέντ᾽, εἰ σαφῶς ἤγγειλά σοι·
τοῦτ᾽ ἄλλ᾽, ἐάν με τῷ τερασκόπῳ λάβῃς   605
κοινῇ τι βουλεύσαντα, μή μ᾽ ἁπλῇ κτάνῃς
ψήφῳ, διπλῇ δέ, τῇ τ᾽ ἐμῇ καὶ σῇ, λαβών.
γνώμῃ δ᾽ ἀδήλῳ μή με χωρὶς αἰτιῶ.
οὐ γὰρ δίκαιον οὔτε τοὺς κακοὺς μάτην

598 Servatur in duobus codd., Γ et L², vera l. πᾶν. Est in L αὐτοῖσ [non αὐτοὺσ] ἅπαν clare scriptum. Nullum post ἅπαν litterae τ vestigium. Consentiunt cum L in ἅπαν codices Vaticani tres, Pal., et Trin.: pluralis ἅπαντ᾽ extat in A et

---

with them. Seneca's Creon says (*Oed.* 687) *Solutus onere regio, regni bonis Fruor, domusque civium coetu viget.* In Greek tragedy the king or some great person is often thus called forth. Cp. Aesch. *Cho.* 663: Orestes summons an οἰκέτης by knocking at the ἑρκεία πύλη, and, describing himself as a messenger, says—ἐξελθέτω τις δωμάτων τελεσφόρος | γυνή τόπαρχος,—when Clytaemnestra herself appears. So in Eur. *Bacch.* 170 Teiresias says—τίς ἐν πύλαισι Κάδμον ἐκκαλεῖ δόμων; 'where is there a servant at the doors to call forth Cadmus from the house?'—ἴτω τις, εἰσάγγιλλε Τειρεσίας ὅτι | ζητεῖ νιν: then Cadmus comes forth. The active ἐκκαλεῖν is properly said (as there) of him who takes in the message, the middle ἐκκαλεῖσθαι of him who sends it in: Her. 8. 19 στὰς ἐπὶ τὸ συνέδριον ἐξεκαλέετο Θεμιστοκλῆα. Musgrave's conj. αἰκάλλουσι is scarcely a word which a man could complacently use to describe the treatment of himself by others. αἴκαλος. κόλαξ Hesych. (for ἀκ-ίαλο ς, from the same rt., with the notion of *soothing* or *stilling*, as ἀκεῖσθαι, ἦκα, ἀκέων, ἄκασκα, ἀκασκαῖος): Ar. *Eq.* 47 ὑποπεσὼν τὸν δεσπότην | ἤκαλλ᾽, ἐθώπευ᾽, ἐκολάκευ᾽, 'fawned, wheedled, flattered': in tragedy only once, Eur. *Andr.* 630 φίλημ᾽ ἐδέξω, πρόδοτιν αἰκάλλων κύνα. 598 τὸ...τυχεῖν sc. ὧν χρήζουσιν. The reading ἅπαντ᾽, whether taken as accus. after τυχεῖν ('to gain all things'), or as accus. of respect ('to succeed in all') not only mars the rhythm but enfeebles the sense. When αὐτοῖσι was corrupted into αὐτοῖς, πᾶν was changed into ἅπαν, as it is in L.

since therein is all their hope of success.   Then why should I
resign these things, and take those?   No mind will become
false, while it is wise.   Nay, I am no lover of such policy, and,
if another put it into deed, never could I bear to act with him.

And, in proof of this, first, go to Pytho, and ask if I brought
thee true word of the oracle ; then next, if thou find that I have
planned aught in concert with the soothsayer, take and slay
me, by the sentence not of one mouth, but of twain—by mine
own, no less than thine.   But make me not guilty in a corner,
on unproved surmise.   It is not right to adjudge bad men good

reliquis plerisque.   Praetulerunt πάντ' Bothius et Burges.   **604** πεύθου A, L
(ex πείθου factum), cum codd. plerisque : πύθου Γ, πυθοῦ Nauck.

ἐνταῦθα = ἐν τῷ ἐκκαλεῖν με, in gaining my ear: cp. O. C. 585 ἐνταῦθα
γάρ μοι κεῖνα συγκομίζεται, in *this* boon I find *those* comprised.   599 πῶς
δῆτ'.   Cp. Her. 5. 106 (Histiaeus to Dareius) βασιλεῦ, κοῖον ἐφθέγξαο
ἔπος; ἐμὲ βουλεῦσαι πρῆγμα ἐκ τοῦ σοί τι ἢ μέγα ἢ σμικρὸν ἔμελλε λυπηρὸν
ἀνασχήσειν; τί δ' ἂν ἐπιδιζήμενος ποιέοιμι ταῦτα; τεῦ δὲ ἐνδεὴς ἐών, τῷ πάρα
μὲν πάντα ὅσαπερ σοί, πάντων δὲ πρὸς σέο βουλευμάτων ἐπακούειν ἀξιεῦμαι ;
600 οὐκ ἂν γένοιτο κ.τ.λ.   Creon has been arguing that *he* has no motive
for treason.   He now states a general maxim.   'No mind would ever
turn to treason, while it was sound.'   As a logical inference, this holds
good only of those who are in Creon's fortunate case.   If, on the other
hand, καλῶς φρονῶν means 'alive to its own *highest* good,' and not merely
to such self-interest as that of which Creon has spoken, then the statement has no strict connection with what precedes: it becomes a new
argument of a different order, which might be illustrated from Plato's
κακὸς ἑκὼν οὐδείς.   It would be forcing the words to render: 'A
base mind could not approve itself wise,' *i.e.* 'such treason as you
ascribe to me would be silly.'   603 ἔλεγχον, accus. in apposition with the
sentence: Eur. H. F. 57 ἡ δυσπραξία | ἧς μήποθ', ὅστις καὶ μέσως εὔνους
ἐμοί, | τύχοι, φίλων ἔλεγχον ἀψευδέστατον.   605 τοῦτ' ἄλλο = τοῦτο δέ.
Soph. has τοῦτο μέν irregularly followed by τοῦτ' αὖθις (*Ant.* 165), by
εἶτα (*Ph.* 1345), by δέ (*Ai.* 670, *O. C.* 440).   τῷ τερασκόπῳ.   This title
(given to Apollo, Aesch. *Eum.* 62) has sometimes a shade of scorn,
as when it is applied by the mocking Pentheus to Teiresias (Eur.
Bacch. 248), and by Clytaemnestra to Cassandra (Aesch. *Ag.* 1440).
608 χωρίς, 'apart': *i.e.* solely on the strength of your own guess (γνώμη
ἄδηλος), without any evidence that I falsified the oracle or plotted with

χρηστοὺς νομίζειν οὔτε τοὺς χρηστοὺς κακούς.   610
φίλον γὰρ ἐσθλὸν ἐκβαλεῖν ἴσον λέγω
καὶ τὸν παρ' αὐτῷ βίοτον, ὃν πλεῖστον φιλεῖ.
ἀλλ' ἐν χρόνῳ γνώσει τάδ' ἀσφαλῶς, ἐπεὶ
χρόνος δίκαιον ἄνδρα δείκνυσιν μόνος,
κακὸν δὲ κἂν ἐν ἡμέρᾳ γνοίης μιᾷ.   615
ΧΟ. καλῶς ἔλεξεν εὐλαβουμένῳ πεσεῖν,
ἄναξ· φρονεῖν γὰρ οἱ ταχεῖς οὐκ ἀσφαλεῖς.
ΟΙ. ὅταν ταχύς τις οὑπιβουλεύων λάθρα
χωρῇ, ταχὺν δεῖ κἀμὲ βουλεύειν πάλιν.
εἰ δ' ἡσυχάζων προσμενῶ, τὰ τοῦδε μὲν   620
πεπραγμέν' ἔσται, τἀμὰ δ' ἡμαρτημένα.
ΚΡ. τί δῆτα χρῄζεις; ἦ με γῆς ἔξω βαλεῖν;
ΟΙ. ἥκιστα· θνήσκειν οὐ φυγεῖν σε βούλομαι
ὡς ἂν προδείξῃς οἷόν ἐστι τὸ φθονεῖν.
ΚΡ. ὡς οὐχ ὑπείξων οὐδὲ πιστεύσων λέγεις;   625
ΟΙ. *   *   *   *   *   *
ΚΡ. οὐ γὰρ φρονοῦντά σ' εὖ βλέπω.   ΟΙ. τὸ γοῦν ἐμόν.
ΚΡ. ἀλλ' ἐξ ἴσου δεῖ κἀμόν.   ΟΙ. ἀλλ' ἔφυς κακός.

623—626 Nemini qui hunc locum diligenter perpenderit dubium fore credo

the seer.   **612** τὸν παρ' αὐτῷ βίοτον κ.τ.λ.: the life is *hospes comesque*
corporis, dearest guest and closest companion : cp. Plat. *Gorg.* 479 B μὴ
ὑγιεῖ ψυχῇ συνοικεῖν: and the address of Archilochus to his own θυμός
as his trusty ally (Bergk fr. 66),—Θυμέ, θύμ' ἀμηχάνοισι κήδεσιν κυκώ-
μενε, | ἐνάδευ, δυσμενῶν δ' ἀλέξευ προσβαλὼν ἐναντίον | στέρνον.   φιλεῖ sc.
τις, supplied from αὐτῷ: Hes. *Op.* 12 τὴν μέν κεν ἐπαινήσειε νοήσας | ἡ δ'
ἐπιμωμητή.   **614** χρόνος: cp. Pind. fr. 132 ἀνδρῶν δικαίων χρόνος σωτὴρ
ἄριστος: *Olymp.* 11. 53 ὅ τ' ἐξελέγχων μόνος | ἀλάθειαν ἐτήτυμον | χρόνος.
615 κακὸν δὲ: the sterling worth of the upright man is not fully appreciated until it has been long tried : but a knave is likely (by some
slip) to afford an early glimpse of his real character.   The Greek
love of antithesis has prompted this addition, which is relevant to
Creon's point only as implying, 'if I *had* been a traitor, you would
probably have seen some symptom of it erenow.'   Cp. Pind. *Pyth.* 2. 90
(speaking of the φθονεροί): στάθμας δέ τινος ἑλκόμενοι | περισσᾶς ἐνέπαξαν

at random, or good men bad.   I count it a like thing for a man
to cast off a true friend as to cast away the life in his own
bosom, which most he loves.   Nay, thou wilt learn these things
with sureness in time, for time alone shows a just man ; but
thou could'st discern a knave even in one day.

CH.   Well hath he spoken, O king, for one who giveth
heed not to fall : the quick in counsel are not sure.

OE.   When the stealthy plotter is moving on me in quick
sort, I, too, must be quick with my counterplot.   If I await him
in repose, his ends will have been gained, and mine missed.

CR.   What would'st thou, then ?   Cast me out of the land ?

OE.   Not so : I desire thy death—not thy banishment—
that thou mayest show forth what manner of thing is envy.

CR.   Thou speakest as resolved not to yield or to believe ?

[OE.   No ; for thou persuadest me not that thou art worthy of belief.]

CR.   No, for I find thee not sane.   OE.   Sane, at least, in
mine own interest.

CR.   Nay, thou should'st be so in mine also.   OE.   Nay,
thou art false.

quin post versum 625 unus desit versus : infra pluribus rem exposui.   Versum 624
Creonti, v. 625 Oedipo tribuunt codd.   In v. 624 pro ὅταν scripsi ὡς ἄν.

ἕλκος ὀδυναρὸν ἐᾷ πρόσθε καρδίᾳ, | πρὶν ὅσα φροντίδι μητίονται τυχεῖν.
Ant. 493 φιλεῖ δ᾽ ὁ θυμὸς πρόσθεν ᾑρῆσθαι κλοπεὺς | τῶν μηδὲν ὀρθῶς ἐν
σκότῳ τεχνωμένων.   **617** The infin. φρονεῖν is like an accus. of respect
(*e.g.* βουλήν) construed with both adjectives : 'in counsel, the quick are
not sure.' Cp. Thuc. I. 70 ἐπινοῆσαι ὀξεῖς.   **618** ταχύς τις χωρῇ, ad-
vances in quick fashion ; nearly = ταχέως πως.   *Ai.* 1266 φεῦ, τοῦ θανόν-
τος ὡς ταχεῖά τις βροτοῖς | χάρις διαρρεῖ, *in what quick sort* does it vanish.
622—626 τί δῆτα χρῄζεις ;...τὸ γοῦν ἐμόν.   A discussion of this passage will
be found in the Appendix, Note 13.   My conclusions are :—(1)
Verse 624, ὅταν προδείξῃς κ.τ.λ., which the MSS. give to Creon,
belongs to Oedipus ; and for ὅταν we must read ὡς ἄν.   (2) Verse 625,
ὡς οὐχ ὑπείξων κ.τ.λ., which the MSS. give to Oedipus, belongs to Creon.
(3) Between 625 and 626 a verse spoken by Oedipus has dropped out,
to such effect as οὐ γάρ με πείθεις οὕνεκ᾽ οὐκ ἄπιστος εἶ.   The
fact of the next verse, our 626, also beginning with οὐ γάρ may have
led to the loss by causing the copyist's eye to wander.   The echoed
οὐ γάρ would suit angry dialogue : cp. 547, 548 ΚΡ. τοῦτ᾽ αὐτὸ

ΚΡ. εἰ δὲ ξυνίης μηδέν ;   ΟΙ. ἀρκτέον γ᾽ ὅμως.

ΚΡ. οὗτοι κακῶς γ᾽ ἄρχοντος.   ΟΙ. ὦ πόλις πόλις.

ΚΡ. κἀμοὶ πόλεως μέτεστιν, οὐχὶ σοὶ μόνῳ.   630

ΧΟ. παύσασθ᾽, ἄνακτες· καιρίαν δ᾽ ὑμῖν ὁρῶ
τήνδ᾽ ἐκ δόμων στείχουσαν Ἰοκάστην, μεθ᾽ ἧς
τὸ νῦν παρεστὸς νεῖκος εὖ θέσθαι χρεών.

ΙΟΚΑΣΤΗ.

τί τὴν ἄβουλον, ὦ ταλαίπωροι, στάσιν
γλώσσης ἐπήρασθ᾽; οὐδ᾽ ἐπαισχύνεσθε, γῆς   635
οὕτω νοσούσης, ἴδια κινοῦντες κακά ;
οὐκ εἶ σύ τ᾽ οἴκους σύ τε, Κρέον, κατὰ στέγας,
καὶ μὴ τὸ μηδὲν ἄλγος εἰς μέγ᾽ οἴσετε ;

ΚΡ. ὅμαιμε, δεινά μ᾽ Οἰδίπους ὁ σὸς πόσις
δυοῖν δικαιοῖ δρᾶν ἀποκρίνας κακοῖν,   640

629 In L ἄρχοντοσ ex ἄρχοντεσ fecit vel prima manus vel διορθωτής.   **631**
καιρίαν A et codd. plerique: cum paucis L κυρίαν praebet; ubi littera υ post rasuram
facta est ex duabus quarum prima legi non potest, altera ι fuit: in marg. γρ. καιρίαν.
635 ἐπήρατ᾽, quod cum multis codd. A habet, vulgatior fuisse lectio videtur.   L
a prima quidem manu habuit ἐπήρασθ᾽ (quod in aliis quibusdam, ut in V et V⁴, extat):

νῦν μου πρῶτ᾽ ἄκουσον ὡς ἐρῶ.   ΟΙ. τοῦτ᾽ αὐτὸ μή μοι φράζ᾽.   **628**
ἀρκτέον = δεῖ ἄρχειν, one must rule : cp. *Ant.* 677 ἀμυντέ᾽ ἐστὶ τοῖς κοσμου-
μένοις.   Isocr. or. 14 § 10 οὐ τῶν ἄλλων αὐτοῖς ἀρκτέον (they ought not
to rule over others) ἀλλὰ πολὺ μᾶλλον Ὀρχομενίοις φόρον οἰστέον.   In
Plat. *Tim.* 48 B ἀρκτέον = δεῖ ἄρχεσθαι, one must begin; in *Ai.* 853
ἀρκτέον τὸ πρᾶγμα = must be begun.   Some understand—'one must be
ruled,' and οὗτοι κακῶς γ᾽ ἄρχοντος, 'No, not *by one* who rules ill': but
(*a*) though ἀρκτέα πόλις might mean, 'the city is to be ruled,' an absolute
passive use of ἀρκτέον is certainly not warranted by such an isolated
example as οὐ καταπληκτέον ἐστίν ('we must not be unnerved') in Dein.
In Dem. § 108: (*b*) ἄρχομαί τινος, 'I am ruled by one' (instead of ἐκ or
ὑπό), could only plead the analogy of ἀκούω τινός, and lacks evidence.
629 ἄρχοντος, when one rules.   ἀρκτέον being abstract, 'it is right to
rule,' there is no harshness in the gen. absol. with τινός understood (cp.
612), which is equivalent to ἐάν τις ἄρχῃ: cp. Dem. or. 6 § 20 λέγοντος
ἄν τινος πιστεῦσαι οἴεσθε ; 'think you that, if any one had said it, they
would have believed?' = οἴεσθε, εἰ τις ἔλεγε, πιστεῦσαι ἂν (αὐτούς); ὦ

CR. But if thou understandest nought? OE. Yet must I rule.

CR. Not if thou rule ill. OE. Hear him, O Thebes!

CR. Thebes is for me also—not for thee alone.

CH. Cease, princes; and in good time for you I see Iocasta coming yonder from the house, with whose help ye should compose your present feud.

IOCASTA.

Misguided men, why have ye raised such foolish strife of tongues? Are ye not ashamed, while the land is thus sick, to stir up troubles of your own? Come, go thou into the house, —and thou, Creon, to thy home,—and forbear to make much of a petty grief.

CR. Kinswoman, Oedipus thy lord claims to do dread things unto me, even one or other of two ills, —

sed mutavit in ἐπῆρατ' corrector antiquus. **637** Κρέων L, A, et reliqui codd. fere omnes: quod tuentur Hermann., Nauck., Blaydes. Κρέον E, probantibus Elmsleio, Dindorf., Campbell. **640** δρᾶσαι δικαιοῖ δυοῖν ἀποκρίνας κακοῖν codd. Quibus causis adductus sim ut δυοῖν...δρᾶν scriberem, infra leges. In T super δυοῖν scripsit συνίζησις librarius quem non effugerat inaudita contractio.

πόλις, πόλις: here, an appeal: in Attic comedy, an exclamation like *o tempora, o mores*: Blaydes cp. Eupolis *ap.* Athen. 424 B ὦ πόλις, πόλις | ὡς εὐτυχὴς εἶ μᾶλλον ἢ καλῶς φρονεῖς: and so Ar. *Ach.* 27. **630** πόλεως. Most of the MSS. have μέτεστι τῆσδ' οὐχί. Had they μέτεστι τῆσδ' οὐ (which appears only in a few inferior MSS.) we should hardly be warranted in ejecting τῆσδ': but, having the choice, we may safely prefer μέτεστιν οὐχὶ to μέτεστι τῆσδ' οὐ. 'I have some right in Thebes, as well as you.' Creon speaks not as a brother of Iocasta, but as a Theban citizen who denies that 'the city belongs to one man' (*Ant.* 737). Plat. *Legg.* 768 B δεῖ δὲ δὴ καὶ τῶν ἰδίων δικῶν κοινωνεῖν κατὰ δύναμιν ἅπαντας· ὁ γὰρ ἀκοινώνητος ὢν ἐξουσίας τοῦ συνδικάζειν ἡγεῖται τὸ παράπαν τῆς πόλεως οὐ μέτοχος εἶναι. **637** οἴκους (the king's palace), acc. after εἰ (cp. 533); κατὰ with στέγας only, referring to the house of Creon, who is not supposed to be an inmate of the palace: see 515, 533. **638** τὸ μηδὲν ἄλγος, the grief which is as nothing (*El.* 1166 δέξαι...|τὴν μηδὲν ἐς τὸ μηδέν): εἰς μέγα φέρειν, make into a great matter: cp. (*Phil.* 259) νόσος | ἀεὶ τέθηλε κἀπὶ μεῖζον ἔρχεται. **640** δυοῖν... ἀποκρίνας κακοῖν. This is the only extant example of δυοῖν scanned as

ἢ γῆς ἀπῶσαι πατρίδος, ἢ κτεῖναι λαβών.
ΟΙ. ξύμφημι· δρῶντα γάρ νιν, ὦ γύναι, κακῶς
εἴληφα τοὐμὸν σῶμα σὺν τέχνῃ κακῇ.
ΚΡ. μή νυν ὀναίμην, ἀλλ' ἀραῖος, εἴ σέ τι
δέδρακ', ὀλοίμην, ὧν ἐπαιτιᾷ με δρᾶν.   645
ΙΟ. ὦ πρὸς θεῶν πίστευσον, Οἰδίπους, τάδε,
μάλιστα μὲν τόνδ' ὅρκον αἰδεσθεὶς θεῶν,
ἔπειτα κἀμὲ τούσδε θ' οἳ πάρεισί σοι.

κομμός.
στρ. α'.   ΧΟ. ¹πιθοῦ θελήσας φρονήσας τ', ἄναξ, λίσσομαι.   649
ΟΙ. ²τί σοι θέλεις δῆτ' εἰκάθω;

---

one syllable, though in the tragic poets alone the word occurs more than 50 times. Synizesis of υ is rare in extant Greek poetry: Pind. *Pyth.* 4. 225 γενὖ͜ων: *Anthol.* 11. 413 (epigram by Ammianus, 1st century A. D.) ὦκιμον, ἡδὖ͜οσμον, πήγανον, ἀσπάραγος. Eur. *I. T.* 970 ὅσαι δ' Ἐρινῦ͜ων οὐκ ἐπείσθησαν νόμῳ, and *ib.* 1456 οἴστροις Ἐρινῦ͜ων, where most editors write Ἐρινῦν, as *ib.* 299 Ἐρινῦς (acc. plur.). Hes. *Scut.* 3 Ἠλεκτρυ͜ωνος. It might be rash to say that Soph. could not have used δυοῖν as a monosyllable; for he has used the ordinary synizesis in a peculiarly bold way, *Ai.* 1129 μή νυν ἀτίμα θεοὺς θεοῖς σεσωμένος: but at least it moves the strongest suspicion. ἀποκρίνας, on the other hand, seems genuine. ἀποκρίνειν is properly *secernere*, to *set apart: e. g.* γῆν (Plat. *Rep.* 303 D): or *to select :* id. *Legg.* 946 A πλήθει τῶν ψήφων ἀποκρίναντας, having selected (the men) according to the number of votes for each. Here, '*having set apart* (for me) one of two ills' is a phrase suitable to the arbitrary rigour of doom which left a choice only between death and exile. For δυοῖν Elms. proposed τοῖνδ' or τοῖνδέ γ': Herm., τοῖνδ' ἕν. I should rather believe that δρᾶν was altered into δρᾶσαι by a grammarian who looked to ἀπῶσαι, κτεῖναι, and perh. also sought a simpler order. But for pres. infin. combined with aor. infin. cp. 623 θνήσκειν...φυγεῖν: *Ant.* 204 μήτε κτερίζειν μήτε κωκῦσαι. See also *O. C.* 732 ἥκω γὰρ οὐχ ὡς δρᾶν τι βουληθείς, where in prose we should have expected δρᾶσαι. The quantity of ἀποκρίνας is supported by Aesch. *P. V.* 24 ἀποκρύψει: ἀποτροπή and its cognates in Aesch. and Eur.: ἐπικρύπτειν Eur. *Suppl.* 296: ἐπικράνων *I. T.* 51. Blaydes conj. δοὺς δυοῖν κρῖναι κακοῖν (*i.e.* 'giving me my choice of two ills'); cp. *O. C.* 640 τούτων...δίδωμί σοι | κρίναντι χρῆσθαι): Dindorf, θάτερον δυοῖν

to thrust me from the land of my fathers, or to slay me amain.

OE. Yea; for I have caught him working evil, by ill arts, against my person.

CR. Now may I see no good, but perish accursed, if I have done aught to thee of that wherewith thou chargest me!

IO. O, for the gods' love, believe it, Oedipus—first, for the awful sake of this oath unto the gods,—then for my sake and for theirs who stand before thee!

CH. Consent, reflect, hearken, O my king, I pray thee!

OE. What grace, then, wouldest thou have me grant thee?

Kommos. 1st strophe.

κακοῖν (where I should at least prefer κακόν): but since, with either of these supposed readings, the construction would have been perfectly clear, it is hard to see how ἀποκρίνας—a far-sought word—could have crept in as an explanatory gloss. **642** δρῶντα κακῶς τοὐμὸν σῶμα would properly describe bodily outrage: here it is a heated way of saying that Creon's supposed plot touched the *person* of the king (who was to be dethroned), and not merely the νόμοι πόλεως. **644** ἀραῖος = ὥσπερ αὐτὸς ἐπαρῶμαι. **647** ὅρκον θεῶν (object. gen.), an oath by the gods (since one said ὀμνύναι θεούς): Od. 2. 377 θεῶν μέγαν ὅρκον ἀπώμνυ: 10. 299 μακάρων μέγαν ὅρκον ὀμόσσαι: Eur. *Hipp.* 657 ὅρκοις θεῶν. But in *O. C.* 1767 Διὸς Ὅρκος is personified. **649—697** The κομμός (see p. 9) has a composite strophic arrangement: (1) *1st strophe*, 649—659, (2) *2nd strophe*, 660—668; answering respectively to (3) *1st antistr.*, 678—688, (4) *2nd antistr.*, 689—697. **649** θελήσας, having consented (πιστεύειν). *O. C.* 757 κρύψον (hide thy woes), θελήσας ἄστυ καὶ δόμους μολεῖν. Isae. or. 8 § 11 ταῦτα ποιῆσαι μὴ θελήσας. Plut. *Mor.* 149 F συνδειπνεῖν μὴ θελήσαντος. φρονήσας, having come to a sound mind. Isocr. or. 8 § 141 καλόν ἐστιν ἐν ταῖς τῶν ἄλλων ἀδικίαις καὶ μανίαις πρώτους εὖ φρονήσαντας προστῆναι τῆς τῶν Ἑλλήνων ἐλευθερίας. **651** εἰκάθω: the aor. subj. is certainly most suitable here: *Phil.* 761 βούλει λάβωμαι; *El.* 80 θέλεις | μείνωμεν; In such phrases the *pres.* subj. (implying a continued or repeated act) is naturally much rarer: βούλει ἐπισκοπῶμεν Xen. *Mem.* 3. 5. 1. As regards the form of εἰκάθω, Curtius (*Verb* II. 345, Eng. tr. 505), discussing presents in -θω and past tenses in -θον from vowel stems, warns us against 'looking for anything particularly aoristic in the θ' of these verbs. In Greek usage, he holds, 'a decidedly aoristic force' for such forms as σχεθεῖν and εἰκαθεῖν 'never

ΧΟ. 3 τὸν οὔτε πρὶν νήπιον νῦν τ' ἐν ὅρκῳ μέγαν καταίδεσαι.
ΟΙ. 4 οἶσθ' οὖν ἃ χρῄζεις; ΧΟ. οἶδα.᾿ ΟΙ. φράζε δὴ τί φῄς.
ΧΟ. 5 τὸν ἐναγῆ φίλον μήποτ' ἐν αἰτίᾳ　　　　　656
　　6 σὺν ἀφανεῖ λόγῳ σ' ἄτιμον βαλεῖν.
ΟΙ. 7 εὖ νυν ἐπίστω, ταῦθ' ὅταν ζητῇς, ἐμοὶ
　　8 ζητῶν ὄλεθρον ἢ φυγὴν ἐκ τῆσδε γῆς.

στρ. β'.　ΧΟ. 1 οὐ τὸν πάντων θεῶν θεὸν πρόμον　　　　　660
　　2 Ἅλιον· ἐπεὶ ἄθεος ἄφιλος ὅ τι πύματον
　　3 ὀλοίμαν, φρόνησιν εἰ τάνδ' ἔχω.
　　4 ἀλλά μοι δυσμόρῳ γᾶ φθίνουσα　　　　　665
　　5 τρύχει ψυχάν, τὰ δ' εἰ κακοῖς κακὰ
　　6 προσάψει τοῖς πάλαι τὰ πρὸς σφῶν.

　　656 τὸν ἐναγῆι φίλον μήποτ' ἐν αἰτίαι | σὺν ἀφανεῖ λόγον ἄτιμον ἐκβαλεῖν L;
litteras γω, lect. λόγῳ indicantes, addidit manus antiqua. λόγῳ praebent A et
plerique codd.: λόγων V cum aliis quibusdam. Lectiones λόγῳ et λόγων commenti
sunt librarii quibus hiatus displicebat, sensus autem loci neutiquam illuxerat.
σ' post λόγῳ primus inseruit Hermannus. In falsa l. ἐκβαλεῖν consentiunt cum
Laurentiano reliqui codd. fere omnes. βαλεῖν tamen, quod Suidas legit, inveni etiam
in cod. T. **659** φυγὴν L, ab antiqua manu factum ex φυγεῖν, quod in aliis

established itself': and he justly cites *El.* 1014 as a place where εἰκαθεῖν
is in no way aoristic. He would therefore keep the traditional accent,
and write σχέθειν, εἰκάθειν, with Buttmann. Now, while believing with
Curtius that these forms were prob. in origin presents, I also think
that in the usage of the classical age they were *often* aorists: as *e.g.*
σχεθεῖν in Aesch. *Theb.* 429 distinctly is. **652** μέγαν, 'great,' *i.e.* strong,
worthy of reverence, ἐν ὅρκῳ, by means of, in virtue of, his oath: Eur.
Tro. 669 ξυνέσει γένει πλούτῳ τε κἀνδρείᾳ μέγαν: for ἐν, cp. *Phil.* 185
ἔν τ' ὀδύναις ὁμοῦ | λιμῷ τ' οἰκτρός. **656** 'that thou shouldest never lay
under an accusation (ἐν αἰτίᾳ βαλεῖν), so as to dishonour him (ἄτιμον),
with the help of an unproved story (σὺν ἀφανεῖ λόγῳ), the friend who
is liable to a curse (ἐναγῆ)': *i.e.* who has just said (644) ἀραῖος
ὀλοίμαν κ.τ.λ. Aeschin. *In Ctes.* § 110 γέγραπται γὰρ οὕτως ἐν τῇ ἀρᾷ· εἰ
τις τάδε, φησί, παραβαίνοι,...ἐναγής, φησιν, ἔστω τοῦ Ἀπόλλωνος, 'let
him rest under the ban of Apollo': as Creon would rest under the ban
of the gods by whom he had sworn. Her. 6. 56 ἐν τῷ ἄγεϊ ἐνέχεσθαι, to
be liable to the curse. ἐν αἰτίᾳ βαλεῖν: [Plat.] *Epist.* 7. 341 A ὡς μηδέποτε

CH. Respect him who aforetime was not foolish, and who now is strong in his oath.

OE. Now dost thou know what thou cravest?

CH. Yea.

OE. Declare, then, what thou meanest.

CH. That thou shouldest never use an unproved rumour to cast a dishonouring charge on the friend who has bound himself with a curse.

OE. Then 'be very sure that, when thou seekest this, for me thou art seeking destruction, or exile from this land.

CH. No, by him who stands in the front of all the heavenly 2nd host, no, by the Sun! Unblest, unfriended, may I die by the strophe. uttermost doom, if I have that thought! But my unhappy soul is worn by the withering of the land, and again by the thought that our old sorrows should be crowned by sorrows springing from you twain.

---

quibusdam codd. mansit. **660** θεῶν θεόν. In L θεὶν paene evanuit, tanquam si librarius eluere voluisset: in A deletum est, relicto inter θεῶν et πρόμον quattuor litterarum spatio. Et plerique quidem codd. θεόν omittunt; minor est numerus eorum qui, ut V, θεῶν reiciunt, θεὸν servant. Integrae l. θεῶν θεὸν pepercit cod. T. **660** καὶ τάδ' codd. Recte delevit Hermannus καὶ, quod versus antistrophicus 695 spurium esse docet. τὰ δ' Kennedius. **668** σφῶϊν (i.e. σφῶν) codd. omnes: interpretatur schol. in E τὰ παρ' ὑμῶν.

βαλεῖν ἐν αἰτίᾳ τὸν δεικνύντα ἀλλ' αὐτὸν αὐτόν, 'so that he may never blame his teacher, but only himself,' equiv. to ἐμβαλεῖν αἰτίᾳ: cp. the prose phrases ἐμβάλλειν εἰς συμφοράς, γραφάς, ἔχθραν, κ.τ.λ. Eur. *Tro.* 305 εἰς ἔμ' αἰτίαν βάλῃ. **660** οὐ τὸν = οὐ μὰ τὸν, as not seldom; usu. followed by a second negative (as if here we had οὐκ ἔχω τάνδε φρόνησιν): 1088, *Ant.* 758, etc. πρόμον, standing foremost in the heavenly ranks, most conspicuous to the eyes of men: the god 'who sees all things and hears all things' (*Il.* 3. 277 ὃς πάντ' ἐφορᾷς καὶ πάντ' ἐπακούεις): invoked *Trach.* 102 as ὦ κρατιστεύων κατ' ὄμμα. **663** ὅ τι πύματόν (ἐστι), (τοῦτο) ὀλοίμαν: schol. φθαρείην ὅπερ ἔσχατον, ἤγουν ἀπώλειαν ἥτις ἰσχάτη. **666 f.** τὰ δ'—σφῷν: and, on the other hand, if the ills arising from you two are to be added to the former ills. Prof. Kennedy gives τὰ δ', rightly, I think: for γᾶ φθίνουσα refers to the blight and plague (25): τάδ' would obscure the contrast between *those* troubles and the new trouble of the quarrel. προσάψει intrans., as perh. only here and in fr.

J. S.   9

ΟΙ. ὁ δ' οὖν ἴτω, καὶ χρή με παντελῶς θανεῖν,   669
    ἢ γῆς ἄτιμον τῆσδ' ἀπωσθῆναι βίᾳ.   670
    τὸ γὰρ σόν, οὐ τὸ τοῦδ', ἐποικτείρω στόμα
    ἐλεινόν· οὗτος δ', ἔνθ' ἂν ᾖ, στυγήσεται.
ΚΡ. στυγνὸς μὲν εἴκων δῆλος εἶ, βαρὺς δ', ὅταν
    θυμοῦ περάσῃς. αἱ δὲ τοιαῦται φύσεις
    αὑταῖς δικαίως εἰσὶν ἄλγισται φέρειν.   675
ΟΙ. οὔκουν μ' ἐάσεις κἀκτὸς εἶ;   ΚΡ. πορεύσομαι,
    σοῦ μὲν τυχὼν ἀγνῶτος, ἐν δὲ τοῖσδ' ἴσος.

672 ἐλεεινὸν codd.: ἐλεινὸν cum Porsono edd.

---

348 καί μοι τρίτον ῥίπτοντι... | ἀγχοῦ προσῆψεν, 'he came near to me.'
Eur. *Hipp.* 188 τὸ μέν ἐστιν ἁπλοῦν· τῷ δὲ συνάπτει | λύπη τε φρενῶν
χερσίν τε πόνος, 'is joined.' It is possible, but harsh, to make προσάψει
act. with γῆ as subject. Since in 695 ἁλύουσαν κατ' ὀρθὸν οὐρίσας is clearly
sound, Herm. rightly struck out καὶ before τά δ' here. See on 696.
669 ὁ δ' οὖν: then *let* him go: *Ai.* 114 σὺ δ' οὖν... | χρῶ χειρί. **672**
ἐλεινόν: tertiary predicate: 'I compassionate thy words, piteous as
they are.' Where a possessive pron. with art. has preceded the subst.,
Soph. sometimes thus subjoins an adj., which really has the predicative
force to which its position entitles it, though for us it would be more
natural to translate it as a mere attributive: *Ant.* 881 τὸν δ' ἐμὸν πότμον
ἀδάκρυτον | οὐδεὶς...στενάζει: *Phil.* 1456 τοὐμὸν ἐτέγχθη | κρᾶτ' ἐνδό-
μυχον: *El.* 1143 τῆς ἐμῆς πάλαι τροφῆς | ἀνωφελήτου. In 1199 (where see
note) τὰν γαμψ. παρθ. χρησμῳδόν is not a similar case. Prof. Kennedy,
placing a comma after ἐποικτείρω, but none after τοῦδ', construes: τὸ
σὸν στόμα ἐλεινόν (ἐστι), οὐκ ἐποικτείρω τὸ τοῦδε. **στυγήσεται**, pass.
Other examples in Soph. are 1500 ὀνειδιεῖσθε: *O. C.* 581 δηλώσεται,
1186 λέξεται: *Ant.* 210 τιμήσεται, 637 ἀξιώσεται: *El.* 971 καλεῖ:
Phil. 48 φυλάξεται: among many found in prose as well as in verse
are ἀδικήσομαι, ἁλώσομαι, ἐάσομαι, ζημιώσομαι, τιμήσομαι, ὠφελήσομαι.
The middle forms of the aorist were alone peculiar to that voice; the
so-called 'future middle,' like the rest, was either middle or passive.
673 στυγνὸς...περάσῃς: 'thou art seen to be sullen when thou yieldest,
but fierce when thou hast gone far in wrath': *i.e., as* thou art fierce in
passion, *so* art thou sullen in yielding. Greek idiom co-ordinates the
clauses, though the emphasis is on στυγνὸς μὲν εἴκων, which the other
merely enforces by contrast: see on 419. **βαρὺς**, *bearing heavily* on the

OE. Then let him go, though I am surely doomed to death,
or to be thrust dishonoured from the land. Thy lips, not his,
move my compassion by their plaint; but he, where'er he be,
shall be hated.

CR. Sullen in yielding art thou seen, even as vehement in
the excesses of thy wrath; but such natures are justly sorest
for themselves to bear.

OE. Then wilt thou not leave me in peace, and get thee
gone?

CR. I will go my way; I have found thee undiscerning,
but in the sight of these I am just.   [*Exit.*

---

object of anger, and so, 'vehement,' 'fierce': *Ai.* 1017 δύσοργος, ἐν γήρᾳ
βαρύς, *ib.* 656 μῆνιν βαρεῖαν: *Phil.* 1045 βαρύς τε καὶ βαρεῖαν ὁ ξένος φάτιν
τήνδ᾽ εἶπε: *Ant.* 767 νοῦς δ᾽ ἐστὶ τηλικοῦτος ἀλγήσας βαρύς. 674 περάσῃς
absol.,= πρόσω ἔλθῃς: *O. C.* 154 περᾷς, (you go too far), *ib.* 885 πέραν |
περῶσ᾽ οἵδε δή. θυμοῦ, partitive gen.: cp. *Il.* 2. 785 διέπρησσον πεδίοιο:
Her. 3. 105 προλαμβάνειν...τῆς ὁδοῦ: sometimes helped by a prep. or
adverbial phrase, as Xen. *Apol.* 30 προβήσεσθαι πόρρω μοχθηρίας: 2 *Epist.*
Tim. 2. 16 ἐπὶ πλεῖον γὰρ προκόψουσιν ἀσεβείας. Others render: 'resentful
[or 'remorseful'] even when thou hast *passed out of* wrath': but (a) περάσῃς
with a simple gen. could not bear this sense: (b) the antithesis pointed
by μὲν and δὲ is thus destroyed. 677 ἀγνῶτος, act., 'undiscerning,' as 681,
1133: pass., 'unknown,' *Ph.* 1008, *Ant.* 1001. Ellendt is not quite
accurate in saying that Soph. was the first who used ἀγνώς in an active
sense, for it is clearly active in Pind. *Pyth.* 9. 58 (478 B.C.) οὔτε
παγκάρπων φυτῶν νήποινον οὔτ᾽ ἀγνῶτα θηρῶν (χθονὸς αἶσαν), 'a portion
of land not failing in tribute of plants bearing all manner of fruit, nor *a*
stranger to beasts of chase.' The passive use was, however, probably
older than the active: compare *Od.* 5. 79 ἀγνῶτες...ἀλλήλοισι (pass.) with
Thuc. 3. 53 ἀγνῶτες ἀλλήλων (act.). ἐν δὲ τοῖσδ᾽ ἴσος: ἐν of the tribunal or
company by whom one is judged: *Ant.* 459 ἐν θεοῖσι τὴν δίκην | δοῦναι:
Eur. *Hipp.* 988 οἱ γὰρ ἐν σοφοῖς | φαῦλοι παρ᾽ ὄχλῳ μουσικώτεροι λέγειν:
and so, more boldly, *O. C.* 1213 σκαιοσύναν φυλάσσων ἐν ἐμοὶ (*me iudice*)
κατάδηλος ἔσται. ἴσος, *aequus*, just: Plat. *Legg.* 975 c τὸν μέλλοντα δικασ-
τὴν ἴσον ἔσεσθαι. [Dem.] or. 7 § 35 (by a contemporary of Dem.) ἴσῳ
καὶ κοινῷ δικαστηρίῳ. So *Ph.* 685 ἴσος ἐν ἴσοις ἀνήρ. The scholiast
explains, παρὰ δὲ τούτοις τῆς ὁμοίας δόξης ἦν καὶ πρώην εἶχον περὶ ἐμέ, *i.e.*
'*of the same repute as before.*' To me such a version of ἴσος appears most

ἀντ. α΄. ΧΟ. 1 γύναι, τί μέλλεις κομίζειν δόμων τόνδ᾽ ἔσω ;			678
    ΙΟ. 2 μαθοῦσά γ᾽ ἥτις ἡ τύχη.					680
    ΧΟ. 3 δόκησις ἀγνὼς λόγων ἦλθε, δάπτει δὲ καὶ τὸ μὴ 'νδικον.
    ΙΟ. 4 ἀμφοῖν ἀπ᾽ αὐτοῖν ; ΧΟ. ναίχι. ΙΟ. καὶ τίς ἦν λόγος;
    ΧΟ. 5 ἅλις ἔμοιγ᾽, ἅλις, γᾶς προπονουμένας,			685
       6 φαίνεται, ἔνθ᾽ ἔληξεν, αὐτοῦ μένειν.
    ΟΙ. 7 ὁρᾷς ἵν᾽ ἥκεις, ἀγαθὸς ὢν γνώμην ἀνήρ,
       8 τοὐμὸν παριεὶς καὶ καταμβλύνων κέαρ ;

ἀντ. β΄. ΧΟ. 1 ὦναξ, εἶπον μὲν οὐχ ἅπαξ μόνον,			689
       2 ἴσθι δὲ παραφρόνιμον, ἄπορον ἐπὶ φρόνιμα
       3 πεφάνθαι μ᾽ ἄν, εἴ σ᾽ ἐνοσφιζόμαν,

684 λόγος L et codd. plerique: ὁ λόγος A, E (cum gloss. ἡ διαφορά), Bodl.
Laud. 54, Barocc. 66. **688** παρίης καὶ καταμβλύνεις cum Hartungio Dindorf.,
posito post ἥκεις interrogationis signo, sublata autem interpunctione post ἀνήρ. Con-

---

strange. 678 Creon leaves the scene. The Chorus wish Iocasta to withdraw Oedipus also, that his excited feelings may be soothed in the
privacy of the house : but the queen wishes first to learn from the
Chorus how the dispute began. 681 δόκησις...λόγων, a *suspicion* resting
on mere *assertions* (those made by Oedipus), and not supported by
facts (ἔργα): hence ἀγνὼς, *unknowing*, guided by no real knowledge.
Thuc. 1. 4 οὐ λόγων...κόμπος τάδε μᾶλλον ἢ ἔργων ἐστὶν ἀλήθεια: 3. 43
τῆς οὐ βεβαίου δοκήσεως. δάπτει δὲ: Oedipus was incensed against
Creon, without proof; on the other hand (δὲ) Creon also (καὶ) was
incensed by the unjust accusation. δάπτει might be historic pres.,
but need not be so taken: Creon is still pained. Aesch. *P. V.* 437 συννοίᾳ
δὲ δάπτομαι κέαρ. The version, 'and *even* injustice wounds,' would make
the words a reflection ;—'An accusation galls, *even* when unfounded':
but this is unsuitable. 683 f. ἀμφοῖν ἀπ᾽ αὐτοῖν sc. ἦλθε τὸ νεῖκος; Thus
far, Iocasta only knew that Oedipus charged Creon with treason. The
words of the Chorus now hint that Oedipus himself was partly to blame.
'So then,' Iocasta asks, 'provocation had been given on *both sides*?'
λόγος, the story (of the alleged treason): for the words of Oed. (642
δρῶντα κακῶς, τέχνη κακή) had been vague. 685 προπονουμένας, '*already*
troubled,' not, 'troubled exceedingly.' προπονεῖν always = to suffer
before, or *for*: Lucian *Iupp. Trag.* § 40 Ἀθηνᾶ Ἄρην καταγωνίζεται, ἅτε
καὶ προπεπονηκότα οἶμαι ἐκ τοῦ τραύματος, *already* disabled. 687 The

Cii. Lady, why dost thou delay to take yon man into the house? 1st antistrophe.

Io. I will do so, when I have learned what hath chanced.

Cii. Blind suspicion, bred of talk, arose; and, on the other part, injustice wounds.

Io. It was on both sides?

Ch. Aye.

Io. And what was the story?

Cii. Enough, methinks, enough—when our land is already vexed—that the matter should rest where it ceased.

Oe. Seest thou to what thou hast come, for all thy honest purpose, in seeking to slack and blunt my zeal?

Cii. King, I have said it not once alone — be sure that I should have been shown a madman, bankrupt in sane counsel, if I put thee away — thee, 2nd antistrophe.

firmat participium παριείς ascripta in L et A interpretatio ἐκλύων. **693** εἴ σε νοσφίζομαι codd., sed repugnat sententiae praesens indicativi. εἴ σ' ἐνοσφιζόμαν coniecerant Hermann., Hartung. (—ην), Badham.; recepit Blaydes.

---

evasive answer of the Chorus has nettled Oedipus by implying that the blame was divided, and that both parties ought to be glad to forget it. He could never forget it (672). ὁρᾷς ἵν' ἥκεις conveys indignant reproach: a grave charge has been laid against your king; instead of meeting it with denial, you are led, by your sympathy with Creon, to imply that it cannot be directly met, and must be hushed up. *Ant.* 735 ὁρᾷς τάδ' ὡς εἴρηκας ὡς ἄγαν νέος: *El.* 628 ὁρᾷς; πρὸς ὀργὴν ἐκφέρει. 688 παριείς with τοὐμὸν κέαρ, seeking to relax, enervate, my resentment: a sense which the close connection with καταμβλύνων interprets, though the more ordinary meaning for παριείς, had it stood *alone* here, would be 'neglecting,' 'slighting' (πόθος παρεῖτο, *El.* 545): cp. Ar. *Eq.* 436 τοῦ ποδὸς παρίει, slack away (some of) the sheet: Eur. *Cycl.* 591 ὕπνῳ παρειμένος: *Or.* 210 τῷ λίαν παρειμένῳ, (neut.) by too great languor. Schneidewin understands, 'neglecting my interest, and blunting (your) feeling': but τοὐμὸν must surely agree with κέαρ. 692 ἐπὶ φρόνιμα: [Dem.] or. 25 § 31 ἐπὶ μὲν καλὸν ἢ χρηστὸν ἢ τῆς πόλεως ἄξιον πρᾶγμα οὐδὲν οὗτός ἐστι χρήσιμος. 693 πεφάνθαι ἄν, oblique of πεφασμένος ἂν ἦν: for the tense cp. Isocr. or. 5 § 56 λοιπὸν ἂν ἦν...εἰ μὴ ἐπεποίητο. The εἰ νοσφίζομαι of the MSS. would necessarily imply that the Chorus *do*

4 ὅς τ᾽ ἐμὰν γᾶν φίλαν ἐν πόνοισιν
5 ἀλύουσαν κατ᾽ ὀρθὸν οὔρισας,   695
6 τανῦν τ᾽ εὔπομπος ἂν γένοιο.

IO. πρὸς θεῶν δίδαξον κἄμ᾽, ἄναξ, ὅτου ποτὲ
μῆνιν τοσήνδε πράγματος στήσας ἔχεις.

OI. ἐρῶ· σὲ γὰρ τῶνδ᾽ ἐς πλέον, γύναι, σέβω·   700
Κρέοντος, οἷά μοι βεβουλευκὼς ἔχει.

IO. λέγ᾽, εἰ σαφῶς τὸ νεῖκος ἐγκαλῶν ἐρεῖς.

OI. φονέα με φησὶ Λαΐου καθεστάναι.

IO. αὐτὸς ξυνειδώς, ἢ μαθὼν ἄλλου πάρα;

694 πόνοις codd.; quod cum versui 665 (φθίνουσα) non respondeat, Dindorf. ibi
φθινὰς legit.   Sed praestat, servato φθίνουσα, hic πόνοισιν legere.   πόνοις τότ᾽ coniecit
Blaydes.   696 τανῦν τ᾽ εὔπομπος εἰ δύναιο γενοῦ L.   Litteram ο voci δύναιο
addidit recentior manus : prima δύναι (i.e. δύνᾳ) scripserat.   Post τανῦν facta est
rasura in τ᾽, quod tamen δ᾽ prius fuisse non ausim dicere.   Deletum est aliquid super

reject Oedipus: *Ant.* 304 εἴπερ ἴσχει Ζεὺς ἔτ᾽ ἐξ ἐμοῦ σέβας. The
change of one letter restores the required ἐνοσφιζόμαν. 694 κ.τ.λ. As
ὅς τε cannot be epic for ὅς, τε goes with οὔρισας: cp. *El.* 249 ἔρροι
τ᾽ ἂν αἰδὼς | ἁπάντων τ᾽ εὐσέβεια θνατῶν. 695 ἀλύουσαν, of one
maddened by suffering, *Ph.* 1194 ἀλύοντα χειμερίῳ λύπᾳ. The conject. σαλεύουσαν would be correct, but tame. 696 ἂν γένοιο. The
MSS. have εἰ δύναιο γενοῦ : for δύναιο, the 1st hand of L had written
δύναι, *i.e.* δύνᾳ. Now, εἰ δύνᾳ γενοῦ is satisfactory in itself, since δύνᾳ
for δύνασαι has good authority in Attic, as Eur. *Hec.* 253 δρᾷς δ᾽ οὐδὲν
ἡμᾶς εὖ, κακῶς δ᾽ ὅσον δύνᾳ. But then we must correct the strophe,
667,—as by writing there τὰ πρὸς σφῷν τοῖς πάλαι προσάψετον, which
I should prefer to Nauck's ingenious προσάψει τοῖς πάλαι τὰ πρόσφατα.
Verse 667, however, seems right as it stands : it gives a better rhythm
for the closing cadence than we should obtain by adding a syllable.
And if so, εἰ δύναιο (or δύνᾳ) γενοῦ here must be reduced to ‿ – ⏒.
(1) If with Hermann we simply omit γενοῦ, the elliptical εἰ δύναιο—
understanding ἴσθι or γενοῦ—is intolerably harsh ; to me it does
not seem even Greek. (2) εἰ γένοιο, ' mayest thou become !' is read by
Bergk and Dindorf ; cp. 863 εἴ μοι ξυνείη. (3) To this I much prefer ἂν
γένοιο, which Blaydes adopts ; but I do so for a reason which he does
not give. I suspect that εἰ δύναιο was a marginal gloss intended to

who gavest a true course to my beloved country when distraught by troubles—thee, who now also art like to prove our prospering guide.

IO.   In the name of the gods, tell me also, O king, on what account thou hast conceived this steadfast wrath.

OE.   That will I ; for I honour thee, lady, above yonder men:—the cause is Creon, and the plots that he hath laid against me.

IO.   Speak on—if thou canst tell clearly how the feud began.

OE.   He says that I stand guilty of the blood of Laïus.

IO.   As on his own knowledge ?   Or on hearsay from another ?

vocem δύναιο, quod σύ fuisse nihil indicat. τανῦν τ' εὔπομπος εἰ δύναιο γενοῦ Α. Repetunt δύναιο omnes quos viderim codd. praeter Bodl. Barocc. 66 qui habet εἰ δύναι ὁ γενοῦ. Numero testimoniorum praevalet τανῦν δ', pondere τανῦν τ', quippe quod et Α et antiquus Laurentiani corrector comprobent.

---

define the sense of ἂν γένοιο, and that ἂν γένοιο was corrupted to γενοῦ when εἰ δύναιο had crept into the text.   (4) Prof. Kennedy acutely conjectures εἰ τό γ' ἕν σοι: 'now also | *with thy best skill* thou ably waftest.' Since the metre of 667 is not certainly sound, no treatment of our verse can be confident.   697 κἄμ': these men know it: allow me also to know it.   ὅτου...πράγματος, causal gen.; *Ant.* 1177 πατρὶ μηνίσας φόνου.   698 στήσας ἔχεις, hast set up, *i.e.* conceived as an *abiding* sentiment, referring to 672 and 689.   Cp. Eur. *I. A.* 785 ἐλπὶς...|οἵαν...|στή- σασαι τάδ' ἐς ἀλλήλας | μυθεύσουσι (Fritzsch).   700 τῶνδ' ἐς πλέον = πλέον ἢ τούσδε, not πλέον ἢ οἶδε.   The Chorus having hinted that Oedipus was partly to blame, he deigned no reply to their protests of loyalty (689 f.).   But he respects Iocasta's judgment more, and will answer *her*.   The Chorus, of course, already know the answer to her question.   701 Κρέοντος, *sc.* στήσας ἔχω τὴν μῆνιν : causal gen. answering to ὅτου πράγματος.   702 λέγ': speak, if you can make a clear statement (εἰ σαφῶς ἐρεῖς) in imputing the blame of the feud: *i.e.* if you are prepared to explain the vague οἶα (701) by defining the provocation.   ἐγκαλεῖν νεῖκός (τινι) = to charge one with (*beginning*) a quarrel: as *Phil.* 328 χόλον (τινὸς) κατ' αὐτῶν ἐγκαλῶν, charging them with having *provoked* your anger at a deed.   704 αὐτὸς ξυνειδώς: *i.e.* does he speak *as* from his own knowledge (of your guilt)?

ΟΙ. μάντιν μὲν οὖν κακοῦργον εἰσπέμψας, ἐπεὶ   705
τό γ' εἰς ἑαυτὸν πᾶν ἐλευθεροῖ στόμα.

ΙΟ. σύ νυν ἀφεὶς σεαυτὸν ὧν λέγεις πέρι
ἐμοῦ 'πάκουσον, καὶ μάθ' οὕνεκ' ἐστί σοι
βρότειον οὐδὲν μαντικῆς ἔχον τέχνης.
φανῶ δέ σοι σημεῖα τῶνδε σύντομα.   710
χρησμὸς γὰρ ἦλθε Λαΐῳ ποτ', οὐκ ἐρῶ
Φοίβου γ' ἀπ' αὐτοῦ, τῶν δ' ὑπηρετῶν ἄπο,
ὡς αὐτὸν ἥξοι μοῖρα πρὸς παιδὸς θανεῖν,
ὅστις γένοιτ' ἐμοῦ τε κἀκείνου πάρα.

713 ἥξει L, sed ex ἥξοι factum. ἥξοι V et L². ἥξει A et codd. plerique, ut

---

705 μὲν οὖν, 'nay.' *El.* 1503. Ar. *Eq.* 13 ΝΙ. λέγε σύ. ΔΗ. σὺ μὲν οὖν
λέγε. Distinguish μὲν οὖν in 483, where each word has a separate force.
706 τό γ' εἰς ἑαυτὸν, in what concerns himself : Eur. *I. T.* 691 τὸ μὲν γὰρ
εἰς ἔμ' οὐ κακῶς ἔχει. πᾶν ἐλευθεροῖ, sets wholly free (from the discredit of
having brought such a charge) : *Ant.* 445 ἔξω βαρείας αἰτίας ἐλεύθερον :
Plat. *Legg.* 756 D ἐλεύθερον ἀφεῖσθαι τῆς ζημίας. 707 ἀφεὶς σεαυτόν, an
appropriate phrase, since ἀφιέναι was the regular term when the natural
avenger of a slain man voluntarily released the slayer from the penalties:
Dem. or. 38 § 59 ἂν ὁ παθὼν αὐτὸς ἀφῇ τοῦ φόνου τὸν δράσαντα : Antiph.
or. 2 § 2 οὐ τὸν αἴτιον ἀφέντες τὸν ἀναίτιον διώκομεν. 708 μάθ' κ.τ.λ. : learn
that·thou canst find no mortal creature sharing in the art of divination.
σοι ethic dat. : ἐστὶν ἔχον = ἔχει (Eur. *Suppl.* 527 τί τούτων ἐστὶν οὐ καλῶς
ἔχον ;): τέχνης, partitive gen. The *gods* have prescience (498) ; but they
impart it to no *man*,—not even to such ministers as the Delphian priests.
Iocasta reveres the gods (647) : it is to them, and first to Apollo, that
she turns in trouble (911). But the shock which had befallen her own
life,—when at the bidding of Delphi her first-born was sacrificed without
saving her husband Laïus—has left a deep and bitter conviction that no
mortal, be he priest or seer, shares the divine foreknowledge. In the
Greek view the μάντις might be (1) first, the god himself, speaking
through a divinely frenzied being in whom the human reason was
temporarily superseded (hence the popular derivation of μαντική from
μανία) : Plat. *Tim.* 71 E μαντικὴν ἀφροσύνῃ θεὸς ἀνθρωπίνῃ δέδωκεν· οὐδεὶς
γὰρ ἔννους ἐφάπτεται μαντικῆς ἐνθέου καὶ ἀληθοῦς : this was much the
same as the Egyptian belief, Her. 2. 83 μαντικὴ δὲ αὐτοῖσι ὧδε διακέεται.
ἀνθρώπων μὲν οὐδενὶ πρόσκειται ἡ τέχνη, τῶν δὲ θεῶν μετεξετέροισι.

OE. Nay, he hath made a rascal seer his mouth-piece; as for himself, he keeps his lips wholly pure.

IO. Then absolve thyself of the things whereof thou speakest; hearken to me, and learn for thy comfort that nought of mortal birth is a sharer in the science of the seer. I will give thee pithy proof of that.

An oracle came to Laïus once—I will not say from Phoebus himself, but from his ministers—that the doom should overtake him to die by the hand of his child, who should spring from him and me.

saepe usu venit cum inter indicativum et optativum pendeat lectio. ἕξει coniecit Canter.; ἕξοι K. Halm., quod receperunt Nauck., Blaydes.

---

(2) Secondly, the μάντις might be a man who reads signs from birds, fire, etc., by rule of mystic science: it was against this τέχνη that scepticism most readily turned: Eur. *El.* 399 Λοξίου γὰρ ἔμπεδοι | χρησμοί, βροτῶν δὲ μαντικὴν χαίρειν λέγω. Iocasta means: 'I will not say that the message came through the lips of a truly god-possessed interpreter; but at any rate it came from the priests; it was an effort of human μαντική.' So in 946, 953 θεῶν μαντεύματα are oracles which *professed* to come from the gods. Others render:—'Nothing in mortal affairs *is connected with* the mantic art': *i.e.* is affected by it, comes within its ken. Then ἐστὶν ἔχον will not stand for ἔχεται (which it could not do), but for ἔχει, as meaning '*is* of,' 'belongs to.' Her. has ἔχειν as = εἶναι *with expressions equivalent to an adverb*, as 2. 91 ἀγῶνα γυμνικὸν διὰ πάσης ἀγωνίης ἔχοντα, '*consisting in* every sort of contest,' as he might have said πολυτρόπως ἔχοντα: so 3. 128 περὶ πολλῶν ἔχοντα πρηγμάτων (=πολλαχῶς): 6. 42 κατὰ χώρην (=ἐμπέδως) ἔχοντες: 7. 220 ἐν ἔπεσι ἐξαμέτροισι ἔχοντα. But such instances are wholly different from the supposed use of ἔχειν *alone* as = εἶναι with a partitive genitive. **711** οὐκ ἐρῶ κ.τ.λ. The exculpation of Apollo *himself* here is obviously not inconsistent with 720, which does not ascribe the prediction to him. And in 853 (ὅν γε Λοξίας | διεῖπε) the name of the god merely stands for that of his Delphian priesthood. **713** ἥξοι is better than the conject. ἕξοι ('constrain'), as expressing the suddenness with which the doom should overtake him. *El.* 489 ἥξει...'Ερινύς. The simple acc. αὐτόν, since ἥξοι = καταλήψοιτο: cp. Her. 9. 26 φαμὲν ἡμέας ἱκνέεσθαι ἡγεμονεύειν, instead of ἐς ἡμέας (2. 29). **714** ὅστις γένοιτ' is oblique for ὅστις ἂν γένηται (whoever may be born), not for ὅστις ἐγένετο (who has been

καὶ τὸν μέν, ὥσπερ γ᾽ ἡ φάτις, ξένοι ποτὲ   715
ληισταὶ φονεύουσ᾽ ἐν τριπλαῖς ἁμαξιτοῖς·
παιδὸς δὲ βλάστας οὐ διέσχον ἡμέραι
τρεῖς, καί νιν ἄρθρα κεῖνος ἐνζεύξας ποδοῖν
ἔρριψεν ἄλλων χερσὶν εἰς ἄβατον ὄρος.
κἀνταῦθ᾽ Ἀπόλλων οὔτ᾽ ἐκεῖνον ἤνυσεν   720
φονέα γενέσθαι πατρός, οὔτε Λάϊον,
τὸ δεινὸν οὐφοβεῖτο, πρὸς παιδὸς θανεῖν.
τοιαῦτα φῆμαι μαντικαὶ διώρισαν,
ὧν ἐντρέπου σὺ μηδέν· ὧν γὰρ ἂν θεὸς
χρείαν ἐρευνᾶι ῥαιδίως αὐτὸς φανεῖ.   725
ΟΙ. οἷόν μ᾽ ἀκούσαντ᾽ ἀρτίως ἔχει, γύναι,
      ψυχῆς πλάνημα κἀνακίνησις φρενῶν.
ΙΟ. ποίας μερίμνης τοῦθ᾽ ὑποστραφεὶς λέγεις;

719 εἰς ἄβατον ὄρος codd.: ἄβατον εἰς ὄρος cum Musgravio Erfurdt., Dindorf., Bothius, Hartung., Seidler.   **722** θανεῖν codd. In A autem γρ. παθεῖν super θανεῖν rubris litteris scripsit manus antiqua; recentior eandem lectionem in marg.

born): Laïus received the oracle before the birth of the child. **715** ξένοι: not Thebans, much less of his own blood. **716** see on 733. **717** διέσχον. 'Three days had not separated the child's birth from us': three days had not passed since its birth. Plut. *Tib. Gracch.* § 18 κελεύσαντος ἐκείνου διασχεῖν τὸ πλῆθος, to keep the crowd off. βλάστας cannot be acc. of respect ('as to the birth'), because διέσχον could not mean 'had elapsed': when διέχειν is intrans. it means (*a*) to be distant, Thuc. 8. 79 διέχει δὲ ὀλίγον ταύτηι ἡ Σάμος τῆς ἠπείρου: or (*b*) to extend, Her. 4. 42 διώρυχα...διέχουσαν ἐς τὸν Ἀράβιον κόλπον. **718** καί = ὅτε (parataxis instead of hypotaxis): Thuc. 1. 50 ἤδη δὲ ἦν ὀψέ...καὶ οἱ Κορίνθιοι ἐξαπίνης πρύμναν ἐκρούοντο. ἄρθρα ποδοῖν = τὰ σφυρά: ἐνζεύξας, fastened together by driving a pin through them, so as to maim the child and thus lessen the chance of its being reared if it survived exposure: Eur. *Ph.* 22 (Iocasta speaks) ἔσπειρεν ἡμῖν παῖδα, καὶ σπείρας βρέφος, | γνοὺς τἀμπλάκημα τοῦ θεοῦ τε τὴν φάτιν, | λειμῶν᾽ ἐς Ἥρας καὶ Κιθαιρῶνος λέπας | δίδωσι βουκόλοισιν ἐκθεῖναι βρέφος, | σφυρῶν σιδηρᾶ κέντρα διαπείρας μέσον (better μέσων), | ὅθεν νιν Ἑλλὰς ὠνόμαζεν Οἰδίπουν. Seneca *Oed.* 812 *Forata ferro gesseras vestigia, Tumore nactus nomen ac vitio pedum.* **719** εἰς ἄβατον ὄρος: the tribrach contained in one word gives a ruggedness which is certainly

Now Laïus,—as, at least, the rumour saith,—was murdered one day by foreign robbers at a place where three highways meet. And the child's birth was not three days past, when Laïus pinned its ankles together, and had it thrown, by others' hands, on a trackless mountain.

So, in that case, Apollo brought it not to pass·that the babe should become the slayer of his sire, or that Laïus should die— the dread thing which he feared—by his child's hand. Thus did the messages of seer-craft map out the future. Regard them, thou, not at all. Whatsoever needful things the god seeks, he himself will easily bring to light.

OE.   What restlessness of soul, lady, what tumult of the mind hath just come upon me since I heard thee speak!

IO.   What anxiety hath startled thee, that thou sayest this?

Laurentiani notavit. Et receperunt quidem παθεῖν Erfurdt., Wunder., Dindorf., Hartung.   Proclivis erat mutatio; nec dubium mihi videtur quin θανεῖν verum sit. **728** ὑπὸ στραφεὶς T, V⁴: quod probat Kayser., recepit Dindorf.

intentional here, as in 1496 τὸν πατέρα πατήρ, *Ai.* 459 πεδία τάδε. A tribrach in the 5th place, always rare, usually occurs either when the penultimate word of the verse is a *paeon primus* (– ◡ ◡ ◡), as *El.* 326 ἐντάφια χεροῖν, or when the last word is a *paeon quartus* (◡ ◡ ◡ –), as *Phil.* 1302 ἄνδρα πολέμιον. Verse 967 below is exceptional. **720** κἀνταῦθ': cp. 582. **722** It is more likely that, as our MSS. suggest, παθεῖν should have been a commentator's conjecture than that θανεῖν should have been a copyist's error (from v. 713). No objection can be drawn from the occurrence of πρὸς παιδὸς θανεῖν so soon after 713: see on 519. **723** τοιαῦτα...διώρισαν, *i.e.* made predictions at once so *definite* and so *false:* φῆμαι, a solemn word used scornfully: cp. 86. The sense of διώρισαν in 1083 is slightly different: here we might compare Dem. or. 20 § 158 ὁ Δράκων...καθαρὸν διώρισεν εἶναι, 'has *laid down* that the man is pure.' **725** ὧν χρείαν ἐρευνᾷ: a bold phrase blended, as it were, from ὧν χρείαν ἔχῃ and ἃ χρήσιμα (ὄντα) ἐρευνᾷ: cp. *Phil.* 327 τίνος... | χόλον...ἐγκαλῶν, instead of τίνος χόλον ἔχων or τί ἐγκαλῶν. **726—754** The mention of '*three roads*' (716) has startled Oedipus.   He now asks concerning (1) the place, (2) the time, (3) the person. The agreement of (1) with (2) dismays him; that of both with (3) flashes conviction to his mind. **727** πλάνημα denotes the fearful 'wandering' of his thought back to other days and scenes; as ἔδοξ' (729) is the word of one who has been in a troubled dream. **728** ποίας μέρ. ὑποστρ., having turned round

ΟΙ. ἔδοξ᾽ ἀκοῦσαι σοῦ τόδ᾽, ὡς ὁ Λάϊος
    κατασφαγείη πρὸς τριπλαῖς ἁμαξιτοῖς.   736

ΙΟ. ηὐδᾶτο γὰρ ταῦτ᾽, οὐδέ πω λήξαντ᾽ ἔχει.

ΟΙ. καὶ ποῦ ᾽σθ᾽ ὁ χῶρος οὗτος οὗ τόδ᾽ ἦν πάθος;

ΙΟ. Φωκὶς μὲν ἡ γῆ κλῄζεται, σχιστὴ δ᾽ ὁδὸς
    ἐς ταὐτὸ Δελφῶν κἀπὸ Δαυλίας ἄγει.

ΟΙ. καὶ τίς χρόνος τοῖσδ᾽ ἐστὶν οὐξεληλυθώς;   735

ΙΟ. σχεδόν τι πρόσθεν ἢ σὺ τῆσδ᾽ ἔχων χθονὸς
    ἀρχὴν ἐφαίνου τοῦτ᾽ ἐκηρύχθη πόλει.

ΟΙ. ὦ Ζεῦ, τί μου δρᾶσαι βεβούλευσαι πέρι;

ΙΟ. τί δ᾽ ἐστί σοι τοῦτ᾽, Οἰδίπους, ἐνθύμιον;

ΟΙ. μήπω μ᾽ ἐρώτα· τὸν δὲ Λάϊον φύσιν   740

730 διπλαῖς, quod habent L aliique complures, mendum est manifestum; neque enim ita explicari potest ut compita significentur ubi via, per quam Laius incedebat, cum *duabus aliis* se coniunxit. Inter paucos qui τριπλαῖς tuentur sunt A et E. **740** φύσιν | τίν᾽ εἶχε φράζε τίνα δ᾽ ἀκμὴν ἥβης ἔχων codd., nulla varietate praeterquam

on account of (= startled by) what care,—like a man whom a sound at his back causes to turn in alarm:—far more expressive than ἐπιστραφείς, which would merely denote attention. For the causal gen., cp. 724 and *Ai.* 1116 τοῦ δὲ σοῦ ψόφου | οὐκ ἂν στραφείην. **731** λήξαντ᾽: the breath of rumour is as a breeze which has not yet fallen: cp. *Ai.* 258 νότος ὡς λήγει, and *O. C.* 517. **733** σχιστὴ δ᾽ ὁδὸς. In going from Thebes to Delphi, the traveller passes by these 'Branching Roads,'—still known as the τρίοδοι, but better as the στενό: from Daulia it is a leisurely ride of about an hour and a half along the side of Parnassus. The following is from my notes taken on the spot:—'A bare isolated hillock of grey stone stands at the point where our path from Daulia meets the road to Delphi, and a third road that stretches to the south. There, in front, we are looking up the road down which Oedipus came [from Delphi]; we are moving in the steps of the man whom he met and slew; the road runs up a wild and frowning pass between Parnassus on the right hand and on the left the spurs of the Helicon range, which here approach it. Away to the south a wild and lonely valley opens, running up among the waste places of Helicon, a vista of naked cliffs or slopes clothed with scanty herbage, a scene of inexpressible grandeur and desolation' (*Modern Greece* p. 79). At this σχιστὴ ὁδός Pausanias saw τὰ τοῦ Λαΐου μνήματα καὶ οἰκέτου τοῦ ἑπομένου: the legend was that Damasistratus

OE. Methought I heard this from thee,—that Laïus was slain where three highways meet.

IO. Yea, that was the story; nor hath it ceased yet.

OE. And where is the place where this befell?

IO. The land is called Phocis; and branching roads lead to the same spot from Delphi and from Daulia.

OE. And what is the time that hath passed since these things were?

IO. The news was published to the town shortly before thou wert first seen in power over this land.

OE. O Zeus, what hast thou decreed to do unto me?

IO. And wherefore, Oedipus, doth this thing weigh upon thy soul?

OE. Ask me not yet; but say what was the stature of

quod ἔσχε pro εἶχε praebet A. Pro τίνα δ' Nauckius dedit τίνος, quod recepi: vide quae infra annotata sunt. Duas fere medendi vias inierunt editores. (1) Servatis εἶχε et τίνα δ', pro ἔχων Brunckius coniecit τότε, Kennedius ἔτι. (2) Servatis τίνα δ' et ἔχων, pro εἶχε Dindorfius coniecit ἦλθε, Hartungius ἔτυχε, Schneidewinus et Blaydesius εἷρπε.

---

king of Thebes had found the bodies and buried them (10. 5 § 4). The spot has a modern monument which appeals with scarcely less force to the imagination of a visitor,—the tomb of a redoubtable brigand who was killed in the neighbourhood many years ago. **735 τοῖσδ'**. For the dat., cp. Her. 2. 145 Διονύσῳ μέν νυν...κατὰ ἑξακόσια ἔτεα καὶ χίλια μάλιστά ἐστι ἐς ἐμέ· Ἡρακλέϊ δὲ...κατὰ εἰνακόσια ἔτεα· Πανὶ δὲ...κατὰ τὰ ὀκτακόσια μάλιστα ἐς ἐμέ. Then from *persons* the idiom is transferred to *things*: Thuc. 3. 29 ἡμέραι μάλιστα ἦσαν τῇ Μυτιλήνῃ ἑαλωκυίᾳ ἑπτά. **736 σχεδόν τι πρόσθεν.** The interval supposed between the death of Laïus and the accession of Oedipus must be long enough to contain the process by which the Sphinx had gradually brought Thebes to despair: but Soph. probably had no very definite conception of it: see on 758. **738 ὦ Ζεῦ.** A slow, halting verse, expressing the weight on his soul: the neglect of caesura has this purpose. **739 ἐνθύμιον:** Thuc. 7. 50 ἡ σελήνη ἐκλείπει...καὶ οἱ Ἀθηναῖοι...ἐπισχεῖν ἐκέλευον τοὺς στρατηγούς, ἐνθύμιον ποιούμενοι. **740** I do not believe that Soph., or any Greek, could have written φύσιν | τίν' εἶχε, φράζε, τίνα δ' ἀκμὴν ἥβης ἔχων, which Herm. was inclined to defend as if τίνα φύσιν εἶχε = τίς ἦν φύσιν. Now τίνος would easily pass into τίνα δ' with a scribe who did not follow the

τίν' εἶχε φράζε, τίνος ἀκμὴν ἥβης ἔχων.

ΙΟ. μέγας, χνοάζων ἄρτι λευκανθὲς κάρα,
μορφῆς δὲ τῆς σῆς οὐκ ἀπεστάτει πολύ.

ΟΙ. οἴμοι τάλας· ἔοικ' ἐμαυτὸν εἰς ἀρὰς
δεινὰς προβάλλων ἀρτίως οὐκ εἰδέναι.   745

ΙΟ. πῶς φής; ὀκνῶ τοι πρὸς σ' ἀποσκοποῦσ', ἄναξ.

ΟΙ. δεινῶς ἀθυμῶ μὴ βλέπων ὁ μάντις ᾖ.
δείξεις δὲ μᾶλλον, ἢν ἐν ἐξείπῃς ἔτι.

ΙΟ. καὶ μὴν ὀκνῶ μέν, ἂν δ' ἔρῃ μαθοῦσ' ἐρῶ.

ΟΙ. πότερον ἐχώρει βαιός, ἢ πολλοὺς ἔχων   750
ἄνδρας λοχίτας, οἷ' ἀνὴρ ἀρχηγέτης;

ΙΟ. πέντ' ἦσαν οἱ ξύμπαντες, ἐν δ' αὐτοῖσιν ἦν
κῆρυξ· ἀπήνη δ' ἦγε Λάϊον μία.

ΟΙ. αἰαῖ, τάδ' ἤδη διαφανῆ. τίς ἦν ποτὲ

742 χνοάζων ... λευκανθὲς L, A, et codd. plerique : χνοάζων ... λευκανθεὶς Γ : χνοάζων...λευκανθὲν Δ. Nullus quod sciam codex χνοάζον habet; L enim, quem unum eius l. testem citat Campbell., nisi me oculi mei fefellerunt, χνοάζων clare scriptum exhibet. Hartungium tamen secutus praetulit Dindorf. χνοάζον...λευκανθεὶς, χνοάζον in χνοάζων propter voc. μέγας mutatum esse credens, λευκανθεὶς vero tum demum in λευκανθὲς transiisse. Mihi quidem vulgatam lectionem et simplicitas et elegantia

construction; and to restore τίνος seems by far the most probable as well as the simplest remedy. No exception can be taken to the phrase τίνος ἀκμὴν ἥβης as = 'the ripeness of what period of vigorous life.' 742 χνοάζων λευκανθὲς κάρα = ἔχων χνοάζον λευκαῖς κάρα: Ar. Nub. 978 χνοῦς ὥσπερ μήλοισιν ἐπήνθει (the down on his chin was as the bloom on apples): here the verb marks the light strewing of silver in dark hair. As Aesch. has μελανθὲς γένος, 'swarthy' (Suppl. 154), so in Anthol. 12. 165 (Jacobs II. 502) λευκανθής = 'of fair complexion' as opp. to μελίχρους. 744 τάλᾶς, as being for τάλανς: Ar. Av. 1494 οἴμοι τάλας, ὁ Ζεὺς ὅπως μή μ' ὄψεται. In Anthol. 9. 378 (Jac. II. 132) καὶ κοιμῶ μεταβάς, ὦ τάλας, ἀλλαχόθι, τάλαν is an easy remedy : but not so in Theocr. 2. 4 ἀφ' ὦ τάλας οὐδέποθ' ἥκει, where πέλας has been conjectured. ἔοικα...οὐκ εἰδέναι = ἔοικεν ὅτι οὐκ ᾔδη : cp. 236 f. 749 καὶ μὴν, 'indeed' I fear (as you do): Ant. 221, El. 556. ἂν δ' is certainly preferable to ἃ δ' ἂν in a poet whose versification is not characterised by any love of unnecessary διάλυσις. Even in prose we find ὃς ἂν δέ instead of ὃς δὲ ἂν,

Laïus, and how ripe his manhood.

IO. He was tall,—the silver just lightly strewn among his hair ; and his form was not greatly unlike to thine.

OE. Unhappy that I am! Methinks I have been laying myself even now under a dread curse, and knew it not.

IO. How sayest thou? I tremble when I look on thee, my king.

OE. Dread misgivings have I that the seer can see. But thou wilt show better if thou wilt tell me one thing more.

IO. Indeed I tremble, but will answer all thou askest, when I hear it.

OE. Went he in small force, or with many armed followers, like a chieftain?

IO. Five they were in all,—a herald one of them ; and there was one carriage, which bore Laïus.

OE. Alas! 'Tis now clear indeed. — Who was he

magis commendant. Nihili est μέλας, quod cum Δ et Pal. habet V, ex μέγας tamen factum. **749** ἁ δ' ἄν L, A, et plerique: ἂν δ' Dresd. 183 (a), ἂν δ' Bodl. Laud. 54. Editorum alii ἁ δ' ἄν, alii ἂν δ' legere maluerunt. Apud Sophoclem ἂν δ' non dubito praeferre, habita ῥυθμοῦ ratione quem Sophoclea poesis in universum dilexit: si autem de Euripidis versu res agaretur, ἁ δ' ἄν cum maiore codd. numero darem.

Her. 7. 8. **750** βαιός identifies the chief with his retinue, the adjective, when so used, suggesting a collective force like that of a stream, full or thin: so πολὺς ῥεῖ, πολὺς πνεῖ of vehement speech, etc.; Eur. *Or.* 1200 ἦν πολὺς παρῇ, if he come in his might: συχνὸν πολίχνιον, a populous town (Plat. *Rep.* 370 D). **751** λοχίτας: cp. Aesch. *Cho.* 766 XO. πῶς οὖν κελεύει νιν μολεῖν ἐσταλμένον; | ...ἢ ξὺν λοχίταις εἴτε καὶ μονοστιβῆ; TP. ἄγειν κελεύει δορυφόρους ὀπάονας (said of Aegisthus). **753** κῆρυξ, as the meet attendant of a king on the peaceful and sacred mission of a θεωρός (114). The herald's presence would add solemnity to the sacrifice and libation at Delphi: Athen. 660 A ἔδρων (= ἔθυον) δὲ οἱ κήρυκες ἄχρι πολλοῦ, βουθυτοῦντες...καὶ σκευάζοντες καὶ μιστύλλοντες, ἔτι δὲ οἰνοχοοῦντες. ἀπήνη ἦγε μία = μία ἦν ἀπήνη, ἢ ἦγε: Pind. *Nem.* 9. 41 ἔνθ' Ἀρέας πόρον ἄνθρωποι καλέοισι = ἔνθα πόρος ἐστὶν ὃν 'Α. καλοῦσιν. The ἀπήνη, properly a mule-car (Pind. *Pyth.* 4. 94) but here drawn by colts (802), and in the *Odyssey* synonymous with ἄμαξα (6. 37, 57), was a four-wheeled carriage used for travelling, as dist. from the two-wheeled war-chariot (ἅρμα): its Homeric epithet ὑψηλή indicates

ὁ τούσδε λέξας τοὺς λόγους ὑμῖν, γύναι;   755

ΙΟ. οἰκεύς τις, ὅσπερ ἵκετ' ἐκσωθεὶς μόνος.

ΟΙ. ἦ κἂν δόμοισι τυγχάνει τανῦν παρών;

ΙΟ. οὐ δῆτ'· ἀφ' οὗ γὰρ κεῖθεν ἦλθε καὶ κράτη
σέ τ' εἶδ' ἔχοντα Λάϊόν τ' ὀλωλότα,
ἐξικέτευσε τῆς ἐμῆς χειρὸς θιγὼν   760
ἀγρούς σφε πέμψαι κἀπὶ ποιμνίων νομάς,
ὡς πλεῖστον εἴη τοῦδ' ἄποπτος ἄστεως.
κἄπεμψ' ἐγώ νιν· ἄξιος γὰρ οἷ' ἀνὴρ
δοῦλος φέρειν ἦν τῆσδε καὶ μείζω χάριν.

ΟΙ. πῶς ἂν μόλοι δῆθ' ἡμὶν ἐν τάχει πάλιν;   765

ΙΟ. πάρεστιν· ἀλλὰ πρὸς τί τοῦτ' ἐφίεσαι;

ΟΙ. δέδοικ' ἐμαυτόν, ὦ γύναι, μὴ πόλλ' ἄγαν

756 ὅσπερ cum ceteris L, facta quidem in o litura, nullo tamen litterae ω
manente vestigio.   **763** ὅ γ' ἀνὴρ L : ὁ Δε γ' ἀνὴρ A, id agente librario ut metro
subveniret, ὅ γ' in ὁ δέ γ' mutato. Et praevaluit in codd. ὁ δέ γ', quanquam cum

---

that it stood higher on its wheels than the ἅρμα : it could be fitted with
a frame or basket for luggage (ὑπερτερίη *Od.* 6. 70, πείρινς *Il.* 24. 190).
756: cp. 118. οἰκεύς = οἰκέτης, as in the *Odyssey* and in a νόμος Σόλωνος in
Lysias or. 10 § 19, who explains it by θεράπων. The *Iliad* has the word
only twice, both times in plur., of 'inmates' (slave or free: 5. 413: 6. 366).
757 ἦ καὶ marks keen interest: *El.* 314 ἦ κἂν ἐγὼ θαρσοῦσα μᾶλλον ἐς
λόγους | τοὺς σοὺς ἱκοίμην ; **758** The poet has neglected clearness on a
minor point, which, so far as I know, has not been remarked.   The
οἰκεύς—sole survivor of the four attendants—had fled back to Thebes
with the news that Laïus had been slain by robbers (118—123).   This
news came before the trouble with the Sphinx began : 126—131.   And
the play supposes an interval of at least several days between the death
of Laïus and the election of Oedipus : see on 736.   Hence κεῖθεν ἦλθε
καὶ...εἶδε cannot mean that the οἰκεύς, on reaching Thebes, found
Oedipus already reigning.   Nor can we suggest that he may have fled
from the scene of the slaughter before he was *sure* that Laïus had been
killed : that is excluded by 123 and 737.   Therefore we must understand :—'when he had come thence, and [*afterwards*] found that *not
only* was Laïus dead, *but* you were his successor.'   (For the parataxis
σέ τε...Λάϊόν τε see on 673.)   I incline to suspect, however, that

who gave you these tidings, lady?

Io. A servant—the sole survivor who came home.

OE. Is he haply at hand in the house now?

Io. No, truly; so soon as he came thence, and found thee reigning in the stead of Laïus, he supplicated me, with hand laid on mine, that I would send him to the fields, to the pastures of the flocks, that he might be far from the sight of this town. And I sent him; he was worthy, for a slave, to win e'en a larger boon than that.

OE. Would, then, that he could return to us without delay!

Io. It is easy: but wherefore dost thou enjoin this?

OE. I fear, lady, that mine own lips have lately uttered

---

paucis V ὅδ' ἀνήρ habet.   οἴ' ἀνὴρ coniecit Hermann., recepit Dindorf.   Coniecerunt alii vel ὡς vel ὥς γ'.

Sophocles was *here* thinking of the man as coming back to find Oedipus already on the throne, and had overlooked the inconsistency. **760** χειρὸς θιγών, marking that the ἱκετεία was formal; as when the suppliant clasped the knees (ἅπτεσθαι γονάτων). Eur. *Hec.* 850 τύχας σέθεν, | Ἑκάβη, δι' οἴκτου χεῖρα θ' ἱκεσίαν ἔχω. **761** ἀγρούς might be acc. of motion to (*O. C.* 1769 Θήβας δ' ἡμᾶς | ...πέμψον); but it is better here governed by ἐπί: for the position of the prep. cp. 734, 1205, *El.* 780 οὔτε νυκτὸς οὔτ' ἐξ ἡμέρας. νομάς: on Cithaeron, or near it, 1127. The man had formerly served as a shepherd (1039), and had then been taken into personal attendance on Laïus (οἰκεύς). **762** τοῦδ' ἄποπτος ἄστεως, 'far from the sight of this town': that is, far from the power of seeing it: whereas in *El.* 1487 κτανὼν πρόθες|...ἄποπτον ἡμῶν = 'far from our eyes': the gen. as after words of 'distance from.' See Appendix, Note 14. **763** οἴ': the ὅ γ' of L (clumsily amended to ὁ δέ γ' in other MSS.) prob. came from οἴ', rather than from ὡς or ὥς γ'. *Phil.* 583 οἴ' ἀνὴρ πένης, '*for* a poor man': Eur. *Or.* 32 κἀγὼ μετέσχον, οἷα δὴ γυνή, φόνου, '*so far as* a woman might.' ὡς, however, is commoner in this limiting sense (1118); οἷα more often = 'like' (751). Here οἷα qualifies ἄξιος, implying that in strictness the faithful service of a *slave* could not be said to create *merit.* **764** φέρειν: cp. 590. **766** πάρεστιν: 'it is easily done.' Eur. *Bacch.* 843 ΠΕ. ἐλθών γ' ἐς οἴκους ἂν δοκῇ βουλεύσομαι. | ΔΙ. ἔξεστι· πάντῃ τό γ' ἐμὸν εὐτρεπὲς πάρα. Not, 'he is here' (nor, 'he is as good as here,' as the schol. explains): in 769 ἵξεται = 'he will come *from the*

J. S.   10

εἰρημέν' ᾖ μοι, δι' ἃ νιν εἰσιδεῖν θέλω.

ΙΟ. ἀλλ' ἵξεται μέν· ἀξία δέ που μαθεῖν
κἀγὼ τά γ' ἐν σοὶ δυσφόρως ἔχοντ', ἄναξ.　　　770

ΟΙ. κοὐ μὴ στερηθῇς γ' ἐς τοσοῦτον ἐλπίδων
ἐμοῦ βεβῶτος. τῷ γὰρ ἂν καὶ μείζονι
λέξαιμ' ἂν ἢ σοὶ διὰ τύχης τοιᾶσδ' ἰών;
ἐμοὶ πατὴρ μὲν Πόλυβος ἦν Κορίνθιος,
μήτηρ δὲ Μερόπη Δωρίς. ἠγόμην δ' ἀνὴρ　　　775
ἀστῶν μέγιστος τῶν ἐκεῖ, πρίν μοι τύχη
τοιάδ' ἐπέστη, θαυμάσαι μὲν ἀξία,
σπουδῆς γε μέντοι τῆς ἐμῆς οὐκ ἀξία.
ἀνὴρ γὰρ ἐν δείπνοις μ' ὑπερπλησθεὶς μέθῃ
καλεῖ παρ' οἴνῳ πλαστὸς ὡς εἴην πατρί.　　　780
κἀγὼ βαρυνθεὶς τὴν μὲν οὖσαν ἡμέραν
μόλις κατέσχον, θἀτέρᾳ δ' ἰὼν πέλας

779 μέθης A et codd. plerique, quos secuti sunt Hermann., Wunder., Hartung.
Sed in L μέθης factum est ex μέθηι: Γ μέθη habet. μέθῃ Nauck., Blaydes.,

pastures.' 768 δι' ἅ. The sense is : 'I fear that I have spoken too
many words ; and on account of those words I wish to see him': cp.
744, 324. Not: 'I fear that my words have given me only too much
cause to desire his presence.' A comma after μοι is here conducive to
clearness. 770 κἀγὼ and που express the wife's sense that he should
speak to her as to a second self. ἐν σοί = within thee, in thy mind (not
'in thy case'): cp. ἐν with the reflexive pronouns, Plat. Theaet. 192 D ἐν
ἐμαυτῷ μεμνημένος : Crat. 384 A προσποιούμενός τι αὐτὸς ἐν ἑαυτῷ διανο-
εῖσθαι. 771 ἐς τοσοῦτον ἐλπίδων : Isocr. or. 8 § 31 εἰς τοῦτο γάρ τινες
ἀνοίας ἐληλύθασιν : Ar. Nub. 832 σὺ δ' ἐς τοσοῦτον τῶν μανιῶν ἐλήλυθας.
The plural of ἐλπίς is rare as = anxious forebodings : but cp. 487. 772
μείζονι : strictly, 'more important': cp. Dem. or. 19 § 248 ἀντὶ...τῆς
πόλεως τὴν Φιλίππου ξενίαν καὶ φιλίαν πολλῷ μείζονα ἡγήσατο αὐτῷ καὶ
λυσιτελεστέραν : as Ant. 637 οὐδεὶς...γάμος | μείζων φέρεσθαι σοῦ
καλῶς ἡγουμένου, no marriage can be a greater prize than your good
guidance. The καὶ with λέξαιμ' ἂν :—could I speak? · Lysias or. 12 § 29
παρὰ τοῦ ποτε καὶ λήψεσθε δίκην; from whom will you ever exact satis-
faction? 773 ἰών, present, not future, part. : Ant. 742 διὰ δίκης ἰών

words too many; and therefore am I fain to behold him.

IO. Nay, he shall come. But I too, methinks, have a claim to learn what lies heavy on thy heart, my king.

OE. Yea, and it shall not be kept from thee, now that my forebodings have advanced so far. Who, indeed, is more to me than thou, to whom I should speak in passing through such a fortune as this?

My father was Polybus of Corinth,—my mother, the Dorian Meropè; and I was held the first of all the folk in that town, until a chance befell me, worthy, indeed, of wonder, though not worthy of mine own heat concerning it. At a banquet, a man full of wine cast it at me in his cups that I was not the true son of my sire. And I, vexed, restrained myself for that day as best I might; but on the next I went

Campbell., recte. Genitivus enim ita demum commode diceretur, si vox μέθη non vinolentiam sed vinum significaret.

πατρί. Xen. *An.* 3. 2. 8 διὰ φιλίας ἰέναι. **775** The epithet 'Dorian' carries honour: Meropè was of the ancient stock, claiming descent from Dorus son of Hellen, who settled in the region between Oeta and Parnassus. The scholiast's comment, Πελοποννησιακή, forgets that the Theban story is laid in times before the Dorian conquest. **776** πρίν μοι ...ἐπέστη. The use of πρίν with the aorist or imperf. indic. is limited to those cases in which πρίν is equivalent to ἕως, 'until': though, where the sentence is negative, πρίν may be otherwise rendered in English: *e.g.* οὐκ ἔγνων πρὶν ἤκουσα, 'I did not become aware *until* I heard'; which we could also render, 'before I heard.' But 'I became aware before I heard' would be ἔγνων πρὶν ἀκοῦσαι (not ἤκουσα). See Prof. B. L. Gildersleeve in the *American Journal of Philology* vol. II. p. 469. ἐπέστη: a verb often used of enemies suddenly coming upon one: Isocr. or. 9 § 58 μικροῦ δεῖν ἔλαθεν αὐτὸν ἐπὶ τὸ βασίλειον ἐπιστάς: Her. 4. 203 ἐπὶ τῇ Κυρηναίων πόλι ἐπέστησαν. **780** παρ' οἴνῳ: Plut. *Mor.* 143C τοὺς τῇ λύρᾳ χρωμένους παρ' οἶνον. Thuc. 6. 28 μετὰ παιδιᾶς καὶ οἴνου. πλαστὸς ὡς εἴην instead of πλαστόν, as if preceded by ὀνειδίζει μοι instead of καλεῖ με. Somewhat similarly ὀνομάζω = λέγω, as Plat. *Prot.* 311 E σοφιστὴν ... ὀνομάζουσι ... τὸν ἄνδρα εἶναι. πλαστὸς, 'feigned (in speech),' 'falsely called a son,' πατρί, 'for my father,' *i.e.* to deceive him. Eur. *Alc.* 639 μαστῷ γυναικὸς σῆς ὑπεβλήθην λάθρα, whence ὑποβολιμαῖος = νόθος. **782** κατέσχον, *sc.* ἐμαυτόν. In classical Attic this use occurs only here: in later Greek it recurs, as Plut.

μητρὸς πατρός τ' ἤλεγχον· οἱ δὲ δυσφόρως
τοὔνειδος ἦγον τῷ μεθέντι τὸν λόγον.
κἀγὼ τὰ μὲν κείνοιν ἐτερπόμην, ὅμως δ'　　　　785
ἔκνιζέ μ' ἀεὶ τοῦθ'· ὑφεῖρπε γὰρ πολύ.
λάθρα δὲ μητρὸς καὶ πατρὸς πορεύομαι
Πυθώδε, καί μ' ὁ Φοῖβος ὧν μὲν ἱκόμην
ἄτιμον ἐξέπεμψεν, ἄλλα δ' ἄθλια
καὶ δεινὰ καὶ δύστηνα προὔφηνεν λέγων,　　　　790
ὡς μητρὶ μὲν χρείη με μιχθῆναι, γένος δ'
ἄτλητον ἀνθρώποισι δηλώσοιμ' ὁρᾶν,
φονεὺς δ' ἐσοίμην τοῦ φυτεύσαντος πατρός.
κἀγὼ 'πακούσας ταῦτα τὴν Κορινθίαν
ἄστροις τὸ λοιπὸν ἐκμετρούμενος χθόνα　　　　795

790 προὔφάνη codd. Est autem in E interpretatio προέδειξε : quo confirmatur Hermanni coniectura προὔφηνεν, a Wundero, Nauckio, Blaydesio, Dindorfio recepta.

Artaxerxes § 15 εἶπεν οὖν μὴ κατασχών. ὑμεῖς μέν κ.τ.λ. Cp. ἔχε, σχές, ἐπίσχες ('stop'), in Plat., Dem., etc. **784** τῷ μεθέντι : the reproach was like a random missile: Menander fr. 88 οὔτ' ἐκ χερὸς μεθέντα κατερὸν λίθον | ῥᾷον κατασχεῖν, οὔτ' ἀπὸ γλώσσης λόγον. The dat., because δυσφόρως τοὔνειδος ἦγον = ὠργίζοντο ἕνεκα τοῦ ὀνείδους. **785** ὅμως δ': cp. 791, and n. on 29. **786** ὑφεῖρπε γὰρ πολύ: so ὑφέρπειν of malicious rumour, Aesch. *Ag.* 450 φθονερὸν δ' ὑπ' ἄλγος ἕρπει | προδίκοις Ἀτρείδαις. Libanius 784 A (quoted by Musgrave) πολὺς τοιοῦτος ὑφεῖρπε λόγος (perhaps suggested by this passage). Pind. *Isthm.* 3. 58 τοῦτο γὰρ ἀθάνατον φωνᾶεν ἕρπει, | εἴ τις εὖ εἴπῃ τι. Cp. *Ant.* 700 τοιάδ' ἐρεμνὴ σῖγ' ἐπέρχεται φάτις. For πολύ cp. *O. C.* 517 τὸ πολύ τοι καὶ μηδαμὰ λῆγον, that strong rumour which is in no wise failing : *ib.* 305 πολύ...τὸ σὸν ὄνομα | διῆκει πάντας. This version also agrees best with 775, which implies that the incident had altered his popular repute. We might render: 'it was ever *recurring to my mind* with force': but this (*a*) is a repetition : (*b*) is less suited to πολύ, which implies diffusion. **788** ὧν ἱκόμην ἄτιμον = ἄτιμον τούτων ἃ ἱκόμην, not graced in respect of those things (responses) for which I had come : Eur. *Andr.* 1014 ἄτιμον ὀργάναν χέρα τεκτοσύνας, not rewarded for its skill. For ἃ ἱκόμην (cogn. accus. denoting the errand, like ἔρχομαι ἀγγελίαν) cp. 1005 τοῦτ' ἀφικόμην: *O. C.* 1291 ἃ δ' ἦλθον...θέλω λέξαι: Ar. *Pl.* 966 ὅ τι μάλιστ' ἐλήλυθας : Plat. *Prot.* 310 E ἀλλ' αὐτὰ ταῦτα καὶ

to my mother and father, and questioned them; and they were wroth for the taunt with him who had let that word fly. So on their part I had comfort; yet was this thing ever rankling in my heart; for it still crept abroad with strong rumour. And, unknown to mother or father, I went to Delphi; and Phoebus sent me forth disappointed of that knowledge for which I came, but in his response set forth other things, full of sorrow and terror and woe; even that I was fated to defile my mother's bed; and that I should show unto men a brood which they could not endure to behold; and that I should be the slayer of the sire who begat me.

And I, when I had listened to this, turned to flight from the land of Corinth, thenceforth wotting of its region by the stars alone,

Vide annot. **791** χρεῖ' ἢ L, paene eraso ι post ἢ: χρεῖ' ἢ A. Ceteri codd. eodem fere modo variant ut in v. 555, q. v.: nullus quod sciam χρείη habet.

νῦν ἥκω παρὰ σέ (where the acc. is cogn. to ἥκω, not object to the following διαλεχθῇς). **790** προὔφηνεν, suggested by Herm., has been adopted by several recent editors. Cp. Herod. 1. 210 τῷ δὲ ὁ δαίμων προέφαινε, and so 3. 65, 7. 37: Plut. *Dem.* § 19 ἐν οἷς ἥ τε Πυθία δεινὰ προὔφαινε μαντεύματα καὶ ὁ χρησμὸς ᾔδετο: *Camill.* § 4 (a man who pretended to μαντική) λόγια προὔφαινεν ἀπόρρητα: Dem. or. 21 § 54 τοῖς ἐφ' ἑκάστης μαντείας προφαινομένοις θεοῖς, the gods announced (as claiming sacrifice) on each reference to the oracle. Yet the fact that προφαίνειν was thus a *vox sollennis* for oracular utterance would not suffice to warrant the adoption of προὔφηνεν, if the προὔφάνη of the MSS. seemed defensible. προὔφάνη λέγων would mean, 'came into view, telling': cp. above, 395, and *El.* 1285 νῦν δ' ἔχω σε· προὐφάνης δὲ | φιλτάταν ἔχων πρόσοψιν. It might apply to the sudden appearance of a beacon (cp. ὁ φρυκτὸς ἀγγέλλων πρέπει, *Ag.* 30): but, in reference to the god speaking through the oracle, it could only mean, by a strained metaphor, '*flashed on me* with the message,' *i.e.* announced it with startling suddenness and clearness. The difficulty of conceiving Sophocles to have written thus is to me so great that the *special* appropriateness of προὔφηνεν turns the scale. **791** γένος δ': see on 29. **792** ὁρᾶν with ἄτλητον, which, thus defined, is in contrast with δηλώσοιμ': he was to show men what they could not bear to look upon. **794** ἐπακούσας (708), 'having given ear'—with the attention of silent horror. **794—797** τὴν Κορινθίαν: 'Henceforth measuring from afar (ἐκμετρούμενος) by the stars

ἔφευγον, ἔνθα μήποτ' ὀψοίμην κακῶν
χρησμῶν ὀνείδη τῶν ἐμῶν τελούμενα.
στείχων δ' ἱκνοῦμαι τούσδε τοὺς χώρους ἐν οἷς
σὺ τὸν τύραννον τοῦτον ὄλλυσθαι λέγεις.
καί σοι, γύναι, τἀληθὲς ἐξερῶ. τριπλῆς   800
ὅτ' ἦ κελεύθου τῆσδ' ὁδοιπορῶν πέλας,
ἐνταῦθά μοι κῆρύξ τε κἀπὶ πωλικῆς
ἀνὴρ ἀπήνης ἐμβεβώς, οἷον σὺ φής,
ξυνηντίαζον· κἀξ ὁδοῦ μ' ὅ θ' ἡγεμὼν
αὐτός θ' ὁ πρέσβυς πρὸς βίαν ἠλαυνέτην.   805
κἀγὼ τὸν ἐκτρέποντα, τὸν τροχηλάτην,
παίω δι' ὀργῆς· καί μ' ὁ πρέσβυς ὡς ὁρᾷ,

797 τελούμενα cum cett. codd. L; erasa tamen post α littera quam ν fuisse conicias. τελούμενον autem an τελουμένων ibi primo stetisset, nescio. Post χρησμῶν particulam γ' addunt B, V, V³, V⁴.   800 Deest in solo L hic versus: accessit

the region of Corinth, I went my way into exile, to some place where I should not see fulfilled the dishonours of [= foretold by] my evil oracles.' ἄστροις ἐκμετρούμενος: *i. e.* visiting it no more, but only thinking of it as a distant land that lies beneath the stars in this or that quarter of the heavens. Schneidewin cp. Aelian *Hist. Anim.* (περὶ ζῴων ἰδιότητος) 7. 48 ἧκε δ' οὖν ('Ανδροκλῆς) ἐς τὴν Λιβύην καὶ τὰς μὲν πόλεις ἀπελίμπανε καὶ τοῦτο δὴ τὸ λεγόμενον ἄστροις αὐτὰς ἐσημαίνετο, προῄει δὲ ἐς τὴν ἐρήμην: 'proceeded to leave the cities, and, *as the saying is, knew their places only by the stars,* and went on into the desert.' Wunder quotes Medea's words in Valer. Flacc. 7. 478 *quando hic aberis, dic, quaeso, profundi Quod caeli spectabo latus?* ἔφευγον might share with ἐκμετρ. the government of τὴν Κορ. χθόνα, but is best taken absolutely. Sense, not grammar, forbids the version :—'I went into exile from the Corinthian land (τὴν Κορινθίαν); thenceforth measuring my way *on earth* (χθόνα) *by the stars.*'   Phrases like ὕπαστρον...μῆχαρ ὁρίζομαι γάμου δύσφρονος | φυγᾷ (Aesch. *Suppl.* 395), ἄστροις τεκμαίρεσθαι ὁδόν (Lucian *Icaromenippus* § 1), are borrowed from *voyages* in which the sailor has no guides but the stars.   Such phrases could be used figuratively only of a journey through *deserts:* as Hesych. explains the proverb ἄστροις σημειοῦσθαι· μακρὰν καὶ ἐρήμην ὁδὸν βαδίζειν· ἡ δὲ μεταφορὰ ἀπὸ τῶν πλεόντων.   796 ἔνθα = ἐκεῖσε ἔνθα. ὀψοίμην after the secondary tense (ἔφευγον) for ὄψομαι: μὴ with the fut. as 1412: *Ai.* 659: *El.* 380, 436:

to some spot where I should never see fulfilment of
the infamies foretold in mine evil doom. And on my way
I came to the regions in which thou sayest that this prince
perished. Now, lady, I will tell thee the truth. When
in my journey I was near to those three roads, there
met me a herald, and a man seated in a carriage drawn
by colts, as thou hast described; and he who was in
front, and the old man himself, were for thrusting me
rudely from the path. Then, in anger, I struck him who
pushed me aside—the driver; and the old man, seeing it,

autem in marg. a manu recentissima. Omissum igitur non animadverterat antiquus
ille codicis corrector qui in supplendo siquid prima manus neglexerat alias Lyncea
se praestabat; unde dubitatio potest incidere, fueritne is versus necne in archetypo
quocum ille Laurentianum contulit.

Trach. 800.   800 καί σοι...τριπλῆς. The fact that this verse is added in
the margin of L only by a late (14th century?) hand has induced Dindorf and Nauck to regard it as due to interpolation. But the trait has
dramatic force. Oedipus is now at the critical point: he will hide
nothing of the truth from her who is nearest to him. It is part of his
character that his earnest desire to know the *truth* never flinches: cp.
1170.   802 κῆρυξ τε, not κῆρύξ τε: see Chandler, *Accentuation* § 971
2nd ed.   803 ἀπήνης: see on 753. οἷον adverbial neut. = ὡς, referring
to Iocasta's whole description; not acc. masc., referring to the person
of Laïus as described by her.   804—812 The κῆρυξ is, I think, identical
with the ἡγεμών, and distinct from the τροχηλάτης. I understand the
scene thus. Oedipus was coming down the steep narrow road when
he met the *herald* (to be known for such by his stave, κηρύκειον) walking
in front of the carriage (ἡγεμών). The herald rudely bade him stand
aside; and Laïus, from the carriage, gave a like command. (With the
imperfect ἠλαυνέτην, 'were for driving,' πρὸς βίαν need not mean more
than a threat or gesture.)   The driver (τροχηλάτης), who was walking at
his horses' heads up the hill, then did his lord's bidding by actually
jostling the wayfarer (ἐκτρέποντα). Oedipus, who had forborne to strike
the sacred herald, now struck the *driver;* in another moment, while
passing the carriage, he was himself struck on the head by Laïus. He
dashed Laïus from the carriage; the herald, turning back, came to the
rescue; and Oedipus slew Laïus, herald, driver, and one of two servants
who had been walking by or behind the carriage; the other servant

ὄχου παραστείχοντα τηρήσας μέσον
κάρα διπλοῖς κέντροισί μου καθίκετο.
οὐ μὴν ἴσην γ' ἔτισεν, ἀλλὰ συντόμως   810
σκήπτρῳ τυπεὶς ἐκ τῆσδε χειρὸς ὕπτιος
μέσης ἀπήνης εὐθὺς ἐκκυλίνδεται·
κτείνω δὲ τοὺς ξύμπαντας. εἰ δὲ τῷ ξένῳ
τούτῳ προσήκει Λαΐῳ τι συγγενές,
τίς τοῦδε νῦν ἔστ' ἀνδρὸς ἀθλιώτερος;   815
τίς ἐχθροδαίμων μᾶλλον ἂν γένοιτ' ἀνήρ;
ὃν μὴ ξένων ἔξεστι μηδ' ἀστῶν τινι

808 ὄχου codd. : est in B gloss. τοῦ ἅρματος. In uno cod. T inveni quod primo aspectu ὄχον videri poterat ; re perpensa tamen illic quoque credo librarium ὄχου dare voluisse. ὄχον coniecit Schaefer.: ὄχους Doederlinus, quod receperunt Hartung., Dindorf., Nauck., Blaydes.   814 Λαΐῳ codd., recte : vide annot. Λαΐου Bothius, Wunder., Hartung., Dindorf., Blaydes.   815 τίς τοῦδέ γ' ἀνδρὸς νῦν ἔστ' ἀθλιώτερος L, paene eluto νῦν, et superscripto a m. rec. gloss. ἄλλως (i. e. ἄλλοσ ?). τίς τοῦδέ γ' ἀνδρὸς ἐστὶν (sic) ἀθλιώτερος A. Ceterorum codd. alii hanc lect., alii illam repetunt. Vocem νῦν, qua priori fortunae repentina calamitas opponitur, pro genuina habeo ; contra, si ἔστ' in ἔτ' mutetur (quod proposuit Dindorf., recepit Nauck.), misere debilitatur comparativus.   Lego igitur, τίς τοῦδε νῦν ἔστ' ἀνδρὸς

(unperceived by Oedipus) escaped to Thebes with the news.   808 ὄχου : '*from the chariot*—having watched for the moment when I was passing— he came down on me, full on my head (μέσον κάρα acc. of part affected), with the double goad.'   The gen. ὄχου marks the point from which the action sets out, and is essentially like τᾶς πολυχρύσου | Πυθῶνος...ἔβας v. 151 : cp. *Od.* 21. 142 ὄρνυσθε... | ἀρξάμενοι τοῦ χώρου ὅθεν τέ περ οἰνοχοεύει, *from* the place.   In prose we should have had ἀπ' ὄχου.   As the verb here involves motion, we cannot compare such a gen. as ἷζεν... τοίχου τοῦ ἑτέρου (*Il.* 9. 219), where, if any prep. were supplied, it would be πρός.   τηρήσας : [Dem.] or. 53 § 17 (contemporary with Dem) τηρήσας με ἀνιόντα ἐκ Πειραιῶς ὀψὲ...ἁρπάζει.   809 καθίκετο governs μου, which μέσον κάρα defines : Plut. *Anton.* § 12 σκύτεσι λασίοις...καθικνούμενοι τῶν ἐντυγχανόντων : Lucian *Symp.* § 16 τάχα δ' ἄν τινος καθίκετο τῇ βακτηρίᾳ : *Icaromenippus* § 24 σφόδρα ἡμῶν ὁ πέρυσι χειμὼν καθίκετο.   This verb takes accus. only as = to *reach*, lit. or fig. (as *Il.* 14. 104 μάλα πώς με καθίκεο θυμόν).   διπλοῖς κέντροισι : a stick armed at the end with two points, used in driving.   Cp. *Il.* 23. 387 (horses)...ἄνευ κέντροιο θέοντες. The τροχηλάτης had left it in the carriage when he got out to walk up the hill.   810 οὐ μὴν ἴσην γ' : not *merely* an even penalty (cp. τὴν ὁμοίαν

watched the moment when I was passing, and, from the carriage, brought his goad with two teeth down full upon my head. Yet was he paid with interest ; by one swift blow from the staff in this hand he was rolled right out of the carriage, on his back ; and I slew every man of them.

But if this stranger had any tie of kinship with Laïus, who is now more wretched than the man before thee? What mortal could prove more hated of heaven? Whom no stranger, no citizen, is allowed

ἀθλιώτερος, particulam γε metri causa intrusam esse credens postquam ἀνδρὸς e sua sede migraverat. Elmsleius coniecerat τἀνδρός, quo recepto Blaydesius dedit τίς τοῦδε τἀνδρὸς ἔστ' ἔτ' ἀθλιώτερος, Campbellius τίς τοῦδε τἀνδρὸς ἔστιν ἀθλιώτερος. Dindorfius olim (ed. 1860) versum e textu eiecerat ; est autem plane necessarius, cum, si deleretur, nihil habiturum esset pronomen ὅν (v. 817) ad quod referretur. Sed iampridem (ed. 1869) poenituit virum doctissimum quod insontem versiculum capitis damnasset : sapit tamen etiamnunc Draconem, reposuit enim τίς τοῦδ' ἀκούειν ἀνδρὸς ἀθλιώτερος, collato v. 1204. **817** ᾧ...τινὰ codd., quod defendit Hermann., interpretans ᾧ μὴ ἔξεστι, ξένων τινὰ δέχεσθαι αὐτόν : 'cui non concessum est ut quisquam eum recipiat.' ᾧ in ὅν mutavit Schaefer., idem τινα servans, ut

---

ἀποδιδόναι, *par pari referre*): Thuc. 1. 35 οὐχ ὁμοία ἡ ἀλλοτρίωσις, the renunciation of such an alliance is *more serious*. συντόμως, in a way which made short work: cp. Thuc. 7. 42 ἠπείγετο ἐπιθέσθαι τῇ πείρᾳ καί οἱ ξυντομωτάτην ἡγεῖτο διαπολέμησιν, the quickest way of deciding the war: Her. 5. 17 ἔστι δὲ σύντομος κάρτα (sc. ὁδός), there is a short cut. The conject. συντόνως (*Tr.* 923 συντόνῳ χερί) would efface the grim irony. 812 μέσης implies that a moment before he had seemed firmly seated: 'right out of the carriage.' Eur. *Cycl.* 7 ἰτέαν μέσην θενών, striking *full* on the shield: *I. T.* 1385 νηὸς δ' ἐκ μέσης ἐφθέγξατο | βοή τις, from within the ship itself: *El.* 965 ἄρκυν εἰς μέσην, right into the net. 814 εἰ συγγενές τι τῷ Λαΐῳ if any tie with Laïus προσήκει τούτῳ τῷ ξένῳ *belongs to this stranger.* συγγενής can take either dat. (akin to) or gen. (kin of): and here several editors give Λαΐου. But the dat. Λαΐῳ, making it verbally possible to identify the ξένος with Laïus, suits the complex suggestiveness with which the language of this drama is often contrived : cp. τῶν in 1167. Again, τῷ ξένῳ τούτῳ might apply to Oedipus himself (452). Had we τι *without* συγγενές, Λαΐου (part. gen.) would then be *necessary.* The constructions of προσήκειν are (1) προσήκω τινί, I am related to: (2) προσήκει μοί τινος, I have a right in, or tie with: (3) προσήκει μοί τι, it belongs to me. Here it is (3). 817 ὅν...τινι. The MSS. ᾧ...τινα must be rendered : 'to whom it is not allowed that any one should receive (him)': but the words would naturally mean : 'to

δόμοις δέχεσθαι, μηδὲ προσφωνεῖν τινα,
ὠθεῖν δ' ἀπ' οἴκων. καὶ τάδ' οὔτις ἄλλος ἦν
ἢ 'γὼ 'π' ἐμαυτῷ τάσδ' ἀρὰς ὁ προστιθείς.   820
λέχη δὲ τοῦ θανόντος ἐν χεροῖν ἐμαῖν
χραίνω, δι' ὧνπερ ὤλετ'. ἆρ' ἔφυν κακός;
ἆρ' οὐχὶ πᾶς ἄναγνος; εἴ με χρὴ φυγεῖν,
καί μοι φυγόντι μῆστι τοὺς ἐμοὺς ἰδεῖν
μηδ' ἐμβατεύειν πατρίδος, ἢ γάμοις με δεῖ   825
μητρὸς ζυγῆναι καὶ πατέρα κατακτανεῖν
Πόλυβον, ὃς ἐξέφυσε κἀξέθρεψέ με.
ἆρ' οὐκ ἀπ' ὠμοῦ ταῦτα δαίμονός τις ἂν
κρίνων ἐπ' ἀνδρὶ τῷδ' ἂν ὀρθοίη λόγον;
μὴ δῆτα μὴ δῆτ', ὦ θεῶν ἁγνὸν σέβας,   830
ἴδοιμι ταύτην ἡμέραν, ἀλλ' ἐκ βροτῶν
βαίην ἄφαντος πρόσθεν ἢ τοιάνδ' ἰδεῖν
κηλῖδ' ἐμαυτῷ συμφορᾶς ἀφιγμένην.
ΧΟ. ἡμῖν μέν, ὦναξ, ταῦτ' ὀκνήρ'· ἕως δ' ἂν οὖν

absolute diceretur ἔξεστι. Coniecit Elmsleius οὖ, quasi attractum esset ad τοῦδε
ἀνδρός, structura sane durissima. Nauckio venit in mentem εἰ μὴ ξένων...τινί, mox
autem, pro τινά in v. 818, ἐμέ. Nihil opus est mutare, modo legas ὄν...τινι cum
Wunder., Hartung., Dindorf. Frequens in codd. hoc genus inversionum; cf. v. 376.
824 μῆστι. L μήτε (correctum a manu antiqua ex μῆστι), A, T (cum γρ. μὴ 'στῖ)
E, V², V³, Bodl. Laud. 54. **825** μῆτ' ἐμβατεύειν L, facto ab antiqua manu μήτε
ex μῆστ', quod prima dederat. μήτ' A quoque et alii. Possis igitur legere (1) ut

whom it is not allowed to receive anyone.' In 376, where σε...γ' ἐμοῦ
is certain, all our MSS. have με...γε σοῦ: much more might the cases
have been shifted here. **818** μηδὲ...τινα, sc. ἔξεστι, absolutely: nor *is it
lawful that* anyone should speak to him. **819** ὠθεῖν δ': the positive δεῖ
must be evolved from the negative οὐκ ἔξεστι: cp. *El.* 71 καὶ μή μ'
ἄτιμον τῆσδ' ἀποστείλητε γῆς | ἀλλ' ἀρχέπλουτον (sc. καταστήσατε). See
above, 241. καὶ τάδ'. And these things—*these curses*—none but I laid
on myself. As the thought proceeds, the speaker repeats τάδε in a
more precise and emphatic form: cp. Plat. *Rep.* 606 B ἐκεῖνο κερδαίνειν
ἡγεῖται, τὴν ἡδονήν. **821** ἐν χεροῖν, not, 'in their embrace,' but, 'by their
agency': *Il.* 22. 426 ὡς ὄφελεν θανέειν ἐν χερσὶν ἐμῇσιν. **822 f.** ἆρ'—ἆρ'
οὐχί. Where ἆρα is equivalent in *sense* to ἆρ' οὐ, this is because it

to receive in his house; whom it is unlawful that any one
accost; whom all must repel from their homes! And this
—this curse—was laid on me by no mouth but mine own!
And I pollute the bed of the slain man with the hands by
which he perished. Say, am I vile? Oh, am I not utterly
unclean?—seeing that I must be banished, and in banishment
see not mine own people, nor set foot in mine own land, or else
be joined in wedlock to my mother, and slay my sire, even
Polybus, who begat and reared me.

Then would not he speak aright of Oedipus, who judged these
things sent by some cruel power above man? Forbid, forbid,
ye pure and awful gods, that I should see that day! No, may
I be swept from among men, ere I behold myself visited with
the brand of such a doom!

CH. To us, indeed, these things, O king, are fraught with fear ;

Elmsleius monuit, μήτε τοὺς ἐμοὺς ἰδεῖν | μήτ' ἐμβατεύειν, subaudito ἔξεστι, sed hoc
durissimum videtur: (2) μῆστι τοὺς ἐμοὺς ἰδεῖν, | μῆστ' ἐμβατεύειν, quod vereor ut
Sophocleae Χάριτες facile patiantur : (3) iam res ad triarios rediit, neque alia superest
ratio quam ut, μῆστι servato, μηδ' ἐμβατεύειν cum Dindorfio scribas. **827**
Huius versus, post Wunderum a Dindorfio fraudis insimulati atque uncis inclusi,
causam orare nullo coram iudice reformidem : vide annot. ἐξέφυσε κἀξέθρεψε L, A,
et codd. plerique. Praeposteram lectionem ἐξέθρεψε κἀξέφυσε tres tantummodo codd.
praebent, praetulit tamen Erfurdt.

means, 'are you satisfied that it is so?' *i.e.* 'is it not abundantly clear?'
(*El.* 614). Here, the transition from ἄρα to ἆρ' οὐχὶ is one from bitter
irony to despairing earnest. **827 Πόλυβον.** Wunder and Dindorf think
this verse spurious. But it is, in fact, of essential moment to the development of the plot. Oedipus fears that he has slain Laïus, but does not
yet dream that Laïus was his father. This verse accentuates the point at
which his belief now stands, and so prepares us for the next stage of
discovery. A few MSS. give ἐξέθρεψε κἀξέφυσε : but the Homeric
πρότερον ὕστερον (*Od.* 12. 134 θρέψασα τεκοῦσά τε) seems out of place
here just because it throws a less *natural* emphasis on ἐξέφυσε.
829 ἐπ' ἀνδρὶ τῷδε with ὀρθοίη λόγον, speak truly in my case. Isaeus or.
8 § 1 ἐπὶ τοῖς τοιούτοις, ὦ ἄνδρες, ἀνάγκη ἐστὶ χαλεπῶς φέρειν, in such
cases. *Il.* 19. 181 σὺ δ' ἔπειτα δικαιότερος καὶ ἐπ' ἄλλῳ | ἔσσεαι, in
another's case. **832 τοιάνδε,** not τοιᾶσδε: cp. 533. **833 κηλῖδα:** cp. ἄγος
1426: *O. C.* 1133 κηλὶς κακῶν. For συμφορᾶς, see on 99. **834 δ' οὖν.** So
where the desponding φύλαξ hopes for the best, Aesch. *Ag.* 34, γένοιτο

πρὸς τοῦ παρόντος ἐκμάθῃς, ἔχ᾽ ἐλπίδα.　　835

ΟΙ. καὶ μὴν τοσοῦτόν γ᾽ ἐστί μοι τῆς ἐλπίδος,
　　τὸν ἄνδρα τὸν βοτῆρα προσμεῖναι μόνον.

ΙΟ. πεφασμένου δὲ τίς ποθ᾽ ἡ προθυμία;

ΟΙ. ἐγὼ διδάξω σ᾽· ἢν γὰρ εὑρεθῇ λέγων
　　σοὶ ταῦτ᾽, ἔγωγ᾽ ἂν ἐκπεφευγοίην πάθος.　　840

ΙΟ. ποῖον δέ μου περισσὸν ἤκουσας λόγον;

ΟΙ. λῃστὰς ἔφασκες αὐτὸν ἄνδρας ἐννέπειν
　　ὥς νιν κατακτείναιεν. εἰ μὲν οὖν ἔτι
　　λέξει τὸν αὐτὸν ἀριθμόν, οὐκ ἐγὼ ᾽κτανον·
　　οὐ γὰρ γένοιτ᾽ ἂν εἷς γε τοῖς πολλοῖς ἴσος·　　845
　　εἰ δ᾽ ἄνδρ᾽ ἕν᾽ οἰόζωνον αὐδήσει, σαφῶς
　　τοῦτ᾽ ἐστὶν ἤδη τοὔργον εἰς ἐμὲ ῥέπον.

ΙΟ. ἀλλ᾽ ὡς φανέν γε τοὔπος ὧδ᾽ ἐπίστασο,

840 ἄγος pro πάθος coniecerunt Blaydes., M. Schmidt., Arndt., al.: recepit
Nauck. 843 κατακτείναιεν L, a manu antiqua; prima manus, quae in hac voce

---

δ᾽ οὖν κ.τ.λ. 835 τοῦ παρόντος, imperf. part., = ἐκείνου ὃς παρῆν: Dem.
or. 19 § 129 οἱ συμπρεσβεύοντες καὶ παρόντες καταμαρτυρήσουσιν, i.e.
οἱ συνεπρέσβευον καὶ παρῆσαν. 836 τῆς ἐλπίδος. The art. is due to the
mention of ἐλπίδα just before, but its force is not precisely, 'the hope of
which you speak.' Rather ἐλπίδα is 'some hope,' τῆς ἐλπίδος is 'hope' in
the abstract: cp. Dem. or. 19 § 88 ἡλίκα πᾶσιν ἀνθρώποις ἀγαθὰ ἐκ τῆς
εἰρήνης γίγνεται, i.e. 'from peace,' not 'the peace.' 838 πεφασμένου, sc.
αὐτοῦ: gen. absol. El. 1344 τελουμένων εἴποιμ᾽ ἄν, when (our plans) are
being accomplished. 840 πάθος, a calamity,—viz. that of being proved
blood-guilty. The conjecture ἄγος is specious. But πάθος shows a finer
touch; it is the euphemism of a shrinking mind (like the phrase ἤν τι πάθω
for θάνω). For perf. with ἄν cp. 693. 841 περισσόν, more than ordinary,
worthy of special note: Her. 2. 32 τοὺς ἄλλα τε μηχανᾶσθαι...περισσά,
i.e. among other remarkable enterprises: Eur. Suppl. 790 τὸ μὲν γὰρ οὐκ
ἤλπιζον ἂν πεπονθέναι | πάθος περισσόν, εἰ γάμων ἀπεζύγην, I had not
deemed it a more than common woe. Iocasta is unconscious of any
point, peculiar to her version, on which a hope could depend: she had
reported the story of the slaughter in the fewest words, 715—716.
844 τὸν αὐτὸν ἀριθμόν, i.e. πλείους and not ἕνα: or, in the phrase of
grammarians, τὸν πληθυντικὸν and not τὸν ἑνικὸν ἀριθμόν. 845 ἴσος: 'one

yet have hope, until at least thou hast gained full knowledge from him who saw the deed.

OE. Hope, in truth, rests with me thus far alone; I can await the man summoned from the pastures.

IO. And when he has appeared—what would'st thou have of him?

OE. I will tell thee. If his story be found to tally with thine, I, at least, shall stand clear of disaster.

IO. And what of special note did'st thou hear from me?

OE. Thou wert saying that he spoke of Laïus as slain by robbers. If, then, he still speaks, as before, of several, I was not the slayer: a solitary man could not be held the same with that band. But if he names one lonely wayfarer, then beyond doubt this guilt leans to me.

IO. Nay, be assured that thus, at least, the tale was first told;

scribenda videtur haesisse, quid dare voluerit dubium est. κατακτείναιεν A et codd. plerique. κατακτείνειαν cum paucis V².

cannot be made to tally with (cannot be identified with) those many': τοῖς πολλοῖς, referring to the plur. λῃστάς (842). **846 οἰόζωνον**, journeying alone. The peculiarity of the idiom is that the second part of the compound is equivalent to a *separate* epithet for the noun: *i.e.* οἰόζωνος, 'with solitary girdle,' signifies, 'alone, and girt up.' *O. C.* 717 τῶν ἑκατομπόδων Νηρῄδων, not, 'with a hundred feet each,' but, countless, and dancing: *ib.* 17 πυκνόπτεροι ἀηδόνες, not, thickly-feathered, but, many and winged: *ib.* 1055 δισσόλους ἀδελφάς, not, separately-journeying sisters, but, two sisters, journeying: *Ai.* 390 δισσάρχας βασιλῆς, not, diversely-reigning kings, but, two reigning kings: Eur. *Alc.* 905 κόρος μονόπαις, not, a youth with one child, but, a youth, his only child: *Phoen.* 683 διώνυμοι θεαί, not, goddesses with contrasted names, but several goddesses, each of whom is invoked. So I understand Eur. *Or.* 1004 μονόπωλον Ἀῶ, 'Eos who drives her steeds alone' (when moon and stars have disappeared from the sky). **847 εἰς ἐμὲ ῥέπον**: as if he were standing beneath the scale in which the evidence against him lies; that scale proves the heavier of the two, and thus descends towards him. **848 ἐπίστασο φανὲν τοῦπος ὧδε**, know that the tale was thus set forth: ἐπίστασο ὡς φανὲν τοῦπος ὧδε, know that *you may take* the story *to have been* thus set forth: where ὡς merely points to the mental attitude which the subject of ἐπίστασο is to assume. *Phil.* 567 ὡς ταῦτ' ἐπίστω δρώμεν', οὐ μέλλοντ'

κοὐκ ἔστιν αὐτῷ τοῦτό γ' ἐκβαλεῖν πάλιν·
πόλις γὰρ ἤκουσ', οὐκ ἐγὼ μόνη, τάδε.　　　　850
εἰ δ' οὖν τι κἀκτρέποιτο τοῦ πρόσθεν λόγου,
οὗτοι ποτ', ὦναξ, τόν γε Λαΐου φόνον
φανεῖ δικαίως ὀρθόν, ὅν γε Λοξίας
διεῖπε χρῆναι παιδὸς ἐξ ἐμοῦ θανεῖν.
καίτοι νιν οὐ κεῖνός γ' ὁ δύστηνός ποτε　　　855
κατέκταν', ἀλλ' αὐτὸς πάροιθεν ὤλετο.
ὥστ' οὐχὶ μαντείας γ' ἂν οὔτε τῇδ' ἐγὼ
βλέψαιμ' ἂν οὕνεκ' οὔτε τῇδ' ἂν ὕστερον.
ΟΙ. καλῶς νομίζεις. ἀλλ' ὅμως τὸν ἐργάτην
πέμψον τινὰ στελοῦντα, μηδὲ τοῦτ' ἀφῇς.　　　860

851 Variam l. καὶ τρέποιτο (quae defendi quidem potest, multo tamen minus est probanda quam κἀκτρέποιτο) praebent A, E, et prima manus in V³.　　**852** τόν

ἔτι, know that you may assume these things to be a-doing, not delayed: and *ib.* 253, 415: below 956. So with the gen. abs.: *Ai.* 281 ὡς ὧδ' ἐχόντων τῶνδ' ἐπίστασθαί σε χρή, these things being so, you must view them in that belief. **849** ἐκβαλεῖν, repudiate: Plat. *Crito* 46 B τοὺς δὲ λόγους οὓς ἐν τῷ ἔμπροσθεν ἔλεγον οὐ δύναμαι νῦν ἐκβαλεῖν. **851** εἰ κἀκτρέποιτο, if he *should* turn aside: see on 772 καὶ...λέξαιμ' ἄν. **852** τόν γε Λαΐου φόνον. Iocasta argues: 'Even if he *should* admit that the deed was done by *one* man (a circumstance which would confirm our fears that the deed was yours), at any rate the death of Laïus cannot be shown to have happened as the oracle foretold; for Laïus was to have been killed by my son, who died in infancy. The oracular art having failed in this instance, I refuse to heed Teiresias when he says that you will yet be found guilty of slaying your father Polybus.' Iocasta, bent on cheering Oedipus, merely *alludes* to the possibility of his being indeed the slayer of Laïus (851), and turns to the comforting aspect of the case—viz., the undoubted failure of the oracle, *on any supposition.* This fine and subtle passage is (to my apprehension) utterly defaced by the conjecture σόν γε Λαΐου φόνον (Bothe), 'it cannot be shown that *your slaying of Laïus* fulfils the oracle.' Herm. reads τόνδε, 'this slaying' (of which you think yourself guilty): but the γε is needed. **853** δικαίως ὀρθόν, in a just sense correct, *i.e.* properly fulfilled: for ὀρθόν see on 503. **854** διεῖπε: *expressly* said: cp. διαδείκνυμι, to

he cannot revoke that, for the city heard it, not I alone. But even if he should diverge somewhat from his former story, never, king, can he show that the murder of Laïus, at least, is truly square to prophecy; of whom Loxias plainly said that he must die by the hand of my child. Howbeit that poor innocent never slew him, but perished first itself. So henceforth, for what touches divination, I would not look to my right hand or my left.

OE. Thou judgest well. But nevertheless send some one to fetch the peasant, and neglect not this matter.

γε codd.: σόν γε Bothius, Dindorf. Lectio τόνδε, quam Γ habet, nihili est. Vide annot.

---

show *clearly* (Her.), διαδηλόω, διαρρήδην, 'in express terms': so above, 394 αἴνιγμα...διειπεῖν = 'to *declare*' (solve) a riddle. **Λοξίας**: a surname of the oracular Apollo, popularly connected with λοξός, 'oblique' (akin to λέχ-ριος, *obliquus, luxus* 'sprained'), as = the giver of *indirect*, ambiguous responses (λοξὰ καὶ ἐπαμφοτερίζοντα, Lucian *Dial. Deor.* 16): Cornutus 32 λοξῶν δὲ καὶ περισκελῶν ὄντων τῶν χρησμῶν οὓς δίδωσι Λοξίας ὠνόμασται, and so Lycophron 14. 1467: to this Pacuvius alludes, Flexa *non falsa autumare dictio Delphis solet.* The association of Apollo with Helios suggested to the Stoics that the idea connecting λοξός with Λοξίας might be that of *the ecliptic:* to which it might be replied that the name Λοξίας was older than the knowledge of the fact. It is not etymologically possible to refer Λοξίας to λυκ, *lux.* But phonetic correspondence would justify the connection, suggested by Mr Fennell, with ἀ-λεξ (Skt. *rak-sh*). Λοξίας and his sister Λοξώ (Callim. *Del.* 292) would then be other forms of Phoebus and Artemis ἀλεξη-τήριοι, ἀλεξίμοροι (above, 164), 'defenders.' Iocasta's utterance here is not really inconsistent with her reservation in 712: see note there. **857 οὔτε τῇδε—οὔτε τῇδε** = οὔτ' ἐπὶ τάδε οὔτ' ἐπὶ θάτερα, neither to this side nor to that: *Phil.* 204 ἤ που τῇδ' ἢ τῇδε τόπων: *Il.* 12. 237 (Hector to Polydamas): τύνη δ' οἰωνοῖσι τανυπτερύγεσσι κελεύεις | πείθεσθαι· τῶν οὔτι μετατρέπομ' οὔτ' ἀλεγίζω, | εἴτ' ἐπὶ δεξί' ἴωσι πρὸς ἠῶ τ' ἠέλιόν τε, | εἴτ' ἐπ' ἀριστερὰ τοί γε ποτὶ ζόφον ἠερόεντα. **859 καλῶς νομίζεις**: he assents, almost mechanically—but his thoughts are intent on sending for the herdsman. **860 στελοῦντα,** 'to summon': στέλλειν = 'to cause to set out' (by a mandate), hence 'to summon': *O. C.* 297 σκοπὸς δέ νιν | ὃς κἀμὲ δεῦρ' ἔπεμπεν οἴχεται στελῶν.

ΙΟ. πέμψω ταχύνασ'· ἀλλ' ἴωμεν ἐς δόμους.
οὐδὲν γὰρ ἂν πράξαιμ' ἂν ὧν οὐ σοὶ φίλον.

ΧΟ. στρ. α'. εἰ μοι ξυνείη φέροντι
2 μοῖρα τὰν εὔσεπτον ἁγνείαν λόγων
3 ἔργων τε πάντων, ὧν νόμοι πρόκεινται   865

μηδὲ τοῦτ' ἀφῇς, 'and do not neglect this.' With à point after στελοῦντα we could render: 'neglect *not even* this': but Oed. does not feel, nor feign, indifference. **862 γάρ**, since ἴωμεν κ.τ.λ. implies consultation. The doubled ἂν gives emphasis: cp. 139. ὧν οὐ σοὶ φίλον = τούτων ἃ πρᾶξαι οὐ σοὶ φίλον ἐστί. *Phil.* 1227 ἔπραξας ἔργον ποῖον ὧν οὔ σοι πρέπον;

863—910 Second στάσιμον. The second ἐπεισόδιον (512—862) has been marked by the overbearing harshness of Oedipus towards Creon; by the rise of a dreadful suspicion that Oedipus is ἄναγνος—blood-guilty for Laïus; and by the avowed contempt of Iocasta, not, indeed, for Apollo himself, but for the μαντική of his ministers. These traits furnish the two interwoven themes of the second stasimon: (1) the prayer for *purity* in word as in deed: (2) the deprecation of that *pride* which goes before a fall;—whether it be the insolence of the τύραννος, or such intellectual arrogance as Iocasta's speech bewrays (λόγῳ, v. 884). The tone of warning reproof towards Oedipus, while only allusive, is yet in contrast with the firm though anxious sympaty of the former ode, and serves to attune the feeling of the spectators for the approach of the catastrophe.

1st strophe (863—872). May I ever be pure in word and deed, loyal to the unwritten and eternal laws.

1st antistrophe (873—882). A tyrant's selfish insolence hurls him to ruin. But may the gods prosper all emulous effort for the good of the State.

2nd strophe (883—896). Irreverence in word or deed shall not escape: the wrath of the gods shall find it out.

2nd antistrophe (897—910). Surely the oracles concerning Laïus will yet be justified: O Zeus, suffer not Apollo's worship to fail.

863 εἰ μοι ξυνείη μοῖρα φέροντι is equivalent to εἴθε διατελοῖμι φέρων, the part. implying that the speaker is *already* mindful of ἁγνεία, and prays that he may continue to be so: whereas εἰ μοι συνείη μοῖρα φέρειν would have been equivalent to εἴθε μοι γένοιτο φέρειν, an aspiration towards

Io. I will send without delay. But let us come into the house : nothing will I do save at thy good pleasure.

Ch. May destiny still find me winning the praise of rever- ent purity in all words and deeds sanctioned by those laws

---

ἀγνεία as not yet attained. Though μοῖρα is not expressly personified (cp. Pind. *Pyth.* 3. 84 τὶν δὲ μοῖρ' εὐδαιμονίας ἕπεται), the conception of it is so far personal that ξυνείη is tinged with the associations of ξυνειδείη, and thus softens any boldness in the use of the participle ; a use which, in principle, is identical with the use after such verbs as διατελῶ, τυγχάνω, λανθάνω. φέροντι (= φερομένῳ, see on 520)...ἀγνείαν, *winning* purity, regarded as a precious κτῆμα (*Ant.* 150): cp. 1190 πλέον τᾶς εὐδαιμονίας φέρει : *El.* 968 εὐσέβειαν...οἴσει (will win *the praise of* piety): Eur. *Or.* 158 ὕπνου...φερομένῳ χαράν. 864 εὔσεπτον, active, 'reverent,' only here : so 890 τῶν ἀσέπτων, also act., 'irreverent deeds,' as in ·Eur. *Helen.* 542 Πρώτεως ἀσέπτου παιδός, impious, unholy : see on 515. 865 ὧν νόμοι πρόκεινται ὑψίπ., 'for which (enjoining which) laws have been set forth, moving on high,'—having their sphere and range in the world of eternal truths : ὑψίποδες being equiv. to ὑψηλοὶ καὶ ὑψοῦ πατοῦντες : see on οἰόζωνον 846, and contrast χθονοστιβῆ 301. The metaphor in νόμοι was less trite for a Greek of the age of Sophocles than for us : cp. Plat. *Legg.* 793 A τὰ καλούμενα ὑπὸ τῶν πολλῶν ἄγραφα νόμιμα —οὔτε νόμους δεῖ προσαγορεύειν αὐτὰ οὔτε ἄρρητα ἐᾶν. πρόκεινται (Thuc. 3. 45 ἐν οὖν ταῖς πόλεσι πολλῶν θανάτου ζημία πρόκειται) strengthens the metaphor : Xen. *Mem.* 4. 4. 21 δίκην γέ τοι διδόασιν οἱ παραβαίνοντες τοὺς ὑπὸ τῶν θεῶν κειμένους νόμους, ἣν οὐδενὶ τρόπῳ δυνατὸν ἀνθρώπῳ διαφυγεῖν, ὥσπερ τοὺς ὑπ' ἀνθρώπων κειμένους νόμους ἔνιοι διαφεύγουσι τὸ δίκην διδόναι : where Socrates speaks of the ἄγραφοι νόμοι which are ἐν πάσῃ χώρᾳ κατὰ ταὐτὰ νομιζόμενοι,—as to revere the gods and honour parents. Arist. *Rhet.* 1. 13. 2 : 'I consider law (νόμον) as particular (ἴδιον) or universal (κοινόν), the particular law being that which each community defines in respect to itself,—a law partly written, partly unwritten [as consisting in local custom]; the universal law being that of nature (τὸν κατὰ φύσιν). For there is a certain natural and universal right and wrong which all men divine (μαντεύονται), even if they have no intercourse or covenant with each other ; as the Antigone of Sophocles is found saying that, notwithstanding the interdict, it is right to bury Polyneices' (*Ant.* 454, where she appeals to the ἄγραπτα κἀσφαλῆ θεῶν νόμιμα). Cp. Cope's

J. S.   11

4 ὑψίποδες, οὐρανίαν
5 δι' αἰθέρα τεκνωθέντες, ὧν Ὄλυμπος
6 πατὴρ μόνος, οὐδέ νιν
7 θνατὰ φύσις ἀνέρων
8 ἔτικτεν, οὐδὲ μάν ποτε λάθα κατακοιμάσει·   870
9 μέγας ἐν τούτοις θεός, οὐδὲ γηράσκει.

ἀντ. α΄. ὕβρις φυτεύει τύραννον·   873
2 ὕβρις, εἰ πολλῶν ὑπερπλησθῇ μάταν,
3 ἃ μὴ 'πίκαιρα μηδὲ συμφέροντα,   875

870 οὐδὲ μήν ποτε L, A, codd. plerique: οὐδὲ μὰν ποτὲ (sic) V: οὐδὲ μήποτε E. Maior ergo codd. auctoritas pro l. οὐδὲ μάν ποτε....κατακοιμάσει facit quam pro l. οὐδὲ μήποτε...κατακοιμάσῃ. Habet certe L κατακοιμάσῃ. Contra legitur κατακοι-

Introd. to Arist. *Rhet.* p. 239. **866 οὐρανίαν δι' αἰθέρα τεκνωθέντες,** called into a life that permeates the heavenly ether (the highest heaven): the metaphor of **τεκνωθέντες** being qualified by its meaning in this particular application to **νόμοι,** viz. that they are *revealed as operative;* which allows the poet to indicate *the sphere throughout which they operate* by **δι' αἰθέρα,** instead of the verbally appropriate **ἐν αἰθέρι**: much as if he had said δι' αἰθέρα ἐνεργοὶ ἀναφανέντες. So, again, when he calls *Olympus,* not *Zeus,* their **πατήρ,** the metaphor is half-fused with the direct notion of 'source.' Cp. Arist. *Rh.* 1. 13. 2 quoted on 865, which continues (illustrating τὸ φύσει δίκαιον): καὶ ὡς Ἐμπεδοκλῆς λέγει περὶ τοῦ μὴ κτείνειν τὸ ἔμψυχον· τοῦτο γὰρ οὐ τισὶ μὲν δίκαιον τισὶ δ' οὐ δίκαιον, Ἀλλὰ τὸ μὲν πάντων νόμιμον διά τ' εὐρυμέδοντος | αἰθέρος ἠνεκέως τέταται διά τ' ἀπλέτου αὖ γῆς (so Scaliger rightly amended αὐγῆς: Emped. 438): where the special reference of Empedocles is to a principle of life common to gods, men, and irrational animals (πνεῦμα τὸ διὰ παντὸς τοῦ κόσμου διῆκον ψυχῆς τρόπον, Sextus Emp. *Adv. Math.* 9. 127: cp. Cope ad loc.). **αἰθέρα**: *Il.* 16. 364 ὡς δ' ὅτ' ἀπ' Οὐλύμπου νέφος ἔρχεται οὐρανὸν εἴσω | αἰθέρος ἐκ δίης: where, Olympus being the mountain, the οὐρανός is above the αἰθήρ, since ἐξ αἰθέρος could not = ἐξ αἴθρας, *after* clear weather: and so *Il.* 2. 458 δι' αἰθέρος οὐρανὸν ἵκει: *Il.* 19. 351 οὐρανοῦ ἐκκατέπαλτο δι' αἰθέρος: cp. *Ant.* 420. Here **οὐρανίαν αἰθέρα**= the highest heaven. **867 Ὄλυμπος**: not the mountain, as in the *Iliad,* but, as in the *Odyssey* (6. 42), the bright supernal abode of the gods: and so = the sky itself: *O. C.* 1654 γῆν τε προσκυνοῦνθ'

of range sublime, called into life throughout the high clear
heaven, whose father is Olympus alone; their parent was no
race of mortal men, no, nor shall oblivion ever lay them to
sleep; a mighty god is in them, and he grows not old.

Insolence breeds the tyrant; Insolence, once vainly
surfeited on wealth that is not meet nor good,   1st antistrophe.

μάσει in A (cui calami fortasse lapsu Campb. aoristum subiunctivi tribuit), et
in reliquis codd. paene omnibus, exceptis L², Δ, Pal., Trin. Quocirca cum fateri
debeamus, lectionem μήποτε...κατακοιμάσῃ sententiae nihilo secius convenire, alteram
tamen, ut multo gravioribus innixam testimoniis, praeferendam duximus.

ὁμοῦ | καὶ τὸν θεῶν Ὄλυμπον. **870 ἔτικτεν**, 'was their parent,' sometimes
used instead of ἔτεκε where the stress is not so much on the fact
of the *birth* as on the *parentage*, 1099, *O. C.* 982, fr. 501: Pind.
P. 9. 15 ὅν ποτε...Ναῒς...ἔτικτεν. (It would be prosaic to render,
'brought forth successively,'—developed.) **οὐδὲ μὰν...κατακοιμάσει**: the
MSS. favour this reading, and οὐδὲ μὰν is suitable as = 'no, nor...' But
I do not see how οὐ μή...κατακοιμάσῃ could be rejected on the ground
which Prof. Campbell assigns, as 'too vehement.' In itself οὐ μή
simply expresses conviction: Plat. *Phaed.* 105 A οὐκοῦν ἡ ψυχὴ τὸ
ἐναντίον ᾧ αὐτὴ ἐπιφέρει ἀεὶ οὐ μή ποτε δέξηται, ὡς ἐκ τῶν πρόσθεν
ὡμολόγηται; **871 μέγας ἐν τούτοις θεός**: the divine virtue inherent in them
is strong and unfailing. Cp. Eur. fr. 188 θεός τις ἐν ἡμῖν. θεός without
art., as 880: *O. C.* 1694 τὸ φέρον ἐκ θεοῦ. Better thus than, 'there
is a great god in these'—which is weak after what has preceded.
873 ὕβρις. The tone of Oedipus towards Creon (esp. 618—672) suggests the strain of warning rebuke. Aeschylus, with more elaborate
imagery, makes ὕβρις the daughter of δυσσεβία and the parent of a
νέα ὕβρις which in turn begets κόρος and θράσος (*Ag.* 764). **τύραννον**,
here not 'a prince,'—nor even, in the normal Greek sense, an uncon-
stitutionally absolute ruler (bad or good),—but, in our sense, 'a tyrant':
cp. Plat. *Pol.* 301 C ὅταν μήτε κατὰ νόμους μήτε κατὰ ἔθη πράττῃ τις εἰς
ἄρχων, προσποιῆται δὲ ὥσπερ ὁ ἐπιστήμων ὡς ἄρα παρὰ τὰ γεγραμμένα
τό γε βέλτιστον ποιητέον, ᾗ δέ τις ἐπιθυμία καὶ ἄγνοια τούτου τοῦ
μιμήματος ἡγουμένη, μῶν οὐ τότε τὸν τοιοῦτον ἕκαστον τύραννον
κλητέον; *Rep.* 573 B ἆρ' οὖν...καὶ τὸ πάλαι διὰ τὸ τοιοῦτον τύραννος ὁ
Ἔρως λέγεται; **874 εἰ...ὑπερπλησθῇ**: Plat. *Rep.* 573 C τυραννικὸς δὲ...
ἀνὴρ ἀκριβῶς γίγνεται, ὅταν ἢ φύσει ἢ ἐπιτηδεύμασιν ἢ ἀμφοτέροις μεθυ-
στικός τε καὶ ἐρωτικὸς καὶ μελαγχολικὸς γένηται. For εἰ with

4 ἀκρότατον εἰσαναβᾶσ'
5 < ἄκρον > ἀπότομον ὤρουσεν εἰς ἀνάγκαν,
6 ἔνθ' οὐ ποδὶ χρησίμῳ
7 χρῆται. τὸ καλῶς δ' ἔχον
8 πόλει πάλαισμα μήποτε λῦσαι θεὸν αἰτοῦμαι.　　880
9 θεὸν οὐ λήξω ποτὲ προστάταν ἴσχων.

στρ. β'. εἰ δέ τις ὑπέροπτα χερσὶν ἢ λόγῳ πορεύεται,　　883

876 seq. ἄκρον in 877 ex mea coniectura supplevi. ἀκροτάταν εἰσαναβᾶσ'
ἀπότομον | ὤρουσεν εἰς ἀνάγκαν L. ἀκροτάταν εἰσαναβᾶσ' ἀπότμον | ὤρουσεν εἰς ἀνάγκαν
A: ubi signum ' post εἰσαναβᾶσ' et litteram o super ἀπότμον rubro charactere usus
corrector addidit. Scilicet in hoc codice prima manus scripserat εἰσαναβᾶσα πότμον :

subj., see on 198. **876** ἀκρότατον is metrically required for correspondence with ὑψίποδες in 866. The MSS. have ἀκροτάταν, possibly due to
ἀνάγκαν. In 877, ἀπότομον ὤρουσεν εἰς ἀνάγκαν, there is a defect of one
long syllable or two short ones, the corresponding verse of the strophe,
866, being δι' αἰθέρα τεκνωθέντες ὧν Ὄλυμπος. ἀπότομον seems unquestionably right: neither ἄποτμον (which occurs as a variant) nor
ἄπορον is nearly so forcible, or so appropriate to this image of the
sudden, headlong fall. If, then, ἀπότομον is kept, these methods of
correction are open:—(1) To prefix ἐξ- to ὤρουσεν. To this the objection, I think, is that ἀκρότατον εἰσαναβᾶσ' must then mean, 'having
climbed to the highest point'; i.e. ἀκρότ. must be a substantive; for,
with εἰσαναβ. (this would not hold of ἀναβᾶσ'), ἀκρότατον could not be
adverbial: cp. *Hom. Hymn.* 19. 11 ἀκροτάτην κορυφὴν μηλόσκοπον εἰσανα-
βαίνων: and so in all places (about 14) where it occurs in the Homeric
poems the verb has an accus. Now, τὸ ἀκρότατον might serve for such:
but surely not ἀκρότατον. (2) To supply before ἀπότομον.a noun agreeing with ἀκρότατον. Arndt conj. αἶπος ('Ἄθθον, Ἀραχναῖον αἶπος Aesch.
Ag. 285, 309). Another possibility is ὄλβον. I propose ἄκρον, which
a scribe ignorant of metre might easily have taken for a redundancy
generated by ἀκρότατον. **877** ἀπότομον...εἰς ἀνάγκαν, to sheer ruin: the
epithet of the *precipice* being transferred to the *abyss* which receives
him: Her. 1. 84 τὸ χωρίον τῆς ἀκροπόλιος...ἐὸν ἄμαχόν τε καὶ ἀπότομον. Cp. αἰπὺν ὄλεθρον (*Il.* 6. 57), θάνατον αἰπύν (Pind. *Ol.* 11.
42). ἀνάγκαν, a constraining doom from the gods: Eur. *Ph.* 1000 εἰς
ἀνάγκην δαιμόνων ἀφιγμένοι. Cp. Plat. *Legg.* 716 A ὁ δέ τις ἐξαρθεὶς
ὑπὸ μεγαλαυχίας ἢ χρήμασιν ἐπαιρόμενος ἢ τιμαῖς ἢ καὶ σώματος εὐμορφίᾳ,

when it hath scaled the crowning height, leaps on the abyss of doom, where no service of the feet can serve. But I pray that the god never quell such rivalry as benefits the State; the god will I ever hold for our protector.

But if any man walks haughtily in deed or word, 2nd strophe.

deinde πότμον voluit corrector in ἀπότομον mutare, hoc cum v. ἀνάγκαν iuncturus. Est autem et in L et in A gloss. ἀπορρῶγα ad v. ἀπότομον. Pro ἀκροτάταν nulla extat in codd. lectionis varietas. Habent item codd. quos viderim omnes ὤρουσεν, excepto T, qui ἀνώρουσεν insulse praebet. Frustra erunt qui ad expediendas huius loci tricas plus opis a codicibus exspectant. Rationes vero quibus coniectura ἄκρον firmatur infra annotatae sunt.

ἅμα νεότητι καὶ ἀνοίᾳ φλέγεται τὴν ψυχὴν μεθ᾽ ὕβρεως...μετὰ δὲ χρόνον οὐ πολὺν ὑποσχὼν τιμωρίαν τῇ δίκῃ ἑαυτόν τε καὶ οἶκον καὶ πόλιν ἄρδην ἀνάστατον ἐποίησε. 878 χρησίμῳ...χρῆται: where it does not use the foot to any purpose: *i.e.* the leap is to headlong destruction; it is not one in which the feet can anywhere find a safe landing-place. For the paronomasia cp. Pind. *P.* 2. 78 κερδοῖ δὲ τί μάλα τοῦτο κερδα-λέον τελέθει; 'but for the creature named of gain (the fox) what so gainful is there here?' 879 τὸ καλῶς δ᾽ ἔχον: but I ask that the god never do away with, abolish, that struggle which is advantageous for the city,—*i.e.* the contest in which citizen vies with citizen who shall most serve the State. The words imply a recognition of the προθυμία which Oed. had so long shown in the service of Thebes: cp. 48, 93, 247. 880 πάλαισμα: cp. Isocr. *Ep.* 7 § 7 τοῖς καλῶς τὰς πόλεις τὰς αὐτῶν διοικοῦσιν ἁμιλλητέον καὶ πειρατέον διενεγκεῖν αὐτῶν. Plut. *Mor.* 820 c ὥσπερ οὐκ ἀργυρίτην οὐδὲ δωρίτην ἀγῶνα πολιτείας ἀγωνιζομένοις (the emulous service of the State), ἀλλὰ ἱερὸν ὡς ἀληθῶς καὶ στεφανίτην (like the contests in the great games). 882 προστάταν: defender, champion: not in the semi-technical sense of 'patron,' as in 411. 883 ὑπέροπτα, adverbial neut. of ὑπέροπτος [not ὑπερόπτα, epic nom. for ὑπερόπτης (*Ant.* 130), like ἱππότα]: cp. *O. C.* 1695 οὔτοι κατάμεμπτ᾽ ἔβητον, ye have fared not amiss. *Il.* 17. 75 ἀκίχητα διώκων | ἵππους: Eur. *Suppl.* 770 ἄκραντ᾽ ὀδύρει: *Ph.* 1739 ἄπειμι...ἀπαρθένευτ᾽ ἀλωμένα: *Ion* 255 ἀνερεύνητα δυσθυμεῖ (hast griefs which I may not explore). χερσὶν, *in contrast with* λόγῳ, merely = ἔργοις, not 'deeds of violence': cp. Eur. *Ph.* 312 πῶς... | καὶ χερσὶ καὶ λόγοισι... | περιχορεύουσα τέρψιν...λάβω, find joy in deed and word of circling dance, *i.e.* in linking of the hands and in

2 Δίκας ἀφόβητος, οὐδὲ   885
3 δαιμόνων ἕδη σέβων,
4 κακά νιν ἕλοιτο μοῖρα,
5 δυσπότμου χάριν χλιδᾶς,
6 εἰ μὴ τὸ κέρδος κερδανεῖ δικαίως
7 καὶ τῶν ἀσέπτων ἔρξεται,   890
8 ἢ τῶν ἀθίκτων θίξεται ματάζων.

890 ἔρξεται L: ubi litteram ξ ex γ ortam esse mihi quidem haud certum videtur. ἔρξεται A. Consentiunt in voce, in spiritu tantum variant ceteri codd.   **891**

song: cp. 864. **885 Δίκας ἀφόβητος**, not fearing Justice: cp. 969 ἄψαυστος ἔγχους, not touching a spear. The act. sense is preferable only because class. Greek says φοβηθεὶς τὴν δίκην, not φοβηθεὶς ὑπὸ τῆς δίκης: the *form* of the adj. would warrant a pass. sense: cp. *Tr.* 685 ἀκτῖνος...ἀθίκτον. With ἄφοβος (*Ai.* 366) ἀφόβητος cp. ἀταρβής (*Tr.* 322) ἀτάρβητος (*Ai.* 197). **886 ἕδη**, *images* of gods, whether sitting or standing; but always with the added notion that they are placed in a temple or holy place as objects of worship. Timaeus p. 93 ἕδος· τὸ ἄγαλμα καὶ ὁ τόπος ἐν ᾧ ἵδρυται: where τόπος prob. denotes the small shrine in which an image might stand. Dionys. Hal. I. 47 uses ἕδη to render *penates*. Liddell and Scott *s. v.* cite the following as places in which ἕδος 'may be a *temple*': but in all of them it must mean *image*. Isocr. or. 15 § 2 Φειδίαν τὸν τὸ τῆς Ἀθηνᾶς ἕδος ἐργασάμενον, i.e. the chryselephantine Athena Parthenos; cp. Plut. *Per.* 13 ὁ δὲ Φειδίας εἰργάζετο μὲν τῆς θεοῦ τὸ χρυσοῦν ἕδος. Xen. *Hellen.* I. 4. 12 Πλυντήρια ἦγεν ἡ πόλις, τοῦ ἕδους κατακεκαλυμμένου τῆς Ἀθηνᾶς: i.e. the ἀρχαῖον βρέτας of Athena Polias in the Erechtheum was veiled in sign of mourning (the death of Aglauros being commemorated at the festival of the Plunteria). Paus. 8. 46. 2 φαίνεται δὲ οὐκ ἄρξας ὁ Αὔγουστος ἀναθήματα καὶ ἕδη θεῶν ἀπάγεσθαι παρὰ τῶν κρατηθέντων (i.e. carry off to Italy): where ἀναθήματα are dedicated objects generally, ἕδη images worshipped in temples. Is Sophocles glancing here at the mutilators of the Hermae in 415 B.C., and especially at Alcibiades? We can hardly say more than this:—(1) There is no positive probability as to the date of the play which can be set against such a view. (2) The language suits it,—nay, might well suggest it; nor does it matter that the Ἑρμαῖ, though ἀναθήματα (Andoc. *De Myst.* § 34), were not properly ἕδη. (3) It cannot be assumed that the dramatic art of Sophocles would exclude such a reference. Direct contemporary

with no fear of Justice, no reverence for the images of gods, may an evil doom seize him for his ill-starred pride, if he will not win his vantage fairly, nor keep him from unholy deeds, but must lay profaning hands on sanctities.

ἕξεται ματᾷζων L. ἕξεται ματάζων (sic) A: deest iota subscriptum in aliis quoque codd., ut B, V, Bodl. Laud. 54. Recepi quod Blaydes. coniecit, θίξεται: vide annot.

---

allusion is, indeed, uncongenial to it. But a light touch like this— especially in a choral ode—might fitly strike a chord of contemporary feeling in unison with the emotion stirred by the drama itself. I do not see how to affirm or to deny that such a suggestion was meant here. **888** δυσπότμου, miserably perverse: *Ant.* 1025 οὐκέτ ἔστ'... | ἄβουλος οὔτ' ἄνολβος. **890** τῶν ἀσέπτων: see on 864. ἕρξεται, keep himself from: *O. C.* 836 εἴργου, 'keep off' (the holy ground): *Her.* 7. 197 ὡς κατὰ τὸ ἄλσος ἐγένετο, αὐτός τε ἔργετο αὐτοῦ καὶ τῇ στρατιῇ πάσῃ παρήγγειλε. Plat. *Legg.* 838 A ὡς εὖ τε καὶ ἀκριβῶς εἴργονται τῆς τῶν καλῶν ξυνουσίας. As to the form, Her. has ἔργω or ἐέργω: in Attic the MSS. give Aesch. *Eum.* 566 κατεργαθοῦ: Soph. *Ai.* 593 ξυνέρξετε: Thuc. 5. 11 περιέρξαντες (so the best MSS., and Classen): Plat. *Gorg.* 461 D καθέρξῃς (so Stallb. and Herm., with MSS.): *Rep.* 461 B ξυνέρξαντος: *Rep.* 285 B ἔρξας. So far as the MSS. warrant a conclusion, Attic seems to have admitted ἐρ- instead of εἰρ- *in the forms with* ξ. The smooth breathing is right here, even if we admit a normal distinction between εἴργω 'to shut out' and εἴργω 'to shut in.' **891** θίξεται. This conjecture of Blaydes seems to me certain. The form occurs Eur. *Hippol.* 1086 κλαίων τις αὐτῶν ἆρ' ἐμοῦ γε θίξεται: *Her.* 652 εἰ δὲ τῶνδε προσθίξει χερί. Hesych. has θίξεσθαι. L has ἕξεται with no breathing. Soph. could not conceivably have used such a phrase as ἔχεσθαι τῶν ἀθίκτων, *to cling to* things which should not even be touched. He himself shows the proper use of ἔχεσθαι in fr. 327 τοῦ γε κερδαίνειν ὅμως | ἀπρὶξ ἔχονται, 'still they cling tooth and nail to gain': fr. 26 τὰ μὲν | δίκαι' ἐπαίνει τοῦ δὲ κερδαίνειν ἔχου. Some explain ἕξεται as 'abstain': *Od.* 4. 422 σχέσθαι τε βίης λῦσαί τε γέροντα: *Her.* 6. 85 ἔσχοντο τῆς ἀγωγῆς. To this there are two objections, both insuperable: (1) the disjunctive ἤ,—with which the sense ought to be, 'unless he gain &c...*or else* abstain': (2) ματᾷζων, which could not be added to ἕξεται as if this were παύσεται. ματᾷζων, acting with rash folly: *Her.* 2. 162 ἀπεματάϊσε, behaved in an unseemly manner: Aesch. *Ag.* 995 σπλάγχνα δ' οὔτι ματᾷζει, my heart does not vainly forebode. The reason for writing ματᾷζων, not ματάζων, is that

9 τίς ἔτι ποτ' ἐν τοῖσδ' ἀνὴρ θεῶν βέλη
10 εὔξεται ψυχᾶς ἀμύνειν;
11 εἰ γὰρ αἱ τοιαίδε πράξεις τίμιαι,   895
12 τί δεῖ με χορεύειν;

ἀντ. β'. οὐκέτι τὸν ἄθικτον εἶμι γᾶς ἐπ' ὀμφαλὸν σέβων,
2 οὐδ' ἐς τὸν Ἀβαῖσι ναόν,   900

892 seq. τίς ἔτι ποτ' ἐν τοῖσδ' ἀνὴρ | θυμῶι βέλη ἐρξεται (sic) ψυχᾶς ἀμύνειν L. Sic etiam A, in quo et θυμῶι et ἐρξεται (sic) clare scripta sunt. Plerique codd. ἐρξεται (sic) habent. Pro θυμῷ, pauci quidam θυμοῦ praebent. Extat θυμῶ (sic) in B, E, T, Pal., V², V³, V⁴. Pro ἐν τοῖσδε, habet E cum paucis aliis ἐν τούτοις, B (omisso ἐν)

---

the form ματαίζω is well attested (Her., Josephus, Hesych., Herodian): while there is no similar evidence for ματάζω, though the latter form *might* have existed, being related to a stem ματα (μάτη) as δικαζ-ω to δικα (δίκη). **892** τίς ἔτι ποτ'...ἀμύνειν; Amid such things (if such deeds prevail), who shall any longer vaunt that he wards off from his life the shafts of the gods? The pres. ἀμύνειν, not fut. ἀμυνεῖν, because the shafts are imagined as already assailing him. ἐν τοῖσδ': 1320: *Ant.* 38 εἰ τάδ' ἐν τούτοις. **893** θεῶν βέλη. The MSS. have θυμῶι, θυμοῦ or θυμῶ: in A over θυμῶι βέλη is written τὴν θείαν δίκην. This points to the true sense, though it does not necessarily presuppose the true reading. The phrase θυμοῦ βέλη, 'arrows of anger,' could mean, 'taunts hurled by an angry man'; but, *alone*, could *not* mean, 'the arrows of the divine wrath.' The readings of the MSS. might have arisen either through the ν of θεῶν being written, as it often is, in a form resembling μ, and ω having then been transposed (so that θυμῶ would have arisen before θυμῶι); or from a gloss θυμοῦ on ψυχᾶς. For βέλη cp. Plat. *Legg.* 873 E πλὴν ὅσα κεραυνὸς ἤ τι παρὰ θεοῦ τοιοῦτον βέλος ἰόν. **894** εὔξεται. This conject. of Musgrave (which Blaydes adopts) involves only the change of one letter from ἐρξεται: and nothing would have been more likely than a change of εὔξεται into ἐρξεται if the scribe's eye or thought had wandered to ἐρξεται in 890, especially since the latter is not obviously unsuited to the general sense. But ἐρξεται here is impossible. For (1) we cannot render: 'will keep off the shafts from himself, so as to ward them from his life': this would be intolerable. Nor (2), with Elmsley: 'who will *abstain from warding off* the shafts of the soul (the stings of conscience, ψυχᾶς βέλη) from his mind (θυμοῦ)?' i.e. who will not become reckless? This most assuredly is not Greek. εὔξεται, on the other hand, gives just the right

Where such things are, what mortal shall boast any more that he can ward the arrows of the gods from his life? Nay, if such deeds are in honour, wherefore should we join in the sacred dance?

No more will I go reverently to earth's central and inviolate shrine, no more to Abae's temple

2nd anti-strophe.

αὐτοῖς: quae mera fudit incuria. θεῶν pro θεῷ coniecit Hermann.; εὔξεται pro ἔρξεται Musgravius. Vide annot. **896** Post χορεύειν habet L in eodem versu haec verba, πονεῖν ἢ τοῖς θεοῖσ: eadem in Pal., M (a correctore), M², M⁵ (omisso ἢ τοῖς θεοῖς) leguntur. Corrupta sunt ex gloss. vocem χορεύειν interpretante, πανη-γυρίζειν τοῖς θεοῖς, quod est in cod. Trin. aliisque.

---

sense: 'If justice and religion are trampled under foot, can any man dare to boast that he will escape the divine wrath?' **896** χορεύειν. The words πονεῖν ἢ τοῖς θεοῖς added in a few MSS. (including L) have plainly arisen from a contracted writing of πανηγυρίζειν τοῖς θεοῖς which occurs in a few others. This gloss correctly represents the general notion of χορεύειν, as referring to the χοροί connected with the cult of Dionysus, Apollo and other gods. The χορός was an element so essential and characteristic that, in a Greek mouth, the question τί δεῖ με χορεύειν; would import, 'why maintain the solemn rites of public worship?' Cp. Polybius 4. 20 (speaking of the youth of Arcadia) μετὰ δὲ ταῦτα τοὺς Φιλοξένου καὶ Τιμοθέου νόμους μανθάνοντες (learning the music of those masters) πολλῇ φιλοτιμίᾳ χορεύουσι κατ' ἐνιαυτὸν τοῖς Διονυσιακοῖς αὐληταῖς ἐν τοῖς θεάτροις, οἱ μὲν παῖδες τοὺς παιδικοὺς ἀγῶνας, οἱ δὲ νεανίσκοι τοὺς τῶν ἀνδρῶν λεγομένους. Eur. Bacch. 181 δεῖ...Διόνυσον... ὅσον καθ' ἡμᾶς δυνατὸν αὔξεσθαι μέγαν· | ποῖ δεῖ χορεύειν, ποῖ καθιστάναι πόδα, | καὶ κρᾶτα σεῖσαι πολιόν; ἐξηγοῦ σύ μοι | γέρων γέροντι, Τειρεσία. The Theban elders need not, then, be regarded as momentarily forget-ting their dramatic part. Cp. 1095 χορεύεσθαι. **898 ἄθικτον**: cp. the story of the Persian attack on Delphi in 480 B.C. being repulsed by the god, who would not suffer his priests to remove the treasures, φὰς αὐτὸς ἱκανὸς εἶναι τῶν ἑωυτοῦ προκατῆσθαι, Her. 8. 36. **ὀμφαλὸν**: see on 480. **900 τὸν Ἀβαῖσι ναόν.** The site of Abae, not far N. of the modern village of Exarcho, was on a hill in the north-west of Phocis, between Lake Copais and Elateia, and near the frontier of the Opuntian Locrians. Her. 8. 33 ἔνθα ἦν ἱερὸν Ἀπόλλωνος πλούσιον, θησαυροῖσί τε καὶ ἀναθήμασι πολλοῖσι κατεσκευασμένον· ἦν δὲ καὶ τότε καὶ νῦν ἐστι

3 οὐδὲ τὰν Ὀλυμπίαν,
4 εἰ μὴ τάδε χειρόδεικτα
5 πᾶσιν ἁρμόσει βροτοῖς.
6 ἀλλ', ὦ κρατύνων, εἴπερ ὄρθ' ἀκούεις,
7 Ζεῦ, πάντ' ἀνάσσων, μὴ λάθοι
8 σὲ τάν τε σὰν ἀθάνατον αἰὲν ἀρχάν.   905
9 φθίνοντα γὰρ Λαΐου < παλαίφατα >
10 θέσφατ' ἐξαιροῦσιν ἤδη,
11 κοὐδαμοῦ τιμαῖς Ἀπόλλων ἐμφανής·
12 ἔρρει δὲ τὰ θεῖα.   910

IO. χώρας ἄνακτες, δόξα μοι παρεστάθη

903 ὀρθὸν L, ὄρθ' A et ceteri codd.   **904** λάθοι L, quod ardenter precantibus potissime convenit. λάθῃ (sic) A, V², V³, V⁴: λάθῃ Brunck., Elmsleius, Blaydes.   **906** φθίνοντα γὰρ λαΐου ∴ θέσφατ' L, adnotato ∴ παλαιὰ in marg. a manu recentiore, παλαιὰ *post* λαΐου inserendum esse significans. Quem ordinem

χρηστήριον αὐτόθι· καὶ τοῦτο τὸ ἱερὸν συλήσαντες ἐνέπρησαν (the Persians in 480 B.C.). Hadrian built a small temple beside the ancient ἱερόν, Paus. 10. 35. 3. **901** τὰν Ὀλυμπίαν, called by Pindar δέσποιν' ἀλαθείας (*Ol.* 8. 2), because divination by burnt offerings (μαντικὴ δι' ἐμπύρων) was there practised on the altar of Zeus by the Iamidae, hereditary μάντεις (Her. 9. 33) : Pind. *Ol.* 6. 70 Ζηνὸς ἐπ' ἀκροτάτῳ βωμῷ…χρηστήριον θέσθαι κέλευσεν (Apollo)· | ἐξ οὗ πολύκλειτον καθ' Ἕλλανας γένος Ἰαμιδᾶν. **902** εἰ μὴ τάδε ἁρμόσει, if these things (the prophecy that Laïus should be slain by his son, and its fulfilment) do not *come right* (fit each other), χειρόδεικτα πᾶσιν βροτοῖς, so as to be signal examples for all men.   Cp. *Ant.* 1318 τάδ' οὐκ ἐπ' ἄλλον βροτῶν | ἐμᾶς ἁρμόσει ποτ' ἐξ αἰτίας, can never be *adjusted* to another,—be *rightly* charged on him.   Prof. Campbell cites Plat. *Soph.* 262 C πρὶν ἄν τις τοῖς ὀνόμασι τὰ ῥήματα κεράσῃ.   τότε δ' ἥρμοσέ τε, κ.τ.λ.,—where I should suppose ἥρμοσε to be transitive : ἥρμοσέ τις τοῖς ὀνόμασι τὰ ῥήματα : if so, it is not parallel. χειρόδ. only here.   **903** ἀκούεις, *audis*, alluding chiefly to the title Ζεὺς βασιλεύς, Xen. *Anab.* 3. 1. 12 ; under which, after the victory at Leuctra in 371 B.C., he was honoured with a special festival at Lebadeia in Boeotia, Diod. 15. 53.   **904** The subject to λάθοι is not definitely τάδε (902), but rather a notion to be inferred from the whole preceding sentence,—'the vindication of thy word.' Elms. cp. Eur. *Med.* 332

or Olympia, if these oracles fit not the issue, so that all men shall point at them with the finger. Nay, king,—if thou art rightly called,—Zeus all-ruling, may it not escape thee and thine ever-deathless power!

The old prophecies concerning Laïus are fading; already men are setting them at nought, and nowhere is Apollo glorified with honours; the worship of the gods is perishing.

Io.   Princes of the land, the thought has come to me

codd. plerique exhibent, quanquam in paucis stat vox παλαιά vel ante Λαΐου vel post θέσφατα plene scriptum (non θέσφατ'). Linwood. autem, qui in v. str. 892 ὦν τοιόσδ' pro ἐν τοῖσδ' coniecerat, hic legit φθίνοντα γὰρ τὰ Λαΐου παλαίφατα: quem sequitur Blaydes. Arndt., qui ipse παλαίφατα coniecerat, τὰ voci Λαΐου non praefixit, cum in v. 892 ἐν τοῖσδ' servaret.

Ζεῦ, μὴ λάθοι σε τῶνδ' ὃς αἴτιος κακῶν.   906 After φθίνοντα γὰρ Λαΐου we require a metrical equivalent for θεῶν βέλη in 893. The παλαιά in the marg. of L and in the text of other MSS. favours παλαίφατα, proposed by Linwood and Arndt, which suits φθίνοντα: cp. 561. Schneidewin conj. Πυθόχρηστα Λαΐου. Λαΐου, object. gen.: cp. Thuc. I. 140 τὸ τῶν Μεγαρέων ψήφισμα (about them).   908 ἐξαιροῦσιν, are putting out of account. This bold use comes, I think, not from the sense of destroying (Xen. Hellen. 2. 2. 19 μὴ σπένδεσθαι Ἀθηναίοις ἀλλ' ἐξαιρεῖν), but from that of setting aside, excluding from consideration: Plat. Soph. 249 B τούτῳ τῷ λόγῳ ταὐτὸν τοῦτο ἐκ τῶν ὄντων ἐξαιρήσομεν, by this reasoning we shall strike this same thing out of the list of things which exist. Cp. Theaet. 162 D θεούς...οὓς ἐγὼ ἔκ τε τοῦ λέγειν καὶ τοῦ γράφειν περὶ αὐτῶν, ὡς εἰσὶν ἢ ὡς οὐκ εἰσίν, ἐξαιρῶ. The absence of a gen. like λόγου for ἐξαιροῦσιν is softened by φθίνοντα, which suggests 'fading from men's thoughts.'   909 τιμαῖς...ἐμφανής, manifest in honours (modal dat.): i.e. his divinity is not asserted by the rendering of such worship as is due to him. Aesch. P. V. 171 (of Zeus) σκῆπτρον τιμάς τ' ἀποσυλᾶται.   910 τὰ θεῖα, 'religion,' both faith and observance: cp. O. C. 1537.

911—1085 ἐπεισόδιον τρίτον. A messenger from Corinth, bringing the news that Polybus is dead, discloses that Oedipus was not that king's son, but a Theban foundling, whom the messenger had received from a servant of Laïus. Iocasta, failing to arrest the inquiries of Oedipus, rushes from the scene with a cry.

911—923 Iocasta comes forth, bearing a branch (ἱκετηρία), wreathed with festoons of wool (στέφη), which, as a suppliant, she is about to lay on the altar of the household god, Apollo Λύκειος, in front of

ναοὺς ἱκέσθαι δαιμόνων, τάδ' ἐν χεροῖν
στέφη λαβούσῃ κἀπιθυμιάματα.
ὑψοῦ γὰρ αἴρει θυμὸν Οἰδίπους ἄγαν
λύπαισι παντοίαισιν· οὐδ' ὁποῖ' ἀνὴρ   915
ἔννους τὰ καινὰ τοῖς πάλαι τεκμαίρεται,
ἀλλ' ἐστὶ τοῦ λέγοντος, ἢν φόβους λέγῃ.
ὅτ' οὖν παραινοῦσ' οὐδὲν ἐς πλέον ποιῶ,
πρὸς σ', ὦ Λύκει' Ἄπολλον, ἄγχιστος γὰρ εἶ,
ἱκέτις ἀφῖγμαι τοῖσδε σὺν κατεύγμασιν,   920
ὅπως λύσιν τιν' ἡμὶν εὐαγῆ πόρῃς·
ὡς νῦν ὀκνοῦμεν πάντες ἐκπεπληγμένον
κεῖνον βλέποντες ὡς κυβερνήτην νεώς.

917 Ἡν φόβουσ λεγᴴ L, i.e. λέγῃ. Post λεγ facta est rasura. Potuit quidem prima manus λέγοι scribere, vel λέγει : nihil tamen superest quod aut hanc l. aut illam firmet. ἢν φόβους λέγῃ (sic) A: eadem lectio in B, E, V, ceteris, nisi

---

the palace. The state of Oedipus frightens her. His mind has been growing more and more excited. It is not that she herself has much fear for the future. What alarms her is to see 'the pilot of the ship' (923) thus unnerved. Though she can believe no longer in *human* μαντική, she has never ceased to revere the *gods* (708); and to them she turns for help in her need. **912** ναοὺς δαιμόνων can only mean the public temples of Thebes, as the two temples of Pallas and the Ἰσμήνιον (20). The thought had come to Iocasta that she should supplicate the gods; and in effect she does so by hastening to the altar which she can most quickly reach (919). **913** στέφη: see on 3. ἐπιθυμιάματα, offerings of incense : cp. 4. In *El.* 634, where Clytaemnestra comes forth to the altar of Apollo προστατήριος, an attendant carries θύματα πάγκαρπα, offerings of fruits of the earth. λαβούσῃ. λαβοῦσαν would have excluded a possible ambiguity, by showing that the δόξα had come before and not after the wreaths were taken up: and for this reason the accus. often stands in such a sentence: Xen. *An.* 3. 2. 1 ἔδοξεν αὐτοῖς προφυλακὰς καταστήσαντας συγκαλεῖν τοὺς στρατιώτας. **916** τὰ καινά, the prophecies of Teiresias, τοῖς πάλαι, by the miscarriage of the oracle from Delphi: 710 f. **917** τοῦ λέγοντος: Plat. *Gorg.* 508 D εἰμὶ δὲ ἐπὶ τῷ βουλομένῳ, ὥσπερ οἱ ἄτιμοι τοῦ ἐθέλοντος,

to visit the shrines of the gods, with this wreathed branch in my hands, and these gifts of incense. For Oedipus excites his soul overmuch with all manner of alarms, nor, like a man of sense, judges the new things by the old, but is at the will of the speaker, if he speak terrors.

Since, then, by counsel I can do no good, to thee, Lycean Apollo, for thou art nearest, I have come, a suppliant with these symbols of prayer, that thou mayest find us some riddance from uncleanness. For now we are all afraid, seeing *him* affrighted, even as they who see fear in the helmsman of their ship.

quod Γ λέγοι praebet. Quae cum ita sint, haud dubie suadent codd. ut ἦν...λέγῃ potius quam εἰ...λέγοι vel εἰ...λέγῃ legamus. **920** κατεύγμασιν codd.: κατάργμασιν Wunder., Hartung., Dindorf., Nauck., Blaydes.

ἄν τε τύπτειν βούληται, κ.τ.λ.—as outlaws are at the mercy of the first comer: *O. C.* 752 τοὐπιόντος ἁρπάσαι. ἦν φόβους λέγῃ has better MS. authority than εἰ λέγοι, and is also simpler: the latter would be an opt. like *Ai.* 520 ἀνδρί τοι χρεὼν (= χρὴ) | μνήμην προσεῖναι, τερπνὸν εἴ τί που πάθοι: cp. *ib.* 1344: *Ant.* 666. But the statement of abstract possibility is unsuitable here. εἰ...λέγῃ has still less to commend it. 918 ὅτε, seeing that, = ἐπειδή: Dem. *or.* 1 § 1 ὅτε τοίνυν οὕτως ἔχει: so ὑπότε Thuc. 2. 60. 919 Λύκει' Ἄπολλον: see on Λύκειε 203. 920 κατεύγμασιν, the prayers symbolised by the ἱκετηρία and offerings of incense. The word could not mean 'votive offerings.' Wunder's conject. κατάργμασιν, though ingenious, is neither needful nor really apposite. That word is used of (*a*) offerings of *first-fruits*, presented along with the εἰρεσιώνη or harvest-wreath, Plut. *Thes.* 22: (*b*) the οὐλοχύται or barley sprinkled on the altar and victim at the *beginning* of a sacrifice: Eur. *I. T.* 244 χέρνιβάς τε καὶ κατάργματα. 921 λύσιν...εὐαγῆ, a *solution without defilement:* i.e. some end to our anxieties, other than such an end as would be put to them by the fulfilment of the oracles dooming Oedipus to incur a fearful ἄγος. For εὐαγὴς λύσις as = one which will leave us εὐαγεῖς, cp. Pind. *Olymp.* 1. 26 καθαροῦ λέβητος, the vessel of cleansing. 923 ὡς κυβερνήτην νεώς, not ὡς (ὄντα) κυβερν. ν., *because* he is our pilot, but ὡς (ὀκνοῖμεν ἄν) βλέποντες κυβερν. ν. ἐκπεπληγμένον: Aesch. *Theb.* 2 ὅστις φυλάσσει πρᾶγος ἐν πρύμνῃ πόλεως | οἴακα νωμῶν, βλέφαρα

ΑΓΓΕΛΟΣ.

ἆρ' ἂν παρ' ὑμῶν, ὦ ξένοι, μάθοιμ' ὅπου
τὰ τοῦ τυράννου δώματ' ἐστὶν Οἰδίπου;   925
μάλιστα δ' αὐτὸν εἴπατ', εἰ κάτισθ' ὅπου.

ΧΟ. στέγαι μὲν αἵδε, καὐτὸς ἔνδον, ὦ ξένε·
γυνὴ δὲ μήτηρ ἥδε τῶν κείνου τέκνων.

ΑΓ. ἀλλ' ὀλβία τε καὶ ξὺν ὀλβίοις ἀεὶ
γένοιτ', ἐκείνου γ' οὖσα παντελὴς δάμαρ.   930

ΙΟ. αὕτως δὲ καὶ σύ γ', ὦ ξέν'· ἄξιος γὰρ εἶ
τῆς εὐεπείας οὕνεκ'. ἀλλὰ φράζ' ὅτου
χρῄζων ἀφῖξαι χὤ τι σημῆναι θέλων.

ΑΓ. ἀγαθὰ δόμοις τε καὶ πόσει τῷ σῷ, γύναι.

ΙΟ. τὰ ποῖα ταῦτα; πρὸς τίνος δ' ἀφιγμένος;   935

926 κάτισθ' A. κάτοισθ' L et codd. plerique. Hinc fortasse, ut Dindorfio
visum est, materiem sumpsit grammaticus in Bachmanni Anecd. vol. 2. p. 358. 20,
qui Sophoclem τὸ οἶσθε ἀπὸ τοῦ οἴδατε κατὰ συγκοπὴν usurpasse tradit.   933 χὤτι

μὴ κοιμῶν ὕπνῳ. 924 When the messenger arrives, Iocasta's prayer
seems to have been immediately answered by a λύσις εὐαγής (921), as
regards part at least of the threatened doom, though at the cost of the
oracle's credit. 926 μάλιστα denotes what stands *first* among one's
wishes: cp. 1466: *Trach.* 799 μάλιστα μέν με θὲς | ἐνταῦθ' ὅπου με
μή τις ὄψεται βροτῶν· | εἰ δ' οἶκτον ἴσχεις, κ.τ.λ.: *Phil.* 617 οἴοιτο μὲν
μάλισθ' ἑκούσιον λαβών, | εἰ μὴ θέλοι δ', ἄκοντα: *Ant.* 327 ἀλλ' εὑρεθείη
μὲν μάλιστ'· ἐὰν δέ τοι | ληφθῇ τε καὶ μή κ.τ.λ. 928 γυνὴ δὲ. Here, and
in 930, 950, the language is so chosen as to emphasise the conjugal
relation of Iocasta with Oedipus. 930 παντελής, because the wife's
estate is crowned and perfected by the birth of children (928). The
choice of the word has been influenced by the associations of τέλος,
τέλειος with marriage. Aesch. *Eum.* 835 θύη πρὸ παίδων καὶ γαμηλίου
τέλους (the marriage rite): *ib.* 214 Ἥρας τελείας καὶ Διὸς πιστώματα:
schol. on Ar. *Thesm.* 973 ἐτιμῶντο ἐν τοῖς γάμοις ὡς πρυτάνεις ὄντες τῶν
γάμων· τέλος δὲ ὁ γάμος: Pindar *Nem.* 10. 18 τελεία μήτηρ = Ἥρα,
who (Ar. *Th.* 976) κλῇδας γάμου φυλάττει. In Aesch. *Ag.* 972 ἀνὴρ
τέλειος = οἰκοδεσπότης: as δόμος ἡμιτελὴς (*Il.* 2. 700) refers to a house
left without its lord: cp. Lucian *Dial. Mort.* § 19 ἡμιτελῆ μὲν τὸν

MESSENGER.

ME. Might I learn from you, strangers, where is the house of the king Oedipus? Or, better still, tell me where he himself is—if ye know.

CH. This is his dwelling, and he himself, stranger, is within; and this lady is the mother of his children.

ME. Then may she be ever happy in a happy home, since she is his heaven-blest queen.

IO. Happiness to thee also, stranger! 'tis the due of thy fair greeting.—But say what thou hast come to seek or to tell.

ME. Good tidings, lady, for thy house and for thy husband.

IO. What are they? And from whom hast thou come?

dubitari non potest quin recte legatur, quanquam L (cum V et Pal.) χῶς τι habet, Γ autem καὶ τί. **935** πρὸσ L, quod tamen ex παρὰ fecit manus vel prima (ut mihi videtur) vel certe antiquissima; paullo recentior addidit δ' post τίνος. παρὰ L² et Pal.: πρὸς A et plerique.

δόμον καταλιπών, χήραν δὲ τὴν νεόγαμον γυναῖκα. **931** αὔτως (*Trach.* 1040 ὧδ' αὔτως ὥς μ' ὥλεσε) can be nothing but adverb from αὐτός (with Aeolic accent), = 'in that very way': hence, according to the context, (*a*) simply 'likewise,' or (*b*) in a depreciatory sense, 'only thus,'—*i.e.* 'inefficiently,' 'vainly.' The custom of the grammarians, to write αὔτως except when the sense is 'vainly,' seems to have come from associating the word with οὗτος, or possibly even with αὐτός. For Soph., as for Aesch. and Eur., our MSS. on the whole favour αὔτως: but their authority cannot be presumed to represent a tradition older than, or independent of, the grammarians. It is, indeed, possible that αὔτως was an instance of old aspiration on false analogy,—as the Attic ἡμεῖς (Aeolic ἄμμες for ἀσμές) was wrongly aspirated on the analogy of ὑμεῖς (see Peile, *Greek and Latin Etymology* p. 302, who agrees on this with Curtius). In the absence of evidence, however, that αὔτως was a like instance, it appears most reasonable to write αὔτως. **932** εὐεπείας, gracious words, = εὐφημίας, in this sense only here: elsewhere = elegance of diction: Isocrates τὴν εὐέπειαν ἐκ παντὸς διώκει καὶ τοῦ γλαφυρῶς λέγειν στοχάζεται μᾶλλον ἢ τοῦ ἀφελῶς (Dionys. *Isocr.* 538). **935** πρὸς τίνος, 'sent by whom,' bringing a message *on the part* of whom: while παρὰ τίνος would be simply 'from whom.' Had παρὰ been genuine, the less obvious πρὸς would not have been likely to supplant it in A and other MSS.

ΑΓ. ἐκ τῆς Κορίνθου. τὸ δ' ἔπος οὐξερῶ τάχα,
ἥδοιο μέν, πῶς δ' οὐκ ἄν; ἀσχάλλοις δ' ἴσως.

ΙΟ. τί δ' ἔστι; ποίαν δύναμιν ὧδ' ἔχει διπλῆν;

ΑΓ. τύραννον αὐτὸν οὐπιχώριοι χθονὸς
τῆς Ἰσθμίας στήσουσιν, ὡς ηὐδᾶτ' ἐκεῖ.   940

ΙΟ. τί δ'; οὐχ ὁ πρέσβυς Πόλυβος ἐγκρατὴς ἔτι;

ΑΓ. οὐ δῆτ', ἐπεί νιν θάνατος ἐν τάφοις ἔχει.

ΙΟ. πῶς εἶπας; ἦ τέθνηκε Πόλυβος, < ὦ > γέρον;

ΑΓ. εἰ μὴ λέγω τἀληθές, ἀξιῶ θανεῖν.

ΙΟ. ὦ πρόσπολ', οὐχὶ δεσπότῃ τάδ' ὡς τάχος   945
μολοῦσα λέξεις; ὦ θεῶν μαντεύματα,
ἵν' ἐστέ· τοῦτον Οἰδίπους πάλαι τρέμων
τὸν ἄνδρ' ἔφευγε μὴ κτάνοι, καὶ νῦν ὅδε
πρὸς τῆς τύχης ὄλωλεν οὐδὲ τοῦδ' ὕπο.

ΟΙ. ὦ φίλτατον γυναικὸς Ἰοκάστης κάρα,   950
τί μ' ἐξεπέμψω δεῦρο τῶνδε δωμάτων;

ΙΟ. ἄκουε τἀνδρὸς τοῦδε, καὶ σκόπει κλύων
τὰ σέμν' ἵν' ἥκει τοῦ θεοῦ μαντεύματα.

---

943 ἦ τέθνηκε Πόλυβος; ΑΓ. εἰ δὲ μὴ | λέγω γ' ἐγὼ τἀληθὲς L et A. Scripsit Triclinius, πῶς εἶπας; ἦ τέθνηκε Πόλυβος γέρων; | ΑΓ. εἰ μὴ λέγω τἀληθές κ.τ.λ. Qua coniectura paullum in melius flexa praebent codd. aliquot recentiores γέρον pro γέρων: nullus autem, quem quidem cognoverim, ὦ γέρον exhibet. Acceperant igitur librarii versum mutilum, πῶς εἶπας; ἦ τέθνηκε Πόλυβος; quem explere placuit aut versu 944 per ineptias distento, aut ratione Tricliniana. Potuit certe poeta ὦ γέρον scribere,

---

L, too, has προσ made from παρὰ by (as I think) the first hand itself; certainly by an early hand. Cp. *Od.* 8. 28 ἵκετ' ἐμὸν δῶ | ἠὲ πρὸς ἠοίων ἢ ἑσπερίων ἀνθρώπων. **936** τὸ δ' ἔπος, 'at the word,' accus. of the object which the feeling concerns: Eur. *El.* 831 τί χρῆμ' ἀθυμεῖς; **937** ἀσχάλλοις, from root σεχ, prop. 'not to hold oneself,' 'to be impatient,' the opposite of the notion expressed by σχο-λή (Curt. *Etym.* § 170): the word occurs in Her., Xen., Dem.; and in *Od.* 2. 193 replaces the epic ἀσχαλάαν. Cp. Aesch. *Ag.* 1049 πείθοι' ἄν, εἰ πείθοι', ἀπειθοίης δ' ἴσως. **941** ἐγκρατὴς = ἐν κράτει: cp. ἔναρχος = ἐν ἀρχῇ, in office, Appian *Bell. Civ.* 1. 14. **943** A defective verse, πῶς εἶπας; ἦ τέθνηκε Πόλυβος; has been patched up in our best MSS. by a clumsy expansion of the next verse (see crit. note). The γέρων supplied by Triclinius (whence some

ME. From Corinth : and at the message which I will speak anon thou wilt rejoice—doubtless ; yet haply grieve.

IO. And what is it? How hath it thus a double potency?

ME. The people will make him king of the Isthmian land, as 'twas said there.

IO. How then? Is the aged Polybus no more in power?

ME. No, verily: for death holds him in the tomb.

IO. How sayest thou? Is Polybus dead, old man?

ME. If I speak not the truth, I am content to die.

IO. O handmaid, away with all speed, and tell this to thy master! O ye oracles of the gods, where stand ye now! This is the man whom Oedipus long feared and shunned, lest he should slay him; and now this man hath died in the course of destiny, not by his hand. [*Enter* OEDIPUS.

OE. Iocasta, dearest wife, why hast thou summoned me forth from these doors?

IO. Hear this man, and judge, as thou listenest, to what the awful oracles of the gods have come.

vel ὦ ξένε. Mihi vero magis arridet Nauckii sententia, restituendum suspicantis πῶς εἶπας; ἢ τέθνηκεν Οἰδίπου πατήρ; Sed utinam vir eximius manum de tabula tollere voluisset, neve versum 944, qui sanus est, hunc in modum refingere; τέθνηκε Πόλυβος· εἰ δὲ μή, ἀξιῶ θανεῖν. Praeeunte Nauckio Dindorfius in Poet. Scenic. ed. v. dedit πῶς εἶπας; ἢ τέθνηκεν Οἰδίπου πατήρ; | ΑΓ. τέθνηκεν· εἰ δὲ μή, αὐτὸς ἀξιῶ θανεῖν. **950** ἡδίστης, quod praebent M et Δ, ineptae tantum coniecturae deberi videtur, ut μέλας pro μέγας in v. 742.

---

late MSS. have γέρον) was plainly a mere guess. Nauck's conj. ἢ τέθνηκεν Οἰδίπου πατήρ; is recommended (1) by the high probability of a gloss Πόλυβος on those words : (2) by the greater force which this form gives to the repetition of the question asked in 941: (3) by the dramatic effect for the spectators. **946** ὦ θεῶν μαντεύματα. Iocasta's scorn is pointed, not at the gods themselves, but at the μάντεις who profess to speak in their name. The gods are wise, but they grant no πρόνοια to men (978). Cp. 712. **947** ἵν' ἐστί: ἵνα as 367, 687, 953, 1311, 1515. O. C. 273 ἱκόμην ἵν' ἱκόμην. τοῦτον τὸν ἄνδρα...τρέμων ἔφευγε, he feared and avoided this man, μὴ κτάνοι (αὐτόν). **949** πρὸς τῆς τύχης, i.e. in the course of nature, and not by the special death which the oracle had foretold. Cp. 977. **951** ἐξέπεμψω, the midd. as in ἐκκαλεῖσθαι (see on 597), μεταπέμπεσθαι, etc., the act. being properly used

ΟΙ. οὗτος δὲ τίς ποτ᾽ ἐστὶ καὶ τί μοι λέγει;

ΙΟ. ἐκ τῆς Κορίνθου, πατέρα τὸν σὸν ἀγγελῶν   955
ὡς οὐκέτ᾽ ὄντα Πόλυβον, ἀλλ᾽ ὀλωλότα.

ΟΙ. τί φής, ξέν᾽; αὐτός μοι σὺ σημάντωρ γενοῦ.

ΑΓ. εἰ τοῦτο πρῶτον δεῖ μ᾽ ἀπαγγεῖλαι σαφῶς,
εὖ ἴσθ᾽ ἐκεῖνον θανάσιμον βεβηκότα.

ΟΙ. πότερα δόλοισιν, ἢ νόσου ξυναλλαγῇ;   960

ΑΓ. σμικρὰ παλαιὰ σώματ᾽ εὐνάζει ῥοπή.

ΟΙ. νόσοις ὁ τλήμων, ὡς ἔοικεν, ἔφθιτο.

ΑΓ. καὶ τῷ μακρῷ γε συμμετρούμενος χρόνῳ.

ΟΙ. φεῦ φεῦ, τί δῆτ᾽ ἄν, ὦ γύναι, σκοποῖτό τις
τὴν Πυθόμαντιν ἑστίαν, ἢ τοὺς ἄνω   965
κλάζοντας ὄρνις, ὧν ὑφηγητῶν ἐγὼ

957 σημάντωρ A et reliqui codd. fere omnes: est autem in B, Bodl. Laud. 54,
aliis gloss. μηνυτής. σημήνασ L a prima manu habuit, quod recentior in σημάντωρ
mutare voluit. Ascripsit antiquus corrector in margine γρ. σημάντωρ. Nulla prae-

---

of the summoner or escort: see on στελοῦντα (860). **954** τί μοι λέγει;
'what does he tell (of interest) for me?' (not 'what does he say to
me?': nor 'what, pray, does he say?'). **956** ὡς: see on 848. **957**
σημάντωρ is, I think, unquestionably right. A is among the MSS.
which have it, and in several it is explained by the gloss μηνυτής.
That the word was not unfamiliar to poetical language in the sense
('indicator,' 'informant') which it has here, may be inferred from *Anthol.*
6. 62 (Jacobs I. 205) κυκλοτερῆ μόλιβον, σελίδων σημάντορα πλευρῆς, the
pencil which makes notes in the margin of pages: Nonnus 37. 551
σημάντορι φωνῇ. On the other hand, σημήνας γενοῦ could mean nothing
but 'place yourself in the position of having told me,' and could only be
explained as a way of saying, 'tell me at once.' But such a use of γενέσθαι with aor. partic. would be unexampled. The only proper use of it
is made clear by such passages as these: *Ai.* 588 μὴ προδοὺς ἡμᾶς
γένῃ, do not make yourself guilty of having betrayed us: *Phil.* 772 μὴ
σαυτόν θ᾽ ἅμα | κἀμὲ...κτείνας γένῃ, do not make yourself guilty of having
slain both yourself and me. **959** εὖ ἴσθ᾽. Dionys. Hal. 1. 41 thus
quotes a verse from the Προμηθεὺς Λυόμενος of Aesch. (Nauck fr. 193. 2)
ἔνθ᾽ οὐ μάχης εὖ οἶδα καὶ θοῦρός περ ὤν, where Strabo p. 183 gives σάφ᾽
οἶδα: and so Pors. here would write σάφ᾽ ἴσθι. But the immediately

ΟΕ. And he—who may he be, and what news hath he for me?

Ιο. He is from Corinth, to tell that thy father Polybus lives no longer, but hath perished.

ΟΕ. How, stranger? Let me have it from thine own mouth.

ΜΕ. If I must first make these tidings plain, know indeed that he is dead and gone.

ΟΕ. By treachery, or by visit of disease?

ΜΕ. A light thing in the scale brings the aged to their rest.

ΟΕ. Ah, he died, it seems, of sickness?

ΜΕ. Yea, and of the long years that he had told.

ΟΕ. Alas, alas! Why, indeed, my wife, should one look to the hearth of the Pythian seer, or to the birds that scream above our heads, on whose showing I

terea nisi codicis Γ auctoritate firmari videtur lectio σημήνας, quam falsam esse mihi persuasum habeo: vide annot. **959** εὖ ἴσθ᾽ codd.: σάφ᾽ ἴσθ᾽ Porson., sed vide infra: κάτισθ᾽ Hartung.: ἔξισθ᾽ Meinekius.

---

preceding σαφῶς is decisive against this. Soph. had epic precedent, *Il.* I. 385 εὖ εἰδὼς ἀγόρευε, etc. Cp. 1071, ἰοὺ ἰού. θανάσιμον βεβηκότα: *Ai.* 516 μοῖρα… | καθεῖλεν Ἅιδου θανασίμους οἰκήτορας: *Ph.* 424 θανών…φροῦδος. **960** ξυναλλαγῇ: see on 34. **961** σμικρὰ ῥοπή, *leve momentum*: the life is conceived as resting in one scale of a nicely poised balance: in the other scale is that which sustains the life. Lessen this sustaining force ever so little, and the inclination (ῥοπή), though due to a slight cause (σμικρά), brings the life to the ground (εὐνάζει). Plat. *Rep.* 556 E ὥσπερ σῶμα νοσῶδες μικρᾶς ῥοπῆς ἔξωθεν δεῖται προσλαβέσθαι πρὸς τὸ κάμνειν,…οὕτω δὴ καὶ ἡ κατὰ ταὐτὰ ἐκείνῳ διακειμένη πόλις ἀπὸ σμικρᾶς προφάσεως…νοσεῖ. **963** Yes, he died of infirmities (νόσοις ἔφθιτο), and of the long years (τῷ μακρῷ χρόνῳ, causal dat.), in accordance with their term (συμμετρούμενος, *sc.* αὐτοῖς, lit. 'commensurably with them'): the part. being nearly equiv. to συμμέτρως, and expressing that, if his years are reckoned, his death cannot appear premature. Cp. 1113, and *Ant.* 387 ποία ξύμμετρος προύβην τύχῃ, 'seasonably for what hap?' **965** τὴν Πυθόμαντιν ἑστίαν = τὴν Πυθοῖ μαντικὴν ἑστίαν, as Apollo himself is Πυθόμαντις, *i.e.* ὁ Πυθοῖ μάντις, Aesch. *Cho.* 1030: cp. Πυθόκραντος, Πυθόχρηστος, Πυθόνικος. ἑστίαν, as *O. C.* 413 Δελφικῆς ἀφ᾽ ἑστίας: Eur. *Ion* 461 Φοιβήιος…γᾶς | μεσόμφαλος ἑστία. **966** κλάζοντας, the word used by Teiresias of the birds when

κτενεῖν ἔμελλον πατέρα τὸν ἐμόν; ὁ δὲ θανὼν
κεύθει κάτω δὴ γῆς· ἐγὼ δ' ὅδ' ἐνθάδε
ἄψαυστος ἔγχους· εἴ τι μὴ τὠμῷ πόθῳ
κατέφθιθ'· οὕτω δ' ἂν θανὼν εἴη 'ξ ἐμοῦ.   970
τὰ δ' οὖν παρόντα συλλαβὼν θεσπίσματα
κεῖται παρ' Ἅιδῃ Πόλυβος ἄξι' οὐδενός.

ΙΟ. οὔκουν ἐγώ σοι ταῦτα προὔλεγον πάλαι;
ΟΙ. ηὔδας· ἐγὼ δὲ τῷ φόβῳ παρηγόμην.
ΙΟ. μή νυν ἔτ' αὐτῶν μηδὲν ἐς θυμὸν βάλῃς.   975

967 κτανεῖν L, A, et ceteri fere omnes: in uno V² κτενεῖν vidi. κτενεῖν tamen cum Dindorfio verum esse duco: plura infra habes. **968** Post κάτω forte omiserat δὴ prima Laurentiani manus, ipsa vero supplevit. Cum autem A et ceteri δὴ ha-

their voice (φθόγγος) had *ceased* to be clear to him, *Ant.* 1001 κακῷ | κλάζοντας οἴστρῳ καὶ βεβαρβαρωμένῳ. **ὧν ὑφηγητῶν** sc. ὄντων, *quibus indicibus:* 1260 ὡς ὑφηγητοῦ τινος: *O. C.* 1588 ὑφηγητῆρος οὐδενὸς φίλων. In these instances the absence of the part. is softened by the noun which suggests the verb; but not so in *O. C.* 83 ὡς ἐμοῦ μόνης πέλας. **967 κτενεῖν.** κτανεῖν, which the MSS. give, cannot be pronounced positively wrong; but it can hardly be doubted that Soph. here wrote κτενεῖν. If κτανεῖν is right, it is the only aor. infin. after μέλλω in Soph., who has the fut. infin. 9 times (*El.* 359, 379, 538: *Ai.* 925, 1027, 1287: *Ant.* 458: *Phil.* 483, 1084): and the pres. infin. 9 times (*El.* 305, 1486: *Ai.* 443: *O. T.* 678, 1385: *O. C.* 1773: *Tr.* 79, 756: *Phil.* 409). Aeschylus certainly has the aor. in *P. V.* 625 μήτοι με κρύψῃς τοῦθ' ὅπερ μέλλω παθεῖν. Excluding the Laconic ἰδῆν in Ar. *Lys.* 117, there are but two instances in Comedy, *Av.* 366 τί μέλλετ'...ἀπολέσαι, and *Ach.* 1159 μέλλοντος λαβεῖν. Cp. W. G. Rutherford, *New Phrynichus* pp. 420—425, and Goodwin, *Greek Moods and Tenses* § 23. 2. The concurrence of tribrachs in the 4th and 5th places gives a semi-lyric character which suits the speaker's agitation. **968 κεύθει,** is hidden. *Ai.* 635 Ἅιδᾳ κεύθων. In *Tr.* 989 σιγῇ κεύθειν may be regarded as transitive with a suppressed acc., 'to shroud (thy thought) in silence.' Elsewhere κεύθω is always trans., and only the perf. κέκευθα intransitive. **δὴ** here nearly = ἤδη: cp. *Ant.* 170 ὅτ' οὖν ὤλοντο... | ἐγὼ κράτη δὴ...ἔχω. **969 ἄψαυστος** = οὐ ψαύσας: cp. ἀφόβητος 885 (with note): *Phil.* 688 ἀμφίπληκτα ῥόθια, billows beating around: *Tr.* 446

was doomed to slay my sire? But he is dead, and hid already
beneath the earth; and here am I, who have not put hand to
spear.—Unless, perchance, he was killed by longing for me:
thus, indeed, I should be the cause of his death. But the
oracles as they stand, at least, Polybus hath swept with him
to his rest in Hades: they are worth nought.

Io.   Nay, did I not so foretell to thee long since?

Oe.   Thou did'st: but I was misled by my fear.

Io.   Now no more lay aught of those things to heart.

beant, nulla de ea voce suspicio inde oriri debet quod deest in codd. Trin. et Γ.
Dindorfius, qui olim κάτωθεν coniecerat, iam κάτω δὴ reposuit. Coniecit Nauckius
κεύθει κάτω γῆς· Οἰδίπους δ'. Dedit autem ex coniectura Blaydesius κάτω κέκευθε γῆς.

μεμπτός, blaming: Eur. *Hec.* 1117 ὕποπτος, suspecting. Cp. note on
ἀτλητῶν 515. εἴ τι μή, an abrupt afterthought :—unless perchance : see
on 124. τὠμῷ πόθῳ: cp. 797 : *Od.* 11. 202 σὸς...πόθος, longing for
thee. 970 εἴη 'ξ: cp. 1075 : *Phil.* 467 πλεῖν μὴ 'ξ ἀπόπτου. ἐξ, as
dist. from ὑπό, is strictly in place here, as denoting the ultimate, not
the proximate, agency. 971 τὰ δ' οὖν παρόντα : but the oracles as they
stand, at any rate (δ' οὖν, 669, 834), Polybus has carried off with him,
proving them worthless (ἄξι' οὐδενός, tertiary predicate), and is hidden
with Hades. τὰ παρόντα, with emphasis : even supposing that they have
been fulfilled in some indirect and figurative sense, they certainly have
not been fulfilled to the letter. The oracle spoke of bloodshed (φονεύς,
794), and is not satisfied by κατέφθιτο ἐξ ἐμοῦ in the sense just explained.
συλλαβών is a contemptuous phrase from the language of common life :
its use is seen in Aristophanes *Plut.* 1079 νῦν δ' ἄπιθι χαίρων συλλαβὼν
τὴν μείρακα, now be off—with our blessing and the girl: *Av.* 1469
ἀπίωμεν ἡμεῖς συλλαβόντες τὰ πτερά, let us pack up our feathers and
be off: Soph. has it twice in utterances of angry scorn, *O. C.* 1383 σὺ
δ' ἔρρ' ἀπόπτυστός τε κἀπάτωρ ἐμοῦ | κακῶν κάκιστε, τάσδε συλλαβὼν
ἀράς, begone...and take these curses with thee: *Phil.* 577 ἔκπλει
σεαυτὸν συλλαβὼν ἐκ τῆσδε γῆς, 'hence in thy ship—pack from this
land!' 974 ηὔδας instead of προὔλεγες: see on 54. 975 νυν, enforcing the
argument introduced by οὔκουν (973), is clearly better than the weak νῦν.
ἐς θυμὸν βάλῃς: Her. 7. 51 ἐς θυμὸν βαλεῦ καὶ τὸ παλαιὸν ἔπος: 8. 68 καὶ
τόδε ἐς θυμὸν βαλεῦ, ὥς κ.τ.λ. 1. 84 ἰδὼν...τῶν τινα Λυδῶν καταβάντα...
ἐφράσθη καὶ ἐς θυμὸν ἐβάλετο. The active in the Βίος Ὁμήρου § 30 ἐς
θυμὸν ἔβαλε τὸ ῥηθέν. In *El.* 1347 οὐδέ γ' ἐς θυμὸν φέρω is not really

ΟΙ. καὶ πῶς τὸ μητρὸς λέκτρον οὐκ ὀκνεῖν με δεῖ;

ΙΟ. τί δ᾽ ἂν φοβοῖτ᾽ ἄνθρωπος, ᾧ τὰ τῆς τύχης
κρατεῖ, πρόνοια δ᾽ ἐστὶν οὐδενὸς σαφής;
εἰκῇ κράτιστον ζῆν, ὅπως δύναιτό τις.
σὺ δ᾽ εἰς τὰ μητρὸς μὴ φοβοῦ νυμφεύματα·   980
πολλοὶ γὰρ ἤδη κἀν ὀνείρασιν βροτῶν
μητρὶ ξυνευνάσθησαν. ἀλλὰ ταῦθ᾽ ὅτῳ
παρ᾽ οὐδέν ἐστι, ῥᾷστα τὸν βίον φέρει.

ΟΙ. καλῶς ἅπαντα ταῦτ᾽ ἂν ἐξείρητό σοι,
εἰ μὴ ᾽κύρει ζῶσ᾽ ἡ τεκοῦσα· νῦν δ᾽ ἐπεὶ   985
ζῇ, πᾶσ᾽ ἀνάγκη, κεἰ καλῶς λέγεις, ὀκνεῖν.

ΙΟ. καὶ μὴν μέγας γ᾽ ὀφθαλμὸς οἱ πατρὸς τάφοι.

976 λέχος οὐκ ὀκνεῖν με δεῖ L, ubi λέκτρον super λέχος corrector scripsit. λέκτρον οὐκ ὀκνεῖν με δεῖ A. Utramque lectionem codd. aliquot firmant: suadent tamen ῥυθμός et ordo verborum ut cod. A potius sequamur quam scribamus οὐκ ὀκνεῖν με δεῖ λέχος. **987** γε post μέγας in codd. deest omnibus. Cuius rei causam

---

similar. **977** ᾧ, 'for whom,' in relation to whom: not, 'in whose opinion.' τὰ τῆς τύχης is here somewhat more than a mere periphrasis for ἡ τύχη, since the plur. suggests successive incidents. τύχη does not here involve denial of a divine order in the government of the world, but only of man's power to comprehend or foresee its course. Cp. Thuc. 5. 104 πιστεύομεν τῇ μὲν τύχῃ ἐκ τοῦ θείου μὴ ἐλασσώσεσθαι. Lysias or. 24 § 22 οὐ μόνον μεταλαβεῖν ἡ τύχη μοι ἔδωκεν ἐν τῇ πατρίδι, the only privilege which Fortune (*i.e.* my destiny) has permitted me to enjoy in my country. **978** πρόνοια. Bentley on Phalaris (XVII, Dyce ii. 115) quotes Favorinus in Laertius *Plat.* § 24 as saying that Plato πρῶτος ἐν φιλοσοφίᾳ ...ὠνόμασε...θεοῦ πρόνοιαν. Bentley takes this to mean that Plato was the first to use πρόνοια of divine providence (not merely of human forethought), and cites it in proof that Phalaris *Ep.* 3 (= 40 Lennep) ἕως ἂν ἡ διοικοῦσα πρόνοια τὴν αὐτὴν ἁρμονίαν τοῦ κόσμου φυλάττῃ is later than Plato. Lennep, in his edition of Phalaris (p. 158), puts the case more exactly. The Stoics, not Plato, first used πρόνοια, *without further qualification*, of a divine providence. When Plato says τὴν τοῦ θεοῦ... πρόνοιαν (*Tim.* 30 C), προνοίας θεῶν (44 C), the phrase is no more than Herodotus had used before him, 3. 108 τοῦ θείου ἡ προνοίη. The meaning of Favorinus was that Plato first established in *philosophy* the conception of a divine providence, though popular language had known such a

ΟΕ. But surely I must needs fear my mother's bed?

ΙΟ. Nay, what should mortal fear, for whom the decrees of Fortune are supreme, and who hath clear foresight of nothing? 'Tis best to live at random, as one may. But fear not thou touching wedlock with thy mother. Many men ere now have so fared in dreams also : but he to whom these things are as nought bears his life most easily.

ΟΕ. All these bold words of thine would have been well, were not my mother living ; but as it is, since she lives, I must needs fear—though thou sayest well.

ΙΟ. Howbeit thy father's death is a great sign to cheer us.

fuisse suspicor, quod cum μέγας scriptum esset μετ́ (ut in A), alterum ρ́, tanquam errore duplicatum, delevit imperitus metri librarius. Restituit autem γε Porsonus, qui ad Eur. *Phoen.* v. 1638 haec dicit : 'Ita postulat metrum...idemque coniecit nescio quis in editione Londinensi a. 1746, sed neglexit Brunckius.'

---

phrase before. Note that in *O. C.* 1180 πρόνοια τοῦ θεοῦ = 'reverence for the god': in Eur. *Phoen.* 637 a man acts θείᾳ προνοίᾳ = 'with inspired foresight': in Xen. *Mem.* 1. 4. 6 προνοητικῶς = not, 'providentially,' but simply, 'with forethought.' **979 εἰκῇ**: cp. Plat. *Gorg.* 503 E οὐκ εἰκῇ ἐρεῖ, ἀλλ' ἀποβλέπων πρός τι (with some definite object in view). **κράτιστον...ὅπως δύναιτο.** Cp. *Ant.* 666 ἀλλ' ὃν πόλις στήσειε τοῦδε χρὴ κλύειν: where χρὴ κλύειν = δικαίως ἂν κλύοι. So here, though ἐστί (not ἦν) must be supplied with κράτιστον, the whole phrase = εἰκῇ κράτιστον ἄν τις ζῴη. Xen. *Cyr.* 1. 6. 19 τοῦ...αὐτὸν λέγειν ἃ μὴ σαφῶς εἰδείη φείδεσθαι δεῖ = ὀρθῶς ἂν φείδοιτο. **980 φοβοῦ.** φοβεῖσθαι ἔς τι = to have fears regarding it: *Tr.* 1211 εἰ φοβεῖ πρὸς τοῦτο: *O. C.* 1119 μὴ θαύμαζε πρὸς τὸ λιπαρές. **981 κἀν ὀνείρασιν**, in dreams *also* (as well as in this oracle); and, as such dreams have proved vain, so may this oracle. Soph. was prob. thinking of the story in Her. 6. 107 that Hippias had such a dream on the eve of the battle of Marathon, and interpreted it as an omen of his restoration to Athens. Cp. the story of a like dream coming to Julius Caesar on the night before he crossed the Rubicon (Plut. *Caes.* 32, Suet. 7). **983 παρ' οὐδέν**: *Ant.* 34 τὸ πρᾶγμ' ἄγειν | οὐχ ὡς παρ' οὐδέν. **984 ἐξείρητο**: the ἐξ- glances at her blunt expression of disbelief, not her frank reference to a horrible subject. **987 ὀφθαλμός**: the idea is that of a *bright, sudden comfort:* so *Tr.* 203 Deianeira calls on her household to rejoice, ὡς ἄελπτον ὄμμ' ἐμοὶ | φήμης ἀνασχὸν τῆσδε νῦν καρπούμεθα (the unexpected news that Heracles has returned). More often this image denotes the 'darling' of

ΟΙ. μέγας, ξυνίημ'· ἀλλὰ τῆς ζώσης φόβος.

ΑΓ. ποίας δὲ καὶ γυναικὸς ἐκφοβεῖσθ' ὕπερ;

ΟΙ. Μερόπης, γεραιέ, Πόλυβος ἧς ᾤκει μέτα.　　990

ΑΓ. τί δ' ἔστ' ἐκείνης ὑμὶν ἐς φόβον φέρον;

ΟΙ. θεήλατον μάντευμα δεινόν, ὦ ξένε.

ΑΓ. ἦ ῥητόν; ἢ οὐχὶ θεμιτὸν ἄλλον εἰδέναι;

ΟΙ. μάλιστά γ'· εἶπε γάρ με Λοξίας ποτὲ
　　χρῆναι μιγῆναι μητρὶ τἠμαυτοῦ, τό τε　　995
　　πατρῷον αἷμα χερσὶ ταῖς ἐμαῖς ἑλεῖν.
　　ὧν οὕνεχ' ἡ Κόρινθος ἐξ ἐμοῦ πάλαι

993 ἢ οὐ θεμιτὸν codd. omnes, quasi librariis hiatum inter ἢ et οὐ legitimum esse arbitrantibus: est tamen in cod. T superscriptum συνίζησις. Veram loci medicinam esse credo non quod Johnsonius proposuit, ἢ οὐ θεμιστὸν, sed quod Brunckius, ἢ οὐχὶ

a family (Aesch. *Cho.* 934 ὀφθαλμὸς οἴκων), or a dynasty that is 'the light' of a land (Σικελίας δ' ἔσαν | ὀφθαλμός, Pind. *Ol.* 2. 9: ὁ Βάττου παλαιὸς ὄλβος,...πύργος ἄστεος, ὄμμα τε φαεννότατον | ξένοισι, *Pyth.* 5. 51). Not *merely* (though this notion comes in) 'a great help to seeing' that oracles are idle (δήλωσις ὡς τὰ μαντεύματα κακῶς ἔχει, schol.). A certain hardness of feeling appears in the phrase: Iocasta was softened by fear for Oedipus and the State: she is now elated. **989** καὶ with ἐκφοβεῖσθε; 772, 851. **991** ἐκείνης, what is there *belonging to* her, *in* her (attributive gen.): Eur. *I. A.* 28 οὐκ ἄγαμαι ταῦτ' ἀνδρὸς ἀριστέως. ἐς φόβον φέρον, tending to fear: cp. 519. **992** θεήλατον, *sent upon us* by the gods: cp. 255. **993** The MSS. having οὐ θεμιτὸν, the question is between οὐχὶ θεμιτὸν and οὐ θεμιστὸν. The former is much more probable, since θεμιτός is the usual form, found in Attic prose, in Eur. (as *Or.* 97 σοὶ δ' οὐχὶ θεμιτόν), and in Soph. *O. C.* 1758 ἀλλ' οὐ θεμιτὸν κεῖσε μολεῖν. On the other hand θεμιστός is a rare poet. form, found once in Pindar (who has also θεμιτός), and twice in the lyrics of Aesch. Had we ἄλλῳ, the subject of θεμιτὸν would be μάντευμα: the accus. ἄλλον shows θεμιτὸν to be impersonal, as in Eur. *Or.* 97, Pind. *Pyth.* 9. 42 οὐ θεμιτὸν ψεύδει θιγεῖν. **996** τὸ πατρῷον αἷμα ἑλεῖν, is strictly 'to achieve (the shedding of) my father's blood.' Classical Greek had no such phrase as αἷμα χεῖν or ἐκχεῖν in the sense of 'to slay.' αἱρεῖν is to *make a prey of*, meaning 'to slay,' or 'to take,' according to the context (*Tr.* 353 Εὔρυτόν θ' ἕλοι | τὴν θ' ὑψίπυργον Οἰχαλίαν). Cp. fr. 726 ἀνδρὸς αἷμα συγγενὲς | κτείνας, which is even bolder than this, but similar, since here we might have had simply τὸν πατέρα ἑλεῖν, 'to *slay*

ΟΕ. Great, I know; but my fear is of her who lives.

ΜΕ. And who is the woman about whom ye fear?

ΟΕ. Meropè, old man, the consort of Polybus.

ΜΕ. And what is it in her that moves your fear?

ΟΕ. A heaven-sent oracle of dread import, stranger.

ΜΕ. Lawful, or unlawful, for another to know?

ΟΕ. Lawful, surely. Loxias once said that I was doomed to espouse mine own mother, and to shed with mine own hands my father's blood. Wherefore my home in Corinth was long

θεμιτὸν. Cum autem in Bodl. Laud. 54 ἄλλοις pro ἄλλον scriptum invenissem, venit mihi in mentem, ut cuivis poterat, ἢ οὐκ ἄλλοισι θεμιτὸν εἰδέναι; Prior in eandem coniecturam inciderat Blaydes.

---

my father': Eur. *Or.* 284 εἴργασται δ' ἐμοὶ | μητρῷον αἷμα, I have wrought the murder of a mother. **997** ἐξ ἐμοῦ, = 'on my part': ἡ Κόρινθος ἐξ ἐμοῦ μακρὰν ἀπῳκεῖτο = 'Corinth was inhabited by me at a great distance,' meaning, 'I took good care not to go near my old home at Corinth.' This implies as the corresponding active form, ἐγὼ μακρὰν ἀπῴκουν τὴν Κόρινθον, I inhabited Corinth (only) at a great distance, *i.e.* shunned inhabiting it at all: where the paradoxical use of ἀποικεῖν has been suggested by contrast with ἐνοικεῖν. The phrase is one of those which, instead of saying that a thing is *not done*, ironically represent it as *done* under a condition which precludes it; as here the condition expressed by ἀπό precludes the act described by οἰκεῖν. See below 1273 ἐν σκότῳ... | ὀψοίαθ'. Cp. *Ant.* 715 ὑπτίοις κάτω | στρέψας τὸ λοιπὸν σέλμασιν ναυτίλλεται, having upset his ship, he makes the rest of his voyage keel uppermost (*i.e.* his voyage comes to an abrupt end): *ib.* 310 ἵν' εἰδότες τὸ κέρδος ἔνθεν οἰστέον | τὸ λοιπὸν ἁρπά-ζητε: where εἰδότες means 'taught by capital punishment': *Ai.* 100 θανόντες ἤδη τἄμ' ἀφαιρείσθων ὅπλα. We must not, then, render: (1) 'Corinth was inhabited (by others) at a great distance from me': where ἐξ ἐμοῦ would be very harsh for ἀπ' ἐμοῦ. When ἐκ denotes distance from, it refers to *things* or *places*. Nor (2) 'Corinth was exchanged by me for a distant home,' as if this were the pass. of ἐγὼ ἀπῴκουν ἐκ τῆς Κορίνθου, 'migrated from': where both the use of the passive and the use of the imperf. tense would be incorrect. ἀποικεῖν is a comparatively rare word. Eur. has it twice (*H. F.* 557: *I. A.* 680: in both with gen., '*to dwell far from*'): Thuc. once with μακρὰν (3. 55) and Xen. once (*Oecon.* 4. 6),—both absol., as = '*to dwell afar*':

μακρὰν ἀπῳκεῖτ᾽· εὐτυχῶς μέν, ἀλλ᾽ ὅμως
τὰ τῶν τεκόντων ὄμμαθ᾽ ἥδιστον βλέπειν.

ΑΓ. ἦ γὰρ τάδ᾽ ὀκνῶν κεῖθεν ἦσθ᾽ ἀπόπτολις;   1000

ΟΙ. πατρός τε χρῄζων μὴ φονεὺς εἶναι, γέρον.

ΑΓ. τί δῆτ᾽ ἐγὼ οὐχὶ τοῦδε τοῦ φόβου σ᾽, ἄναξ,
ἐπείπερ εὔνους ἦλθον, ἐξελυσάμην;

ΟΙ. καὶ μὴν χάριν γ᾽ ἂν ἀξίαν λάβοις ἐμοῦ.

ΑΓ. καὶ μὴν μάλιστα τοῦτ᾽ ἀφικόμην, ὅπως   1005
σοῦ πρὸς δόμους ἐλθόντος εὖ πράξαιμί τι.

ΟΙ. ἀλλ᾽ οὔποτ᾽ εἶμι τοῖς φυτεύσασίν γ᾽ ὁμοῦ.

ΑΓ. ὦ παῖ, καλῶς εἶ δῆλος οὐκ εἰδὼς τί δρᾷς.

ΟΙ. πῶς, ὦ γεραιέ; πρὸς θεῶν δίδασκέ με.

ΑΓ. εἰ τῶνδε φεύγεις οὕνεκ᾽ εἰς οἴκους μολεῖν.   1010

ΟΙ. ταρβῶ γε μή μοι Φοῖβος ἐξέλθῃ σαφής.

ΑΓ. ἦ μὴ μίασμα τῶν φυτευσάντων λάβῃς;

ΟΙ. τοῦτ᾽ αὐτό, πρέσβυ, τοῦτό μ᾽ εἰσαεὶ φοβεῖ.

1001 πατρός τε codd.: πατρός γε Elmsleius, Blaydes., secundum Hermanni coniecturam, quam ipsius δεύτεραι φροντίδες improbaverant. 1002 ἔγωγ᾽ οὐ L,
eraso χὶ post οὐ: ἔγωγ᾽ οὐχὶ A, V, Bodl. Laud. 54: ἔγωγ᾽ οὐ reliqui codd. fere omnes,

as prob. Theocr. 15. 7 (reading ὦ μέλ᾽ ἀποικεῖς with Meineke): Plato
once thus (*Legg.* 753 A), and twice as = to *emigrate* (ἐκ Γόρτυνος, *Legg.*
708 A, ἐς Θουρίους, *Euthyd.* 271 c): in which sense Isocr. also has it
twice (or. 4 § 122, or. 6 § 84): Pindar once (with accus. of motion to a
place), *Pyth.* 4. 258 Καλλίσταν ἀπῴκησαν, they went and settled at Callista.
998 εὐτυχῶς, because of his high fortunes at Thebes. 999 τῶν τεκόντων = τῶν
γονέων: Eur. *Hipp.* 1081 τοὺς τεκόντας ὅσια δρᾶν, and oft.: cp. *H. F.* 975
βοᾷ δὲ μήτηρ, ὦ τεκών [= ὦ πάτερ], τί δρᾷς; 1000 ἀπόπτολις, exile, as *O. C.*
208. 1001 πατρός τε. So the mss., rightly. It is the fear of Oed. regarding
his *mother* by which the messenger's attention has been fixed. In explaining this, Oed. has indeed mentioned the other fear as to his father:
but in v. 1000, ἦ γὰρ τάδ᾽ ὀκνῶν, the messenger means: 'So this, then,
was the fear about her which kept you away?'—alluding to his own
question in 991. As the speaker's tone seems to make light of the
cause, Oed. answers, '*and* that further dread about my father which I
mentioned.' πατρός γε is unsuitable, since it would imply that this was
his *sole* fear. 1002 ἐγὼ οὐχὶ: synizesis, as *Ph.* 551 ἐγώ εἰμι, *O. C.* 998

kept by me afar; with happy event, indeed,—yet still 'tis sweet to see the face of parents.

ME. Was it indeed for fear of this that thou wast an exile from that city?

OE. And because I wished not, old man, to be the slayer of my sire.

ME. Then why did I not free thee, king, from this fear, seeing that I came with friendly purpose?

OE. Indeed thou should'st have guerdon due from me.

ME. Indeed 'twas chiefly for this that I came—that, on thy return home, I might reap some good.

OE. Nay, I will never go near my parents.

ME. Ah my son, 'tis plain enough that thou knowest not what thou doest.

OE. How, old sir? For the gods' love, tell me.

ME. If for these reasons thou shrinkest from going home.

OE. Aye, I dread lest Phoebus prove himself true for me.

ME. Thou dreadest to be stained with guilt through thy parents?

OE. Even so, old man—this it is that ever affrights me.

Brunckius: ἐγὼ οὐχὶ coniecit Porsonus, receperunt edd. plerique. Si ἔγωγ' οὐ genuina lectio fuisset, vix transiturum erat οὐ in οὐχὶ: contra, si οὐχὶ in οὐ semel corrupissent librarii, facillime poterat ἐγὼ in ἔγωγε mutari. **1011** ταρβῶ L, A, codd. reliqui fere omnes: ταρβῶν Erfurdt., Vat. a, c.

ἐγὼ οὐδέ, and *El.* 1281: *Ant.* 458 ἐγὼ οὐκ. **1004** καὶ μὴν, properly 'however'; here, like our 'well indeed' (if you *would* do so). The echoing καὶ μὴν of 1005 expresses eager assent. Cp. *Ant.* 221. **1005** τοῦτ' ἀφικόμην: see on 788. **1008** καλῶς, *pulchre, belle,* thoroughly,—a colloquialism, perh. meant here to be a trait of homely speech: cp. Alciphron *Ep.* 1. 36 πεινήσω τὸ καλόν ('I shall be fine and hungry'): Aelian *Ep.* 2 ἐπέκοψε τὸ σκέλος πάνυ χρηστῶς ('in good style'). **1011** With Erfurdt I think that ταρβῶν is right; not that ταρβῶ could not stand, but Greek idiom distinctly favours the participle. *Ant.* 403 ΚΡ. ἦ καὶ ξυνίης καὶ λέγεις ὀρθῶς ἃ φῄς; ΦΥ. ταύτην γ' ἰδὼν θάπτουσαν. *ib.* 517 ΑΝ....ἀδελφὸς ὤλετο. ΚΡ. πορθῶν γε τήνδε γῆν. Plat. *Symp.* 164 E εἶπον οὖν ὅτι... ἤκοιμι.—καλῶς (*v. l.* καλῶς γ'), ἔφη, ποιῶν. Cp. 1130 ξυναλλάξας. ἐξέλθῃ: cp. 1182 ἐξήκοι σαφῆ, come true. **1013** Cp. *Tr.* 408 τοῦτ' αὖτ'

188 ΣΟΦΟΚΛΕΟΥΣ

ΑΓ. ἆρ' οἶσθα δῆτα πρὸς δίκης οὐδὲν τρέμων;

ΟΙ. πῶς δ' οὐχί, παῖς γ' εἰ τῶνδε γεννητῶν ἔφυν; 1015

ΑΓ. ὁθούνεκ' ἦν σοι Πόλυβος οὐδὲν ἐν γένει.

ΟΙ. πῶς εἶπας; οὐ γὰρ Πόλυβος ἐξέφυσέ με;

ΑΓ. οὐ μᾶλλον οὐδὲν τοῦδε τἀνδρός, ἀλλ' ἴσον.

ΟΙ. καὶ πῶς ὁ φύσας ἐξ ἴσου τῷ μηδενί;

ΑΓ. ἀλλ' οὔ σ' ἐγείνατ' οὔτ' ἐκεῖνος οὔτ' ἐγώ. 1020

ΟΙ. ἀλλ' ἀντὶ τοῦ δὴ παῖδά μ' ὠνομάζετο;

ΑΓ. δῶρόν ποτ', ἴσθι, τῶν ἐμῶν χειρῶν λαβών.

ΟΙ. κᾆθ' ὧδ' ἀπ' ἄλλης χειρὸς ἔστερξεν μέγα;

ΑΓ. ἡ γὰρ πρὶν αὐτὸν ἐξέπεισ' ἀπαιδία.

ΟΙ. σὺ δ' ἐμπολήσας ἢ τυχών μ' αὐτῷ δίδως; 1025

ΑΓ. εὑρὼν ναπαίαις ἐν Κιθαιρῶνος πτυχαῖς.

ΟΙ. ὡδοιπόρεις δὲ πρὸς τί τούσδε τοὺς τόπους;

ΑΓ. ἐνταῦθ' ὀρείοις ποιμνίοις ἐπεστάτουν.

ΟΙ. ποιμὴν γὰρ ἦσθα κἀπὶ θητείᾳ πλάνης;

1025 τεκών codd. Coniecturam procul dubio veram τυχών, quam Bothio Dindorfius, Foertschio Hermannus tribuit, receperunt Herm., Dind., Nauck., Blaydes.

ἔχρηζον, τοῦτό σου μαθεῖν. **1014 πρὸς δίκης**, as justice would prompt, 'justly.' πρὸς prop. = 'from the quarter of,' then 'on the side of': Thuc. 3. 59 οὐ πρὸς τῆς ὑμετέρας δόξης...τάδε, not in the interest of your reputation: Plat. *Gorg.* 459 c ἐάν τι ἡμῖν πρὸς λόγου ᾖ, 'if it is in the interest of our discussion.' *Rep.* 470 c οὐδὲν...ἀπὸ τρόπου λέγεις· ὅρα δὴ καὶ εἰ τόδε πρὸς τρόπου λέγω, 'correctly.' Theophr. *Char.* 30 (= 26 in my 1st ed. p. 156) πρὸς τρόπου πωλεῖν, to sell on reasonable terms. **1016 ἐν γένει**: [Dem.] or. 47 § 70 οὐκ ἔστιν ἐν γένει σοι ἡ ἄνθρωπος, compared with § 72 ἐμοὶ δὲ οὔτε γένει προσῆκεν. **1019 τῷ μηδενί**, dat. of ὁ μηδείς, he who is as if he were not (in respect of consanguinity with me): *Ant.* 1325 τὸν οὐκ ὄντα μᾶλλον ἢ μηδένα. **1023 ἀπ' ἄλλης χειρὸς** sc. λαβών. **1025 ἐμπολήσας...ἢ τυχών**: i.e. 'Did you buy me, or did you light upon me yourself in the neighbourhood of Corinth?' Oed. is not prepared for the Corinthian's reply that he had found the babe on *Cithaeron*. ἐμπολήσας: cp. the story of Eumaeus (*Od.* 15. 403—483) who, when a babe, was carried off by Phoenician merchants from the wealthy house of his father in the isle Syria, and sold to

ΜΕ. Dost thou know, then, that thy fears are wholly vain?

ΟΕ. How so, if I was born of those parents?

ΜΕ. Because Polybus was nothing to thee in blood.

ΟΕ. What sayest thou? Was Polybus not my sire?

ΜΕ. No more than he who speaks to thee, but just so much.

ΟΕ. And how can my sire be level with him who is as nought to me?

ΜΕ. Nay, he begat thee not, any more than I.

ΟΕ. Nay, wherefore, then, called he me his son?

ΜΕ. Know that he had received thee as a gift from my hands of yore.

ΟΕ. And yet he loved me so dearly, who came from another's hand?

ΜΕ. Yea, his former childlessness won him thereto.

ΟΕ. And thou—had'st thou bought me or found me by chance, when thou gavest me to him?

ΜΕ. Found thee in Cithaeron's winding glens.

ΟΕ. And wherefore wast thou roaming in those regions?

ΜΕ. I was there in charge of mountain flocks.

ΟΕ. What, thou wast a shepherd—a vagrant hireling?

Laertes in Ithaca: the Phoenician nurse says to the merchants, τόν κεν ἄγοιμ' ἐπὶ νηός, ὁ δ' ὑμῖν μυρίον ὦνον | ἄλφοι, ὅπῃ περάσητε κατ' ἀλλοθρόους ἀνθρώπους. τυχών is answered by εὑρών (1026) as in 973 προὔλεγον by ηὔδας. Cp. 1039. The τεκών of the mss. is absurd after vv. 1016— 1020. The man has just said, 'Polybus was no more your father than I am'; Oed. is anxiously listening to every word. He could not ask. a moment later, 'Had you bought me, or *were you my father?*' 1025 The fitness of the phrase ναπαίαις πτυχαῖς becomes vivid to anyone who traverses Cithaeron by the road ascending from Eleusis and winding upwards to the pass of Dryoscephalae, whence it descends into the plain of Thebes. 1029 ἐπὶ θητείᾳ, like ἐπὶ μισθῷ Her. 5. 65 etc. θητεία, labour for wages, opp. to δουλεία: Isocr. or. 14 § 48 πολλοὺς μὲν ...δουλεύοντας, ἄλλους δ' ἐπὶ θητείαν ἰόντας. πλάνης, roving in search of any employment that he can find (not merely changing summer for winter pastures, 1137). The word falls lightly from him who is so

ΑΓ. σοῦ δ᾽, ὦ τέκνον, σωτήρ γε τῷ τότ᾽ ἐν χρόνῳ. 1030
ΟΙ. τί δ᾽ ἄλγος ἴσχοντ᾽ †ἐν κακοῖς† με λαμβάνεις;
ΑΓ. ποδῶν ἂν ἄρθρα μαρτυρήσειεν τὰ σά.
ΟΙ. οἴμοι, τί τοῦτ᾽ ἀρχαῖον ἐννέπεις κακόν;
ΑΓ. λύω σ᾽ ἔχοντα διατόρους ποδοῖν ἀκμάς.
ΟΙ. δεινόν γ᾽ ὄνειδος σπαργάνων ἀνειλόμην. 1035
ΑΓ. ὥστ᾽ ὠνομάσθης ἐκ τύχης ταύτης ὃς εἶ.
ΟΙ. ὦ πρὸς θεῶν, πρὸς μητρός, ἢ πατρός; φράσον.
ΑΓ. οὐκ οἶδ᾽· ὁ δοὺς δὲ ταῦτ᾽ ἐμοῦ λῷον φρονεῖ.
ΟΙ. ἦ γὰρ παρ᾽ ἄλλου μ᾽ ἔλαβες οὐδ᾽ αὐτὸς τυχών;

1030 σοῦ δ᾽...σωτήρ γε cum uno cod. Flor. Abb. 152 (Γ) recte probaverunt Elmsleius, Dindorf., Wunder., Campbell. L et ceteri codd. σοῦ γ᾽...σωτήρ γε habent, quod tuentur Brunck., Hermann., Blaydes. Quod Nauckius dare maluit, σοῦ τ᾽...σωτήρ γε, hebetat aciem responsi quo senex regem superbius interrogantem leniter perstringit. 1031 ἐν κακοῖς με λαμβάνεις A et plerique (omisso in duobus codd. Mediolanensibus με): ἐν καιροῖσ με λαμβάνεις L, ἐν καιροῖσ λαμβάνεις Pal. Mirum sane foret si a

soon to be ὁ πλανήτης Οἰδίπους (*O. C.* 3). 1030 σοῦ δ᾽. With the σοῦ γ᾽ of most MSS.: 'Yes, and thy *preserver*' (the first γε belonging to the sentence, the second to σωτήρ). Cp. Her. 1. 187. μὴ μέντοι γε μὴ σπανίσας γε ἄλλως ἀνοίξῃ: where the second γε belongs to σπανίσας. There is no certain example of a double γε in Soph. which is really similar. With σοῦ δ᾽: '*But* thy *preserver*': the γε still belonging to σωτήρ, and δὲ opposing this thought to that of v. 1029. For δέ γε cp. Aesch. *Ag.* 938 ΑΓ. φήμη γε μέντοι δημόθρους μέγα σθένει. ΚΛ. ὁ δ᾽ ἀφθόνητός γ᾽ οὐκ ἐπίζηλος πέλει. 'True, but....' The gentle reproof conveyed by δέ γε is not unfitting in the old man's mouth: and a double γε, though admissible, is awkward here. 1031 τί δ᾽ ἄλγος κ.τ.λ. And in what sense wert thou my σωτήρ? The ἐν κακοῖς of most MSS. is intolerably weak: '*what pain* was I suffering when you found me *in trouble*?' From the ἐν καιροῖσ of L and another good MS. (a most unlikely corruption of so familiar a word as κακοῖς), I conjecture ἐγκυρῶν, 'when you lighted on me': cp. 1026, 1039. Soph. has that verb in *El.* 863 τμητοῖς ὁλκοῖς ἐγκῦρσαι (meet with). 1035 σπαργάνων, '*from* my swaddling clothes': i.e. 'from the earliest days of infancy' (cp. Ovid *Heroid.* 9. 22 *Et tener* in cunis *iam Iove dignus eras*). The babe was exposed a few days after birth (717). *El.* 1139 οὔτε...πυρὸς | ἀνειλόμην...ἄθλιον βάρος. Some understand, 'I was furnished with cruelly dishonouring *tokens of my birth*,' δεινῶς ἐπονείδιστα

ME. But thy preserver, my son, in that hour.

OE. And what pain was mine when thou foundest me in distress?

ME. The ankles of thy feet might witness.

OE. Ah me, why dost thou speak of that old trouble?

ME. I freed thee when thou had'st thine ankles pinned together.

OE. Aye, 'twas a dread brand of shame that I took from my cradle.

ME. Such, that from that fortune thou wast called by the name which still is thine.

OE. Oh, for the gods' love—was the deed my mother's or father's? Speak!

ME. I know not; he who gave thee to me wots better of that than I.

OE. What, thou had'st me from another? Thou did'st not light on me thyself?

vera lectione κακοῖς falsa sed exquisita καιροῖς, metro eadem repugnans, in optimo codice extitisset. Immo ipsum illud ἐν καιροῖς vulneris est antiqui cicatrix. Restituendum credo ἐγκυρῶν με λαμβάνεις: cf. τυχών in vv. 1025, 1039. Vulgata quidem l. ἐν κακοῖς hic magis languet quam ut ferri possit. Coniecit ἐν καλῷ Wunder., ἐν σκάφαισι ('in cunis,' omisso με) Nauck., ἢ κακόν Blaydes., ἐν νάπαις Dindorf.

σπάργανα, alluding to a custom of tying round the necks of children, when they were exposed, little tokens or ornaments, which might afterwards serve as means of recognition (*crepundia, monumenta*): see esp. Plautus *Rudens* 4. 4. 111—126, *Epidicus* 5. 1. 34: and Rich *s. v. Crepundia*, where a wood-cut shows a statue of a child with a string of *crepundia* hung over the right shoulder. Plut. *Thes.* 4 calls such tokens γνωρίσματα. In Ar. *Ach.* 431 the σπάργανα of Telephus have been explained as the tokens by which (in the play of Eur.) he was recognised; in his case, these were ῥακώματα (431). But here we must surely take σπαργάνων with ἀνειλόμην. **1036** ὥστε assents and continues: '(yes,) and so...' ὃς εἶ, *i.e.* Οἰδίπους: see on 718. **1037** πρὸς μητρός, ἢ πατρός; *sc.* ὄνειδος ἀνειλόμην (1035): 'was it at the hands of mother or father (rather than at those of strangers) that I received such a brand?' The agitated speaker follows the train of his own thoughts, scarcely heeding the interposed remark. He is not thinking so much of his parents' possible cruelty, as of a fresh clue to their identity. Not: 'was I so named by mother or father?' The *name*—even if it could be con-

ΑΓ. οὔκ, ἀλλὰ ποιμὴν ἄλλος ἐκδίδωσί μοι.   1040
ΟΙ. τίς οὗτος; ἢ κάτοισθα δηλῶσαι λόγῳ;
ΑΓ. τῶν Λαΐου δήπου τις ὠνομάζετο.
ΟΙ. ἦ τοῦ τυράννου τῆσδε γῆς πάλαι ποτέ;
ΑΓ. μάλιστα· τούτου τἀνδρὸς οὗτος ἦν βοτήρ.
ΟΙ. ἦ κἄστ᾽ ἔτι ζῶν οὗτος, ὥστ᾽ ἰδεῖν ἐμέ;   1045
ΑΓ. ὑμεῖς γ᾽ ἄριστ᾽ εἰδεῖτ᾽ ἂν οὑπιχώριοι.
ΟΙ. ἔστιν τις ὑμῶν τῶν παρεστώτων πέλας
    ὅστις κάτοιδε τὸν βοτῆρ᾽ ὃν ἐννέπει,
    εἴτ᾽ οὖν ἐπ᾽ ἀγρῶν εἴτε κἀνθάδ᾽ εἰσιδών;
    σημήναθ᾽, ὡς ὁ καιρὸς εὑρῆσθαι τάδε.   1050
ΧΟ. οἶμαι μὲν οὐδέν᾽ ἄλλον ἢ τὸν ἐξ ἀγρῶν,
    ὃν κἀμάτευες πρόσθεν εἰσιδεῖν· ἀτὰρ
    ἥδ᾽ ἂν τάδ᾽ οὐχ ἥκιστ᾽ ἂν Ἰοκάστη λέγοι.
ΟΙ. γύναι, νοεῖς ἐκεῖνον ὅντιν᾽ ἀρτίως
    μολεῖν ἐφιέμεσθα; τόνδ᾽ οὗτος λέγει;   1055
ΙΟ. τί δ᾽ ὅντιν᾽ εἶπε; μηδὲν ἐντραπῇς. τὰ δὲ
    ῥηθέντα βούλου μηδὲ μεμνῆσθαι μάτην.

1055 μολεῖν ἐφιέμεσθα τόν θ᾽ οὗτος λέγει; L, A, et codd. plerique, cum τόν θ᾽ illud tanquam pro ὅν θ᾽ dictum librarii acciperent. Itaque super τόν scriptum est in cod. B ὅντινα, in Bodl. Laud. 54 ὅν. Veram l. τόνδ᾽ tres saltem codd. praebent (M,

---

ceived as given before the exposure—is not the sting; and on the other hand it would be forced to take '*named*' as meaning '*doomed to bear* the name.' 1044 βοτήρ: cp. 837, 761. 1046 εἰδεῖτ᾽ = εἰδείητε, only here, it seems: but cp. εἴτε = εἴητε *Od.* 21. 195 (doubtful in *Ant.* 215). εἰδεῖμεν and εἶμεν occur in Plato (*Rep.* 581 E, *Theaet.* 147 A) as well as in verse. In Dem. or. 14 § 27 καταθεῖτε is not certain (κατάθοιτε Baiter and Sauppe): in or. 18 § 324 he has ἐνθείητε. Speaking generally, we may say that the contracted termination -εῖεν for -είησαν is common to poetry and prose; while the corresponding contractions, -εῖμεν for -είημεν and -εῖτε for εἴητε, are rare except in poetry. 1049 οὖν with the *first* εἴτε, as *El.* 199, 560: it stands with the second above, 90, 271, *Ph.* 345. ἐπ᾽ ἀγρῶν: *Od.* 22. 47 πολλὰ μὲν ἐν μεγάροισιν...πολλὰ δ᾽ ἐπ᾽ ἀγροῦ: (cp. *O. C.* 184 ἐπὶ ξένης, *El.* 1136 κἀπὶ γῆς ἄλλης :) the usual Attic phrase was ἐν ἀγρῷ or κατ᾽ ἀγρούς. 1050 ὁ καιρὸς : for the art., cp. [Plat.] *Axiochus* 364 B νῦν ὁ καιρὸς ἐνδείξασθαι τὴν ἀεὶ θρυλουμένην πρὸς

ME. No : another shepherd gave thee up to me.

OE. Who was he ? Art thou in case to tell clearly ?

ME. I think he was called one of the household of Laïus.

OE. The king who ruled this country long ago ?

ME. The same : 'twas in his service that the man was a herd.

OE. Is he still alive, that I might see him ?

ME. Nay, ye folk of the country should know best.

OE. Is there any of you here present that knows the herd of whom he speaks—that hath seen him in the pastures or the town ? Answer ! The hour hath come that these things should be finally revealed.

CH. Methinks he speaks of no other than the peasant whom thou wast already fain to see ; but our lady Iocasta might best tell that.

OE. Lady, wottest thou of him whom we lately summoned ? Is it of him that this man speaks ?

IO. Why ask of whom he spoke ? Regard it not...waste not a thought on what he said...'twere idle.

M² a pr. manu, Δ) ; cod. autem Par. 2884 (E), cui τόνδ' dubitanter imputatum video, τὸν θ' habet.

σοῦ σοφίαν. εὑρῆσθαι: the perf. = 'discovered once for all.' Isocr. or. 15 § 295 τῶν δυναμένων λέγειν ἢ παιδεύειν ἡ πόλις ἡμῶν δοκεῖ γεγενῆσθαι διδάσκαλος, to be the *established* teacher. 1051 Supply ἐννέπειν (αὐτόν), not ἐννέπει. The form οἶμαι, though often parenthetic (as *Trach.* 536), is not less common with infin. (Plat. *Gorg.* 474 A οἶον ἐγὼ οἶμαι δεῖν εἶναι), and Soph. often so has it, as *El.* 1446. 1053 ἄν...ἄν: see on 862. 1054 νοεῖς = 'you wot of,' the man—*i.e.* you understand to whom I refer. We need not, then, write εἰ κεῖνον for ἐκεῖνον with A. Spengel, or νοεῖς; ἐκεῖνον with Blaydes, who in 1055, reading τόνδ', has a comma at ἐφιέμεσθα. Cp. 859. 1055 τόνδ' is certainly right : τὸν θ' arose, when the right punctuation had been lost, from a desire to connect λέγει with ἐφιέμεσθα. Dindorf, however, would keep τὸν θ' : 'know ye him whom we summoned *and* him of whom this man speaks?' *i.e.* 'Can you say whether the persons are identical or distinct ?' But the language will not bear this. 1056 τί δ' ὄντιν' εἶπε; Aesch. *P. V.* 765 θέορτον ἢ βρότειον [γάμον γαμεῖ] ; εἰ ῥητόν, φράσον. ΠΡ. τί δ' ὄντιν'; Ar. *Av.* 997 σὺ δ' εἶ τίς ἀνδρῶν; Μ. ὅστις εἰμ' ἐγώ; Μέτων. Plat. *Euthyphr.*

J. S.   13

ΟΙ. οὐκ ἂν γένοιτο τοῦθ᾽, ὅπως ἐγὼ λαβὼν
σημεῖα τοιαῦτ᾽ οὐ φανῶ τοὐμὸν γένος.

ΙΟ. μὴ πρὸς θεῶν, εἴπερ τι τοῦ σαυτοῦ βίου   1060
κήδει, ματεύσῃς τοῦθ᾽· ἅλις νοσοῦσ᾽ ἐγώ.

ΟΙ. θάρσει· σὺ μὲν γὰρ οὐδ᾽ ἐὰν τρίτης ἐγὼ
μητρὸς φανῶ τρίδουλος ἐκφανεῖ κακή.

ΙΟ. ὅμως πιθοῦ μοι, λίσσομαι· μὴ δρᾶ τάδε.

ΟΙ. οὐκ ἂν πιθοίμην μὴ οὐ τάδ᾽ ἐκμαθεῖν σαφῶς.   1065

ΙΟ. καὶ μὴν φρονοῦσά γ᾽ εὖ τὰ λῷστά σοι λέγω.

ΟΙ. τὰ λῷστα τοίνυν ταῦτά μ᾽ ἀλγύνει πάλαι.

ΙΟ. ὦ δύσποτμ᾽, εἴθε μήποτε γνοίης ὃς εἶ.

ΟΙ. ἄξει τις ἐλθὼν δεῦρο τὸν βοτῆρά μοι;
ταύτην δ᾽ ἐᾶτε πλουσίῳ χαίρειν γένει.   1070

1061 νοσοῦσ᾽ ἔχω consensu satis mirabili codd. praebent omnes, uno excepto, ut
videtur, codice quodam Chigiano, de quo nihil praeterea compertum habeo quam
quod scripsit Dindorfius (ed. 1860): 'ἐγώ ex scholiasta et apographo Chigiano apud
Schowium in libro de charta papyracea Borgiana restitutum pro ἔχω': idem vero in
Poet. Scenic. ed. quinta (1869), nulla cod. Chigiani mentione facta, soli scholiastae
hanc l. tribuit.   1062 οὐδ᾽ ἂν ἐκ τρίτης codd.: in L vocis ἂν accentus a prima
manu, spiritus a recentiore venit.   Primam Hermanni coniecturam, οὐδ᾽ ἐὰν τρίτης,

2 B τίνα γραφήν σε γέγραπται; ΣΩ. ἥντινα; οὐκ ἀγεννῆ. 1058 Since
οὐκ ἔστιν ὅπως, οὐκ ἂν γένοιτο ὅπως mean 'there is, there could be found,
no way in which,' τοῦθ᾽ is abnormal; yet it is not incorrect: 'this thing
could not be attained, namely, a mode in which,' etc. Cp. the mixed
constr. in Ai. 378 οὐ γὰρ γένοιτ᾽ ἂν ταῦθ᾽ ὅπως οὐχ ὧδ᾽ ἔχειν (instead of
ἕξει).   1060 Since the answer at 1042, Iocasta has known the worst.
But she is still fain to spare Oedipus the misery of that knowledge.
Meanwhile he thinks that she is afraid lest he should prove to be too
humbly born. The tragic power here is masterly.   1061 ἅλις (εἰμὶ)
νοσοῦσ᾽ ἐγώ instead of ἅλις ἐστὶ τὸ νοσεῖν ἐμέ: cp. 1368: Ai. 76 ἔνδον
ἀρκείτω μένων: ib. 635 κρείσσων γὰρ Ἅιδᾳ κεύθων: Her. 1. 37 ἀμείνων ἐστὶ
ταῦτα οὕτω ποιεύμενα: Dem. or 4 § 34 οἴκοι μένων, βελτίων: Isae. or. 2
§ 7 ἱκανὸς γὰρ αὐτὸς ἔφη ἀτυχῶν εἶναι: Athen. 435 D χρὴ πίνειν, Ἀντίπα-
τρος γὰρ ἱκανός ἐστι νήφων.   1062 For the genitive τρίτης μητρὸς without
ἐκ, cp. El. 341 οὖσαν πατρός, 366 καλοῦ | τῆς μητρός. τρίτης μητρὸς
τρίδουλος, thrice a slave, sprung from the third (servile) mother: i.e. from
a mother, herself a slave, whose mother and grandmother had also been

OE. It must not be that, with such clues in my grasp, I should fail to bring my birth to light.

Io. For the gods' sake, if thou hast any care for thine own life, forbear this search! My anguish is enough.

OE. Be of good courage; though I be found the son of servile mother,—aye, a slave by three descents,—*thou* wilt not be proved base-born.

Io. Yet hear me, I implore thee: do not thus.

OE. I must not hear of not discovering the whole truth.

Io. Yet I wish thee well—I counsel thee for the best.

OE. These best counsels, then, vex my patience.

Io. Ill-fated one! May'st thou never come to know who thou art!

OE. Go, some one, fetch me the herdsman hither,—and leave yon woman to glory in her princely stock.

receperunt Erfurdt., Elmsleius, Wunder., Hartung., Nauck. Quae haud dubie vera est. Cum enim ἐὰν in formam vulgatiorem ἂν correptum fuisset, praepositionem ἐκ corrector intulit, ut planam faceret genitivi τρίτης rationem; ἂν autem pro ἐὰν accipi voluit, syllabae necessario productae vel ignarus vel oblitus. Postea minus feliciter coniecit Hermannus οὐδ' ἂν εἰ 'κ τρίτης (οὐδ' ἂν εἰ τρίτης Campbell.): ἂν ita explicans ut 'ad suppressum aliquem optativum' pertineret: unde, cum εἰ ad φανῶ iam referatur, structurae duplex insolentia gratuito se intrudit.

---

slaves. No commentator, so far as I know, has quoted the passage which best illustrates this: Theopompus fr. 277 (ed. Müller 1. 325) Πυθονίκην... ἢ Βακχίδος μὲν ἦν δούλη τῆς αὐλητρίδος, ἐκείνη δὲ Σινώπης τῆς Θρᾴττης,... ὥστε γίνεσθαι μὴ μόνον τρίδουλον ἀλλὰ καὶ τρίπορνον αὐτήν. [Dem.] or. 58 § 17 εἰ γὰρ ὀφείλοντος αὐτῷ τοῦ πάππου πάλαι...διὰ τοῦτ' οἰήσεται δεῖν ἀποφεύγειν ὅτι πονηρὸς ἐκ τριγονίας ἐστίν..., 'if, his grandfather having formerly been a debtor,...he shall fancy himself entitled to acquittal because he is *a rascal of the third generation.*' Eustathius *Od.* 1542. 50 quotes from Hippônax Ἀφέω τοῦτον τὸν ἑπτάδουλον (Bergk fr. 75), *i.e.* 'seven times a slave.' For the force of τρι-, cp. also τριγίγας, τρίπρατος (thrice-sold,—of a slave), τριπέδων (a slave who has been thrice in fetters). Note how the reference to the *female* line of servile descent is contrived to heighten the contrast with the real situation. **1063** κακή = δυσγενής, like δειλός, opp. to ἀγαθός, ἐσθλός: *Od.* 4. 63 ἀλλ' ἀνδρῶν γένος ἐστὲ διοτρεφέων βασιλήων | σκηπτούχων· ἐπεὶ οὔ κε κακοὶ τοιούσδε τέκοιεν. **1067** τὰ λῷστα...ταῦτα: cp. *Ant.* 96 τὸ δεινὸν τοῦτο (*i.e.* of which you

ΙΟ. ἰοὺ ἰού, δύστηνε· τοῦτο γάρ σ᾽ ἔχω
μόνον προσειπεῖν, ἄλλο δ᾽ οὔποθ᾽ ὕστερον.

ΧΟ. τί ποτε βέβηκεν, Οἰδίπους, ὑπ᾽ ἀγρίας
ᾄξασα λύπης ἡ γυνή; δέδοιχ᾽ ὅπως
μὴ ᾽κ τῆς σιωπῆς τῆσδ᾽ ἀναρρήξει κακά.   1075

ΟΙ. ὁποῖα χρῄζει ῥηγνύτω· τοὐμὸν δ᾽ ἐγώ,
κεἰ σμικρόν ἐστι, σπέρμ᾽ ἰδεῖν βουλήσομαι.
αὕτη δ᾽ ἴσως, φρονεῖ γὰρ ὡς γυνὴ μέγα,
τὴν δυσγένειαν τὴν ἐμὴν αἰσχύνεται.
ἐγὼ δ᾽ ἐμαυτὸν παῖδα τῆς Τύχης νέμων   1080
τῆς εὖ διδούσης οὐκ ἀτιμασθήσομαι.

1075 ἀναρρήξῃ (sic) L, A, et codd. plerique: ἀναρρήξει V, Bodl. Laud. 54 (cum gloss. εἰς φῶς δείξει), E (ex ἀναρρήξῃ factum): ἀναρήξει Trin.

---

speak). **1072** Iocasta rushes from the scene—to appear no more. Cp. the sudden exit of Haemon (*Ant.* 766), of Eurydicè (*ib.* 1245), and of Deianeira (*Tr.* 813). In each of the two latter cases, the exit silently follows a speech *by another person*, and the Chorus comments on the departing one's *silence*. Iocasta, like Haemon, has spoken passionate words *immediately* before going: and here σιωπῆς (1075) is more strictly 'reticence' than 'silence.' **1074** δέδοικα has here the construction proper to a verb of *taking thought* (or the like), as προμηθοῦμαι ὅπως μὴ γενήσεται,—implying a desire to avert, if possible, the thing feared. **1075** The subject to ἀναρρήξει is κακά, not ἡ γυνή: for (1) ἡ γυνὴ ἀναρρήξει κακά would mean, 'the woman will burst forth into reproaches,' cp. Ar. *Eq.* 626 ὁ δ᾽ ἄρ᾽ ἔνδον ἐλασίβροντ᾽ ἀναρρηγνὺς ἔπη: Pind. fr. 172 μὴ πρὸς ἅπαντας ἀναρρῆξαι τὸν ἀχρεῖον λόγον: (2) the image is that of a storm bursting forth from a great stillness, and requires that the mysterious κακά should be the subject: cp. *Ai.* 775 ἐκρήξει μάχη: Arist. *Meteor.* 2. 8 ἐκρήξας...ἄνεμος. **1076** χρῄζει scornfully personifies the κακά. **1077** βουλήσομαι, 'I shall wish': *i.e.* my wish will remain unaltered until it has been satisfied. Cp. 1446 προστρέψομαι: *Ai.* 681 ὠφελεῖν βουλήσομαι, it shall henceforth be my aim: Eur. *Med.* 259 τοσοῦτον οὖν σου τυγχάνειν βουλήσομαι, I shall wish (shall be content) to receive from you only thus much: (cp. *Ai.* 825 αἰτήσομαι δέ σ᾽ οὐ μακρὸν γέρας λαχεῖν.) *O. C.* 1289 καὶ ταῦτ᾽ ἀφ᾽ ὑμῶν...βουλήσομαι | ...κυρεῖν ἐμοί: Pind. *Olymp.* 7. 20 ἐθελήσω...διορθῶσαι λόγον, I shall have good

Io.   Alas, alas, miserable!—that word alone can I say unto thee, and no other word henceforth for ever.

[She rushes into the palace.

Ch.   Why hath the lady gone, Oedipus, in a transport of wild grief? I misdoubt, a storm of sorrow will break forth from this silence.

Oe.   Break forth what will! Be my race never so lowly, I must crave to learn it. Yon woman, perchance—for she hath a woman's pride—thinks shame of my base source. But I, who hold myself son of Fortune that gives good, will not be dishonoured.

---

will to tell the tale aright. That these futures are normal, and do not arise from any confusion of present *wish* with future *act*, may be seen clearly from Plat. *Phaedo* 91 A καὶ ἐγώ μοι δοκῶ ἐν τῷ παρόντι τοσοῦτον μόνον ἐκείνων διοίσειν· οὐ γὰρ ὅπως τοῖς παροῦσιν ἃ ἐγὼ λέγω δόξει ἀληθῆ προθυμηθήσομαι: and *ib.* 191 c. **1078** ὡς γυνή, in a woman's way: though, as it is, her 'proud spirit' only reaches the point of being sensitive as to a lowly origin. Oedipus himself μέγα φρονεῖ in a higher sense. The sentiment implies such a position for women as existed in the ordinary life of the poet's age. Cp. Eur. *Heracl.* 978 πρὸς ταῦτα τὴν θρασεῖαν ὅστις ἂν θέλῃ | καὶ τὴν φρονοῦσαν μεῖζον ἢ γυναῖκα χρὴ | λέξει: *Hipp.* 640 μὴ γὰρ ἔν γ' ἐμοῖς δόμοις | εἴη φρονοῦσα πλεῖον ἢ γυναῖκα χρή. ὡς is restrictive; cp. 1118: Thuc. 4. 84 ἦν δὲ οὐδὲ ἀδύνατος, ὡς Λακεδαιμόνιος, εἰπεῖν: imitated by Dionys. 10. 31 (of L. Icilius) ὡς Ῥωμαῖος, εἰπεῖν οὐκ ἀδύνατος. See on 763. **1081** Whatever may have been his human parentage, Oed. is the 'son of Fortune' (said in a very different tone from '*Fortunae filius*' in Hor. *Sat.* 2. 6. 49): Fortune brings forth the months with their varying events; these months, then, are his brothers, who ere now have known him depressed as well as exalted. He has faith in this Mother, and will not shrink from the path on which she seems to beckon him; he will not be false to his sonship. We might recall Schiller's epigram on the Wolfians; whatever may be the human paternity of the *Iliad*, 'hat es doch Eine Mutter nur, Und die Züge der Mutter, Deine unsterblichen Züge, Natur.' τῆς εὖ διδούσης, the beneficent: here absol., usu. with dat., as σφῷν δ' εὖ διδοίη Ζεύς, *O. C.* 1435. Not gen. abs., 'while she prospers me,' since the poet. τῆς for αὐτῆς could stand only at the beginning of a sentence or

τῆς γὰρ πέφυκα μητρός· οἱ δὲ συγγενεῖς
μῆνές με μικρὸν καὶ μέγαν διώρισαν.
τοιόσδε δ' ἐκφὺς οὐκ ἂν ἐξέλθοιμ' ἔτι
ποτ' ἄλλος, ὥστε μὴ 'κμαθεῖν τοὐμὸν γένος.　　1085

ΧΟ. στρ.　εἴπερ ἐγὼ μάντις εἰμὶ καὶ κατὰ γνώμαν ἴδρις,
2 οὐ τὸν Ὄλυμπον ἀπείρων,

1084 In L prima manus scripsit τοιόσδ' ἐκφὺς ὡσ οὐκ. Quod cum antiquus διορθωτής intactum transmisisset, dedit recentior manus τοιόσδε δ', ὡς autem punctis notavit, delendum significans. τοιόσδ' ἐκφὺς ὡσ οὐκ A : τοιόσδ' ἐκφὺς οὐκ (omisso ὡσ) B, E, alii : τοιόσδε γ' ἐκφὺς T. Is manifesto fons erroris fuit, quod post τοιόσδε

clause, as 1082. **1082** συγγενεῖς, as being also sons of Τύχη : the word further expresses that their lapse is the measure of his life : cp. 963 : ἀλκᾷ ξύμφυτος αἰών (*Ag.* 107), years with which bodily strength keeps pace. Pind. *Nem.* 5. 40 πότμος συγγενής, the destiny born with one. **1083** διώρισαν: not : '*have determined that I should be* sometimes lowly, sometimes great'; to do this was the part of controlling Τύχη. Rather: 'have *distinguished me as* lowly or great': *i.e.* his life has had chapters of adversity alternating with chapters of prosperity ; and the months have marked these off (cp. 723). The metaphor of the months as sympathetic brothers is partly merged in the view of them as divisions of time : see on 866, 1300. **1084** 'Having sprung of such parentage (ἐκφὺς, whereas φύς would be merely 'having been born such') I will never afterwards prove (ἐξέλθοιμι, *evadam*, cp. 1011) another man' (ἄλλος, *i.e.* false to my own nature). The text is sound. The license of ποτ' at the beginning of 1085 is to be explained on essentially the same principle as μέλας δ' |, etc., (29, cp. 785, 791) at the end of a verse ; viz. that, where the movement of the thought is rapid, one verse can be treated as virtually continuous with the next: hence, too, *Ai.* 986 οὐχ ὅσον τάχος | δῆτ' αὐτὸν ἄξεις δεῦρο; *Ph.* 66 εἰ δ' ἐργάσει | μὴ ταῦτα. So here Soph. has allowed himself to retain ἔτι | ποτέ in their natural connexion instead of writing ἔτι | ἄλλος ποτ'. The genuineness of ποτ' is confirmed by the numerous instances in which Soph. has combined it with ἔτι, as above, 892, below, 1412 : *Ai.* 98, 687 : *Tr.* 830, 922.

1086—1109 This short ode holds the place of the third στάσιμον. But it has the character of a 'dance-song' or ὑπόρχημα, a melody of livelier movement, expressing joyous excitement. The process of

She is the mother from whom I spring; and the months, my kinsmen, have marked me sometimes lowly, sometimes great. Such being my lineage, never more can I prove false to it, or spare to search out the secret of my birth.

CH.   If I am a seer or wise of heart, O Cithaeron, thou 1st strophe. shalt not fail—by yon heaven, thou shalt not!—to know in the

exciderat δ': deinde rudis rei metricae librarius ὡς inseruit (aptam ratus *asseveranti* particulam, cf. *Ai.* 39 ὡς ἔστιν ἀνδρὸς τοῦδε τἄργα ταῦτά σοι), ut versum labantem quomodocunque fulciret. τοιόσδε δὴ φὺς coniecit Blaydes.: τοιόσδε δὴ φὺς οὐκ ἂν ἐξέλθοιμ' ἔτι | ἄτιμος ὥστε μὴ οὐ μαθεῖν Nauck. Dindorf., qui olim coniecerat οὐκ ἂν ἐξέλθοιν ποτὲ | ἀλλοῖος, nunc (ed. 1869) versus 1084, 1085 uncis inclusit.

discovery now approaches its final phase.   The substitution of a hyporcheme for a regular stasimon has here a twofold dramatic convenience.   It shortens the interval of suspense; and it prepares a more forcible contrast.   For the sake of thus heightening the contrast, Soph. has made a slight sacrifice of probability.   The sudden exit of Iocasta has just affected the Chorus with a dark presentiment of evil (1075).   We are now required to suppose that the spirited words of Oedipus (1076—1085) have completely effaced this impression, leaving only delight in the prospect that he will prove to be a native of the land.   A hyporcheme is substituted for a stasimon with precisely similar effect in the *Ajax*, where the short and joyous invocation of Pan immediately precedes the catastrophe (693—717).   The stasimon in the *Trachiniae* 633—662 may also be compared, in so far as its glad anticipations usher in the beginning of the end.

Strophe (1086—1097).   Our joyous songs will soon be celebrating Cithaeron as native to Oedipus.

Antistrophe (1098—1109).   Is he a son of some god,—of Pan or Apollo, of Hermes or Dionysus?

1086 μάντις: as *El.* 472 εἰ μὴ 'γὼ παράφρων μάντις ἔφυν καὶ γνώμας | λειπομένα σοφᾶς: so *O. C.* 1c8ɔ, *Ant.* 1160, *Ai.* 1419: cp. μαντεύομαι = 'to presage.'   1087 κατά with an accus. of respect is somewhat rare (*Tr.* 102 κρατιστεύων κατ' ὄμμα: ib. 379 ἢ κάρτα λαμπρὰ καὶ κατ' ὄμμα καὶ φύσιν), except in such phrases as κατὰ πάντα, κατ' οὐδέν, κατὰ τοῦτο. Cp. Metrical Analysis.   1088 οὐ = οὐ μά: see on 660.   ἀπείρων = ἄπειρος: Hesych. I. 433 ἀπείρονας· ἀπειράτους. Σοφοκλῆς Θυέστῃ.   Ellen c̓t thinks that ἀπειράτους here meant ἀπεράντους ('limitless'): but elsewhere ἀπείρατος always = 'untried' or 'inexperienced.'   Conversely Soph. used ἄπειρος in the commoner sense of ἀπείρων, 'vast,' fr. 481 χιτὼν

3 ὦ Κιθαιρών, †οὐκ ἔσῃ τὰν αὔριον†　　　　1090
4 πανσέληνον, μὴ οὐ σέ γε καὶ πατριώταν Οἰδίπουν
5 καὶ τροφὸν καὶ ματέρ᾽ αὔξειν,
6 καὶ χορεύεσθαι πρὸς ἡμῶν, ὡς ἐπὶ ἦρα φέροντα τοῖς
　　 ἐμοῖς τυράννοις.

1090 οὐκ ἔσῃ τὰν αὔριον codd., cui repugnat versus antistrophici metrum (1101).
Utriusque loci coniunctim habeatur ratio oportet.　Super τὰν αὔριον scriptum est in

---

ἄπειρος ἐνδυτήριος κακῶν.　περά-ω, to go through, πεῖρα (περία), a going-through (*peritus, periculum*), are closely akin to πέρα, beyond, πέρας, πεῖραρ a limit (Curt. *Etym.* §§ 356, 357): in poetical usage, then, their derivatives might easily pass into each other's meanings.　**1090** τὰν ἐπιοῦσαν ἔσῃ would be my correction of the manuscript οὐκ ἔσῃ τὰν αὔριον. Note these points.　(1) In the antistrophe, 1101, ἢ σέ γέ τις θυγάτηρ, though verbally corrupt, seems metrically right.　The measure seems to suit the earnest excitement, just as in *Tr.* 96, 97, where the verse Ἅλιον, Ἅλιον αἰτῶ is followed by τοῦτο καρῦξαι τὸν Ἀλκμήνας πόθι μοι πόθι παῖς: cp. also *Tr.* 500 οὐδὲ τὸν ἔννυχον Ἅιδαν, followed by ἢ Ποσειδάωνα τινάκτορα γαίας.　(2) The phrase τὰν αὔριον πανσέληνον is very singular.　αὔριον (from the same rt. as ἠώς, *aurora*) is always an adverb.　In *Tr.* 945 ἡ αὔριον is opp. to ἡ παροῦσα ἡμέρα: Lysias or. 26 § 6 ἡ αὔριον ἡμέρα: in Eur. *Hipp.* 1117 τὸν αὔριον...χρόνον is acc. of ὁ αὔριον χρόνος, as in *Alc.* 784 τὴν αὔριον μέλλουσαν of ἡ αὔριον μέλλουσα. Thus ἡ αὔριον πανσέληνος can mean only, 'the full-moon *of to-morrow*': not merely the '*coming*' or '*next*' full-moon.　Granting the phrase (as if we should say ἡ αὔριον νύξ), it presupposes that the day on which the Chorus speaks is precisely the eve of a full-moon.　(3)　Now in Par. A τὴν ἐπιοῦσαν is written over τὰν αὔριον: and Par. B has the gloss, κατὰ τὴν αὔριον πάνυ λαμπρὰν ἡμέραν.　The corruption would have happened thus.　Since ἡ ἐπιοῦσα could be used without ἡμέρα as = 'to-morrow' (Polyb. 5. 13. 10), a reader who took τὰν ἐπιοῦσαν here as = '*the coming day*' wrote τὰν αὔριον above it or in the margin; and the more familiar gloss supplanted τὰν ἐπιοῦσαν in the text.　Then πανσέληνον was explained as = πάνυ λαμπράν, and the whole phrase was wrongly interpreted as it is in the gloss of Par. B, '*the all-bright morrow.*'　The οὐκ before ἔσῃ was naturally added to complete the assumed trochaic metre.　πανσέληνον (sc. ὥραν): Her. 2. 47 ἐν τῇ αὐτῇ πανσελήνῳ.　The meaning is: 'At the next full-moon we will hold a joyous παννυχίς,

coming season of full moon that Oedipus honours thee as native to him, as his nurse, and his mother; and that thou art celebrated in our dance and song, because thou art well-pleasing to our prince.

cod. A τὴν ἐπιοῦσαν. Deleto οὐκ, credo reponendum esse τὰν ἐπιοῦσαν ἔσῃ: vide annotationem. οὐκέτι τὰν ἑτέραν dedit Dindorf. **1091** Οἰδίπουν scripsi: Οἰδίπου codd.

---

visiting the temples with χοροί (*Ant.* 153) in honour of the discovery that Oedipus is of Theban birth; and thou, Cithaeron, shalt be a theme of our song.' Cp. Eur. *Ion* 1079, where, in sympathy with the nocturnal worship of the gods, ἀστερωπὸς | ἀνεχόρευσεν αἰθήρ, | χορεύει δὲ Σελάια. The rites of the Theban Dionysus were νύκτωρ τὰ πολλά (Eur. *Bacch.* 486). 1091 πατριώταν, since Cithaeron partly belongs to Boeotia; so Plutarch of Chaeroneia calls the Theban Dionysus his πατριώτην θεόν, *Mor.* 671 c. I read Οἰδίπουν instead of Οἰδίπου. With the genitive, the subject to αὔξειν must be either (1) ἡμᾶς understood, which is impossibly harsh; or (2) τὰν...πανσέληνον. Such a phrase as ἡ πανσέληνος αὔξει σε, i.e. 'sees thee honoured,' is possible; cp. 438 ἥδ' ἡμέρα φύσει σε καὶ διαφθερεῖ: but it is somewhat forced; and the order of the words is against it. The addition of one letter, giving Οἰδίπουν, at once yields a clear construction and a pointed sense. 'Thou shalt not fail to know that *Oedipus* honours thee both as native to him, and as his nurse and mother (*i.e.* not merely as belonging to his Theban fatherland, but as the very spot which sheltered his infancy); and that thou art celebrated in choral song by *us* (πρὸς ἡμῶν), seeing that thou art well-pleasing to *him*.' μὴ οὐ with αὔξειν, because οὐκ ἀπείρων ἔσῃ = a verb of hindrance or denial with a negative: the experience shall not be refused to thee, *but that* he shall honour thee. αὔξειν, not merely by praises, but by the fact of his birth in the neighbourhood: as Pindar says of a victor in the games, *Olymp.* 5. 4 τὰν σὰν πόλιν αὔξων, *Pyth.* 8. 38 αὔξων πάτραν. 1092 τροφόν, as having sheltered him when exposed: τί μ' ἐδέχου; 1391. ματέρ', as the place from which his life rose anew, though it had been destined to be his τάφος, 1452. 1094 χορεύεσθαι, to be celebrated with choral song: *Ant.* 1153 πάννυχοι | χορεύουσι τὸν ταμίαν Ἴακχον. (Not 'danced over,' like ἀείδετο τέμενος, Pind. *Ol.* 11. 76.) 1095 ἐπὶ ἦρα φέροντες: see Merry's note on *Od.* 3. 164 αὖτις ἐπ' Ἀτρείδῃ Ἀγαμέμνονι ἦρα φέροντες. ἦρα was probably acc. sing. from a nom. ἦρ, from rt. ἀρ (to fit), as = 'pleasant service.' After the phrase

7 ἰήιε Φοῖβε, σοὶ δὲ ταῦτ' ἀρέστ' εἴη.

ἀντ. τίς σε, τέκνον, τίς σ' ἔτικτε τᾶν μακραιώνων ἄρα   1098
2 Πανὸς ὀρεσσιβάτα πα-   1100
3 τρὸς πελασθεῖσ'; †ἢ σέ γέ τις θυγάτηρ
4 Λοξίου†; τῷ γὰρ πλάκες ἀγρόνομοι πᾶσαι φίλαι·
5 εἶθ' ὁ Κυλλάνας ἀνάσσων,   1104

1097 σοὶ δὲ] σοὶ δ' οὖν Kennedius.   **1099** τῶν codd., τᾶν Nauck.   ἄρα] ἆρα L : κορᾶν Heimsoeth., Kennedius, J. W. White.   **1100** Πανὸς ὀρεσσιβάτα προσπελασθεῖσ' codd. (προσπελασθεῖσα, sic, L). Syllabae post ὀρεσσιβάτα supplendae causa inseruit τις Hermann., που Heath. (quod recepit Campbell.) : scripsit ὀρεσσιβάταο Wunder., Bothius, Hartung., Blaydes. Coniecit ὀρεσσιβάτα πατρὸς πελασθεῖσ' Lachmann., recepit Nauck. Locum sic refinxit Dindorf.: Νύμφα ὀρεσσιβάτᾳ που | Πανὶ πλαθεῖσ'.   **1101** Conicio ἢ σέ γ' ἔφυσε πατὴρ | Λοξίας pro ἢ σέ γε θυγάτηρ |

ἦρα φέρειν had arisen, ἐπὶ was joined adverbially with φέρειν, ἐπὶ ἦρα φέρειν being equivalent to ἦρα ἐπιφέρειν. Aristarchus, who according to Herodian first wrote ἐπίηρα, must have supposed an impossible tmesis of a compound adj. in the passage of the *Od.* just quoted, also in 16. 375, 18. 56. τοῖς ἐμοῖς τυρ., *i.e.* to Oedipus: for the plur., see on θανάτων, 497. **1096** ἰήιε, esp. as the Healer: see on 154. **1097** σοὶ δὲ: *El.* 150 Νιόβα, σὲ· δ' ἔγωγε νέμω θεόν. ἀρέστ': *i.e.* consistent with those oracles which still await a λύσις εὐαγής (921). **1098** ἔτικτε: see on 870. **1099** τῶν μακραιώνων: here not goddesses (Aesch. *Th.* 524 δαροβίοισι θεοῖσιν) but the Nymphs, who, though not immortal, live beyond the human span; *Hom. Hymn.* 4. 260 αἵ ῥ' οὔτε θνητοῖς οὔτ' ἀθανάτοισιν ἔπονται· | δηρὸν μὲν ζώουσι καὶ ἄμβροτον εἶδαρ ἔδουσιν. They consort with Pan, ὅς τ' ἀνὰ πίση | δενδρήεντ' ἄμυδις φοιτᾷ χοροήθεσι Νύμφαις, *Hymn.* 19. 2. **1100** In Πανὸς ὀρεσσιβάτα προσπελασθεῖσ', the reading of the mss., we note (1) the loss after ὀρεσσιβάτα of one syllable, answering to the last of ἀπείρων in 1087: (2) the somewhat weak compound προσπελασθεῖσ': (3) the gen., where, for this sense, the dat. is more usual, as Aesch. *P. V.* 896 μηδὲ πλαθείην γαμετῇ. L has κοίτῃ written over ὀρεσσιβάτα. I had thought of λέκτροις πελασθεῖσ'. But the gen. is at least tolerable; and on other grounds Lachmann's πατρὸς πελασθεῖσ' is so far better, that πατρὸς, written προσ, would explain the whole corruption. **1101** The words of most mss., ἢ σέ γέ τις θυγάτηρ, probably represent the true metre: see on 1090. But we cannot accept them as meaning 'was a daughter of Apollo thy mother?', since the words τῷ γὰρ πλάκες, κ.τ.λ., leave no doubt that the question intended is, '*Was*

O Phoebus to whom we cry, may these things find favour in thy sight!

Who was it, my son, who of the race whose years are many that bore thee in wedlock with Pan, the mountain-roaming father? Or was Loxias the sire that begat thee? For dear to him are all the upland pastures. Or perchance 'twas Cyllene's lord,

---

Λοξίου, quod L habet. Originem mendi de monstrare infra conatus sum. ἦ σέ γέ τις θυγάτηρ | Λοξίου A et plerique, ubi τις metri explendi gratia manifesto accessit. η σύ γε καὶ γενέτας | Λοξίου dedit Dindorf., cum in versu strophico 1090 οὐκέτι τὰν ἑτέραν exhibeat. Arndt., qui illic οὐκ ἔσῃ τὰν αὔριον servat, hic ἦ σέ γ᾽ εὐνάτειρά τις coniecit, quod receperunt Blaydes., Campbell. Nauckius autem ἦ σέ γ᾽ εὐνάτειρα scribit, omisso τις, cum in v. 1090 τὰν αὖρι pro τὰν αὔριον legat ; et sic Kennedius. ἦ σέ γ᾽ οὔρειος κόρα Hartung.

Apollo thy father?' Dindorf conjectures, ἦ σύ γε καὶ γενέτας | Λοξίου ; I believe that Sophocles wrote ἦ σέ γ᾽ ἔφυσε πατὴρ | Λοξίας ; The corruption would have arisen thus :—(1) The σε of ἔφυσε dropped out, being mistaken for a repetition of the pronoun σέ. (2) Then ΓΕΦΥΠΑΤΗΡ (γεφυπατηρ) would most easily pass into ΓΕΘΥΓΑΤΗΡ (γεθυγατηρ), and τις (which is not found in our best MS., L) would be inserted for sense and metre, the change of Λοξίας to Λοξίου necessarily following. The corruption to θυγάτηρ would have been further assisted by the fact that, after the reference to the Nymph, another feminine noun might have been expected. For σέ γε following σε cp. *Ph.* 1116 πότμος σε δαιμόνων τάδ᾽ | οὐδὲ σέ γε δόλος ἔσχεν. 1103 πλάκες ἀγρόνομοι = πλ. ἀγροῦ νεμομένου, highlands affording open pasturage: so ἀγρον. αὐλαῖς, *Ant.* 785. Apollo as a pastoral god had the title of Νόμιος (Theocr. 25. 21), which was esp. connected with the legend of his serving as shepherd to Laomedon on Ida (*Il.* 21. 448) and to Admetus in Thessaly (*Il.* 2. 766 : Eur. *Alc.* 572 μηλονόμας). Macrobius 1. 17. 43 (Apollinis) *aedes ut ovium pastoris sunt apud Camirenses* [in Rhodes] ἐπιμηλίου, *apud Naxios* ποιμνίου, *itemque deus* ἀρνοκόμης *colitur, et apud Lesbios* ναπαῖος [cp. above, 1026], *et multa sunt cognomina per diversas civitates ad dei pastoris officium tendentia.* Callim. *Hymn. Apoll.* 47 οὐδέ κεν αἶγες | δεύοιντο βρεφέων ἐπιμηλίδες, ᾗσιν Ἀπόλλων | βοσκομένης ὀφθαλμὸν ἐπήγαγεν. 1104 ὁ Κυλλάνας ἀνάσσων, Hermes: *Hom. Hymn.* 3. 1 Ἑρμῆν ὕμνει, Μοῦσα, Διὸς καὶ Μαιάδος υἱόν, | Κυλλήνης μεδέοντα καὶ Ἀρκαδίης πολυμήλου : Verg. *Aen.* 8. 138 *quem candida Maia* | *Cyllenes gelido conceptum vertice fudit.* The peak of Cyllene (now *Ziria*), about 7300 ft. high, in N. E. Arcadia, is visible

6 εἴθ᾽ ὁ Βακχεῖος θεὸς ναίων ἐπ᾽ ἄκρων ὀρέων εὕρημα
　δέξατ᾽ ἔκ του
7 Νυμφᾶν Ἑλικωνίδων, αἷς πλεῖστα συμπαίζει.

OI.　εἰ χρή τι κἀμὲ μὴ συναλλάξαντά πω,　　　　　　1110
　　πρέσβεις, σταθμᾶσθαι, τὸν βοτῆρ᾽ ὁρᾶν δοκῶ,
　　ὅνπερ πάλαι ζητοῦμεν. ἔν τε γὰρ μακρῷ
　　γήρᾳ ξυνᾴδει τῷδε τἀνδρὶ σύμμετρος,
　　ἄλλως τε τοὺς ἄγοντας ὥσπερ οἰκέτας
　　ἔγνωκ᾽ ἐμαυτοῦ· τῇ δ᾽ ἐπιστήμῃ σύ μου　　　　1115
　　προὔχοις τάχ᾽ ἂν που, τὸν βοτῆρ᾽ ἰδὼν πάρος.

1107 εὕρημα] σε κῦμα Kennedius: ἄγρευμα M. Schmidt.　　**1109** Ἑλικωνιάδων
codd.: Ἑλικωνίδων Porson. Et in cod. A quidem prima mánus Ἑλικωνίδος dederat
(hoc enim, non Ἑλικωνίδων, compendiaria scriptura voluit indicare): dein correctoris
ruber stilus litteram a inseruit et signum addidit quo pluralis terminatio denotaretur.

---

from the Boeotian plain near Leuctra, where Cithaeron is on the south
and Helicon to the west, with a glimpse of Parnassus behind it: see
my *Modern Greece*, p. 77.　**1105** ὁ Βακχεῖος θεὸς, not 'the god Βάκχος'
(though in *O. C.* 1494 the MSS. give Ποσειδαωνίῳ θεῷ = Ποσειδῶνι), but
'the god of the Βάκχοι,' the god of Bacchic frenzy; *Hom. Hymn.*
19. 46 ὁ Βάκχειος Διόνυσος: *O. C.* 678 ὁ Βακχιώτας ... Διόνισος.
Some would always write Βάκχειος (like Ὁμήρειος, Αἰάντειος, etc.):
on the other hand, Βακχεῖος is said to have been Attic (cp. Καδμεῖος):
see Chandler, *Greek Accentuation* § 381 2nd ed.　**1107** εὕρημα expresses
the sudden delight of the god when he receives the babe from the mother,
—as Hermes receives his new-born son Pan from the Νύμφη ἐυπλόκαμος,
Hom. Hymn. 19. 40 τὸν δ᾽ αἶψ᾽ Ἑρμείης ἐριούνιος ἐς χέρα θῆκεν | δεξάμενος·
χαῖρεν δὲ νόῳ περιώσια δαίμων. The word commonly = a lucky 'find,'
like ἕρμαιον, or a happy thought. In Eur. *Ion* 1349 it is not '*a foundling*,'
but the box containing σπάργανα found by Ion.　**1109** συμπαίζει: Ana-
creon fr. 2 (Bergk p. 775) to Dionysus: ὦναξ, ᾧ δαμάλης (subduing) Ἔρως
| καὶ Νύμφαι κυανώπιδες | πορφυρέη τ᾽ Ἀφροδίτη | συμπαίζουσιν· ἐπι-
στρέφεαι δ᾽ | ὑψηλῶν κορυφὰς ὀρέων. Ἑλικωνίδων is Porson's correction of
Ἑλικωνιάδων (MSS.), ad Eur. *Or.* 614. Since αἷς answers to δέ in 1097,
Nauck conjectured Ἑλικῶνος αἷσι. But this is unnecessary, as the
metrical place allows this syllable to be either short or long: so in *El.*
486 αἰσχίσταις answers to 502 νυκτὸς εὖ.

or the Bacchants' god, dweller on the hill-tops, that received thee, a new-born joy, from one of the Nymphs of Helicon, with whom he most doth sport.

OE. Elders, if 'tis for me to guess, who never have met with him, I think I see the herdsman of whom we have long been in quest; for in his venerable age he tallies with yon stranger's years, and withal I know those who bring him, methinks, as servants of mine own. But perchance thou mayest have the advantage of me in knowledge, if thou hast seen the herdsman before.

1111 πρέσβει L, erasa post ι littera quae σ haud dubie fuerat. Cum πρέσβυν vel πρέσβυ alii codd. habeant, hoc receperunt Blaydes., Campbell.; illud, Elmsleius, Hartung. Conferri iubet Dindorfius Aesch. *Pers.* 840 (ubi Chorus compellatur), ὑμεῖς δέ, πρέσβεις, χαίρετ'. **1114** δμῶάς τε pro ἄλλως τε ex coniectura scripsit Nauck.; vide tamen annot.

1110—1185 ἐπεισόδιον τέταρτον. The herdsman of Laïus is confronted with the messenger from Corinth. It is discovered that Oedipus is the son of Laïus.

1110—1116 The οἰκεύς who alone escaped from the slaughter of Laïus and his following had at his own request been sent away from Thebes to do the work of a herdsman (761). Oedipus had summoned him in order to see whether he would speak of λῃσταί, or of a λῃστής (842). But meanwhile a further question has arisen. Is he identical with that herdsman of Laïus (1040) who had given up the infant Oedipus to the Corinthian shepherd? He is now seen approaching. With his coming, the two threads of discovery are brought together. **1110** κἀμέ, as well as you, who perhaps know better (1115). μὴ συναλλάξαντά πω, though I have never come into intercourse with him, have never met him: see on 34, and cp. 1130. **1112** ἐν...γήρᾳ: ἐν describes the condition *in* which he is, as *Ph.* 185 ἔν τ' ὀδύναις ὁμοῦ | λιμῷ τ' οἰκτρός: *Ai.* 1017 ἐν γήρᾳ βαρύς. **1113** ξυνᾴδει with τῷδε τἀνδρί: σύμμετρος merely strengthens and defines it: he agrees with this man in the tale of his years. **1114** ἄλλως τε, and moreover: cp. Her. 6. 105 ἀποπέμπουσι...Φειδιππίδην, Ἀθηναῖον μὲν ἄνδρα ἄλλως δὲ ἡμεροδρόμον, an Athenian, and moreover a trained runner. Soph. has ἄλλως τε καὶ == 'especially,' *El.* 1324. 'I know them as servants' would be ἔγνωκα ὄντας οἰκέτας. The ὥσπερ can be explained only by an ellipse: ὥσπερ ἂν γνοίην οἰκέτας ἐμαυτοῦ (cp. 923). Here it merely serves to mark *his first impression* as they come in sight: 'I know those who bring him as

ΧΟ. ἔγνωκα γάρ, σάφ᾽ ἴσθι· Λαΐου γὰρ ἦν
εἴπερ τις ἄλλος πιστὸς ὡς νομεὺς ἀνήρ.

ΟΙ. σὲ πρῶτ᾽ ἐρωτῶ, τὸν Κορίνθιον ξένον,
ἢ τόνδε φράζεις; ΑΓ. τοῦτον, ὅνπερ εἰσορᾷς.   1120

ΟΙ. οὗτος σύ, πρέσβυ, δεῦρό μοι φώνει βλέπων
ὅσ᾽ ἄν σ᾽ ἐρωτῶ. Λαΐου ποτ᾽ ἦσθα σύ;

ΘΕΡΑΠΩΝ.

ἦ, δοῦλος οὐκ ὠνητός, ἀλλ᾽ οἴκοι τραφείς.

ΟΙ. ἔργον μεριμνῶν ποῖον ἢ βίον τίνα;

ΘΕ. ποίμναις τὰ πλεῖστα τοῦ βίου συνειπόμην.   1125

ΟΙ. χώροις μάλιστα πρὸς τίσι ξύναυλος ὤν;

ΘΕ. ἦν μὲν Κιθαιρών, ἦν δὲ πρόσχωρος τόπος.

ΟΙ. τὸν ἄνδρα τόνδ᾽ οὖν οἶσθα τῇδέ που μαθών;

(*methinks*) servants of mine own.' 1117 γάρ, in assent ('you are right, *for*,' etc.), 731: *Ph.* 756: *Ant.* 639, etc. Λαΐου γὰρ ἦν...νομεύς: a comma at ἦν is of course admissible (cp. 1122), but would not strictly represent the Greek construction here, in which the expression of the idea—Λαΐου ἦν πιστὸς νομεύς, εἴπερ τις ἄλλος—has been modified by the addition of the restrictive ὡς before νομεύς. ὡς only means that the sense in which a νομεύς can show πίστις is narrowly limited by the sphere of his work. See on 763: cp. 1078. 1119 τὸν Κορίνθ. ξένον with σέ, instead of a vocative, gives a peremptory tone: *Ant.* 441 σὲ δή, σὲ τὴν νεύουσαν εἰς πέδον κάρα, | φῂς ἢ καταρνεῖ κ.τ.λ., where the equivalent of ἐρωτῶ here is understood. Cp. *Ai.* 71 οὗτος, σὲ τὸν τὰς κ.τ.λ. So in the nomin., Xen. *Cyr.* 4. 5. 22 σὺ δ᾽, ἔφη, ὁ τῶν Ὑρκανίων ἄρχων, ὑπόμεινον. Blaydes thinks that τῷ Κορινθίῳ ξένῳ in Ar. *Th.* 404 comes hence. Surely rather from the *Sthenoboea* of Eur. *ap.* Athen. 427 E πεσὸν δέ νιν λέληθεν οὐδὲν ἐκ χερός, | ἀλλ᾽ εὐθὺς αὐδᾷ, τῷ Κορινθίῳ ξένῳ. 1123 ἦ, the old Attic form of the 1st pers., from ἔα (*Il.* 4. 321, Her. 2. 19): so the best MSS. in Plat. *Phaed.* 61 B, etc. That Soph. used ἦ here and in the *Niobe* (fr. 406) ἦ·γὰρ φίλη 'γὼ τοῦδε τοῦ προφερτέρου, is stated by the schol. on *Il.* 5. 533 and on *Od.* 8. 186. L has ἦν here and always, except in *O. C.* 973, 1366, where it gives ἦ. In Eur. *Tro.* 474 ἦ μὲν τύραννος κεἰς τύρανν᾽ ἐγημάμην is Elmsley's corr. of ἦμεν τύραννοι κ.τ.λ. On the other hand Eur., at least, has ἦν in several places where ἦ is impossible:

CH. Aye, I know him, be sure; he was in the service of Laïus—trusty as any man, in his shepherd's place.

[*The herdsman is brought in.*

OE. I ask thee first, Corinthian stranger, is this he whom thou meanest? ME. This man whom thou beholdest.

OE. Ho thou, old man—I would have thee look this way, and answer all that I ask thee.—Thou wast once in the service of Laïus?

HERDSMAN.

I was—a slave not bought, but reared in his house.

OE. Employed in what labour, or what way of life?

HE. For the best part of my life I tended flocks.

OE. And what the regions that thou didst chiefly haunt?

HE. Sometimes it was Cithaeron, sometimes the neighbouring ground.

OE. Then wottest thou of having noted yon man in these parts—

Hipp. 1012 μάταιος ἄρ' ἦν, οὐδαμοῦ μὲν οὖν φρενῶν: *H. F.* 1416 ὡς ἐς τὸ λῆμα παντὸς ἦν ἥσσων ἀνήρ: *Alc.* 655 παῖς δ' ἦν ἐγώ σοι τῶνδε διάδοχος δόμων: *Ion* 280 βρέφος νεογνὸν μητρὸς ἦν ἐν ἀγκάλαις. **οἴκοι τραφείς**, and so more in the confidence of the master: cp. schol. Ar. *Eq.* 2 (on Παφλάγονα τὸν νεώνητον), πεφύκαμεν γὰρ καὶ τῶν οἰκετῶν μᾶλλον πιστεύειν τοῖς οἴκοι γεννηθεῖσι καὶ τραφεῖσιν ἢ οἷς ἂν κτησώμεθα πριάμενοι. Such *vernae* were called οἰκογενεῖς (Plat. *Men.* 82 B: Dio Chrys. 15. 25 τοὺς παρὰ σφίσι γεννηθέντας οὓς οἰκογενεῖς καλοῦσι), οἰκοτραφεῖς (Pollux 3. 78), ἐνδογενεῖς (oft. in inscriptions, as *C. I. G.* I. 828), or οἰκότριβες [Dem.] or. 13 § 24, Hesych. 2. 766. **1124 μεριμνῶν**: In classical Greek μεριμνᾶν is usu. 'to give one's thought to a question' (as of philosophy, Xen. *Mem.* 4. 7. 6 τὸν ταῦτα μεριμνῶντα): here merely = 'to be occupied with': cp. *Cyr.* 8. 7. 12 τὸ πολλὰ μεριμνᾶν, and so in the *N. T.*, I Cor. 7. 33 μεριμνᾷ τὰ τοῦ κόσμου. **1126 ξύναυλος**, prop. 'dwelling with' (μανίᾳ ξύναυλος *Ai.* 611): here, after **πρὸς**, merely : 'having thy haunts': an instance of that redundant government which Soph. often admits: below 1205 ἐν πόνοις | ξύνοικος : *Ai.* 464 γυμνὸν...τῶν ἀριστείων ἄτερ: *Ph.* 31 κενὴν οἴκησιν ἀνθρώπων δίχα: *Ant.* 919 ἔρημος πρὸς φίλων: 445 ἔξω βαρείας αἰτίας ἐλεύθερον. **1127 ἦν μὲν**, as if replying to χῶροι τίνες ἦσαν πρὸς οἷς ξύν. ἦσθα ; **1128 οἶσθα** with **μαθών**, are you aware of having observed

ΘΕ. τί χρῆμα δρῶντα; ποῖον ἄνδρα καὶ λέγεις;

ΟΙ. τόνδ᾽ ὃς πάρεστιν· ἢ ξυναλλάξας τί πω;　　　1130

ΘΕ. οὐχ ὥστε γ᾽ εἰπεῖν ἐν τάχει μνήμης ὕπο.

ΑΓ. κοὐδέν γε θαῦμα, δέσποτ᾽· ἀλλ᾽ ἐγὼ σαφῶς
ἀγνῶτ᾽ ἀναμνήσω νιν. εὖ γὰρ οἶδ᾽ ὅτι
κάτοιδεν ἦμος τὸν Κιθαιρῶνος τόπον
ὁ μὲν διπλοῖσι ποιμνίοις, ἐγὼ δ᾽ ἑνὶ　　　1135
ἐπλησίαζον τῷδε τἀνδρὶ τρεῖς ὅλους
ἐξ ἦρος εἰς ἀρκτοῦρον ἐκμήνους χρόνους·

1130 ἢ (sic) συναλλάξας L, superscripto συντυχών. Facta est littera λ prior ex
ν, unde vides librarium συναντήσας scribere instituisse. ἢ (sic) συναλλάξας E, Bodl.
Laud. 54, ἢ ξυναλλάξας Vat. a, c: ἢ συνήλλαξας A, T, V, Δ. Cum ἢ in ἢ corruptum
esset, tum demum credo συναλλάξας in συνήλλαξας transiisse. ἢ ξυνήλλαξας Campbell.

---

this man here? Cp. 1142 οἶσθα...δούς; We could not render, 'do you
know this man, through having observed him?' εἰδέναι, implying intuitive
apprehension, is said of knowing facts and propositions, but not persons:
so *scire, wissen, savoir*, Ital. *sapere*: γιγνώσκω, implying a process of
examination, applies to all mediate knowledge, through the senses, of
external objects: so *noscere, kennen, connaître*, Ital. *conoscere*. Cp. Cope
in *Journ. of Philology* I. 79. 1129 καὶ λέγεις: see on 772. 1130 The
constr. is οἶσθα μαθών...ἢ ξυναλλάξας; Oed. takes no more notice of the
herdsman's nervous interruption than is necessary for the purpose of
sternly keeping him to the point. ἢ συνήλλαξας...; 'have you ever met
him?' mars the force of the passage. The testimony of L to συναλλάξας
has the more weight since this is the less obvious reading. Cp. verse 1037,
which continues after an interruption the construction of verse 1035. 1131
οὐχ ὥστε γ᾽ εἰπεῖν: cp. 361. μνήμης ὕπο, at the prompting of memory,—ὑπό
having a like force as in compound verbs meaning to 'suggest,' etc.:
Plut. *Mor.* 813 E λογισμοὺς οὓς ὁ Περικλῆς αὐτὸν ὑπεμίμνησκεν, recalled
to his mind: so ὑποβολεύς (ib.), 'a prompter.' The phrase is more
poetical and elegant than μνήμης ἄπο, adopted by Dind. and Nauck from
the conj. of Blaydes, who compares ἀπὸ τῆς γλώσσης (*O. C.* 936). 1133
ἀγνῶτ᾽ = οὐ γιγνώσκοντα, not recognising me: see on 677. 1134 Soph.
has the epic ἦμος in two other places of dialogue, *Tr.* 531 (answered by
τῆμος) and 154; also once in lyrics *Ai.* 935; Eur. once in lyrics (*Hec.*
915); Aesch. and Comedy, never. τὸν Κιθαιρῶνος τόπον. The sentence
begins as if it were meant to proceed thus: τὸν Κ. τόπον ὁ μὲν διπλοῖς

HE. Doing what?...What man dost thou mean?...

OE. This man here—or of having ever met him before?

HE. Not so that I could speak at once from memory.

ME. And no wonder, master. But I will bring
clear recollection to his ignorance. I am sure that he
well wots of the time when we abode in the region of
Cithaeron,—he with two flocks, I, his comrade, with
one, — three full half-years, from spring to Arcturus;

πω L (post erasum, ut videtur, non πως, sed vel πούς vel ποτε), et codd. plerique:
πως A, M, quod praetulerunt Nauck., Dindorf.: του Blaydes., Kennedius. **1131**
ὑπο] ἀπο Blaydes., Nauck., Dindorf. **1137** ἐμμήνους L, A, cum reliquis codd.
paene omnibus, non excepto E, in quo nihil est quod indicet pr. manum ἐκμήνους
dedisse. Sed ἐκμήνους habet saltem cod. Trin., unde Porson. ἐκμήνους restituit.

ποιμνίοις ἐνέμετο, ἐγὼ δ᾽ ἐνὶ (ἐνεμόμην), πλησιάζων αὐτῷ: but, the verb
ἐνέμετο having been postponed, the participle πλησιάζων is irregularly combined with the notion of ἐνεμόμην and turned into a finite verb,
ἐπλησίαζον: thus leaving τὸν Κ. τόπον without any proper government.
Cp. *El.* 709 στάντες δ᾽ ὅθ᾽ [ὅτ᾽?] αὐτοὺς οἱ τεταγμένοι βραβῆς | κλήρους
ἔπηλαν καὶ κατέστησαν δίφρους, where the change of πήλαντες into ἔπηλαν
καὶ delays (though without superseding, as here) the government of
αὐτούς. For the irregular but very common change of participle into
finite verb cp. *El.* 190 οἰκονομῶ...ὧδε μὲν ἀεικεῖ σὺν στολᾷ | κεναῖς δ᾽
ἀμφίσταμαι τραπέζαις (instead of ἀμφισταμένη): so *Ant.* 810 (ὕμνος ὑμνη-
σεν instead of ὕμνῳ ὑμνηθεῖσαν): *Tr.* 676 ἠφάνισται, διάβορον πρὸς
οὐδενὸς | τῶν ἔνδον, ἀλλ᾽ ἐδεστὸν ἐξ αὐτοῦ φθίνει. Thuc. 4. 100 προσέ-
βαλον τῷ τειχίσματι, ἄλλῳ τε τρόπῳ πειράσαντες καὶ μηχανὴν προσήγαγον.
Though we can have δῶμα πελάζει (Eur. *Andr.* 1167), 'is carried towards the house,' the dat. τῷδε τἀνδρὶ after ἐπλησίαζον here is proof in
itself that the verb does not govern τόπον: further the sense required
is not 'approached,' but 'occupied.' Brunck, taking τῷδε τἀνδρὶ as =
ἐμοί, was for changing ἐπλησίαζον to ἐπλησίαζε: which only adds the
new complication of an irregular μέν and δέ. The text is sound: though
Heimsoeth conjectured νέμων for ὁ μέν, and Nauck ἐν Κιθαιρῶνος νάπαις |
(this with Blaydes) νομεὺς διπλοῖσι ποιμνίοις ἐπιστατῶν | ἐπλησίαζε. This
is to re-write, not to correct. **1137** ἐξ ἦρος εἰς ἀρκτοῦρον: from March to
September. In March the herd of Polybus drove his flock up to
Cithaeron from Corinth, and met the herd of Laïus, who had brought
up his flock from the plain of Thebes. For six months they used to

χειμῶνα δ' ἤδη τἀμά τ' εἰς ἔπαυλ' ἐγὼ
ἤλαυνον οὗτός τ' εἰς τὰ Λαΐου σταθμά.
λέγω τι τούτων, ἢ οὐ λέγω πεπραγμένον;   1140
ΘΕ. λέγεις ἀληθῆ, καίπερ ἐκ μακροῦ χρόνου.
ΑΓ. φέρ' εἰπὲ νῦν, τότ' οἶσθα παῖδά μοί τινα
δούς, ὡς ἐμαυτῷ θρέμμα θρεψαίμην ἐγώ;
ΘΕ. τί δ' ἔστι; πρὸς τί τοῦτο τοὔπος ἱστορεῖς;
ΑΓ. ὅδ' ἐστίν, ὦ τᾶν, κεῖνος ὃς τότ' ἦν νέος.   1145
ΘΕ. οὐκ εἰς ὄλεθρον; οὐ σιωπήσας ἔσει;

1138 χειμῶνα L, χειμῶνι A, facta quidem super ν rasura, nullo tamen relicto litterae a vestigio: χειμῶνι T, V, V². Dativus, utpote facilior, magis invaluit, adiecta nonnunquam (ut in B et Bodl. Laud. 54) interpretatione κατὰ τὸν χειμῶνα: et editorum quoque maiori numero placuit. Eadem quotidianae locutionis appetitio quae

consort in the upland glens of Cithaeron; then, in September, when Arcturus began to be visible a little before dawn, they parted, taking their flocks for the winter into homesteads near Corinth and Thebes. ἀρκτοῦρον, (the star a of the constellation Boötes,) first so called in Hes. *Op.* 566 where (610) his appearance as a morning star is the signal for the vintage. Hippocrates, *Epidem.* 1. 2. 4 has περὶ ἀρκτοῦρον as = 'a little before the autumnal equinox': and Thuc. 2. 78 uses περὶ ἀρκτούρου ἐπιτολάς to denote the same season. See Appendix, Note 15. ἐκμήνους. Plato (*Legg.* 916 B) ἐντὸς ἐκμήνου, sc. χρόνου: the statement in Lidd. and Scott's Lexicon that it is *feminine* seems due to a misunderstanding of the words πλὴν τῆς ἱερᾶς (sc. νόσου) just afterwards. Aristotle also has this form. Cp. ἔκπλεθρος (Eur.), ἔκπους, ἔκπλευρος. The form ἐξμέδιμνον in Ar. *Pax* 631 is an Atticism: cp. ἔξουν Plat. Comicus fr. 36, where Meineke quotes Philemon (a grammarian who wrote on the Attic dialect): Ἀττικῶς μὲν ἔξουν καὶ ἔξκλινον λέγεται, ὥσπερ καὶ παρὰ Σοφοκλεῖ ἐξπηχυστί: adding Steph. Byz. 345 Ἔξγυιος, πόλις Σικελίας, γραφὴν Ἀττικὴν ἔχουσα. Besides ἔκμηνος, Aristotle uses the form ἑξάμηνος (which occurs in a perhaps interpolated place of Xen., *Hellen.* 2. 3. 9); as he has also ἑξάπους. The Attic dialect similarly preferred πεντέπους to πεντάπους, ὀκτώπους to ὀκτάπους, but always said πενταπλοῦς, ἑξαπλοῦς, ὀκταπλοῦς. **1138** The fact that L has χειμῶνα without notice of a variant, while some other MSS. notice it as a variant on their χειμῶνι, is in favour of the accus., the harder reading. It may be rendered '*for* the winter,' since it involves the notion of the time *during* which the flock was to remain in the ἔπαυλα. It is, however, one of

and then for the winter I used to drive my flock to mine own fold, and he took his to the fold of Laïus. Did aught of this happen as I tell, or did it not?

HE. Thou speakest the truth—though 'tis long ago.

ME. Come, tell me now—wottest thou of having given me a boy in those days, to be reared as mine own foster-son?

HE. What now? Why dost thou ask the question?

ME. Yonder man, my friend, is he who then was young.

HE. Plague seize thee—be silent once for all!

χειμῶνα in χειμῶνι deflexit ulterius paullo provecta χειμῶνι mutavit in χειμῶνος (quod, cum gr. χειμῶνι, legitur in Flor. Abb. 152 Γ), quia tempus anni, quo res geruntur (ut ἦρος, θέρους), genitivo potissime designatur. Prompta est tamen, nisi fallor, accusativi defensio.

---

those temporal accusatives which are almost adverbial, the idea of *duration* being merged in that of *season*, so that they can even be used concurrently with a temporal genitive: Her. 3. 117 τὸν μὲν γὰρ χειμῶνα ὕει σφι ὁ θεός ...τοῦ δὲ θέρεος σπείροντες...χρηΐσκοντο τῷ ὕδατι. 2. 95 τῆς μὲν ἡμέρης ἰχθῦς ἀγρεύει, τὴν δὲ νύκτα τάδε αὐτῷ χρᾶται. 2. 2 τὴν ὥρην ἐπαγινέειν σφι αἶγας, 'at the due season.' Hes. *Op.* 174 οὐδέ ποτ' ἦμαρ | παύσονται...οὐδέ τι νύκτωρ. The tendency to such a use of the accus. may have been an old trait of the popular language (cp. ἀωρίαν ἥκοντες Ar. *Ach.* 23, καιρὸν ἐφήκεις Soph. *Ai.* 34). Modern Greek regularly uses the accus. for the old temporal dat.: *e.g.* τὴν τρίτην ἡμέραν for τῇ τρίτῃ ἡμέρᾳ. Classical prose would here use the genit.: Thuc. 1. 30 χειμῶνος ἤδη ἀνεχώρησαν. The division of the year implied is into ἔαρ, θέρος (including ὀπώρα), and χειμών (including φθινόπωρον). **1140** πεπραγμένον, predicate: = πέπρακταί τι τούτων ἃ λέγω; **1141** ἐκ, properly 'at the interval of'; cp. Xen. *An.* 1. 10. 11 ἐκ πλέονος ἢ τὸ πρόσθεν ἔφευγον, at a greater distance: so ἐκ τόξου ῥύματος, at the interval of a bow-shot, *ib.* 3. 3. 15. **1144** τί δ' ἐστί; = 'what is the matter?' 'what do you mean?' *Tr.* 339, *El.* 921, etc. πρὸς τί cannot be connected as a relative clause with τί δ' ἐστί, since τίς in classical Greek can replace ὅστις only where there is an indirect question; *e.g.* εἰπὲ τί σοι φίλον. Cp. *El.* 316. Hellenistic Greek did not always observe this rule: Mark xiv. 36 οὐ τί ἐγὼ θέλω, ἀλλὰ τί σύ. **1145** ὦ τᾶν, triumphantly, 'my good friend.' It is not meant to be a trait of *rustic* speech: in *Ph.* 1387 Neoptolemus uses it to Philoctetes; in Eur. *Her.* 321 Iolaus to Demophon, and *ib.* 688 the θεράπων to Iolaus; in *Bacch.* 802 Dionysus to Pentheus. **1146** οὐκ εἰς ὄλεθρον; see on 430. οὐ σιωπήσας ἔσει; = a fut. perfect,—*at once,*

14—2

ΟΙ. ἆ, μὴ κόλαζε, πρέσβυ, τόνδ', ἐπεὶ τὰ σὰ
δεῖται κολαστοῦ μᾶλλον ἢ τὰ τοῦδ' ἔπη.

ΘΕ. τί δ', ὦ φέριστε δεσποτῶν, ἁμαρτάνω;

ΟΙ. οὐκ ἐννέπων τὸν παῖδ' ὃν οὗτος ἱστορεῖ. 1150

ΘΕ. λέγει γὰρ εἰδὼς οὐδέν, ἀλλ' ἄλλως πονεῖ.

ΟΙ. σὺ πρὸς χάριν μὲν οὐκ ἐρεῖς, κλαίων δ' ἐρεῖς.

ΘΕ. μὴ δῆτα, πρὸς θεῶν, τὸν γέροντά μ' αἰκίσῃ.

ΟΙ. οὐχ ὡς τάχος τις τοῦδ' ἀποστρέψει χέρας;

ΘΕ. δύστηνος, ἀντὶ τοῦ; τί προσχρῄζων μαθεῖν; 1155

ΟΙ. τὸν παῖδ' ἔδωκας τῷδ' ὃν οὗτος ἱστορεῖ;

ΘΕ. ἔδωκ'· ὀλέσθαι δ' ὤφελον τῇδ' ἡμέρᾳ.

ΟΙ. ἀλλ' εἰς τόδ' ἥξεις μὴ λέγων γε τοὔνδικον.

ΘΕ. πολλῷ γε μᾶλλον, ἢν φράσω, διόλλυμαι.

ΟΙ. ἀνὴρ ὅδ', ὡς ἔοικεν, ἐς τριβὰς ἐλᾷ. 1160

ΘΕ. οὐ δῆτ' ἔγωγ', ἀλλ' εἶπον ὡς δοίην πάλαι.

ΟΙ. πόθεν λαβών; οἰκεῖον, ἢ 'ξ ἄλλου τινός;

ΘΕ. ἐμὸν μὲν οὐκ ἔγωγ', ἐδεξάμην δέ του.

ΟΙ. τίνος πολιτῶν τῶνδε κἀκ ποίας στέγης;

ΘΕ. μὴ πρὸς θεῶν, μή, δέσποθ', ἱστόρει πλέον. 1165

ΟΙ. ὄλωλας, εἴ σε ταῦτ' ἐρήσομαι πάλιν.

ΘΕ. τῶν Λαΐου τοίνυν τις ἦν γεννημάτων.

---

or *once for all;* Dem. or. 5 § 50 τὰ δέοντα ἐσόμεθα ἐγνωκότες καὶ
λόγων ματαίων ἀπηλλαγμένοι. So *Ant.* 1067 ἀντιδοὺς ἔσει, *O. C.*
816 λυπηθεὶς ἔσει. The situation shows that this is not an 'aside.'
The θεράπων, while really terrified, could affect to resent the assertion
that his master had been a foundling. **1147 κόλαζε:** of *words, Ai.* 1107
τὰ σέμν' ἔπη | κόλαζ' ἐκείνους. On the Harvard stage, the Theban
at 1146 was about to *strike* the Corinthian (Appendix, Note 1, § 9).
1149 ὦ φέριστε: in tragedy only here and Aesch. *Th.* 39 (Ἐτεόκλεες,
φέριστε Καδμείων ἄναξ): ironical in Plat. *Phaedr.* 238 D. **1151 ἄλλως
πονεῖ:** the theory which he labours to establish is a mere delusion.
1152 πρὸς χάριν, so as to oblige: Dem. or. 8 § 1 μήτε πρὸς ἔχθραν
ποιεῖσθαι λόγον μηδένα μήτε πρὸς χάριν: *Ph.* 594 πρὸς ἰσχύος κράτος,
by main force. **κλαίων:** see on 401. **1154** Cp. *Ai.* 72 τὸν τὰς
αἰχμαλωτίδας χέρας | δεσμοῖς ἀπευθύνοντα (preparatory to flogging): *Od.*

OE. Ha! chide him not, old man—thy words need chiding more than his.

HE. And wherein, most noble master, do I offend?

OE. In not telling of the boy concerning whom he asks.

HE. He speaks without knowledge—he is busy to no purpose.

OE. Thou wilt not speak with a good grace, but thou shalt on pain.

HE. Nay, for the gods' love, misuse not an old man!

OE. Ho, some one—pinion him this instant!

HE. Hapless that thou art, wherefore? what more would'st thou learn?

OE. Didst thou give this man the child of whom he asks?

HE. I did,—and would I had perished that day!

OE. Well, thou wilt come to that, unless thou tell the honest truth.

HE. Nay, much more am I lost, if I speak.

OE. The fellow is bent, methinks, on more delays...

HE. No, no!—I said before that I gave it to him.

OE. Whence hadst thou got it? In thine own house, or from another?

HE. Mine own it was not—I had received it from a man.

OE. From whom of the citizens here? from what home?

HE. Forbear, for the gods' love, master, forbear to ask more!

OE. Thou art lost if I have to question thee again.

HE. It was a child, then, of the house of Laïus.

---

22. 189 σὺν δὲ πόδας χεῖράς τε δέον θυμαλγέι δεσμῷ | εὖ μαλ' ἀποστρέψαντε (of Melanthius the goat-herd); then κίον' ἀν' ὑψηλὴν ἔρυσαν πέλασάν τε δοκοῖσιν: and so left him hanging. 1155 δύστηνος points to the coming disclosure: cp. 1071. 1158 εἰς τόδ' = εἰς τὸ ὀλέσθαι: *Ai.* 1365 αὐτὸς ἐνθάδ' ἕξομαι, *i.e.* εἰς τὸ θάπτεσθαι. 1160 ἐς τριβὰς ἐλᾷ, will push (the matter) to delays (*Ant.* 577 μὴ τριβὰς ἔτι),—is bent on protracting his delay: ἐλαύνειν as in Her. 2. 124 ἐς πᾶσαν κακότητα ἐλάσαι, they said that he *went all lengths* in wickedness: Tyrtaeus 11. 10 ἀμφοτέρων δ' εἰς κόρον ἠλάσατε, ye had taken your fill of both. For the fut., expressing resolve, cp. Ar. *Av.* 759 αἶρε πλῆκτρον, εἰ μαχεῖ. 1161 Remark πάλαι referring to 1157: so *dudum* can refer to a recent moment. 1167 The words could mean either: (1) ' he was one of the children of Laïus ';

ΟΙ. ἦ δοῦλος, ἦ κείνου τις ἐγγενὴς γεγώς;

ΘΕ. οἴμοι, πρὸς αὐτῷ γ' εἰμὶ τῷ δεινῷ λέγειν.

ΟΙ. κἄγωγ' ἀκούειν· ἀλλ' ὅμως ἀκουστέον.   1170

ΘΕ. κείνου γέ τοι δὴ παῖς ἐκλῄζεθ'· ἡ δ' ἔσω
κάλλιστ' ἂν εἴποι σὴ γυνὴ τάδ' ὡς ἔχει.

ΟΙ. ἦ γὰρ δίδωσιν ἥδε σοι; ΘΕ. μάλιστ', ἄναξ.

ΟΙ. ὡς πρὸς τί χρείας; ΘΕ. ὡς ἀναλώσαιμί νιν.

ΟΙ. τεκοῦσα τλήμων; ΘΕ. θεσφάτων γ' ὄκνῳ κακῶν.   1175

ΟΙ. ποίων; ΘΕ. κτενεῖν νιν τοὺς τεκόντας ἦν λόγος.

ΟΙ. πῶς δῆτ' ἀφῆκας τῷ γέροντι τῷδε σύ;

ΘΕ. κατοικτίσας, ὦ δέσποθ', ὡς ἄλλην χθόνα
δοκῶν ἀποίσειν, αὐτὸς ἔνθεν ἦν· ὁ δὲ
κάκ' ἐς μέγιστ' ἔσωσεν. εἰ γὰρ οὗτος εἶ   1180
ὃν φησιν οὗτος, ἴσθι δύσποτμος γεγώς.

ΟΙ. ἰοὺ ἰού· τὰ πάντ' ἂν ἐξήκοι σαφῆ.
ὦ φῶς, τελευταῖόν σε προσβλέψαιμι νῦν,
ὅστις πέφασμαι φύς τ' ἀφ' ὧν οὐ χρῆν, ξὺν οἷς τ'
οὐ χρῆν ὁμιλῶν, οὕς τέ μ' οὐκ ἔδει κτανών.   1185

1170 ἀκούων L, A, et codd. plerique: ἀκούειν Plut. *Mor.* 522 C, et factum est ἀκούων ex ἀκούειν in V, V², V³, V⁴. Est etiam in ipso L ascriptum margini schol., κἀγὼ ὡσαύτως εἰμὶ τῷ νῦν ἀκούειν. Quanquam igitur ἀκούων haud absurde legi potest,

---

or (2) 'he was one of the children of the household of Laïus,' τῶν Λαΐου being gen. of οἱ Λαΐου. The ambiguity is brought out by 1168. See on 814. **1168** κείνου τις ἐγγενὴς γεγώς, some one belonging by birth to his race, the genit. depending on the notion of γένος in the adj., like δωμάτων ὑπόστεγοι, *El.* 1386. **1169** I am close on the horror,—close on uttering it : (ὥστε) λέγειν being added to explain the particular sense in which *he* is πρὸς τῷ δεινῷ, as ἀκούειν defines that in which Oedipus is so. Cp. *El.* 542 τῶν ἐμῶν...ἵμερον τέκνων...ἔσχε δαίσασθαι : Plat. *Crito* 52 B οὐδ' ἐπιθυμία σε ἄλλης πόλεως οὐδ' ἄλλων νόμων ἔλαβεν εἰδέναι. Prof. Kennedy takes λέγειν, ἀκούειν as subst. agreeing with τῷ δεινῷ, 'the dread speaking,' 'the dread hearing.' **1171** While γέ τοι, γε μέντοι, γε μὲν δή are comparatively frequent, γέ τοι δή is rarer: we find it in Ar. *Nub.* 372, Plato *Phaedr.* 264 A, *Rep.* 476 E, 504 A, *Crito* 44 C. **1174** ὡς = 'in her intention': see on 848. πρὸς τί χρείας nearly =

OE.   A slave? or one born of his own race?

HE.   Ah me—I am on the dreaded brink of speech.

OE.   And I of hearing; yet must I hear.

HE.   Thou must know, then, that 'twas said to be his own child—but thy lady within could best say how these things are.

OE.   How? She gave it to thee?   HE.   Yea, O king.

OE.   For what end?   HE.   That I should make away with it.

OE.   Her own child, the wretch?   HE.   Aye, from fear of evil prophecies.

OE.   What were they?   HE.   The tale ran that he must slay his sire.

OE.   Why, then, didst thou give him up to this old man?

HE.   Through pity, master, as deeming that he would bear him away to another land, whence he himself came; but he saved him, for the direst woe. For if thou art what this man saith, know that thou wert born to misery.

OE.   Oh, oh! All brought to pass—all true! Thou light, may I now look my last on thee—I who have been found accursed in birth, accursed in wedlock, accursed in the shedding of blood!   [*He rushes into the palace.*

deductum videtur ab ἀκούειν, lectione minus proclivi, sensum tamen praebente multo graviorem. ἀκούων servat Campbell.: ἀκούειν primus dedit aut Brunckius aut Musgravius, receperunt edd. plerique.   **1172** κάλλιστ'] μάλιστ' coniecit Nauck.

πρὸς ποίαν χρείαν, with a view to what kind of need or desire, *i.e.* with what aim: cp. 1443: *Ph.* 174 ἐπὶ παντί τῳ χρείας ἰσταμένῳ: *Ant.* 1229 ἐν τῷ (= τίνι) ξυμφορᾶς, in what manner of plight.   1176 τοὺς τεκόντας, not, as usually, 'his parents' (999), but 'his father': the plur. as τυράννοις, 1095.   1178 'I gave up the child through pity,' ὡς...δοκῶν, 'as thinking' etc.: *i.e.*, as one might fitly give it up, who so thought. This virtually elliptic use of ὡς is distinct from that at 848, which would here be represented by ὡς ἀποίσοντι. ἄλλην χθόνα ἀποίσειν (αὐτόν): cp. *O. C.* 1769 Θήβας δ' ἡμᾶς | τὰς ὠγυγίους πέμψον.   1180 κάκ': a disyllabic subst. or adj. with short penult. is rarely elided unless, as here, it is (*a*) *first* in the verse, and also (*b*) *emphatic*: so *O. C.* 48, 796: see A. W. Verrall in *Journ. Phil.* XII. 140.   1182 ἂν ἐξήκοι, *must have* come true (cp. 1011), the opt. as Plat. *Gorg.* 502 D οὐκοῦν ἡ ῥητορικὴ δημηγορία ἂν εἴη: Her. I. 2 εἴησαν δ' ἂν οὗτοι Κρῆτες.   1184 ἀφ' ὧν οὐ χρῆν (φῦναι), since he was foredoomed to the acts which the two following clauses express.

ΧΟ. στρ. α΄. ἰὼ γενεαὶ βροτῶν,
2 ὡς ὑμᾶς ἴσα καὶ τὸ μηδὲν ζώσας ἐναριθμῶ.
3 τίς γάρ, τίς ἀνὴρ πλέον
4 τᾶς εὐδαιμονίας φέρει   1190
5 ἢ τοσοῦτον ὅσον δοκεῖν
6 καὶ δόξαντ᾽ ἀποκλῖναι;
7 τὸν σόν τοι παράδειγμ᾽ ἔχων,
8 τὸν σὸν δαίμονα, τὸν σόν, ὦ τλᾶμον Οἰδιπόδα,
   βροτῶν   1195
9 οὐδὲν μακαρίζω·

ἀντ. α΄. ὅστις καθ᾽ ὑπερβολὰν

1186 ἰὼ L (ex ὦ factum), A, al.: ω codd. aliquot, metro reclamante, cum disyllabo
ἰὼ respondeat ὅστις in v. 1197.   1187 In L scripta est interpretatio ἐντάττω super
ἐναριθμῶ, cuius vocis in fine erasa est littera ι, quasi fuisset ἐν ἀριθμῷ.   1193 τὸ

1186—1222 στάσιμον τέταρτον: see Appendix, Note 1, § 10.

1st strophe (1186—1195).   How vain is mortal life !   'Tis well seen
in Oedipus:

1st antistrophe (1196—1203): who saved Thebes, and became its
king:

2nd strophe (1204—1212) : but now what misery is like to his?

2nd antistrophe (1213—1222).   Time hath found thee out and hath
judged.   Would that I had never known thee !   Thou wert our deliverer
once; and now by thy ruin we are undone.

1187 ὡς with ἐναριθμῶ: τὸ μηδὲν adverbially with ζώσας: *i.e.* how
absolutely do I count you as living a life which is no life.   ζώσας should
not be taken as = ' while you live,' or ' though you live.'   We find οὐδέν
εἰμι, 'I am no more,' and also, with the art., τὸ μηδέν εἰμι, 'I am as if I
were not': *Tr.* 1107 κἂν τὸ μηδὲν ὦ: *Ai.* 1275 τὸ μηδὲν ὄντας.   Here
ζώσας is a more forcible substitute for οὔσας, bringing out the contrast
between the semblance of vigour and the real feebleness.   ἴσα καὶ = ἴσα
(or ἴσον) ὥσπερ, a phrase used by Thuc. 3. 14 (ἴσα καὶ ἱκέται ἐσμέν), and
Eur. *El.* 994 (σεβίζω σ᾽ ἴσα καὶ μάκαρας), which reappears in late Greek,
as Aristid. 1. 269 (Dind.).   ἐναριθμῶ only here, and (midd.) in Eur. *Or.*
623 εἰ τοὐμὸν ἔχθος ἐναριθμεῖ κῆδός τ᾽ ἐμόν = ἐν ἀριθμῷ ποιεῖ, if you make
of account.   **1190** φέρει = φέρεται, cp. 590.   **1191** δοκεῖν 'to seem,' *sc.*
εὐδαιμονεῖν: not absol., ' to have reputation,' a sense which οἱ δοκοῦντες, τὰ

CH. Alas, ye generations of men, how mere a shadow do 1st strophe. I count your life! Where, where is the mortal who wins more of happiness than just the seeming, and, after the semblance, a falling away? Thine is a fate that warns me,—thine, thine, unhappy Oedipus—to call no earthly creature blest.

For he, O Zeus, sped his shaft with peerless skill, 1st antistrophe.

σόν τοι codd. (τὸ σόν τϊ B) τὸν σόν τοι Camerarius, quod receperunt Elmsleius, Wunder., Dindorf., Hartung., Nauck., Kennedius, Blaydes.: vide annot. **1196** οὐδένα codd., Brunck., Hartung., Blaydes., Ebner.: οὐδὲν Hermann., Dindorf., Nauck., Campbell.

δοκοῦντα can sometimes bear in *direct antithesis* to οἱ ἀδοξοῦντες or the like (Eur. *Hec.* 291 etc.). Cp. Eur. *Her.* 865 τὸν εὐτυχεῖν δοκοῦντα μὴ ζηλοῦν πρὶν ἂν | θανόντ᾽ ἴδῃ τις: *Ai.* 125 ὁρῶ γὰρ ἡμᾶς οὐδὲν ὄντας ἄλλο πλὴν | εἴδωλ᾽ ὅσοιπερ ζῶμεν ἢ κούφην σκιάν. **1192** ἀποκλῖναι, a metaphor from the heavenly bodies; cp. ἀποκλινομένης τῆς ἡμέρης (Her. 3. 104): and so κλίνει ἡ ἡμέρα, ὁ ἥλιος in later Greek: Dem. or. 1 § 13 οὐκ ἐπὶ τὸ ῥᾳθυμεῖν ἀπέκλινεν. Xen. *Mem.* 3. 5. 13 ἡ πόλις...ἐπὶ τὸ χεῖρον ἔκλινεν. **1193** τὸν σόν τοι κ.τ.λ. The apparently long syllable τὸν (= ἐξ in 1202) is 'irrational,' having the time-value only of ◡: see Metrical Analysis. The τὸ σόν τοι of the MSS. involves a most awkward construction:— 'having thy example,—having thy fate, I say, (*as* an example)': for we could not well render 'having thy case (τὸ σόν) as an example.' Against τὸν σόν, which is decidedly more forcible, nothing can be objected except the threefold repetition; but this is certainly no reason for rejecting it in a lyric utterance of passionate feeling. **1195** οὐδὲν βροτῶν, nothing (*i.e.* no being) among men, a stronger phrase than οὐδένα: Nauck compares fr. 652 οἱ δὲ τῇ γλώσσῃ θρασεῖς | φεύγοντες ἄτας ἐκτός εἰσι τῶν κακῶν· | Ἄρης γὰρ οὐδὲν τῶν κακῶν λωτίζεται, 'no dastard life': *Hom. Hymn.* 4. 34 οὔπερ τι πεφυγμένον ἔστ᾽ Ἀφροδίτην | οὔτε θεῶν μακάρων οὔτε θνητῶν ἀνθρώπων. Add *Ph.* 446 (with reference to Thersites being still alive) ἔμελλ᾽· ἐπεὶ οὐδέν πω κακόν γ᾽ ἀπώλετο, | ἀλλ᾽ εὖ περιστέλλουσιν αὐτὰ δαίμονες· | καί πως τὰ μὲν δίκαια καὶ παλιντριβῆ | χαίρουσ᾽ ἀναστρέφοντες ἐξ Ἅιδου, τὰ δὲ | δίκαια καὶ τὰ χρήστ᾽ ἀποστέλλουσ᾽ ἀεί. The οὐδένα of the MSS. involves the resolution of a long syllable (the second of οὐδὲν) which has an ictus; this is inadmissible, as the ear will show any one who considers the antistrophic verse, 1203, Θήβαισιν ἀνάσσων. **1197** καθ᾽ ὑπερβολὰν τοξεύσας, having hit the answer to the riddle of the Sphinx, when

2 τοξεύσας ἐκράτησε τοῦ πάντ᾽ εὐδαίμονος ὄλβου,
3 ὦ Ζεῦ, κατὰ μὲν φθίσας
4 τὰν γαμψώνυχα παρθένον
5 χρησμῳδόν, θανάτων δ᾽ ἐμᾷ   1200
6 χώρᾳ πύργος ἀνέστα·
7 ἐξ οὗ καὶ βασιλεὺς καλεῖ
8 ἐμὸς καὶ τὰ μέγιστ᾽ ἐτιμάθης, ταῖς μεγάλαισιν ἐν
9 Θήβαισιν ἀνάσσων.

στρ. β΄. τανῦν δ᾽ ἀκούειν τίς ἀθλιώτερος;   1204
2 τίς ἄταις ἀγρίαις, τίς ἐν πόνοις
3 ξύνοικος ἀλλαγᾷ βίου;
4 ἰὼ κλεινὸν Οἰδίπου κάρα,
5 ᾧ μέγας λιμὴν   1208
6 αὑτὸς ἤρκεσεν
7 παιδὶ καὶ πατρὶ θαλαμηπόλῳ πεσεῖν,

1197 ἐκράτησε, **1200** ἀνέστα. Utrique loco tertia persona longe melius convenit quam secunda: vide annot. Secundam tamen in codd. praevaluisse minime mirum est, cum praecederet vocativus Οἰδιπόδα. Veram l. in v. 1197 tuentur M² (ἐκράτησε), Vat. a (ἐκράτησεν): in v. 1200 ἀνέστα vindicant L (σ enim a manu recentiori accessit) et L². Hermannus ἐκράτησε...ἀνέστας dedit. Eiusdem coniecturam secutus scripsit Blaydesius ἐκράτησας ἐς πάντ᾽ pro ἐκράτησε τοῦ πάντ᾽. **1202** Hiatus evitandi causa coniecit Elmsleius βασιλεὺς ἐμὸς | καλεῖ, Blaydesius ἐξ οὗ δὴ βασιλεὺς καλεῖ τ᾽ | ἐμὸς. Immo concessa in hoc genere licentia usus est poeta, ut recte dixit Wunder. Neque opus est ut Hermannum et Blaydesium secuti ἁμὸς legamus,

---

Teiresias and all others had failed: cp. 398: Aesch. *Ag.* 628 ἔκυρσας ὥστε τοξότης ἄκρος σκοποῦ. ἐκράτησε. At 1193 the Chorus addressed Oedipus: at 1197 (ὅστις κ.τ.λ.) they turn to invoke *Zeus* as the witness of his achievements; and so in 1200 L, which here has the corrupt ἐκράτησας, rightly gives ἀνέστα. Then at 1201 (ἐξ οὗ κ.τ.λ.) they resume the direct address to Oedipus, which is thenceforth maintained to the end of the ode. To read ἐκράτησας and ἀνέστας would be to efface a fine trait, marking the passion of grief which turns from earth to heaven, and then again to earth. τοῦ πάντ᾽ εὐδαίμονος: for the adverbial πάντα see on 475; also 823, 1425. **1198** φθίσας, because the Sphinx, when her riddle was solved, threw herself from a rock (Apol-

and won the prize of an all-prosperous fortune; he slew the maiden with crooked talons who sang darkly; he arose for our land as a tower against death.

But now whose story is more grievous in men's ears? Who is a more wretched captive to fierce plagues and troubles, with all his life reversed? 2nd strophe.

Alas, renowned Oedipus! The same bounteous place of rest sufficed thee, as child and as sire also, that thou should'st make thereon thy nuptial couch.

ne longae versus strophici syllabae (τὸν 1195) brevis respondeat; iure enim brevis est haec anacrusis. **1205** τίς ἐν πόνοις, τίς ἄταις ἀγρίαις codd.: τίς ἄταις ἀγρίαις, τίς ἐν πόνοις recte Hermann., metro consulens (cf. v. 1214), receperunt edd. fere omnes. Simplex verumque remedium quo tempore invenerit Hermann., nescio: in ed. tertia (a. 1833) ipse maluit in v. 1214 Δίκα ante δικάζει inserere, hic autem scribere τίς ὧδ' ἐν ἄταις, τίς ἐν ἀγρίοις πόνοις. Hartung., qui in v. 1214 πάλαι delendum censuit, hic scribere voluit τίς ἄταις ἀγρίαις πλέον (omisso τίς ἐν πόνοις): et sic Heimsoeth., nisi quod τόσαις pro πλέον dedit. **1208** ᾧ μέγας λιμήν] πῶς γάμου λιμὴν coniecit Heimsoeth., recepit Nauck. **1209** πατρί] πόσει Blaydes., ex Wunderi coniectura. πεσεῖν] 'μπεσεῖν Hartung.: πέλειν Heimsoeth.

lod. 3. 5): cp. 397 ἔπαυσά νιν. **1199** τὰν γαμψώνυχα κ.τ.λ. The place of the second adj. may be explained by viewing παρθένον-χρησμῳδόν as a composite idea: cp. Ph. 393 τὸν μέγαν Πάκτωλον-εὔχρυσον: O. C. 1234 τό τε κατάμεμπτον... | γῆρας-ἄφιλον. So Pind. Pyth. I. 95, 5. 99 etc. (Fennell, I. xxxvi.). This is not like τὸ σὸν στόμα...ἐλεινόν in 672, where see note. παρθένον: see on κόρα, 508. **1200** θανάτων πύργος: see on 218. **1204** ἀκούειν, to hear of, defining ἀθλιώτερος: Eur. Hipp. 1202 φρικώδη κλύειν. Whose woes are more impressive to others, or more cruel for himself? Cp. O. C. 306 πολὺ...τὸ σὸν | ὄνομα διήκει πάντας. The constr. is τίς ἀθλιώτερος ἀκούειν, τίς (ἀθλιώτερος) ξύνοικος ἐν ἄταις κ. τ. λ., who is more wretched to hear of (whose story is more tragic), who is more wretched as dwelling amid woes (whose present miseries are sharper)? It is not possible to supply μᾶλλον with ξύνοικος from ἀθλιώτερος. **1205** In 1214 the δικάζει τὸν of the mss. should be kept (see Metrical Analysis): here the simple transposition of τίς ἐν πόνοις is far the most probable cure for the metre. ἐν with ἄταις as well as πόνοις: see on 761: for the redundant ἐν...ξύν—, 1126. **1206** The dat. ἀλλαγᾷ might be instrumental, but is rather circumstantial, = τοῦ βίου ἠλλαγμένου. **1208** λιμήν: schol. ὅτι μήτηρ ἦν καὶ γυνὴ ἡ Ἰοκάστη, ἣν λέγει λιμένα. Cp. 420 ff. **1210** πεσεῖν

8 πῶς ποτε πῶς ποθ' αἱ πατρῷαί σ' ἄλοκες φέρειν, τάλας,
9 σῖγ' ἐδυνάθησαν ἐς τοσόνδε;

ἀντ. β'. ἐφεῦρέ σ' ἄκονθ' ὁ·πάνθ' ὁρῶν χρόνος.   1213
2 δικάζει τὸν ἄγαμον γάμον πάλαι
3 τεκνοῦντα καὶ τεκνούμενον.   1215
4 ἰὼ Λάϊειον < ὦ > τέκνον,
5 εἴθε σ' εἴθε σε
6 μήποτ' εἰδόμαν.
7 δύρομαι γὰρ ὥσπερ ἰάλεμον χέων

1214 δικάζει τὸν codd.: δικάζει τ' Hermann., Dindorf., Nauck., Blaydes.,
Kennedius.   Quod autem ὅς ante δικάζει in B aliisque paucis irrepsit, id vocis χρόνος
ultimae syllabae deberi recte iudicat Blaydes.   1216 ἰὼ Λάϊειον τέκνον codd.: ὦ
supplevit Erfurdt.: vide annot.   1217 εἴθε σ' εἴθε codd.: εἴθε σ' εἴθε σε Wunder.

---

here = ἐμπεσεῖν (which Hartung would read, but unnecessarily). Ar.
Th. 1122 πεσεῖν ἐς εὐνὰς καὶ γαμήλιον λέχος. The bold use is assisted
by θαλαμηπόλῳ (bridegroom) which goes closely with πεσεῖν. **1211**
ἄλοκες: cp. 1256, *Ant.* 569, Aesch. *Th.* 753. **1212** σῖγ': cp. Aesch.
Ag. 37 οἶκος δ' αὐτός, εἰ φθογγὴν λάβοι, | σαφέστατ' ἂν λέξειεν. **1213**
ἄκονθ', not as if he had been a criminal who sought to hide conscious
guilt; but because he had not foreseen the disclosure which was to
result from his inquiry into the murder of Laïus. χρόνος, which φύει
ἄδηλα (*Ai.* 647): fr. 280 πρὸς ταῦτα κρύπτε μηδέν, ὡς ὁ πάνθ' ὁρῶν | καὶ
πάντ' ἀκούων (cp. note on 660) πάντ' ἀναπτύσσει χρόνος: see on 614.
Time is here invested with the attributes of the divine omniscience and
justice. **1214** δικάζει (see on 1205), prop. 'tries,' as a judge tries a
cause (δίκην δικάζει): here, 'brings to justice,' punishes: a perhaps
unique poetical use, for in Pind. *Olymp.* 2. 59, which Mitchell quotes,
ἀλιτρά...δικάζει τις = simply 'tries.' Aesch. has another poet. use, *Ag.*
1412 δικάζεις...φυγὴν ἐμοί = καταδικάζεις φυγὴν ἐμοῦ. γάμον πάλαι τεκνοῦντα καὶ τεκνούμενον: one in which ὁ τεκνούμενος has long been identified
with ὁ τεκνῶν: *i.e.* in which the son has become the husband. The ex-
pression is of the same order as τά γ' ἔργα μου | πεπονθότ' ἐστὶ μᾶλλον ἢ
δεδρακότα, *O. C.* 266. **1216** ἰὼ Λάϊειον ὦ τέκνον. Erfurdt's ὦ is the most
probable way of supplying the required syllable, and Reisig's objection
to its place is answered by *Ai.* 395 ἔρεβος ὦ φαεννότατον. Hermann,
however, preferred ὤ, as a separate exclamation: 'Alas, of Laïus (oh

Oh, how can the soil wherein thy father sowed, unhappy one, have suffered thee in silence so long?

Time the all-seeing hath found thee out in thy despite : he judgeth the monstrous marriage wherein begetter and begotten have long been one.   2nd antistrophe.

Alas, thou child of Laïus, would, would that I had never seen thee! I wail as one who pours a dirge from his lips;

1218 ὀδύρομαι codd.: δύρομαι Seidler. Restitui ὥσπερ ἰάλεμον χέων. Vide annot. Habent codices ὡς περίαλλα (non περίαλλ') ἰαχέων (cod. V² ἀχέων). Animadversione dignum est quod in cod. Bodl. Barocc. 66 legitur περίαλα (sic). ἰαχέων servantes participium esse ducunt Nauck., Campbell., adiectivum Elmsleius: ἰακχίων coniecit Erfurdt., receperunt Dindorf., Kennedius.

---

horror!) the son.' Bothe's Λαΐηιον could be supported by Eur. *I. A.* 757 Φοιβήιον δάπεδον: *id.* fr. 775. 64 ὁσίαν βασιλήιον: but seems less likely here. **1218** The MSS. give δύρομαι γὰρ ὡς περίαλλα [sic; in one MS. ὡς περίαλα] ἰαχέων | ἐκ στομάτων. I conjecture δύρομαι γὰρ ὥσπερ ἰάλεμον χέων | ἐκ στομάτων: 'I lament as one who pours from his lips a dirge': *i. e.* Oedipus is to me as one who is dead. Cp. Pind. *Isthm.* 7. 58 ἐπὶ θρῆνον...πολύφαμον ἔχεαν, 'over the tomb they poured forth a resounding dirge.' Every attempt to explain the vulgate is unavailing. (1) ὡς περίαλλ' is supposed to be like ὡς ἐτητύμως, ὡς μάλιστα, 'in measure most abundant.' Now περίαλλα could mean only '*preeminently,*' '*more than others*': Soph. fr. 225 νόμων | οὓς Θάμυρας περίαλλα μουσοποιεῖ, 'strains which Thamyras weaves *with art preeminent*': Ar. *Th.* 1070 τί ποτ' Ἀνδρομέδα | περίαλλα κακῶν μέρος ἐξέλαχον; 'why have I, Andromeda, been dowered with sorrows *above all women*?' Pindar *Pyth.* 11. 5 θησαυρὸν ὃν περίαλλ' ἐτίμασε Λοξίας, honoured *preeminently.* Here, περίαλλα is utterly unsuitable; and the added ὡς makes the phrase stranger still. (2) The MSS. have ἰαχέων. Both ἰαχεῖν and ἰαχεῖν occur: but the latter should, with Dindorf, be written ἰακχέω. Eur. *Her.* 752 ἰακχήσατε: 783 ὀλολύγματα...ἰακχεῖ: *Or.* 826 Τυνδαρὶς ἰάκχησε τάλαινα: 965 ἰακχείτω δὲ γᾶ Κυκλωπία. The participle, however, is unendurably weak after δύρομαι, and leaves ἐκ στομάτων weaker still. (3) ἐκ στομάτων can mean only '*from my lips*' (the plur. as *Tr.* 938 ἀμφιπίπτων στόμασιν, kissing her lips: Eur. *Alc.* 404 ποτὶ σοῖσι πίτνων στόμασιν): it could not mean 'loudly.' (4) Elmsley, doubtless feeling this, took ἰαχέων as gen. of a supposed, but most questionable, ἰαχέος, 'loud,' formed from ἰαχή. Erfurdt conjectured ἰακχίων, 'from lips wild as a bacchant's.' But a Greek poet

8 ἐκ στομάτων. τὸ δ' ὀρθὸν εἰπεῖν, ἀνέπνευσά τ' ἐκ σέθεν
9 καὶ κατεκοίμησα τοὐμὸν ὄμμα.　　　　　　　　　1222

ΕΞΑΓΓΕΛΟΣ.

ὦ γῆς μέγιστα τῆσδ' ἀεὶ τιμώμενοι,
οἷ' ἔργ' ἀκούσεσθ', οἷα δ' εἰσόψεσθ', ὅσον δ'
ἀρεῖσθε πένθος, εἴπερ ἐγγενῶς ἔτι　　　　　　　1225
τῶν Λαβδακείων ἐντρέπεσθε δωμάτων.
οἶμαι γὰρ οὔτ' ἂν Ἴστρον οὔτε Φᾶσιν ἂν
νίψαι καθαρμῷ τήνδε τὴν στέγην, ὅσα

---

would not have brought Iacchos and Thanatos so close together; χωρὶς ἡ τιμὴ θεῶν. (5) ἰάλεμον gives exactly the right force; for them, Oed. is as the dead. ἰάλεμος is *a wail for the dead* in the four places of Eur. where it occurs (*Or.* 1391, *Phoen.* 1033, *Tro.* 600, 1304), in [Eur.] *Rhes.* 895, and in the one place of Aesch., *Suppl.* 115, which is just to our point: the Chorus of Danaïdes say, πάθεα...θρεομένα... | ἰηλέμοισιν ἐμπρεπῆ ζῶσα γόοις με τιμῶ, 'lamenting sorrows meet for funeral wails (*i.e.* the sorrows of those who are as dead), while yet living, I chant mine own dirge.' ἐκ στομάτων fits χέων, since χεῖν was not commonly used absolutely for 'to utter' (as by Pindar, *l. c.* above). (6) The corruption may have thus arisen in a cursive MS.: ἰάλεμον being written ιαλεμο`, the last five letters of ὡσπεριαλεμο῾χεων would first generate αχεων (as in one MS.), or, with the second stroke of the μ, ιαχεων: the attempt to find an intelligible word in the immediately preceding group of letters would then quickly produce the familiar περίαλλα (in one MS. περίαλα). The non-elision of the final α in the MSS. favours this view. **1221** τὸ δ' ὀρθὸν εἰπεῖν, like ὡς εἰπεῖν ἔπος, prefaces the bold figure of speech: I might truly say that by thy means (ἐκ σέθεν) I *received a new life* (when the Sphinx had brought us to the brink of ruin); and now have again *closed my eyes* in a sleep as of death,—since all our weal perishes with thine. The Thebans might now be indeed described as στάντες τ' ἐς ὀρθὸν καὶ πεσόντες ὕστερον (50). ἀνέπνευσα, 'revived,' *i.e.* was delivered from anguish; cp. *Il.* 11. 382 ἀνέπνευσαν κακότητος, had a respite from distress: *Ai.* 274 ἔληξε κἀνέπνευσε τῆς νόσου. **1222** κατεκοίμησα: cp. Aesch. *Ag.* 1293 ὡς ἀσφάδαστος...ὄμμα συμβάλω τόδε: *Ai.* 831 καλῶ θ' ἅμα | πομπαῖον Ἑρμῆν χθόνιον εὖ με κοιμίσαι.

sooth to speak, 'twas thou that gavest me new life, and through thee darkness hath fallen upon mine eyes.

SECOND MESSENGER (*from the house*).

Ye who are ever most honoured in this land, what deeds shall ye hear, what deeds behold, what burden of sorrow shall be yours, if, true to your race, ye still care for the house of Labdacus! For I ween that not Ister nor Phasis could wash this house clean, so many are

---

1223—1530 ἔξοδος. It is told how Iocasta has taken her own life. The self-blinded Oedipus comes forth. Creon brings to him the children his daughters, but will not consent to send him away from Thebes until Apollo shall have spoken.

1223 A messenger comes forth from the house. An ἐξάγγελος is one who announces τὰ ἔσω γεγονότα τοῖς ἔξω (Hesych.), while the ἄγγελος (924) brings news from a distance: in Thuc. 8. 51 (τῷ στρατεύματι ἐξάγγελος γίγνεται ὡς, κ.τ.λ.), one who betrays secrets. **1224** ὅσον δ' : see on 29. **1225** ἀρεῖσθε, take upon you, *i.e.* have laid upon you: like αἴρεσθαι ἄχθος, βάρος : while in *Il.* 14. 130 μή πού τις ἐφ' ἕλκεϊ ἕλκος ἄρηται we may rather compare *Il.* 12. 435 μισθὸν ἄρηται, take up *for* oneself, 'win.' ἐγγενῶς = ὡς ἐγγενεῖς ὄντες, like true men of the Cadmean stock to which the house of Labdacus belonged (261, 273). **1227** Ἴστρον, the Thracian name for the lower course of the river which the Kelts called Danuvius (for this rather than Danubius is the correct form, Kiepert *Anc. Geo.* § 196 *n.*, Byzantine and modern Δούναβις). Φᾶσιν (*Rion*), dividing Colchis from Asia Minor and flowing into the Euxine. ('Phasis' in Xen. *An.* 4. 6. 4 must mean the Araxes, which flows into the Caspian.) Soph. names these simply as great rivers, not with conscious choice as representatives of Europe and Asia. Ovid *Met.* 2. 248 *arsit Orontes | Thermodonque citus Gangesque et Phasis et Ister.* Commentators compare Seneca *Hipp.* 715, *Quis eluet me Tanais? aut quae barbaris Maeotis undis Pontico incumbens mari? Non ipse toto magnus Oceano pater Tantum piarit sceleris*, and Shaksp. *Macbeth* 2. 1 *Will all great Neptune's ocean wash this blood Clean from my hand?*: where, however, the agony of personal remorse renders the hyperbole somewhat more natural than it is here in the mouth of a messenger. **1228** καθαρμῷ, modal dat., 'by way of purification,' so as to purify. νίψαι: Eur. *I. T.* 1191 ἁγνοῖς καθαρμοῖς πρῶτά νιν νίψαι θέλω. The

κεύθει, τὰ δ' αὐτίκ' εἰς τὸ φῶς φανεῖ κακὰ
ἑκόντα κοὐκ ἄκοντα. τῶν δὲ πημονῶν   1230
μάλιστα λυποῦσ' αἱ φανῶσ' αὐθαίρετοι.
ΧΟ. λείπει μὲν οὐδ' ἃ πρόσθεν ᾔδειμεν τὸ μὴ οὐ
βαρύστον' εἶναι· πρὸς δ' ἐκείνοισιν τί φῄς;
ΕΞ. ὁ μὲν τάχιστος τῶν λόγων εἰπεῖν τε καὶ
μαθεῖν, τέθνηκε θεῖον Ἰοκάστης κάρα.   1235
ΧΟ. ὦ δυστάλαινα, πρὸς τίνος ποτ' αἰτίας;
ΕΞ. αὐτὴ πρὸς αὑτῆς. τῶν δὲ πραχθέντων τὰ μὲν
ἄλγιστ' ἄπεστιν· ἡ γὰρ ὄψις οὐ πάρα.
ὅμως δ', ὅσον γε κἀν ἐμοὶ μνήμης ἔνι,
πεύσει τὰ κείνης ἀθλίας παθήματα.   1240
ὅπως γὰρ ὀργῇ χρωμένη παρῆλθ' ἔσω

1231 Veram l. αἴ, quam pauci codd. servant, L a prima manu habuit, sed mutavit in αἴ 'ν corrector. ἀί'ν A et codd. plerique. 1232 ᾔδειμεν L, A, et

idea of *washing off* a defilement belongs to νίζειν (as to its cognates in Sanskrit and Old Irish, Curt. *Etym.* § 439), cp. *Il.* 11. 830 etc. ὅσα (properly referring to a suppressed τοσαῦτα κεύθουσαν) = ὅτι τοσαῦτα: Her. 1. 31 ἐμακάριζον τὴν μητέρα οἵων (= ὅτι τοιούτων) τέκνων ἐκύρησε: Aesch. *P. V.* 908 ἔσται ταπεινός, οἷον ἐξαρτύεται | γάμον γαμεῖν: *Il.* 5. 757 οὐ νεμεσίζῃ Ἄρει... | ὁσσάτιόν τε καὶ οἷον ἀπώλεσε λαὸν Ἀχαιῶν. 1229 The construction is ὅσα κακά (τὰ μὲν) κεύθει, τὰ δὲ αὐτίκα ἐς τὸ φῶς φανεῖ: cp. *El.* 1290 πατρῴαν κτῆσιν...|ἀντλεῖ, τὰ δ' ἐκχεῖ κ.τ.λ. The house *conceals* (κεύθει) the corpse of Iocasta; it will presently *disclose* (φανεῖ) the self-blinded Oedipus: both these horrors were due to conscious acts (ἑκόντα), as distinguished from those acts in which Oed. and Iocasta had become involved without their knowledge (ἄκοντα). ἑκόντα...ἄκοντα for ἑκούσια...ἀκούσια, the epithet of the agent being transferred to the act: see on 1215. 1231 μάλιστα, because there is not the consolation of recognising an inevitable destiny: cp. *Ai.* 260 τὸ γὰρ ἐσλεύσσειν οἰκεῖα πάθη | μηδενὸς ἄλλου παραπράξαντος | μεγάλας ὀδύνας ὑποτείνει: but here λυποῦσι refers rather to the spectators than to the sufferers. αἴ for αἱ ἄν, as oft. in poetry (*O. C.* 395 etc.), rarely in prose, Thuc. 4. 17 οὐ μὲν βραχεῖς ἀρκῶσι, 18 οἵτινες...νομίσωσι. 1232 λείπει, fail: Polyb. 2. 14 ἡ τῶν Ἄλπεων παρώρεια...προκαταλήγουσα λείπει τοῦ μὴ συνάπτειν αὐτῷ, the chain of the Alps, stopping short, fails of touching

the ills that it shrouds, or will soon bring to light,—ills wrought
not unwittingly, but of purpose. And those griefs smart most
which are seen to be of our own choice.

CH. Indeed those which we knew before fall not short of
claiming sore lamentation: besides them, what dost thou an-
nounce?

2 ME. This is the shortest tale to tell and to hear: our
royal lady Iocasta is dead.

CH. Alas, hapless one! From what cause?

2 ME. By her own hand. The worst pain in what hath
chanced is not for you, for yours it is not to behold. Nevertheless, so far as mine own memory serves, ye shall learn that
unhappy woman's fate.

When, frantic, she had passed within the

codd. plerique: ᾔδεμεν Elmsleius, quod multi receperunt editores: vide tamen annot.

(the inmost recess of the Adriatic). μὴ οὐ, because of οὐδὲ with λείπει:
the added τὸ makes the idea of the infin. stand out more independently
of λείπει: cp. 283. ᾔδεμεν, which the MSS. give, should be kept. It was
altered to ᾔδεμεν by Elms. on Eur. *Bacch.* 1345 ὄψ' ἐμάθεθ' ἡμᾶς, ὅτε δ'
ἐχρῆν, οὐκ ᾔδετε: where the εἴδετε of the MSS. is possible, but less probable. Aeschin. or. 3 § 82 has ᾔδειμεν: Dem. or. 55 § 9 ᾔδειτε. See
Curtius, *Verb* II. 239, Eng. tr. 432, who points out that the case of the
third pers. plur. is different: for this, the forms in ε-σαν (as ᾔδεσαν)
alone have good authority. 1235 θεῖον, epic epithet of kings and chiefs,
as in *Il.* of Achilles, Odysseus, Oïleus, Thoas, etc., also of heralds,
and in *Od.* of minstrels, as δῖος *ib.* 16. 1 of Eumaeus: Plat. *Phaedr.*
234 D συνεβάκχευσα μετὰ σοῦ τῆς θείας κεφαλῆς ('your worship').
1236 For πρὸς here see note on 493 *ad fin.* 1238 οὐ πάρα = οὐ
πάρεστιν ὑμῖν: ye have not been eye-witnesses, as I have been.
1239 κἀν ἐμοί, 'e'en in me,'—though *your own* memory, had you been
present, would have preserved a more vivid impression than I can
give: cp. [Plat.] *Alcib.* I. 127 E ἂν θεὸς ἐθέλῃ εἴ τι δεῖ καὶ τῇ ἐμῇ μαντείᾳ
πιστεύειν, σύ τε κἀγὼ βέλτιον σχήσομεν. ἐν—ἔνι (= ἔνεστι), as ἐνεῖναι ἐν
Ar. *Eq.* 1132 etc. 1241 We are to suppose that, when she rushed
from the scene in her passionate despair (1072), Iocasta passed
through the central door of the palace (βασίλειος θύρα) into the
θυρών, a short passage or hall, opening on the court (αὐλή)
surrounded by a colonnade (περιστύλον). Across this court she hurried

θυρῶνος, ἵετ' εὐθὺ πρὸς τὰ νυμφικὰ
λέχη, κόμην σπῶσ' ἀμφιδεξίοις ἀκμαῖς·
πύλας δ', ὅπως εἰσῆλθ', ἐπιρράξασ' ἔσω,
καλεῖ τὸν ἤδη Λάϊον πάλαι νεκρόν,   1245
μνήμην παλαιῶν σπερμάτων ἔχουσ', ὑφ' ὧν
θάνοι μὲν αὐτός, τὴν δὲ τίκτουσαν λίποι
τοῖς οἷσιν αὐτοῦ δύστεκνον παιδουργίαν.
γοᾶτο δ' εὐνάς, ἔνθα δύστηνος· διπλοῦς

1244 Dobraei coniecturam ἐπιρράξασ' confirmat Laurentiani corrector, qui in voce ἐπιρρήξασ' litteram α super η scripsit. Habent ἐπιρρήξασ' A et codd. plerique, quod servant Hermann., Blaydes., Kennedius. Assentior equidem Nauckio, qui lectionem ἐπιρράξασ' non modo probabilem verum etiam necessariam esse iudicat.

to the θάλαμος or bedroom of the master and mistress of the house, and shut herself into it. Presently Oedipus burst into the court with that cry of which we heard the first accents (1182) as he fled from the scene (βοῶν εἰσέπαισεν, 1252). The messenger and others who were in the court watch him in terror as he raves for a sword and asks for Iocasta. Then the thought strikes him that she is in the θάλαμος. He bursts into it (ἐνήλατο 1261). They follow. There they find Iocasta dead, and see Oedipus blind himself. **1242** εὐθύ, 'straight,' is obviously more forcible here than εὐθύς, 'without delay'; a distinction to which Eur. *Hipp.* 1197 τὴν εὐθὺς Ἄργους κἀπιδαυρίας ὁδόν is an exception rare in classical Attic. **1243** ἀμφιδεξίοις here = not simply '*both*,' but '*belonging to both hands*' (for ἀκμαῖς alone would scarcely have been used for 'hands'): so in *O. C.* 1112 ἐρείσατε πλευρὸν ἀμφιδέξιον can mean, 'press your sides to mine *on either hand*.' ἀμφιδέξιος usu. means 'equally deft with either hand' (*ambidexter*), opp. to ἀμφαρίστερος, 'utterly gauche' (Ar. fr. 432): hence 'ambiguous' (of an oracle, Her. 5. 92). The Sophoclean use has at least so much warrant from etymology that δεξιά, from δεκ with added σ, prop. meant merely 'the catcher' or 'receiver': see Curt. *Etym.* §§ 11, 266. **1244** ἐπιρράξασ' from ἐπιρράσσω, Plut. *Mor.* 356 c τοὺς δὲ συνόντας ἐπιδραμόντας ἐπιρράξαι τὸ πῶμα, hastily put the lid on the chest. *Il.* 24. 452 θύρην δ' ἔχε μοῦνος ἐπίβλης | εἰλάτινος, τὸν τρεῖς μὲν ἐπιρρήσσεσκον Ἀχαιοί, | τρεῖς δ' ἀναοίγεσκον κ.τ.λ. (from ἐπιρρήσσω). Hesych. ἐπιρρήσσει. ἐπικλείει. Plato *Prot.* 314 c ἀμφοῖν τοῖν χεροῖν τὴν θύραν...ἐπήραξε (from ἐπαράσσω). In *O. C.* 1503 (χάλαζ') ἐπιρράξασα is intrans. **1245** τὸν ἤδη Λ. πάλαι νεκρόν: for the order cp. Thuc. 7. 23 αἱ πρὸ τοῦ στόματος νῆες ναυμαχοῦσαι: Isocr. or. 4 § 179 τήν τε περὶ ἡμᾶς ἀτιμίαν γεγενημένην:

vestibule, she rushed straight towards her nuptial couch, clutch-
ing her hair with the fingers of both hands; once within the
chamber, she dashed the doors together at her back; then
called on the name of Laïus, long since a corpse, mindful of
that son, begotten long ago, by whom the sire was slain, leaving
the mother to breed accursed offspring with his own.

And she bewailed the wedlock wherein,
wretched, she had borne a twofold brood,

ἐπιρρηγνύναι πύλας num Graece dici poterat? **1245** κάλει codd., Ebner.,
Campbell.: 'κάλει Brunck.: ἐκάλει Blaydes.: καλεῖ Erfurdt., et edd. plerique recte.
Simili mendo codices κύνει pro κυνεῖ praebent in Eur. *Alc.* 183, *Med.* 1141.

Dem. *De Cor.* § 271 τὴν ἁπάντων...ἀνθρώπων τύχην κοινήν: esp. with proper names, as Pind. *Ol.* 13. 53 τὰν πατρὸς ἀντία Μήδειαν θεμέναν γάμον.
1248 παιδουργίαν for παιδουργόν, *i.e.* γυναῖκα τεκνοποιόν (Her. 1. 59),
abstract for concrete: see on 1 (τροφή): cp. *Od.* 3. 49 νεώτερός ἐστιν,
ὁμηλικίη δέ μοι αὐτῷ (= ὁμῆλιξ). Not acc. in appos. with sentence, 'an
evil way of begetting children,' because λίποι | τοῖς οἷσιν αὐτοῦ, 'left *to* (or
for) his own,' would then be very weak. 1249 γοᾶτο. Cp. Curtius, *Verb*
I. 138, Eng. tr. 92: 'It seems to me best on all grounds to suppose that
shortly before the rise of the Greek Epic the [syllabic] augment became
occasionally exposed to the same tendency towards wearing away
(*Verwitterung*) which the ἀ of ἄρα and the ἐ of ἔνερθε could not always
withstand; that there were, in short, pairs of forms then in use, one
with the augment and one without...The omission of the syllabic
augment in Homer was purely a matter of choice...Post-Homeric poetry
adopts the power of dispensing with the syllabic augment as an
inheritance from its predecessor, and makes the greater use of it in
proportion as it is removed from the language of ordinary life. Hence
it is that, as is shown by the careful investigations made by Renner
(*Stud.* i. 2. 18 ff.), the omission of the syllabic augment is extremely
rare in iambic, and far more common in elegiac and lyric verse.
Hence, as is shown (*Stud.* i. 2. 259) by Gerth, in the dialogue of tragedy
the range of this license is very limited indeed, while the majority of
instances of it occur in the slightly Epic style of the messengers'
speeches, or still more commonly in lyric passages.'—The tragic ῥήσεις
here borrow from a practice more marked in epic *narrative* than in
epic *speeches*. In Homer, where augmented and unaugmented forms
are on the whole about equally numerous, the proportion of augmented
to unaugmented is in the speeches about 10 to 3, in the narrative

15—2

ἐξ ἀνδρὸς ἄνδρα καὶ τέκν' ἐκ τέκνων τέκοι. 1250
χὤπως μὲν ἐκ τῶνδ' οὐκέτ' οἶδ' ἀπόλλυται·
βοῶν γὰρ εἰσέπαισεν Οἰδίπους, ὑφ' οὗ
οὐκ ἦν τὸ κείνης ἐκθεάσασθαι κακόν,
ἀλλ' εἰς ἐκεῖνον περιπολοῦντ' ἐλεύσσομεν.
φοιτᾷ γὰρ ἡμᾶς ἔγχος ἐξαιτῶν πορεῖν, 1255
γυναῖκά τ' οὐ γυναῖκα, μητρῴαν δ' ὅπου
κίχοι διπλῆν ἄρουραν οὗ τε καὶ τέκνων.
λυσσῶντι δ' αὐτῷ δαιμόνων δείκνυσί τις·
οὐδεὶς γὰρ ἀνδρῶν οἳ παρῆμεν ἐγγύθεν.
δεινὸν δ' ἀΰσας ὡς ὑφηγητοῦ τινος 1260
πύλαις διπλαῖς ἐνήλατ', ἐκ δὲ πυθμένων
ἔκλινε κοῖλα κλῇθρα κἀμπίπτει στέγῃ.
οὗ δὴ κρεμαστὴν τὴν γυναῖκ' ἐσείδομεν,
πλεκταῖσιν αἰώραισιν ἐμπεπλεγμένην.

1250 ἐξ ἀνδρὸς ἄνδρας A cum codd. plerisque, quibus fraudi fuit pluralis διπλοῦς in v. 1249. In L pr. manus ἄνδρα dederat, recentior litteram σ addidit : ex contrario codicis E corrector ἄνδρας in ἄνδρα mutavit, superscripto τὸν Οἰδίποδα. **1260** ὑφ' ἡγητοῦ mendose L et Aldina : ὑφηγητοῦ ceteri codd., ascripto in A et E gloss. ὁδηγοῦ.

---

about 5 to 7: see Monro, *Hom. Grammar* § 69. διπλοῦς, acc. plur., a twofold progeny, viz. (1) Oedipus by Laïus (ἐξ ἀνδρὸς ἄνδρα), and (2) her four children by Oedipus (τέκνα ἐκ τέκνων, where the poetical plur. τέκνων is for symmetry with τέκνα, as 1176 τοὺς τεκόντας = τὸν πατέρα). **1251** The order (instead of ἀπόλλυται, οὐκέτ' οἶδα) is a bold 'hyperbaton': Blaydes cp. Eur. *Her.* 205 σοὶ δ' ὡς ἀνάγκη τούσδε βούλομαι φράσαι | σῴζειν, where σῴζειν ought to come before βούλομαι. **1255** φοιτᾷ, moves wildly about. Cp. *Il.* 15. 685 ὡς Αἴας ἐπὶ πολλὰ θοάων ἴκρια νηῶν | φοίτα μακρὰ βιβάς—where he has just been likened to a man *jumping* from one horse to another, θρώσκων ἄλλοτ' ἐπ' ἄλλον. So of the sharp, sudden visits of the νόσος, *Ph.* 808 ὀξεῖα φοιτᾷ καὶ ταχεῖ' ἀπέρχεται. *Ai.* 59 φοιτῶντ' ἄνδρα μανιάσιν νόσοις, 'raving.' Curtius (*Etym.* § 417) would refer the word to φυ, φοιτάω coming from φαϝ-ι-τα-ω, 'to be often' (in a place). **1255** πορεῖν is epexegetic of ἐξαιτῶν, which governs a double accus. **1256** (ἐξαιτῶν) τε ὅπου κίχοι, (optative, and not subj., because the pres. φοιτᾷ is historic), representing a deliberative subjunctive, ποῦ κίχω; Xen. *Hellen.* 7. 4. 39 ἠπόρει τε ὅ τι χρήσαιτο τῷ πράγ-

husband by husband, children by her child. And how there-after she perished, is more than I know. For with a shriek Oedipus burst in, and suffered us not to watch her woe unto the end ; on him, as he rushed around, our eyes were set. To and fro he went, asking us to give him a sword,—asking where he should find the wife who was no wife, but a mother whose womb had borne alike himself and his children. And, in his frenzy, a power above man was his guide ; for 'twas none of us mortals who were nigh. And with a dread shriek, as though some one beckoned him on, he sprang at the double doors, and from their sockets forced the bending bolts, and rushed into the room.

There beheld we the woman hanging by the neck in a twisted noose of swinging cords.

1264 seq. πλεκταῖσ ἐώραισ (ex ἐωραῖσ factum) ἐμπεπληγμένην· ὁ δὲ | ὅπως δ' ὁρᾷ νιν, L : ubi δ' post ὅπως docet novam sententiam a versu 1265 exordium duxisse. Scripserat poeta πλεκταῖσιν αἰώραισιν ἐμπεπλεγμένην | ὁ δ' ὡς ὁρᾷ νιν. (1) Primum αἰώραισιν transiit in αἰώραις, quod ipsum legitur in codd. B, V, aliis : (2) deinde, metri

μᾶτι: *i.e.* his thought was, τί χρήσωμαι ; 1257 ἄρουραν: see on 1211. 1259 οὐδεὶς γὰρ ἀνδρῶν: cp. Aesch. *Ag.* 662 ἤτοι τις ἐξέκλεψεν ἢ 'ξητήσατο | θεός τις, οὐκ ἄνθρωπος : *Ai.* 243. 1260 ὡς ὑφηγ.: see on 966. 1261 πύλαις διπλαῖς, the folding doors of the θάλαμος. *Od.* 2. 344 (the θάλαμος of Odysseus) κληισταὶ δ' ἔπεσαν σανίδες πυκινῶς ἀραρυῖαι | δικλίδες. πυθμένων, prop. 'bases': Aesch. *P. V.* 1046 χθόνα δ' ἐκ πυθμένων | αὐταῖς ῥίζαις πνεῦμα κραδαίνοι. Here the 'bases' of the κλῇθρα (bolts) are the staples or sockets which held them. They were on the inner side of the doors, which Iocasta had closed behind her (1244). The pressure of Oedipus on the outer side forces the bolts, causing them to bend inwards (κοῖλα). So Oedipus, within the house, gives the order διοίγειν κλῇθρα, 1287. Others understand : 'forced the doors from their hinges or posts': but this gives an unnatural sense to κλῇθρα. πυθμένες would then mean the στρόφιγγες (Theophr. *Hist. Pl.* 5. 5. 4) or pivots (working in sockets called στροφεῖς) which served as hinges. 1264 αἰώραισιν expresses that the suspended body was still oscillating, and is thus more than ἀρτάναις. αἰώρα (akin to ἀείρω, ἄορ, ἀορτήρ, ἄωρος 'uplifted,' *Od.* 12. 89, Curt. *Etym.* § 518) meant a *swing* (as in Modern Greek), or *swinging movement*: Plat. *Phaed.* 111 E ταῦτα δὲ πάντα κινεῖν ἄνω τε καὶ κάτω ὥσπερ αἰώραν τινὰ ἐνοῦσαν ἐν τῇ γῇ, there is a sort of swinging in the earth which moves all these things up and down ; ...αἰωρεῖται δὴ

ὁ δ' ὡς ὁρᾷ νιν, δεινὰ βρυχηθεὶς τάλας,   1265
χαλᾷ κρεμαστὴν ἀρτάνην. ἐπεὶ δὲ γῇ
ἔκειτο τλήμων, δεινὰ δ' ἦν τἀνθένδ' ὁρᾶν.
ἀποσπάσας γὰρ εἱμάτων χρυσηλάτους
περόνας ἀπ' αὐτῆς, αἷσιν ἐξεστέλλετο,
ἄρας ἔπαισεν ἄρθρα τῶν αὑτοῦ κύκλων,   1270
αὐδῶν τοιαῦθ', ὁθούνεκ' οὐκ ὄψοιντό νιν
οὔθ' οἷ' ἔπασχεν οὔθ' ὁποῖ' ἔδρα κακά,
ἀλλ' ἐν σκότῳ τὸ λοιπὸν οὓς μὲν οὐκ ἔδει

causa, αἰώραις mutatum est in ἑώραις, quod inter alios praebent L et A : (3) ut versus 1264, sexto pede iam mutilus, sarciretur, assumptum est ὁ δὲ ab initio versus sequentis, ὁ δ' ὡς : (4) ὡς denique, metrico muneri iam impar superstes, in ὅπως necessario crevit, vel relicto per incuriam δ', ut in L, vel omisso, ut in A. Similis fuit igitur huius loci fortuna ac versuum 943, 944, quorum prior iam truncatus ab altero pueriliter efferto

καὶ κυμαίνει ἄνω καὶ κάτω, so they swing and surge : *Legg.* 789 D ὅσα τε ὑπὸ ἑαυτῶν (κινεῖται) ἢ καὶ ἐν αἰώραις (in swings) ἢ καὶ κατὰ θάλατταν ἢ καὶ ἐφ' ἵππων ὀχουμένων. Cp. Athen. 618 E ἦν δὲ καὶ ἐπὶ ταῖς ἑώραις τις, ἐπ' Ἠριγόνῃ, ἣν καὶ ἀλῆτιν καλοῦσιν ᾠδήν, 'at the Feast of Swings there was also a song in memory of Erigonè, otherwise called the Song of the Wanderer.' The festival was named ἑῶραι (small images, like the *oscilla* offered to Bacchus, Verg. *G.* 2. 389, being hung from trees) because Erigonè had *hanged herself* on the tree under which she had found the corpse of her father Icarius; the name ἀλῆτις alluding to her wanderings in search of him. Hesych. *s. v.* ἀλῆτις has ἑῶρα : the gloss of Suidas (ἑῶρα· ὕψωσις ἢ μετάρσις) is from the schol. here. ἑώρημα for αἰώρημα (the stage μηχανή) occurs in schol. Ar. *Pax* 77. αἰώρα, however, is the only form for which there is good authority of the classical age. ἐμπεπληγμένην (which L has) would mean 'having dashed herself into...': but this can hardly be justified by the intrans. use of the active, *Od.* 22. 468 f. ὅταν ...πέλειαι | ἕρκει ἐνιπλήξωσι : nor is it appropriate here in reference to the hanging corpse. **1266** γῇ, locative dat.: see on 20: cp. 1451 ναίειν ὄρεσιν. **1269** περόνας (called πόρπαι by Eur. *Ph.* 62), brooches with long pins which could serve as small daggers : one fastened Iocasta's ἱμάτιον on her left shoulder, and another her Doric χιτών on the right shoulder, which the ἱμάτιον did not cover. The Doric χιτών was sleeveless, and usually made with a slit at each shoulder, requiring the use of brooches. (Cp. Guhl and Koner, *Life of the Greeks and Romans*, p. 162 Eng. tr.). In 'The Harvard Greek

But he, when he saw her, with a dread, deep cry of misery, loosed the halter whereby she hung. And when the hapless woman was stretched upon the ground, then was the sequel dread to see. For he tore from her raiment the golden brooches wherewith she was decked, and lifted them, and smote full on his own eye-balls, uttering words like these : 'No more shall ye behold such horrors as I was suffering and working! long enough have ye looked on those whom ye ought never to

supplementum cepit. Vocis ἐμπεπληγμένην super litteram η priorem facta est rasura in L, scriptum est ε in E: ἐμπεπληγμένην habet etiam Bodl. Barocc. 66, nullam prodens eiusmodi suspicionem. Sed ἐμπεπλεγμένην confirmant A, B, V, V², V³, V⁴, reliqui codd. plerique. πλεκταῖς ἑώραις ἐμπεπλεγμένην· ὁ δὲ | ὅπως ὁρᾷ νιν, cum cod. A scribunt Dindorf., Blaydes., Kennedius. πλεκταῖσιν ἀρτάναισιν αἰωρουμένην ex sua coniectura Nauck.

Play' (1882), plate II. p. 26, represents Iocasta with the ἱμάτιον thus worn. Cp. Her. 5. 87, where the Athenian women surround the sole survivor of the expedition to Aegina, κεντεύσας τῇσι περόνῃσι τῶν ἱματίων, and so slay him. Thus too in Eur. Hec. 1170 the women blind Polymestor ; πόρπας λαβοῦσαι τὰς ταλαιπώρους κόρας | κεντοῦσιν, αἱμάσσουσιν. 1270 ἄρθρα can only mean the sockets of the eye-balls (κύκλων). 'He struck his eye-balls in their sockets,' is a way of saying that he struck them full. ἄρθρα could not mean κόρας (pupils), as the schol. explains it. Eur. has another bold use of the word, Cyc. 624 σιγᾶτε πρὸς θεῶν, θῆρες, ἡσυχάζετε, | συνθέντες ἄρθρα στόματος, i.e. shut your lips and be still. 1271 οὐκ ὄψοιντο κ.τ.λ. His words were :—οὐκ ὄψεσθέ με οὔθ' ὁποῖ' ἔπασχον οὔθ' ὁποῖ' ἔδρων κακά, ἀλλ' ἐν σκότῳ τὸ λοιπὸν οὓς μὲν οὐκ ἔδει ὄψεσθε, οὓς δ' ἔχρῃζον οὐ γνώσεσθε: Ye shall not see the evils which I was (unconsciously) suffering and doing [as defiled and defiling], but in darkness henceforth ye shall see those whom ye ought never to have seen [Iocasta and his children], and fail to know those whom I longed to know [his parents, Laïus and Iocasta]. ἔπασχεν...ἔδρα...ἔδει...ἔχρῃζεν can represent nothing but imperfects of the direct discourse: had they represented presents, they must have been πάσχει, etc., or else πάσχοι, etc. ἔπασχεν...ἔδρα mean 'was suffering,' 'was doing' all this time, while ye failed to warn me; and express the reciprocal, though involuntary, wrong of the incestuous relation, with its consequences to the offspring. (Cp. Ant. 171 παίσαντές τε καὶ | πληγέντες αὐτόχειρι σὺν μιάσματι.) 1273 f. ἐν σκότῳ...ὀψοίαθ', i.e. οὐκ ὄψονται: see on 997. The other verbs being plural (with κύκλοι for

ὀψοίαθ᾽, οὓς δ᾽ ἔχρῃζεν οὐ γνωσοίατο.
τοιαῦτ᾽ ἐφυμνῶν πολλάκις τε κοὐχ ἅπαξ   1275
ἤρασσ᾽ ἐπαίρων βλέφαρα· φοίνιαι δ᾽ ὁμοῦ
γλῆναι γένει᾽ ἔτεγγον, οὐδ᾽ ἀνίεσαν
φόνου μυδώσας σταγόνας, ἀλλ᾽ ὁμοῦ μέλας
ὄμβρος χαλάζης αἱματοῦς ἐτέγγετο.
τάδ᾽ ἐκ δυοῖν ἔρρωγεν οὐ μόνου κάτα,   1280
ἀλλ᾽ ἀνδρὶ καὶ γυναικὶ συμμιγῆ κακά.
ὁ πρὶν παλαιὸς δ᾽ ὄλβος ἦν πάροιθε μὲν
ὄλβος δικαίως· νῦν δὲ τῇδε θἠμέρᾳ
στεναγμός, ἄτη, θάνατος, αἰσχύνη, κακῶν
ὅσ᾽ ἐστὶ πάντων ὀνόματ᾽, οὐδέν ἐστ᾽ ἀπόν.   1285
ΧΟ. νῦν δ᾽ ἔσθ᾽ ὁ τλήμων ἔν τινι σχολῇ κακοῦ;

1279 ὄμβρος χαλάζης αἵματος ἐτέγγετο (sic) L, A, codd. plerique. Post αἵματος additum est τ᾽ in E et V²: quam lectionem, quasi χαλάζης αἵματός τ᾽ pro χαλάζης αἱματούσσης dictum esset, receperunt Erfurdt., Musgravius, Elmsleius, Bothius, Linwood., Kennedius. ὄμβρος χαλάζης αἱμάτων ἐτέγγετο cum Hermanno Nauck.: ὄμβρος χάλαζά θ᾽ αἱματοῦσσ᾽ Porson., Dindorf.: ὄμβρος χαλάζης αἱματοῦς Heath., Campbell.: ὄμβρος χαλάζης (i.e. χαλαζήεις, quod Hermann. coniecerat) αἱματοῦς Blaydes. **1280** κάτα restitui pro κακά, quod a fine sequentis versus in codd. omnes irrepsit,

---

subject), the subject to ἔχρῃζεν cannot be ἄρθρα κύκλων, but only Oed. He had craved to learn his true parentage (782 ff.). ὀψοίατο, γνωσοίατο. Ionic, as *O. C.* 945 δεξοίατο: Aesch. *Pers.* 369 φευξοίατο, 451 ἐκσωζοίατο: Eur. *H. F.* 547 ἐκτισαίατο: *Helen.* 159 ἀντιδωρησαίατο. So Thuc. 3. 13 can say ἐφθάραται Ἀθηναῖοι...αἱ δ᾽ ἐφ᾽ ἡμῖν τετάχαται (and 4. 31, 5. 6, 7. 4). **1275** ἐφυμνῶν, of imprecation, as *Ant.* 1305 κακὰς | πράξεις ἐφυμνήσασα τῷ παιδοκτόνῳ: here the idea of *repetition* is also suggested: cp. *Ai.* 292 βαῖ᾽ ἀεὶ δ᾽ ὑμνούμενα: so Lat. *canere, decantare.* **1276** Cp. *Ant.* 52 ὄψεις ἀράξας αὐτὸς αὐτουργῷ χερί. ὁμοῦ = at each blow (hence *imperf.* ἔτεγγον): but in 1278 ὁμοῦ = all at once, not drop by drop (ἀστακτί, and not στάγδην). See on 517 (φέρον). **1279** The best choice lies between Heath's ὄμβρος χαλάζης αἱματοῦς and Porson's ὄμβρος χάλαζά θ᾽ αἱματοῦσσ᾽. The fact that all the MSS. have χαλάζης and that most (including L, A) have αἵματος favours Heath's reading, which is also the stronger. Dindorf prefers Porson's on the ground that such forms as αἱματοῦς, αἱματοῦν are rarer than the feminine forms; but this seems an inadequate reason: Seneca's free paraphrase (*Oed.* 978 *rigat*

have seen, failed in knowledge of those whom I yearned to
know—henceforth ye shall be dark!'

To such dire refrain, not once alone but oft struck he his eyes
with lifted hand; and at each blow the ensanguined eye-balls
bedewed his beard, nor sent forth sluggish drops of gore, but
all at once a dark shower of blood came down like hail.

From the deeds of twain such ills have broken forth, not on
one alone, but with mingled woe for man and wife. The old
happiness of their ancestral fortune was aforetime happiness
indeed; but to-day—lamentation, ruin, death, shame, all earthly
ills that can be named—all, all are theirs.

CH.   And hath the sufferer now any respite from pain?

cum videretur vox μόνου a praepos. ἐκ pendere.   Pro verbis οὐ μόνου κακά coniecit οὐχ
ἑνὸς μόνου Porson.: οὐ μόνου μόνῳ Lachmann.: οὐκ ἀνδρὸς μόνου Arndt.: οὐ μονόστολα
Winckelmann.: οὐ μονοζυγῆ Hermann.: οὐ μόνῳ κακά Nauck.   Servat Kennedius οὐ
μόνου κακά, in fine autem versus sequentis pro κακά scribit πάρα.   Ambo versus
Dindorf., tanquam spurios, e textu eiecit.   1283 τῇδέθ' ἡμέραι L: τῇδε θ'ἡμέραι
codd. plerique.   Sic in Ai. 756 τῇδε θἠμέρᾳ.   Cum Erfurdtio τῇδ' ἐν ἡμέρᾳ praetulerunt Lobeck., Nauck.   1286 ἐν τίνι L, A, cum codd. plerisque: quod praetulerunt Hermann., Wunder., Dindorf., Nauck., Blaydes.: vide tamen annot.

---

ora foedus imber, et lacerum caput Largum revulsis sanguinem venis vomit)
affords no clue as to his text of Sophocles.   μέλας ὄμβρος αἵματος χαλάζης =
a shower of dark blood-drops rushing down as fiercely as hail: cp. O. C.
1502 ὀμβρία | χάλαζ' ἐπιρράξασα.   Pindar has ἐν πολυφθόρῳ...Διὸς ὄμ-
βρῳ | ἀναρίθμων ἀνδρῶν χαλαζάεντι φόνῳ (Isthm. 4. 49) of a slaughter in
which death-blows are rained thick as hail; and so χάλαζαν αἵματος (I.
6. 27): so that the resemblance is only verbal.   1280 f.   Soph. cannot
have written these two verses as they stand; and the fault is doubtless
in 1280.   Porson's οὐχ ἑνὸς μόνου, though plausible, is in sense somewhat
weak, and does not serve to connect 1280 with 1281.   In my conjecture,
οὐ μόνῳ κάτα, the force of the prep. is suitable to the image of a descending torrent which overwhelms: and for its place cp. Ai. 969 τί
δῆτα τοῦδ' ἐπεγγελῷεν ἂν κάτα; ib. 302 λόγους...τοὺς μὲν Ἀτρειδῶν κάτα.
1282 ὁ πρίν, = which they had till lately: παλαιὸς, because the house of
the Labdacidae was ἀρχαιόπλουτος; tracing its line to Cadmus and
Agenor, 268.   1283 δικαίως, in a true sense: cp. 853.   1284 f.   Instead of
κακὰ πάντα, ὅσα ὀνομάζεται, πάρεστιν, we have ὅσα ὀνόματα πάντων κακῶν
ἐστι, (τούτων) οὐδὲν ἄπεστιν: ὄνομα κακοῦ standing for κακὸν ὀνομαζόμενον.
So Aesch. P. V. 210 Γαῖα, πολλῶν ὀνομάτων μορφὴ μία = μορφὴ μία
θεᾶς πολλαχῶς ὀνομαζομένης.   1286 ἔν τινι is right.   Even if τίς σχολὴ

ΕΞ. βοᾷ διοίγειν κλῇθρα καὶ δηλοῦν τινα
τοῖς πᾶσι Καδμείοισι τὸν πατροκτόνον,
τὸν μητρός, αὐδῶν ἀνόσι᾽ οὐδὲ ῥητά μοι,
ὡς ἐκ χθονὸς ῥίψων ἑαυτόν, οὐδ᾽ ἔτι   1290
μενῶν δόμοις ἀραῖος, ὡς ἠράσατο.
ῥώμης γε μέντοι καὶ προηγητοῦ τινος
δεῖται· τὸ γὰρ νόσημα μεῖζον ἢ φέρειν.
δείξει δὲ καὶ σοί. κλῇθρα γὰρ πυλῶν τάδε
διοίγεται· θέαμα δ᾽ εἰσόψει τάχα   1295
τοιοῦτον οἷον καὶ στυγοῦντ᾽ ἐποικτίσαι.

κομμός.   ΧΟ. ὦ δεινὸν ἰδεῖν πάθος ἀνθρώποις,
ὦ δεινότατον πάντων ὅσ᾽ ἐγὼ

κακοῦ could mean 'what form of respite from misery?' τίνι would be less suitable. The Chorus mean: 'and is he now calmer?'—to which the answer is that he is *still* vehemently excited. **1289 μητέρ᾽** (Schneidewin), suggested by Ar. *Vesp.* 1178, would debase this passage. **1291 δόμοις ἀραῖος**, fraught with a curse for the house, making it accursed, **ὡς ἠράσατο**, in terms of his own curse (238 μήτ᾽ εἰσδέχεσθαι μήτε προσφωνεῖν, κ.τ.λ.), according to which anyone who was knowingly ξυνέστιος with the criminal incurred the like curse as he (270). Cp. Eur. *Med.* 608 καὶ σοῖς ἀραία γ᾽ οὖσα τυγχάνω δόμοις, *i.e.* bring a curse on it. *I. T.* 778 (κόμισαί με)...ἢ σοῖς ἀραία δώμασιν γενήσομαι. Aesch. *Ag.* 236 φθόγγον ἀραῖον οἴκοις. Not μενῶν δόμοις, as though the dat. were locative, like γῇ, 1266. **1293 ἢ φέρειν**: Eur. *Hec.* 1107 κρείσσον᾽ ἢ φέρειν κακά: the fuller constr., Her. 3. 14 μέζω κακὰ ἢ ὥστε ἀνακλαίειν. **1294** The subject to δείξει is Oedipus. Cp. *Ai.* 813 χωρεῖν ἕτοιμος, κοὐ λόγῳ δείξω μόνον. *O. C.* 146 δηλῶ δ᾽: 'and I prove it' (viz. that I am wretched), like τεκμήριον δέ. In Ar. *Eccl.* 933 δείξει γε καὶ σοί· τάχα γὰρ εἶσιν ὡς ἐμέ, a person just mentioned is the subject of both verbs, as just afterwards we have, *ib.* 936 δείξει τάχ᾽ αὐτός. On the other hand the verb seems really impersonal in Ar. *Ran.* 1261 πάνυ γε μέλη θαυμαστά· δείξει δὴ τάχα (for the subject cannot well be either μέλη or Aeschylus): and so in Her. 2. 134 διέδεξε, it was made clear: as 2. 117 δηλοῖ, it is manifest. In 3. 82, however, the subject to διέδεξε may be μουναρχίη. Cp. Plat. *Hipp. mai.* 288 B εἰ δ᾽ ἐπιχειρήσας ἔσται καταγέλαστος, αὐτὸ δείξει (the event will show): cp. *Theaet.* 200 E, and see on 341. The central door of the palace is

2 ΜΕ. He cries for some one to unbar the gates and show
to all the Cadmeans his father's slayer, his mother's—the unholy
word must not pass my lips,—as purposing to cast himself out
of the land, and abide no more, to make the house accursed
under his own curse. Howbeit he lacks strength, and one to
guide his steps; for the anguish is more than man may bear.
And he will show this to thee also; for lo, the bars of the gates
are withdrawn, and soon thou shalt behold a sight which even
he who abhors it must pity.

OEDIPUS.

CH.   O dread fate for men to see, O most dreadful of all that Kommos.

---

now opened.   Oedipus comes forth, leaning on attendants; the bloody
stains are still upon his face.   **1293** τοιοῦτον οἷον = τοιοῦτον ὥστε, as we
could have τοιαῦτα εἰπόντες οἷα (instead of ὥστε) καὶ τοὺς παρόντας
ἄχθεσθαι: cp. Madvig *Synt.* § 166 c.   στυγοῦντ', 'while loathing' (the
sight),—not 'hating' Oedipus: ἐποικτίσαι, without ἄν, oblique of ἐποικτί-
σειε, an optat., without ἄν, like κατάσχοι in *Ant.* 605. Cp. fr. 593. 8 φεῦ
κἂν ἀνοικτίρμων τις οἰκτείρειέ νιν.   **1297—1368** A κομμός (see p. 9). The
Chorus begin with anapaests (1297—1306).   The first words uttered
by Oedipus are in the same measure (1307—1311).   Then, after a
single iambic trimeter spoken by the Chorus (1312), (1) *1st strophe*
1313—1320 = (2) *1st antistrophe* 1321—1328; (3) *2nd strophe* 1329—
1348 = (4) *2nd antistrophe* 1349—1368.   Oedipus here speaks in
dochmiac measures blended with iambic; the Chorus, in iambic trimeters,
or dimeters only.   The effect of his passionate despair is thus heightened
by metrical contrast with a more level and subdued strain of sorrow.
Compare *Ai.* 348—429, where the κομμός has in this sense a like
character.   Some regard the κομμός as beginning only at 1313; less
correctly, I think.   Its essence is the antiphonal lament rather than the
antistrophic framework.   **1298** ὅσα...προσέκυρσα: I know no other example of an accus. after προσκυρεῖν, which usu. takes the dat.: but the
compound can at least claim the privilege of the simple κυρεῖν.   The
neut. plur. accus. of *pronouns* and *adjectives* can stand after τυγχάνειν
and κυρεῖν, not as an accus. directly governed by the verb, but rather as
a species of cognate or adverbial accus.: *Ph.* 509 ἀλλ' οἷα μηδεὶς τῶν
ἐμῶν τύχοι φίλων: *O. C.* 1106 αἰτεῖς ἃ τεύξει (which need not be explained by attraction): Aesch. *Cho.* 711 τυγχάνειν τὰ πρόσφορα, *ib.* 714

προσέκυρσ' ἤδη. τίς σ', ὦ τλῆμον,
προσέβη μανία; τίς ὁ πηδήσας   1300
μείζονα δαίμων τῶν μακίστων
πρὸς σῇ δυσδαίμονι μοίρᾳ;
φεῦ, δύστανος·
ἀλλ' οὐδ' ἐσιδεῖν δύναμαί σ', ἐθέλων
πόλλ' ἀνερέσθαι, πολλὰ πυθέσθαι,
πολλὰ δ' ἀθρῆσαι·   1305
τοίαν φρίκην παρέχεις μοι.

ΟΙ. αἰαῖ, αἰαῖ·
φεῦ φεῦ, δύστανος ἐγώ,
ποῖ γᾶς φέρομαι τλάμων; πᾶ μοι

1301 Lectio κακίστων, quam cum aliis aliquot codd. B et V exhibent, inde nata
est, quod litterae κ et μ, ut a librariis scribebantur, formis interdum simillimis erant.
Et in cod. L quidem, qui nunc μακίστων habet, factum est μ ex κ: fortasse etiam in
ccd. A, ubi tamen κ amplius legi non potest.   1303 φεῦ φεῦ δύστανος L, A, et
codd. plerique. Quae verba, tanquam a versu 1308 conflata, reiecerunt Dindorf.,
Wunder., Hartung., Blaydes., consilio, ut mihi quidem videtur, parum considerato.
φεῦ δύστανος Campbell., metro certe non reluctante, cum syllabam brevem (ὄς)
necessaria vocis mora satis excuset.   T φεῦ φεῦ δύσταν' praebet, quod Hermann.
et Elmsleius (δύστην' scribens) receperunt.   σε θέλων L, A, E, al., et sic Ebner.,
Nauck.: σ' ἐθέλων B, quod Hermann., ut 'convenientius anapaestis,' iure praetulit,
edd. plerique.   1304 Verba πόλλ' ἀνερέσθαι, πολλὰ πυθέσθαι, | πολλὰ δ' ἀθρῆσαι,

κυρούντων...τὰ πρόσφορα: Eur. *Ph.* 1666 οὐ γὰρ ἂν τύχοις τάδε: cp. Munro
on *Ag.* 1228 ff. οἶα...τεύξεται in *Journ. Phil.* XI. 134. In *Hipp.* 746
τέρμονα κύρων is not similar, since κύρων = 'reaching,' and the accus. is
like that after ἀφικνεῖσθαι.   1300 ff. ὁ πηδήσας...μοίρᾳ: 'who is the deity
that hath sprung upon thy hapless life with a leap greater than the
longest leap?' *i.e.* 'has given thee sorrow which almost exceeds the
imaginable limit of human suffering?' For μείζονα τῶν μακίστων see on
465 ἄρρητ' ἀρρήτων.   The idea of a malignant god leaping *from above*
on his victim is frequent in Greek tragedy: see on 263.   But here
μακίστων, as in 311 ἵνα, combines the notion of swooping from above
with that of leaping *to a far point*,—as with Pindar μακρὰ...ἄλματα
(*Nem.* 5. 19) denote *surpassing* poetical efforts.   We should then
conceive the δυσδαίμων μοῖρα, the ill-fated life, as an attacked region, *far
into* which the malign god springs.   Here we see a tendency which may
sometimes be observed in the imagery (lyric especially) of Sophocles:

have met mine eyes! Unhappy one, what madness hath come on thee? Who is the unearthly foe that, with a bound of more than mortal range, hath made thine ill-starred life his prey?

Alas, thou hapless one! Nay, I cannot e'en look on thee, though there is much that I would fain ask, fain learn, much that draws my wistful gaze,—with such a shuddering dost thou fill me!

OE. Woe, woe is me!

Alas, alas, wretched that I am! Whither, whither am I borne in my misery? How is my

suppositicia iudicans, uncis seclusit Nauck.: vide tamen annot.   **1307** seqq. In codd. L et A (ut in aliis quibusdam) unus versus est αἶ αἶ αἶ: dein sequitur in L φεῦ φεῦ δύστανος | ἐγώ. ποῖ γᾶσ |; in A unus versus haec continet. T in primo versu αἶ αἶ αἶ αἶ habet: V⁴, αἶ αἶ· φεῦ φεῦ | δύστανος κ.τ.λ. Cum Hermanno servant αἰαῖ, αἰαῖ, δύστανος ἐγώ |, deleto φεῦ φεῦ, Dindorf., Blaydes., Campbell. Sed quare φεῦ φεῦ eiciatur, nihil causae est. Codicum secutus indicia malo cum Nauckio legere αἰαῖ, αἰαῖ | φεῦ φεῦ, κ.τ.λ.   **1309** φέρομαι τλάμων. πᾶι μοι φθογγὰ | διαπέταται φοράδην | L, A, codd. plerique: διέπταται (E), διαπέπταται (quod tres praebent codd.), orta post διαπέταται menda videntur esse. Ipsum illud διαπέταται corruptum esse credo a διαπωτᾶται, quod Musgravius et Seidler. coniecerunt: vide annot. πέταται Kennedius.

---

the *image* is slightly crossed and blurred by the interposing notion of the *thing:* as here he was thinking, 'what suffering *could have gone further?*' See on δι' αἰθέρα τεκνωθέντες, 866. With Aeschylus, on the other hand, the obscurity of imagery seldom or never arises from indistinctness of outline, but more often from an opposite cause,—the vividly objective conception of abstract notions. **1302** πρὸς with dat., after a verb of throwing or falling, is warranted by epic usage: *Od.* 5. 415 μήπως μ' ἐκβαίνοντα βάλῃ λίθακι ποτὶ πέτρῃ | κῦμα μέγ' ἅρπαξαν: *Il.* 20. 420 λιαζόμενον προτὶ γαίῃ, sinking to earth. *Ai.* 95 πρὸς...στρατῷ, 97 πρὸς Ἀτρείδαισιν are different, since no motion is strictly implied. Here the conjecture ἐπὶ is metrically admissible (*Ag.* 66 κάμακος θῆσων Δαναοῖσι, *Pers.* 48 φοβερὰν ὄψιν προσιδέσθαι), but needless. **1303** The pause saves the short final of δύστανος from being a breach of synapheia; cp. *O. C.* 188 ἄγε νῦν σύ με, παῖ, | ἵν' ἄν κ.τ.λ.: *Ant.* 932 ὕπερ. | οἴμοι: Aesch. *Ag.* 1538 ἰὼ γᾶ, γᾶ, εἴθε μ' ἐδέξω: Eur. *Hipp.* 1376 βίοτον. | ὦ: *Ion* 166 Δηλιάδος· | αἱμάξεις. **1304** The fate of Oedipus is a dark and dreadful mystery into which they are fain to peer (ἀνερέσθαι, πυθέσθαι: cp. the questions at 1299 ff., 1327): in its visible presentment it has a fascina-

φθογγὰ διαπωτᾶται φοράδην; 1310
ἰὼ δαῖμον, ἵν' ἐξήλου.

ΧΟ. ἐς δεινόν, οὐδ' ἀκουστόν, οὐδ' ἐπόψιμον.

στρ. α'. ΟΙ. 1 ἰὼ σκότου
2 νέφος ἐμὸν ἀπότροπον, ἐπιπλόμενον ἄφατον,
3 ἀδάματόν τε καὶ δυσούριστον < ὄν. > 1315

1311 ἐξήλου L, A, cum codd. plerisque: ἐξήλω B (ου super ω scripto, cum interpret. προέβης), E, V⁴. Nullus quod sciam codex praebet ἐξήλλου, quod coniecit Hermann., receperunt Dindorf., Campbell., Kennedius. Sed tempus imperfectum hic ferri posse mihi quidem minime persuasit Hermann.: vide annot. Dedit ἐξήλω Blaydes.: Nauckius ex coniectura totum locum sic refinxit, φέρομαι τλάμων· πᾶ μοι

tion (ἀθρῆσαι) even for those whom it fills with horror. 1310 διαπέπαται (MSS.) is unquestionably corrupt. The view that these are anapaests 'of the freer kind' ('ex liberioribus,' Herm.) would not explain the appearance in an anapaestic system of a verse which is not anapaestic at all. Musgrave's and Seidler's διαπωτᾶται, which Blaydes adopts, is far the most probable remedy. The epic πωτᾶσθαι, which Pind. also uses, is admissible in a lyric passage. For the caesura in φθογγὰ διαπωτ|ᾶται φοράδην cp. O. C. 1771 διακωλύσω|μεν ἰόντα φόνον. The wilder and more rugged effect of such a rhythm makes it preferable here to φθογγὰ φοράδην διαπωτᾶται, though the hiatus before ἰὼ is legitimate (see on 1303). To the conjecture πέτεται (or πέταται) it may be objected that the notion of dispersed sound supports the compound with διά. Hermann simply omitted διαπέταται, dividing thus: αἰαι— | δύστανος— | τλάμων; πᾶ μοι φθογγὰ φοράδην; Bergk, πᾶ μοι | φθογγά; διά μοι πέταται φοράδην. Schneidewin (ed. Nauck) πᾶ μοι φθογγά; | φοράδην, ὦ δαῖμον, ἐνήλου. φοράδην = 'in the manner of that which is carried'; here correlative to φέρεσθαι as said of things which are swept onward by a tide or current: thus, of persons deficient in self-restraint, Plat. Theaet. 144 B ἄττοντες φέρονται ὥσπερ τὰ ἀνερμάτιστα πλοῖα, they are hurried away on currents like boats without ballast: Crat. 411 C ῥεῖν καὶ φέρεσθαι: Rep. 496 D πνεῦμα φερόμενον. He has newly lost the power of seeing those to whom he speaks. He feels as if his voice was borne from him on the air in a direction over which he has no control. With the use of the adverb here, cp. βάδην, δρομάδην, σύδην. Elsewhere φοράδην is parallel with φέρεσθαι as = to be carried, instead of walking: Eur. Andr. 1166 φοράδην...δῶμα πελάζει, i.e. borne in a litter: Dem. or. 54 § 20 ὑγιὴς ἐξελθὼν φοράδην ἦλθον οἴκαδε. Such adverbs in -δην, which were prob-

voice swept abroad on the wings of the air? Oh my Fate, how far hast thou sprung!

CH.   To a dread place, dire in men's ears, dire in their sight.

OE.   O thou horror of darkness that enfoldest me, visitant 1st
unspeakable, resistless, sped by a wind too fair! strophe.

φθογγά; | φοράδην, ὦ δαῖμον, ἐνήλου.   **1314** ἐπιπλώμενον L, A, alii codd., inter
quos Bodl. Laud. 54 litteram ο scriptam habet super ω, adiecta interpret. ἐπερχόμενον.
Veram l. ἐπιπλόμενον praebent B, E, V², Bodl. Barocc. 66, al.   **1315** ἀδάμα-
στον codd.: ἀδόματον Hermann.   δυσούριστον codd.: deesse syllabam docet versus
1323.   Coniecit δυσσούριστον ὄν Hermann.: vide annot.

---

ably accusatives cognate to the notion of the verb, are always formed
from the verbal stem, (*a*) directly, like βά-δην, or (*b*) with modified
vowel and inserted α, like φοράδην instead of *φερδην, σποράδην instead
of *σπερδην.   **1311 ἐξῆλου.** In a paroemiac, the foot before the catalectic
syllable is usually an anapaest, seldom, as here (ἐξῆλ—), a spondee: but
cp. Aesch. *Pers.* 33 ἵππων τ᾽ ἐλατὴρ Σωσθάνης: *Suppl.* 7 ψήφῳ πόλεως
γνωσθεῖσαι: *ib.* 976 βάξει λαῶν ἐν χώρῳ: *Ag.* 366 βέλος ἠλίθιον σκήψειεν.
L and A are of the MSS. which give ἐξῆλου: and good MS. authority supports
ἐνήλου in Aesch. *Pers.* 516, ἤλοντο in Xen. *Hellen.* 4. 4. 11. The evidence,
so far as it goes, seems to indicate that, while ἠλάμην (itself rare in prose)
was preferred in the indicative, a form ἠλόμην was also admitted: see
Veitch, *Irreg. Verbs,* ed. 1879.   Blaydes gives ἐξῆλω: Elms. gave ἐξάλω,
'inaudite δωρίζων,' in Ellendt's opinion; but Veitch quotes Theocr. 17.
100 ἐξάλατο.   The imperf. ἐξῆλλον, which Dindorf, Campbell and others
read, was explained by Hermann as = *tendebas,* i. e. 'whither wert thou
purposing to leap?'   To this I feel two objections: (1) the awkwardness
of thus representing the swift act of a moment: (2) the use of ἵνα, which
means *where.* This could not be used with *the imperfect of a verb of
motion* (as ἵνα ἔβαινε, instead of οἷ), but only with the *perfect,* as ἵνα
βέβηκε (*i.e.* where *is* he now), or the aorist when equivalent to the
perfect: as *O. C.* 273 ἱκόμην (I *have* come) ἵν᾽ ἱκόμην. So, here, the
aor. alone seems admissible: ἵν᾽ ἐξῆλου, where *hast* thou leaped to, *i.e.*
where *art* thou? cp. 1515 ἵν᾽ ἐξήκεις, and see on 947.   **1314 ἀπότροπον**
= ὅ τις ἂν ἀποτρέποιτο (Hesych.); and so *Ai.* 608 τὸν ἀπότροπον αἴδηλον
Ἅιδαν, such as all would turn away from, abhorred.   Not 'turning away
from others,' 'solitary,' as Bion *Idyll.* 2. 2 τὸν ἀπότροπον...Ἔρωτα.
ἐπιπλόμενον = ἐπιπελόμενον, pres. part., as *Od.* 7. 261 ἐπιπλόμενον ἔτος
ἦλθε.   **1315 δυσούριστον** is defective by one syllable as compared with

4 οἴμοι,
5 οἴμοι μάλ' αὖθις· οἷον εἰσέδυ μ' ἅμα
6 κέντρων τε τῶνδ' οἴστρημα καὶ μνήμη κακῶν.
ΧΟ. 7 καὶ θαυμά γ' οὐδὲν ἐν τοσοῖσδε πήμασιν
8 διπλᾶ σε πενθεῖν καὶ διπλᾶ φέρειν κακά.   1320

ἀντ. α'.   ΟΙ. 1 ἰὼ φίλος,
2 σὺ μὲν ἐμὸς ἐπίπολος ἔτι μόνιμος· ἔτι γὰρ
3 ὑπομένεις με τὸν τυφλὸν κηδεύων.
4 φεῦ φεῦ.
5 οὐ γάρ με λήθεις, ἀλλὰ γιγνώσκω σαφῶς,   1325
6 καίπερ σκοτεινός, τήν γε σὴν αὐδὴν ὅμως.
ΧΟ. 7 ὦ δεινὰ δράσας, πῶς ἔτλης τοιαῦτα σὰς
8 ὄψεις μαρᾶναι; τίς σ' ἐπῆρε δαιμόνων;

στρ. β'.   ΟΙ. 1 Ἀπόλλων τάδ' ἦν, Ἀπόλλων, φίλοι,
2 ὁ κακὰ κακὰ τελῶν ἐμὰ τάδ' ἐμὰ παθέα.   1330

1320 φορεῖν L, B (cum γρ. φέρειν), V, V³, L², Pal.: φέρειν A, V², V⁴, E, T. Cur φορεῖν non patiatur hic locus, infra monitum est.   **1323** ὑπομένεις ἐμὲ codd.: με restituit Erfurdt. Pro ἔτι γὰρ ὑπομένεις ἐμὲ τὸν τυφλὸν, cod. T habet σὺ γὰρ ὑπομένεις τὸν γε | τυφλὸν, cui coniecturae propositum erat ut metrum sanaret. Hermann., cum in v. 1315 δυσούριστον οἴμοι dedisset, hic scripsit ἔτι γὰρ | ὑπομένεις· τυφλόν τε κήδευε· φεῦ φεῦ. | Pro κηδεύων, coniecit κηδεμών Linwood., recepit Ken-

---

1323 τυφλὸν κηδεύων. Now the second syllable of κηδεύων is 'irrational,' *i.e.* it is a long syllable doing metrical duty for a short one (the third of an antibacchius, – – ◡). Hence in this verse also the penultimate syllable can be either long or short.   Hermann's δυσούριστον ὄν is therefore metrically admissible. It is, however, somewhat weak, and the sound is most unpleasing.   I should rather propose δυσούριστ' ἰόν: for the adverbial neut. plur., cp. ὑπέροπτα...πορεύεται (883, where see note); for the part., Plat. *Legg.* 873 E παρὰ θεοῦ...βέλος ἰόν. Nauck conjectured δυσοιώνιστον. Blaydes gives δυσεξούριστον (not found), in the dubious sense of 'hard to escape from.'   **1318** κέντρων, not literally the pins of the brooches, (which we can scarcely suppose that he still carried in his hands,) but the stabs which they had dealt: as piercing pangs are κέντρα, *Tr.* 840.   **1319** ἐν τοσοῖσδε πήμασιν, when thy woes are so many: cp. 893 ἐν τοῖσδ'.   **1320** πενθεῖν...καὶ φέρειν. The form of the sentence, in dependence on θαῦμα οὐδέν, seems to

Ay me! and once again, ay me!

How is my soul pierced by the stab of these goads, and withal by the memory of sorrows!

CH. Yea, mid woes so many a twofold pain may well be thine to mourn and to bear.

OE. Ah, friend, thou still art steadfast in thy tendance of me,—thou still hast patience to care for the blind man. Thy presence is not hid from me—no, dark though I am, yet know I thy voice full well. *1st antistrophe.*

CH. Man of dread deeds, how could'st thou in such wise quench thy vision? What more than human power urged thee?

OE. Apollo, friends, Apollo was he that brought these my woes to pass, these my sore, sore woes: *2nd strophe.*

nedius. **1330** ὁ κακὰ κακὰ τελῶν ἐμὰ τάδ' ἐμὰ πάθεα A aliique codd. In L prima manus scripserat ὁ κακὰ τελῶν τάδ' ἐμὰ πάθεα: mox alterum κακὰ (ante κακὰ) et ἐμὰ (ante τάδ') addidit corrector antiquus. Est autem in codd. compluribus (ut B, E, T, V, V², V⁴) ὁ κακὰ τελῶν ἐμὰ τάδ' ἐμὰ πάθεα: scilicet interpositum τάδ' causae fuerat ne alterum ἐμὰ deleretur; deletum est alterum κακὰ tanquam διττογραφίᾳ natum. Vide quae annotavimus.

---

exclude the version: 'It is not strange that, *as* you bear, *so* you should mourn, a double pain' (parataxis for hypotaxis). Rather the sense is: 'that you should *mourn* (aloud) and (inwardly) *suffer* a double pain' —*i. e.*, the physical pain of the wounds, and the mental pain of retrospect. I do not agree with Schneid. in referring διπλᾶ πενθεῖν to the double οἴμοι (1316 f.) as = 'make a twofold lament.' The φέρειν of A must be right. φορεῖν can stand for φέρειν 'to carry' when habitual carrying is implied (Her. 3. 34, and of bearers in *Tr.* 965): or fig., of mental habit (ἦθος φορεῖν *Ant.* 705): but φορεῖν κακά could only mean 'to carry ills about with thee'; which is not appropriate here. **1322** μόνιμος, steadfast: Xen. *Cyr.* 8. 5. 11 οἱ μονιμώτατοι πρόσθεν ὄντες (said of hoplites). Cp. *Ai.* 348 ff., where Ajax addresses the Chorus as μόνοι ἐμῶν φίλων, | μόνοι ἐμμένοντες ἔτ' ὀρθῷ νόμῳ. **1325** A distinct echo of *Il.* 24. 563 καὶ δὲ σὲ γιγνώσκω, Πρίαμε, φρεσίν, οὐδέ με λήθεις. Besides λήθω, λήσω, λέληθα, Soph. has ἔληθον (*El.* 1359). **1326** σκοτεινός: cp. *Ai.* 85 ἐγὼ σκοτώσω βλέφαρα καὶ δεδορκότα. **1329 f.** Ἀπόλλων. The memory of Oedipus (cp. 1318) is connecting the oracle given to him at Delphi (789) with the mandate which afterwards came thence (106). Apollo was the author of the doom (τελῶν), but the instrument of execution (ἔπαισε) was the hand of Oedipus. **1330** ὁ κακὰ κακὰ κ.τ.λ.

3 ἔπαισε δ' αὐτόχειρ νιν οὔτις, ἀλλ' ἐγὼ τλάμων.
4 τί γὰρ ἔδει μ' ὁρᾶν,
5 ὅτῳ γ' ὁρῶντι μηδὲν ἦν ἰδεῖν γλυκύ;   1335
ΧΟ. 6 ἦν ταῦθ' ὅπωσπερ καὶ σὺ φῄς.
ΟΙ. 7 τί δῆτ' ἐμοὶ βλεπτόν, ἢ
8 στερκτόν, ἢ προσήγορον
9 ἔτ' ἔστ' ἀκούειν ἡδονᾷ, φίλοι;
10 ἀπάγετ' ἐκτόπιον ὅτι τάχιστά με,   1340
11 ἀπάγετ', ὦ φίλοι, τὸν μέγ' ὀλέθριον,
12 τὸν καταρατότατον, ἔτι δὲ καὶ θεοῖς   1345
13 ἐχθρότατον βροτῶν.
ΧΟ. 14 δείλαιε τοῦ νοῦ τῆς τε συμφορᾶς ἴσον,
15 ὥς σ' ἠθέλησα μηδέ γ' ἂν γνῶναί ποτε.

1339 ἡδονᾷ codd. et edd. plerique: ἀδονᾷ Dindorf.   1341 τὸν ὀλέθριον μέγαν
L, A, codd. plerique: τὸν ὀλέθριον μέγα, B, E, T.   Veram procul dubio l. τὸν μέγ'
ὀλέθριον restituit Erfurdt., receperunt Nauck., Blaydes., Kennedius. Coniecit Tur-
nebus τὸν ὀλέθρον μέγαν, quod miror equidem tot editores (Brunck., Elms., Herm.,
Campbell.) recepisse, praesertim cum ὀλέθρον ne unius quidem codicis fide (quod
sciam) firmetur. Ingeniose magis quam vere Bergkius τὸν ὀλεθρόν με γᾶς. Plura

The dochmiac metre is sound (see Metrical Analysis): it is νομάδος in
the antistrophe (1350) which is corrupt. Prof. Campbell, however,
retaining the latter, here changes the second κακὰ to κακῶς, and the first
ἐμά to ἐμοί.   The iteration of τάδε, κακά, ἐμά is in a style which the
lyrics of tragedy admitted where vehement agitation was expressed.
Euripides carried it to excess.   But here, at least, it is in place.
1331 νιν, τὰς ὄψεις (1328).   οὔτις (ἄλλος), ἀλλ': cp. Od. 8. 311 ἀτὰρ
οὔ τί μοι αἴτιος ἄλλος | ἀλλὰ τοκῆε δύω.   Schneid. cp. Il. 21. 275
ἄλλος δ' οὔτις μοι τόσον αἴτιος οὐρανιώνων | ἀλλὰ [instead of ὅσον]
φίλη μήτηρ.   1337 ff. The simple mode of expression would have
been : τί ἐμοὶ ἡδέως βλεπτόν, ἢ στερκτόν, ἢ ἀκουστόν ἔτ' ἐστίν; what
henceforth can be pleasurably seen, or loved, or heard by me?   But,
instead of the third clause, we have ἢ προσήγορον | ἔτ' ἔστ' ἀκούειν
ἡδονᾷ, 'or what greeting is it longer possible for me to hear with
pleasure?' προσήγορον, passive in Ph. 1353, is here active, as in
Ant. 1185 Παλλάδος θεᾶς | ὅπως ἱκοίμην εὐγμάτων προσήγορος. ἡδονᾷ,
modal dat. adverbially, as ὀργῇ 405. The form ἡδονάν, intermediate
between Attic ἡδονήν and Doric ἀδονάν, is given by L in El. 1277, where

but the hand that struck the eyes was none save mine, wretched that I am! Why was I to see, when sight could show me nothing sweet?

CH. These things were even as thou sayest.

OE. Say, friends, what can I more behold, what can I love, what greeting can touch mine ear with joy? Haste, lead me from the land, friends, lead me hence, the utterly lost, the thrice accursed, yea, the mortal most abhorred of heaven!

CH. Wretched alike for thy fortune and for thy sense thereof, would that I had never so much as known thee!

habes infra. **1348** ὥς σ᾽ ἠθέλησα μηδ᾽ ἀναγνῶναί ποτ᾽ ἄν L et codd. pleiique: pro ποτ᾽ ἄν, ποτε habet A, cum aliis aliquot. ἀναγνῶναι corruptum est ex ἄν γνῶναι, ut ἀναμετρηθεῖεν pro ἄν μετρηθεῖεν praebet A in v. 561. Vere igitur restituit Hermann., ὥς σ᾽ ἠθέλησα μηδέ γ᾽ ἄν γνῶναί ποτε: quam l., cum ad codices paullo propius accedat, praeferendam duco Dindorfianae, ὡς ἠθέλησα μηδέ σ᾽ ἄν γνῶναί ποτε. Idonea est hic particula γε ad augendam vim verborum μηδὲ ἄν γνῶναι: eadem pravae lectionis origini lucis aliquid affert.

Herm. keeps it, but most edd. give ἀδονάν. If right, it was a compromise peculiar to tragedy. The Doricism of scenic lyrics was not thorough-going: here, for instance, we have τλάμων (1333) yet προσήγορον (1338). **1340** ἐκτόπιον: cp. 1411 θαλάσσιον, and see Appendix, Note 11, p. 300. **1341** τὸν μέγ᾽ ὀλέθριον is a certain correction of the MS. τὸν ὀλέθριον μέγαν (or μέγα), a corruption due to the omission and subsequent marginal insertion of μέγα. Cp. *Il.* 1. 158 ὦ μέγ᾽ ἀναιδές: 16. 46 μέγα νήπιος: *Ph.* 419 μέγα | θάλλοντες. The antistrophic words are αὐτὸς ἔφυν τάλας (1363). ὀλέθριον, pass., 'lost,' as *Tr.* 878 τάλαιν᾽ ὀλεθρία. τίνι τρόπῳ θανεῖν σφε φῇς; The objections to the conject. ὄλεθρον μέγαν (metrically admissible as a dochmiac, if the second of ὄλεθρον is made short) are: (1) the awkward necessity of supplying ὄντα in order to defend the position of μέγαν: (2) the phrase ὄλεθρον, which belongs to the colloquial vocabulary of abuse; Dem. or. 18 § 127 περίτριμμα ἀγορᾶς, ὄλεθρος γραμματεύς. **1347** He is to be pitied alike for the intrinsic misery of his fate, and for his full apprehension (συνέσεως, schol.) of it. A clouded mind would suffer less. **1348** ἄν with ἠθέλησα: γε emphasises μηδέ. Oedipus had been the all-admired (8), the 'saviour of the land' (48). But now the Theban elders wish that they had never so much as heard his name or looked upon his face. That bitter cry is drawn from them by the very strength of their sympathy; for his ruin was the

ἀντ. β'. ΟΙ. 1 ὄλοιθ' ὅστις ἦν ὃς ἀγρίας πέδας
2 †νομάδ'† ἐπιποδίας ἔλυσ' ἀπό τε φόνου   1350
3 ἔρρυτο κἀνέσωσέ μ', οὐδὲν εἰς χάριν πράσσων.
4 τότε γὰρ ἂν θανὼν

1349 ἀπ' ἀγρίας L, A, et reliqui codd. fere omnes: ἀγρίας T, recte enim viderat Triclinius spurium esse illud ἀπ', quod illatum est ut clarior fieret genitivi ratio. Maluit tamen Hermann., omisso ἦν, sic legere: ὄλοιθ' ὅστις, ὅς μ' ἀπ' ἀγρίας πέδας. **1350** νομάδος ἐπιποδίας | ἔλυσεν ἀπό τε φόνου | ἔρρυτο κἀνέσωσεν L et A. In L ἔλυσεν radendo factum est fortasse ex ἔλαβέ μ' (non, opinor, ex ἔλαβέν μ'). Cum codd. L et

result of his coming to Thebes. The objections to the reading of the MSS., ὥς σ' ἠθέλησα μήδ' ἀναγνῶναί ποτε, are these: (1) Eur. *Helen.* 290 has the 1st aor. pass., ἀνεγνώσθημεν ἄν, 'we should have been recognised': but ἀναγιγνώσκειν occurs nowhere else in tragedy; and in Attic its regular sense was 'to read,' or in 1st aor. act., 'to persuade.' I have not found a single example of ἀναγιγνώσκω as = ἀναγνωρίζω ('to recognise') in Thuc., Plato, Xen., or the Orators. (2) But the 2nd aor. has that sense in Homer, in Pindar (*Isthm.* 2. 23) and in Herod. (2. 91): may not an Attic poet have followed them? Granted. The sense required here, however, after μηδέ, is to *know*, not to *recognise:* the latter would be pointless. (3) The ellipse of ἄν with the aor. ἠθέλησα would be strangely harsh. Such an ellipse with the *imperf.* sometimes occurs: as Antiphon or. 5 § 1 ἐβουλόμην (and so Ar. *Ran.* 866), *ib.* § 86 ἠξίουν. But if, as seems clear, ἄν is *required* here, then the probability is strengthened that ἀναγνῶναι arose from ἂν γνῶναι. Between Dindorf's ὡς ἠθέλησα μηδέ σ' ἂν γνῶναι and Hermann's ὥς σ' ἠθέλησα μηδέ γ' ἂν γνῶναι the question is: Which is most likely to have passed into the reading of the MSS.? Now they have ὥς σ', and the loss of γ' through a confusion with the same letter in γνῶναι is slightly more probable than the double error of omitting σ' before ἄν and inserting it after ὥς. **1350** The νομάδος of the MSS. is corrupt. It would require an improbable alteration in the strophe (see on 1330); and it yields no good sense. The scholiasts hesitated between rendering it (1) 'feeding on my flesh'! or (2) 'in the pastures.' Reading νομάδ', we have a dochmiac dimeter, agreeing with 1330: see Metrical Analysis. But the use of the word is extraordinary. It must mean ἐν νομαῖς, 'in the pastures'—said of the babe whom the shepherd had been ordered to expose on Cithaeron. Now elsewhere νομάς always means ' *roaming,*' said (*e. g.*) of pastoral tribes, or of animals: *Tr.* 271 ἵππους νομάδας

ΟΕ. Perish the man, whoe'er he was, that freed me in the pas- 2nd anti-
tures from the cruel shackle on my feet, and saved me from death, strophe.
and gave me back to life,—a thankless deed! Had I died then,

A ceteri consentiunt, nisi quod alii ἔρρυτο alii ἔρυτο habent; in paucis autem pro ἔλυσεν
legitur vel ἔλυσέ μ' (E), vel ἔλυσ' ἐμ' (V⁴), vel ἔλαβέ μ' (V). νομάδος procul dubio
falsum est. Coniecit Elmsleius νομάδ'. Sed ne ita quidem huic loco illud vocabulum
posse accommodari spero me iis persuasurum qui infra annotata legerint. Conieci
μονάδ'. Pro κάνέσωσεν Campbellius recte scripsit κάνέσωσέ μ'.

ἐξιχνοσκοπῶν, tracking horses *that had strayed*: fr. 87 νομὰς δέ τις
κερούσσ' ἀπ' ὀρθίων πάγων | καθεῖρπεν ἔλαφος: of waters *wandering* over
the land which they irrigate, *O. C.* 686 κρῆναι...| Κηφισοῦ νομάδες ῥεέθρων.
The idea of wandering movement is inseparable from the word. To
apply it to a babe whose feet were pinned together would have
been indeed a bold use. Prof. Campbell, retaining νομάδος, takes
πέδας as acc. plur. : 'that loosed the cruel clog upon my feet,
when I was sent astray.' But could νομάς, 'roaming,' be said of
the maimed child merely in the sense of '*turned adrift*' by its
parents? The nomin. νομὰς, referring to the roving shepherd (πλάνης
1029) would be intelligible; but the quadruple -ας is against it. Now
cp. Aesch. *Pers.* 734 μονάδα δὲ Ξέρξην ἔρημον, 'Xerxes alone and
forlorn.' Simply transposing ν and μ, I conjecture μονάδ', a word
appropriate to the complaint that the babe, sent to the lonely mountain, had not been left to perish in its solitude. The fact that the
Corinthian shepherd received the child from the Theban is no objection : the child was φίλων μεμονωμένος, desolate and forlorn. ἔλυσ',
which suits the dochmiac as well as ἔλαβέ μ', is more forcible here.
There is a further argument for it. The MSS. give ἀπ' ἀγρίας in 1349,
but the strophe (1329) shows that ἀπ' must be omitted, since 'Απόλ-
λων, φίλοι = δς ἀγρίας πέδας, the first syllable of ἀγρίας being short, as
in 1205, *Ant.* 344, 1124. Now πέδας (*i.e.* πέδης) ἔλαβε, *took from* the
fetter, would be too harsh: we could only do as Schneid. did,
and refer ἀπό back to πέδας: but though Δελφῶν κἀπὸ Δαυλίας (734)
admits of such treatment, the case is dissimilar here. On the other
hand, πέδας ἔλυσ', *loosed from* the fetter, is correct. Thus the metrical
impossibility of ἀπ' confirms ἔλυσ'. The epithet ἀγρία, 'cruel,' is applied
to πέδη as it is to ὀδύνη *Tr.* 975. 1351 ἔρρυτο, a strong aorist of ῥύω,
formed as if there were a present ῥύμι: in *Il.* 18. 515 ῥύατο for ῥύντο is
its 3rd plur. Cp. *Il.* 5. 23 ἔρυτο σάωσε δέ, where the aor. has a like
relation to ἐρύω (the temporal augment being absent). εἰς χάριν: see

5 οὐκ ἦν φίλοισιν οὐδ' ἐμοὶ τοσόνδ' ἄχος.   1355

ΧΟ. 6 θέλοντι κἀμοὶ τοῦτ' ἂν ἦν.

ΟΙ. 7 οὔκουν πατρός γ' ἂν φονεὺς
  8 ἦλθον, οὐδὲ νυμφίος
  9 βροτοῖς ἐκλήθην ὧν ἔφυν ἄπο.

  10 νῦν δ' ἄθεος μέν εἰμ', ἀνοσίων δὲ παῖς,   1360
  11 ὁμογενὴς δ' ἀφ' ὧν αὐτὸς ἔφυν τάλας.

  12 εἰ δέ τι πρεσβύτερον ἔτι κακοῦ κακόν,   1365
  13 τοῦτ' ἔλαχ' Οἰδίπους.

ΧΟ. 14 οὐκ οἶδ' ὅπως σε φῶ βεβουλεῦσθαι καλῶς,
  15 κρείσσων γὰρ ἦσθα μηκέτ' ὢν ἢ ζῶν τυφλός.

ΟΙ. ὡς μὲν τάδ' οὐχ ὧδ' ἔστ' ἄριστ' εἰργασμένα,
  μή μ' ἐκδίδασκε, μηδὲ συμβούλευ' ἔτι.   1370
  ἐγὼ γὰρ οὐκ οἶδ' ὄμμασιν ποίοις βλέπων

1355 Pro ἄχος Faehsius coniecit ἄγος, sed hominis querelae qui se vivum et amicis et sibi gravem esse doleat melius convenit vulgata l.   1360 ἄθλιός codd., 'quo metrum perimitur,' ut ait Erfurdt., ἄθεος restituens. In eandem coniecturam, quae certissima est, inciderant Elmsleius, Seidler. (*De Vers. Dochm.* 59), Reisig.

on 1152.   1356 θέλοντι: Thuc. 2. 3 τῷ γὰρ πλήθει...οὐ βουλομένῳ ἦν... ἀφίστασθαι: Tac. *Agric.* 18 *quibus bellum volentibus erat.*   1357 φονεὺς ἦλθον, have come to be the slayer, a compressed phrase for ἐς τοσοῦτον ηλθον ὥστε φονεὺς εἶναι: cp. 1519, and *Ant.* 752 ἢ κἀπαπειλῶν ὧδ' ἐπεξέρχει θρασύς; *Tr.* 1157 ἐξήκεις δ' ἵνα | φανεῖ. *Il.* 18. 180 εἴ κέν τι νέκυς ᾐσχυμμένος ἔλθῃ, *come to be* dishonoured (where some explain, '*reach thee* dishonoured'): in Xen. *An.* 3. 2. 3 ὅμως δὲ δεῖ ἐκ τῶν παρόντων ἄνδρας ἀγαθοὺς ἐλθεῖν (so the MSS.: τελέθειν G. Sauppe) καὶ μὴ ὑφίεσθαι, the clause ἐκ τῶν παρόντων helps ἐλθεῖν as = *evadere.* In 1433 ἐλθών is not similar. No classical use of *venire* seems really parallel: thus in Iuv. 7. 29 *ut dignus venias hederis, venias* = 'may come forward' (Mayor *ad loc.*).   1359 (τούτων) ἀφ' ὧν, i.e. ταύτης ἀφ' ἧς: plur., as 1095, 1176, 1250.   1360 ἄθεος is a necessary correction of the MS. ἄθλιος, the verse being a dochmiac dimeter, = 1340 ἀπάγετ' ἐκτόπιον ὅτι τάχιστά με. νῦν answers to the *short* first syllable of ἀπάγετ', since the anacrusis can be either long or short: cp. Aesch. *Theb.* 81, where αἰθερία κόνις is metrically parallel to νῦν δ' ἄθεος μέν εἰμ' here. He is ἀνοσίων (*i.e.* ἀνοσίας) παῖς because through him

to my friends and to mine own soul I had not been so sore a grief.

CH. I also would have had it thus.

OE. So had I not come to shed my father's blood, nor been called among men the spouse of her from whom I sprang: but now am I forsaken of the gods, son of a defiled mother, successor to his bed who gave me mine own wretched being: and if there be yet a woe surpassing woes, it hath become the portion of Oedipus.

CH. I know not how I can say that thou hast counselled well: for thou wert better dead than living and blind.

OE. Show me not at large that these things are not best done thus: give me counsel no more. For, had I sight, I know not with what eyes I could e'er have looked on my

---

(*Conject.* 1. 191). **1361** ὁμογενὴς codd.: ὁμολεχὴς Meinekius, Dindorf., Nauck.: ὁμόγαμος Musgravius. **1365** ἔφυ codd.: ἔτι Hermann.: quae emendatio necessaria est, cum respondeant verba ἔτι κακοῦ κακόν verbis strophicis ἔτι δὲ καὶ θεοῖς (v. 1345). **1368** ἦσθ' ἂν Purgold., Hartung.: vide tamen annot.

Iocasta became defiled. **1362 f.** ὁμογενὴς δ' ἀφ' ὧν ἔφυν = κοινὸν γένος ἔχων (τούτοις) ἀφ' ὧν αὐτὸς ἔφυν: *i.e.* having a common brood (a brood born of the same wife) with those (Laïus) from whom he sprang. ὁμογενὴς is usu. taken here as = ὁμοῦ γεννῶν, *begetting with* his mother, or *from the same wife with* his father. But if it is remembered that ὁμογενής is a compound from ὁμο- and the stem of γένος, it will be evident that it could no more mean γεννῶν ὁμοῦ than συγγενής could mean γεννῶν σύν, or ἐγγενής, γεννῶν ἐν. In 460 πατρὸς ὁμόσπορος as = σπείρων τὴν αὐτὴν ἣν ὁ πατήρ is different, since the second part of the compound adj. represents a transitive verb. Meineke's ὁμολεχὴς would be better than Musgrave's ὁμόγαμος: but neither is needed. **1365** πρεσβύτερον, 'older,' then, 'ranking before'; here, 'more serious': Her. 5. 63 τὰ γὰρ τοῦ θεοῦ πρεσβύτερα ἐποιεῦντο ἢ τὰ τῶν ἀνδρῶν : Thuc. 4. 61 τοῦτο...πρεσβύτατον... κρίνας, τὸ κοινῶς φοβερὸν ἅπαντας εὖ θέσθαι. **1368** κρείσσων...ἦσθα μηκέτ' ὢν = κρεῖσσον ἦν σε μηκέτ' εἶναι: see on 1061. ἂν is omitted, as after ἔδει, εἰκὸς ἦν, etc., κρείσσων ἦσθα μὴ ὢν implying the thought, οὐκ ἂν ἦσθα, εἰ τὰ βέλτιστα ἔπασχες: see on 256. **1369** ἄριστ' is adverbial, the construction being οὐχ ὧδε (εἰργασμένα) ἐστὶν ἄριστα εἰργασμένα: that, thus done, they are not done best. So ἄριστα is adverb 407, 1046, *Ai.* 160. **1371** βλέπων = εἰ ἔβλεπον, which is more forcible than to take it with ποίοις

πατέρα ποτ᾽ ἂν προσεῖδον εἰς Ἅιδου μολών,
οὐδ᾽ αὖ τάλαιναν μητέρ᾽, οἷν ἐμοὶ δυοῖν
ἔργ᾽ ἐστὶ κρεῖσσον᾽ ἀγχόνης εἰργασμένα.
ἀλλ᾽ ἡ τέκνων δῆτ᾽ ὄψις ἦν ἐφίμερος,   1375
βλαστοῦσ᾽ ὅπως ἔβλαστε, προσλεύσσειν ἐμοί;
οὐ δῆτα τοῖς γ᾽ ἐμοῖσιν ὀφθαλμοῖς ποτε·
οὐδ᾽ ἄστυ γ᾽, οὐδὲ πύργος, οὐδὲ δαιμόνων
ἀγάλμαθ᾽ ἱερά, τῶν ὁ παντλήμων ἐγὼ
κάλλιστ᾽ ἀνὴρ εἷς ἕν γε ταῖς Θήβαις τραφεὶς   1380

1376 βλαστοῦσ᾽] βλαστόνθ᾽ coniecit Hartung., deleto post ἔβλαστε puncto : sic sensus erit, ἐμοὶ προσλεύσσειν βλαστόντα ὅπως ἔβλαστε, 'ut ego aspicerem liberos tali modo procreatos': sed poetica magis eademque simplicior est codicum lectio.

ὄμμασιν. Cp. *Ph.* 110 πῶς οὖν βλέπων τις ταῦτα τολμήσει λαλεῖν; [Dem.] or. 25 § 98 (the work of a later rhetorician) ποίοις προσώποις ἢ τίσιν ὀφθαλμοῖς πρὸς ἕκαστον τούτων ἀντιβλέψετε; Cp. *Ai.* 462 καὶ ποῖον ὄμμα πατρὶ δηλώσω φανεὶς | Τελαμῶνι 1372 εἰς Ἅιδου. Blind on earth, Oed. will be blind in the nether world. Cp. *Od.* 12. 266 καί μοι ἔπος ἔμπεσε θυμῷ | μάντηος ἀλαοῦ Θηβαίου Τειρεσίαο, where Odysseus is thinking of the blind Teiresias as he had found him in Hades. Cp. 11. 91, where ἔγνω need not imply that the poet of the νέκυια conceived Teiresias as having sight. So Achilles in Hades is still *swift-footed* (11. 546). **1373** οἷν...δυοῖν, a dative of the persons affected, as, instead of the usual ποιῶ ταῦτά σε, we sometimes find ποιῶ ταῦτά σοι: *Od.* 14. 289 τρώκτης, ὃς δὴ πολλὰ κάκ᾽ ἀνθρώποισιν ἐώργει. Plat. *Apol.* 30 A ταῦτα καὶ νεωτέρῳ καὶ πρεσβυτέρῳ...ποιήσω, καὶ ξένῳ καὶ ἀστῷ, μᾶλλον δὲ τοῖς ἀστοῖς. *Charm.* 157 C οὐκ ἂν ἔχοιμεν ὅ τι ποιοῖμέν σοι. Xen. *Hier.* 7. 2 τοιαῦτα γὰρ δὴ ποιοῦσι τοῖς τυράννοις οἱ ἀρχόμενοι καὶ ἄλλον ὄντιν᾽ ἂν ἀεὶ τιμῶντες τυγχάνωσι. Ar. *Vesp.* 1350 πολλοῖς γὰρ ἤδη χἀτέροις αὔτ᾽ εἰργάσω. In Xen. *An.* 5. 8. 24 τούτῳ τἀναντία ποιήσετε ἢ τοὺς κύνας ποιοῦσι, there is warrant for τοῦτον : and in Isocr. or. 16 § 49 μηδὲν ἀγαθὸν ποιήσας τῇ πόλει, for τὴν πόλιν. **1374** κρεῖσσον᾽ ἀγχόνης, not '*worse than* hanging' (such that, rather than do them, he would have hanged himself): but, '*too bad for* hanging' (such that suicide by hanging would not adequately punish their author). Eur. *Hipp.* 1217 εἰσορῶσι δὲ | θέαμα κρεῖσσον δεργμάτων ἐφαίνετο, *too dreadful* to be looked on: Aesch. *Ag.* 1376 ὕψος κρεῖσσον ἐκπηδήματος, *too high* to be leaped

father, when I came to the place of the dead, aye, or on my miserable mother, since against both I have sinned such sins as strangling could not punish. But deem ye that the sight of children, born as mine were born, was lovely for me to look upon? No, no, not lovely to mine eyes for ever! No, nor was this town with its towered walls, nor the sacred statues of the gods, since I, thrice wretched that I am,—I, noblest of the sons of Thebes,

1379 ἱρὰ A, Wunder., Dindorf., Campbell.: ἱερὰ L, B, E, alii; Hermann., Nauck., Blaydes., Kennedius. ἱερὰ hic rhythmum praebet qui flebiliter lamentantis voci paullo melius (ut meae quidem sentiunt aures) videtur convenire; sic etiam in 1428 credo retinendum ἱερὸς, quod, ut hic ἱερὰ, codicum gravior auctoritas commendat.

over. ἀγχόνης: cp. Eur. *Alc.* 229: Ar. *Ach.* 125 ταῦτα δῆτ' οὐκ ἀγχόνη; 'is not this enough to make one hang oneself?' **1375 f.** ἀλλ' introduces (or answers) a supposed objection (the ὑποφορά of technical Rhetoric): Andoc. I § 148 τίνα γὰρ καὶ ἀναβιβάσομαι δεησόμενον ὑπὲρ ἐμαυτοῦ; τὸν πατέρα; ἀλλὰ τέθνηκεν. ἀλλὰ τοὺς ἀδελφούς; ἀλλ' οὐκ εἰσίν. ἀλλὰ τοὺς παῖδας; ἀλλ' οὔπω γεγένηνται. τέκνων ὄψις...βλαστοῦσα = ὁρώμενα τέκνα βλαστόντα: cp. Eur. *Alc.* 967 Θρήσσαις ἐν σανίσιν τὰς | Ὀρφεία κατέγραψεν γήρυς, which the melodious Orpheus wrote down. ὅπως ἔβλαστε: Eur. *Med.* 1011 ἤγγειλας οἷ' ἤγγειλας. **1378** πύργος, the city-wall with its towers and its seven gates (already famous in the *Odyssey*, 11. 263 Θήβης ἕδος ἑπταπύλοιο). Cp. Eur. *Bacch.* 170 Κάδμον... ὃς πόλιν Σιδωνίαν | λιπὼν ἐπύργωσ' ἄστυ Θηβαῖον τόδε. *Hec.* 1209 πέριξ δὲ πύργος εἶχ' ἔτι πτόλιν. **1379** ἀγάλμαθ' ἱερά, the images of the gods in their temples: cp. 20. τῶν = ὧν, as *Ant.* 1086: cp. 1427. Soph. has this use in at least seven other places of dialogue. **1380** κάλλιστ' ἀνὴρ εἰς...τραφείς. εἰς, in connection with a superlative, is strictly correct only where *one* is compared with *several:* as Thuc. 8. 40 οἱ γὰρ οἰκέται τοῖς Χίοις πολλοὶ ὄντες καὶ μιᾷ γε πόλει πλὴν Λακεδαιμονίων πλεῖστοι γενόμενοι: Eur. *Heracl.* 8 πλείστων μετέσχον εἷς ἀνὴρ Ἡρακλέει. So *Tr.* 460 πλείστας ἀνὴρ εἷς...ἔγημε. But here, where the question is of degree in nobility, it merely strengthens κάλλιστ': cp. Thuc. 8. 68 πλεῖστα εἷς ἀνήρ, ὅστις ξυμβουλεύσαιτό τι, δυνάμενος ὠφελεῖν: which, notwithstanding πλεῖστα, is really like our passage, since we cannot suppose a contrast with the collective wisdom of several advisers. ἔν γε ταῖς Θήβαις: the γε, by adding a second limitation, helps, like εἷς ἀνήρ, to emphasise the superlative. If the glories of Thebes can rejoice the sight, no *Theban* at least had a better right to that joy: (and who could have a better right

ἀπεστέρησ' ἐμαυτόν, αὐτὸς ἐννέπων
ὠθεῖν ἅπαντας τὸν ἀσεβῆ, τὸν ἐκ θεῶν
φανέντ' ἄναγνον καὶ γένους τοῦ Λαΐου.
τοιάνδ' ἐγὼ κηλῖδα μηνύσας ἐμὴν
ὀρθοῖς ἔμελλον ὄμμασιν τούτους ὁρᾶν;   1385
ἥκιστά γ'· ἀλλ' εἰ τῆς ἀκουούσης ἔτ' ἦν
πηγῆς δι' ὤτων φραγμός, οὐκ ἂν ἐσχόμην
τὸ μὴ 'ποκλῆσαι τοὐμὸν ἄθλιον δέμας,
ἵν' ἦ τυφλός τε καὶ κλύων μηδέν· τὸ γὰρ
τὴν φροντίδ' ἔξω τῶν κακῶν οἰκεῖν γλυκύ.   1390
ἰὼ Κιθαιρών, τί μ' ἐδέχου; τί μ' οὐ λαβὼν
ἔκτεινας εὐθύς, ὡς ἔδειξα μήποτε
ἐμαυτὸν ἀνθρώποισιν ἔνθεν ἦ γεγώς;

1383 καὶ γένους τοῦ Λαΐου] Sana sunt haec: vide annot. Sed coniecit Hartung., κᾶν γένους τοῦ Λαΐου, i.e. ' *quamvis* sit ille Laii genere ortus.' Arrisit Nauckio quod Herwerden. proposuit, καὶ γένους ἀλάστορα. Benedictus post ἄναγνον plene interpunxit, deinde verba γένους τοῦ Λαΐου tanquam a κηλῖδα pendentia accepit (labem qua Laii gens inficitur). καὶ γένος τὸν Λαΐου (quod ad genus attinet, filium Laii)

than Thebans?) 1381 ἀπεστέρησ' ἐμαυτόν: a regular phrase in reference to separation from civic life: Antiphon or. 5 § 78 εἰ δ' ἐν Αἴνῳ χωροφιλεῖ, τοῦτο οὐκ ἀποστερῶν γε τῶν εἰς τὴν πόλιν ἑαυτὸν οὐδενὸς (not forfeiting any of his relations with Athens) οὐδ' ἑτέρας πόλεως πολίτης γεγενημένος: [Dem.] or. 13 § 22 οὐδενὸς ἔργων τῶν τότε ἀπεστέρησαν ἑαυτούς, the Athenians of those days did not renounce their share in any of the great deeds of the Persian Wars. 1382 τὸν ἀσεβῆ naturally depends on ὠθεῖν. But, if so, it would be very awkward to take τὸν...φανέντα κ.τ.λ. with ἀπεστέρησ' ἐμαυτόν. Rather τὸν φανέντα κ.τ.λ. also depends on ὠθεῖν. ' Bidding all to expel the impious one,—that man who has [*since*] been shown by the gods to be unholy—and of the race of Laïus.' His thought passes from the *unknown* person of the edict to *himself*, precisely as in 1440 f. The words καὶ γένους τοῦ Λαΐου are a climax, since the guilt of bloodshed, which the oracle had first denounced, was thus aggravated by a double horror. 1384 κηλῖδα: see on 832 : μηνύσας ἐμὴν, sc. οὖσαν. 1385 ὀρθοῖς: see on 528. 1386 τῆς ἀκουούσης...πηγῆς, the *source* (viz. the orifice of the ear) from which sounds flow in upon the sense: cp. Plat. *Phaedr.* 245 C ψυχή...πηγὴ καὶ ἀρχὴ κινήσεως. (Not

—have doomed myself to know these no more, by mine own command that all should thrust away the impious one,—even him whom gods have shown to be unholy—and of the race of Laïus!

After baring such a stain upon me, was I to look with steady eyes on this folk? No, verily: no, were there yet a way to choke the fount of hearing, I had not spared to make a fast prison of this wretched frame, that so I should have known nor sight nor sound; for 'tis sweet that our thought should dwell beyond the sphere of griefs.

Alas, Cithaeron, why hadst thou a shelter for me? When I was given to thee, why didst thou not slay me straightway, that so I might never have revealed my source to men?

coniecit Blaydes. **1387** ἂν ἐσχόμην (non ἀνεσχόμην) clare scriptum habet A: sic etiam V: ἀνεσχόμην L, V², V³, al.: ἠνεσχόμην B, E, T, V⁴. **1388** τὸ μὴ ἀποκλεῖσαι codd.: τὸ μὴ ἀποκλῆσαι Elmsleius, Hermann., Nauck., Blaydes., Kennedius: τὸ μάποκλῆσαι Dindorf.: τὸ μήποκλῆσαι Campbell. Prima verbi forma κλήτω fuit, cum ductum sit (velut κονίω, μαστίω, μηνίω) a radice nominali in ι exeunte, κληϜί-s, *clavis*; neque κλείω, sed κλῆω, dicebant Attici veteriores.

the *stream* of sound itself.) **δι' ὤτων** supplements τῆς ἀκουούσης πηγῆς by suggesting the channel through which the sounds pass from the fount. Cp. fr. 773 βραδεῖα μὲν γὰρ ἐν λόγοισι προσβολὴ | μόλις δι' ὠτὸς ἔρχεται τρυπωμένου. ἡ ἀκούουσα πηγή, instead of ἡ πηγὴ τῆς ἀκούσεως, is said with a consciousness that πηγή means the organ of hearing, just as we might have τὰ ἀκούοντα ὦτα. Seneca paraphrases: *utinam quidem rescindere has quirem vias, Manibusque adactis omne qua voces meant Aditusque verbis tramite angusto patet, Eruere possem, gnata:...aures ingerunt, quicquid mihi Donastis, oculi (Phoen.* 226 ff.). **1387 ἐσχόμην,** usu. in this sense with gen., as *Od.* 4. 422 σχέσθαι...βίης. **1388 τὸ μή:** cp. 1232. The simple μή, where (as here) μὴ οὐ is admissible, occurs also in prose, as Antiph. *Tetral.* 3 β § 4 οὐδεὶς ἡμῖν λόγος ὑπελείπετο μὴ φονεῦσιν εἶναι. **1389 ἵν' ἦ.** For ἦ (as 1393) see on 1123. The negative μηδέν here shows how in this construction ἵνα is essentially final, 'so that I might have been'; not = 'in which case I should have been'—for which the negative must have been οὐδέν. So ὡς ἔδειξα μήποτε (1392), that I might never have shown. Eur. fr. 442 φεῦ φεῦ τὸ μὴ τὰ πράγματ' ἀνθρώποις ἔχειν | φωνήν, ἵν' ἦσαν μηδὲν οἱ δεινοὶ λόγοι. **1390 ἔξω τῶν κακῶν,** *i.e.* undisturbed by those sights and sounds from the outer world which serve to recall past miseries. **1391** The imperf. ἐδέχου helps the personification: 'wert ready to shelter me.' **1392 ὡς ἔδειξα:** see on

ὦ Πόλυβε καὶ Κόρινθε καὶ τὰ πάτρια
λόγῳ παλαιὰ δώμαθ', οἷον ἀρά με   1395
κάλλος κακῶν ὕπουλον ἐξεθρέψατε.
νῦν γὰρ κακός τ' ὢν κἀκ κακῶν εὑρίσκομαι.
ὦ τρεῖς κέλευθοι καὶ κεκρυμμένη νάπη
δρυμός τε καὶ στενωπὸς ἐν τριπλαῖς ὁδοῖς,
αἱ τοὐμὸν αἷμα τῶν ἐμῶν χειρῶν ἄπο   1400
ἐπίετε πατρός, ἀρά μου μέμνησθέ τι,
οἷ' ἔργα δράσας ὑμὶν εἶτα δεῦρ' ἰὼν
ὁποῖ' ἔπρασσον αὖθις; ὦ γάμοι γάμοι,
ἐφύσαθ' ἡμᾶς, καὶ φυτεύσαντες πάλιν
ἀνεῖτε ταὐτοῦ σπέρμα, κἀπεδείξατε   1405

1401 ἀρά μου codd.: ἀρ' ἐμοῦ Brunck., Erfurdt.: ἀρα μὴ Blaydes. Optavit ἀρά μοι Linwood.   μέμνησθ' ὅτι L (cum γρ. ὅταν in marg.), A, codd. fere omnes: ἔτι (quod Bodl. Laud. 54, ὅτι praebens, ut variam l. memorat) praebent codd. unus et

---

1389, and cp. Aesch. *P. V.* 776 τί...οὐκ ἐν τάχει | ἔρριψ' ἐμαυτήν...ὅπως πέδῳ σκήψασα τῶν πάντων πόνων | ἀπηλλάγην; **1394** τὰ πάτρια λόγῳ = τὰ λόγῳ πάτρια, an order the less harsh since πάτρια (= of my *fathers*, not πατρῷα, of my *father*) is supplemented by παλαιά. Cp. *Ai.* 635 ὁ νοσῶν μάταν: *El.* 792 τοῦ θανόντος ἀρτίως: Aesch. *P. V.* 1013 τῷ φρονοῦντι μὴ καλῶς: Eur. *Med.* 874 τοῖσι βουλεύουσιν εὖ. **1396** κάλλος κακῶν ὕπουλον, a fair surface, with secret ills festering beneath it (gen. κακῶν as after words of fulness, = κρυπτῶν κακῶν γέμον): because he had seemed most prosperous (775), while the doom decreed from his birth was secretly maturing itself with his growth. κάλλος, concrete, a fair object, Xen. *Cyr.* 5. 2. 7 τὴν θυγατέρα, δεινόν τι κάλλος καὶ μέγεθος, πενθικῶς δ' ἔχουσαν. ὕπουλον, of a sore festering beneath an οὐλή or scar which looks as if the wound had healed: Plat. *Gorg.* 480 Β ὅπως μὴ ἐγχρονισθὲν τὸ νόσημα τῆς ἀδικίας ὕπουλον τὴν ψυχὴν ποιήσει καὶ ἀνίατον, 'lest the disease of injustice become chronic, and render his soul *gangrenous* and past cure' (Thompson). Thuc. 8. 64 ὕπουλον αὐτονομίαν, *unsound* independence opp. to τὴν ἄντικρυς ἐλευθερίαν. Dem. or. 18 § 307 ἡσυχίαν ἄγειν ἄδικον καὶ ὕπουλον, unjust and *insecure* peace. Eustath. *Od.* 1496. 35 Σοφοκλῆς...λέγεται ὕπουλον εἰπεῖν τὸν δούρειον ἵππον, the wooden horse at Troy, as concealing foes. **1397** κἀκ κακῶν like ἀνοσίων παῖς (1360), with reference to the stain incurred by Iocasta. **1398 f.** His memory recalls the scene as if he were again approaching it on his way from

Ah, Polybus,—ah, Corinth, and thou that wast called the ancient house of my fathers, how seeming-fair was I your nursling, and what ills were festering beneath! For now I am found evil, and of evil birth. O ye three roads, and thou secret glen,— thou coppice, and narrow way where three paths met—ye who drank from my hands that father's blood which was mine own,—remember ye, perchance, what deeds I wrought for you to see,—and then, when I came hither, what fresh deeds I went on to do?

O marriage-rites, ye gave me birth, and when ye had brought me forth, again ye bore children to your child, ye created

alter, receperunt Brunck., Blaydes., Kennedius. μέμνησθέ τι Elmsleius, Campbell.: Nauck. autem, vel τι vel ἔτι probans, ὅτι tamen defendi posse censuit. **1405** ταὐτὸν codd. et edd. paene omnes; quod hic ferendum esse iure negans dedit τοὐμὸν Nauck.: immo una tantum littera mutata scribendum est ταὐτοῦ.

Delphi. First, he descries three roads converging in a deep glen or ravine (τρεῖς κέλευθοι—κεκρυμμένη νάπη): then, descending, he comes to a coppice (δρυμός) at a point where his own road narrows (στενωπός) just before its junction with the two others (ἐν τριπλαῖς ὁδοῖς). See on 733. **1400** τοὐμὸν αἷμα, thus divided from πατρός, is more than αἷμα τοὐμοῦ πατρός: 'the same blood which flows in my own veins—the blood of my father.' **1401** For τι, which has a tone of bitterness here, see on 124, 969. The ὅτι of the MSS. must be explained in one of two ways :—(1) as if the construction was irregularly changed by οἷα, ὁποῖα: but the immediate succession of οἷα to ὅτι makes this intolerably harsh: or (2) as if οἷα, ὁποῖα were exclamatory substitutes for δεινά or the like : which seems inadmissible. **1405** ἀνεῖτε ταὐτοῦ σπέρμα. By the change of one letter, we restore sense to the passage. The ταὐτὸν of the MSS. is nonsense. Oedipus was the σπέρμα of Laïus and Iocasta. When Iocasta weds Oedipus, the marriage cannot be said ἀνιέναι ταὐτὸν σπέρμα : for it is absurd to suppose that the *seed sown by Oedipus* could be identified with *Oedipus himself.* But the marriage can be rightly said ἀνιέναι ταὐτοῦ σπέρμα, to yield seed *from the same man* (Oedipus) whom that womb had borne. **1405 ff.** The marriage of Iocasta with Oedipus constituted (ἀπεδείξατε) Oedipus at once *father and brother* (of his children), while he was also *son* (of his wife),—the closest relation in *blood* (αἷμ' ἐμφύλιον) becoming also the *husband.* The marriage made Iocasta the *bride* (νύμφας)—aye, and the child-bearing *wife* (γυναῖκας),—of him to whom she was

πατέρας, ἀδελφούς, παῖδας, αἷμ᾽ ἐμφύλιον,
νύμφας γυναῖκας μητέρας τε, χὥπόσα
αἴσχιστ᾽ ἐν ἀνθρώποισιν ἔργα γίγνεται.
ἀλλ᾽ οὐ γὰρ αὐδᾶν ἔσθ᾽ ἃ μηδὲ δρᾶν καλόν,
ὅπως τάχιστα πρὸς θεῶν ἔξω μέ που   1410
καλύψατ᾽, ἢ φονεύσατ᾽, ἢ θαλάσσιον
ἐκρίψατ᾽, ἔνθα μήποτ᾽ εἰσόψεσθ᾽ ἔτι.
ἴτ᾽, ἀξιώσατ᾽ ἀνδρὸς ἀθλίου θιγεῖν.
πίθεσθε, μὴ δείσητε. τἀμὰ γὰρ κακὰ
οὐδεὶς οἷός τε πλὴν ἐμοῦ φέρειν βροτῶν.   1415
ΧΟ. ἀλλ᾽ ὧν ἐπαιτεῖς ἐς δέον πάρεσθ᾽ ὅδε
Κρέων τὸ πράσσειν καὶ τὸ βουλεύειν, ἐπεὶ
χώρας λέλειπται μοῦνος ἀντὶ σοῦ φύλαξ.
ΟΙ. οἴμοι, τί δῆτα λέξομεν πρὸς τόνδ᾽ ἔπος;
τίς μοι φανεῖται πίστις ἔνδικος; τὰ γὰρ   1420

1414 πείθεσθε, quod praebent codd., defendit Hermann., collato Electrae
v. 1015, ubi tamen πείθου significat, 'sine me tibi persuadere'; hic autem dicere vult

---

also *mother* (μητέρας). Thus, through the birth of children from such a
marriage, complex horrors of relationship arose (ὁπόσα αἴσχιστα ἔργα
γίγνεται). αἷμ᾽ ἐμφύλιον is in apposition with πατέρας ἀδελφοὺς παῖδας,—'a
blood-kinship' standing for 'a blood-kinsman.' It expresses that the
monstrous union confounded the closest tie of *consanguinity* with the
closest tie of *affinity*. The phrase ἐμφύλιον αἷμα, like συγγενὲς αἷμα,
would in Tragedy more often mean 'murder of a kinsman.' But it can,
of course, mean also 'kindred blood' in another sense; and here the
context leaves no ambiguity. Cp. Eur. *Phoen.* 246 κοινὸν αἷμα, κοινὰ
τέκεα | τῆς κερασφόρου πέφυκεν Ἰοῦς. **1410 ff.** ἔξω μέ που | καλύψατ᾽ : the
blind man asks that they will lead him away from Thebes, and *hide* him
from the sight of men in some lonely spot—as amid the wilds of
Cithaeron (1451). We must not transpose καλύψατ᾽ and ἐκρίψατ᾽, as is
done in Schneidewin's ed. (as revised by Nauck), after Burges. **1411** θαλάσσιον: cp. Appendix, Note 11. **1412** ἔνθα μὴ with fut. indic., as *Ai.* 659,
El. 380, *Tr.* 800. **1415** No one can share the burden of his ills. Other
men need not fear to be polluted by contact with him, as with one
guilty of blood. His unwitting crimes and his awful sufferings—alike

an incestuous kinship of fathers, brothers, sons,—brides, wives, mothers,—yea, all the foulest shame that is wrought among men! Nay, but 'tis unmeet to name what 'tis unmeet to do:—haste ye, for the gods' love, hide me somewhere beyond the land, or slay me, or cast me into the sea, where ye shall never behold me more! Approach,—deign to lay your hands on a wretched man;—hearken, fear not,—my plague can rest on no mortal beside.

Ch. Nay, here is Creon, in meet season for thy requests, crave they act or counsel; for he alone is left to guard the land in thy stead.

Oe. Ah me, how indeed shall I accost him? What claim to grace can be shown on my part? For in the

Oedipus, 'parete,' 'voluntati meae obtemperate': quae sententia aoristum flagitat. πίθεσθε restituit Elmsleius, receperunt edd. plerique.

---

the work of Apollo—place him apart. See the passage in which he speaks of all that separates his fate from that of other men stained with guilt, *O. C.* 266—274. And, in illustration of the fear which he seeks to allay, compare the plea of Orestes that, since he has been duly purified from bloodshed, contact with him has ceased to be dangerous (Aesch. *Eum.* 285 ὅσοις προσῆλθον ἀβλαβεῖ ξυνουσίᾳ). **1416** ὧν ἐπαιτεῖς ἐς δέον = seasonably in respect of those things which (ὧν = τούτων ἅ) you ask: the gen. being dependent on the notion of ἐς δέον as = ἐς καιρόν. **1417** τὸ πράσσειν καὶ τὸ βουλεύειν are strictly accusatives of respect, 'as to the doing and the planning,' *i.e.* with a view to doing and planning. So *Ant.* 79, *El.* 1030, *O. C.* 442, *Ph.* 1253, etc. **1418** μοῦνος: see on 304. Kühlstädt (*De Dial. Trag.* 104) thinks that Soph. never uses μοῦνος for μόνος unless with some special emphasis: but, as Ellendt remarks, such instances as *O. C.* 875, 991, *Ant.* 705, fr. 434 refute that view. Rather it was a simple question of metrical convenience. The same is true of ξεῖνος and ξένος, with this exception, that, even where metre admitted ξέν', ξεῖν' occurs as the *first* word of an address: Eur. *I. T.* 798 ξεῖν', οὐ δικαίως. In *O. C.* 928 also, L and A give ξεῖνον παρ' ἀστοῖς. **1420** τίς μοι φανεῖται πίστις ἔνδικος; '*what reasonable claim to confidence* can be produced on my part?' Oedipus had brought a charge against Creon which was false, and had repudiated a charge against himself which was true. He means :—'How can I expect Creon to believe me now,

πάρος πρὸς αὐτὸν πάντ' ἐφεύρημαι κακός.

ΚΡ. οὐχ ὡς γελαστής, Οἰδίπους, ἐλήλυθα,
οὐδ' ὡς ὀνειδιῶν τι τῶν πάρος κακῶν.
ἀλλ' εἰ τὰ θνητῶν μὴ καταισχύνεσθ' ἔτι
γένεθλα, τὴν γοῦν πάντα βόσκουσαν φλόγα   1425
αἰδεῖσθ' ἄνακτος Ἡλίου, τοιόνδ' ἄγος
ἀκάλυπτον οὕτω δεικνύναι, τὸ μήτε γῆ
μήτ' ὄμβρος ἱερὸς μήτε φῶς προσδέξεται.
ἀλλ' ὡς τάχιστ' ἐς οἶκον ἐσκομίζετε·
τοῖς ἐν γένει γὰρ τἀγγενῆ μάλισθ' ὁρᾶν   1430

1422 seq. In L οὔθ' ὡς...οὔθ' ὡs voluit scribere prima manus (quae l. est etiam in Ḅ, V, V², al.) et sic Nauck., Blaydes., Campbell.: οὐχ ὡς...οὐδ' ὡs corrector dedit, quod A quoque et V³ praebent, receperunt Hermann., Dindorf., Kennedius. Quod ad codices attinet, leve est discrimen auctoritatis. Sed habet nescio quid ambitionis rhetoricae duplex illud οὔθ'...οὔθ', quae tali loco parum consentanea videtur: gravius,

---

when I represent myself as the blind victim of fate,—when I crave his sympathy and pity?' πίστις has two main senses, each of which has several shades,—(1) *faith*, and (2) *a warrant for faith*. Here it is (2), essentially as in *O. C.* 1632 δός μοι χερὸς σῆς πίστιν. Not 'a persuasive argument' in the technical sense of Rhetoric, for which πίστεις were 'instruments of persuasion,' whether ἔντεχνοι, provided by the Art itself (λογική, παθητική, ἠθική), or ἄτεχνοι, external to the art, as depositions, documents, etc. **1421 πάντ'**: see on 475. **1422** Cp. the words of Tennyson's Arthur to Guinevere : 'Yet think not that I come to urge thy crimes.' **1424—1431** Nauck gives these verses to Oedipus, making them follow 1415. He regards τοιόνδ' ἄγος κ.τ.λ. as inconsistent with the profession which Creon has just made. Rather may we consider them as showing a kinsman's anxious and delicate concern for the honour of Oedipus and of the house (1430). Creon, deeply moved, deprecates the prolonged indulgence of a painful curiosity (cp. 1304). It is again Creon who says ἴθι στέγης ἔσω (1515) when Oedipus would fain linger. Clearly, then, these verses are rightly placed in the mss. **1425 βόσκουσαν** boldly for τρέφουσαν: cp. Aesch. *Ag.* 633, where the sun is τοῦ τρέφοντος...χθονὸς φύσιν. **1427 f. δεικνύναι** depends on αἰδεῖσθε, for the constr. of which with (1) acc. of persons revered, and (2) infin. of act which such reverence forbids, cp. Xen. *An.* 2. 3. 22 ᾐσχύνθημεν καὶ θεοὺς καὶ ἀνθρώπους προδοῦναι αὐτόν, 'respect for gods

past I have been found wholly false to him.

CREON.

I have not come in mockery, Oedipus, nor to reproach thee with any bygone fault.—(*To the Attendants.*) But ye, if ye respect the children of men no more, revere at least the all-nurturing flame of our lord the Sun,—spare to show thus nakedly a pollution such as this,—one which neither earth can welcome, nor the holy rain, nor the light. Nay, take him into the house as quickly as ye may ; for it best accords with piety

quia simplicius, dicitur οὐχ...οὐδ'. **1424—1431** ἀλλ' εἰ τὰ θνητῶν......ἔχει κακά. Versus hos octo post v. 1415 inserens Oedipo tribuit Nauck.; cur tamen loco moveantur nihil esse causae monstravimus in annot. **1428** ἱερὸς codd. et edd. plerique: ἱρὸς Dindorf., Campbell.; vide supra, v. 1379. **1430** seq. μάλισθ' ὁρᾶν | μόνοις τ' ἀκούειν codd. Coniecit μόνοις θ' ὁρᾶν | μόνοις τ' ἀκούειν Meinekius : μόνοις ὁρᾶν | μόνοις τ' ἀκούειν Dobraeus : μόνοις ὁρᾶν | μόνοις δ' ἀκούειν Blaydes.

and for men forbade us to betray him.' τὸ (= ὅ, see on 1379) μήτε, not οὔτε, since τοιόνδ' ἄγος indicates a *class* of ἄγη : not merely '*which*,' but '*such as*,' earth will not welcome (*quod Terra non* admissura sit): cp. 817, *El.* 654 ὅσων ἐμοὶ | δύσνοια μὴ πρόσεστιν. γῆ—ὄμβρος—φῶς· The pollution (ἄγος) of Oedipus is such that the pure elemental powers—represented by *earth*, the *rain* from heaven, the *light*—cannot suffer it to remain in their presence (προσδέξεται) : it must be hidden from them. Cp. Aesch. *Eum.* 904 f., where the Erinyes, as Chthonian powers, invoke blessings on Attica, γῆθεν—ἔκ τε ποντίας δρόσου—ἐξ οὐρανοῦ τε. ὄμβρος here is not a *synonym* but a *symbol* of water generally, as with Empedocles 282 ὡς τότ' ἔπειτ' ἐδίηνε Κύπρις χθόνα δηρὸν ἐν ὄμβρῳ, | εἴδεα καὶ ποιοῦσα θοῷ πυρὶ δῶκε κρατῦναι: cp. Lucr. I. 714 f. *quattuor ex rebus posse omnia rentur Ex igni terra atque anima procrescere et imbri.* In *Ant.* 1073 the exposure of the unburied corpse is spoken of as a *violence* to οἱ ἄνω θεοί (βιάζονται). It was a common form of oath to pray that, if a man swore falsely, neither earth, nor sea, nor air, might tolerate the presence of his corpse (Eur. *Or.* 1085, *Hipp.* 1030). **1428** The original sense of ἱερός, 'strong' (Curt. *Etym.* § 614), suits a few phrases, such as ἱερὸς ἰχθύς (*Il.* 16. 407). But in such as ἱερὸν ἦμαρ, κνέφας, ὄμβρος, ποταμοί etc. it is more likely that the poet had no consciousness of any other sense than 'sacred.' **1430** The objection to taking μάλιστα

J. S.   17

μόνοις τ' ἀκούειν εὐσεβῶς ἔχει κακά.

ΟΙ. πρὸς θεῶν, ἐπείπερ ἐλπίδος μ' ἀπέσπασας,
ἄριστος ἐλθὼν πρὸς κάκιστον ἄνδρ' ἐμέ,
πιθοῦ τί μοι· πρὸς σοῦ γάρ, οὐδ' ἐμοῦ, φράσω.

ΚΡ. καὶ τοῦ με χρείας ὧδε λιπαρεῖς τυχεῖν;   1435

ΟΙ. ῥῖψόν με γῆς ἐκ τῆσδ' ὅσον τάχισθ', ὅπου
θνητῶν φανοῦμαι μηδενὸς προσήγορος.

ΚΡ. ἔδρασ' ἂν εὖ τοῦτ' ἴσθ' ἂν, εἰ μὴ τοῦ θεοῦ
πρώτιστ' ἔχρῃζον ἐκμαθεῖν τί πρακτέον.

ΟΙ. ἀλλ' ἥ γ' ἐκείνου πᾶσ' ἐδηλώθη φάτις,   1440
τὸν πατροφόντην, τὸν ἀσεβῆ μ' ἀπολλύναι.

ΚΡ. οὕτως ἐλέχθη ταῦθ'· ὅμως δ', ἵν' ἔσταμεν
χρείας, ἄμεινον ἐκμαθεῖν τί δραστέον.

ΟΙ. οὕτως ἄρ' ἀνδρὸς ἀθλίου πεύσεσθ' ὕπερ;

ΚΡ. καὶ γὰρ σὺ νῦν τἂν τῷ θεῷ πίστιν φέροις.   1445

ΟΙ. καὶ σοί γ' ἐπισκήπτω τε καὶ προστρέψομαι,

1437 φανοῦμαι] θανοῦμαι coniecit Meinekius, recepit Nauck.   **1445** τ' ἂν
(i. e. τοι ἂν, τἂν) L, A, codd. plerique: praetulerunt autem γ' ἂν, quod habent L²
et Γ, Hermann., Wunder., Hartung., Blaydes. In τἂν facillime quidem transiisset
γ' ἂν: sed hoc paene irridentis est, illud, maeste recordantis; utrum igitur Creontis

with τοῖς ἐν γένει is not that it follows these words (see on 1394), but
that τἀγγενῆ intervenes.   Rather join it with εὐσεβῶς ἔχει.   ὁρᾶν μόνοις τ'
ἀκούειν = μόνοις ὁρᾶν ἀκούειν τε.   1432 ἐλπίδος μ' ἀπέσπασας, suddenly
plucked me away from (made me to abandon) my uneasy foreboding:
cp. Lat. *revellere* (*falsorum persuasionem*, Sen. *Epist.* 95), and our phrase,
'a revulsion of feeling': *Ai.* 1382 ὡς μ' ἔψευσας ἐλπίδος πολύ.   Con-
versely (*El.* 809) ἀποσπάσας...φρενὸς | αἵ μοι μόναι παρῆσαν ἐλπίδων.
1433 ἄριστος ἐλθὼν πρὸς...ἐμέ, having come to me in so noble a spirit;
cp. 1422 ἐλήλυθα.   This is more natural than to render, 'having
proved thyself most noble towards me' (see on 1357).   1434 πρὸς σοῦ,
in thy interest: Eur. *Alc.* 58 πρὸς τῶν ἐχόντων, Φοῖβε, τὸν νόμον
τίθης: *Tr.* 479 δεῖ γὰρ καὶ τὸ πρὸς κείνου λέγειν, the argument on
his side.   1435 χρείας, request: *O. C.* 1754 προσπίτνομέν σοι.   ΘΗ.
τίνος, ὦ παῖδες, χρείας ἀνύσαι;   1437 μηδενὸς προσήγορος, accosted by
no one: for the gen., cp. *El.* 1214 οὕτως ἄτιμός εἰμι τοῦ τεθνηκότος; *ib.*
344 κείνης διδακτά.   With dat., *Ph.* 1353 τῷ προσήγορος; see on 1337:

that kinsfolk alone should see and hear a kinsman's woes.

OE. For the gods' love—since thou hast done a gentle violence to my presage, who hast come in a spirit so noble to me, a man most vile—grant me a boon:—for thy good will I speak, not for mine own.

CR. And what wish art thou so fain to have of me?

OE. Cast me out of this land with all speed, to a place where no mortal shall be found to greet me more.

CR. This would I have done, be thou sure, but that I craved first to learn all my duty from the god.

OE. Nay, his behest hath been set forth in full,—to destroy the parricide, the unholy one, that I am.

CR. Such was the purport; yet, seeing to what a pass we have come, 'tis better to learn clearly what should be done.

OE. Will ye, then, seek a response on behalf of such a wretch as I am?

CR. Aye, for thou thyself wilt now surely put faith in the god.

OE.   Yea;   and   on   thee   lay   I   this   charge,
      to   thee   will   I   make   this   entreaty:

animo melius congruat, haud dubium videtur.   **1446** προστρέψομαι L, V, V², al.: προτρέψομαι A, V³, V⁴, al., quod receperunt Hermann., Dindorf., Blaydes., Campbell. Sed enixe et summisse supplicanti multo aptius est προστρέψομαι, quod recte servat Nauck.

---

for ὅπου μή with fut. indic., on 1412. **1438** For the doubled ἄν with ἔδρασα, cp. 862; join τοῦτ' with ἴσθι: it could not here go with ἔδρασα. **1440** φάτις (151), the message brought by Creon from Delphi (86): πᾶσ', 'in full,' explicitly: *Ai.* 275 κεῖνος...λύπῃ πᾶς ἐλήλαται. The indefinite person of the φάτις is identified with Oedipus just as in 1382 f. **1442 f.** ἵνα...χρείας, see 367. **1444** οὕτως with ἀθλίου: *Ph.* 104 οὕτως ἔχει τι δεινὸν ἰσχύος θράσος; **1445** The καί belongs to σύ: 'yes, for even thou in sooth would'st now believe in the god (though formerly thou didst not believe his word by the mouth of Teiresias).' This is not spoken in mockery, but with grave sorrow. The phrase πίστιν φέροις as = πιστεύοις (*El.* 735 τῷ τέλει πίστιν φέρων) prob. = 'render belief' (as a tribute due), cp. φόρον, δασμόν, χρήματα φέρειν, and the like figure in Pind. *Ol.* 11. 17 νικῶν | Ἴλᾳ φερέτω χάριν. **1446** καὶ σοί γ': yes [I *am* prepared to abide by Apollo's word], and on *thee*

τῆς μὲν κατ᾽ οἴκους αὐτὸς ὃν θέλεις τάφον
θοῦ· καὶ γὰρ ὀρθῶς τῶν γε σῶν τελεῖς ὕπερ·
ἐμοῦ δὲ μήποτ᾽ ἀξιωθήτω τόδε
πατρῷον ἄστυ ζῶντος οἰκητοῦ τυχεῖν,   1450
ἀλλ᾽ ἔα με ναίειν ὄρεσιν, ἔνθα κλῄζεται
οὑμὸς Κιθαιρὼν οὗτος, ὃν μήτηρ τέ μοι
πατήρ τ᾽ ἐθέσθην ζῶντε κύριον τάφον,
ἵν᾽ ἐξ ἐκείνων, οἵ μ᾽ ἀπωλλύτην, θάνω.
καίτοι τοσοῦτόν γ᾽ οἶδα, μήτε μ᾽ ἂν νόσον   1455

1453 ζῶντε codd.: ζῶντι coniecit Toup., receperunt multi edd.: vide tamen annot.

---

too I lay an injunction, and will now make a prayer to thee; *i. e.* as I turn to the god for what he alone can give (cp. 1519 τοῦ θεοῦ μ᾽ αἰτεῖς δόσιν), so I turn to *thee* for that which lies in thine own power. The midd. προστρέψομαι as in fr. 759 Ἐργάνην (Athene)...προστρέπεσθε: the active has the same sense in *Ai.* 831, *O. C.* 50. On the future, see 1077. There is no cause to desire ἐπισκήψω: each tense has its due force: I now enjoin, and am going on to ask. Just so in Thuc. 2. 44 οὐκ ὀλοφύρομαι μᾶλλον ἢ παραμυθήσομαι, where the conjecture ὀλοφυροῦμαι is needless: 'I *do not* bewail them, but rather *intend to* comfort them.' The reading προτρέψομαι must be judged by the context. With it, the sense is:—yes [*I* am sensible of my duty to Apollo], and I enjoin on *thee*, and will *exhort* thee, to do thine. (Cp. 358 προὐτρέψω: Plat. *Legg.* 711 B πρὸς ἀρετῆς ἐπιτηδεύματα προτρέπεσθαι τοὺς πολίτας.) But this strain of lofty admonition seems little in accord with the tone of the broken man who has just acknowledged Creon's unexpected goodness (1432), and is now a suppliant (cp. 1468). In *Ai.* 831 and *O. C.* 50, where προστρέπω is undoubtedly right, προτρέπω occurs as a variant. **1447** τῆς...κατ᾽ οἴκους: the *name* of Iocasta has not been uttered since 1235. Contrast 950. **1448** τελεῖς, absol., like ἔρδειν, perform rites, *i.e.* the ἐντάφια (Isae. or. 8 § 38). The special term for offerings to the dead was ἐναγίζειν (Isae. or. 3 § 46). **1449** ἀξιωθήτω, *be condemned*: Her. 3. 145 ἐμὲ μέν, ὦ κάκιστε ἀνδρῶν, ...ἀδικήσαντα οὐδὲν ἄξιον δεσμοῦ γοργύρης ἠξίωσας, *doomed* me to a dungeon though I had done no wrong *worthy* of bonds. **1451** ἔα, a monosyllable by synizesis, as in *Ant.* 95 ἀλλ᾽ ἔα με. Cp. *Od.* 9. 283 νέα μέν μοι κατέαξε Ποσειδάων ἐνοσίχθων. ὄρεσιν, locative dative, cp. γῇ, 1266. ἔνθα κλῄζεται κ.τ.λ., lit., 'where my Cithaeron yonder is

—give to her who is within such burial as thou thyself wouldest; for thou wilt meetly render the last rites to thine own. But for me—never let this city of my sire be condemned to have me dwelling therein, while I live: no, suffer me to abide on the hills, where yonder is Cithaeron, famed as mine,— which my mother and sire, while they lived, set for my appointed tomb,—that so I may die by their decree who sought to slay me. Howbeit of thus much am I sure,—that neither sickness

---

famed,'= 'where yonder is Cithaeron, famed as mine,'—*i.e.* made famous by the recent discovery that it is Οἰδίπου τροφὸς καὶ μήτηρ (1092). There is an intense bitterness in the words: the name of Cithaeron is for ever to be linked with his dark story. Statius (quoted by Schneidewin) was doubtless thinking of this place: *habeant te lustra tuusque Cithaeron* (*Theb.* 11. 752). κλήζεται is stronger than καλεῖ-ται, as in *Tr.* 659 ἔνθα κλήζεται θυτήρ means, 'where *fame* (that brought the tidings of his great victory) tells of him as sacrificing.' For the idiom cp. *Il.* 11. 757 Ἀλεισίου ἔνθα κολώνη | κέκληται. **1453** The words ἐξ ἐκείνων form the decisive argument for the ζῶντι of the MSS. against Toup's specious emendation, ζῶντι. His parents in *their life-time* appointed Cithaeron to be his grave. Now they are dead; but, though he can no longer die by their *agency*, he wishes to die ἐξ ἐκείνων, *by their doom*; i.e. by self-exposure in the same wilds to which they had consigned him (cp. 719 ἔρριψεν ἄλλων χερσὶν εἰς ἄβατον ὄρος). The thought of the hostile *dead* bringing death upon the living is one which Sophocles has more than once: *Ai.* 1026 εἶδες ὡς χρόνῳ | ἔμελλέ σ' Ἕκτωρ καὶ θανὼν ἀποφθιεῖν; *Trach.* 1163 (Heracles speaking of Nessus) ζῶντά μ' ἔκτεινεν θανών. The reading ζῶντι, on the other hand, yields nothing but a weak verbal antithesis with τάφον. Had his parents meant him to *live* in lonely misery on Cithaeron, there would be some point in calling it his 'living grave.' But they meant him to die there forthwith (cp. 1174); ζῶντι, then, would mean nothing more than that the grave was chosen before the babe was dead. κύριον, appointed by their authoritative decision: cp. Aesch. *Eum.* 541 ποινὰ γὰρ ἐπέσται· | κύριον μένει τέλος. **1454** ἀπωλλύτην: for the imperf. of intention, cp. Andoc. or. 1 § 41 τὸν πατέρα μου ἀπώλλυε ('*sought* to ruin'), συνειδότα ἀποφαίνων. **1455** οἶδα μὴ (not οὐ) πέρσαι ἄν. οὐ (before infin. no less than in other cases) introduces a negative *statement*, μή a negative *conception*. Where *personal assurance of a fact*

μήτ' ἄλλο πέρσαι μηδέν· οὐ γὰρ ἄν ποτε
θνῄσκων ἐσώθην, μὴ 'πί τῳ δεινῷ κακῷ.
ἀλλ' ἡ μὲν ἡμῶν μοῖρ', ὅποιπερ εἶσ', ἴτω·
παίδων δὲ τῶν μὲν ἀρσένων μή μοι, Κρέον,
προσθῇ μέριμναν· ἄνδρες εἰσίν, ὥστε μὴ   1460
σπάνιν ποτὲ σχεῖν, ἔνθ' ἂν ὦσι, τοῦ βίου·
ταῖν δ' ἀθλίαιν οἰκτραῖν τε παρθένοιν ἐμαῖν,
αἷν οὔποθ' ἡμὴ χωρὶς ἐστάθη βορᾶς
τράπεζ' ἄνευ τοῦδ' ἀνδρός, ἀλλ' ὅσων ἐγὼ
ψαύοιμι, πάντων τῶνδ' ἀεὶ μετειχέτην·   1465
αἷν μοι μέλεσθαι· καὶ μάλιστα μὲν χεροῖν

1458 ὅποιπερ L, codd. et edd. plerique: ὅπηπερ (A, V², al.) praetulerunt Brunck., Erfurdt., Linwood., Blaydes.: sed de termino magis quam de cursu vitae suae proposito loquitur Oedipus.   **1459** Κρέων L, A, T, Brunck., Schneidewin., Kennedius: Κρέον reliqui codd. plerique et edd.   **1460** πρόσθῃ (sic) L, A, et codd. plerique. Accentus non errori sed consilio fortasse debetur, cum inter veteres grammaticos non satis constaret utrum (ut hoc utamur exemplo) πρόσθῃ an προσθῇ

is expressed, μή with infin. can give this emphasis; so Dem. or. 21 § 222 πεπίστευκε τῇ πολιτείᾳ μηδένα ἕλξειν μηδ' ὑβριεῖν μηδὲ τυπτήσειν : [Dem.] or. 40 § 47 αὐτὸς ἑαυτοῦ καταμαρτυρεῖ μὴ ἐξ ἐκείνου γεγενῆσθαι. So μή with infin. occurs after πέποιθα, πέπεισμαι, sometimes also φημί, λέγω, οἴομαι, νομίζω: see Prof. Gildersleeve in *American Journ. of Philology*, vol. 1. p. 49. οὐ πέρσαι ἄν would *also* be right here, as representing the simple statement, ὅτι οὐκ ἂν πέρσειε: cp. [Dem.] or. 49 § 35 οἴεσθε...τὸν πατέρα...οὐκ ἂν φυλάττειν; **1457** with μή understand σωθείς, = εἰ μὴ ἐσώθην ἐπὶ κακῷ τῳ : cp. *Ai.* 950 οὐκ ἂν τάδ' ἔστη τῇδε μὴ θεῶν μέτα, sc. στάντα, = εἰ μὴ ἔστη. **1460** προσθῇ μέριμναν, *take* care *upon thee:* so often of assuming a *needless* burden : Thuc. 1. 78 μή...οἰκεῖον πόνον προσθῆσθε : ib. 144 κινδύνους αὐθαιρέτους μὴ προστίθεσθαι : Plat. *Prot.* 346 D ἔχθρας ἑκουσίας ...προστίθεσθαι. Elmsley's plausible προθῇ (*El.* 1334 εὐλάβειαν...προὐθέμην) would be weaker. ἄνδρες, males (though not ἐξηνδρωμένοι); cp. *Tr.* 1062 θῆλυς οὖσα κοὐκ ἀνδρὸς φύσιν. **1462** ff. ταῖν δ' ἀθλίαιν. Instead of supplying πρόσθου μέριμναν, it is better to regard αἷν in 1466 as an anacolouthon for ταύταιν, arising from the length of the preceding clause. Cp. Antiphon or. 5 §§ 11, 12 δέον σε διομόσασθαι...ἃ σὺ παρελθών, where, after a long parenthetic clause, ἃ has been irregularly substituted for ταῦτα. **1463** f. αἷν *for whom* ἡ ἐμὴ βορᾶς τράπεζα *the table*

nor aught else can destroy me ; for never had I been snatched
from death, but in reserve for some strange doom.

Nay, let *my* fate go whither it will : but as touching my children,—I pray thee, Creon, take no care on thee for my sons ; they
are men, so that, be they where they may, they can never lack the
means to live. But my two girls, poor hapless ones,—who never
knew my table spread apart, or lacked their father's presence,
but ever in all things shared my daily bread,—I pray thee, care
for *them ;* and—if thou canst—suffer me to touch them with my

scribere oporteret: cf. Chandleri librum de accentibus, § 820 edit. alterius. In
Herod. 6. 109 codices προσθῇ praebent. Coniecit Elmsleius προθῇ, receperunt
Wunder., Blaydes.: et inveni quidem πρόθη (sic) in cod. V: praestat tamen vulgata l.
1466 αἷν] ταῖν, quod vidi in cod. V², Blaydesius esse memorat etiam in uno codd.
Parisinorum (2820), ascripto τούτων. Iam Heathius ταῖν coniecerat (quo quidem pro
ταύταιν accepto tollitur anacoluthon), receperunt Brunck., Erfurdt., Hartung., Kennedius.

---

at which I ate οὔποτε χωρὶς ἐστάθη *was never placed apart,* ἄνευ τοῦδ' ἀνδρός
(so that they should be) *without me.* Instead of ἄνευ αὐταῖν, we have
ἄνευ τοῦδ' ἀνδρός, because (αἷν being dat. of persons affected) αἷν οὔποτε
ἡ ἐμὴ τράπεζα χωρὶς ἐστάθη ἄνευ τοῦδ' ἀνδρός is equivalent to αἷ οὔποτε
τὴν ἐμὴν τράπεζαν χωρὶς σταθεῖσαν εἶδον, (ὥστε εἶναι) ἄνευ τοῦδ' ἀνδρός.
This is simpler than to construe : 'for whom the dinner-table, which
was (always) mine, was never placed apart, or without me' : when ἡμὴ
would be a compressed substitute for ἡ ἐμὴ ἀεὶ οὖσα in the sense of
ἀλλὰ ἡ ἐμὴ ἀεὶ ἦν. We cannot take ἡμὴ βορᾶς τράπεζα as merely = ' the
table which I *provided*' : the emphasis on ἡμὴ would alone exclude
this. Prof. Kennedy understands : 'apart from whom (αἷν χωρίς) my
dinner-table ne'er was set *without my bidding,*' *i.e.* never except on
special occasions, when I had so directed. ἄνευ could certainly mean
this (*O. C.* 926 etc.). But can we understand Oedipus as saying, in
effect,—'who always dined with me—except, indeed, when I had
directed that they should *not*'? The attributive gen. βορᾶς is equivalent to an adj. of quality like τρόφιμος, as Eur. *Phoen.* 1491 στολὶς
τρυφᾶς = στολὶς τρυφερά : not like ἅμαξαι σίτου (Xen. *Cyr.* 2. 4. 18)
'waggon-*loads* of grain.' ἐστάθη, because a light table is brought in
for the meal, and removed after it (cp. *Il.* 24. 476, *Od.* 10. 354 etc.).
ἄνευ τοῦδ' ἀνδρός, explaining χωρὶς, as in *Ph.* 31 κενὴν οἴκησιν is explained
by ἀνθρώπων δίχα, *Ai.* 464 γυμνὸν φανέντα by τῶν ἀριστείων ἄτερ. ἄνευ as
in *Tr.* 336 μάθῃς ἄνευ τῶνδ', hear *apart from* these. **1466** μέλεσθαι,

ψαῦσαί μ' ἔασον κἀποκλαύσασθαι κακά.
ἴθ' ὦναξ,
ἴθ' ὦ γονῇ γενναῖε. χερσί τᾶν θιγὼν
δοκοῖμ' ἔχειν σφας, ὥσπερ ἡνίκ' ἔβλεπον.   1470
τί φημί;
οὐ δὴ κλύω που πρὸς θεῶν τοῖν μοι φίλοιν
δακρυρροούντοιν, καί μ' ἐποικτείρας Κρέων
ἔπεμψέ μοι τὰ φίλτατ' ἐκγόνοιν ἐμοῖν;
λέγω τι;   1475
ΚΡ. λέγεις· ἐγὼ γάρ εἰμ' ὁ πορσύνας τάδε,
γνοὺς τὴν παροῦσαν τέρψιν, ἥ σ' εἶχεν πάλαι.
ΟΙ. ἀλλ' εὐτυχοίης, καί σε τῆσδε τῆς ὁδοῦ

1470 σφᾶς, L, A, codd. plerique: σφὰς Pal.: vide annot.   1474 Veram l.
ἐκγόνοιν servant cum paucis codd. B et V⁴: falsam ἐγγόνοιν habent L, A, reliqui fere
omnes.   1477 ἥ σ' εἶχεν L, V, B, E, al.: ἣν εἶχες, quod cum aliis aliquot

---

infin. for imper.: cp. 462. **μάλιστα μέν**: see on 926. **1468 ἴθ' ὦναξ.**
A moment of agitated suspense is marked by the bacchius interrupting
the trimeters, as *Ph.* 749 f. (in an anxious entreaty, as here) ἴθ' ὦ παῖ.
So *O. C.* 1271 τί σιγᾷς; *ib.* 318 τάλαινα. The speech of the agonised
Heracles is similarly broken by short dactylic or choriambic phrases,
Tr. 1081, αἶ αἶ, ὦ τάλας: 1085 ὦναξ Ἀΐδη, δέξαι μ', | ὦ Διὸς ἀκτίς,
παῖσον. But Soph. has used the license most sparingly, and always, it
may be said, with fine effect. **1469 γονῇ γενναῖε**, noble in the grain,—
one whose γενναιότης is γνησία, inbred, true,—referring to the ἀρετή just
shown by Creon (1433). γονῇ here is not merely intensive of γενναῖε,
making it = γενναιότατε, (as the sarcastic γένει seems to be in Plat. *Soph.*
231 B ἡ γένει γενναία σοφιστική, 'the most noble.') Cp. *Ai.* 1094
μηδὲν ὢν γοναῖσιν. **1470 ἔχειν σφας.** σφέας has the accent in Homer when
it is emphatic, as when joined with αὐτούς, being then a disyllable:
Il. 12. 43 σφέας αὐτούς. When non-emphatic and enclitic, it is a
monosyllable: *Od.* 4. 77 καί σφεας φωνήσας. The perispomenon σφᾶς
corresponds to the accented σφέας, as in σφᾶς αὐτούς: the enclitic
σφας to the enclitic σφεας. Thus in *O. C.* 486 we must write ὡς
σφας καλοῦμεν with Herm.; where Elmsley gave ὡς σφᾶς, holding
(against the grammarians) that this form was never enclitic. Here,
as in 1508, the pronoun is non-emphatic. According to the rule

hands, and to indulge my grief. Grant it, prince, grant it, thou noble heart! Ah, could I but once touch them with my hands, I should think that they were with me, even as when I had sight...

[CREON'S *Attendants lead in the children* ANTIGONE and ISMENE.]

Ha? O ye gods, can it be my loved ones that I hear sobbing, —can Creon have taken pity on me and sent me my children— my darlings? Am I right?

CR. Yea: 'tis of my contriving, for I knew thy joy in them of old,—the joy that now is thine.

OE. Then blessed be thou, and, for guerdon of this errand,

praebet A, ex· moneta correctoris est sermonem pedestrem diligentis. Ab uno deterioris notae libro (Laur. 32. 2) ἤ σ᾿ ἔχει receperunt Wunder. (πάλαι cum ἔχει iungens), Hermann., Blaydes. (πάλαι ad γνοὺς referentes). Pro παροῦσαν Blaydes. coniecit πάροιθε.

---

now generally received, a *monosyllabic* enclitic stands unaccented after a paroxytone word, the latter remaining unaffected: we therefore write ἔχειν σφας. But, according to Arcadius and Herodian, a paroxytone word followed by an enclitic *beginning with* σφ took the acute on its last syllable, as ἔχείν σφας: see Chandler, §§ 965, 966 2nd ed. 1471 τί φημί; the cry of one startled by a sound or sight, as *Tr.* 865: *O. C.* 315 τί φῶ; Aesch. *P. V.* 561 τίς γῆ; τί γένος; τίνα φῶ λεύσσειν; 1472 τοῖν...φίλοιν | δακρυρροούντοιν. The use of the masc., referring to the two girls, is distinct from the poetical use by which a woman speaking of herself can use the masc. *plural*, but exemplifies the Attic preference for the masc. to the fem. *dual* in participles, and in some adjectives and pronouns: cp. Xen. *Cyr.* I. 2. 11 μίαν ἄμφω τούτω τὼ ἡμέρα λογίζονται. Plat. *Phaedr.* 237 D ἡμῶν ἐν ἑκάστῳ δύο τινέ ἐστον ἰδέα ἄρχοντε καὶ ἄγοντε, οἷν ἑπόμεθα. So τὼ θεώ, τοῖν θεοῖν (Demeter and Persephone). 1474 τὰ φίλτατ᾿ ἐκγ. ἐμοῖν, my chief treasure, (consisting in) my two daughters: cp. on 261 κοινῶν παίδων κοινά: *El.* 682 πρόσχημ᾿ ἀγῶνος, a glory (consisting in) a contest. 1475 λέγω τι; see Plat. *Crat.* 404 A κινδυνεύεις τι λέγειν, compared with *Symp.* 205 D κινδυνεύεις ἀληθῆ λέγειν. Ar. *Eq.* 333 νῦν δεῖξον ὡς οὐδὲν λέγει τὸ σωφρόνως τραφῆναι, 'what nonsense it is.' 1477 γνοὺς...πάλαι: aware of the delight which you now feel, —as you ever felt it: *i.e.*, taught by the past to foresee that you would thus rejoice. 1478 Soph. may have been thinking of Aesch. *Cho.* 1063 ἀλλ᾿ εὐτυχοίης, καί σ᾿ ἐποπτεύων πρόφρων | θεὸς φυλάττοι καιρίοισι συμφοραῖς. τῆσδε τῆς ὁδοῦ, causal gen.: *El.* 626 θράσους | τοῦδ᾿ οὐκ ἀλύξεις:

δαίμων ἄμεινον ἢ 'μὲ φρουρήσας τύχοι.
ὦ τέκνα, ποῦ ποτ᾽ ἐστέ; δεῦρ᾽ ἴτ᾽, ἔλθετε   1480
ὡς τὰς ἀδελφὰς τάσδε τὰς ἐμὰς χέρας,
αἲ τοῦ φυτουργοῦ πατρὸς ὑμὶν ὧδ᾽ ὁρᾶν
τὰ πρόσθε λαμπρὰ προὐξένησαν ὄμματα·
ὃς ὑμίν, ὦ τέκν᾽, οὔθ᾽ ὁρῶν οὔθ᾽ ἱστορῶν
πατὴρ ἐφάνθην ἔνθεν αὐτὸς ἠρόθην.   1485
καὶ σφὼ δακρύω· προσβλέπειν γὰρ οὐ σθένω·
νοούμενος τὰ λοιπὰ τοῦ πικροῦ βίου,
οἷον βιῶναι σφὼ πρὸς ἀνθρώπων χρεών.
ποίας γὰρ ἀστῶν ἥξετ᾽ εἰς ὁμιλίας,

1481 ὡς codd.: εἰς Elmsleius, Wunder., Hartung.: ἐς Blaydes.   **1487**
Habent codd. aliquot (in quibus sunt B, E, L², V⁴) τὰ πικρὰ τοῦ λοιποῦ βίου, quod
recepit Blaydes.; eo usque enim aetatis Oedipi filiolas non acerbe degisse.   Qua ipsa

---

Eur. *Or.* 1407 ἔρροι τᾶς ἀσύχου προνοίας. **1479** ἢ 'μὲ is required here, since
with ἢ με the stress would fall wholly on **φρουρήσας.** On the other hand
in 1478 **καί σε** is right, because, after **εὐτυχοίης,** the *person* does not need
to be at once emphasised again.   This is not, however, like *Il.* 23. 724
ἤ μ᾽ ἀνάειρ᾽ ἢ ἐγὼ σέ, where με suffices because the sense is, '*slay,* or *be
slain.*'   In *El.* 383, 1213 με and σοι are justified by the stress on ὕστερον
and προσήκει respectively. **1481** ὡς τὰς...χέρας.   As the sense is so plainly
equivalent to ὡς ἐμέ, we are scarcely justified in changing ὡς to εἰς (with
Elmsley), or ἐς (with Blaydes).   *Tr.* 366 δόμους | ὡς τούσδε is a slightly
stronger case for such change, yet not a conclusive one.   ἐς is now
read for ὡς in Ar. *Ach.* 242 (ὡς τὸ πρόσθεν) and in Thuc. 8. 36 (ὡς τὴν
Μίλητον), 103 (ὡς τὴν Ἄβυδον).   Soph. has ὡς ὑμᾶς *Tr.* 366. **1482 f.**
Construe : αἲ προὐξένησαν ὑμὶν who *have effected* for you τὰ πρόσθε λαμπρὰ
τοῦ φυτ. πατρὸς ὄμματα ὧδε ὁρᾶν that the once bright eyes of your sire
should see thus, *i.e.* should be sightless : cp. his own phrase quoted in
1273 ἐν σκότῳ τὸ λοιπὸν...ὀψοίατο.   *Ph.* 862 ὡς Ἀΐδᾳ παρακείμενος ὁρᾷ,
he sees as the dead, *i.e.* not at all.   Cp. Xen. *Apol. Socr.* § 7 ὁ θεὸς δι᾽
εὐμένειαν προξενεῖ μοι οὐ μόνον τὸ ἐν καιρῷ τῆς ἡλικίας καταλῦσαι τὸν βίον,
ἀλλὰ καὶ τὸ ᾗ ῥᾷστα, the god's kindly offices grant to me that I should
close my life etc.   προξενεῖν = (1) to be a πρόξενος : then (2) fig., to lend
one's good offices : either (*a*) absol., as *O. C.* 465 προξένει, stand my
friend : or (*b*) with dat. and acc., or acc. and infin., to *effect* a thing,

may heaven prove to thee a kinder guardian than it hath to me! My children, where are ye? Come hither,—hither to the hands of him whose mother was your own, the hands whose offices have wrought that your sire's once bright eyes should be such orbs as these,—his, who seeing nought, knowing nought, became your father by her from whom he sprang! For you also do I weep—behold you I cannot—when I think of the bitter life in days to come which men will make you live. To what company of the citizens will ye come,

ratiocinatione suspicor adductos fuisse librarios ut verba transponerent, nisi si mera negligentia id fecerint: sed nota est antiquae Graecitatis consuetudo qua dicitur τὰ λοιπὰ τοῦ πικροῦ βίου pro τὸν λοιπὸν βίον τὸν πικρόν.

---

or result, for one: Xen. *An.* 6. 5. 14 ἴστε...με...οὐδένα πω κίνδυνον προξενήσαντα ὑμῖν: Plut. *Alex.* 22 αὐτῷ...τοιαῦτα ὀνείδη προξενῶν (said of one who panders to vices): Soph. *Tr.* 726 ἐλπὶς ἥτις καὶ θράσος τι προξενεῖ. In particular, προξενεῖν τινά τινι = συνιστάναι, to *introduce* one person to another. So Prof. Kennedy understands here: 'which introduced to you your father's once brilliant eyes, that you should thus behold them'—*i.e.* presented them to you in this state. But ὧδ' ὁρᾶν seems thus to lose its force : and the ordinary usage of προξενεῖν confirms the version given above. **1484** οὔθ' ὁρῶν οὔθ' ἱστορῶν: *i.e.* neither *recognising* his mother when he saw her, nor *possessing any information* which could lead him to suspect that she was such. ἱστορεῖν is (1) to be, or (2) to become, ἴστωρ, a knower: *i.e.* (1) to have information, or (2) to seek it. Sense (2) is more frequent : but Aesch. has (1) in *Eum.* 455 and *Pers.* 454, Soph. probably in *Tr.* 382, though οὐδὲν ἱστορῶν there *might* mean ὅτι οὐδὲν ἱστόρει (imperf.), 'did not ask.' Here (1) is best, because it would be almost absurd to say that he had wedded Iocasta 'without asking any questions'—as if he could have been expected to do so. Cp. *O. C.* 273 νῦν δ' οὐδὲν εἰδὼς ἱκόμην ἵν' ἱκόμην. **1485** ἠρόθην: cp. 1257, 1210. **1489 f.** ὁμιλίας...ἑορτάς. The poet is thinking of his own Athens, though the language is general. ὁμιλίας comprises all occasions on which Attic women could appear in public,—as at the delivery of ἐπιτάφιοι (Thuc. 2. 45): ἑορτάς suggests such festivals as the Thesmophoria, the Panathenaea, or the Dionysia (when women were present in the theatre, at least at tragedy). To feel the force of this passage, we must remember how closely the Greek festivals were bound up with the life of the *family*. Kinsfolk took part in them together : and at such

ποίας δ᾽ ἑορτάς, ἔνθεν οὐ κεκλαυμέναι   1490
πρὸς οἶκον ἵξεσθ᾽ ἀντὶ τῆς θεωρίας;
ἀλλ᾽ ἡνίκ᾽ ἂν δὴ πρὸς γάμων ἥκητ᾽ ἀκμάς,
τίς οὗτος ἔσται, τίς παραρρίψει, τέκνα,
τοιαῦτ᾽ ὀνείδη λαμβάνων, ἂν τοῖς ἐμοῖς
γόνοισιν ἔσται σφῷν θ᾽ ὁμοῦ δηλήματα;   1495

1491 In L factum est ἵξεσθ᾽ ex ἥξετ᾽ (non, opinor, ex ἥξεθ᾽,) et habent ἥξετ᾽ B, F., V⁴. Natum est illud haud dubie ex ἥξετ᾽ in v. 1489. Contrario errore T in v. 1489 ἵξετ᾽ praebet, cum praecurrerent scribentis oculi ad ἵξεσθ᾽ in 1491. **1493** τίς οὗτος ἔσται γ᾽ ὃς E: τίς οὗτός ἐστιν ὃς παραρρίψει coniecit Elmsleius, quod

---

moments a domestic disgrace, such as that which the sisters inherited, would be most keenly felt. In Athenian law-courts the fact of association at festivals could be cited in evidence of family intimacy: Isocr. or. 19 § 10 ἕως μὲν γὰρ παῖδες ἦμεν, περὶ πλέονος ἡμᾶς αὐτοὺς ἡγούμεθα ἢ τοὺς ἀδελφούς, καὶ οὔτε θυσίαν οὔτε θεωρίαν (public spectacle) οὔτ᾽ ἄλλην ἑορτὴν οὐδεμίαν χωρὶς ἀλλήλων ἤγομεν. Isae. or. 8 § 15 καὶ εἰς Διονύσια εἰς ἀγρὸν ἦγεν ἀεὶ ἡμᾶς, καὶ μετ᾽ ἐκείνου τε ἐθεωροῦμεν (in the theatre) καθήμενοι παρ᾽ αὐτόν, καὶ τὰς ἑορτὰς ἤγομεν παρ᾽ ἐκεῖνον πάσας. It was the Attic custom for a bridegroom Θεσμοφόρια ἑστιᾶν τὰς γυναῖκας, to provide a banquet at the next Thesmophoria for the women of his deme (Isae. or. 3 § 80), and also φράτορσι γαμηλίαν εἰσφέρειν, to provide a banquet for his clansmen when his bride was introduced into his φρατρία (or. 8 § 18). **1490** κεκλαυμέναι, only poet.: later poets and Plut. have κέκλαυσμαι: the poet. δεδακρυμένος also occurs in later prose, Plut., Lucian, etc. The festivals were religious celebrations, which would be polluted by the presence of persons resting under an inherited ἄγος (cp. note on 240). Some word or act reminds the daughters of Oedipus that they are thus regarded, and they go home in tears. Greek sensitiveness to public notice on such occasions might be illustrated by the story in Her. of the affront offered to the deposed king Demaratus by his successor Leotychides at the Spartan festival of the γυμνοπαιδίαι (6. 67). Demaratus drew his robe over his head, and left the theatre: κατακαλυψάμενος ᾔιε ἐκ τοῦ θεήτρου ἐς τὰ ἑωυτοῦ οἰκία. Contrast the effusive public greeting which Electra imagines herself and Chrysothemis as receiving ἔν θ᾽ ἑορταῖς ἔν τε πανδήμῳ πόλει (El. 982). **1491** ἀντὶ τῆς θεωρίας, in place of the sight-seeing (for which they had looked). θεωρία is (1) subjectively, a sight-

to what festival, but ye shall go home bathed in tears, instead
of sharing in the holiday? But when ye are now come
to years ripe for marriage, who shall he be, who shall be the
man, my daughters, that will hazard taking unto him such
reproaches as must be baneful alike to my sons and to you?

languere dicit Hermann., neque iniuria.   **1494** τοῖς ἐμοῖς] τοῖς πάλαι coniecit
Dindorf., τοῖς νέας Blaydes., τοῖς γάμοις Hartung., qui pro δηλήματα proposuit
'κμεμαγένα.   **1495** γονεῦσιν codd., mendo, ut mihi quidem videtur, manifesto:
vide annot. Coniecturam γόνοισιν, quam Nauckio deberi credo, veram esse non
dubito. γαμβροῖσιν acute magis quam apposite coniecit Arndt.

---

seeing: (2) objectively, *a spectacle.* In sense (1) the article is added here
because a definite occasion is meant; usually, the art. is absent: Thuc.
6. 24 πόθῳ ὄψεως καὶ θεωρίας: Plat. *Rep.* 556 C ἢ κατὰ θεωρίας ἢ κατὰ
στρατείας (on *travels* or *campaigns*): Isocr. or. 17 § 4 ἅμα κατ' ἐμπορίαν
καὶ κατὰ θεωρίαν. In Her. 1. 30 τῆς θεωρίης ἐκδημήσας...εἵνεκεν, the art.
is added as in ἡ εἰρήνη ('peace') etc., because 'seeing the world' is
spoken of generically. **1493** τίς οὗτος ἔσται, τίς, κ.τ.λ., is more animated
for τίς οὗτος ἔσται, ὅστις. Theocr. 16. 13 τίς τῶν νῦν τοιόσδε; τίς εὖ
εἰπόντα φιλασεῖ; is compared by Jacobs there, and by Schneidewin
here, but is not really similar, since τοιόσδε there refers back to v. 5 f.,
τίς γάρ...ὑποδέξεται (κ.τ.λ.); **1494** λαμβάνων instead of the infin. with
παραρρίψει, as Plat. *Legg.* 699 A οὐδεὶς τότε ἐβοήθησεν οὐδ' ἐκινδύνευσε
ξυμμαχόμενος. **1495** γόνοισιν. The disgraces of the polluted house
will be ruinous not only to the *sons* of Oedipus—who, as men, will still
be able to cope with the disadvantage so far at least as to win their
bread (1460)—but also to his helpless *daughters*, on whom the inherited
dishonour will entail destitution (1506). The γονεῦσιν of the MSS. yields
no tolerable sense, whether it is referred to Laïus and Iocasta or to
Iocasta alone. δήλημα is a hurt, bane, mischief, in a physical or
material sense: *Od.* 12. 286 ἄνεμοι χαλεποί, δηλήματα νηῶν: Hom. *Hom.*
Hymn. Apoll. 364 (of the dead monster) οὐδὲ σύ γε ζώουσα κακὸν δήλημα
βροτοῖσιν: Aesch. fr. 119 ὁδοιπόρων δήλημα χωρίτης δράκων (the serpent
in the fields, a bane of wayfarers). The disgraces are δηλήματα to the
sons and daughters as involving their ruin in life: but could not be called
δηλήματα to the *dead* in the remote figurative sense of *marring their*
memories. Nor would there be any fitness in the conjunction of
harm to the dead with harm *of another kind* to the living. Oedipus
here thinks of the living, and of the future, alone. The conject. γαμβροῖσιν, besides being far from the MSS., presumes the event which he

τί γὰρ κακῶν ἄπεστι; τον πατέρα πατὴρ
ὑμῶν ἔπεφνε· τὴν τεκοῦσαν ἤροσεν,
ὅθεν περ αὐτὸς ἐσπάρη, κἀκ τῶν ἴσων
ἐκτήσαθ᾽ ὑμᾶς ὧνπερ αὐτὸς ἐξέφυ.
τοιαῦτ᾽ ὀνειδιεῖσθε. κᾆτα τίς γαμεῖ;　　　　　1500
οὐκ ἔστιν οὐδείς, ὦ τέκν᾽, ἀλλὰ δηλαδὴ
χέρσους φθαρῆναι κἀγάμους ὑμᾶς χρεών.
ὦ παῖ Μενοικέως, ἀλλ᾽ ἐπεὶ μόνος πατὴρ
ταύταιν λέλειψαι, νὼ γάρ, ὣ 'φυτεύσαμεν,
ὀλώλαμεν δύ᾽ ὄντε, μή σφε περιίδῃς　　　　　1505
πτωχὰς ἀνάνδρους ἐγγενεῖς ἀλωμένας,
μηδ᾽ ἐξισώσῃς τάσδε τοῖς ἐμοῖς κακοῖς·
ἀλλ᾽ οἴκτισόν σφας, ὧδε τηλικάσδ᾽ ὁρῶν
πάντων ἐρήμους, πλὴν ὅσον τὸ σὸν μέρος.
ξύννευσον, ὦ γενναῖε, σῇ ψαύσας χερί.　　　　1510
σφῷν δ᾽, ὦ τέκν᾽, εἰ μὲν εἰχέτην ἤδη φρένας,

1497 τὴν τεκοῦσαν spurium esse censet Nauck., verba ὅθεν...ἐσπάρη nihil aliud
significare posse existimans quam 'a quo (patre) satus est.' Quid vero obstat quin
ὅθεν ἐσπάρη significet 'unde,'—id est ἐξ ἧς,—'satus est'? Reicit etiam verba τῶν
ἴσων Nauck., cum Sophoclem credat ita scripsisse: ὑμῶν ἔπεφν᾽, ὅθενπερ αὐτὸς
ἐσπάρη, | κἀκτήσαθ᾽ ὑμᾶς ὧνπερ αὐτὸς ἐξέφυ.　　**1505** μή σφε παρίδῃς codd.: μή

---

regards as impossible. **1496** πατέρα: for the tribrach see on 719. **1498**
τῶν ἴσων is poetically equivalent to τῶν αὐτῶν, i.e. τῆς αὐτῆς: it is like
saying, 'from a source which was even as that whence he sprang,'
instead of, 'from the same source whence he sprang.' Cp. 845 οὐ γὰρ
γένοιτ᾽ ἂν εἰς γε τοῖς πολλοῖς ἴσος, and note. **1500** ὀνειδιεῖσθε: see on
672. **1501** δηλαδὴ: prosaic, but also in Eur. Or. 789, I. A. 1366.
1503 ἀλλ᾽ after the vocative, like σὺ δέ, but stronger, as introducing an
appeal: as O. C. 1405 ὦ τοῦδ᾽ ὅμαιμοι παῖδες, ἀλλ᾽ ὑμεῖς...μή μ᾽ ἀτιμά-
σητέ γε: and ib. 237. **1505** δύ᾽ ὄντε, both of us: cp. Eur. Ion 518 σὺ
δ᾽ εὖ φρόνει γε καὶ δύ᾽ ὄντ᾽ εὖ πράξομεν. περιίδῃς: on Porson's objection, see Appendix, Note 16. **1506** ἐγγενεῖς, your kinswomen as they are
(where in prose we should have οὔσας added). The word was full of
meaning for an Attic audience, who would think of Creon as placed by
Oedipus in the position of ἐπίτροπος (guardian) and κύριος (representative before the law) of the unmarried girls who are here viewed as

For what misery is wanting? Your sire slew his sire, he had
seed of her who bare him, and begat you at the sources of his
own being! Such are the taunts that will be cast at you; and
who then will wed? The man lives not, no, it cannot be, my
children, but ye must wither in barren maidenhood.

Ah, son of Menoeceus, hear me—since thou art the only
father left to them, for we, their parents, are lost, both of us,—
allow them not to wander poor and unwed, who are thy kinswomen, nor abase them to the level of my woes. Nay, pity
them, when thou seest them at this tender age so utterly forlorn, save for thee. Signify thy promise, generous man, by the
touch of thy hand! To you, my children, I would have given

σφε περιίδης Dawes.: μὴ παρά σφ' ἴδης Porson.: μὴ περὶ σφ' ἴδης Fritzschius: μή
σφ' ἀτιμάσῃς Erfurdt., qui prius μὴ σφε δὴ προδῷς coniecerat. **1506** ἐγγενεῖς
codd. (in L prima manus ἐνγενεῖς scripserat): ἐκγενεῖς ex sua coniectura Dindorf.,
vocem alias non inventam, quacum conferri iubet ἔκβιος, ἔκτιμος, ἐξούσιος. Coniecit
ἀστέγους Hermann., ἐκστεγεῖς Schneidewin. **1511** εἰχέτην codd.: εἰχετόν γ'
Brunck., Blaydes.; sed vide annot.

orphans (1505); their brothers not being of age. Cp. Isae. or. 5 § 10;
[Dem.] or. 46 § 18. 1507 ἐξισώσῃς τάσδε, do not put them on the level of
my miseries: cp. 425: for τάσδε instead of τὰ τῶνδε κακά, cp. note on
467. 1508 τηλικάσδ', at their age, i.e. so young: Ant. 726 οἱ τηλι-
κοίδε (so old) καὶ διδαξόμεσθα δὴ | φρονεῖν πρὸς ἀνδρὸς τηλικοῦδε (so
young) τὴν φύσιν; 1509 πλὴν ὅσον τὸ σὸν μέρος, except in so far as,
on thy part, οὐκ ἔρημοι εἰσί. 1511 εἰχέτην, 2nd pers. dual, with
the form proper to the 3rd (μετειχέτην, 1465). Before the Attic
period, the Greek language had attained to this regular distinction of
active dual forms:—(1) primary tenses, 2nd pers. -τον, 3rd pers. -τον;
(2) secondary tenses, 2nd pers. -τον, answering to Skt. tam: 3rd pers.
-την, Skt. tām. As regards (2), two classes of exceptions occur: (a)
Homeric 3rd pers. in -τον instead of -την: three instances, διώκετον
(Il. 10. 364), ἐτεύχετον (13. 346), λαφύσσετον (18. 583). These Curtius
refers to 'the want of proper linguistic instinct on the part of some
late rhapsodist.' (b) Attic 2nd pers. in -την instead of -τον. Our εἰχέτην here is the only instance proved by metre: but 8 others are established. Against these fall to be set at least 13 Attic instances of the
normal -τον. Curtius regards the 2nd pers. in -την as due to a false
analogy. In the third person dual -την was distinctive of the secondary

πόλλ' ἂν παρῄνουν· νῦν δὲ τοῦτ' εὔχεσθέ μοι,
οὗ καιρὸς ἐᾷ ζῆν, τοῦ βίου δὲ λῴονος
ὑμᾶς κυρῆσαι τοῦ φυτεύσαντος πατρός.

ΚΡ. ἅλις ἵν' ἐξήκεις δακρύων· ἀλλ' ἴθι στέγης ἔσω. 1515

ΟΙ. πειστέον, κεἰ μηδὲν ἡδύ. ΚΡ. πάντα γὰρ καιρῷ καλά.

ΟΙ. οἶσθ' ἐφ' οἷς οὖν εἶμι; ΚΡ. λέξεις, καὶ τότ' εἴσομαι
κλύων.

ΟΙ. γῆς μ' ὅπως πέμψεις ἄποικον. ΚΡ. τοῦ θεοῦ μ' αἰτεῖς
δόσιν.

1512 εὔχεσθέ μοι codd. : εὔχεσθ' ἐμοί Wunder. : τοῦθ' ἐν εὔχομαι Blaydes., qui
etiam τοῦτ' ἐπεύχομαι, Nauckio probante, coniecit: ηὔχθω μόνον Dindorf. ; sed
nusquam alibi reperitur imperativus perfecti ηὖγμαι, quanquam Soph. *Trach.* 610
ηὔγμην ('voveram') dixit, et Plato *Phaedr.* 279 c ηὖκται ('facta sunt vota'). 1513
οὗ καιρὸς ἀεὶ ζῆν τοῦ βίου δὲ λῴονος codd. Tres fere corrigendi rationes tentatae sunt.
(1) Omisso ζῆν, Elmsleius sic explicat : εὔχεσθε κυρῆσαι τοῦ βίου οὗ καιρὸς ἀεὶ (κυρῆσαί
ἐστι), λῴονος δὲ τοῦ φυτ. πατρός. Hermann. autem, ζῆν pariter omittens, εὔχεσθε pro
passivo habet : i. e., De vobis id fiat a me votum, quod cuique tempori conveniat.

tenses. Attic speech sometimes extended this distinction to the *second*
person also. (Curtius, *Verb* I. 80, Eng. tr. 53.) 1512 ff. Oedipus now
turns from Creon to the children. The few words which he addresses
to them are spoken rather to the older hearers and to himself. τοῦτ'
εὔχεσθέ μοι, 'make this prayer, as I bid you': not, 'pray on my account'
(in which sense Wunder reads ἐμοί). In these words Oedipus is thinking solely of his children : he has now passed away from the thought of
self (1458). ὑμᾶς in 1514 is no argument for understanding με as
subject to ζῆν: rather it is added to mark the contrast with πατρός.
1513 I prefer οὗ καιρὸς ἐᾷ ζῆν, τοῦ βίου κ.τ.λ. to οὗ καιρὸς ἀεὶ ζῆν, βίου
κ.τ.λ. on these grounds. 1. τοῦ before βίου, though not required,
is commended, by Greek idiom; it also gives a decidedly better
rhythm ; and it is not likely to have crept into the text, since
the occurrence of ἀεί with the α long was not so uncommon that
it should have suggested the need of supplementing the metre by
τοῦ: but, apart from metrical motive, there was no other for *intruding*
the article. 2. οὗ καιρός, without any verb, though a possible phrase, is
a harsh one. 3. From εαι to αει would be an easy transition. And
καιρὸς ἐᾷ is quite a natural expression: cp. Eur. *I. A.* 858 δοῦλος· οὐχ
ἁβρύνομαι τῷδ'· ἡ τύχη γὰρ οὐκ ἐᾷ. The foreboding of Oedipus is

much counsel, were your minds mature; but now I would have this to be your prayer—that ye live where occasion suffers, and that the life which is your portion may be happier than your sire's.

CR. Thy grief hath had large scope enough: nay, pass into the house.

OE. I must obey, though 'tis in no wise sweet. CR. Yea: for it is in season that all things are good.

OE. Knowest thou, then, on what conditions I will go? CR. Thou shalt name them; so shall I know them when I hear.

OE. See that thou send me to dwell beyond this land. CR. Thou askest me for what the god must give.

(2) Omisso τοῦ, scribit Hartung. οὐ καιρός, αἰεὶ ζῆν, βίου δὲ λῴονος: quod recipiunt Blaydes., Campbell., ἀεὶ tamen tuentur, neque post καιρὸς distinguunt. (3) In v. ἀεὶ mendum vident alii. οὐ καιρὸς ἐᾷ ζῆν, τοῦ βίου δὲ λῴονος coniecit Dindorf., quem secuti sunt Wunder., Nauck., Kennedius: οὐ καιρός ᾗ ζῆν, Meinekius: οὐ καιρός, εὖ ζῆν Blaydes. 1517 εἰμι codd.: εἶμι Brunck. 1518 πέμψεις L (πέμψῃσ corrector) A, codd. plerlque: πέμψῃς (sic) T, V², alii. ἀπ' οἴκων L (ου rubris litteris a manu recenti superscripto), A (superscripto γρ. ἀποικον), codd. plerique: ἀποίκων V²: veram l. ἄποικον habet B.

---

that his daughters must become homeless exiles (1506) unless Creon shelters them at Thebes. 'To live where occasion allows' means in his inner thought, 'to live at Thebes, if that may be—if not, in the least unhappy exile that the gods may grant you.' The monosyllabic ἔα (1451, Ant. 95) and ἐᾷ (Il. 5. 256 τρεῖν μ' οὐκ ἐᾷ Παλλὰς Ἀθήνη) go far to remove the metrical objection. Meineke's conjecture, ᾗ, gives a more prosaic phrase, and is too far from the ἀεὶ of the MSS. 1515 ἐξήκεις: see on 1357. 1516 καιρῷ = ἐν καιρῷ. In Thuc. 4. 59 most MSS. give εἰ μὴ καιρῷ τύχοιεν ἑκάτεροι πράσσοντες: Classen reads ἐν καιρῷ on the ground that Thuc. so has it in 1. 121, 5. 61, 6. 9. 1517 The words οἶσθ' ἐφ' οἷς οὖν εἰμι; were said with some return of his former agitation: λέξεις κ.τ.λ. is said by Creon with calm, grave courtesy; they have nothing in them of such irony as, 'I shall know when you are pleased to tell me.' So Aesch. Theb. 260 ET. αἰτουμένῳ μοι κοῦφον εἰ δοίης τέλος: 'would that thou could'st grant me a light boon.' XO. λέγοις ἂν ὡς τάχιστα, καὶ τάχ' εἴσομαι (i.e. and then I shall know if I can serve thee). 1518 ὅπως πέμψεις: sc. ὅρα: Xen. An. 1. 7. 3 ὅπως οὖν ἔσεσθε ἄνδρες, 'see that ye be': Plat. Rep. 337 A ὅπως μοι, ὦ

J. S.   18

ΟΙ. ἀλλὰ θεοῖς γ' ἔχθιστος ἥκω. ΚΡ. τοιγαροῦν τεύξει
τάχα.

ΟΙ. φῂς τάδ' οὖν ; ΚΡ. ἃ μὴ φρονῶ γὰρ οὐ φιλῶ λέγειν
μάτην. 1520

ΟΙ. ἄπαγέ νύν μ' ἐντεῦθεν ἤδη. ΚΡ. στεῖχέ νυν, τέκνων
δ' ἀφοῦ.

ΟΙ. μηδαμῶς ταύτας γ' ἕλῃ μου. ΚΡ. πάντα μὴ βούλου
κρατεῖν·

καὶ γὰρ ἁκράτησας οὔ σοι τῷ βίῳ ξυνέσπετο.

ΧΟ. ὦ πάτρας Θήβης ἔνοικοι, λεύσσετ', Οἰδίπους ὅδε,
ὃς τὰ κλείν' αἰνίγματ' ᾔδει καὶ κράτιστος ἦν ἀνήρ, 1525
οὗ τίς οὐ ζήλῳ πολιτῶν ταῖς τύχαις ἐπέβλεπεν,

1521 νῦν bis L, A, B, E, al.: νῦν—νυν T : νυν bis Brunck. **1523** τῷ
βίῳ] διὰ βίου ex sua coniect. dedit Nauck. **1524—1530** Hos versus choro
recte tribuunt codd.; Oedipo scholiasta et Blaydes. Scholiasta versu 1523 fabulam
melius finiri iudicat : τὰ γὰρ ἑξῆς ἀνοίκεια, γνωμολογοῦντος τοῦ Οἰδίποδος. Errorem inde
natum esse monet Dindorf., quod in Phoenissis similes versus (1758 seqq.) Oedipo
tribuit Euripides, duo quidem priores prope ad verbum de Sophocleis expressos :
ὦ πάτρας κλεινῆς πολῖται, λεύσσετ', Οἰδίπους ὅδε, | ὃς τὰ κλείν' αἰνίγματ' ἔγνω καὶ
μέγιστος ἦν ἀνήρ. Delendos vv. 1524—1530 censuit Fr. Ritter., quibus si caremus,
curto nimis exitu fabula praeciditur. **1526** ὅστις οὐ ζήλῳ πολιτῶν καὶ τύχαις
ἐπιβλέπων codd. Nulla lectionis varietas nisi quod ἐν pro οὐ praebent V, M, M⁵

ἄνθρωπε, μὴ ἐρεῖς. Not (εἶμι ἐπὶ τούτοις), ὅπως κ.τ.λ. 1519 ἀλλὰ θεοῖς γ' :
i.e. 'Nay, the *gods*, who hate me, will not be displeased that I should be
thrust forth.' For the synizesis in θεοῖς see on 640. ἥκω, 1357. Creon's
reply, τοιγαροῦν τεύξει τάχα, means : 'if the gods *do* desire thy banishment, thou wilt soon have thy wish'—when the oracle at Delphi
is consulted (1443). According to the story which Soph. follows,
Oedipus was at first detained at Thebes against his own wish. But
when some time had elapsed, and that wish had given place to a calmer
mood, the Thebans, in their turn, demanded his expulsion; and Creon
then yielded (*O. C.* 433 ff.). 1520 ἃ μὴ φρονῶ. Cp. 569. Creon cannot tell how Apollo may decide. 1522 ἕλῃ μου: cp. 1022 χειρῶν λαβών.
1524—1530 See critical note. These verses are spoken by the Chorus,
as Creon turns with Oedipus to enter the house. The calm close which
the tragedy requires would be wanting if they were spoken by the
chief sufferer himself. Of extant Greek tragedies, the *Prometheus* and
the *Agamemnon* are the only ones which end with words spoken by one

OE. Nay, to the gods I have become most hateful. CR. Then shalt thou have thy wish anon.

OE. So thou consentest? CR. Nay, 'tis not my wont to speak vain words when I lack knowledge.

OE. Then 'tis time to lead me hence. CR. Come, then,— but let thy children go.

OE. Nay, take not these from me! CR. Crave not to be master in all things: for the mastery which thou didst win hath not followed thee through life.

CH. Dwellers in our native Thebes, behold, this is Oedipus, who knew the famed riddle, and was a man most mighty; on whose fortunes what citizen did not gaze with envy?

a pr. manu; βίῳ pro ζήλῳ habet M; quae nihili sunt. ὃν τίς οὐ ζήλῳ πολιτῶν τῆς τύχης ἐπέβλεπεν; Musgravius, et sic Blaydes. Unde ἐπέβλεπεν mutuatus cum Martini coniectura οὗ, Ellendtii ταῖς coniunxit Hartung., ut ita legat : οὗ τίς οὐ ζήλῳ πολιτῶν ταῖς τύχαις ἐπέβλεπεν, quod recepit Nauckius. ὥς τις οὐ ζήλῳ πολιτῶν καὶ τύχαις ἐπιβλέπων Kennedius. πᾶς ὃν ἐξήλου πολιτῶν καὶ τύχαις ἐπέβλεπον (sic, non ἐπέβλεπεν) Dindorf. in Poet. Scen. ed. quinta (1869). πρῶτος ἐν ζήλῳ πολιτῶν καὶ τύχαις ἐπιφλέγων Campbell.: errat autem vir doctissimus cum gloss. ἐπαιρόμενος ad ἐπιβλέπων non solum in M verum etiam in E esse tradit ; nam in cod. E pag. 110, qua continentur versus 1518—1530, neque illud est glossema neque aliud quicquam.

---

of the actors; and in each case this is justified by the scheme of the trilogy to which the play belonged. **1525** Here, as elsewhere, the MSS. fluctuate between ᾔδει and ᾔδη. The Attic ᾔδη, as *first* pers. sing., is contracted from ᾔδεα: in the *third*, the classical form was not ᾔδη but ᾔδει, or, before a vowel, ᾔδειν (as it *must* be in Eur. *Ion* 1187, Ar. *Pax* 1182 etc.). No 3rd sing. in εα, from which η could come, is said, or can be supposed, to have existed. Aristarchus, indeed, is quoted by the schol. on *Il.* 5. 64 in favour of the η. But the Doric 3rd sing. ἀπολώλη in *Tab. Heracl.* 1. 39 is the only such form which is beyond question. Curtius (*Verb* II. 237, Eng. tr. 431 ff.) therefore agrees with those textual critics who, like La Roche, Cobet, and Kontos (Λόγιος Ἑρμῆς p. 61) would always write the 3rd sing. ᾔδει (or ᾔδειν). Cp. Rutherford, *New Phrynichus*, pp. 229 ff. ᾔδει αἰνίγματα (*plur.* with reference to the hexameter ἔπη in which it was chanted) = knew *instinctively*, by the intuition of genius : in Eur. *Phoen.* 1759 the adapter of this verse has altered ᾔδει (perhaps by a slip of memory) to the more natural but less forcible ἔγνω, 'read aright,' solved. **1526** οὗ τίς οὐ ζήλῳ ... ταῖς τύχαις ἐπέβλ., 'on whose fortunes what citizen did

18—2

εἰς ὅσον κλύδωνα δεινῆς συμφορᾶς ἐλήλυθεν.
ὥστε θνητὸν ὄντ᾽ ἐκείνην τὴν τελευταίαν ἰδεῖν
ἡμέραν ἐπισκοποῦντα μηδέν᾽ ὀλβίζειν, πρὶν ἂν
τέρμα τοῦ βίου περάσῃ μηδὲν ἀλγεινὸν παθών. 1530

1528 ὄντα κείνην scripserat pr. manus in L; corrector ε ante κ addidit. **1529**

---

not look with emulous admiration?' To me it appears certain that we should here read the interrogative τίς with ἐπέβλεπεν instead of ἐπιβλέπων. Cp. *O. C.* 1133 ᾧ τίς οὐκ ἔνι | κηλὶς κακῶν ξύνοικος; 871 ὅπου τίς ὄρνις οὐχὶ κλαγγάνει; Eur. *Phoen.* 878 ἀγὼ τί δρῶν οὔ, ποῖα δ᾽ οὐ λέγων ἔπη, | εἰς ἔχθος ἦλθον. Dem. or. 18 § 48 ἐλαυνομένων καὶ ὑβριζομένων καὶ τί κακὸν οὐχὶ πασχόντων πᾶσα ἡ οἰκουμένη μεστὴ γέγονεν. Then the καὶ of the MSS. should be ταῖς. The argument for this depends primarily on the usage of the verb ἐπιβλέπω, which nowhere occurs in the sense of *invidere alicui*, 'to look *jealously* upon.' See Appendix, Note 17. 1529 The use of ἐπισκοποῦντα is peculiar. I take the exact sense to be :—'*fixing one's eye on* the final day (as on a point towards which one is moving), *that one should see it*,' *i.e.* 'until one shall have had experience of it.' Thus ἐπισκοπεῖν is used in a sense closely akin to its common sense of 'attentively considering' a thing: and the whole phrase is virtually equivalent to, '*waiting meditatively to see* the final day.' For the added infin., cp. Thuc. 3. 2 νεῶν ποίησιν ἐπέμενον τελεσθῆναι, καὶ ὅσα ἐκ τοῦ Πόντου ἔδει ἀφικέσθαι. Cp. Plin. 7 § 132 *alius de alio iudicat dies*, et tamen supremus de omnibus, *ideoque nullis credendum est.* Hartung proposed to replace ἰδεῖν by γε δεῖ (where γε would be intolerable), and Nauck by χρεών. But the infin. ὀλβίζειν as a 'sententious' imperative (see on 462) is appropriate in this γνώμη. μηδέν᾽ ὀλβίζειν. Eur. *Androm.* 100 ff. partly reproduces the language of this passage: χρὴ δ᾽ οὔποτ᾽ εἰπεῖν οὐδέν᾽ ὄλβιον βροτῶν, | πρὶν ἂν θανόντος τὴν τελευ-

Behold into what a stormy sea of dread trouble he hath come!

Therefore, while our eyes wait to see the destined final day, we must call no one happy who is of mortal race, until he hath crossed life's border, free from pain.

Voces quattuor quae in L super μηδέν' ὀλβίζειν πρὶν ἂν deletae sunt ad interpretationem aliquam potius quam ad variam l. videntur pertinuisse.

ταίαν ἴδῃς | ὅπως περάσας ἡμέραν ἥξει κάτω. He has the thought again in *Tro.* 510, *Heracl.* 866, *I. A.* 161, as Soph. again in *Trach.* 1. The maxim, 'Call no man happy before death,' first appears in Greek literature as a set γνώμη in Aesch. *Ag.* 928 ὀλβίσαι δὲ χρὴ | βίον τελευτήσαντ' ἐν εὐεστοῖ φίλῃ· but Aristotle recognises the popular tradition which ascribed it to Solon (Her. 1. 32, where Solon says that a man may be called εὐτυχής *in* life, but ὄλβιος only *after* a life exempt from reverse). Cp. Iuv. 10. 274 f. *Et Croesum, quem vox iusti facunda Solonis Respicere ad longae iussit spatia ultima vitae*, where Mayor refers to the proverbs Λυδὸς (Croesus) ἀποθνῄσκει σοφὸς ἀνήρ, and τέλος ὅρα βίου (Paroemiogr. II. 187, I. 315 n.), and to notices of the saying in Cic. (*De Fin.* 2 § 87, 3 § 76), Diog. Laert. (1 § 50 τὰ θρυλούμενα), Ovid (*Met.* 3. 135), Seneca (*De Tranq. An.* 11 § 12), Josephus (*Bell. Iud.* 1. 5. 11 = 29 § 3), Arrian (7 § 16. 7), Lucian (*Charon* 10): cp. Ecclus. 11. 28. Does Solon mean, Aristotle asks, (1) that a man *is* happy when he is dead? Or (2) that, after death, he *may be said to have been* happy? If (1), Arist. declines to allow that the dead are positively happy; and popular opinion, he says, denies that they are always negatively so, *i.e.* free from unhappiness. If (2), then is it not absurd that at the time when he *is* happy we are not to call him so? The fallacy, he concludes, consists in treating 'happiness' as dependent on bright *fortunes*: οὐ γὰρ ἐν ταύταις τὸ εὖ ἢ κακῶς, ἀλλὰ προσδεῖται τούτων ὁ ἀνθρώπινος βίος, καθάπερ εἴπαμεν, κύριαι δ' εἰσὶν αἱ κατ' ἀρετὴν ἐνέργειαι τῆς εὐδαιμονίας, αἱ δ' ἐναντίαι τοῦ ἐναντίου. (*Eth. Nic.* I. 11.)

APPENDIX.

NOTE I.

The Oedipus Tyrannus at Harvard.

In the Introduction, I have referred to the memorable performance of the *Oedipus Tyrannus* by members óf Harvard University in May, 1881. The thorough scholarship, the archæological knowledge and the artistic skill which presided over that performance invest the record of it with a permanent value for every student of the play. Where the modern imagination most needs assistance, this record comes to its aid. Details of stage-management and of scenic effect, which a mere reading of the text could suggest to few, become clear and vivid. Mr H. Norman's 'Account of the Harvard Greek Play'—illustrated by excellent photographs—is, in fact, a book which must always have a place of its own in the literature of the *Oedipus Tyrannus*. I select those passages which relate to the principal moments of the action; and, for more convenient reference, I arrange them in successive sections.

§ 1. *Opening Scene.* 'Account,' p. 65. 'The scene behind the long and narrow stage is the palace of Oedipus, king of Thebes,—a stately building with its frieze and columns. There is a large central door with two broad steps, and two smaller side doors; all three are closed. In the centre of the stage in front is a large altar; beside each of the smaller doors of the palace is another altar. A flight of steps leads from the stage at each side. The sound of the closing doors has warned the audience that the long-expected moment is at hand, and an immediate silence ensues. Under these circumstances the first notes of the orchestra come with great effect, and the entire prelude is unusually impressive. As it closes, the spectators are sympathetic and expectant.

'Slowly the crimson curtains on the right-hand side below the stage are drawn apart, and the Priest of Zeus enters, leaning on a staff, a venerable and striking figure....Behind him come two little children. They are dressed in soft white tunics and cloaks, their hair is bound with white fillets, and they carry in their hands olive branches twined with wool,—

ἐλαίας θ' ὑψιγέννητον κλάδον,
λήνει μεγίστῳ σωφρόνως ἐστεμμένον.

This shows that they come as suppliants. Behind the children come boys, then youths, and then old men. All are dressed in white and carry suppliant boughs; in the costumes of the men, the delicate fabric of the undergarment, the χιτών, contrasts beautifully with the heavy folds of the ἱμάτιον. With grave, attentive faces the procession crosses the front of the stage, and mounts, the steps; the suppliants lay down their branches and *seat themselves on the steps of the altars.* The priest alone remains standing, facing the palace door.

'The first impression upon the spectators was fortunate. The innocent looks of the children, the handsome figures of the men, the simplicity and solemnity of their movements, set off as they were by the fine drapery of their garments and the striking groups around the altars, had an instant and deep effect. It is safe to say that fears of crudeness or failure began rapidly to vanish. The spectacle presented at this moment was one of the most impressive of the play.

'After a short pause the great doors of the palace are thrown back, and the attendants of Oedipus enter and take up their positions on each side. They wear thin lavender tunics reaching nearly to the knee. Their looks are directed to the interior of the palace, whence, in a moment, Oedipus enters. His royal robes gleam now with the purple of silk and now with the red of gold; gold embroidery glitters on his crimson tunic and on his white sandals; his crown gives him dignity and height.

'For an instant he surveys the suppliants, and then addresses them.'

§ 2. *Arrival of Creon from Delphi:* verses 78 ff. 'Account,' p. 69. 'While Oedipus is speaking, the children on the [spectators'] left of the stage have descried some one approaching, and one of them has pointed him out to the priest. It is Creon, who enters with rapid strides, wearing a wreath of bay leaves sparkling with berries, the symbol of a favorable answer. He is dressed in the short salmon-colored tunic and crimson cloak, with hat and staff. A hasty greeting follows; and

Oedipus, the priest, and the suppliants wait for the answer of the oracle.'

§ 3. *Withdrawal of the Suppliants, and Entrance of the Chorus:* vv. 143—151, p. 71. 'With the assurance of speedy aid [for the Thebans] he [Oedipus] leads Creon into the palace, and the attendants follow and close the doors. Slowly the white-robed suppliants rise ; the petition being granted, each one takes his bough, and led by the priest they descend the steps and disappear.

'As the last figure passes out of sight the notes of the orchestra are heard once more, this time with a measured beat which instantly attracts attention, and the Chorus of old men of Thebes issues from the same entrance. They are men of various ages, dressed in tunics reaching to the instep, and full ἱμάτια, of harmonious soft warm colors. The excellence of the costumes was marked ; each man seemed to have worn his dress for years, and to exhibit his individuality in the folds of it. They enter three deep, marching to the solemn beat of the music ; and as the first rank comes in sight of the audience the strains of the choral ode burst from their lips.

Shoulder to shoulder and foot to foot the old men make their way to the altar on the floor of the theatre and take up their positions around it. This entrance of the Chorus was surpassed in dramatic effect by few features of the play : the rhythmical movements, the coloring and drapery, the dignity of the faces, the impressive music sung in unison by the fifteen trained voices,—all these combined to produce a startling effect on the audience.'

§ 4. *Entrance of Teiresias*, v. 297, p. 75. 'At this moment Teiresias enters, a towering venerable figure, with long white hair and beard. He is guided to the stage by a boy, whose blue cloak contrasts with the snowy draperies of the old man.' *His exit*, v. 462, p. 79. 'The two men part in deadly anger, Oedipus going within the palace and the boy leading Teiresias down the steps [from the stage, see § 1]....Once more the music sounds, and the Chorus gives voice to its feelings concerning the strange scene which has just been enacted.'

§ 5. *Entrance of Creon, when he comes to repudiate the charge of treason brought against him by Oedipus:* v. 512, p. 81. 'As the strains of [choral] music die away, Creon is seen hastily ascending the steps [to the stage] on the right [of the spectators: cp. § 2]. He is no longer dressed as a traveller, but in garments suited to his high rank. His tunic is of delicate dark crimson material, with a gold border; his ἱμάτιον is of bright crimson cashmere, with a broader gold border; his sandals are of crimson and gold. He strides to the centre of the stage and bursts out in indignant denial of the charges that Oedipus has made against him.'

§ 6. *Iocasta enters while high words are passing between Oedipus and Creon:* v. 631, p. 83. 'Just as this [altercation] reaches its height the doors of the palace are seen to open, and the Chorus bids both angry speakers cease, as Jocasta is approaching. The attendants of Jocasta enter and place themselves on each side of the door, and a moment later the queen herself stands upon the threshold. Oedipus turns to her with welcome, and Creon with a gesture of appeal.

'Her dress consists of a richly trimmed silvery undergarment, and an ἱμάτιον of crimped pale yellow silk. She wears a crown, bracelets, and necklace, and white sandals embroidered with gold.'

It was upon this group—the first complex one in the play—that Mr F. D. Millet based his scheme of the costumes, to which he gave long study, both from the historical and from the artistic point of view, and which he has described in the *Century Magazine* of Nov., 1881. From this article, Mr Norman (p. 83) quotes the following passage:—

'It was part of the original scheme that in each group the most prominent character should, as far as possible, be the focus, not only of interest in the text, but from the point of view of costume. Let us see how the first complex group fulfilled this condition. On the stage left stood Oedipus, in rich but deep-toned red; on the right, Creon, equally in red, but of a color entirely different in scale; the attendants of the king, in lavender tunics bordered with gold-embroidered white, flanked the doorway; and the two attendants of Jocasta, in delicate blue and salmon, brought the eye by a pleasing graduation in intensity of color and strength of tone up to the figure of the queen, clothed in lustrous and ample drapery.'

§ 7. *Arrival of the Messenger from Corinth:* v. 924, p. 89. 'As the Chorus closes, Jocasta enters [v. 911] in a new state of mind. She has comforted Oedipus by ridiculing all oracles; but she is not without faith in the power of Gods, and she brings frankincense and garlands, and lays them with a prayer upon the altar.

'While she is speaking, an old man has entered on the left below the stage. He is dressed as a common traveller, in a tunic and short cloak, his hat slung over his shoulder, and a stout staff in his hand. It is the messenger from Corinth. He looks round as if in search of something, and as soon as the queen has finished her prayer he inquires of the Chorus where the home of Oedipus, or, better still, the king himself, can be found. He is promptly informed that the mansion he sees is the palace of Oedipus, and that the lady before it is the queen. With a profound salutation as he ascends to the stage, he declares himself to be the bearer of news at once good and bad. Old Polybus, king of Corinth, is dead, and the citizens are about to make Oedipus king. This is indeed news to Jocasta. Oedipus has long avoided Corinth lest he should slay his father, Polybus; now he can return, as king, all fear dispelled. Oedipus enters in response to her summons. His royal robes have been exchanged for simpler ones of white and gold. He, too, learns the news with triumph.'

§ 8. *Iocasta divines the worst :—her final exit;* vv. 1040—1072, p. 92. 'But Jocasta? At the other end of the stage the queen is writhing in anguish. The deep-red cloak which she wears is twisted about her; now she flings her hands up and seems about to speak, then her hands are pressed on her mouth to stop the cries which rise, or on her bosom to silence the beating of her heart. She rushes toward the king, but stops half-way; her face shows the tortures of her soul. The truth is all too clear to her. The spectator feels that this suspense cannot last, and relief comes when the Chorus suggests that perhaps Jocasta can tell something about the shepherd of Laius. When appealed to by Oedipus, she forces the suffering from her face and turns with a smile. But Oedipus has gone beyond recall. Her last appealing words are scorned, and with the language and the gesture of despair she rushes from the stage.'

§ 9. *The Herdsman of Laïus is brought in: the whole truth is extorted from him:* vv. 1110—1185, pp. 94 ff. 'As the music ceases the attendants of Oedipus appear at the entrance on the right, supporting a strange figure between them. It is an aged man, with grizzled hair and beard, clothed in coarse homespun cloth, and with a rough, untanned sheepskin over his shoulders. He supports himself on a sapling staff which he has cut in the woods. He mounts the steps with difficulty, and faces the king. He is no stranger to the errand on which he has been brought, and with the greatest difficulty he is made to speak. The contrast between the eagerness of the messenger from Corinth to tell all he knows, and the silence of the tender-hearted old shepherd, is very striking. The shepherd cannot bear the other's telltale chatter, and with the words, " Confusion seize thee and thine evil tongue !" he swings his staff to strike him. At a gesture from Oedipus the attendant stops the blow. The old man must be made to speak. The muscular attendants spring forward and seize him. Then the truth is wrung from him, word by word. He gave the child to the Corinthian ; it came from the palace ; they said it was the son of Laius ; Queen Jocasta herself placed it in his hands ; they said that an oracle had declared that it should kill its father. The truth is out ; the oracles are not falsified ; his father's murderer, his mother's husband, Oedipus faces his doom. With a fearful, choking cry he pulls his robes over his head and face, and bursts into the palace.

' This scene...was the dramatic climax of the play. The acting led up to it gradually by the excited conversation and the shepherd's blow. When Oedipus burst through the doors of the palace, his attendants quickly followed him ; the horror-stricken messengers turned with despairing gestures and descended the steps, the one to the right, the other to the left, and a profound silence fell upon the theatre.'

§ 10. *Effect of the fourth stasimon*, vv. 1223—1530, p. 98. ' In the opening strains of the last choral ode, which now ring out, the emotions of the scene are wonderfully expressed. Each one recognizes the solemnity and depth of his own feelings in their pathetic tones.'

§ 11. *The Messenger from the House: the entrance of the blinded Oedipus*, 1223—1296, pp. 98 f. ' As the ode [just mentioned] closes, the palace doors are opened violently from within, and the second messenger rushes on the stage. He is a servant from the palace, clad, like the attendants, in a short light tunic. He brings a tale of horror : Oedipus, on entering, had called for a sword, and demanded to know where Jocasta was. No one would tell him ; but at last, seeing the doors of the bedchamber shut, he had broken through them and disclosed the body of the queen hanging by the bed. Tearing down the body, he had snatched from the shoulders the golden clasps and had thrust them into his eyes.'......' In a moment Oedipus himself appears, leaning on his attendants, his pale face marred by bloody stains. The dismayed Chorus hide their faces in their robes, and the king's voice is broken with sobs as he cries, αἰαῖ, αἰαῖ, δύστανος ἐγώ.'

§ 12. *Closing scene,* vv. 1416—1530, pp. 101 ff. 'As Oedipus is begging to be slain or thrust out of the land, the approach of Creon, who has resumed his royal powers, is announced. The memory of all his injustice to Creon overwhelms Oedipus, and he cannot bear to meet him. But he is blind and unable to flee, so he hides his face and waits in silence. Creon enters, crowned, followed by two attendants... His first words are reassuring; the new king does not come with mocking or reproach, but directs that a sight so offensive to earth and heaven be hidden within the palace. Oedipus asks the boon of banishment, but is informed by the cautious Creon that the God must be consulted. Then the blind man begs that his wife be buried decently, and reiterates his prayer that he may be permitted to leave the city which he has afflicted. And one thing more he asks,—that he may embrace his daughters again. By a sign Creon despatches his own attendants to bring them, and while Oedipus is still speaking their voices are heard.

'Antigone and Ismene now enter, led by the attendants of Creon, and are placed in the arms of Oedipus, who falls on his knees beside them, and addresses them with saddest words. The children are too young to appreciate the horror of the scene, but they are filled with pity for their father's pain. There is a look of genuine sympathy on the two bright faces which watch the kneeling figure. Creon has retired to the right of the stage and has wrapped his robe round him, unable to bear the sight of the terrible farewell. He is summoned by Oedipus to give his hand in token of his promise to care for the helpless girls. The children fall back, the blind man waits with outstretched hand, and Creon slowly and sadly walks across the stage and gives the sign. Then Oedipus turns again to his little ones. The painful scene, however, has lasted long enough, and Creon orders Oedipus to leave his children and withdraw. It is a dreadful separation, but the king's order is imperative. So Oedipus tears himself away, his attendants throw open the doors, the attendants of Creon take the children by the hand, and Creon himself leads Oedipus up the steps and into the palace....The children and the second messenger follow; the attendants of Oedipus enter last and gently close the doors.

'The music sounds again in pathetic tones, and the Coryphaeus expresses for his fellows the lesson of life.'

NOTE II.

Verse 2.

On the meaning of θοάζετε.

The points of the question are these.　1. θοάζειν, from θο-ό-ς swift (rt. θεϜ, θέω; Curt. *Etym.* § 313), occurs ten times in Eur., four times transitively, 'to impel,' 'urge,' as *Bacch.* 66 θοάζω Βρομίῳ πόνον ἡδύν: six times intransitively, as *Troad.* 349 μαινὰς θοάζουσ'. If it is the same word here, what would θοάζειν ἕδρας mean? (*a*) Not, I think, 'to urge, press your supplication,'—referring to the eager gestures or aspect of the suppliants: for *rapid motion*, and not merely eagerness, is implied by θοάζω. Rather (*b*) 'to come with eager haste as suppliants': as Herm. explains Erfurdt's 'cur hanc sessionem festinatis?'—'cur tanto studio hic sessum venitis?' Now I can conceive Sophocles saying σπεύδειν or ἐπείγειν or even θοάζειν ἱκετείαν: but could he have said θοάζειν ἕδρας? The primary notion of a *fixed attitude* stands out too clearly above the secondary notion of *a supplication*.

2.　For another θοάζειν, 'to sit,' only two passages are cited.　(i) Empedocles 52 θάρσει καὶ τότε δὴ σοφίης ἐπ' ἄκροισι θόαζε. This *might* mean 'hasten on to the heights of wisdom': though, when ἐπί with dat. denotes motion, it usually means 'against,' as in *Od.* 10. 214 οὐδ' οἵ γ' ὡρμήθησαν ἐπ' ἀνδράσιν. But the more natural sense would be, 'sit on the heights of wisdom.' (ii) Aesch. *Suppl.* 595 ὑπ' ἀρχᾶς [L ἀρχὰς] δ' οὔτινος θοάζων | τὸ μεῖον κρεισσόνων κρατύνει· | οὔτινος ἄνωθεν ἡμένου σέβει κάτω. Hermann renders the first words: '*hasting* at no one's bidding,' *nullius sub imperio properans*. So Mr Paley: 'Himself *urged to action* (θοάζων) by no authority.' But the scholiast is right, I· believe, in rendering θοάζων by καθήμενος. Only ὑπ' ἀρχᾶς οὔτινος θοάζων does not mean 'sitting *under* no other's rule,' but 'sitting *by* no other's mandate.' (I should prefer ὕπαρχος.) For the Aeschylean image of Zeus *throned* on high, cp. Aesch. *Agam.* 182 δαιμόνων δέ που χάρις | βιαίως σέλμα σεμνὸν ἡμένων.

3.　Ancient tradition recognised θοάζειν as = θάσσειν nere. Plut. *Mor.* 22 E says, τῷ **θοάζειν** ἢ τὸ κινεῖσθαι σημαίνουσιν, ὡς Εὐριπίδης ... ἢ τὸ καθέζεσθαι καὶ θαάσσειν, ὡς Σοφοκλῆς,—quoting this passage. So the *Etym. Magn.* 460. 10 διὰ τί προσθακεῖτε τάσδε τὰς ἕδρας; τί προσχρῄζετε ταύταις ταῖς ἕδραις; If ἢ had stood before τί, the last clause would have seemed to glance at the other explanation. So the Schol. θοάζετε, κατὰ διάλυσιν ἀντὶ τοῦ θάσσετε· but adds, ἢ θοῶς προσκάθησθε.

4. Buttmann would connect θοάζω *to sit* with θε, the stem of τίθημι. θοάζω cannot be obtained *directly* from θε. It is possible, however, that a noun-stem, from which θοάζω *to sit* came, may itself have been derived from a secondary form of θε. It might be said that θαα-, θοω-, suggest a θεϝ or θαϝ or θυ akin to θε: cp. φαν (πιφαύσκω) with φα, στυ (στῦλος) with στα.

5. To sum up :—Emped., Aesch. and Soph. seem to have used θοάζειν as = θάσσειν. We can only say that (i) the sound and form of θοάζω may have suggested an affinity with θαάσσω, θόωκος: (ii) as a purely poetical word, θοάζω belonged to that region of language in which the earlier Attic poets—bold manipulators of old material—used a certain license of experiment, not checked by scientific etymology, and so liable to be occasionally misled by false or accidental analogies.

NOTE III.

Verses 44, 45.

ὡς τοῖσιν ἐμπείροισι καὶ τὰς ξυμφορὰς
ζώσας ὁρῶ μάλιστα τῶν βουλευμάτων.

It is not without careful consideration that I have given the view of this passage which appears in my text. A different interpretation has the support of scholars whose opinions justly carry the greatest weight, first among whom must be named my honoured friend, the Regius Professor of Greek in the University of Cambridge. If any such question could be decided by the authority of a master's instinct, it would be so for me by the judgment of Dr Kennedy; and as in this case I am unable to concur with it, I can only state my reasons, in the assurance of a candid and friendly hearing. In his brilliant edition of this play Professor Kennedy renders the passage thus (p. 58):—

'ὡς *since* τοῖσιν ἐμπείροισιν *to men of experience* ὁρῶ *I see that* (not only counselling but) καὶ *also* τὰς ξυμφορὰς τῶν βουλευμάτων *comparisons of their counsels* μάλιστα ζώσας *are in most lively use.*' In a note on τὰς ξυμφορὰς τῶν πραγμάτων (Thuc. 1. 140 § 3) Shilleto wrote thus :—

'Interpreting here (see § 1) "events, issues, results," I disagree with such rendering of Soph. *Oed. T.* 44 ὡς τοῖσιν ἐμπείροισι καὶ τὰς ξυμφορὰς | ζώσας ὁρῶ μάλιστα τῶν βουλευμάτων. I have long thought that 'comparisons of counsels' was there meant and have compared Æschyl. *Pers.* 528 quoted above on 128, 9. (I am rejoiced to find that Prof. Kennedy and I have independently arrived at the same conclusion. See *Journal of Philology*, Vol. I. p. 311, 312.) καὶ seems thus to have more significance. Men of experience may receive suggestions from not only gods but from other men (εἴτ' ἀπ' ἀνδρὸς οἶσθά που). Collations also of counsels are most effective. It is not improbable that Sophocles had in view the adage σύν τε δύ' ἐρχομένω καί τε πρὸ ὃ τοῦ ἐνόησεν Hom. *Il.* 10. 224.'

It will be seen that Mr Shilleto agreed with Professor Kennedy in taking ξυμφοράς as = 'comparisons,' but differed from him (1) in taking ζώσας—as I do—to mean '*effective*,' not 'in vogue' (an old schol. in L has ζώσας, ἀντὶ τοῦ ἐνεργεστέρας): (2) in taking the καὶ ('also') to imply 'independently of hints from the *gods*,' and not 'in addition to' *offering* counsels.'

The explanation of ξυμφοράς as 'comparisons' seems to have been first proposed by John Young, Professor of Greek in the University of Glasgow from 1774 to 1821; but it occurred to Mr Shilleto and Dr Kennedy independently both of him and of each other. Mr Verrall, the editor of the *Medea*, has added his sanction to this rendering of ξυμφοράς.

In Aesch. *Pers.* 528 we have ξυμφέρειν βουλεύματα, 'to compare counsels.' Hence it is inferred that 'a comparison of counsels' could be expressed by ξυμφορὰ βουλευμάτων. On the other side I would submit two considerations.

1. συμφορά is a word of very frequent occurrence, and yet in the extant literature of the classical age it is never found except in one of two senses,—(i) an event, issue: (ii) a calamity. That is, usage had restricted this very common noun to senses parallel with the intransitive συμφέρειν as meaning 'to happen' (Thuc. 6. 20 ξυνενέγκοι μὲν ταῦτα ὡς βουλόμεθα, ita *eveniant*). The limit imposed by usage can be illustrated from Lucian. His *Lexiphanes* is a burlesque of euphüism. There (§ 6) we have the phrase τὸ μὲν δὴ δεῖπνον ἦν ἀπὸ συμφορῶν, 'the repast was furnished from contributions.' The point is that the learned speaker has employed συμφορά in a sense which derivation warranted, but which sounded strangely, as parallel with the *transitive* συμφέρειν, 'to bring together': the ordinary phrase would have been ἀπὸ συμβολῶν.

2. Next, we will suppose that Sophocles intended to hazard an exceptional use of the noun, relying on the context to show that ξυμφοράς meant 'comparisons.' Convenience prescribes the general rule that, when a strange use of a word or phrase is risked in reliance on an explanatory context, this context should not follow at an interval, but

should either precede or closely accompany the word or phrase which would otherwise be obscure. A rough illustration—the first that occurs to me—from our own language will serve to show what I mean. 'Many of the visitors were afterwards present at a collation, and did ample justice to the difference of hands in the MSS.' If we heard that read aloud, we should be apt to suppose—down to the word 'to'—that 'collation' meant luncheon; and a certain degree of discomfort would attend the mental process of apprehending that it meant a comparison of documents. This inconvenience would not arise if the mention of the MSS. preceded, or closely accompanied, the word 'collation.' Such an argument applies *a fortiori* to συμφορά, since the literary sense of the word 'collation' is at least thoroughly recognised, while συμφορά nowhere else occurs in the sense of 'comparison.' Consider now the two verses,

ὡς τοῖσιν ἐμπείροισι καὶ τὰς ξυμφορὰς
ζώσας ὁρῶ μάλιστα τῶν βουλευμάτων.

When the first verse was spoken, would any hearer in the theatre doubt that ξυμφορὰς meant 'issues,' or divine that it was going to bear the unexampled sense of 'comparisons'? And the indispensable clue, τῶν βουλευμάτων, is postponed to the end of the next line. In the circumstances, it is hard to imagine any good writer arranging his words thus; it is, to me, altogether inconceivable that a skilled writer for the stage should so arrange them. If Sophocles had intended to suggest ξυμφέρειν βουλεύματα, he would at least have given ξυμφορὰς βουλευμάτων.

It is justly maintained that the interpretation which we are discussing (1) explains the καί, (2) is logical. Certainly: but, as I have endeavoured to show in the commentary, my version also satisfies these two conditions. And while, on the other view, the sense is logical, I must confess that to me it does not seem appropriate. The general spirit and tone of the speech appear adverse to it. The Priest of Zeus salutes Oedipus, not, indeed, as a god, but as unique and supreme among mortals. Can we imagine him giving his peerless sovereign so strong a hint to consult other men? Oedipus *himself* afterwards mentions casually that the suggestion to send for Teiresias had come from Creon (279), but that is a very different thing.

For ζώσας, Mr Verrall has proposed to read σώσας, from σάω to sift, —a verb found only in Her. 1. 200 σῶσι διὰ σινδόνος, 'they strain through linen.' He renders: 'Since I see that among the experienced comparison (or conference) of counsels does in a manner (μάλιστα) sift them.' As μάλιστα could mean 'most' or 'best,' it was unnecessary to invest it with a sense of which there is (I think) no example: yet even those who are unable to entertain this conjecture must appreciate its striking ingenuity. Commenting on it in a valuable paper read before the Cambridge Philological Society (*University Reporter*, March 14, 1883), Professor Kennedy observes that Greek literature presents no example of a metaphor from 'straining' (ἠθέω, διηθέω), or from 'sifting' (κοσκινίζω, διαττάω, more rarely σάω, σακεύω, σήθω), while in Latin the nearest approach is the use of *cernere*, of which *cribrare*, 'to sift,' is a derivative.

Mr Fennell, the editor of Pindar, has tentatively suggested another version which I may mention before closing this note. 'For I see that, in the case of men who have been tried in action, their practical experiences (τὰς ξυμφοράς) are *also* (*i.e.* in relation to the *future* too) more effectual than any counsels' (offered by men without such experience). Now (*a*) while agreeing with the version of ζώσας, I feel that its figurative sense is here rendered extremely bold by the separation of τὰς ξυμφοράς from τῶν βουλευμάτων, since, in my version, it is τῶν βουλευμάτων which determines the relation in which ζώσας means 'effective'; (*b*) I should also venture to question whether μάλιστα τῶν βουλευμάτων could stand for μᾶλλον ἢ τὰ βουλεύματα in a case where συμφοραί, as 'the lessons of life,' are *contrasted* with βουλεύματα as *merely theoretic* counsels.

NOTE IV.

Verses 198 f.

τελεῖν γάρ, εἴ τι νὺξ ἀφῇ,
τοῦτ' ἐπ' ἦμαρ ἔρχεται.

Before adopting τελεῖν, I had weighed the various interpretations of τέλει, and had for some time been disposed to acquiesce in Elmsley's as the least strained. He renders '*omnino*,' '*absolute*,' comparing Eur. *Bacch.* 859 ff. γνώσεται δὲ τὸν Διὸς | Διόνυσον ὃς πέφυκεν ἐν τέλει θεὸς | δεινότατος, ἀνθρώποισι δ' ἠπιώτατος. On Elmsley's view, ἐν τέλει there means *omnino*, 'in fulness'; and here the sense would be 'in fulness— if night spare aught—day attacks this': *i.e.* so as to make the tale of havoc full. Yet I think with Professor Tyrrell that in *Bacch.* 860 ἐν τέλει could not bear the sense which Elmsley gave to it. I should prefer there to render it, as Mr Sandys did, 'in the end'—*i.e.*, when his wrath has been aroused. I now believe, however, that Munro's brilliant emendation in that place is right,—ὃς πέφυκεν ἐν ἀτελεῖ θεὸς | δεινότατος: 'who is a god most terrible towards the uninitiated' (*Journ. Philol.* Vol. XI. p. 280). If, then, τέλει is to mean 'in fulness' here, it must dispense with even such support as might have been derived from the passage in the *Bacchae*. And, at the best, the sense obtained by such a version is hardly satisfactory. Still less would it be so, were τέλει joined with ἀφῇ, as = 'spare anything at all': εἴ τι τέλει ἀφῇ could not possibly mean εἰ ὁτιοῦν ἀφῇ. Nor could τέλει go with ἀφῇ as = 'remit anything *in regard to completeness*': nor again, as Hermann proposed, 'remit anything *to the completion*'—*i.e.*, fail to complete.

Others have rendered—'if night *at its close* spare anything.' The objections to this are,—(i) the weakness of the sense: (ii) the *simple* dative in this meaning: for 'at the end' is ἐπὶ τῷ τέλει (Plat. *Polit.* 268 D), or πρὸς τέλει (*Legg.* 768 C). The scholiast who explains τέλει as ἐπὶ τῷ ἑαυτῆς τέλει begs the question by his addition of ἐπὶ τῷ. Of proposed emendations, the obvious τελεῖν—which Hermann merely suggested, himself preferring the bolder cure mentioned below—is at once the simplest and the best. Dindorf spoils it (in my judgment) by taking it with ἀφῇ instead of ἐπέρχεται:—'Fortasse igitur scribendum, τελεῖν γὰρ εἰ (vel ᾖ) τι νὺξ ἀφῇ, *i.e. nox si* (vel *ubi*) *quid malorum perficiendum reliquerit, id dies aggreditur et perficit.*'

Among other conjectures are: (1) Kayser, τελεῖ γάρ· εἴ τι κ.τ.λ. 'for Ares will finish his work.' (2) Hermann, μέλλει γάρ· εἴ τι νὺξ δ᾽ ἀφῇ κ.τ.λ.: 'Cunctatur enim (sc. Mars): si quid nox autem dimiserit, id invadit dies': μέλλει, 'delays,' meaning, I suppose, 'tarries too long among us.' (3) Arndt would change τέλει into ἀεί, and in the 5th ed. of Schneidewin (revised by Nauck) this is approved, τέλει being pronounced 'clearly wrong.'

NOTE V.

Verses 219—221.

ἀγὼ ξένος μὲν τοῦ λόγου τοῦδ᾽ ἐξερῶ,
ξένος δὲ τοῦ πραχθέντος· οὐ γὰρ ἂν μακρὰν
ἴχνευον αὐτός, μὴ οὐκ ἔχων τι σύμβολον.

Professor Kennedy understands οὐ γάρ κ.τ.λ. as referring to a suppressed clause. 'On my having been a foreigner at the time of the deed, I lay no stress; for had I been no foreigner, but one of the citizens, I myself, whatever my native shrewdness, as in guessing the riddle of the Sphinx, should not have traced the matter far, seeing that I had not (μὴ οὐκ ἔχων) any token (*i.e.* any clue to guide me).'

The difficulties which I feel in regard to the above interpretation are these. (*a*) I do not see how the hearer could be expected to supply mentally such a suppressed clause as 'That, however, matters not; for even if I had been a citizen'... (*b*) The σύμβολον lacking to Oed. is some way of obtaining such a clue. We should not expect him, then, to say that, even if he had been a citizen of Thebes at the time, he could not have made much progress in the investigation, because he would have had no clue.

According to Professor Campbell, the suppressed clause is εἰ ἴχνευον, and the sense is: 'I have remained a stranger to the matter, for, if I *had* undertaken an inquiry, I could not have followed it far, since I had no clue to guide me.' 'He offers this excuse for having hitherto neglected what he now feels to be an imperative duty.' But Sophocles assumes that Oed. has just heard, *for the first time*, of the mysterious murder (105—129). On hearing of it, Oed. straightway asked why the Thebans themselves had not at the time made a search (128). Here, then, we cannot understand him to speak as if he had all along shared the knowledge of the Thebans, or as if he were apologising for having neglected to act upon it sooner.

Mr Blaydes understands: 'For (were it otherwise, had I not been thus ignorant), I should not have had to investigate it (αὐτό, the foul deed) far, without finding (quin haberem) some clue.' To this the objections are that (1) μὴ οὐκ ἔχων = 'unless I had,' and could not mean 'without finding': (2) the remark would be suitable only if Oed. had already for some time been engaged in a fruitless search, whereas he is only about to commence it.

Schneidewin formerly conjectured ἦ [for οὐ] γὰρ ἂν μακρὰν | ἴχνευον αὐτός, οὐκ [for μὴ οὐκ] ἔχων τι σύμβολον: 'for [if I had *not* appealed to you], I should have searched long indeed by myself, seeing that I have no clue.' In the 5th ed., revised by Nauck, οὐ is wisely replaced instead of ἦ (though οὐκ for μὴ οὐκ is kept), and the sense is given substantially as I give it.

Much of the difficulty which this passage has caused seems attributable (1) to a prevalent impression that οὐ γάρ...ἄν in such a sentence always means, 'for *else*,' etc.: (2) to want of clearness regarding μὴ οὐ.

Now, as to (1), it depends on the context in each case whether οὐ γὰρ ἄν means, 'for *else*,' etc. When it has that force, it has it because there is a *suppressed protasis*. Such is the case in v. 82 ἀλλ' εἰκάσαι μὲν ἡδύς· οὐ γὰρ ἄν...εἷρπε: *i.e.* εἰ μὴ ἡδὺς ἦν. Such is also the case in 318 διώλεσ'· οὐ γὰρ ἂν δεῦρ' ἱκόμην: *i.e.* εἰ μὴ διώλεσα. But when the protasis is *not* suppressed, then, of course, there is no such ellipse as our word 'else' implies. Thus Xen. *Anab.* 7. 7. 11 καὶ νῦν ἄπειμι· οὐδὲ γὰρ ἂν Μήδοκός με ὁ βασιλεὺς ἐπαινοίη, εἰ ἐξελαύνοιμι τοὺς εὐεργέτας: 'and now I will go away; for Medocus the king would not commend me, *if I should drive out our benefactors.*' Had the protasis εἰ ἐξελαύνοιμι τοὺς εὐεργ. been suppressed, then οὐδὲ γὰρ ἄν...ἐπαινοίη must have been rendered, 'for *else* he would not commend me': but, since it is given, we do not need 'else.' So Dem. *De Cor.* § 228 ὡμολόγηκε νῦν γ' ἡμᾶς ὑπάρχειν ἐγνωσμένους ἐμὲ μὲν λέγειν ὑπὲρ τῆς πατρίδος, αὐτὸν δ' ὑπὲρ Φιλίππου. οὐ γὰρ ἂν μεταπείθειν ὑμᾶς ἐζήτει, μὴ τοιαύτης οὔσης τῆς ὑπαρχούσης ὑπολήψεως περὶ ἑκατέρου: 'he has admitted that, as matters stand, we start from the conviction that I speak in our country's cause, and he in Philip's; *for* he would not have been seeking to bring you over to his view, *were not such the existing impression with regard to each.*' Here, μὴ τοιαύτης οὔσης represents the protasis, εἰ μὴ τοιαύτη ἦν, exactly as here in *O. T.* 221 μὴ οὐκ ἔχων represents the protasis εἰ μὴ εἶχον: and we do not insert 'else' after 'for.'

(2) As regards μὴ οὐ with the participle, the general principle may, I think, be stated thus. Every sense possible for (*e.g.*) μὴ ποιῶν is possible for μὴ οὐ ποιῶν when the principal verb of the sentence is negative. Take the sentence ῥᾴδιον ἡμῖν ζῆν μὴ πονοῦσι. The participial clause here could represent, according to the sense intended, any one of four things, viz. (1) εἰ μὴ πονοῦμεν, 'if,—as is the fact,—we are not labouring': (2) ἐὰν μὴ πονῶμεν, 'whenever we do not labour,' *or*, 'if we shall not labour': (3) εἰ μὴ πονοῖμεν, 'if we should not labour': (4) εἰ μὴ ἐπονοῦμεν, 'if we had not (then) been labouring, (as in fact we then were,)' *or*, 'if we were not (now) labouring, (as in fact we now are.)' So in the negative sentence, οὐ ῥᾴδιον ἡμῖν ζῆν μὴ οὐ πονοῦσι, the participial clause can equally represent any one of the same four things.

But from the very fact that μὴ οὐ can stand only in a *negative* sentence it follows that a participial clause with μὴ οὐ will, in practice, most often express an *exception* to a negative statement. This must not, however, make us forget that μὴ οὐ with the participle is still equivalent to the protasis of a conditional sentence. Thus :—

Her. 6. 9 πυθόμενοι τὸ πλῆθος τῶν Ἰάδων νεῶν καταρρωδήσαν μὴ οὐ δυνατοὶ γένωνται ὑπερβαλέσθαι, καὶ οὕτω οὔτε τὴν Μίλητον οἷοί τε ἔωσι ἐξελεῖν μὴ οὐκ ἐόντες ναυκράτορες κ.τ.λ.: where μὴ οὐκ ἐόντες = εἰ μὴ εἰσι, (or ἢν μὴ ἔωσι,) the negative condition. Her. 6. 106 εἰνάτῃ δὲ οὐκ ἐξελεύσεσθαι ἔφασαν μὴ οὐ πλήρεος ἐόντος τοῦ κύκλου, *i.e.* εἰ μὴ πλήρης ἐστὶν ὁ κύκλος, 'if (as is the case) the moon is not full' (they are speaking on the εἰνάτῃ itself). Plat. *Lysis* 212 D οὐκ ἄρα ἐστὶ φίλον τῷ φιλοῦντι μὴ οὐκ ἀντιφιλοῦν, *i.e.* ἐὰν μὴ ἀντιφιλῇ, unless it love in return. Soph. *O. C.* 359 ἥκεις γὰρ οὐ κενή γε, τοῦτ' ἐγὼ σαφῶς | ἔξοιδα, μὴ οὐχὶ δεῖμ' ἐμοὶ φέρουσά τι: 'thou hast not come empty-handed, *without* bringing,' etc.: where the participial clause, epexegetic of κενή, implies εἰ μὴ ἔφερες, (οὐκ ἂν ἧκες,)—'hadst thou not been bringing (as thou *art* bringing), thou wouldst not have come.'

In all the above passages, it is the present participle which stands after μὴ οὐ, as it is also in *O. T.* 13, 221. Now compare (1) Dem. *De Coron.* § 34 μὴ κατηγορήσαντος Αἰσχίνου (= εἰ μὴ κατηγόρησεν Αἰσχίνης) μηδὲν ἔξω τῆς γραφῆς οὐδ' ἂν ἐγὼ λόγον οὐδένα ἐποιούμην ἕτερον. (2) *De Falsa Legat.* § 123 οὐ γὰρ ἐνῆν μὴ παρακρουσθέντων ὑμῶν (= εἰ μὴ παρεκρούσθητε ὑμεῖς) μεῖναι Φιλίππῳ. Here, though the sentences are negative, we have μή, not μὴ οὐ, with the *aorist* partic., representing the protasis. In (1) the *order* of clauses affects the question, but not in (2). Owing to the comparative rarity of μὴ οὐ with the participle, generalisation appears unsafe; but it looks as if prevalent usage had accustomed the Greek ear to μὴ οὐ with partic. chiefly in sentences where the protasis so represented would have been formed with (1) imperf. indic., or (2) pres. subjunct., or (3) pres. optat. In conditional sentences with the *aor.* indicative, even where the negative form admitted μὴ οὐ, there may have been a preference for μή. The instances cited seem at least to warrant the supposition that, in such a sentence as οὐκ ἂν ἀπέθανεν εἰ μὴ ἔπεσε, Demosthenes would have chosen μή (rather than μὴ οὐ) πεσών as the participial substitute for the protasis.

NOTE VI.

Verses 227 f.

κεἰ μὲν φοβεῖται, τοὐπίκλημ' ὑπεξελὼν
αὐτὸς καθ' αὑτοῦ.

With this, the common reading, it is necessary to suppose some ellipse. I believe ὑπεξελὼν and αὐτός to be indefensible. If they were to be retained, I should then, as the least of evils, translate thus:—
'And if he is afraid,—when (by speaking) he will have removed the danger of the charge from his own path,—[*let him not fear*].' Such an

ellipse—though, to my mind, almost impossibly harsh—would at least be mitigated by the following πείσεται γὰρ ἄλλο μὲν | ἀστεργὲς οὐδέν, which we might regard as an irregular substitute for an apodosis in the sense of μὴ φοβείσθω, γάρ being virtually equivalent to 'I tell him.'

Among the interpretations of the received text which have been proposed, the following claim notice.

1. Professor Kennedy renders (the italics are his): 'and if he fears, and hides away the charge | against himself, *let him speak out*.' Here ὑπεξελὼν = 'having suppressed,' and μὴ σιωπάτω is mentally supplied from v. 231 (three verses further on).

2. Professor Campbell gives the preference to the following version (while noticing two others):—' And let the man himself, if he be touched with fear, inform against himself, by taking the guilt away with him': *i.e.* ὑπεξελὼν = 'having withdrawn,' and 'the words καθ' αὐτοῦ are to be construed κατὰ σύνεσιν with v. 226, *sc.* ποιείτω τάδε, self-banishment being in this case equivalent to self-impeachment.' This is tantamount (if I understand rightly) to supplying σημαινέτω from σημαίνειν in 226.

3. Schneidewin: 'And if he is afraid, *because he will have revealed* (ὑπεξελὼν) a charge against himself,—*let him not fear*' (*sc.* μὴ φοβείσθω). So Linwood, only supplying σημαινέτω.

4. Elmsley: 'And if he is afraid, (still let him denounce himself, *sc.* σημαινέτω,) thus extenuating the guilt (by confession),'—*crimen confitendo diluens*. To say nothing of the sense given to ὑπεξελὼν, the *aorist* part. seems strange on this view.

5. Matthiae regards the construction as an irregular form of what might have been more simply put thus: κεἰ μὲν φοβεῖται, τὸ ἐπίκλημα αὐτὸς καθ' αὐτοῦ ὑπεξελὼν (ἀπελθέτω ἐκ τῆς γῆς)· πείσεται γὰρ οὐδὲν ἄλλο ἀστεργές: 'If he is afraid, (let him leave the country,) thus *taking away* the charge against himself.' He explains ὑπεξελὼν by '*subripiens*,' *i.e. subterfugiens, declinans*, 'evading the danger of being accused.' Neither this nor the ellipse of ἀπελθέτω seems possible. Wunder nearly agrees with Matthiae.

6. Hermann (3rd ed.) translates v. 227 'Si metuit, subterfugiens accusationem sui ipsius,' and supposes the apodosis to be γῆς ἄπεισιν ἀβλαβής,—μὲν and δὲ having been added because the clause πείσεται γὰρ has been put first. Thus he agrees with Matthiae as to ὑπεξελὼν, but takes it with φοβεῖται, not with a supposed ἀπελθέτω.

7. Dindorf also takes Matthiae's view of ὑπεξελὼν, but wishes (ed. 1860) for ὑπεξέλοι in an imperative sense: 'crimen subterfugiat': 'let him evade the charge against himself' (by going into exile).

Under one or another of the above interpretations those given by most other commentators may be ranged.

Among emendations, the palm for ingenuity seems due to Hartung's κεἰ μὲν φοβεῖται, τοὐπίκλημ' ἐπεξίτω | αὐτὸς καθ' αὑτοῦ: 'and if he is afraid, still let him *prosecute* the charge against himself.' This is, however, more brilliant than probable.

Mr Blaydes in his note proposes to read κεἰ μὲν φοβεῖται τοὐπίκλημ' ὑπεξελεῖν (*to draw forth* from the recesses of his own mind), and supplies, 'let him feel assured.' For this view of ὑπεξελεῖν, cp. above, no. 3. In his text, however, he gives (on his own conjecture) καὶ μὴ φοβείσθω τοὐπίκλημ' ὑπεξελεῖν | αὐτὸς καθ' αὑτοῦ.

NOTE VII.

The proposed transposition of verses 246—251, κατεύχομαι...ἠρασάμην.

Otto Ribbeck suggested that these six verses should stand immediately after 272 (ἐχθίονι). He thought that their displacement in the MSS. arose from a confusion between ὑμῖν δὲ in 252 and the same words in 273. He argued that 251, παθεῖν ἅπερ τοῖσδ' ἀρτίως ἠρασάμην, has no meaning unless it follows 269—274, καὶ ταῦτα τοῖς μὴ δρῶσι κ.τ.λ. Dindorf and Nauck adopt the transposition. Against it, and in favour of the MSS., I would submit these considerations. (1) The transposition destroys the natural order of topics. The denunciation of a curse on the *murderer* must stand in the fore-front of the speech, whereas the transposition subjoins it, as a kind of after-thought, to the curse on those who disobey the edict. It thus loses its proper emphasis. (2) The transposition enforces an awkward separation between ταῦτα τοῖς μὴ δρῶσιν (269) and τοῖς ἄλλοισι (273). The latter depends for its clearness on juxtaposition with the former: but six verses are now inserted between them. (3) In 251 Ribbeck's objection would fail if we had τῷδ' instead of τοῖσδ': but τοῖσδ' is used to include the hypothesis of *several* murderers (247, cp. 122).

NOTE VIII.

Verse 305.

εἰ καί *and* καὶ εἰ.

(1) εἰ καί, in its normal usage, = '*granting that*...,' where the speaker admits that a condition *exists*, but denies that it is an obstacle: above, 302 : 408, εἰ καὶ τυραννεῖς : *El.* 547, εἰ καὶ σῆς δίχα γνώμης λέγω.

(2) In our passage (as in *Ai.* 1127, *Trach.* 71), the καί has a slightly stronger sense, — 'if *indeed*—though I should be surprised to hear it.'

(3) Both these uses differ from that in which εἰ καί has the sense which properly belongs to καὶ εἰ, '*even supposing that...*,' where the speaker refrains from granting the existence of the alleged condition: *Tr.* 1218 εἰ καὶ μακρὰ κάρτ᾽ ἐστίν, ἐργασθήσεται, 'even if the favour is a very large one, it shall be granted.'

For the regular distinction between εἰ καί and καὶ εἰ, see *Il.* 4. 347 καὶ εἰ δέκα πύργοι Ἀχαιῶν | ὑμείων προπάροιθε μαχοίατο, compared with *Il.* 5. 410 Τυδείδης, εἰ καὶ μάλα καρτερός ἐστιν.

The normal use of καὶ εἰ occurs below, 669, 1077: *O. C.* 306 κεἰ βραδύς | εὕδει: *Ant.* 234 κεἰ τὸ μηδὲν ἐξερῶ: 461 κεἰ μὴ σὺ προὐκήρυξας: *El.* 617 κεἰ μὴ δοκῶ σοι.

Conversely, we have καὶ εἰ for εἰ καί in *Ai.* 692, 962 : *O. C.* 661 : below, 986, 1516.

(4) All the foregoing uses, in which εἰ καί forms a single expression, must be distinguished from those cases in which καί belongs closely to the *following* word, as 283 εἰ καὶ τρίτ᾽ ἐστί: *Ant.* 90 εἰ καὶ δυνήσει γ᾽.

Similarly, for καὶ εἰ, distinguish those cases in which καί = 'and': *O.C.* 1323 ἐγὼ δὲ σός, κεἰ μὴ σός, ἀλλὰ τοῦ κακοῦ | πότμου φυτευθείς.

NOTE IX.

Verses 328 f.

οὐ μήποτε
τἄμ᾽ ὡς ἂν εἴπω μὴ τὰ σ᾽ ἐκφήνω κακά.

Prof. Kennedy takes the passage thus :—ἐγὼ δ᾽ οὐ μήποτε εἴπω τἀμά, *I will never speak my things*, ὡς ἂν (εἴπω), *however I may call them* (whatever they may deserve to be called), μὴ τὰ σ᾽ ἐκφήνω κακά, *lest I disclose your things as evil.* Or, as he renders it in verse, 'but mine I ne'er will speak, | however named, lest I display thine — evil.' For ὡς ἄν as = 'in whatever way,' he compares *Il.* 2. 139 ὡς ἂν ἐγὼν εἴπω, πειθώμεθα πάντες: Soph. *Ai.* 1369 ὡς ἂν ποιήσῃς, πανταχοῦ χρηστός γ᾽ ἔσει: Dem. *De Cor.* 292 [§ 192] τὸ...πέρας, ὡς ἂν ὁ δαίμων βουληθῇ, πάντων γίγνεται: and adds : 'We might place commas before and after ὡς ἄν, to indicate the quasi-adverbial character which it acquires by the ellipse [of εἴπω], in reality not more abnormal than that of ἥδοιο in 900 [937], ἥδοιο μέν, πῶς δ᾽ οὐκ ἄν ;' (*Oed. Tyr.*, pp. 76 f.).

As Prof. Kennedy has well said elsewhere (*Stud. Soph.* p. 62), if any emendation were to be admitted, the simplest would be εἰπὼν for εἴπω (a change which Hermann also once suggested), with a comma after τἄμ' : ἐγὼ δ' οὐ μήποτε (εἴπω) τἀμά, ὡς ἂν εἰπὼν (*by* telling them) μὴ...ἐκφήνω. But with him (though our interpretations differ) I believe that the words are sound as they stand.

Hardly any passage, however, in Sophocles has given rise to so large a number of conjectures. Most of these have been directed to the same general object—some such alteration of the words τἄμ' ὡς ἂν εἴπω as shall make it easier to take the *second* μὴ with ἐκφήνω. The following may be mentioned : (1) Wolff, τἄμ' ὄψαν' εἴπω, 'my visions,'—ὄψανον having that sense in Aesch. *Cho.* 534. (2) Hartung, τὰ θέσφατ' εἴπω. (3) C. F. Hermann, τὰ μάσσον' εἴπω. (4) Campbell, εἴπω τάδ', ὡς ἂν μὴ τά σ' ἐκφήνω κακά. (5) Nauck, approved by Bonitz, ἄνωγας εἴπω. (6) Campe, *Quaest. Soph.* I. 18, ἄγνων ἀνείπω. (7) Arndt, τἄλλων ἀνείπω. (8) Seyffert, Weismann, Ritter, τἄμ' ὡς ἀνείπω. (9) Wecklein, τἄμ' ὧδ' ἀνείπω. (10) Papageorgius, τἄμ ἐς σ' ἀνείπω. See his *Beiträge zur Erklärung und Kritik des Sophokles*, p. 22, Iena, 1883.

NOTE X.

Verse 361.

The forms γνωτός *and* γνωστός.

γνωτός is regularly formed from the verbal stem γνω with the suffix το : cp. Skt. *ǵnâ-t-as*, Lat. *notus*. In the form γνωστός, the origin of the σ is obscure : Curtius remarks that we might suppose a stem γνωσ expanded from γνω, but also a present *γνωϳω, which might be compared with O. H. G. *knâu*. In the case of καυστός (Eur.), κλαυστός (Soph.), the σ is explained by καϝϳω (καίω), κλαϝϳω (κλαίω). The existing data do not warrant us in assigning the forms with or without σ to certain periods with such rigour as Elmsley's, for example, when he regarded εὔγνωτος as the only correct Attic form. ἄγνωστος occurs in *Odyssey*, Thucydides, Plato (who has also γνωστός); in Pindar *Isthm.* 3. 48 ἄγνωστοι is doubtful; Mommsen gives ἄγνωτοι, and so Fennell, who remarks *ad loc.* that in *Ol.* 6. 67 for ἄγνωτον (as against ἄγνωστον) Mommsen has the support of two good MSS. We have ἄγνωτος in Sophocles and Aristophanes ; εὔγνωστος in Sophocles, Euripides, Lysias, etc.

With regard to the meaning of these verbals, it has been held that, where such forms as γνωτός and γνωστός existed side by side, Attic writers appropriated the *potential* sense to the *sigmatic* form, distinguishing γνωστός, as 'what *can* be known,' from γνωτός, 'what *is* known.' Nothing in the sigmatic form itself could warrant such a distinction. However the σ be explained, γνωστός, no less than γνωτός, must have primarily meant simply 'known,' as καυστός 'burnt' and κλαυστός 'wept.' And we find ἄκλαυστος as = 'unwept' (not, 'what cannot be wept for'), πολύκλαυστος as = 'much-wept' (not, 'worthy of many tears'). When the modal idea of 'may' or 'can' attached itself to these verbals, it was merely by the same process as that which in Latin brought *invictus*, 'unconquered,' to the sense of 'unconquerable.' Yet I would suggest, on the other hand, that the special attribution of a potential sense to the sigmatic forms may have thus much ground. When two forms, such as γνωτός and γνωστός, were both current, regular analogies would quicken the sense that γνωτός had a participial nature, while γνωστός, in which the σ obscured the analogy, would be felt more as an ordinary adjective, and would therefore be used with less strict regard to the primary participial force. Thus it might be ordinarily *preferred* to γνωτός, when 'knowable' was to be expressed. At the same time, it would always remain an available synonym for γνωτός as = 'known.' And we have seen in the commentary that Sophocles is said to have used γνωστός, as well as γνωτός, in the sense of 'well-known.'

NOTE XI.

Verse 478.

The reading of the first hand in the Laurentian MS., πετραῖος ὁ ταῦρος.

This reading raises one of those points which cannot be lightly or summarily decided by any one who knows the rapid transitions and the daring expressions which were possible for the lyrics of Greek Tragedy. Hermann—who was somewhat more in sympathy with the manner of Aeschylus than with that of Sophocles—characteristically adopted the reading,—which he pronounces 'multo vulgata fortiorem.' The mere substitution of metaphor for simile is not, indeed, the difficulty. Euripides, for instance, has (*Med.* 184) ἀτὰρ φόβος εἰ πείσω | δέσποιναν ἐμήν'... καίτοι τοκάδος δέργμα λεαίνης | ἀποταυροῦται δμωσίν. But the boldness of λεαίνης so closely followed by δμωσίν is not comparable to that which we must assume here, if τὸν ἄδηλον ἄνδρα were so immediately followed by πετραῖος ὁ ταῦρος : nor can I persuade myself that Sophocles would have so written.

The further verbal question, whether φοιτᾷ πετραῖος could be said in the sense, '*wanders among rocks*,' is one which must be considered in the light of Sophoclean usage. We have below 1340 ἀπάγετ᾽ ἐκτόπιον: 1411 θαλάσσιον | ἐκρίψατ᾽: *Antig.* 785 φοιτᾷς δ᾽ ὑπερπόντιος ἔν τ᾽ ἀγρονόμοις αὐλαῖς: *El.* 419 ἐφέστιον | πῆξαι ..σκῆπτρον: *Ant.* 1301 βωμία... | λύει...βλέφαρα (she closes her eyes at the altar): and perh. fr. 35 καὶ βωμιαῖον ἐσχάρας λαβών, for Steph. Byz. 191. 8, citing it, says, τὸ τοπικὸν βώμιος καὶ κατὰ παραγωγὴν βωμαῖος. Given these examples, we could scarcely refuse to Sophocles such a phrase (for instance) as φοιτᾷ ὀρεινός. My own feeling in regard to πετραῖος is that it is decidedly bolder—not to say harsher—than any phrase of the kind which can be produced; but, on the other᾽hand, I certainly am not prepared to say that, in lyrics, Sophocles could not have used it. It is the extreme abruptness of the metaphor in this context, rather than the singularity of the phrase, that has decided me against reading πετραῖος ὁ ταῦρος.

NOTE XII.

Verse 508.

πτερόεσσα κόρα. *The Sphinx.*

The Sphinx, with lion's body and human head, has a unique place among the most ancient symbols of an irresistible daemonic might, at once physical and mental. The Egyptian type was *wingless*, and of male sex. The Sphinx of Ghizeh—oldest and largest of extant examples—dates from the age of the Fourth Dynasty (perhaps from *circ.* 2400 B.C.), as Mariette's latest results have established (*Revue archéol.*, new series 26, 1873, pp. 237 ff.), and was the object of a cultus, which does not appear to have been the case with any other Egyptian Sphinx.

The *winged* type occurs first in the lands of the Euphrates. The earliest example which can be approximately dated is afforded by the palace of Esharaddon, which belongs to the seventh century B.C. Here the winged and crouching Sphinx is female (Milchhoefer, *Mitth. des deutschen archaeol. Institutes in Athen*, fourth year, 1879, p. 48,—the best authority for the present state of knowledge on the subject). Phoenicia was in this case, as in so many others, the point at which Egyptian and Asiatic influences converged. A stele from Aradus (*Musée Napoléon* III. xviii. 4) shows a Sphinx with Egyptian head-gear and on a pedestal of Egyptian character, but with the Assyrian wings.

The wingless Sphinx was not unknown to the earlier art of Hellenic countries. Such a Sphinx (female, however, and in this respect not Egyptian) occurred on the Sacred Way at Miletus (Newton, *Travels* Vol. II. p. 155). At Thebes, singularly enough, was found a terracotta figure, about 4 inches long, of a wingless crouching Sphinx (Milchhoefer, *l. c.*, p. 54). As is well known, it was maintained by Voss in his *Mythologische Briefe* that the Greek Sphinx, being borrowed from Egypt, was wingless until the influence of the Attic dramatists popularised the winged type. Aeschylus, indeed, like Hesiod, does not mention wings in his brief description of the Sphinx on the shield of Parthenopaeus (*Theb.* 541), nor in his only other notice of the monster (fr. 232): but the Sphinx of Euripides, like that of Sophocles, is winged (*Phoen.* 1022 ff.). Gerhard argued as far back as 1839 (*Abhandl. der k. Akad. der Wissensch. z. Berlin*) that the Greek winged Sphinx was probably much older than the age of the dramatists, and this fact has long been placed beyond discussion. The oldest representations of the Sphinx found on the soil of Greece Proper are presumably the relievo-figures in gold, ivory, etc., of the graves at Spata in the Mesogaia of Attic, and at Mycenae: and these have the wings. Three round figures of winged Sphinxes, in Parian marble, have also been found in Greece (two in Attica, one in Aegina): a round terracotta figure of a winged Sphinx, which possibly served as akroterion of a heröon, has been found at Olympia, and a similar figure is reported to have been found at Corinth. These Sphinxes are regarded by Milchhoefer as the oldest and most complete Greek examples of polychromy applied to round figures. The feathers of the Sphinx's wings were, in two cases at least, painted red and dark-green (or blue?), and in one instance a brownish-red colour had been given to three corkscrew ringlets which fell on the Sphinx's breast and shoulders.

It was not in connection with Thebes and Oedipus that the Sphinx was most generally familiar to Greek art. By far her most frequent appearance was on sepulchral monuments, as an emblem of the unconquerable and inscrutable power which lays man low,—as the Seiren, from another point of view, was similarly applied. But the Oedipus myth illustrates in a very striking manner the essential traits both in the Asiatic and in the Hellenic conception of the Sphinx.

(1) *The Sphinx oppresses the Thebans.* This belongs to the original essence of the Sphinx idea, as a manifestation, in mind and body, of a force with which mortals may not cope. A grave of the Egyptian Thebes shows a bearded Sphinx, with one of its feet on three men

(Lepsius, *Denkm.* v. 3. 76 c). An Attic vase shows two Sphinxes, with a prostrate man between them. A bowl found at Larnaka represents winged griffins and Sphinxes, with a man held captive (Milchhoefer *l. c.* 57, 51). The pitiless female Sphinx of Greek mythology belongs to the same order of winged pursuers as the Harpies and the Gorgons.

(2) *The Sphinx asks a riddle.* Here we seem to have a purely Hellenic graft on the Egyptian and Asiatic original. To the Greek mind, the half-human, half-leonine shape was itself a riddle, and—*given the notion of oppressor*—could have suggested the story. The Centaur was not characteristically an oppressor of man; in the Chimaera, nothing was human; but in the Sphinx these conditions met, and the crouching posture suggested grim expectancy.

(3) *The Sphinx sits on the Φίκειον ὄρος near Thebes.* In the Hesiodic *Theogony* the Sphinx is called Φίξ (Φῖκ' ὀλοήν, 326). Which was older,— the name of the hill, or Φίξ as a name for the monster? If the former, then we might well suppose that the localising of the myth had been suggested by the accident of a hill with such a name existing near a town in which Phoenician and Egyptian influences had long been present.

(4) *The Sphinx is vanquished by Oedipus.* This is hyperbole clothed in myth. 'He is so acute that he could baffle the Sphinx.' For it is a distinction of the monumental Sphinx that it never appears as tamed or vanquished. The man-headed lions and bulls of Assyria, as Layard pointed out, are symbols of hostile forces which have been subdued and converted to the service of the conqueror. It is never so with the Sphinx of Egyptian, Asiatic, or Hellenic art.

In conclusion, I may notice the most recent addition—a brilliant one—which has been made to the known examples of the Greek winged Sphinx. Under the auspices of the Archaeological Institute of America, the site of the ancient Assos, opposite Lesbos, on the south coast of the Troad, has within the last two years been thoroughly explored by a mission of American scholars and archaeologists[1]. On Oct. 4, 1881, was found the fragment of a relief with winged Sphinxes, belonging to the Doric temple of Athene, which crowned the acropolis of Assos. The date of the temple may be referred to the early years of the 5th century B.C. The Assos relief exhibits two Sphinxes crouching face to face, and must have decorated the lintel above the central inter-columniation of the temple-front—having a heraldic significance, as the

[1] In the *Fortnightly Review* (April, 1883) I gave some notes of a tour in the Troad (Sept. 1882) which included a visit to Assos.

civic emblem of Assos, like the two crows of the Thessalian Crannon, the two axes of the Carian Mylasa, the two heads of Tenedos, and the like. Mr J. T. Clarke, in his excellent Report on the investigations at Assos, of which he has been the director, (p. 111) writes:—

'Of all the sculptures of Assos discovered by the present expedition, and in the Louvre'—[those namely given to France in 1838 by Mahmoud II., of which the most striking are the bas-reliefs of Centaurs] —'the magnificent Sphinxes are by far the best preserved, they alone having been taken from a hard bed of mortar, which had long saved them from weathering. The carving of this relief is of a delicacy and vigour comparable to the best works of fully developed Greek art. Throughout the body the firm muscles and yielding cushions of flesh are indicated with an appreciation of natural forms which shows a distinct advance beyond the art of Mesopotamia, successful as were its representations of animals; while the decorative character of the composition is maintained by the admirable outline of paws, wings, and tail. The heads are of that archaic type familiar in Attic sculptures dating near the beginning of the fifth century B.C. The eye, though shown nearly in profile, is still too large,—the corners of the mouth drawn up to a meaningless smile. The Egyptian derivation of the Sphinx is more evident than is elsewhere the case upon Greek works, by the closely fitting head-dress, welted upon the forehead and falling stiffly behind the ears.'

NOTE XIII.

Verses 622—626.

KP. τί δῆτα χρῄζεις; ἢ με γῆς ἔξω βαλεῖν;
ΟΙ. ἥκιστα· θνῄσκειν οὐ φυγεῖν σε βούλομαι
    ὡς ἂν προδείξῃς οἷόν ἐστι τὸ φθονεῖν.
KP. ὡς οὐχ ὑπείξων οὐδὲ πιστεύσων λέγεις;
ΟΙ.   *   *   *   *   *   *
KP. οὐ γὰρ φρονοῦντά σ' εὖ βλέπω.   ΟΙ. τὸ γοῦν ἐμόν.

In discussing this passage, I take first the two points which seem beyond question.

1. v. 624 ὅταν...φθονεῖν, which the MSS. give to Creon, belongs to Oedipus. The words προδείξῃς οἷόν ἐστι τὸ φθονεῖν can mean nothing but '*show forth* [by a terrible example] *what manner of thing it*

is to envy,'—how dread a doom awaits him who plots to usurp a throne (cp. 382). *Ant.* 1242 δείξας ἐν ἀνθρώποισι τὴν δυσβουλίαν | ὅσῳ μέγιστον ἀνδρὶ πρόσκειται κακόν. *El.* 1382 καὶ δεῖξον ἀνθρώποισι τἀπιτίμια | τῆς δυσσεβείας οἷα δωροῦνται θεοί. Thuc. I. 76 ἄλλους γ' ἂν οὖν οἰόμεθα τὰ ἡμέτερα λαβόντας δεῖξαι μάλιστα εἴ τι μετριάζομεν. 6. 77 προθυμότερον δεῖξαι αὐτοῖς ὅτι οὐκ Ἴωνες τάδε εἰσίν. (For the *tone* of the threat, cp. also *Ant.* 308, 325, *Trach.* 1110.) Eur. *Heracl.* 864 τῇ δὲ νῦν τύχῃ | βροτοῖς ἄπασι λαμπρὰ κηρύσσει μαθεῖν, | τὸν εὐτυχεῖν δοκοῦντα μὴ ζηλοῦν (said of the captive Eurystheus). It is a mere accident that προδείκνυμι does not elsewhere occur as = to show *forth:* that sense is as natural for it as for προδηλόω, προφαίνω, προκηρύσσω, etc. I do not think that ὅταν can be defended by rendering, '*when* thou shalt *first* have shown,'—a threat of torture before death. This strains the words : and death would itself be the essence of the warning example. Read ὡς ἂν, in order that : as *Phil.* 825 ὡς ἂν εἰς ὕπνον πέσῃ.

2. v. 625, ὡς οὐχ ὑπείξων...λέγεις, which the MSS. give to Oedipus, belongs to Creon. Spoken by Oed., ὑπείξων must mean 'admit your guilt,' and πιστεύσων 'obey' me (by doing so): but the only instance of πιστεύειν in this sense is *Trach.* 1228 πείθου· τὸ γάρ τοι μεγάλα πιστεύσαντ' ἐμοὶ | σμικροῖς ἀπιστεῖν τὴν πάρος συγχεῖ χάριν : with 1251 σοί γε πιστεύσας. But there (*a*) the sense of 'obeying' verges on that of *taking one's word* as warranty for the act : and (*b*) πείθου, ἀπιστεῖν help it out. Here, Creon speaking, ὑπείξων means 'consent to give me a fair hearing,' —under the tests which Creon himself proposed (603 f.),—and πιστεύσων, 'believe' my solemn assurances.

3. Verse 624 having been given to Oedipus, and v. 625 to Creon, will the passage have been healed if vv. 625 and 624 change places? I think not. For v. 624 will then mean : '[I will yield, and believe you, *only*] when you have been made an example of envy': to which Creon will reply, 'Nay, I find you mad' (*i.e.* what you call my *envy* is but remonstrance with your *folly*). This is too disjointed. I have long thought, and still think, that a verse spoken by Oed. has dropped out after 625, as is explained in the commentary.

NOTE XIV.

Verse 762.

ἄποπτος.

I believe that ἄποπτος has two distinct uses, and that a neglect of the distinction has made some confusion. (1) As a verbal adject. of passive sense : *seen, though at a distance:* Arist. *Pol.* 2. 12 ὅπως ἄποπτος ἔσται ἡ Κορινθία ἐκ τοῦ χώματος : (2) in poetry and later prose, as an adject. meaning, '*away from* the sight of' : implying either (*a*) 'seen *only* afar,' '*dimly* seen,' as *Ai.* 15 : or (*b*) '*out* of sight of,' as here : *i.e.* not seen, or not seeing, according as the ὄψις is that of object or subject. Dionys. Hal. 2. 54 ἐν ἀπόπτῳ τίθενται τὸν χάρακα (of an ambuscade), '*in a place out of sight*' (not, 'in a place seen afar'). ἄποπτος does not occur in the *active* sense parallel with (1), as = 'seeing, though at a distance' : analogy would, however, warrant it : see on 515. Ast strangely gives 'τὸ ἄποπτον, *specula*,' quoting the Platonic *Axiochus* 369 A, and Lidd. and Scott, referring to the same passage, give 'τὸ ἄποπτον, *a look-out place, watch-tower*' *:* but there ἐξ ἀπόπτου θεώμενος = 'seeing *afar off.*' In this adverbial phrase (*Phil.* 467 ἐξ ἀπόπτου σκοπεῖν, Galen 3. 222 ἐξ ἀπόπτου θεασάμενος) the word has sense (1), meaning, 'so that the place at which you look is ἄποπτος to you.'

NOTE XV.

Verse 1137.

ἐξ ἦρος εἰς Ἀρκτοῦρον. *The significance of Arcturus in the popular Greek calendar.*

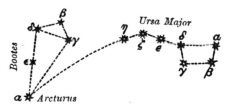

Arcturus is from ἄρκτος and οὖρος, 'watcher'. (akin to ὁράω, and to our *ward*)—the 'bear-ward,' the keeper, or *leader*, of *Ursa Maior*. This name was also given to the whole constellation Βοώτης ('ploughman') of which Arcturus is the brightest star : Cic. *Arat.* 96 *Arctophylax, vulgo qui dicitur esse Boötes.* Greek writers speak of ἀρκτούρου ἐπιτολή not in a geometrical sense, but as meaning 'earliest visibility'; and this in two distinct applications.

(1) The season when Arcturus first begins to be visible, after sunset, as an evening star, shortly before the vernal equinox (March 20—21). This is sometimes termed the 'acronychal' rising (from ἀκρόνυχος, on the verge of night). Hippocrates, who was the contemporary of Sophocles,

J. S. 20

and who illustrates the popular reckoning by Arcturus more clearly than any other writer, uses ἀρκτούρου ἐπιτολή in this sense without any qualifying epithet, leaving the context to show what he means : περὶ διαίτης 3. 68 (vol. VI. p. 598 ed. Littré) μετὰ δὲ ταῦτα [viz. when 44 days have elapsed from the winter solstice] ὥρη ἤδη ζέφυρον πνέειν, καὶ μαλακωτέρη ἡ ὥρη·...εἶτα δὲ [15 days later] ἀρκτούρου ἐπιτολή, καὶ χελιδόνα ὥρη ἤδη φαίνεσθαι, τὸν ἐχόμενον δὲ χρόνον ποικιλώτερον ἤδη διάγειν μέχρις ἰσημερίης [the vernal equinox] ἡμέρας τριάκοντα δύο.

(2) Far more commonly, ἀρκτούρου ἐπιτολή denotes the season when Arcturus begins to be visible as a morning star. This is termed the 'heliacal' rising (ἡλιακή), because Arcturus is then visible before sunrise. In the age of Hippocrates and Sophocles (say in 430 B.C.), Arcturus began to be thus visible about a week before the autumnal equinox, which falls on Sept. 20—21; and, in the popular language of that age, '*the rising of Arcturus*' commonly meant, 'shortly before the autumnal equinox.' Cp. Hippocr. περὶ διαίτης 3. 68 (VI. 594 Littré, before the passage cited above) τὸν μὲν ἐνιαυτὸν ἐς τέσσαρα μέρεα διαιρέουσιν, ἅπερ μάλιστα γινώσκουσιν οἱ πολλοί, χειμῶνα, ἦρ, θέρος, φθινόπωρον. καὶ (1) χειμῶνα μὲν ἀπὸ πλειάδων δύσιος ἄχρι ἰσημερίης ἠαρινῆς, (2) ἦρ δὲ ἀπὸ ἰσημερίης μέχρι πλειάδων ἐπιτολῆς, (3) θέρος δὲ ἀπὸ πλειάδων μέχρι ἀρκτούρου ἐπιτολῆς, (4) φθινόπωρον δὲ ἀπὸ ἀρκτούρου μέχρι πλειάδων δύσιος. Here he tells us that, according to the reckoning with which the Greeks of the 5th century B.C. were most familiar, the year was divided into four parts, thus : (1) *Winter*—from the setting of the Pleiads to the vernal equinox : (2) *Spring*—from the vernal equinox to the rising of the Pleiads : (3) *Summer*—from the rising of the Pleiads to the rising of Arcturus : (4) *Autumn*—from the rising of Arcturus to the setting of the Pleiads. In the sevenfold division of the year (noticed by Hippocrates in his περὶ Ἑβδομάδων), summer was subdivided into θέρος, early summer, and ὀπώρα, late summer : and the latter ended with the 'heliacal' rising of Arcturus, as Galen 5. 347 says : ὅσοι τὸν ἐνιαυτὸν εἰς ἑπτὰ τέμνουσιν ὥρας, ἄχρι μὲν ἐπιτολῆς τοῦ κυνὸς (Sirius) ἐκτείνουσι τὸ θέρος, ἐντεῦθεν δὲ μέχρις ἀρκτούρου τὴν ὀπώραν. Hippocrates says that, in watching the course of maladies, particular attention should be paid to the stars, especially to the rising of Sirius and of *Arcturus*, and to the setting of the Pleiads ; for these are the critical seasons at which diseases most often mend, cease, or enter on new phases : περὶ ἀέρων, ὑδάτων, τόπων 11 (vol. II. p. 52 ed. Littré). The short phrase of Sophocles, εἰς ἀρκτοῦρον, can be matched with several of his medical contemporary, showing how familiar the sign was : ἐπιδημ. 1. 2. 4 περὶ ἀρκτοῦρον (= a

little before the autumnal equinox), *ib.* 1. 2. 7 πρὸ ἀρκτούρου ὀλίγον καὶ ἐπ᾽ ἀρκτούρου (*before*, and *at*, his 'heliacal rising'): περὶ ἀέρων κ.τ.λ. 10 μήτε ὑπὸ κύνα μήτε ἐπὶ τῷ ἀρκτούρῳ (neither just before Sirius rises, nor just when Arcturus does so). For the Roman writers, though Arcturus had no longer the same importance as a mark of the people's calendar, he is especially the symbol of equinoctial storms in September: Plaut. *Rudens* prol. 69 *Nam Arcturus signum sum omnium acerrimum: Vehemens sum exoriens: cum occido, vehementior.* Cp. Horace *Carm.* 3. 1. 27 *saevus Arcturi cadentis Impetus.* Plin. 18. 74 (Arcturus rises) *vehementissimo significatu terra marique per dies quinque* (indicated as Sept. 12—17).

A passage of curious interest is Plin. 2. 47 *usque ad sidus Arcturi, quod exoritur undecim diebus ante aequinoctium auctumni.* Here Pliny treats the 'heliacal rising' of Arcturus as an event of fixed date, occurring annually about Sept. 9 or 10. But, owing to the precession of the equinoxes, this 'heliacal rising' becomes progressively later,—as will be seen below, about one day later in every 70 years. In Pliny's time (about 70 A.D.) the earliest time at which Arcturus could have been seen before sunrise would have been considerably later than Sept. 9 or 10. It would seem, then, that Pliny had taken his date from a literary source long anterior to his own age. On this point, Professor G. H. Darwin has kindly given me the subjoined note:—

'A rough calculation gives the following results with respect to the rising of Arcturus in the latitude of Athens (38° N.):—

'In 430 B.C. the rising of Arcturus (R.A. 185°, decl. 32°) preceded that of the sun

on 7 Sept. (N. S.) by 22 minutes,
and on 15 Sept. by 61 minutes.

'In 70 A.D. the rising of Arcturus (R. A. 191°, decl. 29°) preceded that of the sun

on 15 Sept. by 23 minutes,
and on 22 Sept. by 62 minutes.

'After a star has risen it remains invisible for some time on account of mist on the horizon, but if the climate be clear the interval of invisibility after geometrical rising is short. It is of course also invisible in the day time and shortly after sunset or before sunrise. If therefore a star only rises in the geometrical sense a short time before sunrise, it will remain altogether invisible. From the above results we see that on Sept. 7, 430 B.C. and on Sept. 15, 70 A.D. Arcturus though really above the horizon before sunrise must have been invisible on account of the brightness of the twilight. On the 15 Sept.

20—2

430 B.C. and on the 22 Sept. 70 A.D. it must have been visible after geometrical rising, and before there was so much daylight as to extinguish stars of the first magnitude. It is likely that Arcturus would have thus been first visible as early as 12 Sept. 430 B.C., and as 20 Sept. 70 A.D. The first visibility of Arcturus took place between seven and eight days earlier in the month in 430 B.C. than in 70 A.D. In a clear climate like that of Greece the first visibility, after the period of invisibility due to the nearness of the sun, would fix the time of year within two or three days. At this season the rapid decrease of the sun's declination conspires with the increase of his right ascension to produce a rapid increase in the interval by which the rise of Arcturus precedes that of the sun. As above stated, this interval would increase from 22 to 61 minutes between Sept. 7 and 15, 430 B.C. In a week after Sept. 15 the star would have risen long before sunrise, and the appearance of the star in the east and the rapidity of its extinction by the rays of the sun would cease to be a remarkable phenomenon.'

NOTE XVI.

Verse 1505.

μή σφε περιΐδης.

Porson on *Med.* 284 holds that Tragedy *never* admitted περί before a vowel (whether the prep. stood alone or was compounded with another word) in senarii, in trochaics, or in a regular system of anapaests. In Ar. *Th.* 1070 περίαλλα occurs in an anapaestic verse from Eur., but this, says Porson, seems to have belonged to a free or irregular system (systema illegitimum). In Soph. 225 περίαλλα belongs to lyrics: so περιόργως (not a certain reading) in Aesch. *Ag.* 216: περιώδυνος *ib.* 1448: and περιώσια Soph. fr. 611. Where a compound of περί occurs elsewhere than in lyrics, Tragedy, Porson says, used tmesis: as Eur. *Bacch.* 619 τῷδε περὶ βρόχους ἔβαλλε : fr. *ap.* Cornut. *De N. D.* 184 κορυφὴ δὲ θεῶν ὁ περὶ χθόν' ἔχων | φαεινὸς αἰθήρ. Similarly such a form as ἠμφιεσμένος (Ar. *Eccl.* 879) belongs to Comedy, not Tragedy. Here, then, he would write παρά σφ' ἴδης (the MSS. having παρίδης) : Fritzsche, περί σφ' ἴδης. But it may be urged : (1) such a tmesis is alien from the style of ordinary tragic dialogue: (2) the extant remains of Attic Tragedy justify Porson's remark that compounds of περί were avoided, but are too small to warrant a rule absolutely excluding them: (3) the probability of such a rule, intrinsically slight, is further lessened by the περίαλλα of the Euripidean anapaest : (4) one *reason* why περί before a vowel should be usually avoided is evident : a compound with ἀμφί would in most cases express the same notion, without resolving the foot : *e.g.* ἀμπέχω, ἀμφίστημι dispensed with need for περιέχω, περιΐστημι. A single example like our passage goes far to break down the assumed universality of the exclusion.

NOTE XVII.

Verse 1526.

οὗ τίς οὐ ζήλῳ πολιτῶν ταῖς τύχαις ἐπέβλεπεν.

Lucian once uses the verb ἐπιβλέπω with a dative, *Astrol.* 20 (where he is imitating an Ionic style) καί σφισι γιγνομένοισι τῷ μὲν ἡ Ἀφροδίτη τῷ δὲ ὁ Ζεὺς τῷ δὲ ὁ Ἄρης ἐπέβλεψαν (looked favourably upon). Plutarch (*Caes.* 2) has τοῖς χρήμασιν ἐποφθαλμιῶντος, 'eyeing the money' (covetously), but that proves nothing for ἐπιβλέπω. ἐπιβλέπω usually takes either (*a*) an accus. with preposition of an object towards whom one looks,—εἰς ἡμᾶς Plato *Phaedr.* 63 A, ἐπὶ τὴν Θηβαίων πόλιν Deinarch. or. 1 § 72 : or (*b*) a simple acc. of a thing which one mentally considers : as λόγους Plat. *Legg.* 811 D, ἀτυχίας, συμφοράς Isocr. or. 1 §§ 21, 35. Are we warranted, then, in rendering, ' not *looking jealously* on the prosperity (ζήλῳ, or as Prof. Kennedy translates it, the aspiring hopes) and fortunes of the citizens'?

I take ζήλῳ as a dative of manner with ἐπέβλεπεν. Thebans viewed Oedipus, not with jealousy, but with ζῆλος, *i.e.* with a sense that he was the type of perfect good fortune, the highest model for aspiring effort. ζῆλος is felt by one who is impelled to lift himself towards the level of a superior; φθόνος, by one who would depress that superior to his own; when they are mentioned together, it is because baffled ζῆλος often breeds φθόνος: Plat. *Menex.* 242 A πρῶτον μὲν ζῆλος, ἀπὸ δὲ ζήλου φθόνος. Cp. Eur. *Suppl.* 176 ff. σοφὸν δὲ πενίαν τ' εἰσορᾶν τὸν ὄλβιον, | πένητά τ' ἐς τοὺς πλουσίους ἀποβλέπειν | ζηλοῦνθ', ἵν' αὐτὸν χρημάτων ἔρως ἔχῃ, *i.e.* that his ζῆλος of the prosperous man may spur him to honourable exertion. The chief reason for preferring οὗ...ταῖς τύχαις to Musgrave's ὅν...τῆς τύχης is that the latter is so much further from the MSS.: the usage of ἐπιβλέπειν also favours the former. The reading of the MSS., ὅστις...καὶ τύχαις ἐπιβλέπων, is nonsense. We cannot *supply* ἦν with the participle.

Prof. Kennedy, reading ὡς τις, renders: 'mighty man he was, for one who never eyed jealously the aspiring hopes and fortunes of the citizens': *i.e.* he was as powerful as a τύραννος could be who refrained from jealously suppressing all eminence near him. This version raises the question noticed above—as to whether ἐπιβλέπων would have been used, without any addition, in the sense of *invidens*. As regards the sense, we scarcely seem to need here a clause which qualifies and restricts the former *might* of Oedipus, even though this clause at the same time implies a tribute to his moral greatness.

INDICES.

I. GREEK.

The number denotes the verse, in the English *note* on which the word or matter is illustrated. When the reference is to the Latin critical note, cr. is added to the number. When the reference is to a *page*, p. is prefixed to the number.)(means, 'as distinguished from.'

A

ἀβλαβής as a cretic, 229
ἀγηλατεῖν, ἄγος, 402
ἀγκύλη, 204
ἀγνώς, act. and pass., 677
ἀγροί, opp. to πόλις, 1049
ἀγρόνομοι πλάκες, 1103
ἀγύρτης, 387
ἀγχόνης κρεῖσσον, 1374
ἀδύπολις, 510
ἀελλάδες ἵπποι, 466
ἄζομαι, 155
ἀθέως, 254
ἄθικτος, of Delphi, 898
ἄθλιος, of folly, 372
αἰδοῦμαι with (1) accus. of pers., (2) infin. of act, 1427
αἰθήρ)(οὐρανός, 866
αἰκάλλειν, 597
αἷμα αἱρεῖν, 996
αἷμα ἐμφύλιον, 1406
αἱματοῦς, 1279
αἱρεῖν, to 'take,' or 'slay,' 996
αἵρεσθαι πένθος, 1225
αἰσυμνήτης)(τύραννος, pp. 4 f.
αἰώρα, 1264
ἀκούειν, to be called, 903
ἀκτὴ (βώμιος), edge of, 182
ἄκων = ἀκούσιος (of an act), 1229
ἀλέξομαι as future, 539

ἄληθες; 350
ἀλλά, puts and meets a supposed objection, 1375
ἄλλος, ὁ, idiomatic use of, 290
ἄλλος redundant, 7
ἄλλος omitted (οὔτις, ἀλλά), 1331
ἄλλως τε, 'and moreover,' 1114
ἄλοκες, in fig. sense, 1211
ἀλύειν, 695
ἀμφιδέξιοι ἀκμαί, 1243
ἀμφιπλήξ ἀρά, 417
Ἀμφιτρίτης μέγας θάλαμος, 194
ἄν = ἃ ἄν, 281, 749
ἄν, ellipse of with imperf. (ἐβουλόμην), 1348; (ἔδει), 256, 1368
ἄν omitted after ὅς with subjunct., 1231
ἄν with infin. or partic., 11
ἄν with partic. or infin., limit to use of, 523
ἄν repeated, 139, 339, 862, 1438
ἄν before verb corrupted to ἀνα-, 1348
ἀναγιγνώσκειν not found in Attic prose as = 'to recognise,' 1348
ἀνάγκη, a constraining doom, 877
ἀνακηρύσσειν, 450
ἄναξ, of a god and of a seer, 284
ἀναπλάκητος, 472
ἀναπνεῖν, to revive, 1221
ἀναρρηγνύναι, intrans., in fig. sense, 1075
ἄνδρα, accus. *before* infin., in a γνώμη, 314

ἀνδρηλατεῖν, 100
ἄνευ, senses of, 1463
ἀνήκεστον, of a μίασμα, 98
ἀνθ' ὦν=ἀντὶ τούτων, 264
ἀνύειν with adj., to _make_ such or such, 166
ἀξιοῦσθαι, to be condemned (with infin.), 1449
ἀπαυδᾶν in commands, 236
ἀπείρων=ἄπειρος, 1088
ἀπευθύνειν, to steer aright, 104
ἀπήνη, 753
ἁπλοῦν, εἰς, 519
ἀπό)(ἐκ, of source, 395
ἀπό, sense of in compound adjectives, 196
ἀπό)(παρά or πρός τινος, 42
ἀποικεῖσθαι, pass., bold use of, 997
ἀποκλίνειν, intrans., 1192
ἀποκρίνειν, 640
ἀπονοσφίζειν, 480
ἀπόξενος, 196
ἀπόπτολις, exile, 1000
ἄποπτος, two senses of, p. 304
ἄποπτος ἄστεως, 762
ἀποσπᾶν ἐλπίδος τινά, 1432
ἀποστερεῖν ἑαυτὸν τῆς πόλεως, 1381
ἀποστρέφειν χέρας, 1154
ἀπότομος ἀνάγκη, 877
ἀπότροπος, 1314
ἀποφάσκειν, 483
ἆρα equiv. in sense to ἆρ' οὐ, 822
ἀρά=ἐρινύς, 417
ἀραῖος, bound by an oath, 276
ἀραῖος δόμοις, sense of, 1291
ἀραῖος ὀλοίμην, 644
ἀργός, senses of, 287
ἄρθρα ποδῶν, 718 ; κύκλων, 1270
ἀριθμός, of plural number as opp. to singular, 844
ἄριστα, adv., 1369
ἀρκτέον, ' one must rule,' 628
ἁρμόζειν, absol., of oracles, to come true, 902
ἄρουρα, fig. sense of, 1257
ἄρρητ' ἀρρήτων, 465
Ἄρτεμις ἀμφίπυρος, 207
ἄρχειν)(κρατεῖν, 54

ἄστροις ἐκμετρεῖσθαι γῆν, 795
ἀσχάλλειν, 937
ἀτελεύτητος, 336
ἄτιμος with genit., 788
αὐθαδία, not necessarily stupid, 550
αὔξειν, to reflect honour upon, 1091
αὔριον always adv., 1090
αὐτός, 'unaided,' 221, 341
αὐτός='at once' (ἀδελφὸς καὶ πατήρ), 458
αὐτός='unaltered in opinion,' 557
αὐτοῦ=ἐμαυτοῦ, 138
αὔτως, sense and accent of, 931
ἀφανὴς (λόγος), unproved, 656
ἀφιέναι ἑαυτόν, to absolve oneself, 707
ἀφικνεῖσθαι ἐπὶ πάντα, 265
ἀφόβητος, 'not fearing,' with genit., 885
ἄψαυστος=οὐ ψαύσας, 969
ἄψορρος, 431

B

βαιός =with few attendants, 750
βακχεῖος θεός, 1105
βάλλειν ἐν αἰτίᾳ, 656
βάλλειν ἐς θυμόν, 975
βαρύς, of vehement wrath, 673
βάσανος, 493
βασιλεύς, title of Zeus, 903
βέλη θυμοῦ, θεῶν, 893
βουλήσομαι, 1077
βούνομος)(βουνόμος, 26
βόσκειν=τρέφειν, 1425

Γ

γαιάοχος=guarding the land, 160
γάρ, merely prefacing statement, 277
γάρ, in elliptical sentences, 582
γάρ, in assent, 1117
γάρ, in negation, 1520
γε, scornful (σύγε), 445
γε...γε, 1030
γε, added to a repeated pron. (σέ...σέ γε), 1101
γε μέντοι, 442
γέ τοι δή, 1171
γένεθλα (πόλεως), her 'sons,' 180
γενέτας, senses of, 470
γνωτός and γνωστός, 361, p. 298
γονῇ γενναῖος, 1469

I. GREEK. 313

δάϊος, 214
δάπτειν, of mental pain, 681
δαφναφόρος, 21
δέ, introducing a γνώμη, 110
δέ, introducing objection, 379
δέ, after σέ, etc., in addresses, 1097
δέ, of apodosis after concessive protasis, 302
δέ, when attention is turned to a new point, 319
δέ...γε, 1030
δὲ οὖν, 669, 834
δείκνυμι, of a warning example, p. 304
δεῖμα, δείματα, 294
δεινά, adv., 483
δεινόπους ἀρά, 418
δείξει, δηλοῖ, etc., sometimes impersonal, 1294
δεξιά, first sense of, 1243
δεύτερα, τά, the second-best course, 282
δή, as nearly = ἤδη, 968
δηλαδή, 1501
δήλημα, sense of, 1495
δην, adverbs in, 1310
δῆτα, in assent, 445
δι' αἰθέρα τεκνωθέντες, 866
διὰ τύχης ἰέναι, 773
διαφέρειν, 'bear to the end,' 321
διδακτός, opp. to ἄρρητος, 300
δίδωμι λόγον ἐμαυτῷ, 583
διειπεῖν, 394, 854
διέχειν, trans. and intrans., 717
δικάζειν, peculiar use of, 1214
δικαίως = 'in a strict sense,' 853
Δίκη, 274
διολλύναι, to forget, 318
διορίζειν, 723, 1083
διπλαῖ πύλαι, 1261
δοκεῖν, to approve, 483
δοκεῖν, (1) with infin. understood, (2) 'to have repute,' 1191
δυοῖν, never a monosyllable, 640
δυσούριστον, 1315
δύσποτμος, of folly, 888

E

ε elided after η (εἴη 'ξ), 970

ἔα, ἑᾷ, a monosyllable, 1451, 1513
ἐγγενῶς, 1225
ἐγκαλεῖν νεῖκος, sense of, 702
ἐγκρατής = ἐν κράτει, 941
ἐγκυρῶν (conjectured), 1031
ἔγχος φροντίδος, of a device, 170
ἐγὼ οὔτ', 322
ἕδος, sense of, 886
ἕδρα, of supplication, 2
εἰ with subjunctive, 198, 874
εἰ with fut. indic., 702
εἰ...εἴτε = εἴτε...εἴτε, 92
εἰ καί and καὶ εἰ, p. 296
εἰ καί, 305
εἴ τι μή, in diffident expressions, 124
εἰδεῖτε = εἰδείητε, 1046
εἰδώς, with sure knowledge, 119
εἰκάθω, 651
εἰκῇ, sense of, 979
εἰκός, τό, of a reasonable estimate, 74
εἰμί understood with an adject., 92
εἰμί with partic., instead of pres. or imperf., 126
εἴργομαι, to abstain from, 890
εἷς = continuous, 374
εἷς, with superlat. (κάλλιστ' ἀνὴρ εἷς), 1380
εἰς ἑαυτόν, τό, in what concerns himself, 706
εἰς καλόν, 78
εἰς πάντας (αὐδᾶν), 93
εἷς τι φοβεῖσθαι, 980
εἶτ' οὖν...εἴτε, 1049
ἐκ in adverbial phrases (ἐξ ὑπαρχῆς), 132
ἐκ, of a former state (τυφλὸς ἐκ δεδορκότος), 454
ἐκ, of ultimate cause, 590, 1453
ἐκ (μακροῦ), 'at a long interval,' 1141
ἐκ = 'since' (ἐξ οὗ), 1197
ἐκ τῶνδε = μετὰ τάδε, 282
ἐκβάλλειν, to repudiate a statement, 849
ἐκγενής (conjectured by Dind.), 1506 cr.
ἐκδημεῖν, to be abroad, 114
ἐκκαλεῖν, 597
ἐκκινεῖν (ῥῆμα), 354
ἐκλύειν δασμόν, 35
ἐκμετρεῖσθαι γῆν ἄστροις, 795
ἔκμηνος, 1137

ἐκπειρᾶσθαι, 360
ἐκπέμπομαι, midd., 951
ἐκτείνομαι, fig. sense of, 153
ἐκτόπιος ἄγεται (instead of ἐκ τόπων), 1340
ἐκτρίβειν, 428
ἐκών = ἑκούσιος (of an act), 1229
ἐλαύνειν ἄγος, 98
ἐλαύνειν ἐς τριβάς, 1160
ἐλευθεροῦν στόμα, sense of, 706
ἐμπέφυκε, of prophecy, 299
ἐμπλήσσειν, 1264
ἐν = 'in the case of,' 388
ἐν, of pursuit or calling (ἐν τῇ τέχνῃ), 562
ἐν ἀργοῖς (πράσσεσθαι), 287
ἐν γένει, 1016
ἐν δέ, adverbial, 27, 181
ἐν (δικασταῖς), 'before judges,' 677
ἐν ὅρκῳ, 652
ἐν σοί, penes te, 314
ἐν σοί, 'in thy mind,' 770
ἕν τινι ὁρᾶν and ἐνορᾶν τινι, 537
ἐν τύχῃ, γήρᾳ, 80, 1112
ἐν χεροῖν, by his hands, 821
ἐναγής, 'liable to a curse,' 656
ἐναριθμῶ, 1187
ἐνδατεῖσθαι, 205
ἔνθα = ἐκεῖσε ἔνθα, 796
ἐνθύμιος, 739
ἐνταῦθα = 'in that point,' 598
ἐξαγγέλλομαι, 148
ἐξάγγελος, 1223
ἐξαιρεῖν, to put out of account, 908
ἐξελθεῖν, to be fulfilled, 88
ἐξεστεμμένοι, said of suppliants, 3
ἐξισοῦν, to bring to a (lower) level, 425, 1507
ἐξισωτέον, 408
ἑός as = 'thine,' p. 6
ἐπ' ἀγρῶν and like phrases, 1049
ἐπακούειν, 794
ἐπεί = 'for else,' 390
ἐπεύχομαι, 249
ἔπι, adverb, 181
ἐπὶ ἦρα φέρειν, 1095
ἐπὶ ἠθέων λεκτοί (conject.), 13 cr.
ἐπὶ τῷ ἀνδρί = in his case, 829
ἐπὶ φρόνιμα ἄπορος, 692
ἐπιβλέπειν, classical use of, p. 309

ἐπίκουρος, 'avenging,' 497
ἐπιοῦσα, ἡ, 1090
ἐπιρράσσω, 1244
ἐπισκοπεῖν, sense of, 1529
ἐπιστροφή, 134
ἐπιτολὴ ἀκρόνυχος and ἡλιακή, p. 305
ἐπιών, ὁ, the first comer, 391
ἔπος, of an oracular response, 89
ἔπουρος, 194
ἐπῳδός, ἡ, distinguished from ὁ ἐπῳδός, p. lxviii
ἐπώνυμος, uses of, 210
ἔργω, ἔρξω, ἔρξας, &c., 890
ἐρρύμην, aor. of ῥύω, 1351
ἔρχομαι, to come to be (φονεὺς ἦλθον), 1357
ἕσπερος θεός = Ἅιδης, 178
ἑστία, of Delphi, 965
εὖ, 'carefully,' 308
εὖ διδόναι, to give good, 1081
εὖ ἴσθ' with hiatus, 959
εὐαγὴς λύσις, 921
εὐέπεια, senses of, 932
εὐθύ)(εὐθύς, 1242
Εὔκλεια, title of Artemis, 161
εὕρημα, 1107
εὔσεπτος, act., 'reverent,' 864
εὔχομαι, constr. of, 269
εὐῶψ, epith. of comfort, 189
ἐφυμνεῖν, of imprecation, 1275
ἔφυν, of a natural claim, 9
ἔχομαι, uses of, 891, 1387
ἔχω, with aor. partic., 577, 698
ἔχω, intrans. with adv. (Herod.), 708
ἐῶραι, αἱ, the festival, 1264

Z

ζῆλος)(φθόνος, p. 309
ζῆν, to be operative, 45

H

ἦ, 1st pers. sing. imperf. of εἰμί, 1123
ἤ...ἤ, where the first ἤ might be absent, 487
ἢ καί = than even, 94
ἢ καί, in question, 368, 757
ἢ οὐκ as one syllable, 555
ἤ...τε instead of ἤ...ἤ, 539
ᾔδει, 3rd sing., 1525

ἤδειμεν, ἤδειτε, ἤδεσαν, 1232
ἡδονά, form of, 1337
ἡδύς = εὐάγγελος, 82
ἤθεος, 18
ἡλόμην and ἠλάμην, 1311
ἦμος, in tragic dialogue, 1134
ηὖγμαι, 1512 cr.

Θ

θάλαμος, 1241
θανάσιμος βεβηκώς, 959
θεῖα, τά, religion, 910
θεῖος, epithet of kings, &c., 1235
θελήσας, 649
θεμιτός and θεμιστός, 993
θεός, said of λοιμός, 27
θεός, without art., 871
θεσπιέπεια, a really pleonastic form, 463
θεωρία, uses of, 1491
θεωρός, to Delphi, 114
θητεία)(δουλεία, 1029
θίξομαι, 891
θοάζειν, as = θάσσειν, 2, p. 286
θυρών, 1241
θω, verbal forms in, 651

I

Ἰάκχιος, 1218
ἰάλεμος, 1218
ἰάχεῖν, ἰακχεῖν, 1218
ἰέναι ἐπί (accus.), to attack, 495
ἱερός, epith. of ὄμβρος, 1428: and ἱρός,
    1379 cr.
Ἰήιος, 154, 1096
ἴθι, in entreaty, 1468
ἱκνεῖσθαι εἴς τι, to incur a fate, 1158
ἱκτήριοι κλάδοι, 3
ἵνα, 'where,' 367 (with genit.), 687 (with
    ἥκειν), 947 : limit to its use, 1311
ἵνα, final, with imperf. and aor. indic.,
    1389
ἵνα μὴ εἴπω, 328
ἴσα καί = ἴσα ὥσπερ, 1187
ἴσα, τά, poet. for τὰ αὐτά, 1498
ἴσος, adjectival compounds with, 478
ἴσος, 'just,' 677
ἰσοῦσθαι, passive, 31
ἱστάναι ἐλπίδα, 698

ἱστορεῖν, senses of, 1484
ἰῶ and -ίσω, futures in, 538
ἰών, pres., not fut., partic., 773

K

καθ' ὑπερβολήν, 1197
καθικνεῖσθαι, construct. of, 809
καί, emphasizing verb, 851, 989, 1129
καί, 'e'en,' where the speaker is diffident
    (κἂν ἐμοί), 1239
καί = adeo, 347
καί = ὅτε, 718
καί (δεῦρ' ἔβημεν) = 'in the first instance,'
    148
καί...καί = 'both, and (yet),' 413
καὶ μήν, 'indeed,' 749, 1004
καὶ μήν γε, 345
καὶ σύ, 'thou on thy part,' 342
καὶ ταῦτα, 37
καιρός, with art., 1050
καιρῷ = ἐν καιρῷ, 1516
κακός = δυσγενής, 1063
κάλλος, concrete, a fair thing, 1396
καλῶς, colloquial use of, 1008
κατά, with acc. of respect, 1087
κατά, after its case, 1280
κατὰ ἑαυτόν, = 'alone,' 62
κατὰ στέγας ἰέναι, 637
κατακοιμᾶν ὄμμα (of deathlike anguish),
    1222
κάταργμα, sense of, 920
κατάφημι)(ἀπόφημι, 507
κατεύχομαι, 246
κατέχω, intrans. (to restrain oneself), 782
κεκλαυμένος, 1490
κέντρα διπλᾶ, 809
κέντρα, fig., 1318
κέρδος, material gain, 595
κεύθειν, to be hidden, 968
κήδευμα, of a brother-in-law, 85
κηλὶς συμφορᾶς, 833
Κῆρες)(Μοῖραι, 472
κλάζειν, of birds, 966
κλαίων, 'to thy cost,' 401
κλήχομαι)(καλοῦμαι, 1451
κλῇθρα, door-bolts, 1261
κοινός = κοινωνός, 240

κολάζειν, of verbal reproof, 1147
κρ, vowel long before, 640
κρείσσων εἰ μὴ ὤν=κρεῖσσόν ἐστί σε μὴ
εἶναι, 1368
κτῆμα, of mental or moral qualities, 549
κυκλόεις ἀγορᾶς θρόνος, 161
κύων, said of the Sphinx, 391
κωφὰ ἔπη, 290

Λ

λαμβάνειν (ἀραῖον), 276
λάμπειν, said of sound, 186
λέγειν, of *mere* talk, 360
λέγω δέ, as an exordium, 412
λέγω τι; 1475
λείπειν, intrans., to stop short, 1232
λήγειν, fig., of rumour, 731
λήθω, parts of used by Soph., 1325
λιμήν, poet. for ὑποδοχή, 420, 1208
λόγων δόκησις, κόμπος, 681
Λοξίας, 854
λοχῖται, a king's body-guard, 751
λύειν, with simple genit., 1350
λύειν τέλη=λυσιτελεῖν, 317
Λύκειος, epith. of Apollo, 203

M

μάγος, 387
μακραίωνες, αἱ, the Nymphs, 1099
μαλερός, 190
μάλιστα, of one's *first* wish, 926
μάντις, said of (1) god, (2) man, 708
μάντις, 'prescient,' 1086
ματάζω, ματάζω, 891
μέγα, adv. with adj., 1341
μεγάλη θάλασσα, ἡ, 194
μέγας=in a strong (moral) position, 652
μεθιέναι λόγον, 784
μείζονα τῶν μακίστων, 1300
μείζων, 'nearer and dearer,' 772
μέλλω, fut. or aor. after, 967
μεμνώμεθα, subjunct., 49
μέν, clause with, without expressed antithesis, 18
μὲν οὖν, where each word has a separate
force, 483
μὲν οὖν, as='nay rather,' 705

μεριμνᾶν, uses of, 1124
μέσης (ἐξ ἀπήνης), '*right* out of,' 812
μεσόμφαλος, of Delphic oracle, 480
μέτεστί μοι πόλεως, sense of, 630
μέτοικος, sense of in poetry, 452
μή where μὴ οὐ could stand, 1388
μή before the infin., where οὐ could
stand, 1455
μή, in a saving clause (with partic. understood)=εἰ μή, 1457
μὴ οὐ, with partic., 13, 221, p. 293
μὴ οὐ, τό, with infin., 1232
μὴ)(οὐ παρὼν θαυμάζεται, 289
μηδέ, irregularly equiv. to μὴ καί, 325
μηδείς, ὁ, 'he who is as nought,' 1019
μηδέν, τό, 'what is as nought,' 638
μηδέν, τό, adverbial with ζώσας, 1187
μηδὲν εἰδώς, ὁ (instead of οὐδέν), 397
μήτε, understood, 239
μία ῥώμη=ἑνὸς ῥώμη, 122
μοι='as I bid you,' 1512
μοῖρα, how far personified, 863
μονάς, 1350
μόνιμος, 1322
μόνος, not 'alone,' but 'pre-eminently,'
299
μονῳδίαι, structure of, p. lxxx
μοῦνος, in dialogue, 304
μοῦνος, supposed limit to its use by Soph.,
1418

N

ναίειν ὁμοῦ (said of feelings, &c.), 337
νέμω, of sway, 579
νηλής)(ἄνοικτος, 180
νίζειν, special sense of, 1228
νιν, accus. plur., 1331
νεμάς, use of, 1350
νόμος ἴδιος and κοινός, 865
νῦν δέ, with aor. equiv. to perf., 263
νωμάω, senses of, 300
νωτίζειν, 192

Ξ

ξεῖνος for ξένος in dialogue, 1420
ξένη=ξένη γῆ, 455
ξυμφοράς, τάς, τῶν βουλευμάτων, p. 287

O

οἷα impossible after ὅτι in 1401

οἷα (δοῦλος, '*for* a slave '), rarer than ὡς..., 763

οἶδα)(γιγνώσκω, 1128

Οἰδίπους as vocative, 405 cr.

οἰκεύς = οἰκέτης, 756

οἶμαι, only sometimes parenthetic, 1051

οἷον (after τοιοῦτον) instead of ὥστε, 1293

οἶσθ' ὡς ποίησον; 543

ὀλέθριος, pass., 'lost,' 1341

ὄλεθρος, colloquial use of, 1341

Ὄλυμπος, the sky, 867

ὄμαυλος)(σύμφωνος, 186

ὄμβρος, symbol of water generally, 1427

ὁμιλίαι ἀστῶν, sense of, 1489

ὁμογενής, sense of, 1362

ὁμόσπορος, 260, 460

ὁμόστολος, ' roaming with,' 212

ὁμοῦ, senses of, 1276

ὀμφαλός, the Delphic, 480, 898

ὄνομα κακοῦ = κακὸν ὀνομαζόμενον, 1284

ὄντες, etc., with a numeral (δύ' ὄντε), 1505

ὀπίσω, of the future, 486

ὅπως μή, after verb of fearing, 1074

ὅπως πέμψεις, '(see) that you send,' 1518

ὁρᾶν τὰ αὐτά, sense of, 284

ὁρᾷς; in reproach, 687

ὀρθός, 'justified,' 506

ὅρκος θεῶν, 647

ὄρμενος, aor. part., 'sped,' 177

ὄρνιθι αἰσίῳ, 52

ὅς ἄν δέ instead of ὅς δὲ ἄν (in prose), 749

ὅσον μή, with partic., 347

ὅσος with causal force (=ὅτι τοσοῦτος), 1228

ὅστις with superl., εἰμί being understood, 344, 663

οὐ γὰρ ἄν, with protasis suppressed or expressed, p. 292

οὐ (τὸν θεόν) = οὐ μά, 660

οὐδ' ἄν εἷς, 281

οὐδὲ μήν, 'no, nor,' 870

οὐδεὶς ὃς οὐχί = πᾶς τις, 373

οὐδὲν (instead of οὐδεὶς) βροτῶν, 1195

οὐκ εἰς ὄλεθρον; 430

οὐκ ἴσος, *more than* equal, 810

οὔπω instead of οὔποτε, 105

οὔπω ironically, 594

οὐρανία αἰθήρ, 866

ὅτε, 'seeing that,'=ἐπειδή, 918

οὗτις, ἀλλά, for οὗτις ἄλλος, ἀλλά, 1331

οὗτος σύ, 532

οὕτως divided from its adjective, 1444

ὀφθαλμός, fig. sense of, 987

Π

πάγκαρπος, epith. of laurel, 83

πάθος, euphemistic, 840

παθών, by bodily pain, 403

Παιάν, of Apollo, 154

παιδουργία for παιδουργός, 1248

πάλαι, of a *recent* moment, 1161

παλαιός, joined with ὁ πρίν (not a pleonasm), 1282

πάλαισμα, of civic emulation, 880

πάλιν, redundant, 430

πάλλω, trans. and intrans., 153

πᾶν δρᾶν, etc., 145, 265

πανσέληνος (ὥρα), 1090

πάντα, adv. neut. plur., 475, 1197

παντελής, of a wife, 930

παρ' οἴνῳ, 780

παρ' οὐδέν, 983

παρά in τὸν παρ' αὑτῷ βίοτον, 612

παραμείβειν, to outstrip, 504

παραρρίπτω, with partic., 1494

παραχορήγημα, p. 7

πάρεστιν, impers., 'it can be done,' 766

παρέχειν)(ἔχειν, 567

παρήχησις, rhetorical, 370

παριέναι κέαρ, 688

πάροδος of Chorus, 151

πάτριος)(πατρῷος, 1394

πατριώτης, said of a place in one's native land, 1091

πέλας, adv., with παραστατεῖν, 400

πελασθῆναι, usu. with dat. in conjugal sense, 1100

περᾶν (θυμοῦ), to go far *in*, 673

περί, compounds with, in tragic verse, p. 308

περίαλλα, use of, 1218

περιβόατος, 191

περισσός, 'of special note,' 841

περιτελλομέναις ὥραις, 156

περόνη, a brooch, 1269
πέτομαι, aorist forms of, 16
πετραῖος, a doubtful use of, p. 300
πηγή, ἡ ἀκούουσα, 1386
πημονή, quasi-colloquial use of, 363
πίθεσθε)(πείθεσθε, 1414 cr.
πίπτειν = ἐμπίπτειν (as on a bed), 1210
πίστιν φέρειν τινί, 1445
πίστις, senses of, 1420
πλάνης, 1029
πλάνος, πλάνη, 67
πλαστός, 780
πλέον τι, 'some advantage,' 37
πλησιάζειν = πλησίον εἶναι, 91: with dat.,
    1134
Πλούτων, name for Hades, 30
ποικιλῳδός, chanting riddles, 130
ποῖος Κιθαιρών = ποῖον μέρος Κιθαιρῶνος,
    421
πόλις, the, exists where its men are, 56
πόλις, indignant appeal to, 629
πόλις, adjectives compounded with, 510
πολύζηλος, senses of, 381
πολύς, of strong rumour, 785
πολὺς ῥεῖ, etc., of vehement speech, etc.,
    750
πομπός, 288
πόποι, 167
ποτέ = tandem aliquando, 335
ποῦ; 'on what ground?' 355
ποῦ; 'in what sense?' 390
πράσσειν, 'put into act,' 69
πράσσειν, of intrigue (pass.), 124
πράσσεσθαι, midd., senses of, 287
πρεσβύτερον, 'more serious,' 1365
πρίν, with indic., limit to use of, 776
πρό)(ἀντί, ὑπέρ, πρός with gen., 10, 134
προδείκνυμι, of a warning example, p. 304
προδεικνύναι γαῖαν, 456
προδείσας)(ὑπερδείσας, 89
πρόμος θεῶν, of the Sun, 660
πρόνοια, classical use of, 978
προξενεῖν, senses of, 1482
προπηλακίζω, 427
προπονεῖν, senses of, 685
πρός following its case, 178
πρός, with dat., after verb of throwing or
    falling, 1302

πρὸς δίκης, 1014
πρὸς ποσί, τό, 131
πρὸς σοῦ, 'in thy interest,' 1434
πρός τινος, 'on one's side,' 134
πρὸς τίνος αἰτίας; 1236
πρός τινος)(παρά τινος, 935
πρὸς (τῷ δεινῷ), close to it, 1169
πρὸς χάριν, 1152
προσάγεσθαι, 131
προσάπτειν, intrans., 666
προσήγορος, act. and pass., 1337, 1437
προσήκην, constructions of, 814
προσθήκη, aid, 38
προσκεῖσθαι, 232
προσκυρεῖν with accus., 1298
προσταθέντα, said of βέλεα, 206
προστάτην ἐπιγράφεσθαι, 411
προστατήριοι θεοί, 203
προστάτης, champion, 882
προστάτης νόσου, 303
προστείχειν for προσστείχειν (MSS.), 79 cr.
προστίθεσθαι μέριμναν, 1460
προστρέπεσθαι, 1446
πρόσωπον, τὸ σόν, 'thy frown,' 448
πρότερον ὕστερον, the so-called figure,
    827
προφαίνειν, said of an oracle, 790
προφαίνεσθαι, 395
πυθμένες, sockets of bolts, 1261
Πυθόμαντις ἑστία, 965
πύματον (ὅ τι) ὀλοίμαν, 663
πύργος (city-walls with towers), 56, 1378
πυρφόρος, of pestilence, 27
πῶς βλέπων; 1371
πωτᾶσθαι, 1310

Ρ

ῥαψῳδός, of the Sphinx, 391
ῥέπειν εἴς τινα, 847
ῥοπή = momentum, 961
ῥύεσθαι (μίασμα), 312

Σ

σ', elided, though emphatic, 64
σαφής = 'proved,' 390
σεμνόμαντις, ironical, 556
σημάντωρ, 957
σκοτεινός, of blindness, 1326

σοί, not σοι, required, 435
σπάργανα, fig. for infancy, 1035
στάσιμον, Arist.'s definition of, p. 8
στέγειν, classical use of, 11
στέλλειν)(στέλλεσθαι, 434, 860
στέρξας, having formed a desire, 11
στέφη = ἱκετηρία, 911
στόλος = λαός, 170
στόμα, of a prophet, 429
στόματα, said of one mouth, 1218
συγγενής, with genit. or dat., 814
συγγενής, said of πότμος, etc., 1082
συλλαβών, colloquial force of, 971
σύμμαχος, of gods, 274
συμμετρεῖσθαι, 73, 963
σύμμετρος, strengthens ξυνάδειν, 1113
σύμμετρος ὡς κλύειν, 84
συμφορά, classical uses of, p. 288
συμφορά, euphemistic for guilt, 99
συμφορά, of a happy event, 454
συμφοραὶ βουλευμάτων, 45
συμφυτεύειν, 347
σύν, 'by means of,' 566
σὺν ἀνδράσιν = ἄνδρας ἔχων, 55, 123
σὺν γήρᾳ βαρύς, 17
συναλλαγαὶ δαιμόνων, 34
συνέρχομαι, to conspire with, 572
συνέστιος, implying a share in family worship, 249
συντιθέναι, to concoct a plot, 401
συντόμως, 810
σφας, σφέας, accent of, 1470
σχιστὴ ὁδός, the, 733, 1398
σχολῇ, adv., 434
σῶμα δρᾶν κακῶς, sense of, 642
σωτήρ, as epithet of τύχη, 80

T

τὰ δέ, answering to τὰ μέν *understood* (after ὅσα), 1229
τὰ λῷστα ταῦτα (of which you speak), 1067
τάλας, last syllable long, 744
τε, irregularly placed, 258, 528, 694
τε, linking the speaker's words to those of a previous speaker, 1001
τε καί where καί alone would suffice, 487

τεκόντες, οἱ = οἱ γονεῖς, 999
τεκόντες, οἱ = ὁ πατήρ, 1176.
τέλει, proposed versions for in 198, p. 290
τελεῖν (absol.), to perform (funeral) rites, 1448
τελεῖν εἰς, 222
τέλειος, τέλος, of marriage, 930
τερασκόπος, 605
τέχνη, human skill, 380
τῇδε...τῇδε (βλέπειν), to right or to left, 857
τηλικόσδε, 'so young,' 1508
τηρήσας, 808
τι, adv., 'perchance,' 969, 1401
τί δ' ἔστιν; 319, 1144
τί δ' ὄντιν' εἶπε; 1056
τί φημί; a startled cry, 1471
τί χρείας = τίς χρεία, 1174
τιμωρεῖν, 'to punish,' 107
τίς and ὅστις combined, 72
τις, indef., after noun with definite art. (ὁ κύριός τις), 107
τις with adv. force (ταχύς τις = ταχέως πως), 618
τις for ὅστις only in indirect question, 1144
τίς (ἔβας); 'in what spirit?' 151
τίς οὐ = πᾶς τις, 1526
τίς οὗτος, τίς...; for τίς οὗτος, ὅς, 1493
τοιόσδε, after noun with ὁ σός, 295
τοιόσδε, in appos. with explanatory adj., 435
τόκοι, labours of child-bed, 26
τόσος, rare in Soph., 570
τοῦ λέγοντος εἶναι, 917
τοῦτ' αὐτό, τοῦτο, 1013
τοῦτο μέν...τοῦτ' ἄλλο, 605
τρέφειν, said of the concomitants of one's life, 374
τρίδουλος, 1062
τρίτος, added, 581
τυραννίς, of the king as embodying kingship, 128
τύραννος, earliest occurrences of the word, p. 5
τύραννος, probable etymology of, *ib.*
τύραννος = a 'tyrant' in our sense, 873
τύχη, idea of, 977

Y

ὕβρις, personified, 873
ὑμέναιος)(ἐπιθαλάμιον, 422
ὑπεξαιρεῖν, 227
ὑπεξελών, proposed versions for in 227, p. 295
ὑπὲρ ἄτας, 'to avert' ruin, 165, 188
ὑπερμάχεσθαι, ὑπερμαχεῖν, 265
ὑπηρετεῖν νόσῳ, 217
ὑπὸ μνήμης, 1131
ὑπόρχημα, p. lxxxvii
ὑποστρέφεσθαι μερίμνης, 728
ὕπουλος, 1396
ὑποφορά, rhetorical, 1375
ὑφέρπειν, of rumour, 786
ὑφιέναι, to suborn, 387
ὑψίποδες, epith. of νόμοι, 865

Φ

φαίνω, to set forth a story, 525
φάσκειν, = 'be confident,' 462
φάτις, of a divine message, 151
φέρειν)(φορεῖν, 1320
φέρειν πίστιν τινί, 1445
φέρεσθαι πλέον, to achieve more, 500
φέριστε, ὦ, rare in trag., 1149
φέρω = φέρομαι, 590
φέρω ἀγνείαν, 863
φεύγειν τι, to escape the penalty of it, 355
φῆμαι μαντικαί, 723
φήμη)(ὀμφή and κληδών, 43
φθερεῖσθαι, 272
φίλοι, powerful friends, 541
φοβεῖσθαι ἔς τι, 980
φοίνιος, poet. for θανάσιμος, 24
φοιτᾶν, sense of, 1255
φοράδην, form and senses of, 1310
φρονεῖν, senses of, 326, 1520
φρονήσας, 'having become sane,' 649
φυλάσσεσθαι παρά τινι, sense of, 382
φύσις (πέτρου, etc.), 334

X

χαίρω πᾶσι, sense of, 596
χάλαζα, fig. uses of, 1279
χεῖν, of song, etc., 1218
χειρὶ τιμωρεῖν, as opp. to a fine or to ἀτιμία, 107
χειρόδεικτος, a ἅπαξ λεγόμενον, 902
χείρωμα, 560
χέρνιψ, 240
χερσίν = simply ἔργοις, opp. to λόγῳ, 883
χηρεύειν, 479
χθονοστιβής, 301
χιασμός, rhetorical, 538
χνοάζειν, 742
χορεύειν, typifying public worship generally, 896
χορεύεσθαι, 1094
χρεία, 'request,' 1435
χρείαν τινὸς ἐρευνᾶν, 725
χρυσέα, epith. of Hope, 157
χρυσομίτρας, epith. of Bacchus, 209
χωρίς = 'without evidence,' 608

Ω

ὥς, final, with aor. indic., 1392
ὡς, as prep., 1481
ὡς, marking the mental attitude of the subject to the verb, 848, 1174
ὡς and ὥσπερ, in comparison, with ellipse of a verbal clause, 923, 1114, 1178
ὡς, added to a genit. absol., 11, 145
ὡς, with accus. absol., 101
ὡς ἄν, as = 'in whatever way,' p. 297
ὡς ἂν μή, 328
ὡς γυνή, 'in a woman's way,' 1078
ὡς (δοῦλος, 'for a slave'), 763, 1117
ὡς τεθραμμένον, 'which (he says) has been,' etc., 97
ὥστε, confirms and continues the last speaker's words, 1036
ὥστε γε, οὐχ, in reply, 1131
ὦ τᾶν, 1145

II. MATTERS.

A

Abae, temple at, 900
abstract for concrete (τροφή = θρέμματα),
  1, 1248, 1396
'accent' defined, p. lxv.
  ,, of Βακχεῖος, 1105
  ,, of κῆρυξ (not κῆρύξ) τε, 802
  ,, of προσθῇ, 1460 cr.
  ,, of verbal derivatives with short
  penult., 460
accented forms of pers. pron. preferable,
  435, 574, 1479
accus. absol., 101
  ,, after κυρεῖν, τυγχάνειν, 1298
  ,, after notion equiv. to transitive
  verb, 31
  ,, at beginning of sentence, without
  any regular government, 216, 278, 1134
  ,, before infin., where dat. could
  stand, 913
  ,, before infin. with εὔχομαι, 269
  ,, cognate, 192, 264, 340, 422
  ,, cognate, denoting one's errand
  (ἔρχομαι ἀγγελίαν), 788
  ,, cogn. to verb of feeling (τὸ ἔπος
  ἥδομαι), 936
  ,, double, after στέλλεσθαι, 434
  ,, in appos. with σέ, instead of a
  vocative, 1119
  ,, in appos. with whole sentence, 603
  ,, of antecedent, prefixed to relative
  clause, 449
  ,, of *person*, after ἥκειν, 713
  ,, of place to which, 1178
  ,, temporal, almost adverbial in reference to a *season*, 1138
acting, probable style of old Greek,
  p. xxxiv.
adj. agreeing with pers., instead of subst.
  with prep. (ἐκτόπιος ἄγομαι), 1340, p. 300
  ,, and adv. co-ordinated (τί ἢ νέον ἢ
  πάλιν ὁρᾷς;), 155

adj., comparative, to be carried on to a
  second clause, 1204
  ,, compounded with noun of like sense
  with the subst. (βίος μακραίων), 518
  ,, compound, equiv. to two distinct
  epithets (οἰόζωνος), 846, 965
  ,, instead of adv. (ὕστερος), 222
  ,, instead of proper name in genit.
  (Λαβδάκειος παῖς), 267, 451, 1216
  ,, or pron., as epith. of a compound
  phrase (τοὐμὸν φρενῶν ὄνειρον, not τῶν
  ἐμῶν), 108
  ,, second, as epithet, following subst.
  (τὰν γαμψώνυχα παρθένον χρησμῳδόν),
  1199, 1245
  ,, simple, instead of adj. with ὤν, 412,
  1506
  ,, transferred from subst. in the gen.
  to its dependent subst. (τοσόνδε τόλμης-
  πρόσωπον), 532, 832, 1375
  ,, verbal, in -όs, used as fem., 384
  ,,   ,, sigmatic form of, p. 298
  ,,   ,, with act. sense (ἄψαυστος),
  969
adv., neut. plur., 883
Aeschylus, apparent reminiscence of, 1478
  ,,   Theban trilogy of, p. xviii.
Agenor, 268
alliteration, rhetorical, 370
altars on the stage, p. 10
ambiguity of phrase, intended by the
  dramatist, 137, 261, 572, 814, 1167
anacolouthon (dat. for accus.), 353
  ,,   (plur. subject, sing. verb), 60
  ,,   through change of construction (κεκλόμενος...προφάνητέ μοι), 159
'anacrusis,' p. lxvii.
anapaestic paroemiae, spondees in, 1311
anapaests, excluded by Arist. from στάσιμα, p. 8
antecedent, attracted into case of relative
  (accus.), 449

aor. part., of a wish, hope, etc., 11, 649

,,   ,,   with γίγνομαι, 957

,,   ,,   with ἔσομαι, 1146

aor. referring to a moment just past, 337

Apollo, προφήτης of Zeus, 151

,,   with attributes of Zeus, 470

,,   as a pastoral god, 1103

aposiopesis, 1289

Arcturus, in Greek calendar, 1137, p. 305

Ares, the Destroyer, 190

Aristophanes of Byzantium, ὑποθέσεις ascribed to, p. 4

Aristophanes, parodies tragic altercation, 548

Aristotle's criticisms on the *Oed. Tyrannus*, p. xxvi.

,,   Κυμαίων πολιτεία, pp. 4 f.

'arsis,' p. lxvi.

Artemis Εὔκλεια and Ἀγοραία, 161

,,   with a torch in each hand, 207

·art. as relative, 1379

,,   as relat. pron., 200

,,   with abstract noun (ἡ ἐλπίς, 'hope'), 836

,,   with infin. in dependent clause, 1232, 1388

,,   with καιρός, 1050

,,   referring to a previous mention, 845

article, with interr. pron., in repeated question (τὸ τί;), 120, 291

Asclepiades of Tragilus, p. 6

Assos, the American exploration of, p. 302

Atlantic, the, w. limit of earth, 194

augment, syllabic, omitted, 1249

,,   temporal, omission of, 68

B

blight, threefold, 25

'Branching Roads,' the, 733, 1398

brooches (women's) used as daggers, 1269

bull, the, type of a savage wanderer, 478

C

Cadmeia, the, of ancient Thebes, 20

caesura, irregular, in anapaests, 1310

children bought, to be sold as slaves 1025

choral ode, relation of to preceding ἐπεισόδιον, 463

choreic rhythm, p. lxxii.

choriambic verse, p. lxxviii.

chorus almost always close a play, 1524

Cithaeron, the glens of, 1025

clauses, 1st and 2nd contrasted, and 3rd repeating 1st, 338

colloquial phrases, 336, 363, 971, 1008

comparison, elliptical form of (οἰκίαν ἔχει μείζω τοῦ γείτονος), 467

condensed expression (μία ἀπήνη ἦγε = μία ἦν, ἢ ἦγε), 753, 1451

conditional statement of probable fact (τάχ' ἂν ἦλθε = probably came), 523

conjectures by the editor, p. lxi.

,,   of former critics, adopted in this ed., p. lx.

construction changed (in answering a question which prescribed a different form), 1127

'contraction,' metrical, p. lxvi.

co-ordination of clauses, where we should subordinate one to the other, 419

Corneille's *Oedipe*, p. xxxviii.

Creon, the, of Sophocles, p. xxxi.

crepundia (Roman), 1035

Cyllene, mount, 1104

Cyprian Lays, reference to Oedipus in, p. xvi.

D

dative after ὁ αὐτός, 284

,,   after ὄρνυμαι (as = 'to attack'), 165

,,   alone, in sense of dat. with πρός, 175

,,   ethic (πᾶσι κλεινός), 8, 40, 596

,,   local, 20

,,   locative, 381, 422, 1266, 1451

,,   modal (ἀσφαλείᾳ), 51, 909, 1228, 1526

,,   ,,   cognate to idea of verb (ὕπνῳ εὕδειν), 65

Daulia in Phocis, p. xxi., 733

'deed and word,' 72

'Delian,' epith. of Apollo, 154
deliberative subjunct., indirect forms of,
  72, 1256
Delphi, wealth of temple at, 152
  ,,   topography of, 463
Dionysus, epithets of, 209 ff.

E

echo, of one speaker's words by another,
  570, 622, 1004
elemental powers, the, profaned by an
  impure presence, 1427
elision of σέ, etc., though emphatic, 64
  ,, of δ' at end of verse, 29
ellipse of verbal clause after ὡς, 923
entrance, stage, for one coming from the
  country, 78
epexegetic clause, after an adject., 57
'episode,' Arist.'s definition of, p. 8
epithet of agent transferred to act (γάμος
  τεκνῶν καὶ τεκνούμενος), 1214, 1229
  ,,   placed *after* a subst. which has
  art. and adv. phrase *before* it (τὸν ἤδη
  Λάϊον πάλαι νεκρόν), 1245
'epode' in choric songs, p. lxviii.
Eubulus, the comic poet, the *Oedipus* of,
  p. xxxv.
Euripides, the *Oedipus* of, p. xviii.
  ,,   *Phoen.*, 1788 ff., 1524 cr.
'exodus,' Arist.'s definition of, p. 9
expansion of verses in MSS., 1264 cr.

F

'falling' verse or sentence, p. lxx.
false characters soon betray themselves,
  615
festivals, Greek, bound up with family
  life, 1489
figurative and literal expression half-
  blended, 866, 1300
Fortune, Oedipus the son of, 1081
fusion of two modes of expression, 725
fut. indic. after ἔνθα μή, 1412
  ,,   ,,   of wish, resolve, etc. (βουλήσομαι), 1077, 1160, 1446
  ,, in -ισω and ιῶ, 538
  ,, interrog., with οὐ, commands, 430,
  1140

fut. 'middle' as pass., 672
  ,, optative, 538, f. 792, 796, 1271 ff.
  ,, partic. with art., 297
  ,, perfect, 411, 1146

G

genitive, absol. of subst. without partic.,
  966—1260
  ,, absol., with subject understcod
  (ἄρχοντος, when one rules), 629, 838
  ,, after adj. of active sense, 885
  ,, after ἄτιμος, 788
  ,, after compound adj. denoting
  lack (ἄχαλκος ἀσπίδων), 190
  ,, after ἐπώνυμος, 210
  ,, after νόμοι (laws *prescribing*
  things), 865
  ,, after πολυστεφής, 83
  ,, after προστάτης, etc., 303
  ,, after verb of rising or raising, 142
  ,, after verb of taking (ἕλῃ μου),
  1522
  ,, attributive, forming one notion
  with a subst. which has an epithet
  (τοσόνδε τόλμης πρόσωπον), 532
  ,,   ,,   (γῆς τις, one *of* the land),
  236
  ,,   ,,   (προστάτου γράφε-
  σθαι), 411
  ,,   ,,   (τί ἐστιν ἐκείνου; *in*
  him...?), 991
  ,,   ,,   with infin. (οὐ παντός
  ἐστι ποιεῖν), 393, 917
  ,, causal (τῆς προθυμίας), 48, 697,
  701, 1478
  ,,   ,,   (ἰκτὴρ πόνων), 185, 497
  ,, depending on subst. implied in
  adj. (ὧν ἀνάριθμος), 179, 1168
  ,, =an adj. of quality (στολὶς τρυφᾶς,
  i.e. τρυφερά), 1463
  ,, objective (ἀλκὴ κακοῦ) 93, 218, 647
  ,, of constituent (τὰ φίλτατ' ἐκγόνοιν), 1474
  ,, of source (φροντίδος ἔγχος), 170,
  312, 473, 681
  ,, of parent (μητρός), 1062
  ,, of place *from which* an act is
  done (ὄχου), 808

genitive, of place *whence*, 152, 192
  ,,   of things needed, after εἰς δέον, 1416
  ,,   partitive, 240
  ,,   ,, after ἔχειν, 708
  ,,   ,,   ,, περᾶν, 673
  ,,   ,, in ὡς ὀρχῆς ἔχω, 345
  ,,   ,, of point to which (εἰς τοῦτ᾽ ἀνοίας), 771
  ,,   simple, after λύειν, 1350
goad, driver's, with two points, 809
god, an unseen, the agent, 1259
Greeks, their unity expressed in religious rites, 240

H

happiness, to be predicated of no one before death, 1529
Harvard, *Oedipus Tyrannus* at, p. l., p. 279
Helicon, nymphs of, 1109
herald, sacred functions of, 753
Hermae, supposed reference to mutilation of, 886
Hermes, 1104
Hesiod, reference by, to Oedipus, p. xv.
hiatus (εὖ ἴσθ᾽, as if F preceded ι), 959
Hippocrates, references of, to Arcturus, p. 306
Homer, an echo of, 1325
Homeric poems, notices of Oedipus in, p. xiv.
Homeric practice as to syllabic augment, 1249
'honesty the best policy,' 600
house of Oedipus, general plan of, 1241
'hyperbaton,' 1251
'hyporcheme,' defined, p. lxxxvii.
hyporcheme in place of stasimon, 1086

I

iambic trimeters interrupted by short phrases, 1468
imperfect, not admissible in 1311
  ,, of intention or menace, 805, 1454
  ,, of τίκτω, instead of aor., 870
  ,, of willingness (ἐδέχου), 1391
  ,, partic. (ὁ παρών = ὃς παρῆν), 835

imperfect, referring to a result of effort (εὕρισκον, was able to find), 68
  ,, and aor. joined in a condit. sentence, 125
  ,, indic., of obligation etc. (ἔδει), 256, 1368
improbability, element of, in the plot, noticed by Aristotle, p. xxvii.: how treated by the moderns, p. xlvii.
incense in propitiation, 4, 913
indefin. pronoun (τις) after noun with art., 107
indirect discourse turned into direct, 1271
infin. after ἐξευρίσκειν, 120
  ,, after ἐπισκοπεῖν, 1529
  ,, after λέγω etc. as = *iubeo*, 350
  ,, alone, instead of infin. with ὡς (τὸ δ᾽ ὀρθὸν εἰπεῖν), 1221
  ,, and accus. in prayer (*subaud.* δός, etc.), 190
  ,, defining an adj. (ἄτλητος ὁρᾶν), 792, 1204
  ,,   ,, a phrase, 1169
  ,, epexegetic (ἐξαιτῶ σε τοῦτο πορεῖν), 1255
  ,, = an accus. of respect (φρονεῖν ταχύς), 617
  ,, for imperat., 462, 1466, 1529
  ,, of plup. with ἄν, 693
  ,, of purpose, with verb of 'going,' etc., 198
  ,, understood after χρῆν, 1184
  ,, with art. = an accus. of respect, 1417
  ,, without ἄν, representing an optat. without ἄν, 1296
  ,, without ὥστε (εἰκάσαι), 82
  ,, with τὸ μή (οὐ), 1232, 1388
interrogative (τίς) and relative (ὅστις) pronouns combined, 71
Iocasta, the Sophoclean, character of, p. xxx.
Ionic 3rd plur. (ὀψοίατο), 1273
  ,, verse, p. lxxix.
Ionicisms in trag. dialogue, 304
'irrational syllable,' p. lxvi.
Ismenus, Ismenion, 21
Ister, the river, 1227
iteration of a word, rhetorical, 370

J

Julius Caesar wrote an *Oedipus*, p. xxxv.

K

king, etc., summoned forth by visitors, 597
'kommos,' a, defined, p. 9
  ,,   structure of the 1st, p. lxxx.
  ,,   the 2nd, almost a monody, p. xciii.

L

laurel, worn by θεωροί returning from Delphi, 83
Laurentian MS., general relation of to the others, p. lvi.
laws, the 'unwritten,' 865
leaping from above,—fig. of an evil δαίμων, 263, 1300
life, the, the guest of the body, 612
logaoedic verse, p. lxxii. *n.*
logographers, the, references of, to Oedipus, p. xvii.
Loxias, 894
Lycia, haunt of Artemis, 208
lyrics, relation of the form to the matter of, p. xcvii.

M

Maenads, 212
manuscripts used in this edition, p. lii.
market-place, statue of Artemis in, 161
masc. subst. used as fem. adject. (σωτὴρ τύχη), 80
  ,,   dual instead of fem., 1472
mesode in choric songs, p. lxviii.
metaphor, a trait of Sophoclean, 866, 1300
  ,,   substituted for simile, p. 299
'monodies' in Tragedy, p. lxxx.

N

Nero fond of acting Oedipus, p. xxxv.
neut. adj. or pron. referring to masc. or fem. noun, 542
  ,,   referring to men (οὐδὲν κακόν for οὐδεὶς κακός), 1195
Nymphs, the, 1099

O

Oedipodeia, the, a lost epic, p. xv.
Oedipus—feels his own fate as separating him from human kind, 1415
  ,,   the Sophoclean, character of, p. xxix.
Olympia, μάντεις at, 901
Olympus, the sky, 867
optat., after secondary tense, replacing subj. with ἄν, 714
  ,,   in dependent clause, by attraction to optat. of wish, etc., 506
  ,,   instead of subj. with ἄν, after primary tense, 315, 979
  ,,   representing a deliberative subjunct. after a secondary tense, 72, 1256
  ,,   simple, where optat. with ἄν is more usual, 1296
  ,,   with ἄν, deferential, 95, 282, 343
  ,,   with ἄν, expressing one's conviction, 1182
oratio obliqua, 1271
order of words, abnormal (τὸν ἤδη Λάϊον πάλαι νεκρόν), 1245
  ,,   (ὅπως, οὐκέτ' οἶδ', ἀπόλλυται), 1251
  ,,   (ὁρᾶν μόνοις τ' ἀκούειν), 1430
  ,,   (τὰ πάτρια λόγῳ, for τ.λ.π.), 1394
oscilla (Roman), 1264
oxymoron, 196

P

paeon, the, in metre, p. lxxxiii.
Pallas, Theban shrines of, 20
paradoxical phrases such as ἐν σκότῳ ὁρᾶν, 997, 1482
Parnassus, snow-crowned, 473
paronomasia (χρησίμῳ χρῆται), 878
partic. as tertiary predicate, 1140
  ,,   *continuing* a question which another speaker has interrupted, 1130
  ,,   epithet of agent, transferred to his act, 1214
  ,,   equiv. to protasis of a sentence, 117
  ,,   imperf. (ὁ παρών = ὃς παρῆν), 835
  ,,   )(infin., after εἴ μοι ξυνείη μοῖρα, 863
  ,,   in nomin., instead of accus. and infin. (ἅλις νοσοῦσ' ἐγώ), 1061, 1368

partic., irregularly replaced by finite verb, 1134
,, modal, answering to a modal dative, 100
,, (ὤν) omitted, 412, 966
,, or adj. equiv. to an adv., 963
,, = protasis with εἰ, 1371
,, with γε, instead of finite verb, in a reply, 1011
,, with μέμνημαι, 50
,, with παραρρίπτω, 1494
parts, cast of the dramatic, p. 7
pastoral epithets of Apollo, 1103
patrons of μέτοικοι, 411
pause, prevents a breach of synaphea, 1303
pauses, metrical, p. lxvii.
perf. of final result (εὑρῆσθαι, 'found once for all'), 1050
Phasis, the river, 1227
Pherecydes of Leros on Oedipus, p. xvii.
Philocles, traditional defeat of Sophocles by, p. xxxii.
Pindar, reference of to Oedipus, p. xvi.
plague at Athens, supposed allusion to, p. xxxii.
pleonasm, 408
Pliny, references of to Arcturus, p. 307
Plunteria, festival of the, 886
pluperf. infin. with ἄν, 693
plural, allusive, for singular, 366, 497, 1091, 1359, 1405
,, neuter as adverb, 883
pollution, feared from contact with the blood-guilty, 1415
Polus, the tragic actor, p. xxxiii.
position, irregular, of a *second* epithet, 1199
,, unusual, of words, giving emphasis, 139, 278, 525
positive and negative joined (γνωτὰ κοὺκ ἄγνωτα), 58
,, (verb) to be evolved from negative, 241
power, the substance of, better than the show, 599
predicate, adj. as, after subst. with art., 672, 971

prep., following its case, 178, 525
,, between two nouns, governing both, 761, 1205
,, needlessly added (ξύναυλος πρὸς χώροις), 1126
present infin. after εὔχομαι, 892
,, indic. or partic., denoting a permanent character, 437
,, historic, 113
'prologue,' Arist.'s definition of, p. 8
pronoun in appos. with following subst. (τάδε...τάσδ' ἀράς), 819
,, possessive, for genit. of pers. pron. (σὸς πόθος), 969
,, redundant, 248, 385, 407
proöde in choric songs, p. lxviii.
prophecy, Greek view of, 708

Q

'quantity,' metrical, defined, p. lxv.
,, of vowels before κρ, 640

R

rain, symbol of water generally, 1427
recognition of children by tokens, 1035
redundant expression, 1126, 1463
relative pron. instead of demonstrative, after a parenthesis, 264
,, with causal force (ὅσα = ὅτι τοσαῦτα), 1228
repetition (ἀστὸς εἰς ἀστοὺς), 222, 248, 261
,, in euphemism (βλαστοῦσ' ὅπως ἔβλαστε), 1375
,, in lyric lament, 1193, 1330
,, of one speaker's words by another, 548
resident-aliens at Athens, and their patrons, 411
'resolution,' metrical, p. lxvi.
revivals, recent, of Greek plays, p. xlix.
rhetoric, figures of, 370, 538, 1375
,, πίστεις of, 1420
rhythm defined, p. lxv.
rhythmical 'sentence,' the, p. lxvii.
,, 'period,' the, p. lxviii.
riddle of the Sphinx, pp. 6, 302

'rising' rhythmical sentence, p. lxxiv.
rivers, representative, 1227

S

sacrifices, excommunication from, 240
seasons, the, Greek reckoning of, by the
stars, p. 306
Seneca's *Oedipus*, p. xxxv.
sentence, structure of, changed as it proceeds, 159, 587
'sifting,' no classical Greek metaphor
from, p. 290
slaves, home-bred, most trusted, 1123
Solon's saying, 1529
Sophocles, and the modern dramatisers of
the story—essential difference between
them, p. xlv.
  ,, general characteristics of his
style, p. lviii.
  ,, new traits of the story invented by, p. xx.
Sphinx, death of, 1198
  ,, Egyptian, Asiatic and Hellenic
types of, p. 300
  ,, relation of, to the Oedipus-myth,
p. 301
  ,, riddle of, p. 6
  ,, winged, 508, pp. 300 f.
stars, the wanderer's guides, 694
stasimon, Arist.'s definition of a, p. 8
State, rivalry in service of the, 880
subject of verb indefinite, 904
subjunct. after ὅς without ἄν, 1231
  ,, deliberative, 364, 651
  ,, ,, (usu. aorist), 485
  ,, without ἄν, 317
suppliants, their branches, 3
  ,, touch the hand, 760
syllabic augment omitted, 1249
synaphea, saved by a pause, 1303
'syncope,' p. lxvi.
synizesis, 555, 1002, 1451, 1518
  ,, of υ rare, 640
synonym used, instead of repeating the
same word, 54

T

table brought in for a meal, 1463
Teiresias, the, of Sophocles, p. xxxi.

text, deviations from Laurentian MS. in,
p. lvii.
  ,, of Sophocles, general condition
of, p. lix.
Théâtre Français, the, *Oedipe Roi* at, p.
li.
Thebaid, the 'cyclic,' fragment of, p.
xvi.
Thebes, topography of ancient, 20, 1378
'thesis,' p. lxvi.
'Thracian,' epith. of Euxine, 196
time the test of worth, 614, 1213
title of the *Oedipus Tyrannus*, p. 4
tmesis, 27, 199
tribrach, apparent, for cyclic dactyl, p.
xcii.
  ,, in senarii, usual limits to use of,
537, 719
trochaics, in what sense excluded from
στάσιμα, p. 9
tunic, women's Doric, 1269
tyrannis, the Greek, 541

V

verb, left to be understood, 683, 1037
  ,, (or partic.) to be supplied from a
cognate notion (νομίσας from ἰδών), 538
  ,, referring to two subjects, though
appropriate only to one, 116
verbal adjective, sigmatic form of, p.
298
verse, beginning with word which closely
adheres to preceding verse (ποτ'), 1084
  ,, rhythm of, suited to the thought,
332, 719, 738, 1310
vocative of Οἰδίπους, 405 cr.
Voltaire's *Oedipe*, p. xlii.
  ,, criticisms, p. xliv.

W

west, the region of the Death-god, 178
women, position of, 1078
  ,, presence of, at festivals, etc. 1489

Y

year, popular division of, by the stars,
p. 306

Z

zeugma of verb, 116

LaVergne, TN USA
26 May 2010
183968LV00002B/16/P